Additional Praise

"The story of Mormons and blacks shares much with the history of race in America. The Mormon tale is further laden with entanglements peculiar to itself—often fraught, sometimes inspiring. *For the Cause of Righteousness* breaks new ground with its mix of international scope, comprehensive chronology, and theoretical vision. It recognizes that notions of race are not merely dictated from the pinnacles of hierarchy, and it offers a complement of narrative analysis and illuminating primary documents. This is a notable study."

— Philip Barlow, author of *Mormons and the Bible: The Place of the Latter-day Saints in American Religion*

"This deeply-researched volume attending to race in the broad sweep of Mormon history—both in the United States and internationally—performs a singular scholarly service. Attuned to the complexities in this sweeping, dynamic story, Stevenson shows the ongoing negotiations between church leaders and ordinary members, as well as an ever-changing spectrum of opinion amongst those leaders. His choice of documents allows him to tell a story at once of continuities, glacial change, and dramatic turning points that will provoke discussion as well as enlighten readers."

— Matthew Mason, Associate Professor of History, Brigham Young University

"Global in scope and local in detail, this deeply-researched history is relevant for all seeking to understand the complicated interactions between doctrine and culture, and leader and congregant, as Mormonism moves into the 21st century. Told through the voices of women and men in the United States, Nigeria, Ghana, South Africa, Brazil, and beyond as they attempted to understand the role of race in the LDS Church and its teachings, this work is a crucial reminder for all of us that whatever our differences, 'all are alike unto God.' The stories Stevenson brings out of archival obscurity are going to be with us for a long time. As they should be."

— Robert Tabor, National Director of Mormons for Obama

"*For The Cause of Righteousness* is an honest look at an often misunderstood subject within the LDS Church. Russell Stevenson creates an easy to understand narrative that takes the reader from casual observer of the Church's past to well-rounded historian. Bold and thought provoking, it approaches a difficult subject with the sensitivity and respect it deserves."

— Richie T. Steadman, founder of The Cultural Hall Podcast

"Russell Stevenson has provided an impeccable collection of research to shed light on the historical space where two nineteenth-century minorities—Mormons and Blacks—converged and co-existed. This documentary reader reveals the struggle of the fledgling church to navigate the difficult territory between its vision, its emerging doctrine, and the widely-held social and cultural prejudices of its day. The documents show that the Church's maturation process subsumed pain, progress, shame, yearning, and increased clarity over time. For the Cause of Righteousness offers a balanced and thorough compilation of the available research. The text begs the reader to acknowledge, reflect, and reconcile the sometimes disappointing tendencies of human nature."

— Stephanie Sorenson, author of *Covenant Motherhood: Reflecting the Role of Christ in Our Lives*

"As I teach on this subject around the world, the most common and consistent question coming out of the significant shift in paradigm is 'How could this have happened?' Russell has done a wonderful job pulling together an incredible amount of historical accounts sufficient for every reader to clearly understand how this could have and indeed did happen. I applaud this great effort and attention to this much needed topic and history. This work will become a resource for many to come and find a wealth of stories and history upon which they can expand both their knowledge and research efforts."

— Marvin Perkins, co-author of the *Blacks in the Scriptures*

For the Cause of Righteousness

For the Cause of Righteousness

A Global History of Blacks and Mormonism,
1830–2013

Russell W. Stevenson

GREG KOFFORD BOOKS
SALT LAKE CITY, 2014

Greg Kofford Books
P.O. Box 1362
Draper, UT 84020
www.gregkofford.com
facebook.com/gkbooks

ISBN 978-1-58958-529-4 (paperback)
978-1-58958-530-0 (hardcover)
Also available in ebook.

2018   17   16   15   5   4   3   2   .

Library of Congress Cataloging-in-Publication Data
available upon request

Dedicated to Stewart Stanley Stevenson
(October 31, 1980–November 1, 1980).

Hope we're making you proud, Stew.

Contents

Acknowledgments

Only a knave would suggest that a book he authored rested solely on his own laurels. Books take time, infrastructure, documents, and legwork from people whose names could easily remain unseen by the reading public. But they do it all the same.

I owe a tremendous debt to the personnel at the LDS Church History Library. Librarians such as Brittany Chapman, Ronald Romig, and Jay Burrup make the work of any serious researcher of Mormonism possible. Similarly, the team of digital historians at the Church History Library have made a generous collection of documents available to historians who live far from the Archives. Those who have generously reviewed my manuscript also deserve high praise. And to those who have pointed me toward important sources, I pay particular thanks. Men and women such as Steven Densley, Stephanie Sorenson, James Egan, Julianne Gough, and Lavina Fielding Anderson, Loyd Ericson, and Christian Larsen have provided consistent and life-giving encouragement and feedback as I labored on this project. The story is more complex, compelling, and intriguing due to your generosity.

And my family—those ranging from my siblings (Natalie, Travis, Brady, Clint, and Stewart) to my parents (Kent and Nancy) to my grandfather, Stanley Walker Stevenson—have all played a role in motivating me to embark on this project. Even when we have disagreed (moments that have proven to be few and far between), such things matter little compared to rolling, generally-unseen, strength that strong family bonds provide.

In this book, I seek only to tell a story. Nothing more and nothing less. I owe it all to the black Saints who have toiled, pressed, and endeavored to live out their faith, even when faced with considerable opposition—whether from mob attacks or interpersonal microaggressions. At times, it is a difficult story. And at others, it moves and edifies. No decent history is so simple that it can only appeal to one of the human emotions. It demands that we explore the full spectrum of human existence: frustration, joy, grief, anger, mourning, depression, and love.

Growing Up White

It is my church as much as it is yours.
—Bishop Edwin Woolley[1]

*The Lord our God hath put us to silence, and given us water of gall
to drink, because we sinned against the Lord.*
—Jeremiah 8:14

A confession: I am a white Mormon man.

I grew up in the white wilderness: Lincoln County, Wyoming. There are no stoplights, and the nearest department store is two hours away. In 2010, demographers identified all counties with fewer than six people per square mile as "frontier counties." In Lincoln County, racial diversity cropped up spontaneously and served primarily as interesting novelties for my whiteness–drenched Mormon community. My family's idea of an engaging night at home was looking up various headings in Bruce R. McConkie's *Mormon Doctrine* (second edition, of course). I, like myriad others, accepted the pre–1978 priesthood ban as advertised. I didn't really bother to engage the doctrinal issues undergirding it. One of the tragic luxuries of living a white narrative is the ability to entertain the delusion that non–white populations and their struggles are, at best, irrelevant.

My hometown was one of the last Mormon colonies settled in the nineteenth century. Made up of hard–working, stolid folk, my community exuded the qualities Mormonism values in its white pioneer tradition. Year after year, cattle ranchers and farmers powered through –40 °F winters, even as they worked

---

1. This quotation has also been attributed to Robert Gardner, though Woolley almost certainly uttered it. Both the Gardner and the Woolley families quote it proudly as a defining aspect of their relationship to the institutional LDS Church. Laurel Thatcher Ulrich, Woolley's great–niece, observed: "The sense that this is 'my church, as well as the 'the Lord's church' permeates my family scriptures" and explains "my own commitment to the institution even when I have been most aware of the problems in it." Laurel Thatcher Ulrich, "Family Scriptures," 123. Brigham Young once quipped that "if Bishop Woolley should fall off his horse while crossing the Jordan River on the way to his pasture, those searching for him should not expect him to be floating downstream; they would more likely find him swimming upstream, obstinately contending against the current." Leonard J. Arrington, *From Quaker to Latter–day Saint: Bishop Edwin D. Woolley,* 449; Arrington, *Brigham Young: American Moses,* 200. For the Gardner (mis)attribution, see William R. Palmer, qtd. in "Pioneers of Southern Utah: Robert Gardner," 384.

a second–day job for The Man to make ends meet. Exposure to urban issues or most ethnic diversity came through the media or through the handful of students of color (generally adopted) through the school system. And for the rural poor, the "media" amounted to three television stations received by erecting the rabbit–ears antennae. We lived in a modern–day Mayberry where boys could play football in the streets and a local drive–in provided the best food in town.

The information age resounded in America's small towns. My home received internet service in the mid–90s, and it unleashed a wave of information upon our cloistered community. Even with my parents' controversy–free book collection, I had worked through the various Mormon narratives I had been raised with: the Mormon narrative of Sunday School, of home evenings, and of Ivan Barrett's Joseph Smith and the Restoration. The internet opened up an entirely new conversation for me. I learned not only of seer stones but also polygamy, polyandry, and, most importantly for this book, Elijah Ables, a black priesthood holder lauded for his "zeal for the cause of righteousness."[2] I could not square Elijah's experiences with what I thought I knew, so I put his memory aside in my box of what I thought were irrelevant but interesting curiosities.

Mormon missions can do a lot of things to Mormon young people. They give some confidence and others humility. My mission rewired my racial make-up. As a Hmong–speaking missionary in California, my active engagement with the white community was limited; I spent my time interpreting for paramedics, eating pig brains, and explaining that the bearded man with the red robe was Jesus of Nazareth. I came to believe that Zion—including the institutional church—should be a safe haven and a refuge for the downtrodden and oppressed. Zion looks a little different—and perhaps a little truer—in the slums.

My mission experience mirrored Elijah Ables's Mormonism a little more than that of my parents. I spoke regularly with African Americans and struggled to look them in the eye as they quoted Acts 10:34 ("God is no respecter of persons"). I sorted through various explanations, often preferring what I call the dispensationalist explanation: that is, that in God's grand scheme of things, he planned for different races to receive priesthood blessings at different times. It was neat, clean, and precedented in holy scripture. As Joseph Smith would tell Orson Hyde when Hyde postulated a theory, there was but "one serious objection to it": "it is not true."[3]

Mormonism celebrates the idea of resounding revelations and overflowing visions. How could the Saints have stumbled so badly on a matter so important to the salvation of the human family? Would not a prophet have sought to correct his people from excluding a large percentage of the human family from his blessings? That the Mormon collective could influence the leadership has been

---

2. Kirtland Elders Certificates, CD, CR 100 41, 75, LDS Church History Library.

3. "Minutes of Council of the Twelve in Upper Room of Historian's Office," qtd. in Gary J. Bergera, "The Orson Pratt–Brigham Young Controversies: Conflict within the Quorum, 1853–1868," 31.

a recurring theme throughout Mormon scripture and modern Latter–day Saint history.

Religion is made on the ground as well as it is revealed from Mount Sinai. That godly communities can render themselves unworthy of revelation is a well–established tradition in Judeo–Christian and Mormon texts. In the Book of Mormon, an ancient prophet in America taught that "he that will harden his heart, the same receiveth the lesser portion of the word," a proviso that does not exclude word received from Mormon Church leadership. In another episode, God's people had become so wicked that their commander, Mormon, felt they had been "left to ourselves, that the Spirit of the Lord did not abide in us." They had "become weak like unto our brethren" (Mormon 2:26). God commands Mormon, their prophet and military commander, to withhold counsel from his followers, ordering him to "stand as an idle witness" while he watches them self–destruct (Mormon 3:16). In the Old Testament, the Israelites requested that Moses speak with them but, they continued, "Let not God speak with us, lest we die"; and they "stood afar off" while Moses spoke with the Lord. In another text, the Lord silences the prophet Ezekiel from speaking to the people of God because they were "a rebellious house." God continued with details: "I will make thy tongue cleave to the roof of thy mouth, that thou shalt be dumb, and shalt not be to them a reprover" (Ezek. 3:26). In modern times, Joseph Smith, speaking on behalf of the Lord, declared that "vanity and unbelief have brought the whole church under condemnation" (D&C 84:55).

As the Saints developed their racial attitudes, they were also a profoundly small minority struggling to survive in an America ill–disposed to welcoming them. A wide corpus of literature has demonstrated that minority religious groups must develop strategies to navigate within the larger community. In J. Kameron Carter's magisterial work, *Race: A Theological Account*, he concludes that race and racism were a "social arrangement" that allowed Christianity to co–exist with the rise of Western civilization.[4] Mormonism shared this impulse: an almost existential need to negotiate and compromise in a futile effort to survive. Joseph once quipped that "getting anything into the heads of this generation . . . has been like splitting hemlock knots with a corn–dodger for a wedge and a pumpkin for a beetle."[5] Yet as resistant as they were to Joseph Smith's teachings, they felt entirely comfort-able adopting the racial attitudes prevalent in nineteenth–century America. Even Joseph Smith entertained it on occasion. When Church leaders released Official Declaration #2 in 1978, it was not only the dawning of a "long–promised day"; it was also the close of a very long night.

In assessing the origins of Mormonism's racial doctrines and policies, the question of power and agency inevitably enter the conversation. As Michel

---

4. J. Kameron Carter, *Race: A Theological Account*, 8.

5. Andrew F. Ehat and Lyndon W. Cook, comps. and eds., *The Words of Joseph Smith: The Contemporary Accounts of the Nauvoo Discourses of the Prophet Joseph Smith*, 319.

Foucault observes, the prison system shifted from a system of violence to a system of surveillance. Surveillance, Foucault argues, "does not link forces together in order to reduce them; it seeks to bind them together in such a way as to multiply and use them." This system of surveillance did not function as a "triumphant power" based on omnipotence but as a "modest, suspicious power, which functions as a calculated, but permanent economy."[6]

The Mormon race question is, at its roots, a question of power: who wields it, to whom it is delegated, and who must partake of its fruits. The tight–knit and cloistered communities of Mormon society created the perfect environment in which Mormons could establish for themselves a self–regulating community, one in which all could be watchful for threats to their own whiteness. As Foucault noted, modern constructions of power no longer relied on brute force but "via the actions of individuals as they discipline themselves, in accordance with dominant norms and ideals." The discipline of oneself "assures the automatic functioning of power." Foucault noted that power in perfected form "should tend to render its actual exercise unnecessary." In Foucault's history, the civil authorities directed the building of this structure. Armed with financial resources and armaments, the government could—and did—exercise brute force when self–regulation broke down.[7] In 1861, N. B. Johnson complained to Mormon President Brigham Young that his uncertain racial status had "rather embarrast [him] on the account of some who pretend to understand all mysteries."[8] Haunted by Missouri, racialization discourse infected the Mormon community, ultimately evolving to become a self–perpetuating strand of the Mormon people's cultural DNA. As Foucault sorrowfully noted: "We all have some element of fascism inside our heads."[9]

Questions surrounding the Mormon hierarchy's power have been some of the most enduring queries in its history. In the nineteenth century, describing Brigham Young as an all–powerful dictator was stock–in–trade discourse for the Eastern establishment.[10] Brigham Young "is a complete tyrant," the *National Aegis* raged. "Every man holds his life at the will of Brigham Young."[11] "His sway is now effectually undisputed in the territory," one commentary noted as the Mormons inched towards war with the United States in spring 1857.[12] A widely published report cast Young as "the most brutal tyrant now on earth and in point

---

6. Michel Foucault, *Discipline and Punish: The Birth of the Prison*, 201.

7. Ibid., 170.

8. N.B. Johnson, Letter to Brigham Young, January 1, 1861, Brigham Young Office Files, Reel 38.

9. Michel Foucault, *"Society Must Be Defended": Lectures at the College de France*, 30.

10. For a treatment of anti–Mormon rhetoric directed at Brigham Young, see J. Spencer Fluhman, *"A Peculiar People": Anti–Mormonism and the Making of Religion in Nineteenth–Century America*, chaps. 3–4.

11. "The Condition of Utah," *National Aegis*, April 1, 1857, 2.

12. "Details of Utah News," *Boston Post*, June 8, 1857, 2.

of treasonous designs without an equal."[13] The *Boston Courier* complained that Church leadership "controls all the actions of the people."[14]

Indeed, several modern commentators have also employed this rhetoric in describing Brigham Young, the leader most often associated with the origins of Mormonism's policy of racial exclusion. In 1978 skeptics often asked Sonia Johnson and her supporters how she dodged excommunication for supporting the Equal Rights Amendment. Johnson "said all the right things," assuring them that "the Church is not a totalitarian organization." But she admitted that her arguments exhibited "a certain lack of real conviction."[15] Historian David Roberts notes that Brigham Young used Stalin–like tactics to eliminate his rivals.[16] Another historian, John J Hammond, has felt that Brigham Young's relationship to Joseph Smith could be compared to "that between Lenin and Stalin." Whereas "Lenin created Bolshevism," Stalin "institutionalized it." Similarly, "Smith created Mormonism," and "Young institutionalized it."[17] In 2012, a youth group in Russia called for the expulsion of Mormon missionaries, declaring them to be "a totalitarian sect."[18]

Chronologically and geographically, they are vastly different disciplines— one deriving from a bloc of land covering almost a fourth of the earth's land mass and the other from a sliver of territory in the remote Intermountain West. Certainly, exerting political control over a small region such as territorial Utah would be a much simpler task, making it easier to believe that Brigham exerted greater control over the territory and certainly Mormon society.

But we can take the comparisons of our several commentators and engage them on their merits. If Brigham Young could be considered a tyrant, how did he go about building the racial wing of his empire? At whose feet do we lay the blame? Who directed the building of this edifice? Who surveyed it, managed its keeping, and guarded it from interlopers? And when the walls began to come down in 1978, who played the role of Gorbachev in allowing free passage into the outside world? In what had become a global faith community, the ability to concentrate this power into the hands of a single man or group of men would be an awesome talent indeed. But boiled down, these comparisons evoke a crucial question: Who bears the responsibility for pulling the trigger?

An examination of how scholars have answered the question for the Soviet Union reveals how elusive the issue of culpability can be. In the rich corpus of

---

13. " From Utah," *Newark Daily Advertiser*, April 6, 1857, 2; "Outrages of Brigham Young," *Rock River Democrat*, April 14, 1857, 2; "From Utah," *Weekly Wisconsin Patriot*, April 18, 1857, 1.

14. "Utah," *Boston Courier*, May 14, 1860, 2.

15. Sonia Johnson, Letter to Alvin and Ida Harris, July 20, 1978, Box 42, fd. 12, Sonia Johnson Papers.

16. David Roberts, *Devil's Gate: Brigham Young and the Great Mormon Handcart Tragedy,* 67.

17. John J Hammond, *A Divided Mormon Zion: Northeastern Ohio or Western Missouri*, 389.

18. "'A Totalitarian Sect': Youth Group Wants to Kick Mormons Out of Russia," October 31, 2012, http://www.rferl.org/content/pro–kremlin–group–wants–mormons–out–of–russia/24757052.html (accessed December 5, 2013).

literature on the Soviet purges of the 1930s, three distinct approaches have surfaced. One of the first scholars to assess the origins of the Soviet massacres was
Robert Conquest, who centered the responsibility for the massacres on Vladimir
Lenin and Josef Stalin. Lenin, Conquest argued, "established within the Party all
the seeds of a centralized bureaucratic attitude." The Communist Party did not
represent the populace "as it existed, but the future and real interests of that proletariat." "Loyalty and solidarity" stemmed largely from "the ideas in the minds
of [the Party's] leading members."[19] As for the second instrument of Soviet slay-
ing, Conquest quotes Hungarian philosopher Georg Lukacs's depiction of Stalin
as "the apex of a pyramid which widened gradually towards the base and was
composed of many 'little Stalins.'" From above, "they were objects." From below,
they were the "creators and guardians of the cult of personality." By Conquest's
reckoning, "loyalties and solidarities" in Stalinism "worked in one direction
only—upward."[20]

In the 1970s, a new wave of scholars began to reassess the analysis of Robert
Conquest. Led by historians such as Stephen Cohen, Jerry Hough, and Sheila
Fitzpatrick, they attacked Conquest's approach as simplistic. "I thought the
suggestion absurd that any political regime could control a society," Fitzpatrick
declared. It was a "value–laden" system that played all too easily into the hands
of Western historians seeking to undermine Soviet claims to Eastern Europe.
Fitzpatrick and others concluded that the politics were more complicated than
"simple 'top down' repression." Many "people and groups were pushing competing agendas." Fitzpatrick began to "see a 'from below' pattern" that was "driving
the politicians further than they might otherwise have gone." She and other revi-
sionists sought to understand the degree to which "social support" existed for the
Bolshevik regime, while acknowledging that critics disparaged her efforts merely
as "an attempt to justify Stalinism."[21]

J. Arch Getty's analysis of the Soviet purges attacked those who cast Stalinism
as monolithic even more potently: "Was it necessary," he asked, "to attribute every initiative and policy to the Great Teacher?" He warns readers that it would
"naïve to be taken in by Stalin's cult of personality and to accept Stalinist protestations of unity." Indeed, he concludes, "it may well be that where one finds
the loudest affirmations of unity are the places where unity is most lacking."
Getty criticizes the Western view that casts Soviet power as flowing from "top to
bottom, from the center to the localities."[22] The reality, he concludes, is that the
"chain of command collapsed more often than it functioned." The Communist
Party was "more an undisciplined and disorganized force" than "a sophisticated
order of totalitarianism."[23] As Stephen Kotkin has argued, in the Stalinist state,

---

19. Robert Conquest, *The Great Terror: A Reassessment,* 7.
20. Ibid., 446–47.
21. Sheila Fitzpatrick, "Revisionism in Retrospect: A Personal View," 683–84, 689, 694.
22. J. Arch Getty, *Origins of the Great Purges: The Soviet Communist Party Reconsidered,* 27.
23. Ibid.

"mechanisms of power—such as mutual surveillance and self–identification" existed in the Soviet state "on a much more ordinary level." The Soviet central state "understood that its power rested on the characteristics and behavior of the people."[24] Crafting Mormonism's racial consensus, therefore, has been a much more involved process than sending out First Presidency circulars or making speeches. Foucault has insisted that "the power isn't localized in the state apparatus," and societal change is impossible "if the mechanisms of power that function outside, below and alongside the State apparatuses, on a much more minute and everyday level, are not also changed."[25]

The comparison invites us to reassess who has controlled the defining of Mormon discourse on racism through the decades. In Harvard business professor Ronald Heifetz's groundbreaking study on leadership, he argues that figures within an organization often wield "leadership without authority." Such leaders, Heifetz argues, have the capacity to be "both more bold and subtle."[26] They can "raise hard questions and generate distress."[27] We find that in the creation of Mormon racial identity, there was an intricate interplay between voices such as the "authoritative" Brigham Young and the informal (though, in the end, equally provocative and attitude–defining) white mob at Winter Quarters. We find that while David O. McKay may have held the pulpit, African Saints held the imagination, both to their hope and to their doom.

Mormonism's racial prison housed both executive suites and dungeons alike. Thomas Coburn, a victim of racial violence in territorial Utah, lived in a different wing than Jane Manning James, the faithful black Saint who labored tirelessly (and failed) to receive Mormonism's temple rituals. Spencer W. Kimball, who acknowledged the soul–searing personal obstacles he overcame in granting blacks the priesthood, lived in a very different cell than Caleb Shreeve, the retired army general whose efforts to uphold the priesthood ban bordered on the fanatical. Yet prison walls encased them all the same.

By the time the Saints had settled in the Intermountain West, they had achieved a state of—to adopt Heifitz's language—racial equilibrium. As an overwhelmingly white community with few racial outsiders, the Mormon community could labor under the notion that racial Otherness was a foreign—and irrelevant—element to the Intermountain Mormon community. As Heifitz notes, "A society may operate without increasing levels of stress, quite oblivious to the bankruptcy that lies ahead." If a society lacks a "general climate of urgency—the feeling that something must change—the society may do nothing until it is too late."[28]

---

24. Stephen Kotkin, *Magnetic Mountain: Stalinism as a Civilization*, 23.

25. Foucault, "BodyPower," in Colon Gordon, ed., *Power/Knowledge: Selected Interviews and Other Writings, 1972–1977*, 60.

26. Heifetz, *Leadership without Easy Answers*, 207.

27. Ibid., 128.

28. Ibid., 35.

In our wandering through the black–Mormon milieu, it becomes hard not to wonder when—or if—Mormon leaders in fact led the Mormon people. The conventional scholarship on the essence of leadership has, as Heifetz has observed, used influence as "the mark of leadership." By this model, a "leader gets people to accept his vision, and . . . if something goes wrong, the fault lies with the leader." This model of leadership is an oversimplification, Heifitz argues. It is the duty of the leader not merely to give directives to community—to which they respond with a rigid goose–step. Leadership requires "giving clarity and articulation to a community's guiding values."[29] And one need not hold the prophetic mantle to find success in this responsibility.

Leonard Arrington has warned Mormon historians to be aware of "the unanimity bias"—the "notion that Mormon society has, from the earliest years, been characterized by concert in thought and behavior, by cooperation, concord, and consensus."[30] On racial issues, it took nearly a century before significant pushback against the consensus developed; the degree of unanimity in the Saints' position is shocking. Until the mid–twentieth century, few Saints made the effort to dissent on racial issues. Factions and dissenters had mobilized based on the claims of visionaries, capitalists, and fundamentalists. A paltry few of these voices based their dissent on a desire for racial equality. Indeed, the most notable group to dissent based on racial issues expressed concerns that Church leaders had erred in granting blacks the priesthood in 1978.

This volume seeks to explore the story of blacks and Mormonism through an intimate lens, focusing not only on the experiences of Church leaders but also the ordinary Latter–day Saint: the day laborer nervous about his African ancestry, the West African woman establishing her own "Mormon" congregation, the Pat Boone–loving Mormon missionary in Africa, the death–defying explorer, John M. Goddard, ruminating on his affection for African dance, and the Black Panther musing on the Mormons' wasted potential. Robert Orsi has argued that religion "comes into being in an ongoing, dynamic relationship with realities of everyday life."[31] This drama played in several theatres: West Africa, the United States, Brazil, and South Africa. This volume seeks to explore the story of blacks and Mormonism through an intimate lens in each of these locales. Race was both a spoken and lived experience. The Mormon people witnessed it, felt it, and absorbed it. But for the Mormon people, racism was a conscious decision—and one that exacted a heavy toll during their epoch in the wilderness.

---

29. Ibid., 23.

30. Leonard Arrington, "The Search for Truth and Meaning in Mormon History," 7.

31. Robert Orsi, "Everyday Miracles: The Study of Lived Religion," 3–21.

Part 1

The History

Chapter 1

Black and White, Bond and Free, 1830–47

"Don't let a single corner of the earth go without a mission."
—Joseph Smith

Mormonism's earliest narratives took pains to include blacks. Racial narratives attempt to explain the origin, state, and destiny of a grouping of people. Even if its first adherents were uniformly Anglo-Saxon, its earliest scriptural texts were unequivocal concerning the spiritual unity of all mankind. Joseph Smith's Book of Mormon insisted that the gospel of Jesus Christ was available to "both black and white, bond and free, male and female" (2 Ne. 26:33). In 1831, Joseph Smith declared in the name of the Lord that "it is not right that any man should be in bondage one to another" (D&C 101:79).

Establishing a global Mormonism became something of an obsession for the young prophet. In 1843, he told members of the Church's governing body: "when you meet with an Arab, send him to Arabia, when you find an Italian, send him to Italy. & a french man, to France; or an Indian, that is suitable, send him among the Indians. & this and that man send them. to the different places where they belong.—Send somebody to Central America and to Spanish America & don't let a single corner of the earth go without a mission."[1] By the time of his death, he and his followers had transformed his movement from a band of the disenchanted to a movement he promised would "revolution[ize and] civilize the world."[2] Lyman Littlefield felt Joseph's vision enabled " mankind . . . to see the gospel eye to eye and travel together the strait and narrow path."[3]

Joseph Smith's Racial Coalition

The grand designs of Mormonism's vision make for a strange fit with its provincial origins. Mormonism's founder Joseph Smith started as little more than

---

1. Andrew H. Hedges, Alex D. Smith, and Richard Lloyd Anderson, eds., *Journals 2: December 1841–April 1843*, April 19, 1843, 370.

2. Andrew F. Ehat and Lyndon W. Cook, eds., *The Words of Joseph Smith: The Contemporary Accounts of the Nauvoo Discourses of the Prophet Joseph Smith*, July 23, 1843, 234.

3. Lyman O. Littlefield, *Reminiscences of Latter-day Saints,* 53.

a village seer in upstate New York. His more urbane contemporaries would have called him a huckster, hardly distinguishable from the myriad self-proclaimed prophets teeming throughout New England.

As a boy, Joseph participated in a debating club at the schoolhouse on Durfee Street in Palmyra. Joseph's neighbor, Orasmus Turner, recalls that his intellect "occasionally shone out . . . especially when he used to help us solve some portentous questions of moral or political ethics."[4] However, Palmyra's free black population was limited: forty-six blacks in a population of 3,724.[5] The neighboring Rochester had but eighteen in a population of 1,502.[6]

While slavery was considered to be a moral evil, upstate New Yorkers had little incentive to grapple with the problems of racism and slavery directly. Furthermore, the Smith family generally had had other issues pressing upon them: leg infections, crop failures, and the occasional treasure hunt. Still, Joseph's mother thought him a pensive boy inclined to "meditation and deep study" rather than "the perusal of books."[7]

Living in a predominantly white agrarian community, Joseph saw little of the abolitionist furor developing in northern cities. He had probably heard of the debate over Missouri's entrance into the Union as a slave state. In 1820, a local paper editorialized that "friends of a free government" should "stand to their posts and put at defiance the gasconading threats of southern slave-holders."[8] In 1819 a Palmyra newspaper published Patrick Henry's letter on slavery, despairing over the plight of the enslaved: "I believe a time will come when an opportunity will be offered to abolish this lamentable evil. Everything we can do is to improve it, if it happens in our day; if not, let us transmit to our descendants together with our slaves, a pity for their unhappy lot, and abhorrence for slavery."[9] When a black man was dragged through the street "like a dog" in the South, the story reached upstate New York. The scene repulsed Yankee pundits: "Is humanity and sympathy for our fellow beings selfishly confined to our own color only?"[10]

As early as 1820, Joseph began claiming to receive visions from God the Father and Jesus Christ. In 1827, according to Joseph, an angel directed him to a hill in which he unearthed plates that had the appearance of gold. Joseph translated these plates into a text of more than five hundred pages that he and

---

4. Orasmus Turner, *History of the Pioneer Settlement of Phelps & Gorham's Purchase and Morris' Reserve*, 214.

5. Horatio Gates Spafford, ed., *A Gazetteer of the State of New York*, 400.

6. British visitor James Silk Buckingham observed: "There were fewer people of colour in the streets [of Rochester] than in any town we had visited." Qtd. in Diane Shaw, *City Building on the Eastern Frontier: Sorting the New Nineteenth-Century City*, 190 note 44.

7. Lucy Smith, *Biographical Sketches of Joseph Smith the Prophet and His Progenitors for Many Generations*, 84.

8. "Missouri and Slavery," *Palmyra Register*, December 6, 1820, 3.

9. Patrick Henry, "Letter on Slavery," *Palmyra Register*, December 29, 1819, 3.

10. "A Most Barbarous Scene," *Rochester Telegraph*, August 1, 1820, 3. For another example see "Barbrous" [sic], *Palmyra Register*, August 18, 1819, 2.

others interpreted to be an account of America's ancient inhabitants known as the "Nephites" and the "Lamanites."[11] Having completed the translation, he officially founded the Church in April 1830.

The black populations of Joseph Smith's and the Saints' settlements never amounted to more than a few hundred at most. In 1839, Mormon apostle Parley P. Pratt observed that "one half dozen negroes or mulattoes, never have belonged to our Society, in any part of the world, from its first organization to this day."[12] But some Saints experienced a limited degree of interracial dialogue in their youth. Sarah DeArmon Pea Rich had grown up with a black slave in her intimate family circles.[13] Levi Hancock recalls that "the first time in my life I saw some negroes" was during his childhood when he listened to their stories. Years later, he still remembered that one confided that "he wished he had been white as I was."[14] Martha P. Jane Thomas was proud to call herself a "southern woman . . . raised in a slave state."[15] The wife of Joseph Smith's first cousin by marriage, Bathsheba Bigler Wilson Smith from Tennessee remembers that her family had either "given freedom to their slaves . . . from conscientious motives" or eschewed slavery outright.[16]

In 1831, Joseph received a revelation assuring him that Missouri was the "land of promise . . . appointed and consecrated for the gathering of the Saints" (D&C 57:1). In his official 1838 history, Joseph Smith's scribe, W.W. Phelps, initially identified "Negroes as descendants of Ham" and Native Americans as "Lamanites." Someone—likely Joseph Smith himself—ordered that any genealogical identifiers be stricken from the record. Mulholland either removed the scriptural names or replaced them with modern terms such as "Indians" or, in the case of Missouri whites, identified them as descendants of the biblical Japheth, "pioneers of the west."[17] Joseph had received revelations identifying the Missouri borderlands with Zion, locating the Garden of Eden in its far-western Jackson County. A wave of Mormons began to flow into the region. When Joseph visited the region in summer 1831, he freely preached to a "respectable number of negroes."[18]

---

11. For the best scholarly work on the Book of Mormon, see Terryl L. Givens, *By the Hand of Mormon: The American Scripture that Launched a New World Religion.*

12. Parley P. Pratt, *Late Persecutions of the Church of Jesus Christ, of Latter-day Saints; Inflicted by the State of Missouri upon the Mormons* (1839), 11. In the 1840 edition, Pratt increases the number to "one dozen," suggesting that approximately six blacks joined the Saints between 1839 and 1840. See also Pratt, *Late Persecutions of the Church of Jesus Christ, of Latter-day Saints; Ten Thousand American Citizens Robbed, Plundered, and Banished; Others Imprisoned, and Others Martyred for their Religion. With a Sketch of Their Rise, Progress and Doctrine* (1840), 28.

13. Sarah DeArmon Pea Rich, "Journal of Sarah De Armon Pea Rich," transcribed by Alice M. Rich, 14–15.

14. Levi Ward Hancock, "The Life of Levi W. Hancock," typescript, 2, Perry Special Collections.

15. Martha Pane Jones Thomas, in Daniel Stillwell Thomas Family History, 23.

16. Bathsheba B. Wilson Smith, Autobiography, photocopy of holograph, 1.

17. "Manuscript History of the Church," A–1, 129

18. Ibid.

The Saints also saw their associations with the African Americans as reflective of their condition as struggling colonists. Emily Dow Partridge Young recalled her gratitude for local blacks' willingness to provide housing for the impoverished Saints. Despite their meager resources, her family could at least "have a good fire, and so kept from freezing."[19] When Heber C. Kimball saw blacks in Richmond, Missouri, he found it a novelty to "hear them call the cows 'sook cherry' and see them tote . . . the pails or tubs of milk on the heads."[20] Though the Saints sought to be friendly, they nevertheless saw the black population as an exotic race living under conditions unworthy of respectable whites.

The center of Mormonism continued to be in upstate New York. But as missionaries traveled to Missouri, they established small Mormon communities along the way, the largest being in Kirtland, Ohio, a village in the wilderness of the Western Reserve. But after the missionaries left the town, the newly converted Saints forged their own faith without the guiding influence of Church authorities.

The new community's version of Mormonism indicated that they drew from eclectic sources. Lacking the structure that Joseph Smith established in upstate New York, charismatic preachers took control of the Mormon community. A leading figure in the newly formed Mormon community was a preacher called "Black Pete." Raised in northern Ohio by a woman named Kino (a name that suggests a retention of her African heritage and identity), "Black Pete" riveted the Kirtland Mormons with visions and song. Reuben Miller recalled that Pete "used to get the power and writhe around in various contortions on the floor." He "r[a]n over the hills and [said] he saw holes of fire." Young white women burst into ecstasy while listening to his preaching.[21] Charismatic and commanding, Pete wielded considerable influence in defining the lived religion of the newly converted Kirtland Mormons.

When Methodists began to teach northern blacks like Pete in the late eighteenth-century, they drew on their tradition of Islam even as they embraced the tenets of Christianity. After Pete was baptized in 1830, he fashioned a hybrid Mormonism that reflected both his Islamic heritage and newly embraced Methodist faith. When Joseph Smith moved his followers to the region in early 1831, he cracked down on the hybrid Mormonism, declaring that the Lord had revealed it to be the product of "false spirits" (D&C 50:2).

Mormon editor W. W. Phelps quickly became the leading voice for the Mormon community in Jackson County by publishing *The Evening and the*

---

19. "Reminiscences of Emily Dow Young Partridge," April 7, 1884, typescript, 9, Perry Special Collections. Her sister, Eliza, expressed discomfort at having to "go through the room occupied by the Negroes" in order to get to her room. The Diary of Eliza Maria Partridge Lyman, 2, MSS 1217, Perry Special Collections.

20. "Extract from Heber C. Kimball's Journal," *Woman's Exponent* 10, no. 2 (June 15, 1881): 9.

21. Reuben Harmon, in *Naked Truths about Mormonism*, 1, no. 2 (April 1888): 201. For a fuller treatment of "Black Pete," see Mark Lyman Staker, *Hearken O Ye People: The Historical Setting of Joseph Smith's Ohio Revelations*, chaps. 1–4, 8.

Morning Star. Bombastic and witty, Phelps never considered his rhetoric particularly offensive nor did he take himself too seriously. Most Saints took Phelps's language in stride. But their Missouri neighbors were less casual.

Missouri had played a central role in the country's debate over slavery since its entrance into the union in 1820. Phelps promoted western Missouri as a land belonging to the American Indians, "the Lamanites." Phelps—and presumably others—dared to embrace Mormonism's anti-slavery impulse publicly. Calling the abolition of slavery a "wonderful event of the age," Phelps exaggerated Mormonism's anti-slavery impulse. When Phelps tried to urge moderation in allowing free blacks to enter Missouri, the locals recoiled at the idea of free blacks coming at all. By summer 1833, it was clear that the Saints had crossed too many lines for the Missourians to countenance.

Pundits freely assailed Phelps and the Saints with racial epithets, with one newspaper editor labeling them as "Black Mormons" whose impulse for race-mixing would incite havoc on the state's racial order.[22] "They have been tampering with our slaves, and endeavoring to sow dissension and raise sedition among them."[23] A Jackson County vigilance committee observed that the Saints had "reached the low condition of the black population" and were taking measures to "drive us to emigrate" through an "indirect invitation to the free brethren of color in Illinois, to come like the rest to the land of Zion."[24] These accusations were serious; the charge of abolitionism was akin to the charge of terrorism. The Missourians accused the Saints of "conniving . . . with the Indians, and stirng [sic] up the negroes to rebel against their masters."[25] Apostle George A. Smith later observed that "when it came to the cool discretion necessarily intrusted to an editor in control of public opinion," Phelps was "deficient." Joseph agreed, laughing that he "would be willing to pay Phelps for editing a paper, provided nobody else should have the privilege of reading it but myself."[26]

Slavery was more symbolic than substantive to the residents of Jackson County; in 1830, the county had only 2,822 residents with but 193 black slaves.[27] Church leaders still warned members to "have nothing to say to the slaves whatever, but to mind our own business."[28] Making matters worse, Phelps spoke freely about Jackson County being "the land of Zion" consecrated for God's kingdom. Phelps longed for the day when this "wilderness and desert" would "become like Eden or

---

22. "Grand Instigators of the New York Riots," *Liberator*, July 26, 1834, 119.

23. Bruce N. Westergren, ed., *John Whitmer: From Historian to Dissident* , 104.

24. "'Regulating the Mormonites," *Niles' Weekly Register* 9, no. 3 (September 14, 1833): 48.

25. Sidney Rigdon, et al., Petition Draft, circa 1838–39, http://josephsmithpapers.org/paperSummary/sidney-rigdon-js-et-al-petition-draft-tothe-publick-circa-1838%E2%80%931839#5 (accessed August 11, 2013).

26. "History of Joseph Smith," *Millennial Star* 21, no. 7 (February 12, 1859): 107.

27. Lyle W. Dorsett, "Slaveholding in Jackson County, Missouri," 26.

28. "The Life and Testimony of Mary E. Lightner," 195.

the garden of the Lord."[29] He wrote a hymn highlighting the apocalyptic vision that the Missouri Saints entertained:

> When Jesus comes in burning flame
> To recompense the just
> The world will know the only name
> In which the Saints can trust.[30]

The "wilderness will soon blossom as a rose," Phelps promised, and "Zion shall arise and put on her beautiful garments and become the joy of the world."[31]

By August 1833, the Saints had been evicted from their homes, left to fend for themselves against the anger of the *vox populi*. Phelps immediately issued an extra edition of the *Evening and the Morning Star* assuring the locals that he actually had wanted to "prevent [blacks] from being admitted as members of the Church."[32] Phelps assured Missourians that the Saints had no interest in inviting blacks to the area: "The introduction of such a cast [sic] among us would corrupt our blacks and instigate them to bloodshed."[33]

But it was too late. The mob destroyed the *Evening and the Morning Star*'s press and forcibly expelled the Saints from Jackson County. The Saints relocated to Clay County, but the reception was lukewarm, at best, even when they moved farther north into Daviess County. When Mormon Samuel Brown attempted to vote in Gallatin, an election worker refused him, snarling that the Mormons had "no more right to vote than the d----d negro."[34] After the Saints' were finally removed from Missouri in 1838, Apostle Parley P. Pratt denounced claims that the Mormons supported racial integration: "The statement concerning our invitation to them to become Mormons, and remove to this state, and settle among us, is a wicked fabrication, as no such thing was ever published . . . by our people."[35] Over twenty years later, Brigham Young could still feel the sting: "When we went to Missouri, the government feared that we would set the Negroes free—a thing that we never thought of—our views are known on that point."[36]

The Saints gleaned many lessons from Jackson County. Not only did they come to recognize the inhospitality of civil society to religious sects making exceptional claims; they also learned that they needed to be cautious about becoming too close to the black community. In summer 1836, Missouri Governor Daniel Dunklin wrote

---

29. "The Elders in the Land of Zion to the Church of Christ Scattered Abroad," *Evening and Morning Star* 1, no. 2 (July 1832): 12.

30. "New Jerusalem," *Evening and the Morning Star* 1, no. 5 (October 1832): 39.

31. "The Gathering," *Evening and the Morning Star* 1, no. 6 (November 1832): 45.

32. W. W. Phelps, Extra of *Evening and the Morning Star*, July 1833.

33. John Whitmer and W. W. Phelps, Letter to Brethren, July 29, 1833.

34. Samuel Brown, Affidavit, September 5, 1838, in Sidney Rigdon, *An Appeal to the American People: Being an Account of the Persecutions of the Church of Latter-day Saints; and the Barbarities Inflicted on Them by the Inhabitants of the State of Missouri*, 17.

35. Pratt, *Late Persecutions of the Church of Jesus Christ*, 11.

36. John Pulsipher, Notebook, February 18, 1855.

Phelps: "Your neighbors accuse your people . . . of being opposed to slavery. You deny. Whether the charge, or the denial, is true, I cannot tell." But "whether true or false," Dunklin continued, "the consequences will be the same . . . unless you can by your conduct and arguments convince them of your innocence."[37] For the remainder of Joseph Smith's life, Joseph was forced to perform an awkward negotiation between his own expansive vision for Zion, the racial prejudices of his own people, and the real consequences that could come from being labeled an abolitionist. His movement had attracted a broad coalition: abolitionists, slave-owners, and the indifferent. And he fielded attacks from all fronts. As a minority religious movement, he feared taking a strong position on the violently divisive topic of race relations.

Indeed, the Saints had endured their share of racial attacks while settling in Missouri. Once the Saints had been expelled from Jackson County, a reporter believed that the impoverished Saints had "reached the low conditions of the black population."[38] The Saints' willingness to harbor antislavery sentiment in Missouri won them, an overwhelmingly white religious group, the epithet of "black Mormons"; the title received so much circulation that it was used to describe some New York City white antislavery activists who dared come to a respectable establishment with blacks alongside them. Surely, a New York paper concluded, the sight was "intended to outrage public taste and feeling."[39] A local paper feared that the Mormons would invite "degraded and corrupted free negroes and mulattos" to be "fit companions" for Missourians's "wives and daughters." Introducing "such a cast [sic]," they feared, would surely "corrupt" their slave population and "instigate them to bloodshed."[40]

Joseph's positions on slavery reflected the immediate pressures he faced. No, "we do not believe in setting the Negroes free," he published in one Church newspaper in 1838.[41] Later, he told Orson Hyde that blacks have souls and should be "put . . . on a national equalization."[42] But on occasion, Joseph also made black men the target of jokes.[43] He annoyed pro-slavery factions while alienating abolitionists. During his ill-fated presidential run of 1844, Joseph Smith called for an end to slavery but still proposed compensating slave owners for their lost property.[44]

---

37. Daniel Dunklin, Letter to W. W. Phelps, July 28, 1836, in "Manuscript History of the Church," A–1, 748.

38. "The Mormonites—Nullfication," *National Gazette* (Philadelphia), August 22, 1833, 3.

39. "Grand Instigators of the New York Riots," *Liberator*, July 26, 1834, 119.

40. "The Outrage in Jackson County," *Evening and the Morning Star* 2, no. 17 (February 1834): 128. For a fuller treatment of racialization rhetoric in 1830s Mormonism, see Russell Stevenson, *Black Mormon: The Story of Elijah Ables,* chap. 2; and T. Ward Frampton, "'Some Savage Tribe': Race, Legal Violence, and the Mormon War of 1838," 175–207.

41. "Answers to Sundry Questions," *Elders' Journal of the Church of Jesus Christ of Latter-day Saints* 1, no. 2 (May 1838): 29.

42. Hedges, Smith, and Anderson, *Journals 2, December 1841–April 1843,* January 2, 1843, 212.

43. Ibid., April 7, 1843, 344.

44. For Joseph Smith's plan to compensate a slave owner "a reasonable equivalent for his property," see Joseph Smith, *General Smith's Views of the Powers and Policy of the Government of the United States,* 11.

Still, Joseph took measures to strengthen his black membership while attempting to avoid being pigeonholed. Joseph ordained Elijah Ables to the priesthood in March 1836, only to applaud black slavery a month later.[45] By December 1836, Ables had been ordained to be a Seventy.[46] In 1838, Joseph directed Elijah to serve a mission to Upper Canada, which had become the largest colony of runaway slaves in North America. After the mission, Ables's missionary associates tried to indict him for a number of spurious charges ranging from the petty to the outrageous. Joseph listened patiently and then ignored the complaint.[47] In April 1841, Ables was issued a new certificate attesting to his status as a Seventy.[48]

Black women joined the Saints as well. As Connell O'Donovan has discovered, missionary Stephen Post baptized the wife of Samuel Francis, a free black living in upstate New York. This unnamed wife was the first recorded black woman who joined Mormonism.[49] In April 1842, John D. Lee baptized Mark Young as well as "Milla and Cynthia" whom he identified as "two servants" that belong to Young. They both likely stepped away from the Mormon community when Young returned to Methodism the following month.[50]

In Connecticut, Jane Manning joined the faith and led a family of free blacks nearly a thousand miles to Nauvoo in order to join the main body of the Saints. When Joseph Smith welcomed them, their feet bloodied from the trek, he expressed amazement: "Is this not faith?" he exclaimed, as he looked at her tattered band.[51] Joseph and his wife, Emma, forged such a strong bond with Jane that they offered to seal them to her as an adopted daughter. While she initially refused, Jane never forgot the promise.

Confidants such as associates Orson Hyde and Zebedee Coltrin expressed alarm; had Joseph forgotten the lessons of Missouri?[52] Hyde warned Joseph that pro-black racial policies could lead to the decline of the white race. Joseph scoffed: The

---

45. Joseph Smith, Letter to Oliver Cowdery, in *Messenger and Advocate* 2, no. 7 (April 1836): 229–31.

46. Roll, First Council of the Seventy, December 27, 1836, CR 3 123, LDS Church History Library.

47. Meeting Minutes, June 1, 1839, quoted in Lester E. Bush, "Mormonism's Negro Doctrine," 52.

48. Elijah Abel Priesthood Certificate, April 4, 1841.

49. Stephen Post, Journal, September 23, 1836, LDS Church History Library. Many thanks to Connell O'Donovan for directing scholars to this journal entry.

50. John D. Lee, Journal, April 12, 1842, MS 2092, LDS Church History Library. O'Donovan also has been kind enough to make this information available on his blog post, "Three Newly Discovered Early Black Mormon Women," http://rationalfaiths.com/three-newly-discovered-early-black-mormon-women (accessed February 11, 2014).

51. Jane Manning James, Autobiography, 1893, transcribed by Elizabeth Roundy, 17, LDS Church History Library.

52. Later in life, Zebedee Coltrin recalls resisting Joseph Smith's directive to administer ritual washings and anointing to Elijah Ables; he complied only because he had been "commanded by the Prophet to do so" and told himself that he would "never again Anoint another person who had Negro blood in him." Coltrin qtd. in L. John Nuttall, Diary, May 31, 1879, typescript, Perry Special Collections.

"slaves in Washington [are] more refined than the presidents." Shocked at Joseph's position, Hyde emphasized what a black-friendly policy would mean: "They will rise above me." Joseph agreed, but, doubtless to Hyde's dismay, expressed sympathy with aspiring blacks rather than status-conscious whites: "If I . . . attempted to oppress you, would you not be indignant, & try to rise above me?"[53]

Soured by the mob violence of Missouri, Joseph had no tolerance for men seeking to inflict vigilante justice on Nauvoo's black population. In the weeks preceding the assassinations of Joseph and Hyrum Smith, a free black named Chism was accused of stealing approximately $1,500 dollars. A "lawless banditti, under the pretence of a legal process" kidnapped him and "hurried out some distance into the woods, where he was tied, stripped, and most inhumanely beaten." One of the assailants was arrested but "for want of evidence . . . he was fined but five dollars and the [court] cost." Outraged, Joseph "stated that he believed that it was a plot . . . [to] screen the prisoner from the condemnation he justly deserves." "Lynch law," Joseph declared, "will not do in Nauvoo." It was no coincidence, Apostle John Taylor editorialized, that the assailant "hails from Missouri."[54] A week later, Taylor lauded the Saints' willingness to "stand up in defence of the oppressed, of whatever country, nation, color, or clime . . . no matter whether it was an Indian, a negro or any other man."[55] Joseph drew the line at black-and-white intermarriage,[56] but Joseph held firm in his commitment to protect the rights of Nauvoo's black residents—even if they numbered but twenty.[57]

Race relations had always taken a back seat in the Mormon community; even Joseph Smith was willing to distance himself from the extremities of contemporary abolitionism. But his commitment to qualified racial inclusion checked the influence of hardliners Orson Hyde and Zebedee Coltrin. The strength of his will and personality compelled them to hold their peace, in spite of their disgust.

53. Hedges, Smith, and Anderson , *Journals 2, December 1841–April 1843*, January 2, 1843, 212.

54. "Robbery and Lynching," *Nauvoo Neighbor*, 1, no. 4 (April 3, 1844): 2.

55. "Conference Minutes," *Times and Seasons* 5, no. 13 (July 15, 1844): 1.

56. Scott H. Faulring, ed., *An American Prophet's Record: The Diaries and Journals of Joseph Smith*, February 8, 1844, 445.

57. Newell G. Bringhurst, *Saints, Slaves, and Blacks: The Changing Place of Blacks within Mormonism*, 222.

Chapter 2

Cursed, 1845–90

Its nothing to do with the blood for of one blood has God made all flesh.
—Brigham Young, March 26, 1847

If no other Prophet ever spake it Before I will say it now in the name of Jesus Christ. I know it is true & they know it. The Negro cannot hold one particle of Government
—Brigham Young, January–February 1852

In June 1844, Joseph Smith was murdered in Carthage Jail. In his absence, the Mormon community lay vulnerable to the ghosts of racism then brooding in the land. Facing possible dissolution seemed to solidify the Mormons' racial identity. The time for racial experimentation was over. However longsuffering the Saints felt Joseph Smith to be toward the black community, they had no more patience for such things. Now seeing Nauvoo, Illinois—even America—as a tinderbox set to explode in the light of a looming millennial day, the Saints closed ranks. "We will leave this wicked nation to themselves," Brigham Young told a gathering of Saints at the Nauvoo temple, "for they have rejected the gospel, and I hope and pray that the wicked will kill one another and save us the trouble of doing it."[1] Though the Saints reacted with relative calm to the murder of their Prophet, their memory of him stewed, firing a hope for vengeance. In June 1845, Willard Richards and others gathered to pray "that God would avenge the murders of Joseph & Hyrum."[2]

After his death, a battle over succession threatened to tear apart the Church. Several men jockeyed for position. Between Joseph Smith's first counselor, Sidney Rigdon, the lawyer-visionary James Strang, and Brigham Young, president of Joseph Smith's Quorum of the Twelve, there appeared little hope of reconciliation. Elijah Ables, now a member of the First Quorum of the Seventy living in Cincinnati, cast his lot with Brigham Young and carried out his duties aggres-

---

1. George D. Smith, *An Intimate Chronicle: The Journals of William Clayton*, 251.

2. Willard Richards, Journal, June 27, 1845, Willard Richards Papers, holograph in Richard E. Turley, *Selected Collections from the Archives of the Church of Jesus Christ of Latter-day Saints*, 1:31 (hereafter cited as *Selected Collections*).

sively. He routed out dissent in the struggling branch and called for the excommunication of troublemakers and dissidents.[3]

In April 1845, Orson Hyde attacked Sidney Rigdon's claims to authority by charging that those who remained undecided between Brigham Young and Rigdon resembled premortal spirits whose wavering assured them birth into black bodies in mortality: "Those spirits in heaven that lent an influence to the devil, thinking he had a little the best right to govern, but did not take a very active part any way, were required to come into the world and take bodies in the accursed lineage of Canaan; and hence the Negro or African race."[4] Even as prospective leaders appealed to the Prophet's name, they left behind Joseph Smith's racial innovations in the blood spattered on the floors of the Prophet's Carthage jail cell.

The small population of black Mormons needed to navigate their way as a minority in a predominantly white church, itself on the brink of falling apart. In T. H. Breen's and Stephen Innes's book on blacks in seventeenth-century Virginia, they argue that colonial blacks adopted a "transactional" approach to interacting with the white population. Free blacks achieved a degree of social mobility by acknowledging whites' rules and power structures. Like the blacks in white northern Virginia, black Mormons also felt impelled to follow the cues of the white Mormon power structure to achieve financial independence. Quincy Newell also highlights the fluidity of religious expression when she argues that Jane Manning's religious identity demonstrates the "variety of religious options available to black people" in ante- and postbellum America.[5] Ronald Coleman concludes that the black Saints who achieved respectability within the Mormon communities benefited from the "paternalism that governed interactions between Euro-Americans and African Americans" in American society more broadly.[6] Indeed, in Lowell, Massachusetts, Mormonism produced two notable black Mormon leaders: Q. Walker Lewis and Joseph T. Ball. Church leaders questioned Ball's legitimacy and morality, but Lewis won the respect of all as an "example for his more whiter brethren to follow."[7]

---

3. Conference Minutes, June 1, 1845, *Times and Seasons* 6, no. 10 (June 1, 1845): 915. For other evidence of the Cincinnati excommunications, see John Crippin, Letter to Brigham Young, March 14, 1845, Reel 29, Brigham Young Office Files, LDS Church History Library. Correspondence to and from Brigham Young, unless otherwise noted, is from this collection.

4. Orson Hyde, *Speech of Elder Orson Hyde, Delivered before the High Priests Quorum of Nauvoo, April 27th, 1845, upon the Course and Conduct of Mr. Sidney Rigdon and upon His Merits to His Claim to the Presidency of the Church of Jesus Christ of Latter-day Saints*, 30.

5. Quincy Newell, ed., "The Autobiography and Interview of Jane Manning James," 251.

6. Ronald Coleman, "'Is There No Blessing for Me?' Jane Elizabeth Manning James, a Mormon African American Woman," 155.

7. For Wilford Woodruff's concerns regarding Ball, see Wilford Woodruff, Letter to Brigham Young, November 16, 1844, Young Office Files, Reel 56. For Lewis, see William Appleby, Journal, May 19, 1847, LDS Church History Library.

Young also felt the sting of Missouri; however, his loyalty to Joseph Smith ruled all. Only months before the McCary episode, Young received a vision from Joseph Smith, a vision including directives on how to provide guidance to the Saints in the wilderness. "I took him by the right hand," Brigham Young recorded, "and kist him many times." Brigham felt insecure about his ability to lead the Saints: "Brother Joseph," he said, "you know well better than I due you rased them up and brought the Priesthood to us."[8] Three months later, Brigham Young brooded over his failings as a leader, confiding in his colleagues: "I feel my weakness, my bitterness. I hurt in the Almighty. I shall yet be a Mormon."[9] While the better part of the Nauvoo Saints had sustained his leadership, no one labored under any pretenses that Young commanded the same stature as Joseph Smith.

Yet this same insecurity also left Brigham Young poorly positioned to lead the Saints. As they prepared to travel west, the Saints resisted obedience to his directions. In May 1846, Brigham Young tried to order the Saints to start going West immediately; a "part voted in favor, and a part did not vote either way." Brigham Young insisted that "the time had come when I should command them what to do" and that he would give them "a slap of revelation" to make them move.[10] Frustrated, he tried to convince them that he would not be as longsuffering as Joseph Smith. While Joseph was "a merciful man [who] bore with these things untill it took his life," he (Brigham) would "not do it." Brigham Young knew that he had not yet won control of his Saints.[11]

The troubled relationship Brigham Young had with the Saints had ramifications for the future of race relations in the Mormon community. In 1846 Orson Hyde baptized and ordained an African American, William McCary, and performed his marriage to Daniel Stanton's daughter, Lucy. Identifying himself as an "Indian Prophet," McCary followed the Saints to Winter Quarters. When McCary called for a meeting of Church leaders to determine his lineage, Young responded warmly: "Its nothing to do with the blood for of one blood has God made all flesh." Brigham drew on the example of Walker Lewis to defend racial inclusion: "We [have] one of the best Elders an African in Lowell."[12] McCary left the meeting contented with this ruling and a little richer; Brigham Young and other apostles had donated $12.50 to help him and Lucy get on their feet.

The good feelings did not last long. After Young left Winter Quarters in early April, McCary began to practice polygamy with several white women in the settlements. The Saints ran the McCarys out of town in a fit of racial outrage.[13]

---

8. Vision of Brigham Young, February 17, 1847, Young Office Files, Reel 87.

9. General Church Meeting Minutes, May 23, 1847, Box 1, fd. 53, in Turley, *Selected Collections,* 1:18

10. Brigham Young quoted in John Turner, *Brigham Young: Pioneer Prophet,* 146.

11. Ibid., 162.

12. General Church Meeting Minutes, March 26, 1847, Box 1, fd. 52, in Turley, *Selected Collections,* 1:18.

13. Nelson Whipple, "History of Nelson Whipple," 70–72.

The McCarys assumed the Indian names of Warner/Okah Tubbee and Laah Ceil, calling themselves members of Choctaw royalty. McCary performed "on the fife, flute, and other musical instruments" for audiences throughout the region. Observers glamorized McCary's talents; he could reportedly "play on over *one hundred* different musical instruments, (!) and is a master of *seventeen* (!) languages."[14] However, in 1851, the same newspaper identified "the celebrated Indian chief, 'Okah Tubbee,' as "none other than Carey, a negro, or rather mulatto."[15]

McCary's philandering rocked the Winter Quarters community. Orson Hyde was livid; after all, McCary seemed to prove what most Saints already suspected about black people. The Saints who had listened to McCary were not merely dim-witted but depraved. If they wanted to apostatize, they might have at least followed Strang, whom Hyde considered to be an "honorable imposter" when compared to McCary.[16]

An enraged Parley P. Pratt, who remained in Winter Quarters while Young led the vanguard company west in April 1847, delivered the first on-the-record statements connecting black skin color to priesthood exclusion. Pratt castigated the Saints for following a "black man who has got the blood of Ham in him which lineage was cursed as regards the priesthood."[17] Dissident William Smith delighted in McCary's antics, which provided a perfect excuse for Smith to mock the Twelve. Smith's newspaper snarled that blacks "belong[ed] to that class of spiritual beings that transgressed in heaven and became devils."[18]

In the fall of 1847, Brigham Young returned to Winter Quarters. The McCary incident struck a chord and triggered his impulse toward violent rhetoric. Making matters worse, a messenger came to his camp to inform him that Walker Lewis's son had married a white woman. Young exclaimed in disgust: "They wd. av [sic] to be killed." Interracial marriage was a crime against the human race that would lead to humankind's ultimate demise: "Mulattos r [sic] like mules" and "can't have children," he asserted. But in a striking moment of circumspection, Young backpedaled; could any priesthood leader deny "a black man & white woman" if they "come to you and demand baptism?" Moments after calling for their death,

14. "Dr. Okah Tubbee, Chief of the Choctaws," 1; emphasis in original.

15. Ibid.; see also "The Celebrated Indian Chief," *Alexandria Gazette*, July 10, 1851, 1; "Okah Tubbee," *Telescope* (Manchester, N.H.), January 20, 1849; "At a recent Temperance meeting," *Illinois Weekly Journal*, November 22, 1848, 3; "Tremont Temple Hall," *Boston Evening Transcript*, November 16, 1848, 3. McCary also made public appearances before civic societies; in Boston, he appeared before a temperance society, declaring that temperance had saved his tribe "at least *six hundred thousand dollars*, which they had appropriated for educational purposes." "Correspondence of Albany Argus," *Sun* [Pittsfield, Mass.], November 7, 1848, 3. For a biography by Lucy McCary, see Laah Tubbee, *A Sketch of the Life of Okah Tubbee*.

16. Orson Hyde, Speech, May 30, 1847, in Selected Collections, DVD 18.

17. General Church Minutes, April 25, 1847, Box 1, fd. 53, in *Selected Collections*, 1:18.

18. William Smith, "Judas Iscariot's Lineage," *Melchisedek and Aaronic Herald*, 1, no. 8 (February 1850): 2.

he conceded that an interracial couple "may have a place in the Temple" if they promised to be "eunuchs for the Kingdom of Heaven's sake."[19]

Unlike many of his associates, Brigham Young experienced a radical transition in his views toward blacks. Orson Hyde and Parley P. Pratt had both expressed longstanding resentment against the black community. Hyde had tried to convince Joseph Smith to be more careful about his support for blacks in Nauvoo. Pratt had attempted to distance the Saints from the black community after the Missouri crucible. Embittered by years of racial epithets, the Saints had grown to see "blackness" as a ghost from their past that could threaten their very lives.

The act of moving to Utah created the space for the solidification of a white Mormon identity. Wilford Woodruff recalls taking a bath in the Salt Lake for the first time; "one of our number was a negro," he wrote, "and when he came out and the salt water had dried upon him he was almost white." Joseph Smith's old New York friend, Porter Rockwell, joked that the "sudden change in the negro's color was the first miracle that had been performed in this part of the country."[20] By spring 1849, Young began drawing a firm line, making his first comments explicitly denying priesthood ordination and temple blessings to those he considered to be tainted with the blood of Cain.[21] These comments formed the theological foundations for the LDS Church's race-based restriction ban for nearly 130 years.

As Governor Young and the Utah Territorial Legislature crafted their first draft of a proposed state constitution—one Young called a shrewdly written "clever" document[22]—it had become apparent that achieving statehood would require the support of southern senators.

Furthermore, several southern converts brought their slaves with them, forcing Young and the legislature to render a decision. In 1849, Brigham Young indicated that he "wish[ed] not to meddle with this subject but leave things to their natural course."[23] He advised the Saints' Congressional delegate, John Bernhisel, that the Utah Territory would embrace slavery, but only if necessary for "the good of the General Government."[24]

National politics were such that open alliances could mean political suicide and even bodily harm. During one session, in March 1850, Bernhisel saw slavery provoke "noise and confusion [that] beggars all discription [sic]." Congressmen delivered 'very inflammatorry speeches" and "threats were freely made by Southern members of disolving [sic] the union." Bernhisel watched as Virginia Representative Richard K. Meade "rushed toward [New York Representative

---

19. General Church Minutes, December 2, 1847, Box 1, fd. 59, in Turley, *Selected Collections,* 1:18.

20. Matthias Cowley, ed., *Wilford Woodruff: History of His Life and Labors as Recorded in His Daily Journals,* 620.

21. General Church Minutes, February 13, 1849, Box 2, fd. 8, in Turley, *Selected Collections,* 1:18.

22. John Pulsipher Notebook, February 15, 1849, LDS Church History Library.

23. Brigham Young, Letter to Orson Hyde, July 19, 1849, Box 16, fd. 17, Young Office Files.

24. Brigham Young, Letter to John Bernhisel, October 14, 1849 Box 16, fd. 18, Young Office Files.

William] Duer." Other Congressmen intervened, preventing a fistfight from occurring on the House floor.

So Bernhisel hedged. Utah must be seen as a free territory, if its petition for statehood could make it past the judging eyes of antislavery Northerners. In September, Bernhisel rejoiced that the federal government had finally granted Utah's petition for a territorial government, but their decision was based on a deception: "Had it been believed that slavery existed or would ever be tolerated, our bill never would have passed the House."[25] He urged Brigham Young to wipe Utah clean from any outward signs of slavery: "I beg leave respectfully," he pleaded, "to suggest that no person of African descent be reported as a slave" on the 1850 census.[26] At this stage, slavery had to remain Utah's secret. Since Bernhisel's arrival in Washington he had "made it a point… not to make slavery nor politics a point."[27] Brigham Young and other Church leaders never saw themselves as supporters of slavery, even if they felt blacks should fill subservient societal roles.

With a growing population of Southern slaveholders in the territory, a decision needed to be made concerning the status of the slave population. In 1849, Young instructed Territorial Representative John M. Bernhisel that the Saints were "naturally averse" to slave systems, but they were not "strenuous upon this question."[28] Now officially a U.S. territory, the Saints craved the autonomy that statehood would grant them. They needed friends. The 1850 California compromise allowed Utah to enter the Union and decide its own position on slavery. The Mormons had never been fond of slavery, and Utah soil was ill equipped for a slave economy. In the fall of 1851, the *Deseret News* reprinted Joseph Smith's presidential platform, which included a plan for the abolition of slavery.[29] Still, Young viciously opposed any efforts to force Utah's position: "It is none of their damned business what we do or say here. What we do it is for them to sanction, and then for us to say what we like about it."[30]

In 1852, George A. Smith presented a bill before the Utah Territorial Legislature legalizing bonded "service" in the territory. Young and the legislators saw such servitude as honorable and benevolent. Several legislators had personal and family connections to slave owners or southern interests, even if they hailed from Northern states.[31] While they found the slave states' political power tyrannical and inflated, they did not question the place of blacks in American society.

---

25. John M. Bernhisel, Letter to Brigham Young, September 12, 1850, Reel 70, Young Office Files.

26. John M. Bernhisel, Letter to Brigham Young, July 3, 1850, Reel 70, Young Office Files.

27. John M. Bernhisel, Letter to Brigham Young, March 21, 1850, Reel 70, Young Office Files.

28. Brigham Young, Letter to John Bernhisel, October 14, 1849, Box 16, fd. 18, Young Office Files.

29. Joseph Smith, "Views of the Powers and Policy of the Government of the United States," reprinted in *Deseret News*, August 19, 1851, 2, 8.

30. Brigham Young, January 5, 1852, in Richard Van Wagoner, ed., *The Collected Discourses of Brigham Young*, 1:471.

31. Nathaniel Ricks, "A Peculiar Place for a Peculiar Institution: Slavery and Sovereignty in Early Territorial Utah," 100–102.

Young exhorted the Saints not to "abuse the Negro & treat him Cruel." Southern slavery was barbaric and wasteful, he argued: if southern states "abolish[ed] slavery and institute[d] free labor . . . they would be much richer than they are." But the social strata were firm: "The Negro Should serve the seed of Abram."[32] The "Act in Relation to Service" passed with limited debate.[33] In 1854, Parley P. Pratt blasted American society for its "treatment of the Mormons, the Indians, and the negroes."[34] But if admission to the Union required embracing slavery, it was a price Young and the Legislature were willing to pay.[35]

Young endorsed the new law with enthusiasm and then began spelling out the theological ramifications: "If there never was a prophet or apostle of Jesus Christ [that] spoke it before, I tell you, this people that are commonly called Negroes are children of Cain." And he knew "that they cannot bear rule in the Priesthood, for the curse on them was to remain upon them until the residue of the posterity of Michael and his wife" received the priesthood blessings."[36] Neither could "the Africans . . . hold one particle of power in government."[37] Wilford Woodruff recorded that only "one drop" of African blood would disqualify a man from receiving priesthood blessings, a comment that would later serve as the defining aspect of Young's racial theology.[38]

Young expressed even less tolerance for interracial sexuality, a threat that could undermine the strength of the Mormon experiment. If Mormons engaged in sexual relationships with Africans during their "unguarded moment[s], the Church "must go to destruction," and they would "receive the curse which has been placed upon the seed of Cain, and never more be numbered with the children of Adam who are heirs to the priesthood until that curse be removed."[39] So grave were the ramifications of interracial sexuality that he cast it as a matter of life and death, a crime worthy of execution. If a guilty party "would walk up and say cut off my head, and kill man, woman and child it would do a great deal towards atoning for the sin. Would this be to curse them? No, it would be a blessing to them; it would do them good that they might be saved with their brethren. A man would shudder should hear us talk about killing folk, but it is one of the greatest blessings to some to kill them, although the true principles of it are not understood."[40]

---

32. Scott G. Kenney, ed., *Wilford Woodruff's Journal, 1833–1898*, January–February 1852, 4:97–99.

33. For a thorough discussion of the passage of the 1852 act, see Ricks, "A Peculiar Place for a Peculiar Institution," chap. 3.

34. Terryl L. Givens and Matthew J. Grow, *Parley P. Pratt: The Apostle Paul of Mormonism*, 356.

35. For Young's willingness to negotiate on slavery, see Brigham Young, Letter to Orson Hyde, July 19, 1849, Young Office Files, Box 16, fd. 17; and Brigham Young, Letter to John Bernhisel, October 14, 1849, Box 16, fd. 18, both in Young Office Files.

36. Young, January 5, 1852, 1:471.

37. Ibid.

38. Kenney, *Wilford Woodruff's Journal,* January–February 1852, 4:97.

39. Young, January 5, 1852, 1:470.

40. Ibid., 1:468–69.

In spite of Young's violent rhetoric, one observer considered Young's speech to be antagonistic to slavery, noting "the Governor remarked to the Assembly that he was opposed to the system of slavery" and that "its cruelties and abuses were obnoxious to humanity."[41] Young did not insist that execution be included in the proviso that illegalized interracial sexuality, contrary to the speech given to the territorial legislature. In fact, some Saints—particularly those from the British Isles—opposed slavery more vigorously. While Brigham Young was protecting slavery in Utah, the British Empire had abolished slavery nearly two decades earlier. As British stonemason James Moyle traveled through the Louisiana bayous en route from Liverpool to Salt Lake City, he saw the slave markets: "It was revolting to my feelings to think of the men women and children that we saw there, where [were] going to be sold like cattle or horses." Even if they "had a black skin yet they where [were] human beings." Moyle often felt more comfortable "hav[ing]a good chat with the negroes at the Quarter" than when faced with the "tall, fine looking" Southern gentleman who "looked so clean with his white clothes and straw hat so different from my clothes which was for a cooler climate."[42]

Young appeared to recognize that his views were hardly normative: "I may vary in my view from others, and they may think I am foolish in the things I have spoken and think that they know more than I do, but I know [that] I know more than they do."[43] Though his public hostility to federal authority, Young could not pretend that these were anything other than perilous waters. Hoping to keep slavery both "safe, rare, and legal," Young considered himself to be pragmatic, reasonable, and humane; "averse" though the Saints might have been, only the occasional voice dared--or cared--to attack it. Cognizant of the delicacy of the political act he faced, Young adjusted his posture as circumstances dictated. And the sheer absence of slaves—the 1850 census identifies only 26—enabled the Saints to accept slavery without facing it directly. [44]

Mormons previously opposed to slavery became more open to its presence in the Utah Territory. As a young man, W. W. Phelps had made a crusade out of attacking slavery and had almost singlehandedly inflamed the Missourians to violence by trumpeting the Mormons' anti-slavery credentials. In Utah, Phelps extolled the territory as a land where "the Jehovah smitten Canaanite [would] bow in humble submission to his superiors, and prepare himself for a mansion of glory when the black curse of disobedience shall have been chased from his skin by a glance from the Lord."[45]

---

41. William L. Knecht and Peter L. Crawley, eds., *History of Brigham Young*, 113.
42. James H. Moyle, "Reminiscences, 1886," n.p., LDS Church History Library.
43. Young, January 5, 1852, 1:471.
44. Randall M. Miller and John David Smith, Dictionary of Afro-American Slavery, 506.
45. "The Celebration of the Twenty-Fourth of July," *Deseret News*, July 26, 1851, 1.

Brigham Young defended slavery in Utah by pointing out its distinctiveness from the slavery of Southern plantations: "It is essentially purchasing them into freedom, instead of slavery. . . . [Here] they could find that consideration pertaining not only to civilized but humane and benevolent society." Utah slavery would be a form of emancipation: "a people will be released from servile bondage both mental and physical, and placed upon a platform upon which they can build; and extend forth as far as their capability and natural rights will permit." While they would "inevitably carry the curse which was placed upon them," they were part of a long and illustrious heritage: "Service is honorable; it exists in all countries, and has existed for ages; it probably will exist in some form in all time to come."[46] Mormon poetess Eliza R. Snow agreed:

> Japhet shall dwell within the tents of Shem
> And Ham shall be his servant; long ago
> The prophet said: "'Tis' being now fulfill'd
> The curse of the Almighty rests upon
> The colored race; In his own time, by his
> Own means, not yours that curse will be remov'd.[47]

In 1853, Orson Pratt expanded on Orson Hyde's earlier formulation concerning blacks' preexistent state, giving Mormonism its first arguments suggesting that the race-based priesthood ban had been implemented due to premortal unworthiness; "Some spirits take bodies in the lienage [sic] of the chosen seed through whom the Priesthood is transferred, others receive bodies among the African negroes, or in the lineage of Canaan, whose descendants were cursed, pertaining to the priesthood."[48] Blacks had little choice but to act out their social role as servants to Utah's white population. Brigham Young hoped that white slave owners would "reach over them and round about them and treat them as kindly, and with that human feeling necessary to be shown to mortal beings of the human species," drawing on their labors "as they would their own children."[49]

Slavery never would be a central aspect of Utah life; in 1860, there were approximately two hundred black slaves living in the territory. While their experience in territorial Utah did not mirror the brutality or scope of Southern plantations, it revealed the contradictions the Saints experienced in negotiating their religion with a once-foreign slave system. Brought to the territory by Southern Mormon slaveowners such as John Crosby and John Holladay, black slaves were forced to reckon with their new life in a white Zion.[50] In 1861, Brigham Young

---

46. Governor's Message, *Deseret News*, January 10, 1852, 2.

47. Eliza R. Snow, "The New Year, 1852," in Jill Mulvay Derr and Karen Lynn Davidson, eds., *Eliza R. Snow: The Complete Poetry*, 420–21.

48. Orson Pratt, "The Pre-Existence," 56.

49. Young, January 5, 1852, 1:470.

50. William E. Parrish, "The Mississippi Saints," 489–506.

considered purchasing Jerry Smoot in order to grant him his freedom.[51] The slave was later sold to Abraham Smoot and died in 1861.[52]

Slaveholding Saints often exerted the same kinds of coercion over their slaves that marked slavery in the South. In 1850, some slaveholding Saints planned to travel to San Bernardino, California, to reap the rewards of the California gold rush. California had been admitted to the Union as a free state, thus endangering the status of the Saints' slave property. William Crosby accused a Utah "servant," Green Flake, of being "disafected [and] saucy" to Agnes Flake, his late master's wife who had traveled to California. Crosby urged Young to prevent Flake from leaving the territory, even appealing to Young's known-hatred of interracial unions: "[Flake] would leave his Black wife and git him a white woman" the moment he set foot in California.[53]

Though the number of slaves in the territory was small, anxiety about racial status troubled some of Utah's white population. The same year as Young's proposed slave purchase, a Payson man nervously wrote Young to inquire about the implications of his own racial background. He had African ancestry and wanted to know how far "any legal seed could mix with the Canaanite & then clame [sic] an heirship to the Priesthood." He had spoken with "three different bishop[s] for an answer & they told me they were not able to answer such a question."[54] In the *Deseret News,* a columnist warned young white women to avoid wearing their hair curly; it would "make people believe you have negro blood in your veins."[55]

Following the Civil War, the Utah Territory was the first territory to ratify, albeit symbolically, the thirteenth, fourteenth, and fifteenth amendments.[56] Years later, freed slave Marinda Bankhead recalled "the joyful expressions which were upon the faces of all the slaves, when they ascertained that they had acquired their freedom through the fortunes of war."[57] The completion of the transcontinental railroad brought a new class of blacks into the territory. Newly emancipated blacks came to the Territory to work with the railroad and escape the horrors of the postbellum South. But when black laborer Thomas Coburn allegedly flirted with a white woman, he was found murdered a few days later with a note warning all blacks to avoid white women.[58] When a reporter asked Brigham Young about the status of blacks in the territory, he said the Saints "consider and treat them as what

---

51. Brigham Young, Letter to Mrs. Lewis, January 3, 1860.
52. Donna T. Smart, ed., *Mormon Midwife: The 1846–1888 Diaries of Patty Bartlett Sessions,* 286.
53. Turner, *Brigham Young,* 224.
54. N. B. Johnson, Letter to Brigham Young, January 1, 1861.
55. "Girls Who Want Husbands," *Deseret News,* April 18, 1855, 5.
56. Thomas L. Kane, Letter to Brigham Young, October 13, 1869; Brigham Young, Letter to Thomas L. Kane, October 26, 1869.
57. "Slavery in Utah," *Broad Ax,* March 25, 1899, 1.
58. "The Killing of Thos. Coleman Monday Night," *Union Vedette,* December 15, 1866, 2.

they are, the sons of Cain."[59] What had once been an opportunistic response to win the support of the southern states and even the Winter Quarters Saints had metastasized into hard-boiled racial prejudice.

Meanwhile, while the first Mormon missionaries set foot in British South Africa in 1853, their efforts represented the hope to cull the faithful from the Commonwealth. From the English, Joseph once declared, "many hundreds have of late been added to our numbers; but so, even so, it must be" for "the Savior he hath said 'My sheep hear my voice.' In the late 1830s, Dutch immigrants in South Africa had moved inland to distance themselves from British efforts to abolish slavery throughout the empire. Deeply religious, the Dutch accused the British of trampling on the laws of God. Dutch immigrant Anna Steenkamp declared that the Dutch were rebelling against the slaves "being placed on an equal footing with Christians, contrary to the laws of God and the natural distinctions of race and religion.[60] By the end of the century, the Dutch successfully terminated British rule over the region and transformed it into a Dutch colonial state controlled by the Dutch settlers, now called "Afrikaaners"—and to be so for the next 90 years.

In South Africa, Mormonism entered a world of sharpening divides between the British, the Dutch, and the black population. South Africa's black population suffered under the country's new pharaohs. The American Mormons saw South Africa's race relations as indicative of an apocalypse looming on the horizon. One missionary in South Africa prophesied that "in a few short years . . . God will stir up the Kaffirs and make them the instruments of his anger."[61] By the end of the century, the *Telegraph* noted that "the people at the Cape [in South Africa] are troubled with a few fanatics who have introduced Mormonism into Africa." It "suppose[d] that the new men are Americans or English" since the editors "cannot understand how the polygamy of natives could . . . offend Europeans."[62]

The Saints' racial assumptions extended across the Atlantic as well. During the first mission to South Africa, Jesse Haven projected the racial notions then gaining traction among the Saints. He approved of "the Kaffirs hav[ing] a plurality of wives," since it ensured that "there is more virtue among the sexes, with them, than there is among the whites." But he dismissed other Christians' efforts to proselytize them as, at best, futile and, at worst, harmful: "They [the missionaries] have succeeded in introducing among them some of the licentious customs of our refined cities." Ultimately, the black tribes "have too much of the blood of

---

59. "A Talk with Brigham Young," *Charleston Courier*, August 9, 1869, 4.

60. Joseph Smith, Letter to Isaac Galland, September 11, 1839; John W. De Gruchy, The Church Struggle in South Africa, 18.

61. "Correspondence," *Millennial Star* 26 (December 10, 1864): 797.

62. "Mormonism in South Africa," *Millennial Star* 32, no. 42 (October 18, 1870): 668–69.

Elijah Ables, ca. 1860s, was ordained to the Melchizedek Priesthood in March 1836; his ordination was authorized by Joseph Smith. Courtesy LDS Church History Library.

Cain in them, for the Gospel to have much effect on their dark spirits."[63] But this did not prevent him from baptizing a handful of "colored women" and "administer[ing] to a colored girl" who was "troubled with a lameness." In September 1854, one "colored" convert "wanted her name taken off "the records; she "thought her daughter would want hers taken off likewise."[64]

Both Brigham Young and Ables's wife, Mary Ann, died in 1877, allowing black Saints in Utah a glimmer of hope that Young's successors would have more moderate views on race. Ables's family had largely left him abandoned as a renter in the house of the Salt Lake City dog-catcher.[65] In 1879, he approached the Church leadership, petitioning them for his endowment. Young had denied him in 1853, and Ables, now in his late sixties, felt it was time to revisit the issue. This request forced Church leaders to grapple directly with the status they had taken for granted. Brigham Young's successor, John Taylor, treated Elijah Ables as a stranger, though he had been known and treated with affection by Joseph Smith.

Taylor launched an investigation and traveled to Provo to discuss the matter with Zebedee Coltrin and Abraham Smoot, two former confidantes of Joseph Smith. Both claimed to have had conversations with the Prophet about the place of blacks in the Church. Coltrin informed Taylor that Joseph Smith revoked the priesthood from Ables. "Brother Joseph kind of dropped his head and rested it on his hand for a minute," Coltrin remembered, "and then said, 'Brother Zebedee is right, for the Spirit of the Lord saith the Negro has no right to the Priesthood.'" Taylor returned to Ables with his decision: he could not receive his endowment. Ables protested, declaring that he had two priesthood certificates authorized by well-known Church leaders. Joseph F. Smith also acknowledged that Ables had been a "stalwart" member for decades. Troubled by the 1879 Supreme Court de-

---

63. Jesse Haven, Letter to Franklin D. Richards, May 13, 1856, *Millennial Star* 18, no. 23 (June 7, 1856): 367.

64. Jesse Haven Diaries, August 2, 1853, March 19, 1854, September 15, 1854, LDS Church History Library.

65. Russell Stevenson, *Black Mormon: The Story of Elijah Ables,* 64.

cision directed against the Mormon practice of polygamy, Church leaders spent little time on Ables's claims before dismissing them. President John Taylor finally concluded that Ables must have "been ordained before the word of the Lord was fully understood."[66]

Not only had Young and Taylor denied Ables his endowment blessings, but the shift marked an increased hardening of explanations for the priesthood ban. The idea that the black skin was a sign of premortal unworthiness dated back to Orson Hyde's 1845 comments; however, by the late 1860s, Church leaders had still not generally sought to explain the priesthood ban using this same logic.

Mormon doctrine on the premortal life generally held that spirits had choosen sides between God's plan of free agency and Lucifer's plan of coerced righteousness well before they were born—indeed, well before the earth's creation. In 1870, Godbeite John S. Lindsay of the *Salt Lake Tribune*—also a noted actor at the Salt Lake Theater—produced a polemic piece attacking the growing tendency to associate black skin with premortal unworthiness. Lindsay argued that the Mormon "belief in the origin of the black race is so closely interwoven with the doctrine of the pre-existence of man as a spirit that, in examining one theory, touching upon the other will be to some degree unavoidable." By the *Salt Lake Tribune's* account, Mormon folk theology held that blacks had been "*a-straddle the fence*" and now had been "condemned to suffer on this earth and pay the penalty of their disloyalty by dwelling in bodies inferior to those of their more loyal brethren—us white folks." And the Cain narrative made no sense. Lindsay remarked: "Wherever Cain found his wife, she must have been a *fair* daughter of the earth, no curse of blackness resting on *her.*"[67]

Yet Lindsay's attacks revealed as much about his background as it did about Mormonism's racial ideas. He believed that even in cases of "amalgamation," the "best and noblest blood . . . keeps the ascendancy, and where advantages are equal it never resolves itself into meaner conditions." Lindsay's attacks were based not on standards of racial equality but "the lessons of nature and science on the subject."[68] He was tired of the "ignorance, superstition, and idolatry." Lindsay had been raised to believe Mormonism was a "blaze" of glory but it was nothing more than "sparks." After visiting the outside world, he found that Mormonism failed to live up to the standards of truth. After joining with the Godbeites, he promised to venerate "no creed or dogma old or new that does not fasten its claims to truth directly on my reason and common sense."[69]

---

66. John Taylor, quoted in L. John Nuttall, Diary, May 31, 1879; Newell G. Bringhurst, "Elijah Abel and the Changing Status of Blacks in Mormonism," 31.

67. "The Origin of Races," *Salt Lake Tribune*, April 23, 1870, 130.

68. In the late 1860s, William S. Godbe led a faction supporting big business capitalism and, eventually, spiritualism against Brigham Young's policies of economic protectionism. See Ronald W. Walker, *Wayward Saints: The Godbeites and Brigham Young.*

69. Ibid., 172.

But only fifteen years later, the doctrine had been enshrined as conventional wisdom when, in 1885, Mormon intellectual Brigham H. Roberts of the First Council of the Seventy described "the seed of Ham" as the race designated to bear "those spirits that were not valiant in the great rebellion in heaven."[70] These comments framed and informed the next era of theology attempting to explain black-white racial difference in Mormonism.

Brigham Young had never been particularly interested in supporting his racial opinions for such intricate theology. Race, to him, was part of the natural order, a product of a fallen world which must be endured until the human family could be redeemed at the resurrection. When a reporter asked Brigham Young in 1869 about the status of blacks in the territory, he said the Saints "consider and treat them as what they are, the sons of Cain."[71]

But the narrative remained fluid. Was the priesthood ban due to ancestry or to premortal unworthiness? Church leaders couldn't decide. Wilford Woodruff recorded a conversation between Brigham Young and his brother, Lorenzo, also in 1869, when Lorenzo was bishop of Salt Lake Twentieth Ward. He had known Elijah Ables at least as early as 1845 when he represented the Cincinnati Branch, of which Elijah had been an active member for at least [two?] years: [72]

> Lorenzo Young asked if the Spirits of Negroes were Nutral in Heaven. He said someone said Joseph Smith said they were. Preside[n]t Young said No they were not. There were No Nutral spirits in Heaven at the time of the Rebelion. All took sides. He said if any one said that He Herd the Prophet Joseph Say that the spirits of the Blacks were Nutral in Heaven He would not Believe them for He herd Joseph Say to the Contrary. All spirits are pure that Come from the presence of God. The posterity of Cane are Black Because He Commit Murder. He killed Abel & God set a Mark upon his posterity But the spirits are pure that Enter their tabernacles & there will be a Chance for the redemption of all the Children of Adam Except the Sons of perdition.[73]

In 1889, two decades later and a decade after John Taylor had replaced Brigham Young as Church president, the topic still bemused Church leaders. That same year, while Matthias Cowley and Lorenzo Snow were in Preston, Idaho for a Church conference, Snow privately mentioned that an early convert, likely Harvey Whitlock, "turn[ed] black" after apostatizing from the Church.[74] Cowley's next question was logical: Were blacks neutral in the premortal life?

Snow responded that he "did not believe that the Negroes were born into black bodies because of neutrality in their pre-existent state"—a position that accorded

---

70. Brigham H. Roberts, "To the Youth of Israel," 297.

71. "A Talk with Brigham Young," *Charleston Courier*, August 9, 1869, 4.

72. "Conference Minutes," *Times and Seasons* 6, no. 5 (March 15, 1845): 842.

73. Kenney, *Wilford Woodruff's Journal*, December 25, 1869, 6:510–11.

74. Blackness was fairly often associated with demonic possession. For example, when the Kirtland converts began to experience visions, Levi Hancock noted that Edson Fuller would "fall and turn black in the face." Quoted in Matthew Bowman, *The Mormon People: The Making of an American Faith*, 44.

with Brigham Young's as far as it went, but rather "he believed that they were born in the Negro Race because of a Pre-existent arrangement that Cain should be their progenitor in the flesh." But Cowley's account, added two new elements to the premortality narrative. First, this "arrangement" amounted to a type of covenant. Just as Abraham's male offspring, even before experiencing mortality, were assigned as heirs to the priesthood through a similar covenant-family arrangement reaching back into premortal life, an unrighteous lineage was prepared, also before mortality, for unrighteous spirits. Second, and significantly, although Snow accepted that blacks were Cain's descendants, this designation family arrangement predated Cain's murder of Abel. Following the murder, the racial "order or condition was not changed, notwithstanding the awful crime of which Cain was guilty." In other words, Snow believed that black-skinned peoples retained their black skin regardless of, not because of, Cain's sin.[75] Snow was one of the few apostles with an education at an avowedly abolitionist institution, so it is hardly surprising that he sought to reconcile Mormon principles with racial justice.

Brigham H. Roberts was bolder: "How do you reconcile [the black exclusionary ban] with the justice of God? I reconcile it by the knowledge which comes to us through the doctrine of the pre-existence of man's spirit and I believe that conditions in this life are influenced and fixed by the degree of faithfulness by the degree of development in the pre existent state." He felt assured that black skin was no indication of divine displeasure but in fact of divine confidence: "The favored sons of God are not those furthest removed from trial from sorrow from affliction," he said, referencing the black population. "It is the fate apparently of those whom God most loves that they suffer most, that they might gain the experience for which men came into this world."[76]

But conservative leaders hesitated to make this doctrinal position either so public or so definitive, certainly when the conversation centered on premortality. In 1907 Church Historian Joseph Fielding Smith observed that this belief in premortal neutrality had become "quite general" among the Saints. When a young man in Tooele asked Smith about the rationale for the priesthood ban, Smith attempted to debunk the "premortal neutrality" explanation completely, answering that "there is nothing in our standard works, nor any authoritative statement to the effect that one third of the hosts of heaven remained nuteral [sic] in the great conflict and that the colored races are of that neutral class." This position, Smith assured him, is "not the official position of the Church, merely the opinion of men." He admitted that a "tradition" attributed to Joseph Smith a declaration that "the reason why the children of Cain [blacks] cannot receive the Priesthood is that Cain cut his brother Abel off from the

---

75. Matthias F. Cowley, qtd. in Dennis Horne, *Latter Leaves in the Life of Lorenzo Snow*, 11. According to Cowley, Snow made these comments during a trip from Preston to Malad, Idaho. He had been called upon to assist the stake presidency in deciding where to build the new Oneida Stake Academy. "A Location Selected," *Utah Journal*, July 27, 1889, 4, indicates that this decision was made in the summer of 1889.

76. Brigham H. Roberts, "Discourse by Elder B. H. Roberts," *Millennial Star* 57 (July 11, 1895): 435.

Jane Manning James, ca. 1860s, spent years urging Church leadership to seal her as a daughter to Joseph Smith, as she insisted had been promised to her. She was eventually sealed as a "servant." Courtesy LDS Church History Library.

earth before he had seed." Blacks, this tradition stated, could not "hold the Priesthood until such time and place as Abel shall have posterity, which of course will not be in this mortal life." Though a tradition it was—and a tradition that Smith accepted—"the fact remains that the children of Cain cannot hold the Priesthood."[77] The only evidence Smith proposed was the Book of Abraham text indicating that the Pharoah of Egypt had been "cursed . . . as pertaining to the priesthood" since he was "of that lineage by which he could not have the right of Priesthood" (Abr. 1:26–27). Although Smith was then the official Church Historian, he did not explain how this traditional explanation squared with justice.

Most black Saints from the Joseph Smith era clung to their faith, even as they wrestled with the hardening doctrinal posture. In 1884, Jane James urged President John Taylor to grant her temple rituals reserved for "others who are white." She acknowledged the well-accepted belief that her "race & color" had been "handed down through the flood" and thus disqualified her from receiving temple blessings in the avenue open to any other worthy woman. But James countered with an alternative theology: "God promised Abraham that in his seed all the nations of the earth should be blest." This promise exists in both the Old and New Testaments. Genesis 18:18 is the Lord's own announcement to Abraham that "all the nations of the earth shall be blessed in him," while the Apostle Paul reminded the Galatians (3:8) that "God would justify the heathen through faith, [and] preached before the gospel unto Abraham, saying, In thee shall all nations be blessed." White Saints had an obligation to offer blessings to her, urged Jane, even though she had been born outside the covenant lineage. Indeed, Joseph and Emma Smith had offered to adopt her as a part of their eternal family.

As Taylor had with Ables, he first ignored, then denied her requests. After Taylor's death, Jane applied again to Wilford Woodruff. In denying her request, he did not cite premortal unworthiness. Like Young, he explained the curse of Cain: "It was against the Law of God. As Cain killed Abel, all the seed of Cain

---

77. Joseph Fielding Smith, Letter to Alfred M. Nelson, January 31, 1907.

would have to wait for redemption until all the seed that Abel would have had that they may Come through other men Can be redeemed."[78]

So Woodruff offered a compromise: the creation of a special ordinance in which Jane was sealed to Joseph and Emma—but as a servant, not as a daughter.[79] In what seems to be an excess of concern about purity, Jane was not allowed into the Endowment House to receive this unique ordinance on her own behalf. Rather, Joseph F. Smith served as the proxy for his uncle, Joseph Smith, and George A. Smith's widow, Bathsheba W. Smith, served as Jane's proxy. Temple recorder John Nicholson recorded this uncomfortable ordinance.[80] Not fully satisfied, Jane applied again after this proxy ordinance for her own sealing blessings, but was, not surprisingly, again refused.[81]

Another example during this period was the experience of former slave Samuel Chambers, who came to Utah with his wife, Amanda, also African American, following the Civil War. At that point, the Mormons were not performing new ordinations of African American men, and Chambers was never ordained to the priesthood. He acquired significant land holdings in east Salt Lake City and proved a tenacious and committed Church member. In 1913, Booker T. Washington, while visiting Salt Lake City, met Samuel Chambers, then about age eighty-two, and described him as a "fine looking old fellow, a kind of colored Brigham Young."[82]

In 1896, an avowedly Democratic black news editor in Salt Lake City, Julius F. Taylor, said that "the Little Dictator of Salt Lake City," apparently a persona he created to express his political opinions, wanted Chambers to serve as a Republican member of the Utah State Legislature. He felt confident that Chambers "would have received the nomination, at the very sound of his name." The nominating convention "would have went [sic] wild with enthusiasm." The "Little Dictator" thought him a "gentleman of great ability . . . held in the highest esteem by all classes of his fellow citizens."[83]

This "insignificant looking autocrat," the editor maintained, "run[s] the Methodist Church and dictated to the Minister how to preach and pray." He "hurl[s] sinners and all others headlong into Perdition who refuse to acknowledge me as the Little Dictator." The Little Dictator "started the Baptist Church and was one of the Elders" and "own[s] and have a perpetual chattel mortgage on all the members of our race in Salt Lake and when I order them to do anything, they

---

78. Kenney, *Wilford Woodruff's Journal,* 9:322 [October 16, 1894].

79. Franklin D. Richards, Journal, August 22, 1895, in Turley, *Selected Collections,* 1:35. See also Quorum of the Twelve, Meeting Minutes, January 2, 1902.

80. Michael Souders, "Preaching the Restored Gospel: John Nicholson's Homiletic Theories for Young Mormons," 420–46.

81. Franklin D. Richards, Journal, August 22, 1895, in Turley, *Selected Collections,* 1:35. See also Quorum of the Twelve, Meeting Minutes, January 2, 1902, George A. Smith Family Collection, Box 78, fd. 7, Marriott Special Collections.

82. Louis R. Harlan and Raymond W. Smock, eds., *The Booker T. Washington Papers: 1912–1914,* 12:153.

83. "The Little Dictator of Salt Lake," *Broad Ax,* March 14, 1896, 1.

all obey me like little children."[84] At one point, Julius Taylor accused "the Little Dictator" of pressing a prominent Democrat for money: "We honestly believe that he wanted to be in a position to say good Lord and good devil."[85] Chambers, Taylor claimed, was at best an easy pawn for the Republican establishment.

For the previous generation, the Mormon people had sought to shed the racial discourse assigned to them by Eastern pundits, politicians, and the burgeoning class of anthropologists. The Mormon embrace of polygamy had invited the press to label Mormons with "Asiatic" and "Oriental" attributes—some anthropologists argued that Mormon polygamy had spawned a new race—the Saints felt impelled to redefine their own whiteness in the eyes of the press.[86] The range of racial identities attributed to the Mormons spanned the globe. They were negatively compared and/ or contrasted to Indian *thuggees*,[87] Chinese immigrants,[88] Turks,[89] "Hottentots,"[90] and, on occasion, African Americans.[91] In 1881, a Mississippi paper posited that "if Mormonism could be induced to go to 'polygamist Africa,' where it "would find a congenial home, it would be a good riddance for the civilized world."[92]

Mormonism's racial Otherness came under attack in popular art forms as well. In Jack London's 1914 novel, *Star Rover*, the hero transports himself into past lives, one of them being a young boy slain during the Mountain Meadows Massacre.

---

84. "The Little Dictator of Salt Lake," *Broad Ax*, February 15, 1896, 4.

85. "The Little Dictator of Salt Lake," *Broad Ax*, April 11, 1869, 1.

86. There is a sizable and growing body of research on how racial constructs influenced anti-Mormon and anti-polygamy discourse. J. Spencer Fluhman, *"A Peculiar People:" Anti-Mormonism and the Making of Religion in Nineteenth-Century America*; Sarah Barringer Gordon, *The Mormon Question: Polygamy and Constitutional Conflict in Nineteenth-Century America*, chap. 2; Terryl L. Givens, *The Viper on the Hearth: Mormons, Myths, and the Construction of Heresy*, 55–85; Nathan Oman, "Natural Law and the Rhetoric of Empire: *Reynolds v. United States*, Polygamy, and Imperialism"; Russell Stevenson, "Mo-rientalism: Mizra Khan and Mormon Identity in India," June 2013, unpublished manuscript.

87. In the early nineteenth century, the *thuggee* were considered to be a band of religious fanatics living in the mountains of India who ambushed passersby—especially Europeans—and killed them using elaborate Hindu rituals. "Against Mormonism," *Daily Inter Ocean* (Chicago), January 25, 1887, 4; "Thuggee and Mormonism," *Salt Lake Tribune*, January 6, 1877, 2; "The News," *Salt Lake Tribune*, October 6, 1893, 5; "Cannon's Volley at Supreme Court," *Salt Lake Tribune*, July 19, 1879, 4; "Johnny Young's Plea," *New York Herald*, February 17, 1881, 6; "What Is Religion," *New York Herald*, May 11, 1879, 10; "Utah," *American Traveller*, May 15, 1857, 4; "The Mormons in Utah," *Boston Traveler*, April 14, 1857, 2; "A Free Country," *Constitution* (Middletown, Conn.), June 18, 1856, 2; "Utah Territory—Mormonism," *Weekly Advocate* (Baton Rouge, La.), March 25, 1860, 4.

88. "Mormons," *Daily Inter Ocean* (Chicago), October 27, 1889, 4.

89. The *Washington Sentinel* observed that the Mormons "are Turks in all save the matter of wearing turbans and eating opium." See "The Turks and the Mormons," *Washington Sentinel*, May 7, 1854, 2.

90. "The Naturalization of Mormons," *Salt Lake Tribune*, July 13, 1889, 6; "Mormonism in Africa," *Salt Lake Tribune*, January 11, 1879, 6; "The Mormon Problem," *San Francisco Bulletin*, March 16, 1869, 1.

91. "Negro Mormons," *Galveston [Texas] Tri-Weekly News*, March 16, 1870, 2.

92. "A Good Suggestion," *Saginaw [Michigan] News*, August 27, 1881, 1.

When the boy sees that white men accompany the Indian attackers, he has no trouble with overlapping racial categories: "They ain't whites. . . .They're Mormons."[93]

In 1903, Senator-elect and Apostle Reed Smoot angered onlookers when he directed white waitresses to serve a doorkeeper and Julius F. Taylor at a dinner; several of the waitresses refused to comply with the senator's directions.[94] He cited President Theodore Roosevelt's 1901 invitation for Booker T. Washington to join him at the White House: "If President Roosevelt isn't too good to entertain a colored man at the White House, I don't see why I shouldn't have colored people as my guests."[95] The act enraged Southerners. One correspondent accused both Smoot and Roosevelt of "hav[ing] negro blood" and that "the head of the peanus [sic] of both, are black." Smoot, the man fumed, deserved to "kiss each [black] squarely on the ass" and "should be castrated."[96]

In 1905, Raymond Browne, a popular songwriter (he once placed a commercial advertisement calling for "song poems, all kinds wanted. . . . I made fortunes for others and can aid you"[97]) penned the lyrics to "The Mormon Coon," recorded on a brittle 78 rpm record. Its cover jacket shows a black man in a formal, ecclesiastical suit, with a long flowing beard that echoed caricatures of Joseph F. Smith, who had been voluminously cartooned during his testimony in the Smoot Senate hearings just the year before. The "Mormon Coon" celebrates his life in Utah and his large harem of wives:

> I've got a big brunette, and a blonde to pet
> I've got 'em short, fat, thin, and tall
> I've got a Cuban gal, and a Zulu pal
> They come in bunches when I call
> And that's not all
> I've got 'em pretty too
> Got a homely few
> I've got 'em black to octoroon
> I can spare six or eight
> Shall I ship 'em by freight?
> For I am the Mormon coon.[98]

The piece was circulated throughout the country and was a favorite of minstrel shows throughout the United States and even among the military in the Panama Canal Zone.[99] Drawing on the interest in polygamy that had died down after

---

93. Jack London, *The Star Rover*, 135.

94. "Indignant at Smoot's Action," *Pittsburgh Press*, February 13, 1903, 11.

95. Ibid.

96. Qtd. in Jonathan H. Moyer, "Dancing with the Devil: The Making of the Mormon-Republican Pact," 307.

97. "Classified Advertising," *National Magazine*, 25, no. 6 (March 1907): 691.

98. James P. Leary, ed., *Wisconsin Folklore*, 218.

99. Advertisement, *Arizona Republican* (Phoenix), June 30, 1905, 6; "Minstrels Entertain," *Daily News-Democrat* (Huntington, Ind.), February 18, 1905, 1; "Elks Minstrels Fun," *Evening Bulletin* (Honolulu), March 9, 1906, 3; Advertisement, *Chicago Daily Tribune*, February 20,

"The Mormon Coon" was a popular song in turn-of-the-century America suggesting that Mormonism resembled black and "Oriental" hypersexuality. Courtesy Johns Hopkins University Special Collections.

Woodruff's 1890 Manifesto but had been revived by the 1904–07 Smoot hearings, the piece placed white Mormons, polygamy, and interracial sexuality into one cultural construct of comic depravity.[100]

The "Mormon Coon" was obvious satire, but it had a special bite, since Mormons in Utah advertised their mountain home as a refuge for those seeking racial purity and generally avoided teaching blacks, a fact that did not go unnoticed by the Eastern press.[101] In 1882, a Mormon missionary assailed Southerners for countenancing interracial sexuality, much of it consisting of slave owners' exploitation of enslaved women; it was "bad enough to call down a similar destruction as that which befell the cities of the plain."[102] The Utah State Legislature sought to bolster its lily-white image by passing anti-miscegenation legislation in 1888. It thus sought to close a loophole left by the 1852 Utah Territorial law banning interracial sexual relations from which interracial marriage had been omitted.[103] In 1893, George Q. Cannon boasted in an editorial that the Utah Saints were "not a mongrel breed" and had "comparatively few of what are known as the inferior races."[104] In 1905, Brigham H. Roberts

1905, 12; "Songs, Jokes, Sketches, and Dances by Elks," *Indianapolis News*, March 2, 1907, 13; "Social Life of the Zone," *Canal Record* (Ancon, Panama Canal Zone), April 13, 1910, 261.

100. For a thorough contextualization of this song against the social and political currents of early twentieth-century America, see Martha M. Ertman, "Race Treason: The Untold Story of America's Ban on Polygamy," 351–54.

101. "Society in the South," *Deseret News*, November 18, 1885, 14; "The Next Senator from Missouri," *Washington Sentinel*, September 9, 1854, 2; "Tweedle," *Plain Dealer* (Cleveland, Ohio), November 16, 1853, 2; "No Negro Need Apply," *Columbus [Ga.] Daily Enquirer*, April 14, 1883, 1.

102. A. H. [Alphonzo Houtz] Snow, Letter to Editor, March 15, 1882, "Voice from the Southern States," in Deseret News, April 19, 1882, 7. See "Fifty-First Annual Conference," Salt Lake Herald April 7, 1881, 3 and "Association Intelligence," The Contributor 4 (June 1883): 359. Snow was acting mission president when the president, John Morgan, was absent. See "History of the Southern States Mission," Latter-day Saints Southern Star 1, no. 18 (April 1, 1899), 138.

103. For a thorough treatment of miscegenation law in Utah, see Patrick Q. Mason, "The Prohibition of Interracial Marriage in Utah, 1888–1963," 108–31.

104. "An Ex-Editor's Saturday Talk," *Deseret News*, February 25, 1893, 14.

quipped, quoting pundit William B. Smith: "Let not man join together what God hath put asunder."[105]

The debate on the precise line between black and white continued into the twentieth century. In a January 1902 meeting of the Quorum of the Twelve Apostles, John Henry Smith, son of Apostle George A. Smith, expressed his views that "persons in whose veins the white blood predominated should not be barred from the temple,"[106] but, in the same meeting, Joseph F. Smith, by now Church president, countered flatly: "In all cases where the blood of Cain showed itself, however slight, the line should be drawn there."[107]

In spite of the racial purity rhetoric, the Saints struggled to know exactly what the place of the black man should be within their evolving worldview. In *The Contributor*, an anonymous author wrote an in-depth portrait of "Our Coloured Brethren," giving life to these stereotypes in a thick tapestry of racial stereotypes and assumptions. Blacks, this observer noted, "were highly emotional in their natures" and "inclined to look upon the funny side of things." Freeing the blacks, he noted, had been "not only a curse to the country but to the colored race" as they had been "much better cared for in slavery than they can care for themselves." But perhaps, he continued, emancipation served a greater end after all. Blacks could now "be thrown upon their own resources" and could learn "that they must do something for themselves, and for the general good, as God designed that all should, instead of being pampered in idleness." [108]

But this anonymous writer also noted that blacks had tremendous potential. Though emancipation had reduced blacks to "selling their votes for bad whiskey" or "playing the part of the petty politician, with little show of success," they had the potential to fulfill a "higher and holier mission": the redemption of Africa, a continent of "men and women of their own flesh and blood sunk in ignorance, barbarism, and idolatry . . . groping for the light." Having been trained

---

105. B. H. Roberts, *The Seventy's Course in Theology: First Year,* 163. Dr. William B. Smith was a professor of mathematics at Tulane University. He argued: "If we sit with the negroes at our tables, if we entertain them as our guests and social equals, if we disregard the color line in all other relations, is it possible to maintain it fixedly in the sexual relation, in the marriage of our sons and daughters, in the propagation of our species? Unquestionably, No! It is as certain as the rising of tomorrow's sun that, once the middle wall of social partition is broken down, the mingling of the tides of life would begin instantly and proceed steadily. . . . If the race barrier be removed, and the individual standard of personal excellence be established, the twilight of this century will gather upon a nation hopelessly sinking in the mire of mongrelism." William B. Smith, *The Color Line: A Brief in Behalf of the Unborn,* xiv.

106. Quorum of the Twelve, Meeting Minutes, January 2, 1902, George A. Smith Family Papers.

107. Ibid.

108. "Our Coloured Brethren," *The Contributor* 7, no. 1 (October 1885): 32–33. This piece was also published under the same title in *The Phrenological Journal and Science of Health* 81, no. 52 (November 1885): 260–62.

in America, the African American could bring the blessings of America to his "benighted countryman," thus becoming a "benefactor to his race."[109]

Whiteness became a device for negotiating power relations between the Mormon and American populations. As W. Paul Reeve has demonstrated, the Latter-day Saints felt it necessary to "prove" their whiteness to the American population. The Saints' had established themselves as a racial Other through by practicing a form of marriage that Americans viewed with "holy horror." Well-aware of their Otherness, the Saints attempted to compromise with the white American establishment by adopting the racial values they celebrated.[110] President Theodore Roosevelt celebrated the Mormons' ability to build up the Anglo-Saxon population through their high birthrates, since he feared that whites would lose their preeminence in the modern world. A *New York Herald* political cartoon depicted Roosevelt learning of Mormon President Joseph F. Smith's forty-two children and bellowing in delight: "That's Bully! No race suicide there!"[111] Polygamy had once been caricatured as a "relic" of a backwards community. It was now seen as the means by which the Mormon population could prove its worthiness by producing strapping Anglo-Saxon offspring to build up America's white population.

In 1890, Church President Wilford Woodruff issued the Manifesto, withdrawing Church sanction for new plural marriages in the United States and thereby deflecting an even harsher round of legislative sanctions. Although cohabitation did not stop—nor did secretly authorized new plural marriages—the date marked the beginning of a shift in how the public portrayed the "Mormon question." The press became less inclined to racialize the Mormon people, preferring to compare them to the religiously zealous Boer colonizers of South Africa. Staunchly religious and hard-boiled frontier wayfarers, the Boers shared some of their narrative with the Mormon people. The Mormons' alleged "narrowness," "ignorance of the world," "fanaticism," and "bigotry" made them a fellow religion with the Dutch Boers in the eyes of the American Protestant mainstream.[112] When a group of Idaho Mormons relocated to Wyoming in 1901, they were said to "emulate Boers."[113] Mormon suffragist Ruth May Fox ran a boarding house in Salt Lake City where she met some "strange people," including "a Negro family [who] got in one of the housekeeping apartments by sending the white mother to apply for the vacancy." She listed the incident in her memoirs alongside a lurid story involving the arrest of a sex trafficker and a pregnant dwarf "who later gave

109. "Our Coloured Brethren," *The Contributor*, 33.

110. Paul Reeve, "From Not White to Too White: The Historical Evolution of a 'Mormon Race,'" 2013.

111. Michael H. Paulos, "'Horribly Caricatured and Made Hideous in Cartoons,'" 132.

112. "Growing Power of Mormonism," *Oregonian*, (Portland), June 17, 1902, 12.

113. "2,000 Mormons to Trek," *Omaha World Herald*, April 13, 1901, 1. See also "The Trouble in the Transvaal," *New Haven [Conn.] Register*, September 5, 1899, 6; "Bryan and the Boers," *New York Tribune*, October 20, 1899, 8; Roger Pocock, "My Most Exciting Adventure," *Denver Post*, December 11, 1910, 59.

birth to a child nearly as big as its mother and received pictured notoriety in the Salt Lake Daily Papers."[114] Fox quickly "discovered the evil" in her own home "and . . . got rid of the mess" before journalists linked the sensational incident to her as the sexually exploited dwarf's Mormon landlady.[115]

The Mormon community's racial narrative had reoriented itself radically over the past two generations. Transforming itself from a group of "black Mormons" struggling to navigate the complex racial politics of American society to become a group of genealogically unchallengeable Anglo-Saxons was not a simple process. But having written out or marginalized the narratives of black Saints such as Elijah Ables and Jane Manning James, the Saints could solidify their standing as Anglo-Saxon Americans, well-distanced from the ghosts of men like Elijah Ables.

114. The "dwarf" was likely Bessie Riley, a pregnant teenager living as a bonded servant to Mrs. Artiburn. Officials attempted to have Artiburn arrested for abusing the girl, but Riley would not support the charges. She testified in court that she "let [Artiburn] have her way." In February 1902, Riley gave birth to a 7.5 pound girl whom the *Salt Lake Tribune* described as "physically perfect." See "Mrs. Artiburn Discharged," *Deseret News*, November 21, 1901, 8, and "Performed Caesarian Section," *Salt Lake Tribune*, February 28, 1902, 3.

115. Brittany Chapman, ed., *Carry On: The Personal Writings of Ruth May Fox*. My thanks to Ms. Chapman for providing early access to her manuscript.

Chapter 3

The Long Night, 1890–1960

"A series of sights which make civilization ooze up in the human breast."
—A Salt Lake City reporter's description
of the film, *Birth of a Nation* (1923)

"We are striving to get to Zion if it be the will of our Heavenly Father."
—Alice Daniels, a black South African Mormon (1923)

"Just 10 years ago there was no segregation whatsoever and now Negroes are segregated a la Georgia everywhere except on street cars. A taxi man even refused to drive me home from the depot!!!"
—Black novelist Wallace Thurman (1929)

While the white Saints solidified their racial identity, the African American community in Salt Lake City also began to have a voice. Building on the foundation of the past generation, racial identity came to identify American Saints more than ever before. White Saints drank deeply of the virtues and values white American society valued. Once Elijah Ables and Jane Manning James had died, the Saints had but few tokens of the old days. In matters of race, white Mormons had come to pass for much of white America for the next generation.

And race had come to be not merely a problem for Mormons in America but Mormons abroad as well. As the Church began to expand into South Africa and Brazil, the Saints came to recognize that race was not merely an inheritance from a parochial past but also a potential impediment to a global future. Committed as they were to upholding their hard–won racial identity, Utah Mormons were not inclined to sacrifice their white identity in order to become a global church. Racial inclusion was too great a sacrifice for a people who had suffered being white, black, and everything else for far too long.

Good Servants

Strident though the white Saints had become, black Utahans also began to gain their voice in white Mormon society. In 1895, former slave Julius Taylor established the Salt Lake City African American newspaper, *Broad Ax* in hopes of "infus[ing] a spirit of liberal and honest enquiry into the living questions of the day" in hopes of "lead[ing] the minds of the colored people away from false notions, old prejudices, and disagreeable memories." The paper differed from many African American outlets by openly allying itself with the Democratic Party.[1] "It is time," *Broad Ax* declared for "the colored people [to] act from reason, and not from impulse and prejudice." No "logical reason" existed for a black man in Utah to be a Republican "any more than he should be a Mormon, a Methodist, or a Baptist."[2] The Republican Party had betrayed blacks. "Negro haters" controlled the Utah party and felt that "every member of the race must forever praise . . . and forever worship these leaders."[3] Drawing on the intellectual currents of Social Darwinism, *Broad Ax* cast black history as a steady progression toward civilization: "Originating in the jungles of a savage continent, [blacks] have been brought to civilization through the portals of servitude, and at last through the survival of the fittest they have finally reached the goal of liberty and equality before the law."[4]

The Saints also began to recreate their collective memory of Elijah Ables to fit with the prevailing attitudes. In 1903, a Salt Lake patriarch named Miner spoke at the Baptist funeral of Eugene Burns, Elijah Ables's grandson. According to the *Salt Lake Tribune*, the patriarch lavished praise on Elijah, suggesting that he was "the only one of his race who ever overcame the conditions of his bondage."[5] The souls of the black man had been "doomed before his birth." The patriarch concluded that, thankfully, Joseph Smith's teachings allowed that "the negro may step up into the preliminary state of exaltation."[6]

Even the white Mormons found such comments offensive. The *Deseret News* angrily editorialized that the *Tribune* had only "vilif[ied] and misrepresent[ed]" the Saints' position on blacks' spiritual fate, countering: "'The Mormons do not believe any such rubbish."[7]

But when black intellectual William Pickens visited Utah more than twenty–five years later to inquire about the state of race relations, the Saints he interviewed recalled that Elijah had overcome his racial status by being a "good servant."[8] In his 1920 biographical sketch of Ables, Assistant Church Historian Andrew Jenson made no secret of his priesthood status, recording that he was "the only colored man who is known to have been ordained to the Priesthood."[9] The *Deseret News* and the *Salt Lake Tribune* agreed on one key fact: Ables, had, in fact, been ordained to the Melchizedek Priesthood. This historical fact problematized the genealogical narrative that Mormons had crafted and accepted for over

---

1. "To the Colored People of Utah," *Broad Ax*, August 31, 1895, 1.
2. Ibid.
3. "The Little Dictator of Salt Lake," *Broad Ax*, March 14, 1896, 1.
4. Ibid.
5. "No Room for Blacks," *Salt Lake Tribune*, November 1, 1903, 8.
6. Ibid.
7. "Negroes and Heaven," *Deseret News*, December 17, 1903, 4.
8. William Pickens," "One Negro in Heaven Mormons Tell Pickens," 6.
9. Andrew Jenson, *Latter-day Saint Biographical Encyclopedia: A Compendium of Biographical Sketches of Prominent Men and Women in the Church of Jesus Christ of Latter-day Saints*, 3:577.

a generation. Everyone knew it. The question was not whether it had happened; the question was whether it mattered.

Individual members occasionally lauded Southern blacks for their commitment to Church activity. In 1912, Alan Strong, a returned missionary from the Southern states, recalled that "some of the colored people were the most religious he had seen, and that a number of them had been baptized into the church."[10] President Joseph F. Smith lauded black "polished gentlemen . . . who have been unfortunate enough not to be white . . . in their skin; but in their hearts and in their manners, in their courtesy and conduct, they were far superior to many of their boasting white brothers."[11] That the priesthood ban existed at all seemed to be something of an open secret in most circles. Apostle David O. McKay did not face his first moral crisis over the policy until 1921 when, touring the world missions with Hugh J. Cannon, he met an unnamed faithful black man living with his Polynesian wife and children in Hawaii. He asked President Heber J. Grant "if he would please make an exception so we could ordain that man to the Priesthood." Grant wrote back: "David, I am as sympathetic as you are, but until the Lord gives us a revelation regarding that matter, we shall have to maintain the policy of the Church."[12]

Mormon discourse towards blacks also came to exhibit troubling contradictions. For example, defensive LDS writers showed increasing tendencies to detach the skin color of African Americans from their eternal and social identities. Mormon poet C. Frank Steele wrote a sentimental poem for the *Juvenile Instructor* in 1920 entitled "Little Nigger Baby," musing on the black mother–child relationship; "beneath that dusky skin a guileless heart I see / Alovin' just like white folks' babies do." Steele seemed to suggest that black skin color was something to overlooked rather than embraced.[13]

Steele's fixation on the black body extended beyond mere curiosity. When Mormon reformers began to call for the use of the individual cup for use in the sacrament ritual, they used the black body to emphasize the threat of disease. After a Mormon physician, David L. McDonald, observed a black man drinking from a public fountain in spring 1912, he warned that while "the negro *per se* is harmless," the "tubercle germs in a large percentage of their mouths are deadly to the one who drinks after them." After traveling onward to Baltimore, McDonald "realized that some two hundred thousand negroes share the public fountain cup with their white brethren." McDonald urged the Saints to give up the then common communal sacrament cup in an effort to promote good hygiene and prevent the spread of disease. "The Latter-day Saints above all," McDonald admonished, "should hold

---

10. Salt Lake City Tenth Ward Minutes, March 10, 1912, LR 9051 11, Reel #2, LDS Church History Library. Many thanks to Joseph Soderburg for directing me to this source.

11. President Joseph F. Smith, *Conference Report*. April 1905, 86.

12. Gregory A. Prince and Wm. Robert Wright, *David O. McKay and the Rise of Modern Mormonism*, 74.

13. "Little Nigger Baby," 44.

themselves ready to accept scientific truths."[14] And "scientific truth," it was believed to be; at the 1908 International Congress on Tuberculosis in Washington, one of the lecturers warned that blacks had "become affected with this malady to such a degree as to imperil whites who are associated with them."[15]

More overt racial hostility surfaced in the early twentieth-century Mormon West. While Utah blacks were not subject to the same degree of racial terrorism that haunted Southern blacks, they were not safe from it. During the Klan's Reconstruction days, their violence had repelled the Mormons, a people with three generations of inherited revulsion toward mob rule. But in the 1920s, the national Klan spilled out of the South in a national recruitment campaign that successfully papered over the Klan's reputation. Branding itself as protectors of simple patriotism, "plain talk" and "one hundred percent Americanism," the Klan presented itself less as an aggressor and more as supporters of faith, family, and country.[16] A Klan editorial in Georgia lobbied for schools to "teach the girl how to make a home, and the boy how to make [a] living and be honest and clean."[17]

The Klan established two major chapters in Salt Lake City and Ogden.[18] According to Larry Gerlach, the Klan in Utah did not have one distinctive characteristic; indeed, "local variation" was the "distinguishing feature of Beehive Klankraft."[19] Its Salt Lake chapter issued a statement warning that "certain elements in our community defy our laws with impunity." "We serve notice," it warned, "to this element that such an attitude will no longer be tolerated." They were willing to issue threats and intimidate when necessary. The Klan cast itself as a mysterious crime-fighting organization, committed to "the support of law and order, and to the stern punishment, without fear or favor, of offenders."[20] In Salt Lake City, reports circulated that the Klan had threatened local gambling den organizers such as Ike Bernstein and "Gentleman Jim" Donaldson with tar and feathers, "one of the greatest remedies for curbing gambling and other habits." The letters were dismissed as a hoax by the authorities, and the recipients made little effort to leave town.[21] But the movement in Utah failed to achieve

---

14. David L. McDonald, "The Individual Sacrament Cup," 216–17.

15. "The White Plague and Weak Bodies," 696.

16. For extensive treatments of the Ku Klux Klan in 1920s America, see Thomas Pegram, *One Hundred Percent American: The Rebirth and Decline of the Klan in 1920s America;* Kathleen M. Blee, *Women of the Klan: Racism and Gender in the 1920s;* and Nancy K. MacLean, *Behind the Mask of Chivalry: The Making of the Second Ku Klux Klan.*

17. Quoted in Pegram, *One Hundred Percent American,* 103.

18. "Blames K of C. for Broadside against Klan," *Salt Lake Telegram,* October 8, 1923, 2; "Klan Lecture Given Here," *Ogden Standard-Examiner,* March 26, 1924, 2; "Articles Are Filed by Ku Klux Klan," *Salt Lake Telegram,* November 8, 1924, 2.

19. Larry Gerlach, *Blazing Crosses in Zion: The Ku Klux Klan in Utah,* 140.

20. "Ku Klux Klan, Fully Organized in Salt Lake; Serves Public Notice That Lawless Element Will Be Punished," *Salt Lake Telegram,* February 7, 1922, 2.

21. "Salt Lake Ku Klux Officers Deny Threats," *Salt Lake Telegram,* March 9, 1922, 2. For Bernstein's and Donaldson's involvement in Utah gambling rings, see "Stop Gambling Here!"

the Klan's popularity in the Midwest. In Ogden, city administrators denied the Klan's request to participate in the local Fourth of July Parade.[22] Utah Democrats and Republicans alike condemned the Klan's activities.[23] In Boise, Klan members took it upon themselves to launch a statewide campaign against bootleggers.[24]

In 1925, the Klan's violent streak surfaced when Klansmen conspired to lynch black miner Robert Marshall after he shot and killed Officer J. Milton Burns in Price, Utah.[25] The mob included a number of the town's blue-collar professionals, ranging from a barber to an electrician. Eleven men were charged with the murder.[26] The men were eventually freed on bail.[27] Over a hundred witnesses were questioned, but the grand jury failed to issue any indictments. Frustrated, District Attorney Fred W. Keller asked Judge George Christensen to drop all charges. When Christensen found "that there was no objections to the dismissal," he struck the case from the docket, assuring all that "no blame should be placed on the attorney for the dismissal of the case.[28]

Though many Utahans found the Klan distasteful in practice, its history struck Utah Saints as romantic and alluring. The D. W. Griffith film, *Birth of a Nation*, first released in 1913, depicted the origins of the Klan as romantic and chivalrous with the hopes of saving the nation from the onslaught of black empowerment during the post-bellum era. The film found wide popularity in Utah theaters. Utah Mormons found *Birth of a Nation* an enthralling depiction of love, war, and rec-onciliation—all the while taking for granted its depiction of blacks as lazy and sexually aggressive. In Fillmore, a movie reviewer compared *Birth of a Nation* to *Abraham Lincoln; Abraham Lincoln* had enchanted the *St. Petersburg [Florida] Evening Independent* into believing it to be "one of the most important pictures ever brought to the screen" and "the sensation of the movie world."[29] The *Salt Lake Telegram* thought the film a "masterpiece" that should be "of marked interest to school children." A local school principal arranged for the theater to "set aside

Salt Lake Telegram, July 16, 1916, 2.

22. "News Notes from All Parts of Utah," *Davis County Clipper* (Bountiful, Utah), July 4, 1924, 2.

23. ""Things Politically," *Park [City] Record* (Utah), August 29, 1924, 1; "The Klan in a Day's Uproar," *Ogden Standard*, June 26, 1924, 4.

24. "Idaho Klan to Go after Bootleggers," *Ogden Standard*, January 1, 1923, 1.

25. "Murder Victim Is Buried at Former Home in Sanpete," *News Advocate* (Price, Utah), June 25, 1925, 1.

26. "Eleven Arrested on Charge of Murder in Lynching of Negro," *News Advocate* (Price, Utah), June 25, 1925, 1.

27. "Alleged Leaders of Lynching Mob Freed upon Bail," *News Advocate* (Price, Utah), July 2, 1925, 1.

28. "Murder Victim Is Buried at Former Home in Sanpete," *News Advocate* (Price, Utah), June 25, 1925, 1; "Thirty Citizens to Be Summoned for Grand Jury," *News Advocate* (Price, Utah), July 9, 1925, 1; "Charges Against Accused Lynching Leaders Dropped," *News Advocate* (Price, Utah), September 10, 1925, 1.

29. "Boy Scout Drive for Second Ward Monday and Tuesday," *Millard County Progress*, March 12, 1926, 1. The Lynn Theatre promised to contribute the proceeds from *Abraham Lincoln* to the local Boy Scout troop. See also "Theater Gossip," *The Evening Independent* [St. Petersburg, Florida], July 19, 1927, 4.

Monday afternoon as a special matinee" in celebration "of the birth of Abraham Lincoln."[30] In Park City, a reviewer thought it "high and commanding."[31] A Salt Lake reviewer called the film "a series of sights which make civilization ooze up in the human breast."[32] In a Salt Lake City school district, children staged a theatrical production of the film for a Parent-Teacher Association meeting.[33] Another reviewer lauded the film for its historically accuracy in its "painfully realistic . . . depictions of the trials and tribulations of the South in the reconstruction." Its "value from an educational standpoint," he declared, "cannot be overestimated," and the "large numbers of children" who viewed it would receive "beautiful, yet stern lesson[s] of patriotism and citizenship."[34]

Social columns in outlying Utah settlements reported when residents made the trip to Salt Lake to view this film.[35] One advertisement urged Utahns to see it if only "as a matter of instructive or educational interest."[36] While the Civil War spectacle scenes mesmerized viewers, its racial commentary remained in center focus.[37] In Cedar City, the *Iron County Record* praised the film for "portray[ing] conditions and sentiments in the Southern states" and the "racial problem with which this nation still has to cope," all "without being offensively partisan."[38] A Logan newspaper praised the film for portraying the "rides and rescues of the . . . original right-enforcing organization of true sons of the Old South."[39] The film, an Ogden editorialist observed somewhat defensively, had "a deeper purpose than the justification of the organization of the 'Ku Klux Klan' or 'Night-riders.' This . . . is to deepen the inborn love of Americans for their country."[40] The *Grand Valley Times* concluded that "Shakespeare . . . has not surpassed or even approached" Griffith in linguistic beauty.[41]

Segregation also grew in strength during the 1920s. Famed Harlem Renaissance author Wallace Thurman was born and raised in west Salt Lake City. Nathan Gray, a classmate, recalled that Thurman had both black and white friends. In 1926, Thurman expressed less sentimental memories about Utah: "There are no Negro professional men. There are no Negro publications, not even a church bulletin. There are no Negro business houses. There are no Negro stores. There are no Negro policemen, no Negro firemen, no Negro politicians,

---

30. "'Birth of a Nation' Opens Today at Gem," *Salt Lake Telegram*, February 12, 1922, 14.

31. "At Theatre Next Week," *Park [City, Utah] Record*, February 6, 1925, 6.

32. "Birth of a Nation at State Saturday," *Salt Lake Telegram*, May 24, 1923, 17.

33. "Children to Stage 'Birth of a Nation,'" *Salt Lake Telegram*, November 9, 1926, 13.

34. "'Birth of a Nation' Scores at American," *Salt Lake Telegram*, December 23, 1921, 6.

35. "Lehi Locals and Personals," *American Fork Citizen*, March 11, 1916, 5.

36. "Two Big Attractions Coming to Milford," *Beaver County News*, November 9, 1917, 1.

37. "'The Birth of a Nation' Is a Soul-Stirring Spectacle," *Box Elder News*, January 23, 1917, 2.

38. "'Birth of a Nation' Has Big Run in Cedar," *Iron County Record*, February 15, 1918, 1.

39. "'Ku Klux Klan's Warning to Its Victims," *Logan Republican*, March 25, 1916, 5.

40. "Birth of a Nation Is a Production of Great Merit," *Ogden Standard*, March 27, 1916, 5.

41. "'The Birth of a Nation' Greatest of All Pictures, Coming to Ides," *Grand Valley Times* (Moab, Utah), May 10, 1918, 8.

save some petty bondsmen."[42] He did not attribute their position to *de jure* segregation but to individual laziness: "There has been certainly nothing about [them] to inspire anyone to do anything save perhaps drink gin with gusto, and develop new techniques for the contravention of virginity."[43] When Thurman visited Salt Lake City three years later, he was shocked to see segregated facilities: "Here in Salt Lake," he wrote a friend, "just 10 years ago there was no segregation whatsoever and now Negroes are segregated a la Georgia everywhere except on street cars. A taxi man even refused to drive me home from the depot!!!"[44] When Elijah Ables's grandson, Lawrence, held his white grandchild, he said to his daughter: "We finally got the black out of the Ables."[45] White Mormon congregations freely enjoyed performing "negro skit[s]" and "negro minstrel shows."[46] While often meant in good humor, the shows relied on stereotypes that belittled and demeaned Utah's black minority population.

Like much of America, the Mormons—a people devoted to self-reliance—reeled after the economic crash of 1929. With the rise of federal welfare assistance, Church leaders responded by constructing local alternatives to government-sponsored aid, especially its much-touted Welfare Plan, which endures to this day. The welfare program had a limited impact on the Depression-era Utah economy. Cognizant of Mormons' limited capacity for self-help, state government officials turned to Franklin D. Roosevelt's federal programs for relief. The federal government established a robust public industrial and educational sector in Utah, making it the ninth-greatest recipient of federal aid in the 1930s.[47]

Mormon attitudes toward the black population continued unchanged through the Great Depression and World War II. During the 1920s, a pattern had developed of blacks moving from the urban centers of Salt Lake City and Ogden to mines in Carbon and Emery counties. New Deal relief and employment programs gave African American job opportunities otherwise unavailable to them. The Civilian Conservation Corps (CCC) was the federal government's program devised to employ men in making wilderness trails, building dams, and planting trees. It carried out most of the federal projects prompting an influx of black workers into the state.

Utahans reacted with quiet hostility toward these new blacks. In May 1935, a company from the Ninth Corps unit that employed black workers found their

---

42. Wallace Thurman, "Quoth Brigham Young: This Is the Place," reprinted in Tom Lutz and Susanna Ashton, eds., *These "Colored" United States: African American Essays from the 1920s*, 266–67.

43. Ibid., 262.

44. Wallace Thurman, Letter to William Rapp, ca. April 1929, quoted in Eleonore Van Notten, *Wallace Thurman's Harlem Renaissance*, 80.

45. Boyd Ables [the grandchild mentioned in the text above], email to Russell Stevenson, June 19, 2013.

46. "M.I.A. Road Show Proves Pleasing," *Iron County Record*, January 31, 1935, 4; see also "Lions Club Planning Minstrel Show," *Iron County Record*, October 14, 1935, 4.

47. Dean L. May, *Utah: A People's History*, 178.

stay sufficiently unpleasant that they asked to be returned to California.[48] Another black CCC worker recalled that they "didn't like being segregated, but we expected that sort of thing in Utah."[49] However, segregation was a national policy; CCC director Robert Fechner had witnessed "vigorous resentment shown by some communities where a considerable number of negro enrollees were placed." He decided that "negro and white enrollees should be segregated and this policy was generally followed in all Corps areas."[50]

The presence of blacks roused greater ire in some communities than others. Mrs. Leland Larsen of Brigham City complained to Governor Henry Blood: "The War Department has stationed a very undesirable class of men, such as Mexicans, Phillipians [sic] and, worst of all, Negroes. Imagine the social problems this incurs in our city. As a mother of two growing daughters whose property and home joins this camp, I implore your support and influence in having this group of men moved from our community."[51] Blood promised that the problem would be promptly resolved; the racially integrated company was relocated and replaced with Company 2539, an all-white unit.[52]

In 1939, realtor and Mormon bishop Sherman Brewster in Salt Lake City blamed plunging tourism rates and urban blight on African Americans. He initiated a campaign to remove all black residents from the neighborhoods near the City and County building—a popular site for tourists. Outraged, Salt Lake City's black community marched to the Capitol to protest Brewster's campaign, but the city commissioners denied Brewster's petition. That same year, realtors adopted a restrictive covenant, a common development in American suburbs during this period, in which signatory realtors collectively decided that no real estate would be "sold, transferred granted, or conveyed to any person not of the Caucasian race."[53]

The onset of World War II further invited racial integration. Black soldiers came to Utah military bases such as Hill Air Force Base in Ogden and the Dugway Proving Grounds in the west desert.[54] More than two thousand blacks from the South came to work at the Naval Depot in Clearfield.[55] Based on past experience, the War Manpower Commission anticipated that many defense-contracting firms, including those in Utah, would express "reluctance to hire nonwhites because of the difficulty in amalgamation with the white workers." Blacks were generally hired as a group rather than as individual workers, and the

---

48. Olen Cole, *The African-American Experience in the Civilian Conservation Corps*, 19.

49. Ibid., 68.

50. Ibid., 26.

51. Mrs. Leland Larsen, Letter to Henry H. Blood, April 26, 1935, Henry H. Blood Papers, Utah State Archives, qtd. in Kenneth W. Baldridge, "Nine Years of Achievement: The Civilian Conservation Corps in Utah," 338.

52. Henry H. Blood, Letter to Mrs. Leland Larsen, May 2, 1935, Henry H. Blood Papers, Utah State Archives, qtd. in ibid., 338.

53. Eileen Hallet Stone, *Hidden History of Utah*, 55.

54. Richard O. Ulibarri, "Utah's Ethnic Minorities: A Survey," 217.

55. Antonette C. Noble, "Utah's Defense Industries and Workers in World War II," 372.

best jobs they could find tended to be as "porters, waiters, and other railroad and smelter employees."[56] While most blacks left Utah after the war, a few stayed and began to focus their efforts on correcting the racial injustice that had existed in Utah Mormonism for the past generations.[57]

A Branch of Love

While blacks in Mormon America had little choice but to deal with the legacy their faith community had inherited from white America's larger society, observers could find a counter-narrative in an unlikely locale: black South Africa. In 1865, Brigham Young closed the South African mission due to brewing Xhosa conflicts with the British government. The mission remained closed until 1903, when Warren H. Lyon reopened the mission and started anew the South African Mormon mission.[58]

For most of the twentieth-century, the relationship between blacks and Mormons in South Africa remained largely segregated, with the white American Mormons acknowledging blacks as a relic of a past or, at best, as symbols of "savage nobility." But a handful of blacks did manage to become members of the Mormon community. When they did, they revealed the tensions that white Mormons faced as they sought to reconcile the priesthood exclusionary ban with their notions of fraternity and brotherhood.

When the Mormons came into contact with South African blacks, they brought with them the racial consensus they had inherited from over two generations of race construction in the Intermountain West. Mormons had no interpretive tools to understand the origins of black people, as they did with Native Americans. Quoting the words of an old Mormon hymn, Elder Orson M. Rogers said they could ask "our Indian": "At home we can say to our Indian: 'O, stop and tell me, Red man/Who are you, why you roam/And how you get your living/Have you no God no home." And the Book of Mormon, he declared, could give them answers.[59]

But Mormons had "no such book that can tell us much about our colored brethren on this hemisphere . . . so recourse to ethnologists must be had." The first theory he cited offered no scripture, attributing the dark skin to the "climate, environment, and custom." It was possible, he believed, that "thousands of years of tropical sun beating down on our naked bodies would be sufficient to produce a change in the color of the skin that would eventually be inherited from generation to generation." Rogers distanced himself and the Saints from the "theory which has been advanced by a few, and not upheld by many . . . that the dark skin is the result of a curse from the Almighty God."[60]

---

56. Ibid.

57. Ronald Coleman, "African-Americans in Utah," 3–5.

58. Francis M. Lyman, "To the Ministry and Saints of the European Mission," 2.

59. Orson M. Rogers, "Native Tribes of South Africa," 625.

60. Ibid., 625–26.

Rogers came to South Africa with a clear set of racial assumptions: "When I first came here I thought every one was a negro who had a dark skin and kinky hair...but I found that there are different classifications made by Colonials." Though rare, he had learned that 'the true negro[es]" were "fine specimens of humanity, with large sinewy bodies, well-shaped and agile." But "pure negro[es] were "so rare in Cape Colony" that his theorizing was based on sheer speculation. By contrast, Rogers considered the "Bushmen" to be "the lowest type of the human family...much like intelligent beasts." The "Hottentots" are a "filthy people" who "gladly live on the refuge of rubbish heaps" and "sort[ed] out the garbage barrels." He found "the morals of the natives" to be "terrible...in fact they have little sense of wrong." When it came to missionary work, Rogers made no overt reference to a priesthood ban, saying only that the Elders "do very little work among the colored people, as we consider that our message is more important to the whites at present." But Rogers tired of seeing so many blacks and looked forward to the day where they "are seen only in Pullman cars or in restaurants."[61] Christianity had made the natives "very arrogant and smart." If one tries to correct them, the reply comes, 'I have the same heaven as you' and such things." The Boers "handle the natives better than the English, because they are strict with them," Rogers concluded. "As it is the nature of a native to serve, he likes a Boer."[62]

Generally, missionaries were more interested in the building of Western economic infrastructure: after one missionary gave a detailed accounting of the country's civic buildings and transportation facilities, he "trusted that what has been said will show that African cities are modern and up-to-date, rivaling those found in other new cities."[63]

In 1913, Nicholas Groesbeck Smith, George Albert Smith's half-brother, accepted the calling to be the new mission president for the South African mission, replacing President Frank J. Hewlett who had served there for the past two years.[64] Since his childhood, Smith had expressed sympathies for local blacks, even if he did not necessarily support a change in the ban. One friend, Abner Howell, had long suffered persecution from other Mormons: "Before I was in my teens," he wrote Mormon chronicler Kate Carter, "I wondered many times why I was a different color to the other boys. Little by little I was told that I was cursed and could not go to heaven when I died, but was doomed to go to hell with the devil and burn forever." One day, Nicholas's father, John Henry Smith, found Howell crying about the things he had heard. Smith "comforted me with a few kind words and took me to his house. . . . He got the Book of Mormon and turned to the 26th chapter of 2nd Nephi and last verse." The text moved Howell: "When I was through reading, a great load was lifted from my heart and mind, and my eyes were opened, and I read more and more. I thought how great that was! The words: 'all are alike unto

---

61. Ibid., 630–31, 634–35.
62. Ibid., 634–35.
63. Evan P. Wright, *A History of the South African Mission, 1903,–1944,* 3 vols. (1986), 2:52.
64. "New President for the African Mission," 900.

An unidentified man (left), likely a missionary, rides with Pres. Nicholas G. Smith (middle) in a rickshaw pulled by a tribal African man (right), likely in Durban, South Africa, ca. mid-1910s. Courtesy Nicholas and Marion Smith family.

God.'"[65] Only a few years later, Nicholas would try to convince President Joseph F. Smith to allow some of those Africans to receive their temple ordinances.[66] Nicholas's son, Gerald Gay Smith, recalls when an Ogden restaurant told Howell that he could not dine with the rest of the team but had to eat in the kitchen. Smith allegedly told the manager that "we'll all eat in the kitchen with him."[67]

His experiences relate the complicated relationship white Mormons created with South African blacks. Nicholas's wife, Florence, fretted over Smith's calling. When Florence first learned of the location, she exclaimed: "Oh that horrid black place!"[68] Florence later said that "all I could think of was black people and all those animals."[69] But she went. Worse, the Smiths were so poor that their first home was in Woodstock, a racially integrated community a little east of Capetown. Their home was robbed in November 1915. But they grew to appreciate the humanity of their black neighbors. One of Smith's sons recalls that when his mother lost her watch, it was a "black boy" that "returned the watch to us." The Smiths "always felt it was a direct answer to prayer." Their sentiments only went so far; a year later, Smith finally managed to raise the money to rent a location in Rosebank, a suburb "where only white folks live."[70] Two years later, they purchased a home in Mowbray on land that "included grass[,] trees, and flowers." Smith thought it a "beautiful home, ample in size to accommodate living quarters for the mission president and missionaries living there."[71]

---

65. Kate B. Carter, *The Story of the Negro Pioneer,* 57.

66. Lavina Fielding Anderson, "A Ministry of Blessing: Nicholas Groesbeck Smith," 59.

67. Ibid., 61 note 3.

68. Lavina Fielding Anderson, *Nicholas Groesbeck Smith, 1881-1945: A Documentary History,* 72.

69. Ibid., 74.

70. Ibid., 81.

71. Ibid., August 27, 1916.

Though the Smiths moved away from their racially-integrated neighborhood, Mormon blacks enjoyed a congenial relationship with white Mormon authorities. Paul T. Harris and William P. Daniels were two South African black men who joined the Mormons in the early twentieth-century. Harris, an African American cook for the Fordsberg police, was a faithful tithe-payer and won the friendship of Smith. Smith regularly associated with Harris and mentions eating, lodging, and holding special testimony meetings with him.[72] When some missionaries visited Harris's home "for supper the old colored man made us welcome."[73] Elder June B. Sharp, then a missionary serving in South Africa, recalls visiting Harris during a raging thunderstorm:

> Brother Harris told the missionaries not to be concerned; they got down on their knees and prayed; he asked the Lord to stop the storm until the elders could return to their quarters. The rain stopped immediately but started as soon as the elders returned home.[74]

Smith also forged a particularly strong relationship with William P. Daniels, a "coloured" man whom he met while living in Woodstock.[75] Born in Stellenbosch, Daniels's sister had joined the Mormons before the Smiths arrived and gave William rave reviews about the American sect.[76] When missionary Alfred J. Gowers taught Daniels at his shop, Daniels was impressed by Gowers's dedication: "He had come 13,000 miles to preach the Gospel, and was not receiving a penny. . . . This struck me very forcibly, and I compared his position with that of my minister who was earning a comfortable if not fat salary and was living in a house given him free by the congregation."[77]

Daniels visited Utah, accepted Mormonism, and received a blessing from Joseph F. Smith, then President of the Church, assuring him that he would receive the priesthood at some point. Missionary Evan Wright observed that "hundreds of latter-day missionaries and local members have heard Brother Daniels testify that he had received such a blessing." With "tears running down his cheeks and dropping off his chin," Daniels knew that "someday, perhaps in the next life, he would be able to hold the priesthood."[78] Daniels asked President Smith what he should tell them in South Africa. Smith enjoined him to "tell them the truth." Daniels listened; when an article came out in the *Cape Argus*, he effused about his interactions with the Utah Mormon population: "I saw nothing that hurt my religious susceptibilities, but everything that caused me to admire and strive to follow the standard

---

72. Ibid., 160.

73. Ibid., January 13, 1919.

74. Ibid., 161.

75. Ibid., September 20, 1916. In South Africa, "coloured" was a separate legal category for mixed-race blacks.

76. For his birth place, see "Cape District," Cumorah's Southern Cross 7, no. 3 (March 1933): 46.

77. Nicholas Smith, Manuscript, 162.

78. Ibid., 162.

of their faith."[79] President Smith noted that for Daniels, "nothing was too good to be said about Utah & the Mormons."[80] From that time forward, the Daniels family hoped to join the Saints in the Rockies. In 1921, Mission President J. Wyley Sessions counseled them against it: he "read [to them]…an article about the Saints not to gather yet under present conditions in Zion."[81] In July 1923, William's wife, Alice, expressed her hope of leaving South Africa for Utah: "We are striving to get to Zion if it be the will of our Heavenly Father."[82]

Daniels went out of his way to be hospitable to the Mormon missionaries. One evening, Daniels prepared "a banquet of about ten courses" for the Smith family and the missionaries in Cape Town. Another evening, Nicholas recorded that he and his family had dined with the Daniels family and "had a most delightful time nearly eating our heads off."[83] Nicholas appreciatively recorded Daniels's gift to them on another occasion of "a basket of pairs [sic] and apples."[84] Smith also had no qualms about taking his family and the elders to help Daniels celebrate his fifty-third birthday where they "had a pleasant time but ate too much."[85] On another "most delightful day," the Smith family accepted the Daniels'es invitation to spend the day with them "visiting with colored people and riding around the town eating strawberries."[86]

The racial climate of South Africa made it difficult, if not impossible, for Daniels to attend church regularly. When a member "brought up the question of color" during an evening class, Smith noticed that "Daniels [was] the only

Pres. William P. Daniels, ca. 1930s, served as Branch President over the "Branch of Love" from early 1932 until the time of his death in 1936. Dalton called him "one of my loyalist, kindest, sweetest, friends." Courtesy LDS Church History Library.

---

79. Ibid., 164.

80. Ibid., April 15, 1917.

81. Mowbray Cottage Meeting Minutes, October 10, 1921, LDS Church History Library.

82. Ibid., July 9, 1923.

83. Anderson, Nicholas G. Smith, February 7, 1917 and June 4, 1918.

84. Ibid., April 19, 1917.

85. Ibid., August 19, 1917.

86. Ibid., December 11, 1917.

colored man present" and "felt somewhat hurt" by the member's comment.[87] But Daniels persisted. On South Africa's Union holiday over a month later, "Daniels & a young lady were the only ones who came to Bible class."[88]

Daniels devised his own solution. Though denied priesthood privileges by Joseph F. Smith, Daniels formed an *ad hoc* congregation based out of his home. The study group began in January 1921. Made up primarily of his family and missionaries, Daniels' group studied the scriptures together and held "testimony meetings" every Monday evening. Fellow black member Paul T. Harris also attended on occasion.[89] Daniels's Mormonism was rigorous and exacting. On June 13, 1921, Daniels presented a lesson entitled "Sincerity of belief not enough," quoting Matthew 15:8: "This people draweth nigh unto me with their mouth, and honoureth me with their lips; but their heart is far from me."[90]

At one of the early meetings, Daniels "introduced the Gospel" to all attending. The Daniels group saw the expansion of Mormonism into South Africa as a sign of the apocalypse; his wife, Alice, quoted Matthew 24:14: "this gospel of the kingdom shall be preached in all the world for a witness unto all nations; and then shall the end come."[91] Their lessons touched on topics associated with American Mormonism, including titles such as "American Indians of Israel."[92] Hymns included American Mormon classics such as "Redeemer of Israel," "Ye Elders of Israel," "Joseph Smith's First Prayer" and "Oh My Father."[93]

Initially, the congregation accepted Daniels as the presiding authority over the small group, even when the mission president was present.[94] On October 10, Nicholas Smith's successor, J. Wyley Sessions, motioned that the Daniels family branch should be "establish[ed] [as] a Regular Meeting under the authorities of the Church in South Africa to be presided by an Elder or any other authorized person sent by the Mission President and in charge of Bro. Daniels." The Monday evening study sessions would "still be continued as usual." The motion "was voted for and unanimously carried" by all present.[95] The following week, Elder Golden Harris was assigned to preside over the Daniels branch.[96] Other missionaries, such as Clarence W. Jones, Clinton M. Black, and Chester A. Engstrom took turns presiding over the meeting, and the mission president continued to attend with some frequency. But Daniels almost always conducted the meetings.[97] The Daniels family appeared to have accepted the

---

87. Ibid., April 26, 1917.

88. Ibid., May 31, 1917.

89. Mowbray Cottage Meeting Minutes, April 25, 1921.

90. Ibid., June 13, 1921.

91. Ibid., January 16, 1921. These minutes are near the back of the first volume. See also Mowbray Cottage Branch Minutes, July 11, 1921.

92. Mowbray Cottage Meeting Minutes, May 15, 1922.

93. Ibid., July 11, 1921, February 5, 1922, May 15, 1922, and May 18, 1925.

94. Ibid., April 25, 1921, May 16, 1921, May 23, May 30, 1921, July 11, 1921.

95. Ibid., October 10, 1921.

96. Ibid., October 17, 1921.

97. Ibid., October 22, 1922, November 13, 1922, February 5, 1923, April 16, 1923.

new arrangement without reservation; in June 1923, both William and Alice Daniels gave a "short talk on some instant of obeying the authority of the priesthood." They opened the meeting by singing the hymn: "We Thank Thee Oh God for a Prophet" and closed with: "Come Listen to a Prophet's Voice."[98]

No conversations about racial issues were recorded in the existing meeting minutes. During the lesson on "the pre-existence of spirits," Willie Daniels, the scribe, recorded no comments noting the racial component of many Mormons' discussions on premortality. Regardless, Daniels had likely come to grips with the exclusion. Daniels' son, Willie posed a situation in which "an old man . . . and also a young child" were baptized; which, Willie asked, "would have the greater reward"? Daniels pointed his son to "the parable of the labourers who came to work at different hours yet received. . . the same pay."[99] Daniels and his wife consistently testified to their commitment to the Mormon Church and its tenets. During one meeting Alice Daniels declared to all "as to how the gospel ha[d] improved her." At another, Daniels bore "a strong testimony on how a latter-day Saint can by faith accomplish his duties with a good heart and mention some instances on how he tried to promote the gospel by <his> example as a Latter-day Saint."[100]

Their meetings were not always rigorous explorations of Mormon doctrine. A week before St. Patrick's Day, "Irish jokes and stories were related by members of the family."[101] On Alice Daniels's birthday, Willie Daniels recorded, "President and Sister Sessions . . . were here and had a good time." Later in the evening, "the Saints came and spent an enjoyable evening" celebrating the birthday festivities.[102] The Daniels often hosted "Home nights" that not only encouraged discussion of gospel doctrine but also "games and refreshment."[103] During one light-hearted evening, Daniels sang a rendition of "You're a Dangerous Girl," a jazz ballad by Russian American singer Al Jolson. Still feeling the romantic spirit, both William and Alice shared the story of their courtship. Willie recorded that William told "how Father met mother" and Alice followed up William's story with "how Father proposed."[104]

As Daniels conducted meetings under the auspices of the Church, white Saints in South Africa continued to say what had been said for generations about black ineligibility to hold the priesthood. In July 1927, the *Cumorah Monthly Bulletin* observed that the question of "who may hold the priesthood" was a "subject of frequent inquiry" in South Africa "where so many good people are unable to declare, with certainty, a genealogy pure from the Hamite or Canaanitish blood." The mission president, then Samuel Martin who served from 1926 to

98. Ibid., June 11, 1923.
99. Ibid., July 25, 1921.
100. Ibid., August 8, 1921.
101. Ibid., March 10, 1921.
102. Ibid., September 5, 1921.
103. Ibid., June 11, 1923.
104. Ibid., July 9, 1923.

1929, struggled to articulate the Church's position. When faced with the Old Testament-based racial thought so entrenched in Mormon dogma, he assured the South African Saints that he was "not unmindful of the fact that we are living under very different conditions today" than those that existed in Old Testament times. "We are living in a day of grace and not under the rigid ceremonial laws of the Mosaic dispensation." The law was a strange one, Martin seemed to say: "we may not fully comprehend all the meaning contained in the prophetic declarations of God to His prophets on first reading, nor are we always able to realize their awful literalness."

When presented with a priesthood candidate who could not definitively identify himself as non-African, the "servants of God dare not presume to confer it, but humbly submit to His judgment." For each race, Martin promised, "there is a kingdom, a mansion prepared in exact harmony with the laws we obey, irrespective of our colour, wealth, or education in a worldly sense." But still, Martin concluded, "the Priesthood is only for those whom God shall so call and choose out of the various races." All should partake of the gospel blessings, even if they could not participate in church administration; to refuse activity "would be like a drowning man refusing to enter the life boat because he is not allowed to row or drive it into port himself." Ultimately, Martin concluded: "All the human race are not called to be kings."[105]

But Daniels's faithfulness fit awkwardly, at best, into this racial narrative. In 1929, Don M. Dalton replaced Martin as mission president. Unlike Martin, Dalton could not help but notice the commitment of Daniels's small band. Between 1929 and 1932, William P. Daniels was set apart in what was an unprecedented calling in Mormon history: the first black branch president never ordained to the priesthood. On President Don Dalton's photograph of Daniels, he jotted a note indicating that Daniels began his service as branch president in 1929. However, in March 1932, *Cumorah's Southern Cross* called Daniels' congregation a "new Branch."[106]

Called the "Branch of Love," it was, to South African Church leaders, an auxiliary not unlike the Relief Society or Primary.[107] While they enjoyed an inferior status in relation to the other Church units, the arrangement was well regarded by other members; after one branch conference, *Cumorah's Southern Messenger* observed that the branch was "thriving," even if it consisted wholly of the Daniels family.[108]

The branch read complex theological works like *Jesus the Christ* by James E. Talmage. Daughter Alice Daniels later remembered that they would "read a line and then discuss it." It "took [the family] 20 years to get through the

---

105. Samuel Martin, "Who May Bear the Priesthood," 1-5.

106. "Cape District," *Cumorah's Southern Cross* 6, no. 3 (March 1932): 46.

107. "Cape District," Cumorah's Southern Cross 6, no. 12 (November 1932): 203. For a very brief discussion of the Branch of Love, see Newell Bringhurst, "Mormonism in Black Africa: Changing Attitudes and Practices, 1830-1981," 21 note 26.

108. "Cape District," *Cumorah's Southern Cross* 6, no. 3 (March 1932): 46.

book."[109] A tremendous cook, Daniels prepared "wonderful roast beef dinners with yellow rice" in a "spotlessly clean home" for the missionaries.[110] Daniels also liked to welcome new elders "into the missionary work…with one of those famous Daniels' dinners, including the 'Penguin Eggs.'"[111] In 1929, Daniels led the Saints in their Book of Mormon reading, going through the text sixteen times in a year.[112] Dalton publicly congratulated Daniels for being one of fourteen Latter-day Saints for reading the Book of Mormon twice in six months.[113]

In his later years, Daniels fell ill with heart difficulties and neuritis.[114] When President Dalton learned of Daniels's affliction, he "wept bitterly" and gathered his family at the Daniels home to "say farewell." Daniels recalls that the family "knelt at my bedside, and prayed, even the youngest, little George Edward, who was only five." Dalton administered a blessing to the ailing Daniels and "promised me I would return to Cumorah," the name of the South African Mission home. Nearly three weeks later, Dalton "fetched me in his car, and took me to Sunday School" where Daniels bore testimony of his "wonderful recovery due to faith and prayer." All "present from the oldest, to the very youngest, came and shook hands with me and welcomed me back in their midst."[115] Alice always felt that Church leadership "accepted us as good, wholesome Latter-day Saints."[116] After Daniels's death, Dalton remembered Daniels as "one of my loyalist, kindest, sweetest, friends."[117] His obituary in *Cumorah's Southern Messenger* praised his home as a "shrine of hospitality" where "scores of missionaries have been . . . to partake of the sweet spirit which won for the little branch the name, 'the Branch of Love.' "[118]

The relationship between the Daniels family and white South African Mormons indicates the several layers of racial thought that made up Mormonism in South Africa in the early twentieth century. All who knew Daniels acknowledged him to be a first-rate Latter-day Saint, even to the point that he compelled white Saints to make space for him. John Smith, then a child, remembered that the Danielses "would come into our meetings, then they would sneak out" for fear of embarrassing the white Mormons. When Daniels saw Nicholas G. Smith in public, Daniels "would try to dodge him because you didn't associate with and greet blacks." But President Smith "would cut across anyway and put his

---

109. Hal King, "Touching Temple Fulfills a Dream for Aged Woman," 10.

110. Anderson, Nicholas Groesbeck Smith, 166.

111. "Resting Now from Care and Sorrow," *Cumorah's Southern Messenger* 10, no. 10 (October 1936): 153.

112. "Roll of Honour," *Cumorah's Southern Cross* (September 1929): 5.

113. "East London Wins Book of Mormon Reading Competition," *Cumorah's Southern Cross* 6, no. 4 (April 1932): 62.

114. "Cape District," *Cumorah's Southern Cross* 7, no. 3 (March 1933): 46.

115. Anderson, Nicholas Groesbeck Smith, 167.

116. King, "Touching Temple Fulfills a Dream for Aged Woman," 10.

117. Notation on back of photograph of William P. Daniels, Don and Myrtle Dalton Mission Papers, Box 1, fd. 3, LDS Church History Library.

118. "Resting Now from Care and Sorrow," 153.

Nicholas G. Smith and wife, Florence, visiting a tribal dwelling during his tenure as Mission President in South Africa, ca. mid-1910s. Courtesy LDS Church History Library.

arm around him. That was our Dad."[119] When Daniels died in 1936, Alice remembered her father urging her: "Whatever you do, Alice, stand by the Church."[120] In 1981, the *LDS Church News* lauded the Danielses as "the only LDS black family in that nation" for "more than half a century."[121]

After his death, the Mormon-black relationship remained began to show signs of deterioration. In 1941, Utah-born immigrant Zola Schaer relocated to South Africa in an effort "to recuperate after a long illness." On the way to her new home, the city of Maun, Schaer traveled with her party of family and close friends through a native settlement. When their car broke down nearby, Schaer and Foster "walked around the village taking in the places of interest." After taking in the animal life, they set up camp in the natives' settlements. The women "undressed for bed regardless of the natives who were sitting around enjoying the fire." Foster's two boys played shirtless with the native children; she took a picture of them and submitted it to *Cumorah's Southern Messenger*. The editor joked that the boys were "go[ing] native." [122] When President June Sharp's car broke down in Basutoland, they stayed the night with a Mormon trader, Norman Halse. The next morning, Halse "led the natives who came to trade in a few of their own dances," a moment that the missionaries were quick to capture on film.[123]

The Native Boys

Ida Sharp, wife of mission president June Sharp, made only passing references to the black population in 1947, seeing them either as a sea of street vendors or perhaps as "the native boy[s]" who carried their luggage and did their ironing.[124]

But the rise of apartheid reified the racial sentiments already brewing within the Mormon community. Beginning in 1949, the Afrikaner government began to implement a series of draconian laws forbidding whites and non-whites from

119. Anderson, Nicholas Groesbeck Smith, 165.

120. King, "Touching Temple Fulfills a Dream for Aged Woman," 10.

121. Ibid.

122. Zola Schaer, "N'Gamiland Adventure," *Cumorah's Southern Messenger*, vol. 15, no. 2 (February 1941): 22–23, 30.

123. "On Tour with the President," *Cumorah's Southern Messenger* 23, no. 11 (November 1948): 114.

124. Ida Sharp, Notebook, September 20–21, 1947, LDS Church History Library.

living in the same area of town, having sexual relationships, and marrying. Each resident was also required to be classified according to his or her race: white, colored (i.e., mixed-race), black, or another ethnicity entirely (e.g., Indian).[125] In 1952, Prime Minister Daniel Malan defended white efforts to retain political control of the Cape: "To do what world opinion demands would mean suicide by white South Africa."[126]

Like Malan, the Mormons took care to ensure that the Church in South Africa was governed exclusively by leaders of white ancestry. When mission president Evan P. Wright took office in 1948, the First Presidency, then consisting of George Albert Smith, J. Reuben Clark, and David O. McKay directed him that "no man was to be ordained to or advanced in the priesthood until he had traced his genealogy out of Africa." Past mission presidents like Smith, Sessions, and Dalton had too freely socialized with families like the Daniels. In 1949, the editor of *Cumorah's Southern Messenger* noted that "there is a great deal of genealogy work being done in South Africa [so] that those who have been baptized into the church may trace their genealogy out of the country and be ordained to the priesthood."[127]

The burdens of the genealogical program were becoming increasingly apparent; by July 1950, two more full-time missionaries were appointed to work as genealogical researchers, in hopes of "increase[ing] the Priesthood holders among the male members of the Church."[128] President Wright assigned "six missionaries" to spend "much of their time doing genealogical work both instructing the members in connection with this work and assisting in family research."[129] Special trips were made to locate archival collections in Paarl, Stellenbosch, and private collections.[130]

The genealogical program incited considerable complaint. "It is an unfortunate situation that one's genealogy must be traced out of the country before a worthy person can hold the priesthood," South African genealogist Harold Lundstrom, a Mormon, acknowledged, "but that is the way that has been decreed by revelation through the Prophets that have been called to direct the Kingdom of God on earth." The future of the Church could depend upon it, for "the time may come when the Elders will be recalled just as they have been in the past." Otherwise, the members would "be left to themselves for leadership," and if they do not "possess the Priesthood and exercise the Priesthood righteously, the Church will not prosper here, just as it won't prosper in many of the other

125. Deborah Posel, The Making of Apartheid, 1948-1961.

126. Alex Thomson, *U.S. Foreign Policy towards Apartheid South Africa, 1948–1994*, 23.

127. Marriner K. Norr, "Genealogy in South Africa," *Cumorah's Southern Messenger*, 24, no. 12 (December 1949): 180.

128. "Two Elders Appointed to Work Genealogy," *Cumorah's Southern Messenger* 25, no. 7 (July 1950): 107.

129. Prince and Wright, *David O. McKay*, 75–76.

130. "Genealogy Message," *Cumorah's Southern Messenger* 27, no. 8 (August 1952): 124.

countries where mankind will 'come not unto this Priesthood.'"[131] The very existence of the work appeared to depend on one's ability to demonstrate a "pure" non-African ancestry.

President Wright expressed similar frustration: "We are doing a lot of genealogical research but many of our people haven't been able to trace their lines out of Africa and therefore are not eligible for ordination to the Priesthood. Other individuals have run into slave lines from three to six or seven generations ago. . . . [M]any questions have been raised which will seriously effect [sic] future missionary work in South Africa." In June 1952, Wright expressed his anxiety about the sustainability of the priesthood infrastructure: "We are badly in need of leadership through the priesthood, and I am most anxious to ordain men as fast as we possibly can." Admittedly, this program also annoyed white members. They felt that the Americans were challenging their whiteness. "This is the only mission in the Church where it is necessary for a man to trace his genealogy to establish his eligibility for the priesthood," Wright pointed out in correspondence with the First Presidency. "As a result, the members of the Church in this country feel penalized."[132]

White South African Saints also expressed their dismay to Church leaders above the mission level. In an address at the April 1952 general conference, Apostle Matthew Cowley reassured the South African Saints "who have never had a visit from one of the leaders of this Church" that their "prayers will one day be answered."[133] David O. McKay responded by visiting South Africa in early 1954, the first trip made by any General Authority to Africa. He visited in large part to address whites' concerns that they did not have pure European ancestry. During his trip, he echoed the longstanding—though far from scriptural—wisdom that the priesthood ban could be dated to premortality. Curtis Tracy, one of the young missionaries present, found it "so beautiful and clear" that it made "you want to get out and shout this gospel, the message of ours, from the housetops."[134] Tracy "wished I could remember the exact words," but he remembered McKay explaining "things so perfect and lovely that you know no one but a prophet of God could utter them." McKay reportedly claimed that, "like certain molecules attract each other," premortal spirits "were attracted to certain parents because of a likeness or spiritual attraction. The spirits that came through the lineage of Cain chose it freely and were willing to give up certain privileges."[135] McKay concluded that "white men who had no outward signs of negro blood . . . could receive the priesthood" with the approval of the mission president.[136]

---

131. "Ancestral Data Gathered over 100 Years," *Cumorah's Southern Messenger* 25, no. 7 (July 1950): 103.

132. Prince and Wright, *David O. McKay*, 75–76.

133. Matthew Cowley, "You Are the Leaven," in *Conference Report*, (April 1952): 102 and *Cumorah's Southern Messenger* 27, no. 7 (July 1952): 105.

134. Curtis Tracy, Journal, January 17, 1954, LDS Church History Library.

135. Ibid.

136. Ibid.

Despite this important step toward local autonomy, even after McKay's visit, a "pure" genealogy was still equated with premortal worthiness and access to the priesthood. In 1960, missionary Claude Richards chastised the "complacent attitude of some people towards their costly birth-right, well-earned in the spirit world." Too many Saints "neglect covenant birth as of little consequence" and "do not value their church membership, nor the priesthood conferred upon them."[137]

Most religious organizations in South Africa had segregated congregations, in deed if not in word. In 1957, the National Party, South Africa's ruling white minority, passed the Native Law Amendment Act, which, among other provisions, prohibited blacks from meeting or assembling with whites in areas where their presence would be deemed a "nuisance."[138] Anglican Archbishop Geoffrey Clayton resisted this law. Though sympathetic to the plight of ethnic minorities, Clayton had long hesitated to directly challenge the government's policies, instead allowing a few minorities to attend church with white Anglicans and administer limited humanitarian aid. But the "church clause" pushed Clayton beyond his habitual restraint. In March 1957, he warned Minister Hendrik Verwoerd that the Anglican Church would be "unable to obey it or counsel our clergy and people to do so." The Baptist Union, often more moderate on church-state, warned the government that the new act will "compel law-abiding Baptists to violate the law . . . . [W]here conscience and legislation conflict we must take our stand with our conscience, whatever the consequences may be."[139]

The act was never seriously enforced, except for a handful of cases where a black congregation tried to gather in white areas. Even the racially minded Dutch Reformed Congregation in the conservative Pinelands suburb invited a black minister to preach a sermon to its members; Dr. A. J. van der Merwe, a Dutch Reformed Church official, thought the act to be politically unwise: "Any practical advantage which it may have does not weigh up against its propaganda value against the minister." Committed though the Dutch Reformed Church was to racial segregation, they had "tried to completely honest and sincere." They "credit our brother Churches with the same sincerity in arriving at an opposite conclusion, and where we do not see eye to eye in this matter we must agree to differ in brotherly love."[140]

While other denominations sought out legislative change, the Saints accepted the routine, at least partly because black members were so few. In 1953, President Leroy Duncan "found that many things have not changed" since he

<hr />

137. "Protect Your Birthright," *Cumorah's Southern Messenger* 35, no. 4 (April 1960): 97.

138. Steven Gish, *Desmond Tutu: A Biography,* 24.

139. De Gruchy, *The Church Struggle in South Africa,* 59.

140. John W. DeGruchy, *The Church Struggle in South Africa,* 59–60. See also William Sachs, *The Transformation of Anglicanism: From State Church to Global Communion,* 316.

served in South Africa as a young man.[141] In 1961, President Hugh B. Brown praised the Saints for their "sturdy and rugged personalities," a quality that South African Mormon leaders felt mirrored the early Saints.[142] The underlying message was not resistance in the name of freedom of religion but instead clinging to what had become the status quo and which increasingly harmonized with the Afrikaaner nationalistic narrative then prevalent in the country. *Cumorah's Southern Messenger* acknowledged: "Here is the native African who was the first one to inhabit the continent and next to him is the white man."[143] But whiteness was linked to social progress. The article about the history of the "Mysterious Dark Continent" told the white narrative as the story of the "real Africa." The "real" country began only with "the increase of [colonist] population that continued to flow in." The immigrants "trekked into the wilderness and formed several colonies further inland." Though the colonists had "many troubles to overcome with the ever threatening native tribes," the blacks "were eventually overruled" and the whites "began to take complete control of the country."[144] In the early 1950s, the Saints could count only about two thousand members, only four hundred of them active participants.[145] Their appropriation of South African nationalism was a manifestation of the Mormons' hardwired survival instincts coupled with generations of racialized discourse—discourse that itself had been adopted as the Saints struggled to survive the racial currents of American society.

In the 1950s and 1960s, Church leaders struggled to expand the membership base. Under the direction of Mission President Leroy Duncan, chapel construction increased throughout the country. "One of the principle [sic] needs in the South African mission," *Cumorah's Southern Messenger* observed, "is for adequate and beautiful chapels where members of the Church may assemble."[146] As of 1949, Mowbray had the only chapel in the entire mission, a chapel considered to be "a real blessing in the lives of the people in Cape Town."[147] Now, drawing primarily on member donations, the Saints pushed for new chapels to be built in Johannesburg, Springs, and Ramah, among others.[148] It was a daunting struggle, and branches failed to retain youth. A generation later, Mission President Ben De Wet ruefully remembered: "Dances, regular films shows, concerts, picnics, sports

---

141. "Mission President's Message," *Cumorah's Southern Messenger* 28, no. 2 (February 1953): 18. For Duncan's earlier missionary service, see "Elders in the South African Mission," *Cumorah's Monthly Bulletin* 1, no. 5 (October 15, 1927): front matter.

142. Hugh B. Brown, "A Message to the Saints of the South African Mission," 120.

143. "Building the Kingdom," *Cumorah's Southern Messenger* 36, no. 10 (October 1961): 265.

144. "The Mysterious Dark Continent," *Cumorah's Southern Messenger* 36, no. 10 (October 1961): 260–61.

145.Sister Smith, "God, Grant Us Strength," 132.

146. "Beautiful Chapels—A Pressing Need," *Cumorah's Southern Messenger* 24, no. 12 (December 1949): 174.

147. Ibid.

148. "Adieu, Kind Friends, Adieu," *Cumorah's Southern Messenger* 28, no. 2 (February 1953): 22; "Ramah Branch," *Cumorah's Southern Messenger* 30, no. 2 (February 1955): 31.

events, you name it, all were tried only to learn that Satan was smarter in his field of activity than we were."[149]

South African Saints maintained a close bond with their American mother church. Branches occasionally held square dances to raise funds for chapel construction, an American-style activity that brought "the Church into the limelight" and aroused nonmember interest. Between dances, the members were "kept busy answering questions and explaining principles of the Gospel."[150] In December 1950, one of the branches sponsored a Gold and Green Ball, in which the Saints "transformed . . . the hall into a scene of sylvan beauty" with ballroom dancing and a royalty contest. [151] In Durban, a Relief Society member, Alma Jones, regularly lectured on American authors like Herman Melville and Walt Whitman.[152] Missionaries showed films that "included slides of scenery in the state of Utah, a picture history of the Book of Mormon and reproductions of archaeological remains in Central America." Two branches—Cumorah and Ramah—were given Book of Mormon names.[153]

South African mission leadership demonstrated a remarkable ability to compartmentalize the apartheid system from the teachings of Mormonism. "Injustice is [a] great evil," Fisher instructed the mission; "we must be concerned with the justice and welfare of all people, because the membership of this Church is made up of people from all nations." He also condemned "intolerance" as "another self-destroying evil," reminding the Saints that "brotherhood, like charity, begins at home" and "must be resident in our hearts, on our streets, in our towns."[154]

On rare occasions, *Cumorah's Southern Messenger* spoke out against racial policies. In August 1947, Vivien Meik, a widely syndicated reporter and longtime resident of Africa, quoted Haile Selassie, the Emperor of Ethiopia: "[Europe] let my helpless country be ravaged with gas and bombs. She called it civilizing blacks but your own white nations will yet live to admit the stark truth—that by distorting the Father's teaching Europe was blackening civilization." Saving Europe, Meik argued, "lies not in Europe." On the contrary, in Mormonism's "teaching, in the practice of its precepts it is showing the world that Christianity that . . . I learnt in the simple prayers at my mother's knee. The Christianity of Christ—not the mere 'Churchianity' of Europe today."[155] Meik eventually joined the Mormons and became a columnist with the *Deseret News*.

---

149. Ben De Wet, "South Africa: A Different View," 8, LDS Church History Library.

150. For instances of Mormon dances in South Africa, see, "South African Mission," *Cumorah's Southern Messenger* 27, no. 3 (March 1952): 38; "The Members and the Mission," *Cumorah's Southern Messenger* 32, no. 8 (August 1957): 122; "Branch Notes—Ramah Branch," *Cumorah's Southern Messenger* 32, no. 12 (December 1957): 189.

151. "Cumorah G and G Ball," *Cumorah's Southern Messenger* 25, no. 12 (December 1950): 187.

152. Relief Society Minutes, Durban Branch, July 11 and August 15, 1963, LR 2382 14, LDS Church History Library.

153. "A Peculiar People," *Cumorah's Southern Messenger* 32, no. 7 (July 1957): 101.

154. "Priesthood Corner," *Cumorah's Southern Messenger* 32, no. 3 (March 1957), 39.

155. Vivien Meik, "Is Mormonism the Remedy," 111-12.

Such instances were rare. It was more frequent for LDS publications in South Africa to caricature blacks, highlighting their allegedly "primitive" natures. In May 1949, a group of singing Elders called "the Mormonaires" toured the townships, observing "native life in its true primitive form." The black audience (called "a pack of dirty natives" by the news writer) was "enthusiastic" to hear the Elders to sing American songs, but after one of them "pos[ed] for a picture with a rather sticky, black baby," he "couldn't stand himself until he'd scrubbed, sterilized, and de-odorised his hands."[156] The cover of the magazine featured a black native wearing feathers and a loincloth, while he held a tribal shield.[157] That fall, the elders continued their singing tour in Zululand and found that the Zulus were "the most intent listeners" and "thoroughly enjoyed the popular strains of American music as rendered by their 'white brothers.'"[158] In December 1952, the cover incorporated a caricaturized version of a native alongside a depiction of Santa Claus, both holding a large present offering "Greetings" to the readers.[159]

White South African Mormons were much more willing to entertain Asian cultural customs. American missionaries had long commented on how trying "real" Indian cuisine was one of the treats of serving in South Africa.[160] In March 1952, the youth of the Mowbray Branch arranged to have Pandit Rishiraim deliver a presentation on India that offered a "vivid picture of conditions in his own country and was prepared to answer questions relating to the similarities and differences between the administration of India and South Africa." President Wright added his thoughts on "the unique opportunity" the Saints had "of hearing the views of the Indian to-day."[161] Nearly two decades later in May 1970, the Bulawayo Branch sponsored a "Chinese Dinner" in which the chapel's recreation hall was a "fairyland with Chinese lanterns swaying between red curtains, the walls beautifully decorated with Chinese scrolls surrounded by dozens of fans and Chinese lamps." Waitresses were "dressed in white Chinese costumes and carried pink sunshades" while Chinese music played in the background.[162] The Relief Society in Johannesburg arranged for a "charming Indian girl, Sarena" modeling her sari. Though "several very beautiful saries were displayed . . . time did not permit the model[ing] of them all." A few weeks later, the Pretoria Relief Society arranged for a "cultural evening" in which "Pretoria will represent India." The sisters were asked "to dress in saries," and the Relief Society "will take curry and rice."[163]

156. "Gospel Preached through Music," *Cumorah's Southern Messenger* 24, no. 5 (May 1949): 70.

157. Cover of *Cumorah's Southern Messenger* 24, no. 5 (May 1949).

158. "'Mormonaires' Attract Bloemfontein Audiences," *Cumorah's Southern Messenger* 24, no. 9 (September 1949): 128.

159. Cover of *Cumorah's Southern Messenger* [2]7, no. 12 (December 1952).

160. "District Highlights," *Cumorah's Southern Messenger* 13, no. 10 (October 1939): 157.

161. "District Highlights," *Cumorah's Southern Messenger* 27, no. 5 (May 1952): 76.

162. "Your Ward and Branch Activities," *Cumorah's Southern Messenger* 45, no. 5 (May 1970): 130.

163. Pretoria Relief Society Minutes, Transvaal Stake, June 1 and 13, 1972, LR 7191 14, LDS Church History Library.

Other Christian denominations reflected the hardening racial legislation. Journalist Can Themba, a writer for the urban black magazine, *Drum,* visited various churches in Johannesburg to assess their openness to integration. "The Presbyterian Church in Noord Street allowed me in, yet the one in Orange Grove refused me admittance." The Orange Grove clergy physically pushed him, saying that the owners of the building opposed integration; they "also said something about the laws of the country." He found South Africa's Dutch Reformed Church, the state church, even less sympathetic. It had long offered scriptural justification for apartheid. When Themba approached a Kensington meetinghouse, "an aged church official . . . shoved me violently, shouting for me to get away."[164] In 1962, a small Presbyterian congregation of nine experimented with integration, but this denomination died out quickly.[165] Some racially integrated congregations like the Anglicans ignored the law and continued to meet without disturbance. While the government did not repeal the law, few efforts were made to enforce it.[166]

But Mormon leadership accommodated the government's demands. In the mid-1960s, Moses Mahlangu learned about the Book of Mormon and was intrigued to find that it could settle points of doctrine dividing South African Christians: "People will have no need to fight if they read both the Bible and the Book of Mormon," he argued.[167] According to Andrew Clark, an American expatriate living in South Africa, Mission President Howard Badger[168] "applied to the government in Pretoria and received special permission to baptize blacks," including Mahlangu. But shortly before his baptism, "President Badger learned from America that the gospel was to be preached first to the whites and then to the blacks." "What are we going to do?" Mahlangu asked Badger. "I don't know what to do," Badger responded, "because I tried to baptize you, but now I can't go against instructions."[169] For the next fourteen years, Mahlangu came anyway,

---

164. Cam Themba, *The Will to Die,* 77.

165. "First Integrated Church," *Florence [Fla.] Times Daily,* November 3, 1962, 2.

166. DeGruchy, *The Church Struggle in South Africa,* 60.

167. "Moses Mahlangu—The Conversion Power of the Book of Mormon," https://www.lds.org/pages/moses-mahlangu-the-conversion-power-of-the-book-of-mormon?lang=eng&country=afe (accessed December 29, 2013).

168. In the 1930s, Mission President Don McCarroll Dalton started a Mormon missionary baseball club; this club played a significant role in exposing South African whites to Mormons. Booker T. Alston, "The Cumorah Baseball Club: Mormon Missionaries and Baseball in South Africa," *Journal of Mormon History,* 40, no. 2 (Summer 2014): 93-127. Howard Badger, then a missionary to South Africa, played ball at the *Winderbosch* commons of Capetown. The club organized its teams strictly on racial lines. See Howard Pearson, "Mormon Missionary Baseball Team Makes Friends in South Africa," *Deseret News,* January 23, 1937, 3; "The History of the South African Mission," *Cumorah's Southern Messenger* 32, no. 10 (October 1957): 156; Pett Yus, quoted in Alan Klein, *Growing the Game: The Globalization of Major League Baseball,* 202.

169. Moses Mahlungu, "I Waited Fourteen Years," 159.

listening to LDS services through an open window in the Johannesburg Chapel. He was baptized in 1980.[170]

"Happier Races": Mormonism in Brazil and Cuba

In Brazil, widespread race-mixing and inadequate genealogical records gave Church leaders considerable anxiety. How could they ensure "pure" lines for priesthood holders and endowed members? Throughout the early twentieth century, missionaries regularly focused their teaching on Brazil's German population. Until Mormonism lifted its priesthood ban, there could be no hope of Mormonism becoming a self-sustaining institution in Latin America or Africa.

Nevertheless, Argentina's first converts—German immigrants—implored Church leaders to send missionaries to Buenos Aires. When the mission's first president, Elder Melvin J. Ballard dedicated the continent for proseletyzing in 1925, he noted that the American immigration laws had forced European immigrants to come to South America. Ballard mused that he did not know "what purpose God may have in their being in that great southland, the other part of Zion."[171] Ballard only hoped that "they who are from Gentile nations may also, with others, have this privilege of hearing the gospel and come into the fold of Christ." In his dedicatory prayer, he further prayed that "the Indians of this land . . . [would] receive the gospel" and "would again become a white and delightsome people."[172]

Missionaries actively sought out converts who exhibited "white" characteristics of European peoples. When missionaries attempted to proselyte some Indian populations in Argentina and Bolivia, they took note that natives living in La Paz were "very light of complexion" and were "not downtrodden in any sense, and all seem to be happy . . . not a bit like slaves as is the case in Argentina."[173]

Language use among missionaries in Brazil varied by region. They regularly held meetings in both German and Spanish, though it was acknowledged that "practically all the work done in the South American mission is performed in the Spanish language."[174] An early German missionary in Joinville, Brazil, Emil Schindler, wrote his home branch in Germany that 95 percent of the city's inhabitants spoke German. Mission president Reinhold Stoof actively networked with

170. Ibid., 153. For Church leaders' use of the law as rationale, see "Moses Mahlungu—The Conversion Power of the Book of Mormon," http://www.lds.org/pages/moses-mahlangu-the-conversion-power-of-the-book-of-mormon?lang=eng&country=afe (accessed October 5, 2013); and Andrew Clark, "The Fading Curse of Cain: Mormonism in South Africa," 50.

171. Melvin J. Ballard, "Answering the Call," 166.

172. Andrew Jenson, "South American Mission, Manuscript History and Historical Reports, 1925–35," December 25, 1925.

173. Ibid., ca. spring 1926.

174. Jenson, South American Mission Manuscript History, February 6, 1926. For other instances of bilingual teaching, see also January 20, 1926, January 24, 1926, February 3, 1926,

clubs and societies of the elite German population, such as the Teachers Society, the German Scientific Society, and a Socialistic Society.[175] Another pair of missionaries visited the town of Merlo thinking it would be a German stronghold; when they found that "there are few Germans living there," they decided that it would be a "good country place in which to do missionary work among the Spanish speaking people."[176]

According to Mark Grover, the "German colonies of southern Brazil provided a perfect environment for Mormonism."[177] German Mormons gave their allegiance, not to Brazil, but to their ancestral land of Germany, even expressing strong sympathies for the Nazi regime. Rulon Howells, who was called a mission president in Brazil in 1935, noted that "all they heard was pro, so they were in more or less agreement with what was going on in Germany."[178] But sympathy with Germany had another advantage for Mormon missionaries. The First Presidency expressed their fears to the newly called president about "the negro problem in South America" and instructed him to concentrate on proselytizing Germans. In fact, "one of the most pleasing features" of Brazilian society was that "the Germans have refrained from intermingling with the negroes of that land."[179] After Mormon Senator William King openly criticized Hitler's regime on the U.S. Senate floor, Howells wrote an article for a local paper emphasizing Mormon support for the Nazis.[180] In 1949, Howells blamed the limited growth in the town of Piracicaba on its black presence: "None of the other churches," he explained "had a meeting where black and white had mingled together completely, so they weren't used to it." Piracicaba would need to have racially segregated units. When the black members protested Howells's imposition of racially segregated units, Howells dug in his heels; he would not allow blacks to "force the white people to meet with them." Angered by this resistance from a usually compliant and cooperative membership, President Howells directed the missionaries to "make a new start among the white population" by "going to the city from a neighboring city to hold cottage meetings with white members and friends." In 1953, Howells implemented a strict lineage-screening team to ensure that baptized members were free from "the blood."[181]

---

175. *Der Stern,* January 27, 1929, qtd. in ibid., November 14, 1929. See also July 13 and July 15, 1926.

176. Jenson, South American Mission Manuscript History, May 17, 1926.

177. Mark L. Grover, "The Mormon Church and German Immigrants in Southern Brazil: Religion and Language," 299.

178. Ibid., 302.

179. Jenson, "South American Mission Manuscript History," February 1935. For the First Presidency's comments, see First Presidency, Letter to Rulon Howells, June 29, 1935, Rulon Howells Missionary Papers, LDS Church History Library.

180. Grover, "The Mormon Church and German Immigrants in Southern Brazil: Religion and Language," 302 note 15.

181. Mark L. Grover, "Religious Accommodation in the Land of Racial Democracy: Mormon Priesthood and Black Brazilians," 26–27.

This position put the Church crosswise with the growing strength of Brazilian nationalism. In 1938 the government of Getúlio Vargas eventually banned German-language meetings and threatened the German Saints with jail time if they persisted.[182] Mission President John Bowers ordered all German-language meetings to cease; four years later, his successor, William Seegmiller, directed the burning of all Church literature in German as an act of patriotism toward not only Brazil but also the United States.[183] Watching the books burn, missionary Asael Sorenson later recalled, was "like tearing part of the soul out of the German Saints."[184] Convert baptisms among Germans remained sparse. Although the missionaries were "received kindly," they had little success "in trying to lead the colonists to a better life."[185]

Lineage tests continued for the next generation essentially unabated. In 1964, the president of the Ipiranga Branch in São Paulo discovered what he believed to be an African ancestor. The mission president released him from all priesthood duties. After seven years of non-priesthood holding activity, he forwarded his information to Salt Lake City where the First Presidency nullified the decision and reinstated his priesthood.[186] In another case, a Brazilian missionary's mother informed him that because his father was a "mulatto," he had no right to the priesthood. Troubled, the young missionary returned home. However, the branch president reassured him that, because his patriarchal blessing designated him a member of the house of Israel, he was free of African ancestry.[187]

Cuba posed similar problems. For over four hundred years, most of the blacks, Spaniards, and Native Americans had intermarried freely, making it difficult to determine the racial status of any given Cuban. While a few Cubans maintained the veneer of whiteness, it was generally a façade. Genealogical records for the mixed-race population were scanty at best and inevitably recent; census enumerators used visual indicators to identify Cubans as "black" or "white." In July 1947 the First Presidency commissioned Heber Meeks, president of the Southern States Mission, to investigate whether the Cuban racial milieu would allow for Mormon proselytizing.[188] Born and raised in Salt Lake City, Meeks had little exposure to ethnic diversity. His friend, Nicholas G. Smith, the former mission president over South Africa, might have been able to offer insight, but there is no known evidence of their having a conversation on racial issues.[189]

---

182. For a personal account of a German Mennonite immigrant in Brazil during the Vargas crackdown, see Hans Kasdorf, *Design of My Journey: An Autobiography*, 161–62.

183. Grover, "The Mormon Church and German Immigrants in Southern Brazil," 305.

184. Ibid., 306.

185. Jenson, "South American Mission Manuscript History," ca. September 1932.

186. Ibid., 31.

187. Ibid., 32.

188. Heber C. Meeks, Autobiography, 1980-82, 204.

189. Nicholas G. Smith records Meeks's name and address in his personal notebook as "Heber Meeks, 2280 Lake Street" without further comment. The *Deseret News* confirms that this address belonged to the Heber Meeks of our story. Nicholas G. Smith, Notebook, MS

In summer 1947, Meeks visited Cuba to assess the question. He consulted a team of government officials and academics, analyzed the skimpy racial data provided by the Cuban census office, and drew on high-profile LDS acquaintances to establish Cuban contacts, including William Dobson, a regional representative for the Boy Scouts of America and "a prominent lawyer in Cuba." Meeks, his wife, and three staff members, checked into "one of the prominent hotels" in Havana.[190]

After a brief investigation, Meeks's initial impression was unfavorable. Although the newly installed Raul Lopez del Castillo government was stable, its "officials are corrupt and the government very inefficiently managed."[191] An 1947 visitor from Utah at about the same time found Havana to be "a clean city with narrow streets . . . some white folks but mostly Cubans and Spanish."[192] Meeks had estimated the "white element" in Cuba as numbering about a million. It was "made up largely of the professional and business class in urban centers," which he considered positive, "maintain[ed] a strict segregation from the colored race," and their associations did "not permit membership to anyone with colored blood." Meeks visited some of Havana's elite civic clubs for whites and saw "no one who possessed any of the colored characteristics." Even more encouraging to Meeks, club advisors informed Meeks that "genealogies were carefully checked for all members."[193] As Meeks drafted his report, he noted that "we are doing missionary work in South American countries where there is little or no discrimination against the negro." Yet we "are successfully teaching the gospel to groups free from negro blood." If missionaries were sent to Cuba, he concluded, the same sensitivity to racial background "would of necessity be our only approach and our work limited to this group." It would require "sending missionaries with a fine educational background who could meet and present the gospel to the professional and business groups of the white race."[194]

But the "negro situation" was another matter. In the South, Meeks commented bluntly, "we do not proselyte among the negroes because of race discrimination." Missionaries were forbidden from "socializ[ing] with them even to conducting meetings because of public sentiment." Blacks "cannot attend white meetings for the same reasons." And they "cannot carry on Church activities among themselves because they cannot hold the Priesthood." In Cuba, the middle and lower classes tended to have the physical attributes of stereotypical African ancestry. "Whites and colored would attend the same meetings," and

---

8861, Reel #3, LDS Church History Library; and "Summoned," *Deseret News*, November 16, 1940, 9.

190. Meeks, Autobiography, 204.

191. Heber C. Meeks, "Report on Visit to Cuba," not paginated.

192. W.W. Willey, Letter to Editor, *Davis County Clipper*, April 4, 1947, 5.

193. Meeks, "Report on Visit to Cuba."

194. Ibid.

"they would socialize in all their religious activities," a situation he obviously considered undesirable.[195]

But despite Meeks's concerns about "inject[ing] the program of the Church and its philosophy into the Cuban situation," he acknowledged the broadbased proselytizing approach's venerable history in the Church. "Jonah argued himself out of going to Ninevah because it seemed to him to be a very undiplomatic thing to do, to go into the capital city of the most powerful nation on the face of the earth, and tell them of their sins." Yet he went and found success. As a second example, "Paul went to Rome." While he considered that "the sins of the people (mixing white and colored blood through marriage)" had disqualified "them [from] the blessings of the gospel," Meeks could not "bring myself to recommend . . . that we stay out of Cuba." The Cubans—black and white alike—"are entitled to the truth."[196] "Would it be a tragedy to teach them the truth," he asked the First Presidency. "Would it be a disfavor to teach them racial purity?" If blacks "had . . . known the truth," then "the cursed negro blood would not be in their veins." Surely, "the negro would be a happier race if they knew their racial status and enjoyed the blessings of membership in the Church, its purifying influence in their lives—without holding the Priesthood—than in their present tragic plite [sic] in the world." The Mormon message had "helped the American Negro," and Meeks felt certain that "many of the [Cuban] negroes would accept the gospel and be happy in the church."[197] The First Presidency ultimately decided against Meeks's proposal; as of today, missionaries have still not been assigned to work in Cuba although, for the past forty years, the barrier has been more political than racial.

Upon returning from his trip, Meeks asked internationally renowned sociologist Lowry Nelson in 1947 whether missionary work could be viable in Cuba in spite of its large Afro-Cuban population. When Meeks informed Nelson of the priesthood ban, Meeks hardly thought twice about it, thinking it a matter of common knowledge. "I would appreciate your opinion," Meeks wrote, "knowing, of course, our concept of the Negro and his position as to the Priesthood." Perhaps Nelson knew of "groups of white blood in the rural sections" that had "maintain[ed] segregation from the Negroes?" Meeks was worried that "it would probably be difficult to find, with any degree of certainty, groups of pure white people."[198]

Born and raised in Utah, Nelson had an impressive record as a scholar of rural life in the Mormon corridor; as one contemporary newspaper described him, Nelson "knows the problems of the rural boy and rural parent probably as well as any man in the state."[199] He had received his Ph.D. in rural sociology in 1929 from the University of Wisconsin and immediately became Dean of Applied Sciences

195. Ibid.

196. Ibid.

197. Ibid.

198. Heber Meeks, Letter to Lowry Nelson, June 20, 1947, Lowry Nelson Papers, Box 4, fd. 2, Special Collections, Merrill-Cazier Library, Utah State University, Logan.

199. "Lowry Nelson to Preside Over Timp. Council," *Manti Messenger*, October 10, 1930, 1.

at Brigham Young University.[200] In 1934, Nelson took leave from his position to be the social service director for the Utah Emergency Relief Administration; in 1936, he became head of Utah Agricultural College's experimental station.[201] He also became involved in federal projects in Utah, serving on Franklin D. Roosevelt's Rural Resettlement Administration board (1935–36) when he was appointed to serve as the head of the Utah Agricultural Experiment Station sponsored by Utah State Agricultural College (now Utah State University) in Logan.[202] More relevant to Meeks's query, he had spent 1946 studying the rural Cuban population and came away feeling increasingly sympathetic toward peoples of African descent. It was Cuba that exposed him to the problems of racial inequality.

Nelson's experience with African American populations had been virtually nonexistent up to that point. His childhood hometown had no black residents of record.[203] Even Madison, Wisconsin, was made up primarily of northern Europeans. When called upon to speak at an LDS seminary graduation in 1931, he proclaimed that tolerance "is our greatest need today" and warned students against intolerance as "the progeny of ignorance."[204]

When Meeks informed Nelson of the priesthood ban and sought his advice, Nelson was shocked. Although he was aware of the cultural uneasiness with mixed-race proselytizing, he never knew "that there was a fixed doctrine on this point." The exchange forced Nelson to "come face to face with the issue."[205] Though aware of "certain statements made by authorities regarding the status of the Negro," he had assumed them to be cultural narrow-mindedness, not that "they constituted an irrevocable doctrine."[206] Meeks quoted Nelson that if missionaries were "to go into a situation like that and preach a doctrine of 'white supremacy,'" it would be a "tragic disservice."[207]

Nelson had never considered himself to be opposed to to Church leadership. Though agnostic on certain doctrinal issues,[208] he supported the Church's general

200. Ibid.; "Leadership Fete Planned at B.Y.U.," *Milford News*, January 25, 1934, 1; "Nelson to Head U.S.A.C. Station," *Salt Lake Telegram*, December 12, 1935, 13.

201. "Nelson to Head USAC Station," 13. For his initial "leave," see "B.Y.U. Adds Major in Agricultural Economics," *Washington County News* (Saint George), August 15, 1935, 1.

202. "Officials of Resettlement Administration," *Salt Lake Telegram*, August 15, 1935, 13.

203. The 1900 U.S. Census designated whether a person was "white," "black," or mulatto. I have examined the entirety of Emery Precinct for this year and have found that it contained only white residents U.S. Census, 1900, Utah, Emery Precinct, https://familysearch.org/pal:/MM9.3.1/TH-266-11930-42134-49?cc=1325221&wc=M94Y-1B7:1508065709 (accessed January 11, 2014).

204. "Dr. Lowry Nelson Speaker at Seminary Commencement," *Iron County Record*, April 18, 1931, 1.

205. Lowry Nelson, Letter to First Presidency, October 8, 1947, Merrill-Cazier Library.

206. Lowry Nelson, Letter to Heber Meeks, June 26, 1947. For Meeks's quotation, see Meeks, "Report on Visit to Cuba."

207. Meeks, "Report on Visit to Cuba."

208. While working for BYU, Nelson told a fellow LDS professor in 1934 that immortality was "an hypothesis, which cannot be tested by any method we know, whether it is true or not."

mission. In summer 1947, he assured President George Albert Smith and his coun-selors that he believed "our Church could perform a great service in Cuba" but added that "it would be better that we not go in at all, than to go in and promote racial distinction."[209] Smith and his counselors chastised Nelson, noting that racial intermingling was "repugnant to most normal-minded people."[210] They respected Nelson's scholarship but felt he was "too fine a man to permit yourself to be led off from the principles of the Gospel by worldly learning." They hoped that he could "reorient your thinking and bring it in line with the revealed word of God."[211]

Meeks and Nelson strongly felt that the Church's policy should be more flex-ible; but in 1949, Presidents George Albert Smith, J. Reuben Clark, and David O. McKay released a statement affirming that blacks would continue to be excluded from priesthood ordination. This position was "not a matter of the declaration of a policy but of direct commandment from the Lord."[212] This statement was the most rigid racial statement to become public to that point. It now stated without qualification that "the conduct of spirits in the pre-mortal existence has some deter-mining effect upon the conditions and circumstances under which these spirits take on mortality." But most of all, it claimed agnosticism: "Why the Negro was denied from the days of Adam is not known." The statement's audience, though strong, was limited in dissemination. James Clark did not include it in his six-volume *Messages of the First Presidency*. Lester Bush found the statement in the LDS Church Archives; however, the document's purpose remains unknown. It was likely a doctrinal response to quash the growing strain of racial liberalism among scholars such as Nelson.[213] The earliest published and circulated version is in John J. Stewart's volume, *Mormonism and the Negro,* a venue that did not typically serve as the First Presidency's means of issuing official statements.[214] The document is obviously authentic; however, its contents would not have been as well-known as they are if Stewart had not included it in his book.

But Nelson resisted both the stated and tacit criticism. In 1952, he read a *Deseret News* article about the Church's genealogical records program in South Africa, which reported the plight of a dying woman who needed to prove non-African genealogy before she could receive temple endowment even vicariously.

Qtd. in Gary J. Bergera and Ronald Priddis, *Brigham Young University: House of Faith,* 57.

209. Lowry Nelson, Letter to First Presidency, June 26, 1947, Merrill-Cazier Library.

210. George Albert Smith, J. Reuben Clark, and David O. McKay, Letter to Lowry Nelson, July 17, 1947, Merrill-Cazier Library.

211. First Presidency, Letter to Lowry Nelson, November 12, 1947, Merrill-Cazier Library.

212. John J. Stewart, *Mormonism and the Negro,* 78–82.

213. "First Presidency Statement," August 17, 1949, Lester E. Bush Papers, Box 4, fd 4. Marriott Special Collections. In 1953 BYU President Ernest L. Wilkinson criticized Dr. Lowry Nelson of Minnesota, who "think[s] that the problem should be approached from a Sociological point of view." See Ernest L. Wilkinson, Letter to David O. McKay, January 31, 1953, Adam S. Bennion Papers, Box 9, fd. 7.

214. John J. Stewart, *Mormonism and the Negro* (1960), 16–18. Subsequent editions (published in 1967, 1970, and 1978) included the document.

Nelson still felt loyalty to Church leadership, so he requested permission from Church leaders to critique the policy. The First Presidency's secretary, Joseph Anderson, responded, noting that McKay gave him permission "to publish any article you wish." But, Anderson warned him, "when a member of the Church sets himself up against doctrines preached by the Prophet Joseph Smith and by those who have succeeded him in the high office which he held, he is moving into a very dangerous position."[215]

Sincerely troubled, Nelson sent a carefully written article to *The Nation*, exposing the priesthood ban before the American public: "According to Mormon theology, the status of the Negro on earth was determined in the 'pre-existent' state," he observed. "I have heard it said" that the group supporting God's plan "was no more than one-third" while the "other third 'sat on the fence,' refusing to take sides." Nelson linked this racial lore with the priesthood ban, affirming that, as a youth, he had been taught that these "fence-sitters" could be "identified as the Negro." Mormon doctrine left them in a "sort of never-never land, a twilight zone between the Satanic hosts and those who were ready to be counted" on God's side.

He felt that "there would never be any change in the Negro policy until the facts were widely known and pressure could be brought to bear from without as well as within."[216] Nelson was leery of even putting his views in print: "discussions by interested persons are largely sub rosa" and "might be said to constitute a 'Mormon underground.'" Confident that these false assumptions could be rooted out with comparative ease, Nelson wrote: "Theoretically the Church has a means by which its doctrines may be modified. It was founded upon the idea of 'progressive revelation,' that as God spoke to the people in Bible days, so He continues to do today through the head of the church." Few Christian denominations "have the procedures for change that the Mormon church has." Church leaders are "men of good will" who certainly were "troubled by the ethical problem which this bit of dogma presents."[217] He assured all that he spoke "in a spirit of constructive criticism and in the conviction that his church, with so many admirable qualities and achievement to its credit, is faced by a challenge to place itself alongside those other groups which are laboring against racial bigotry."[218]

There was no documented response from the First Presidency, but BYU religion professor Roy W. Doxey wrote a letter to *The Nation* challenging Nelson's interpretation of Mormon theology. Doxey argued that Nelson was incorrect in claiming that "the Negro...was not neutral" in premortality. But in that case, what *did* blacks do? Doxey could not say, except that the "the Mormon teaching is in accord with justice, contrary to what Dr. Nelson wrote." Blacks' failure to support God's plan rendered them unworthy of priesthood ordination. It was

215. Joseph Anderson, Letter to Lowry Nelson, May 23, 1952, Merrill-Cazier Library.

216. Lowry Nelson, *In the Direction of His Dreams*, 350.

217. Lowry Nelson, "Mormons and the Negro," 488.

218. Ibid.

not racism, he argued; it was a simple matter of choices and consequences. If anything, the LDS Church was more expansive than others, since the priesthood "is conferred on *all* worthy males, unlike other Christian churches." Blacks, by their very nature, were deemed unworthy.[219]

He ticked off the ways in which blacks could participate in Church life: they could be baptized, partake of communion, and ultimately be resurrected in the highest kingdom of glory (of which there were three in Mormon theology). Since "we are all children of God," he acknowledged, "we should be interested in the social and economic welfare of the Negro." Doxey assured readers that "in the ultimate and final purpose of God . . . the Negro will 'possess the priesthood, and receive all the blessings which we [white men] are now entitled to.'"[220] But the exact doctrinal claims undergirding the priesthood ban were still in dispute.

In Brazil, the premortal explanation still dominated the discourse in race discussions among the Saints. When missionary Frank Meyer Jr. asked mission president Asael Sorenson how to explain the priesthood ban, Sorenson quoted a 1947 McKay speech in which he stated that "the real reason" for racial inequality "dated back to our pre-existent life." Blacks, Sorenson told Meyer with Joseph Smith's earlier quote, "should be CONFINED TO THEIR OWN SPECIES—separate but not equal."[221] Further, even the Savior "made it quite clear that those who had the blood of Cain were not to receive the gospel." Equating Cain with the women of Canaan "[who] came out" to Jesus seeking help for a "daughter . . . grievously vexed with a devil," Sorenson pointed out that "the Saviour would not even speak to her." After this rebuff, her continued further inquiries of the apostles were but an "annoy[ance]." Christ "knew that before this life this woman had not been valiant in his service and had even lent her influence to Satan because of which she was entitled to no better earthly lineage than that of the—cursed—race." Only when the woman willingly accepted her place—to "eat of the crumbs which fall from the master's table"—did the Savior laud her faith.[222] It was a difficult doctrine to be sure, and mission leadership had "tried to the best of our ability to explain their lot." But ultimately, blacks "should be thankful that they have not this responsibility in this life, for where much is given, much is expected."[223]

However awkward these explanations felt—and Sorenson knew entirely well how poorly they were received—Sorenson felt that blacks had little room to complain. They enjoyed membership in Christ's Church. Protests should be dismissed out-of-hand; the word of the Lord had been revealed, and calls for reform should not be taken seriously. The Savior had set the example for how to treat blacks, Sorenson maintained: with a tolerant condescension, at best as

---

219. Roy W. Doxey, "The Mormons and the Negro," inside front cover.

220. Ibid.

221. Asael Sorenson, Letter to Frank Meyers, June 7, 1956.

222. Ibid.

223. Ibid. Sorenson directed the missionaries to "place this letter in the Branch files for future reference," indicating that the document was to serve as a standard response throughout the mission.

men and women who had listened for a little bit too long to the devil in the life before. The racial dogma had metastatized well beyond the provincial quarters of the Intermountain West and a handful of missionaries in South Africa. It had become a global system.

While Mormon leadership in Brazil locked into a racial dogma dismissive of any claims to racial equality, a new movement began to brood over the lands of West Africa that would impel men like Sorenson to revisit their very core of their racial theology. The days were numbered for Mormonism's haphazardly crafted white consensus.

Chapter 4

Dawning: From Aba to Detroit, 1946–75

"I don't know how we can keep the Church and eventually the priesthood from them."
—LaMar S. Williams, Church representative,
Nigeria (1961)

"Problems like hunger and want can be solved and man's status in life can be elevated and made Godlike, creative, resourceful, holy, and happy."
—Nigerians Charles Agu and Anie D. Obot, on what
Mormonism could do for Nigeria (1963)

Dr. Virginia Cutler was smart and savvy, the kind of woman everyone wanted on their team. As one of the Church's leading representatives for international development and former dean of Brigham Young University's College of Family Living, she taught at the University of Ghana as a visiting professor and had attended several meetings with blacks. A Cornell University graduate and a sharp administrator, Cutler had orchestrated the construction of her own complex on the university campus and had spearheaded numerous educational programs in developing countries such as Indonesia and Thailand as a part of the State Department's global effort to buttress the Third World against Communism.[1]

When A. A. Kwapong, a vice-chancellor from the University of Ghana, visited Cornell, he asked the administrators who had the talent to set up his home economics program. "There is only one person who can do it," they said. "Virginia Cutler at Brigham Young University."[2] After being left as a young widow and mother of two, she "felt that I should get the very best education possible and that I must do everything I could for my family as well as for my church."[3] She urged the American Saints to gain deeper knowledge of the world: "It used to be that it didn't

---

1. "Women Cited for Accomplishments in '56," *Deseret News*, December 11, 1956, 28; "Home Economist Slates 2-Year Indonesian Stay," *Deseret News*, March 8, 1957, 8; "By Their Fruits," *Deseret News*, May 29, 1965, 17.

2. "Virginia Cutler—Her Heart Is Where the Home Is," *Ensign,* July 1985, 36

3. "People We Want to Know More About—Dr. Virginia Cutler," *Improvement Era,* February 1970, 51.

matter if you knew anything about what was going on in Ghana or in South Africa, but today we need to expand our knowledge as far as we can."[4]

Big World

At the end of World War II, the First Presidency began to think more seriously about expanding missionary efforts in the developing world, particularly Latin America. Between 1945 and 1950, it launched renewed missionary efforts in Brazil, Guatemala, Ecuador, and El Salvador. Because these efforts occurred under the umbrella erected by Joseph Smith that defined these populations, despite their heavy infusion of Europeans, as "Lamanites," native populations received special outreach as a part of missionary service.[5] At a meeting of the wives of the Bountiful Kiwanis, Farmington banker Dale Clark suggested "a new approach" to international diplomacy: "the use of technicians instead of striped pants diplomats" to assist "backward and war ravaged countries."[6] Cutler alerted the Saints that they had an obligation "to make his world very, very big."[7] But making the world "very big" was an impossibility for the Mormon community and its leaders under the existing racial strictures.

As early as 1946, some Nigerians began to petition June B. Sharp, now a mission president in South Africa, for missionaries and literature.[8] Over the next fifteen years, hundreds of Nigerians created independent congregations and implored Mormon headquarters for missionaries and Church literature. They received pamphlets, copies of the Book of Mormon, and James E. Talmage's *Articles of Faith*—but no missionaries. The prospects for mass conversion were lush; Pastor Itah Akpan of Abak, Nigeria, wrote Mark E. Petersen promising that "all my 18 churches agree to affiliate with you. . . . Sir I want the church here in Nigeria please."[9]

True, some African Christians resented the presence of foreign missionaries; Mormon proselyte Harry Akpan reported that he had heard "a lot of peoples" complain about "having foreign missionaries in our midst." Akpan countered by saying that "it is the lack of missionaries in our midst" that prevented the Nigerians from receiving "more enlightenment" from the "gospel of our Lord

---

4. Ibid., 52.

5. For a discussion of Mormonism's expansion into Latin America, see Nestor Curbelo, *The History of the Mormons in Argentina*, and Henri Gooren, "The Dynamics of LDS Growth in Guatemala, 1948–1998," 55–75; Mark L. Grover, "The Maturing of the Oak: The Dynamics of LDS Growth in Latin America," 79–104, and Grover, "Religious Accommodation in the Land of Racial Democracy: Mormon Priesthood and Black Brazilians," 23–34. For personal accounts, see John Forrest O'Donnal, *Pioneer in Guatemala: The Personal History of John Forrest O'Donnal,* chap. 5; and Seth Mattice, Journal, 1946–47.

6. "Kiwanis Will Hear 'Des. News.' Editor," *Davis County Clipper* (Bountiful, Utah), July 15, 1955, 1.

7. Rich Boyer and Jim Jardine, "People Want to Know More About Dr. Virginia Cutler," 52..

8. Council of the Twelve Meeting Minutes, October 24, 1946, Adam Bennion Papers, qtd. in Lester E. Bush Jr., "Mormonism's Negro Doctrine: An Historical Overview," 67 note 204. See also Bringhurst, "Mormonism in Black Africa," 17–18.

9. Itah Akpan, Letter to Mark E. Petersen, August 28, 1960.

Jesus Christ."[10] In 1960, the First Presidency (David O. McKay, J. Reuben Clark, and Henry D. Moyle) tasked President Glen G. Fisher of the South African Mission with investigating the commitment of these African petitioners to the Church. 'Some of the letters that we have received from these people," the First Presidency warned him, "lead us to question . . . whether or not they are really sincere in their desires to become members of the Church and are truly converted to the truths of the Gospel, or if they merely wish to become affiliated with a American church in order that they might thereby be the recipients of help in the way of contributions."[11] One correspondent had mentioned to Mission Department official LaMar S. Williams that "what we really want from you is to give us aid financially," since "there are many poor, needy and widows who require help within the Church."[12]

Typically, mission presidents over African areas had urged members and missionaries to avoid the natives entirely. Within months of Fisher's visit to Nigeria, white Latter-day Saint expatriates living in Eritrea (generally part of the State Department's Point Four development initiative) "discussed teaching gospel to Eritrean people when requested." Citing a letter written by William S. Erekson, president of the Swiss Mission who had jurisdiction over areas without missions of their own, they "decided . . . to go ahead while making certain that they understand they are not allowed to hold the priesthood for the curse of Ham."[13] But the relationship was already strained; the Saints sometimes felt it necessary to relocate their ward activities due to "problems with the natives."[14]

When Fisher arrived in Lagos, he found a newly independent Nigeria enveloped in organizational chaos. The waiting rooms at the airport were "crowded, with people" trying to return to their country of origin; it was a "sight never to be forgotten." But when he met the would-be Mormons, Fisher was "impressed with their sincerity and also the knowledge they had of the church." Fisher "felt sure that more visits would be made and promised that I would recommend that missionaries be sent to their country."[15]

LaMar Williams had already been answering questions from Nigerian inquirers and uncomfortably warned the Nigerians that they might not like what they found in Mormonism: "There are some things about this church which may be difficult for you to understand," he warned Charles Udo-Ete, a postal worker in Aba.[16] When Itah Akpan asked for missionaries, Williams spelled out that missionary work in Nigeria presented "some serious problems . . . that are under

---

10. Minutes of the General Conference of the Church in Nigeria, March 10, 1961.

11. First Presidency (David O. McKay, J. Reuben Clark, Henry D. Moyle), Letter to Glen Fisher, March 21, 1960.

12. Timothy Udoh, Letter to LaMar Williams, August 25, 1960.

13. Alvin R. Dyer, "A Fulfillment of Prophecy," *Conference Report* (October 1960): 58.

14. Asmara Branch, Manuscript History, Quarterly Historical Report, July–September 1962.

15. Glen Fisher, Reminiscences, n.d.

16. LaMar S. Williams, Letter to Charles Udo-Ete, January 31, 1961

consideration," although he did not mention that the problem was priesthood ordination.[17] Williams told the First Presidency that he did not wish "to handle this situation through the mail," since "on this issue they are deserving of personal representation and explanation so that there would be no misunderstanding on this delicate subject."[18]

Pleased with Fisher's optimistic report, the First Presidency agreed to allow Williams and a young missionary, Marvin Jones, who was en route to his assignment in the South African Mission, to spend two weeks visiting the congregations in Nigeria and investigating the situation. A Nigerian member, M. U. Ekpo, felt confident that "our affiliation is accepted by the Church of Jesus Christ of Latter-day Saints (Utah)" even if it was "not openly reveal[ed] to me." He knew "through the spiritual signs that is in me that our affiliation application is granted."[19]

Nigeria had long been teeming with American religions. A generation earlier, Port Harcourt was home to "the Methodists, the Niger Delta Branch of the Church Missionary Society, the Roman Catholics, the Faith Tabernacle, the Baptists, the African Church, the Salvation Army, the African Methodist Episcopals (Zion branch), the African Methodist Episcopals (Bethel branch), the New Church (Swedenborg), the Apostolic Mission, the Seventh-day Adventists, the First Century Gospel (an offshoot of the Faith Tabernacle), and up a side street, a [Muslim] mosque" with "badly printed pamphlets."[20] Several Nigerians had been members of the Salvation Army, known for its crack team of school administrators and medical professionals. The Mormons faced stiff competition.[21]

When Jones first set foot in Nigeria, the anthills, lizards, and the deformed beggars transfixed the young man. He had "never seen so many deformations."[22] He saw "twisted arms and legs, club feet, blind men, burnt flesh and any other you can think of. Even leprosy . . . you just can't imagine it unless you've seen it." The markets bemused him. He asked his girlfriend at home: "How would you like a stuffed allegator [sic] . . . or lizard or snake (boa constrictor) skin purse?"[23]

Over the duration of their short stay in Nigeria, Williams and Jones lived with their Nigerian contacts, rather than seeking out Western-style hotels. Charles Agu, one of the leaders urging for missionaries to come, lauded the pair for "the finest example of Christian living, patience, love, humility and devotion." They had "travelled to the darkest corners of Eastern Nigeria," "lived in huts," and "slept on hard beds," all while going "without food and water for many days, and

17. LaMar S. Williams, Letter to Itah Akpan, November 16, 1960.
18. Williams, Letter to First Presidency, May 3, 1961.
19. Nigerian General Conference Minutes, March 10, 1961, 3.
20. Howard Wolpe, *Urban Politics in Nigeria: A Study of Port Harcourt*, 78.
21. John Ilife, *The African Poor: A History*, 196.
22. Marvin Jones, Letter to Dorothy Buckley, November 2, 1961.
23. Ibid., October 28, 1961.

shar[ing] in the poverty of the people." Surely, Agu told them, these ambassadors of Mormonism would "have laid down your lives for these people."[24]

In their first meeting with the American missionaries, the Nigerian converts bore their testimony of the message they had received. "No other Church has taught us these things before," was the refrain. Several expressed unbounded confidence in the doctrines of Mormonism: "Without the teaching you sent to us I would never have known the truth. I have nothing more to say. I have received the truth." They seemed to accept the Church's position on blacks and the priesthood. The Mormon message was too compelling for them to do otherwise: "Consequently," one pastor wrote, "we therefore will not refuse this Church because the priesthood is denied us." It was the Lord testing their fortitude: "Who knows what the Lord will do for a people who repent & live righteously before him."[25] A group of Nigerian men assured Williams of their commitment, even if they never could receive the priesthood: "His plans and blessings will not restore His priesthood to us in this world or in the world to come; therefore, we will not reject His gospel among us because of priesthood."[26]

The Ikot Nsung congregation showered warmth on Williams, even producing an acrostic in his honor:

W Willing: You are willing to nurse our churches
I   Indispensable: Your presence with us will always be indispensable
L   Loving: You are loving to our churches and to us old and young
L   Loyal: You are loyal to our home mission
I   Intelligent: Your intelligence appeals to our senses
A Alert: You are alert to our spiritual needs
M Mild: You are mild and gentle
S   Shepherd: You are the shepherd we have longed for

But Jones also felt skeptical. For all their warmth, the people seemed mostly interested in financial assistance: "I'm beginning to believe that is the reason why the Chief & the others are so willing to accept our teachings & the fact that they cant hold the priesthood. . . . [I]t is so hard to tell what their underlying motives are."[27] They "very badly want financial help from the Church," Jones wrote, but they "realize that [it] will have to come through their efforts."[28]

While the Mormon message intrigued the rural African congregations—proselytes often walked over twenty miles to attend a meeting—urban proselytes in Lagos found the priesthood ban repulsive. "Why not have a prophet in Africa?" one Nigerian asked the young Marvin. The Lagos congregation saw the ban as a fundamental barrier to progress. One man told Williams and Jones

---

24. Charles Agu, Welcome Address, December 1962.
25. Marvin Jones, Diary, November 9, 1961.
26. A.D. Obot, S.U.E. Ekanem, O. Usoroh, M. E. Akpan, Letter to LaMar S. Williams, November 15, 1961.
27. Jones, Diary, October 24, 1961.
28. Ibid., October 22, 1961.

that "if we are to have a foundation the priesthood will be a serious problem." All members must "be equal in all things."[29] One Nigerian suggested: "We need to come to America and teach you Christianity." The comment rattled the young missionary: "I think that maybe he's right."[30]

In spite of these pockets of resistance, the Nigerians generally "all agreed that they still wanted the church to be established here in Nigeria."[31] "These people are just hungry for the truth," Jones wrote. "Their minds are open and receptive and take things for what they are worth. I can't see how the church could possibly keep from coming here and start missionary work among the Negroes."[32] Williams felt compelled to go further: "I don't know how we can keep the Church and eventually the priesthood from them."[33] Udo-Ete was adamant about his membership: "If the Church of Jesus Christ decides to reject me that is up to them, but I must continue in the teachings of the Church."[34]

When their investigatory tour was completed in early November 1961, Jones continued onward to his full-time mission in South Africa,[35] and Williams returned to Salt Lake City where he gave a positive report to the First Presidency. Within the week, the First Presidency decided to pursue missionary work within West Africa, albeit confidentially. Williams urged Jones to "keep this as quiet as possible until we know where we are going from here."[36] In 1963, McKay announced that Williams, Forrest Goodrich, Urban Bench, and Walter Atwood, accompanied by their wives, would serve as the first full-time missionaries in Nigeria.[37] McKay made sure that Williams understood the import of the mission: "This is a new appointment, a new assignment, not only to you individually but to the entire Church." Though the Nigerians were "a people not entitled to hold the priesthood," McKay spelled out that they were "entitled to other blessings

---

29. Anonymous man, quoted in ibid., October 25, 1961.

30. Marvin Jones, Letter to Dorothy Buckley, October 28, 1961.

31. Ibid.

32. Ibid.

33. LaMar Williams, Journal, October 29, 1961.

34. LaMar Williams, Statement, n.d.

35. Jones returned to Utah in 1963 and graduated with a bachelor's degree in business and economics from Weber State University in Ogden, Utah. A bright student, he received a perfect 4.0. grade point average. "Weber College Lists High Honor Students," *Ogden Standard-Examiner*, July 1, 1964, 19; "College to Award Degrees during Ceremony June 11," *Ogden Standard-Examiner*, June 5, 1966, 11.

36. LaMar Williams, Letter to Marvin Jones, November 8, 1961.

37. "The Church Moves On," *Improvement Era* 66, no. 3 (March 1963): 195; "Called on Mission," *Uintah Basin Standard*, April 25, 1963, 1. Goodrich was a prominent member of his small town, Tridell, Utah, and often hosted foreign visitors. He also served a midlife mission in the Central States Mission as a part of his calling as local Seventy. See "English Family to Live in Tridell," *Vernal Express*, June 15, 1949, 1; "Greek Student Learns American Way of Farming," *Vernal Express*, November 2, 1950, 1; "Forrest Goodrich Chosen for LDS Mission," *Vernal Express*, October 4, 1951, 8; "F. Goodriches Receive New Assignment," *Vernal Express*, January 17, 1963, 13.

of the Church, including eternal life in the Celestial Kingdom."[38] He warned Williams that "the enemy knows the significance of your mission" and that "Satan will be determined to thwart you in every way possible."[39] When Williams returned to Nigeria, this time accompanying N. Eldon Tanner, a counselor in the First Presidency, another congregation greeted them in song:

> Welcome Elder Tanner and Elder Williams to our country
> With warm hearts we raise.
> Oh welcome, welcome in our midst
> Strength and health and life we pray
> Oh Christ their portion be
> To do thy will and win lost souls to thee—to thee
> Oh Lord of Hosts, Jesus Christ the crucified
> Go and preach to all the nations
> Was our Lord's command, Lo
> Will be with you to guide your footsteps on your way
> Onward then your banners fly
> Our land the gospel spread
> God give you true and His own rare reward we pray
> He gives the best more than we can now afford

McKay was resolute in his support for the Nigerian mission: "We shall help them build their meetinghouses and these meetinghouses will soon be used as schools in helping their children to read."[40] The Nigerians shared McKay's vision for Mormonism in their homeland. In the Constitution for Charles Agu's congregation in Aba, it stated that one of the goals of LDS Church in Nigeria was "to build hospitals, dispensaries, and other health centres to meet the health needs of members and the community in general." It would also "build schools and other institutions of learning for the purpose of imparting knowledge to members and the community in general." [41] Leaders were to be "elected at a General Meeting . . . by secret ballot."[42] Another congregation reminded Williams that "our Country is just emerging to a full Nation-hood and your timely visit therefore is a desideratum."[43] In a welcome address signed by Aba's church leaders, the Saints gloried in the "opportunities for advancement of man in Industry, Politics, Education, Social and Cultural life [that] have . . . emerged" after decolonization. The Saints would become a new social network consisting of churches, schools, training centres, orphanages, and old mens [sic] homes."

But such things, they insisted, "can never be complete without the opportunity to know the truth and see the light of Jesus Christ as revealed by God to

---

38. "A Blessing upon the Head of Elder LaMar Stevenson Williams," November 21, 1962.

39. Ibid.

40. David O. McKay, Diary, October 11, 1962, cited in Gregory A. Prince and Wm. Robert Wright, *David O. McKay and the Rise of Modern Mormonism*, 85.

41. *The Constitution and Bye[Sic]-Laws of the Church of Jesus Christ of Latter-day Saints*, 3.

42. Ibid., 10.

43. Welcome Address, Ikot Nsung Congregation, November 3, 1961.

prophet Joseph Smith."[44] The Saints must "propogate [sic] Christianity and the Gospel of Jesus Christ as revealed to Prophet Joseph Smith and as directed by the first presidency and present day Prophets of the Church in Salt Lake City."[45] One Nigerian leader wanted complete autonomy from the Salt Lake City headquarters: "I don't have to wait for revelation to know that I am the natural head in Nigeria," wrote self-proclaimed Mormon bishop Anie Dick Obot. "Nigerian priests will run their own branch. This is their creation, and they are in their own country."[46]

Blue Flowers and Bright Stars

The Nigerian congregations were, like the Mormon missionaries, on the look-out for frauds. When Reverend Samuel Uba Oti asked Agu about the beliefs of the LDS Church, Agu reminded him that Agu himself was neither a "man of letters or position." Instead, he was "quite an ordinary man" with a "small business of my own." The LDS Church had no professional clergy, Agu was happy to say: "Members give their services free, and every member of the Church is a worker in the Church, and by this collective effort much is accomplished by all."[47]

The very name of the Church came to be a sign of perceived institutional integrity. In the earliest days of the Church, it had functioned under the name, United Apostolic Church.[48] But after receiving Fisher's correspondence, the Nigerians became aware of the Utah Church's name and adapted accordingly. In June 1960, E. J. Okpong, the Nigerian Saints' "General Secretary," notified the government of "the existence of the Church of Jesus Christ of Latter-day Saints" in Nigeria.[49]

After the name change, another Nigerian Saint, Reverend Ottoman Akpan, learned that the "United Apostolic Church" had been using literature from the LDS Church. Akpan knew full well that the United Apostolic Brethren were no longer affiliated with the Church of Jesus Christ of Latter-day Saints. They were "not for your said Divine Mission but the United Apostolic Churches." Akpan finally exploded, commanding Williams: "DO NOT WASTE OUR GOOD LITERATURE THAT WAY TO HIM AGAIN."[50]

Membership was a sacrificial act for Nigerian Mormons. There was never enough money. A Sunday School teacher pled with Church headquarters for an English Bible: "I have no money yet I beg you to help me with a copy I hope you being immaculate in Gods work will not fail to send me one."[51] The Nigerians saw the Utah Church as the geographic center of their faith and the source of providential blessings. Elijah Esien "seize[d]" an "opportunity in reporting to

---

44. Charles Agu, B. O. Akpan, E. B. Owo, and Onyedike, Welcome Address, October 1961.
45. *The Constitution and Bye[Sic]-Laws of the Church*, 3.
46. "Mormons: The Black Saints of Nigeria, " *Time*, June 18, 1965, 72.
47. Charles Agu, Letter to Samuel Uba Oti, November 13, 1964.
48. Inaugural Minutes, June 12, 1960.
49. E. J. Okpon, Letter to District Office, June 24, 1960.
50. Ottoman Akpan, Letter to LaMar S. Williams, February 16, 1961.
51. Gaskon Umah, Letter to LaMar Williams, January 10, 1961.

you [LaMar Williams] about my enemies from my village," hoping only that the Church would "put me and my family in prayers daily and through our Almighty God, we will [be] free in any difficulties."[52] The branch's only typewriter wasn't functioning, they had no transportation, and they had "no money at present" to pay for either.[53] But Moses Okoro, a polygamist believer, urged the Saints to endure: "The beginning of anything is hard," he assured them, and "no flower wears so lovely a blue as those which grow at the foot of the frozen glacier. . . . [N]o stars gleam so brightly as those which glisten in the polar sky."[54]

Voices from within Church headquarters urged the First Presidency to act aggressively in claiming the eager West African converts. In 1963, Williams wrote Nigerian premier I. A. Emeludamu to assure him that the Mormons "have no intentions of dominating or segregating our members in Nigeria." Williams tried to explain that the lack of proselytizing efforts was merely due to a lack of opportunity as a "relatively young church" that has "neither the man power nor means to spread the gospel of our Master to every land at one time." Williams insisted that "the teachings of the church have not generally appealed to the Negro people." He enjoined Emeludamu to believe that Williams did "not believe in racial discrimination" and was "working for the day when the members in Nigeria will have all the blessings we enjoy."[55]

Meanwhile, McKay felt it necessary to position this missionary effort within a larger political context. George Romney was running for his second term as governor in Michigan, and McKay felt that "certain politicians might take the view that it was done to influence the negro vote in [his] favor."[56] A civil rights statement from Salt Lake City would have had limited—if any—influence in Michigan. Though the black vote turned out overwhelmingly for incumbent Governor John Swainson, Romney won wide acclaim for his support of civil rights legislation.[57] In June 1963, he surprised an NAACP rally in Detroit by "walk[ing] casually to the head of the group," even though the organization had made no request for his attendance.[58] The following year, he walked out of the GOP National Convention in protest of the Republicans' antipathy towards civil rights, though he also refused to join Nelson Rockefeller in his civil rights platform. Rockefeller quipped: "George, you really are a damn loner, aren't you?"[59] Romney's reputation as a supporter of the civil rights movement not only won

---

52. Elijah Esiem, Letter to LaMar Williams, May 30, 1960.

53. Nigerian General Conference Minutes, March 10, 1961, 4.

54. Moses Okoro, Speech transcript, November 12, 1961.

55. LaMar Williams, Letter to I. A. Emeledamu, July 23, 1963.

56. McKay, Diary, October 18, 1962, qtd. in Prince and Wright, *David O. McKay*, 84.

57. "Signs Point to Romney as Victor in Michigan," *Dallas Morning News*, October 9, 1962, 5.

58. "Romney Heads 'Rights' March," *Plain Dealer* (Cleveland, Ohio), June 30, 1963, 5-AA. Romney headed another march in March 1965. See "Violence Hit by Thousands" [sic], *San Diego Union*, March 10, 1965, 1.

59. "I Can't Let You Talk to Them, George. You'll Snow Them," *Life*, May 5, 1967, 823. See also J. B. Haws, *The Mormon Image in American Mind*, 42.

him no favors among Church leadership but it also forced them to calculate the potential political fallout of moving forward on the Nigerian program.

In 1963, the Nigerian missionary program ran into further obstacles when a Cal Polytech Nigerian student, Ambrose Chukwu, learned of the Church's race policy. He had just heard of the Mormon people and visited a congregation out of curiosity. While visiting with the ward bishop, he saw a world map out of the corner of his eye, showing where young men and women were serving their missions. But the African continent lacked missionaries. "Why have you no missions anywhere in Africa, except in South Africa?" he asked. The bishop responded that his "reply would wound your feelings." When Chukwu pressed, the bishop finally told him that "it is our article of faith that the Negro was cursed by God and this makes him unworthy to hold the office of a priest or elder in our church." The two talked "for over three hours," and the bishop let him borrow what Chukwu incorrectly called "one of the most important books of their religion": John J. Stewart's volume, *Mormonism and the Negro*. [60]

John J. Stewart was a well-known author on a variety of LDS topics. As a professor of communications at Utah State University, he could also claim academic legitimacy. [61] Stewart urged readers to understand the doctrine of racial exclusion lest "we place ourselves in much the same position as churches that favor blind faith." [62] Is it "just or unjust," Stewart asked, for God to "enable people to be born under those circumstances and with those opportunities consistent with their conduct in the spirit world?" [63] The answer, Stewart declared, was an unequivocal yes; the priesthood ban was "reasonable doctrine." [64] It had to be; otherwise, Mormons had no choice but to "admit in effect that all Gospel doctrine is not sound." [65] He scorned efforts to cast the ban as the product of early Mormons' efforts to accommodate Missourians: the "Prophet Joseph . . . was not afraid of

---

60. John J. Stewart, *Mormonism and the Negro: An Explanation and Defense of the Doctrine of the Church of Jesus Christ of Latter-day Saints in regard to Negroes and Others of Negroid Blood, with a Historical Supplement* (1960), 9. This first edition was self-published (under the name of Bookmark), but Community Press acquired it that same year, publishing two editions. In 1967, a third edition, jointly authored by John J. Stewart and William E. Berrett, was published under the title of *Mormonism and the Negro: An Explanation and Defense of the Doctrine of the Church of Jesus Christ of Latter-day Saints in Regard to Negroes and Others of Negroid Blood, with a Historical Supplement* (1967). In fall 1978, Horizon Publishers issued a fourth edition after the receipt of the priesthood revelation. In this chapter, I cite only the Bookmark first edition.

61. A selected list of Stewart's published works includes *The Eternal Gift: The Story of the Crucifixion and Resurrection of the Christ; Joseph Smith: Democracy's Unknown Prophet; Mormonism v. Communism; How You Gain a Testimony; The Glory of Mormonism; The Miracles of Christmas; For God So Loved the World; George Washington and the Mormons; Remembering the McKays: A Biographical Sketch with Pictures of David O. and Emma Ray McKay.*

62. Stewart, *Mormonism and the Negro*, 9.

63. Ibid., 25.

64. Ibid., 9.

65. Ibid.

persecution nor public censure nor ridicule."[66] Supposing that he would "curry the favor of the world by manifesting a prejudice against the Negro is an affront to this courageous man and to the known facts of history."[67] In a vague reference to Elijah Ables, Stewart noted that Joseph "had Negro servants and friends who were devoted to him, recognizing in him a champion of their race and rights."[68]

But Stewart went further. Premortality explained why much of the world's population lived in "squalor, filth, poverty, and degradation," particularly the "lowest classes of society in Africa" who "live[d] out their lives in a fashion akin to that of the animals."[69] They did so "through their own free agency, to penalize themselves as to their circumstances in the world."[70] This was not to say that whites would always outperform blacks, only that "we [white-skinned peoples]" were "ahead of [blacks] in the first lap of the race."[71] Denying the priesthood to blacks was "an act of mercy." Given "the social prejudice against him, imagine the obstacles that the Negro would encounter in attempting to honor and magnify the Priesthood." In fact, the "very fact that God would allow those spirits who were less worthy . . . to partake of a mortal body" was evidence of "His infinite mercy and charity."[72] Those who dared distance themselves from the doctrinal foundations for the ban were dismissed as mere "apologizers."[73] Blacks should thank God that they existed at all when he could have cast them out with Satan and his angels.[74]

Upon reading Stewart's volume, Chukwu was livid. Given Stewart's stature, he identified the volume with official LDS doctrine and fired off an enraged article to the Biafran newspaper, *Nigerian Outlook*, including several of the more inflammatory excerpts from Stewart's volume.[75] Chukwu "did not eat or sleep until I finished reading the book," concluding that Mormons supported "religious apartheid." Chukwu considered Nigeria to be "a godly country," and "such a collection of madmen have no right to go under the name Christian." Mormonism's God "is not our God," for he did not "believe in a God whose adherents preach the superiority of one race over the other." The Nigerians could not "receive them with open arms" and "grant them freedom and passage to tell us in our own homes that even the most eminent and saintly 'Negro' is . . . inferior even to the least admirable white person." Mormonism "belittl[ed] the intelligence of Nigerians" and "is godlessness." Allowing the Mormons to enter

---

66. Ibid., 15.
67. Ibid.
68. Ibid., 18.
69. Ibid., 29–30, 44.
70. Ibid., 30.
71. Ibid., 33.
72. Ibid., 50.
73. Ibid., 9, 13, 15, 19, 26, 35.
74. Ibid., 50.
75. The *Nigerian Outlook* became the *Biafran Sun* during the civil war. See Gunilla Faringer, *Press Freedom in Africa*, 29.

Nigeria would do "irreparable damage . . . to Nigeria's good name." For the Mormons "even to dream of proselytizing in Nigeria, let alone to express it" was "the height of impudence." Blacks had no hope for achieving the highest level of salvation of blacks in Mormonism, Chukwu declared: "As a Negro . . . you are only considered fit to sweep the congregation hall."[76]

Chukwu's piece was not the first time the paper had revealed racial injustice in the United States; in 1962, the newspaper's editor, Gabriel Indigo, was turned away from several American commercial establishments. Though the State Department issued its regrets, Indigo made sure that *Nigerian Outlook* readers knew about it.[77]

The Nigerian government was not necessarily opposed to foreigners; Western capital had long been a mainstay of the Nigerian economy. But accusing the Mormons of "importing godlessness" was no small thing, and the Nigerian government issued blocks on the four missionary couples seeking to enter the country. They were assigned to other missions while Church leaders tried to perform damage control. The Goodriches, for example, awaited developments on an Indian reservation in upstate New York.[78] When Lowell Bennion learned of the newspaper account, he "blush[ed] in shame and anger to read it." We "have sown the wind," he commented, "and are reaping the whirlwind."[79]

So serious was the blowback that LaMar Williams flew to San Luis Obisbo to mend fences with the journalist. While he made some headway in establishing warmer relations with Chukwu, the Nigerian unsurprisingly held his ground.

While the Church worked with the government to acquire visas, President N. Eldon Tanner sent a letter to the Nigerian Saints acknowledging the local leaders' legitimacy and promised them "that when they were able to obtain government permission for the church to enter their country representatives would be sent to assist them with their church program."[80] Tanner assigned the distribution of leadership capabilities to the local level, rather than to headquarters, tacitly assigning stewardship—if not priesthood—to the Nigerian church leaders.

Charles Agu and Anie Dick Obot followed up by issuing a statement of belief in the *Nigerian Outlook*, taking care to note that they both had been "recognized as Leaders of the Church." They reminded readers that the Saints believed in the resurrection of Jesus Christ and that "life hereafter has something to do with the

---

76. Ambrose Chukwu, "They're Importing Ungodliness," *Nigerian Outlook,* March 5, 1963, 3, FN 1907, Butler Library, Columbia University. Many thanks to Elizabeth Harwood for assisting me in acquiring an original scan of this document.

77. Richard Glen Lentz and Karla K. Gower, *The Opinions of Mankind: Racial Issues, Press, and Propaganda in the Cold War,* 150.

78. "Tridell," *Vernal [Utah] Express,* May 16, 1963, 12.

79. Lowell Bennion, Letter to George Boyd, October 21, 1963, quoted in Mary Bradford, *Lowell L. Bennion: Teacher, Counselor, Humanitarian,* 246.

80. James B. Allen, "Would-Be Saints: West Africa Before the 1978 Priesthood Revelation," 230.

degree of perfection man attains in this life," including "the perfection of mind and body." Agu and Obot promised that with "the weapons of true Christian living which is manifest in the lives of Latter-day Saints, human problems like hunger and want can be solved and man's status in this life can be elevated and made Godlike, creative, resourceful, healthy, and happy."[81]

Agu begged Williams to cooperate with the government; could not "some good, clean Negro person be given the priesthood so that our work may go forward?"[82] He feared that political difficulties would prompt Church leaders to "call off the whole arrangement as not worth all the trouble." But Agu thought the possibilities transcended politics: "This is a question of people and their salvation. It is a matter of life and death with us. . . . I think this should be more important to the church than the confusion of color."[83] In spite of the government's resistance, a small band of Nigerian Saints promised their "unflinching support in continuing our activities in the church, even more than before, in hope that whether it takes us a whole lifetime to achieve our objective, our unborn generation will live to glorify and bless us for our devotion and thirst after righteousness."[84]

In fall 1964, Williams obtained a tourist visa and traveled to Nigeria to negotiate with government officials. The work appeared to progress, albeit at a snail's pace. He arranged for a cooperative scholarship fund that would assist Nigerian students in attending Brigham Young University. Williams also reached out to Anie Dick Obot's group. Though Obot knew "that no one could hold the priesthood [and] that there would be no salaried ministers," he was ready to support the Utah church. Williams arranged for Obot's congregation to be granted the official title of the Church of Jesus Christ of Latter-day Saints.[85]

One Nigerian convert, Sensen Asianya, a Nigerian Boy Scout leader, had discovered Church literature while taking his troop on a field trip to the library. Intrigued, he contacted his friend, Charles Agu, for more information. Agu responded that he had seen a copy of the Book of Mormon while in Lagos. Agu and Asianya began to study the literature, much to the anger of Asianya's Catholic leaders. They rented a public structure in which they held a study group that attracted about twelve families.[86] In the summer of 1963, Williams visited Asianya's group. While they were generally receptive, the word, "Mormon" "confused" them because they thought he was saying "mammon."[87] According to Asianya, Tanner attempted to assure the government that, even if they were not allowed to

---

81. "What You Ought to Know about the Church of Jesus Christ of Latter-day Saints," *Nigerian Outlook*, June 26, 1963, 5. Allen, "Would-Be Saints," 231, mistakenly dates this article as June 16, 1963. Many thanks to Kent Larsen for his efforts in acquiring this newspaper clipping.

82. Ibid.

83. Allen, "Would-Be Saints," 232.

84. Ibid., 232–33.

85. Ibid., 234.

86. Sensen Asianya, Fireside Address at Cedar Rapids, Iowa, August 3, 1966.

87. Ibid.

proselyte, they "would help . . . at least to promote agricultural skills."[88] But the Nigerians were "getting a bit too impatient" while waiting for the missionaries.[89]

In the late 1950s, oil was discovered in Biafra, Nigeria's southeastern province and home to most of the Nigerian Mormon proselytes. The discovery prompted talk of sectional divides with threats of violence from all parties.[90] McKay likely learned of the internal unrest and, deciding that "the time has not yet come to go into Nigeria," sent Williams a telegram: "Discontinue negotiations, and return home immediately." Williams met with the First Presidency upon his return home, but the reception was awkward. Presidents McKay, Brown, and Tanner were "almost silent" during the debriefing, while Thorpe B. Isaacson, a newly called counselor to the First Presidency, directed the conversation. "I was not really informed as to why I'd been called home," noted the disappointed Williams. But Isaacson clearly communicated that a mission was "just asking for a lot of problems."[91]

In 1967, the Biafran region of Nigeria declared independence. Saints living in Lagos saw little of the trouble. Sonia Johnson, who would acquire fame in the future as an Equal Rights Amendment activist, was then living in Lagos with her husband, Richard, a statistician for the American Institute for Research. She reported that whites who had left the North were "astonished to see people sitting so nonchalantly in Lagos as if we weren't all on top of an active volcano."[92] Johnson shrugged it off: "I don't think we were ever in danger (except of being shot by accident, as a couple of expatriates were)."[93] In one letter home, Johnson mentioned the Biafran conflict in one breath, only to transition seamlessly to: "The biggest news is that we have a cat" in the next.[94]

Williams's work had been "in the very area" of the war's worst violence.[95] A bloody civil war ensued for the next three years, threatening to rip the fledgling Mormon community apart. "It wasn't until then," he recalled, "that I felt that the Lord had something to do with getting me out of Nigeria."[96]

Before the war began, Asianya left for the United States on an exchange program to study agriculture in Iowa. He visited a Mormon congregation in Cedar Rapids, Iowa, and gave an address on the growing strength of Nigerian Mormonism. Entirely unaware of Nigerian culture or history, the attendees peppered him with questions. When Asianya told the Americans that Nigerians

---

88. Ibid.

89. Ibid.

90. Samuel E. Belk, Memo to McGeorge Bundy, December 30, 1964, in *Foreign Relations of the United States, 1964–1968: Africa,* edited by Nina Howland, 612.

91. Allen, "Would-Be Saints," 236.

92. Sonia Johnson, Letter to Harrises, November 28, 1966.

93. Sonia Johnson, Letter to Harrises, August 6, 1966. For a brief treatment of Sonia Johnson's correspondence, see Heather M. Kellogg, "Shades of Gray: Sonia Johnson's Life through Letters and Autobiography," 77–86.

94. Sonia Johnson, Letter to Harrises, February 5, 1966, Sonia Johnson Papers, Box 3, folder 11.

95. Prince and Wright, *David O. McKay,* 91.

96. Williams, quoted in ibid., 94.

spoke several languages, someone wondered aloud if the Nigerians had adopted a universal sign language like the American Indian.[97] When the Muslim Prime Minister was assassinated in 1966, Asianya hoped that new leadership would be friendlier to Church missionary efforts. "Members of our Church really believe that we will have a chance now." His hope was in vain. By 1969, he had returned to his home to find it devastated. He wrote a letter to a Mormon contact begging for assistance: "The enormity of our problems should evoke humanitarianism in every man and woman, regardless of creed, colour or race."[98]

Another Biafran man named Anthony Obinna had grown up an ardent anti-colonialist, so he told the official LDS magazine after his conversion: "Our people detested Western education and hated anyone who talked to them about sending their children to school or taking them to church." In Obinna's community of Umuelem Enyiogugu, Nigerians "were always afraid of white men and never wanted to appear before them or go near them." In fact, Obinna would later label his parents and grandparents as "idol worshippers" who regularly "promised their gods such animals as goats, sheep, hens and fowls, and many other things . . . to protect their lives and those of their families." But Obinna's father was a practical man; after realizing that he could not understand English visitors, he sent Anthony to school where Anthony studied English and considered entering the ministry.[99]

In 1965, Obinna had a "dream" in which "a tall person carrying a walking stick in his right hand" appeared to him. The man asked Obinna if he had read John Bunyan's classic Christian devotional work, *Pilgrim's Progress*. He had, but years earlier. The man directed him to "read it again." Some months later, the man "appeared to me again" and "took me to a most beautiful building and showed me everything in it."[100]

During the war, Obinna discovered a *Reader's Digest* article entitled: "March of the Mormons" in which he saw a picture of the Salt Lake Temple—a picture that mirrored the image he saw in his dream. The "new discovery" intrigued him, and he "rushed out immediately to tell my brothers, who were all amazed and astonished to hear the story." Obinna could not contact headquarters, as there was a "blockade all over Nigeria."[101]

The Nigerian Saints attributed their survival to Providence. Mennie Udorn, a war widow from northern Nigeria, wrote Church leaders in 1976 to assure them that the "All Mighty God, the God who created Joseph Smith Spiritually to the world to reveal the ways of salvation to those that will seek" would be "saved." After Biafran soldiers had "captured and carried away" her husband, she herself was taken captive; she could not return to her home until 1972. She was pleased to find a "few

97. Asianya, Fireside Transcript, August 3, 1966.
98. Sensen Asianya, Letter to Mary Cain, February 1, 1969.
99. Anthony Obinna, "Voice from Nigeria," Ensign (December 1980): 28.
100. Ibid., 29.
101. Ibid.

members who came back safely" and had "started the reorganization again."[102] One member, Sampson Upkong, traversed the country by bicycle to provide support to some twenty pockets of members throughout Nigeria; by February 1966, transportation costs had skyrocketed from 18 to 600 naira.[103] But the war devastated most of the Mormon groups. Williams remembered that "all we could do later was go back and kind of bring the pieces back together again."[104] Isolated from the Church and the outside world, it had appeared that Mormonism would be ripped apart by the horrors of war. And the hopes for resuscitation were slim.

Members like Udorn had little familiarity with the Utah Church. Her husband had run an independent "Mormon" congregation and refused to join other LDS restoration groups such as the Bickertonites, then active in northern Nigeria. She wanted her children to attend the Bickertonite school, but the administration refused to provide the assistance that was available to other students unless Udorn's congregation merged with the Bickertonites. When they turned her away for lack of tuition, she rummaged through her husband's belongings to see if he had "corresponden[ce] with the Overseas International Headqrts." Pests had eaten away most of the documents, but she believed that "the Spirit of my husband made the left hand side address of the duplicate of your letter to remain undamaged." She only wanted to see if the "Latter-day Saints of Utah is still functioning."[105] Above all, she wanted to "remain independently in the name of THE REAL CHURCH OF JESUS CHRIST OF LATTER DAY SAINTS."[106]

In 1975, Charles Agu assured Lorry Rytting, an analyst visiting from the Church's Public Communications Department that they had informed Church headquarters of "their happy survival," but "no words of congratulation was received."[107] Rytting performed the first baptisms of Nigerians in their homeland.[108] But to the Nigerians, the Church still felt conspicuously absent. The following year, Joseph Ereba begged the Missionary Department for answers: "I am much worried why the church has not functioned as early as 1972, up til these times." His converts felt betrayed: "People whom I have spent long time all night and day in campaigning to join me for the organization of this church have been failed woefully; all my preaching in vain, and my words have been proved a liar."[109] Perhaps the Utah church could just send them "Mormon Bibles, plus doctrinal statements and belie[fs]."[110]

102. Mennie Udorm, Letter to First Presidency, December 3, 1976.

103. Sonia Johnson, Letter to Harrises, February 5, 1966, Box 3, fd. 10, Sonia Johnson Papers.

104. Allen, "Would-Be Saints," 238.

105. Udorm to First Presidency, December 3, 1976.

106. Ibid.

107. Charles Agu, "Welcome Address to Dr. and Mrs. Rytting," June 14, 1975. See also Haws, *The Mormon Image in the American Mind*, 75.

108. Reed Clegg, "Friends of West Africa: An Opportunity for Service," 95.

109. Joseph Ereba, Letter to Missionary Department, November 30, 1976.

110. Udorm to First Presidency, December 3, 1976.

Williams believed that Mormons were predominantly Biafrans, but the war found Mormons on sides of the line. In Abak, Biafran soldiers took one Mormon proselyte and her family captive, eventually killing the husband. Yet the organization endured. In 1972, "the few members who came back started the organization again."[111] Asianya became politically active, hoping to mobilize American Mormons in support of the Biafran refugees.[112]

Like the Nigerians, some Ghanaians also heard the Mormon message in a variety of ways and found it appealing. In 1964, Dr. Raphael Abraham F. Mensah, a young schoolmaster, became acquainted with Mormonism while visiting Lilian Clark, a Sufi Indian living in St. Agnes, England. Clark had been visiting with the sister missionaries and was impressed by the missionaries' "sincerity and spontaneous friendliness."[113] Clark told the missionaries that she had seen Joseph Smith and the angel Moroni in vision. The missionaries dismissed her claims out of hand; one sister missionary noted in her journal: "Talk about weird experiences!"[114] Clark had befriended Mensah during his visit to Great Britain and, according to one account, gave Mensah the missionaries' materials.[115] Mensah returned to Buabasha, Ghana, and cultivated a small following based on Mormon teachings. He attracted other investigators, including Joseph Johnson, Clement Osekre, and M. K. Koomson, whom he assigned leadership positions in the movement. It spread to Sekondi and Cape Coast while the headquarters remained in Accra. In 1969, the group drew up a constitution stating their new religion's aims, organization, and bylaws.[116] Mormons like Virginia Cutler played a key role in supporting the congregations, even as they felt personal uncertainty about the congregations' viability. Joseph Dadzie's official history of Mormonism recalled Cutler fondly for bringing "much warmth and a ray of hope" for the struggling Saints.[117]

The male-dominated constitution notwithstanding, one of the earliest followers of Mormonism was Rebecca Ghartney Mould, who quickly founded one of Ghana's first congregations. She built a meetinghouse on her own land in

---

111. Mennie Udorm, Letter to First Presidency, November 9, 1976.

112. Sensen Asianya, Letter to Mary Cain, February 1, 1969, LDS Church History Library.

113. Lilian Clark, Letter to Loretta Johnson, June 3, 1962.

114. Loretta Johnson, Journal, March 24, 1962.

115. "One Baptism May Eventually Lead to Many Conversions," *Church News*, June 14, 1980, 23; Karin Brown, Letter to Lori Kennard. Accounts differ on the particulars of Mensah's conversion. According to Joseph Dadzie, "Timeline," Joseph K. Dadzie Papers, MS 16034, LDS Church History Library, Mensah was "a baptized member of the Church [who] returned from America." According to Joseph Johnson, Mensah affiliated with the Mormons when he met Lilian Clark in England, who gave him Mormon literature which he brought back to Ghana. See Johnson, "History of the Church of Jesus Christ of Latter-day Saints in Ghana," ca. 1985, LDS Church History Library,

116. Constitution of the Church of Jesus Christ of Latter-day Saints, April 27, 1969, Dadzie Papers.

117. "A Short Report on the Ghana Mission," September 10, 1973, in Ghana and Nigeria Files," MS 16493, LDS Church History Library.

the village of Kweikuma, initially patronized by curiosity seekers. "As soon as they would fill the meeting place with new members . . . they would be down again to a small number of people," one of her early converts recalled. But stories of miracles circulated. "Crippled children [and] blind people" were "healed completely through the power of fasting, prayer, and faith."[118] Mould's meetings were lively religious experiences that blended Mormonism, Pentecostal Christianity, and native ritual. The first hour of her meetings "consisted mostly of songs praising the Lord," including "drumming, dancing [and] clapping of hands."[119] One convert described how the ecstatic Saints "came to the center of the chapel and moved in circles."[120] She administered ritualistic washings that promised to cleanse her followers from all their sins.[121] Mormon scripture played little role in the services, since Mould was the only one who owned a copy of the Book of Mormon and only "occasionally mentioned it when preaching."[122]

Joseph B. Johnson and Raphael Abraham Frank Mensah preach Mormonism in Ghana in 1971, seven years prior to the arrival of official Mormon missionaries. Courtesy LDS Church History Library.

Though Mould preached distinctively Mormon doctrine, her blend of ritual anointings, personality-centered leadership, and music represented a syncretic tradition of Western Christianity and traditional Ghanaian spirituality typical to West African independent churches. Most of her adherents had previously joined Anglican, Roman Catholic, and Methodist groups.[123] Harmonizing with traditional Mormon teachings, though perhaps alarming to the more sedate contemporary missionaries, was the Pentecostal emphasis on restoration—an effort to recapture the faith of the New Testament apostles.[124]

Called "the Prophetess" and "leader" by men such as Mensah, Johnson, and Osekre, Mould's authority was striking. One young convert, Samuel Bainson, was impressed by her "powerful and influential" testimony "of the Prophet Joseph

118. Samuel Bainson, "An African's Journey," self-published, n.d., 10.

119. Ibid., 7; See also Joseph Dadzie, "The History of the 'Church of Jesus Christ of Latter Day Saints in Ghana,'" n.d., Dadzie Papers.

120. Bainson, "An African's Journey," 7.

121. Program for "The Devine [sic] Order of Mount Tabborar Service," August 22, 1971, Dadzie Papers.

122. Joseph Dadzie, "The History of the 'Church of Jesus Christ of Latter Day Saints in Ghana,'" Dadzie Papers..

123. Steven J. Salm and Toyin Falola, *Culture and Customs of Ghana*, 48.

124. Ogbu Kalu, *African Pentecostalism: An Introduction*, 7.

Smith and the Book of Mormon, and the fact that there is a living Prophet today, even Spencer W. Kimball."[125] Despite the blistering heat of the iron-roofed hut, Bainson committed himself to "Mother Mould" and "wouldn't have missed a meeting for anything."[126]

Mould played a significant role in governing the young church in Ghana. When Mensah wanted to establish a "steering committee" to organize the Church's affairs, he requested that the Prophetess "elect three members" to the council.[127] That same year, Mould was appointed to the Ghanaian church's "High Council or in other words, the Twelve Apostles"—the only woman serving in that unit.[128] In the summer of 1972, native LDS leaders in Accra entertained a proposal for "seizing [prohibiting] women from giving revelations and prophecies," but the plan was quickly scuttled. But the revelatory channels were placed on a tighter leash: all "dreams [and] revelations, etc. must first [be] reported to the Pastor."[129]

Although women-headed congregations were not unusual in Ghana, Mormonism could not accommodate them in its existing structure; and they also encountered resistance from other members and men. Joseph Johnson established an LDS congregation in Moree. Martha Mills and a man named Koomson headed a prayer group nearby and became familiar with the Mormon version. Mills was converted to Mormonism and wanted to apply the Mormon name to her congregation, but Koomson rejected the Mormon message and resorted to "force, beating her with a club and wounding her in the face." Johnson praised her refusal to break while she "kept the flock together with her strong testimony."[130]

Explorers and Educators

By the 1950s, the white consensus had seeped throughout the body of the Intermountain Mormon populace. Whiteness had been hard-won—and its benefits had proven intoxicating for some and necessary for others. Having allowed themselves to be locked into an Intermountain cell of racial thought, there would need be no immediate hope for redemption from within the nation's borders. For the Saints' racial redemption, they would need to turn elsewhere. But who would refashion Mormonism's racial contours? That responsibility rested not only on the shoulders of dogged West African Mormon proselytes but also on the shoulders of a cadre of adventurers and humanitarians who began to envision Africa as something other than a "dark continent."

Some unabashedly perpetuated well-established stereotypes Americans used in talking about Africa. In 1955, Rendell N. Mabey, later one of the first mis-

125. Bainson, "An African's Journey," 8.
126. Ibid., 10.
127. Clement Osekre, Letter to Rebecca Mould, September 11, 1972, Dadzie Papers.
128. High Council Meeting Minutes, ca. fall 1972, Dadzie Papers.
129. Ibid.
130. Janath Russell Cannon, Diary, September 9, 1979, LDS Church History Library.

sionaries to Ghana and Nigeria, embarked on an elephant hunt in Zambia. His diary—published in the *Davis County Clipper* in Bountiful, Utah—concentrates on local color: mosquitoes, tsetse flies, and myriad animal life.[131] "The best shot" at an elephant, he told Davis County readers, "is the center of the front leg just where the ear falls on the body and half way to the lower body line." He called the party's native assistants "boys" and found their superstitions worthy of ridicule: "we were told that tomorrow an old man would have to remove the nerve from the tusks and no unmarried boy or girl must watch for 'if they do it will make them infertile.'"[132] He criticized the mothers' methods of child-rearing: "Women in [the United States] have far better ways of caring for their children than carrying them on their backs or holding them in their arms."[133] He admitted that elephant hunts were immensely wasteful. After a kill by the white hunter, villagers came to their camp to butcher the elephant and take the meat back to their village. He vividly described how "the women placed their baskets" on their heads, "strapped their babies on their backs and trudged off through the forest and back to their home" with "blood streaming down their faces and bodies from the baskets above." They probably wondered "why some foolish hunter was content with two tusks and a tail."[134] Mabey and his companion, Harold Calder, showed the footage they produced at a Bountiful Ward Christmas party.[135] The following year, he embarked on a second hunt, this time to "collect specimens for the Los Angeles Museum." His particular assignment was to bring back "an elephant skull."[136] By 1960, he had completed two more big game hunts.[137] One observer cast Mabey's "on the spot, yet uncut and unedited film" as a story of "man pitted against desert land and highly dangerous plants and animals."[138]

A Bountiful couple, Paul and Delores Seifert, traveled to Morocco to teach school at a U.S. Air Force base and, in a letter to the *Davis County Clipper*, admitted that "it will take a little while to become acquainted with the inhabitants."[139] Three years later in Rabot, Delores Seifert gave birth to a son who died a week later.[140] Africa remained a strange and foreign land to most Mormons.

But it took another explorer and filmmaker to expand American Mormon interest in Africa beyond elephant hunts or Peace Corps volunteers hacking their

---

131. "Safari in Africa," *Davis County Clipper* (Bountiful, Utah), November 11, 1955, 1.

132. "Safari in Africa," *Davis County Clipper* (Bountiful, Utah), November 18, 1955, 1.

133. "Safari in Africa," *Davis County Clipper* (Bountiful, Utah), November 25, 1955, 1.

134. Ibid.

135. "Bountiful News," *Davis County Clipper [Bountiful, Utah]*, December 23, 1955, 15.

136. "Rendell Mabey Sets Second African Trip," *Davis County Clipper* (Bountiful, Utah]) August 8, 1958, 1.

137. "Mabey Shows African Safari," *Davis County Clipper* (Bountiful, Utah), December 9, 1960, 10.

138. Ibid.

139. "Local Couple to Teach School in Morocco," *Davis County Clipper* (Bountiful, Utah), September 26, 1958, 4.

140. "Seifert Rites," *Davis County Clipper [Bountiful, Utah]*, February 12, 1960, 6.

way through the jungle: John M. Goddard, world traveler and filmmaker.[141] As a fifteen-year-old boy, he famously composed a list of 127 goals, most of which involved travel to exotic countries. By age twenty-three, he had traversed over 250,000 miles and was the youngest member of the Adventurers Club, a club for explorers of developing regions.[142] While serving a mission in the Northern States, which included Winnipeg, Canada, he delivered lectures at the local LDS chapels.[143] He was a restless spirit: "I may have been born in Salt Lake City," he wrote while traveling through Italy, "but I really grew up in Foggia."[144] Goddard believed in living deliberately. When he visited a gambling hall ("the glittering den of iniquity") in Monte Carlo, he "wandered from room to room watching the fashionably dressed 'gamers'" and pitied them for their "immoderate and purposeless living."[145] Yet he valued the cultivation of the "impressionable mind," one that "notes and records everything of worth." He hoped to "foster a love that demands nothing but the privilege of its own expression—a love that clothes every vista with beauty, discloses a friend in every contact, an inspiration in every scene of nature."[146]

A war veteran and returned missionary, Goddard garnered wide acclaim for his travels throughout the African continent throughout the 1950s. In 1951, he became the first person to cruise the Nile in a kayak, an excursion that became a documentary film, *Kayaks down the Nile*. During his travels, he met Ugandan royalty and saw, as the *Omaha World Herald* styled them, "the pygmies of Central Africa."[147] Billed as a "famous world explorer" who was "trim and hardy in middle age," Goddard sold well as a media personality.[148] Giving presentations became a career that eventually earned him up to $50,000 annually.[149]

Goddard's extensive correspondence from the trip and journals reveal the complicated views he harbored concerning the African continent and its peoples. His first arrival in Africa reveals his youthful, yet cultivated, sense of himself: "Ah! Africa le Magnifique! Can it really be true?" It was to be "a trip of unparalleled adventure . . . covering a territory which is an abridged edition of the world."[150] When he first caught sight of Africans in October 1950, they were part of a scene in which "a rusty antique of a tug-boat [was] crammed to the smoke-stack with a mass of black humanity"[151]

141. For Goddard's awards, see "Goddard Film to Feature Scenic Trip," *University of Utah Daily Chronicle*, March 25, 1955, 1.

142. "L.D.S. Missionary to Speak Wednesday," *Winona [Minn.] Republican-Herald,* May 14, 1949, 13.

143. "Mormon Elder to Give Talk on Foreign Tour," *Winnipeg Tribune,* January 11, 1949, 7; "Club Members," *Winona Republican-Herald,* May 17, 1949, 4.

144. John M. Goddard, Letter to Family, September 21, 1950.

145. Goddard to Family, September 20, 1950.

146. Goddard to Family, October 12, 1950.

147. "Yank, 2 Pals End Up Nile Dinghy Trip," *Omaha World Herald,* June 27, 1951, 16.

148. "First Time in Ventura County," *Press-Courier* (Oxnard, Calif.), June 2, 1958, 6.

149. "One Man's Life of No Regrets," *Life,* March 24, 1972, 66.

150. John M. Goddard, Letter to Family, n.d. (ca. October 1950).

151. Goddard to Family, October 3, 1950.

Initially, he noted that some of the blacks he encountered were "a mixture of Hamitic and Bantu" and "are some of the most primitive people in the world."[152]

After a few months on the Nile, he assured his parents that he was "completely happy": "Africa seems familiar and like home to me after studying about it so much and living it in my mind for so many years." He "love[d] the natives" for their serenity and cheerfulness: "Whites can learn a lesson from these so-called primitive people."[153] When he encountered one of his first African villages, he thought it to be an "African Shangri La."[154] He found the women's dancing to be enchanting: "I have never seen women dance with such beauty and grace yet with such economy of movement. . . . [T]heir heads bobbed and nodded rhythmically in an almost Balinese-like technique; eyes closed and faces an expressionless yet beautiful mask."[155] Goddard felt real affection for the natives, though it was born of virtues he projected on them: "his reserved politeness, his hearty sense of humor, his child-like curiosity and wonderment, his faith in the ultimate triumph of good over bad, right over wrong[.] His jolly laziness, His soft—'Jambo, Bwana' (Hello, Sir)."[156]

Goddard fully accepted the superiority of Western civilization and technology. He was amused when tribal members "run off into the bush or immediately cover their fine jewelry and beadwork with their togas" at the sight of his camera: "This same situation was repeated in every village we visited during the journey. The people were scared to death of the camera and usually fled if they saw it being pointed their way."[157] He scoffed at the gendered division of labor: "Only the women of the tribe worked while the men sat before their mud walled huts and gossiped. Ah these primitive societies![158]" In 1950, he had delighted in speaking with a British doctor about his "wonderful experiences as a healer of the black man's physical and spiritual ills."[159] When he happened across a village racked with a variety of ills, his "heart went out to the poor wretches and I found myself

---

152. Goddard to Family, January 4, 1951.

153. Goddard to Family, n.d. (ca. October 1950).

154. Goddard to Family October 25, 1950.

155. Goddard to Family, April 27, 1951.

156. Goddard to Family, October 26, 1950, holograph. A typescript version of the letter includes this passage: "When I reminisce over my experiences during the past two weeks they have the peculiar fabric of a dream; I see the sinewy, black, greased and dusted bodies of my African friends; the bone and bead ornaments on arms, legs, ears, nose, and lips; I hear the catchy syncopation of their chanting; the soul-deep throb of their drums in the deep night; I am sitting with them again smiling back at the circle of beaming faces around the camp fire; smelling the dried fish, banana beer, the mingled odors of man and beast that cling to their villages; I laugh at their clownish dancing, so uninhibited and appealing, dressed in Edenic ballet skirts of fresh leaves distended by malarial spleens. Their lives are a never ending succession of merriment and misery, faith and famine, bravery and barbarism, humor and hookworm, dignity and death." Goddard to Family, October 26, 1950, typescript. The holograph does not contain this quoted passage.

157. Goddard to Family, January 11, 1951.

158. Goddard to Family, December 30, 1950.

159. Goddard to Family, November 1, 1950.

trying to figure out some way to help them." But he was certain his efforts would fail: "These primitive people rarely trust white men's medicine preferring to put their faith in their worthless witch-doctors—the greatest 'quacks' in the world."[160] However, by 1956, his views of African medicine had changed, probably due to coursework in anthropology at the University of Southern California. Rather than scorning African medicine, he was determined to find the African roots for Western medicine: "We will be on the lookout for everything of this nature that we can find," he told the *Deseret News* on the eve of his departure.[161] By the 1980s, he had "developed a deep respect for [medicine men]. Most of them are not phonies or charlatans but are sincerely desirous of helping their people."[162]

Though raised in the depths of Utah racial thought, his exposure to Africa prompted him to question his childhood assumptions. "Why do people always refer to Africa as the 'Dark Continent' when it's a land of blazing sunshine," he wondered to his family.[163] Goddard found his exploration "worthwhile just for the wonderful people I have met." He had "made life-long friendships with individuals of 15 nationalities and races."[164] He was cognizant of the ambiguity that Westernization forced upon the native people, observing that the "big problem with the learned negro in Africa is that he is neither accepted by whites or blacks but is treated impersonally by both races."[165]

Goddard's presentations presented Africa as a rich, life-giving world, filled with images of "the beautiful terrain of the hitherto impenetrable country [and] glimpses into the lives of the natives of the area, and views of the wildlife of the jungle area."[166] The reviewer of his presentation at the University of Utah noted that Goddard and his companions "fought jungle fever, wild beasts, savage tribesmen, and 130-degree heat." Goddard's film had it all: "strange tribesmen, queer animals, [and] odd jungle life . . . and most of it has been caught in his wonderful color films."[167] His story was one of defying death, fighting "32 different diseases, hostile natives, rampaging hippos, and crocodiles."[168]

The dangers were real but due more to natural forces than "strange tribesmen." On the Nile, his kayak hit a patch of river vegetation and turned over with Goddard "under the kayak being dragged along upside down with my legs all

---

160. Goddard to Family, January 10, 1951.

161. "Elder Goddard Sets Congo Exploration," *Deseret News*, May 12, 1956, 6.

162. Gary Stockdale and Patricia Campbell, "Interview: John Goddard," *Metamorphisis* 4, no. 2 (Summer 1986): 62.

163. Goddard to Family, January 10, 1951.

164. Goddard to Gamily, January 4, 1951 (December–January inclusive).

165. Goddard to Family, n.d. (ca. October 1950).

166. "Nile River Film to Be Shown in Cedar City," *Iron County Record* (Cedar City, Utah), March 12, 1953, 1.

167. "African River Adventure Scheduled for ULAS," *University of Utah Daily Chronicle*, February 17, 1954, 1.

168. "Film to Portray Eventful Trip down Nile River," *Ogden-Standard Examiner*, March 17, 1953, 12.

fouled up in the lashings." Until he could extricate himself, he suffered "the most hellish and unforgettably horrible minutes of my life." Making matters worse, he was weakened after "suffering for several days from a mild attack of dysentery." Even when he was free of the kayak, the water "churned me around like a mouse caught in a washing machine."[169]

"Just as my lungs seemed about to explode," he wrote his parents, "I broke the surface just long enough to gulp in great draughts of delicious, resuscitating oxygen before being sucked under again." The air infused bolstered his spirits, enabling him to make his way to shore. He laid there, "panting and half dead with fatigue " like a "floating mass of rotting vegetation giving thanks to our Father-in-Heaven for having once again spared my life."[170] He had outsmarted the Grim Reaper once again.

By the end of his trek, he had dodged drowning, trampling, and execution. His trek received national press coverage.[171] In 1951, he returned to the United States and married a Provo model and ward organist, Pearlyne Crowley.[172]

In 1956, Goddard and Jack Yowell, a South African journalist living in Kenya, commenced another expedition to travel the entirety of the Congo River. The Glendale West Ward had him speak shortly before leaving.[173] Though Goddard adored the African wilderness, his Congo travels celebrate Western industrialization and global capitalism. He found the Belgian Congo to be "the brightest spot on the Dark C[ontinent]." Congolese industry—uranium in particular—was "a big business which boasts proudly of its black shareholders & its black ledger figures" and was "solidly rooted in the hard facts of economics." Its promise was tremendous: "It has minerals galore, water, forest products, labor—& a rare commodity called peace." If one wanted to see a Congolese work hard, Goddard maintained, "just give one of these boys a Sears & Roebuck Catalogue."[174]

---

169. Goddard to Family, May 15, 1951.

170. Ibid.

171. "Three Paddle down the Nile for 9 Months," *Anniston [Ala.] Star*, July 29, 1951, 16; "Yank Will Make Record Canoe Trip," *Miami [Okla.] Daily News-Record*, August 1, 1950, 1; "Ex-Pilot Tours Africa in Canoe," *Pampa Daily News*, August 1, 1950, 2; "Trio in Canoe Explore Entire Nile for First Time in 4,200-Mile Trip," *Kane [Penn.] Republican*, September 6, 1951, 10; "To Explore Nile," *Greeley [Colo.] Daily Tribune*, September 6, 1950, 11.

172. A wedding photograph of Goddard and Crowley includes the date of their wedding, http://gatheringgardiners.blogspot.com/2012/05/1920–1970-glendale-ca.html (accessed January 21, 2014). See also "Holiday Week Marked by Parties and Numerous Get-Togethers," *Ogden-Standard Examiner*, November 26, 1950, 2B . Pearlyne was the subject of an award-winning photo portrait by Provo photographer, Robert W. Stum. "Photographer Wins Office, Awards with State Group," *[Provo] Daily Herald*, September 10, 1954, 4.

173. Glendale West Ward, Manuscript History and Historical Reports, October 28, 1956. When the party encountered rough rapids, Yowell fell off the raft and drowned. "Colored Film on Congo at College Tonight," *Los Angeles Tribune*, April 8, 1960, 8. Goddard returned the body to Yowell's family in Nairobi and commenced his trip again.

174. John M. Goddard, Congo Journal, May 27, 1956.

John M. Goddard poses with tribesmen in the Congo, ca. 1956. Goddard used the proceeds from his subsequent lectures to help with various congregations raise funds for chapels and missionary efforts. Courtesy BYU Special Collections.

Goddard believed that "the Belg[ians] themselves can be credited with creating peace on a continent where unrest is the rule," an end game that amounted to the dissolution of tribal societies.[175] The "peace" Goddard witnessed was actually the merciless crack-down on any form of political dissent, with the Belgian government using American funds and weapons. But for Goddard, civilization had triumphed: "Men whose fathers practiced cannibalism & who may still wear grotesque tribal markings on their faces now operate complex mining machinery, cranes, steam shovels, locomotives & diesel powered boats."[176]

The Congo expedition also resulted in a documentary, *Bongos down the Congo*. The film received national publicity;[177] and both the *Deseret News* and *Cumorah's Southern Messenger* (the South Africa Mission magazine) referred to him as "Elder John Goddard," though it had been several years since his missionary service.[178] Goddard made regular presentations at Brigham Young University and Boy Scout events in Utah.[179] At his lecture in Panguitch, Utah, proceeds

175. Ibid.

176. Ibid.

177. "20th century Reveals Program for 1956–1957," *Oshkosh [Wisc.] Daily Northwestern*, August 23, 1956, 24.

178. For instances of this title appearing in print, see "Sets Congo Expedition," *Cumorah's Southern Messenger* 31, no. 6 (June 1956): 83 and "Elder Goddard Sets Congo Exploration," *Deseret News*, May 12, 1956, 6.

179. "1960 Annual Merit Badge Pow-Wow," *[Provo] Daily Herald*, March 3, 1960, 9; "Exploring African Wonderlands," *[Provo] Daily Herald*, March 23, 1969, 10.

from the lecture were earmarked to purchase "an organ for the South Ward Chapel."[180] He spoke for similar building fund events at the Provo Tabernacle and San Bernardino, California.[181] In 1975, he delivered a presentation at the Los Angeles Stake that brought in an audience of over 400 people at $2.50 per person. "You greatly enlarged our coffers," the local Seventies Council said warmly, "all of which, of course, is for His cause." Goddard donated the proceeds to the stake's missionary fund.[182]

Goddard's fame extended well beyond the Mormon corridor. In 1955, he penned "Kayaks down the Nile" for *The National Geographic Magazine*, the first time his story made it into print.[183] He gave presentations at educational institutions in major cities such as Los Angeles, Chicago, and Lansing, Michigan.[184] During a Chicago show, he "introduce[d] the audience to an incredible fire-walking and glass-eating ceremony performance by the descendants of escaped African slaves in Surinam."[185] His film found widespread viewership upon release, even earning a spot on the ABC television network's series *Bold Journey* in May 1959.[186] When *Bold Journey* had a lottery contest for a trip to Africa, they arranged for the winner, a schoolteacher named Billie-Marie Gannon, to travel with Goddard as her guide.[187]

Battling dysentery, whitewater, wild hippos, and the "*kamikaze* attacks of the Bug Air Corps," Goddard's story exuded the spirit of daring-do and rugged naturalism. One evening, he wrote his family, "we were lulled to sleep by the throaty 'music' of several Hippo bases,—our next door neighbors."[188] When he came face-to-face with a large elephant, he attempted to point the "camera right at him (a little shakily I'm afraid) with it running at a fast and furious 24 frames." Within moments the elephant "lunge[ed] forward a few feet then stopping suddenly coming closer and closer" and then decided to "get down to business to eradicate the pest annoying him." The elephant "came lumbering toward me in

180. "Famed Explorer to Speak and Show Movies," *Garfield County News* (Panguitch, UT), January 28, 1954, 1.

181. "Troop Sponsors Church Benefit," San Bernardino County Sun, September 29, 1955, 48; "Goddard Congo Films Scheduled for Building Fund," Sunday Herald (Provo, Utah) March 20, 1960, 9A..

182. The Seventies Council of the Los Angeles Stake, March 8, 1975, Goddard Papers, Box 3, fd. 9.

183. John M. Goddard, "Kayaks down the Nile," *National Geographic Magazine* 72, no. 5 (May 1955): 697–723.

184. Kent Stevenson, interviewed by Russell W. Stevenson, December 27, 2013, notes in my possession. For his Lansing visit, see "Exploring African Wonderlands," *[Provo] Daily Herald*, March 23, 1969, 10. For Iowa, see "Goddard to Narrate Film Here Sunday," *Carroll [Iowa] Daily Times Herald*, March 15, 1963, 1. For Chicago, see "Andes to Amazon Is Second Film," *[Chicago] Daily Herald*, November 14, 1963.

185. "Andes to Amazon is 2nd Film," *[Chicago] Daily Herald*, November 14, 1963, 64.

186. "TV Last Night," *Boston Daily Record*, May 12, 1959, 18.

187. Goddard's wife, Pearlyne, also accompanied them on the trek. See "City Teacher Wins Long Foreign Trip," *Seattle Daily Times*, April 26, 1958.

188. Goddard to Family, January 10, 1950.

a fast rush." Goddard "flung myself into the canoe and pushed off almost in the same motion—and none too soon." He assured his family that "this is the very last time that I will put myself in a position to be 'discombabblelated' by a big game animal."[189]

LDS publications for youth embraced Goddard as an exemplar of righteous masculinity. In 1959, Goddard wrote "Kayaks down the Nile" for the Church's official magazine, the *Improvement Era*. Billing Goddard as "one of the country's foremost explorers," the magazine cast Goddard as a shining son of Mormon America willing to grapple with even the most formidable of natural forces. Wendell Phillips, president of the American Foundation for the Study of Man, called Goddard's efforts one of the "great feats of exploration and physical endurance of all time."[190] He also taught courses in the Cultural Anthropology Department at Brigham Young University.[191] The LDS youth magazine, *New Era,* received a question about whether Mormons should "consider skydiving, auto racing, skin diving, mountain climbing, motorcycle riding, and so forth, risks that we should not expose ourselves to?" Goddard assured the young readers that "in each of these adventures there has been a deep and enduring enrichment of body, mind, and spirit, a warm sense of communion with our Heavenly Father through contact with the beauty of his creations."[192]

In addition to Goddard's explorations, he became the fastest flying civilian (excluding test pilots), reaching 1,420 miles per hour at 63,000 feet.[193] He hosted his own, short-lived television show, *This Exciting World,* which offered an "intimate full-color look at the incredible contrasts of life in Venezuela, Surinam (Dutch Guiana), Brazil, and Peru."[194] In 1973, Weber State University and Brigham Young University both showed *Kayaks.*[195] That same year, he published a memoir, *Kayaks down the Nile,* through Brigham Young University Press. He continued to deliver presentations for groups throughout southern California: the Lions' Club, [196]

---

189. Goddard to Family, December 30, 1950.

190. John M. Goddard, "Kayaks down the Nile, Part I," Improvement Era 62, no. 10 (October 1959): 735.

191. "Shapley Teacher on Her Way to Big Adventures," *Corsicana Daily Sun [Navarro, Tex.],* June 25, 1958, 7.

192. John M. Goddard, "Q&A response," *New Era,* July 1974, 10.

193. "Exploring African Wonderlands," *[Provo] Daily Herald,* March 23, 1969, 10.

194. "Travelogue Program," *Press Telegram* (Pasadena, Calif.), October 4, 1967, 70; "Television," *Redlands Daily Facts* (Redlands, Calif.), September 1, 1965, 16; "Travelogue Program," *Independent* (Long Beach, Calif.), October 5, 1967, P2; "Forum Will Show Film on Turkey," *Tucson [Ariz.] Daily Citizen,* February 9, 1967, 29; "Travel Film to Be Seen by Forum," *Tucson Daily Citizen,* February 7, 1964, 44.

195. "John M. Goddard Presents," *[Provo] Daily Herald,* March 25, 1973, 23. Film screenings continued for several years after their initial release, sometimes with Goddard in attendance. "WSC Plans Travelogue on Nile Trip," *Ogden-Standard Examiner,* April 4, 1973, 9B.

196. Myron D. Clayton, Letter to John Goddard, February 29, 1972, John M. Goddard Papers, Box 3, fd. 9, Perry Special Collections.

Pasadena City College,[197] San Diego Union High School,[198] the Rotary Club of Los Angeles,[199] and the Women's Auxiliary of the Los Angeles Medical Association.[200] Observers often felt "spellbound" as they watched his presentations.[201]

However, Goddard's constant absence proved too much for Pearlyne, and they divorced in the early 1960s.[202] He remarried and again divorced. In 1986, *Life* reporter Anne Fadiman interviewed his first two wives and reported that they "shared the opinion that he would someday outgrow his adolescent fantasies."[203]

Goddard said little of his religion in either public presentations or in private correspondence. His Church activity amounted to an occasional public prayer or talk. Though he never claimed divine commission for his efforts, he felt that God had protected him. In November 1950, he wrote his family that they had seen "the hand of God in all our undertakings and I know that the solicitations of you, the family, and our dear friends have been primarily responsible for our constant guidance and protection."[204] After his trip, he reflected that "our Heavenly Father didn't make our trip easy for us but He did instill in us courage, faith and strength to overcome any and all obstacles and hardships in our path, so that in meeting and conquering our tribulations we became stronger, wise, and better men."[205]

Throughout the 1970s, Goddard turned his stories of adventure into morality tales on the need for racial tolerance, environmentalism, and understanding. "Get to know the peoples of the world," he implored a Utah audience in 1975, "no matter the color of their skin or their religion." The "brain has no color and intelligence is equally distributed throughout the peoples of the world."[206] One school administrator lauded Goddard for his "witty dialogue with its interesting vocabulary." She found his "values and philosophy refreshing . . . not only because they agree with mine, but because it is now very 'in' to consider these kinds of references as 'corny,' etc." Even more important, she was glad the male students "had the opportunity to hear a very masculine person of note reveal sensitivities for other people, the environment, our systems etc. There is a real need for this

---

197. Laura Davies, Letter to John Goddard, June 1, 1975, holograph, John M. Goddard Papers, Box 3, fd. 9.

198. Peter Rowe, Letter to John Goddard, March 2, 1975.

199. Earl R. Lingle, Letter to John M. Goddard, March 7, 1972.

200. Maryann Attalla, Letter to John M. Goddard, June 10, 1975.

201. Phyllis Perkins, Letter to John M. Goddard, May 15, 1975; Bill Brown, Letter to John M. Goddard, September 15, 1975.

202. Stephanie Hales, a daughter born to Pearlyne Crowley in her second marriage, discusses John's and Pearlyne's divorce in a Facebook post, August 24, 2013, https://www.facebook.com/stephanie. hales.39/posts/322956557850322 (accessed January 22, 2014), screenshot in my possession

203. Fadiman, "John Goddard: 108 adventures down, 19 to go," 22.

204. John M. Goddard, Letter to Family, November 20, 1950.

205. John M. Goddard, Letter to Family, July 20, 1951.

206. "A Man of Little Monkey Business," *Monday Magazine* (Provo, Utah), April 7, 1975, 17. For a brief discussion of *Monday Magazine*, see Bryan Waterman and Brian Kagel, *The Lord's University: Freedom and Authority at BYU*, 81.

kind of balance in young people."[207] So popular was Goddard that BYU Motion Picture Studios commenced plans to re-enact scenes from his Nile kayaking experience.[208] Some Mormons who saw Goddard's presentation thanked him for showing his "love for God's many children," love that "can't help but open many doors and avenues unto you to further your understanding of the world and the Lord's ecumenical enterprise of winning souls to his eternal verities."[209]

Sonia Johnson also experienced a transformation. By most accounts, she was a conservative Mormon housewife. She poked at the Communists who were "pretty glum" after the "madman" Ghanaian President Kwame Nkrumah was deposed in Ghana: "Tough luck!" she said, sharing in the "general rejoicing" of the Ghanaian community. Johnson grew excited upon hearing that a temple might be constructed in Mormonism's "promised land" of Jackson County: "I'd love to think that it was really starting to wind itself up, this old world of ours, but I'll just have to have patience, I guess."[210]

Though she had personally never fostered racial bigotry, she grew up in a family that had; upon arrival, she urged her mother—but no one else—to visit them: "The rest of you can't come because you don't like Negroes, and there are a few of them around!"[211] she ribbed her family. But she had never seriously engaged racial issues: "I've certainly led a protected, uninformed, uninvolved life," she confessed to her mother. "Basically, I'm a selfish, thoughtless brute . . . an uneducated, crass mortal, and I need lots of polishing and perfecting."[212] On March 24, 1966, she had learned "from a complicated thought process I've just been through in the last few seconds" that race would be the defining issue of her times, that "living among negroes, in a land composed of little else, causes one to ponder the question much more often and much more seriously than ever before." Blacks were among "the finest, most intelligent, most moral, most level-headed persons" she had ever known. After experiencing Africa firsthand, the priesthood ban "just doesn't make sense to me."[213] But even then, Johnson allowed that there must be a timetable for these things: "It's not President McKay's function to deal with this," but she hoped that "the next President of the Church will receive some revelation about it."[214]

Other Utahns also engaged Africa through humanitarian, educational, and government programs. Conventional wisdom dictated that "black African states remain pro-western or at least neutral" in the Cold War struggle, making it an ap-

---

207. JeanAnne Turner, Letter to John M. Goddard, April 30, 1975.

208. "Actors Sought to Re-enact Goddard's Nile Adventure," *[Provo] Daily Herald*, October 22, 1975.

209. The Seventies Council of the Los Angeles Stake, Letter to John M. Goddard, March 8, 1975.

210. Sonia Johnson, Letter to Harrises, August 28, 1966.

211. Johnson to Harrises, October 23, 1965.

212. Johnson to Harrises, July 16, 1966.

213. Sonia Johnson, Letter to Harrises, March 24, 1966.

214. Ibid.

pealing site for Mormons committed to preserving American hegemony.[215] Some Latter-day Saints went to Africa as a part of the Point Four development program sponsored by the State Department. State Department employee and humanitarian worker Rex Ottley had long participated in African development missions; in 1960, he and a number of Mormons were working in the State Department's Point Four development program in Ethiopia. In 1969, Ottley and a handful of Mormon expatriates were living in Kampala, while they worked as agricultural advisers in the brewing political storm of Uganda. By January 1971, Idi Amin Dada had overthrown the government and controlled Kampala. Within months, he had killed several thousand former supporters of his predecessor, Milton Obote. While Dada cracked down, the small Mormon congregation discussed lessons with titles such as "The Mormon Communities along the American Frontier," and "The Saints Are Driven Out of the State of Missouri."[216] In September 1972, the *Deseret News* published a light-hearted article about the Mormon experience in Uganda, telling a story of Ottley's wife, Bernell, who traditionally went fishing on her birthday and "traditionally . . . catches the biggest fish." After she landed a seventy-pound Nile perch on the river by Lake Victoria, Rex reportedly wanted Bernell to "consider having a suspension of natal days—as most women do."[217] The report said little of Ottley's extensive work teaching livestock techniques to African villagers and nothing about teaching the gospel.

Utah universities engaged in cooperative efforts with West Africa as the U.S. government developed international aid and student exchange programs, and Nigeria's oil potential seemed particularly promising.[218] Prominent Vernal resident A. R. Pierce took a position in Nigeria with Kerr McGee Oil.[219] Dr. Joseph Fillerup of the Education Division at the College of Southern Utah (now Southern Utah University) taught for two years in Nigeria under the auspices of Columbia Teachers College.[220] "Mrs. John Bede," a Vernal middle-school teacher, spent two years teaching in Nigeria.[221] Davis County native Vincent Mayer spent two years "help[ing] to build bridges, school houses, reading rooms, and water

215. "New Africa Means Diplomacy Problems," *[University of] Utah Daily Chronicle*, February 27, 1963, 2.

216. Kampala, Uganda Group, General Minutes, November 15, 1970, and March 14, 1971.

217. "The Trouble with Birthdays," *Deseret News*, September 28, 1972, 1E.

218. "Babson's Point of View," *Vernal Express*, July 10, 1969, 10; "Business and the Stock Market," *Vernal Express*, February 5, 1970, 3.

219. Pierce's work in Nigeria was recorded in "Linda Pierce Will Marry Ted C. Olsen," *Vernal Express*, May 26, 1966, 4.

220. "Escalante Chit-Chat," Garfield County News (Panguitch, Utah) , September 19, 1963, 1; "USU Board Names Division Head at Cedar City," Sunday Herald (Provo, Utah), September 15, 1963, 8.

221. "Club Members Hear Reports on Foreign Visits," *Vernal Express*, April 11, 1968, 5. See also "West Bountiful," *Davis County Clipper* (Bountiful, Utah), December 25, 1964, 11, and "North Notes," *Ephraim Enterprise*, December 3, 1970, 9; "Blanding Boy Starts Peace Corps Work," *Times Independent* (Moab, Utah), November 21, 1963, 4.

wells" in the "bush country" of Central Africa.[222] Utah State University's Evan Thompson served with the Near East Foundation to advise Tanzania on the improved agricultural techniques he claimed to have learned at the "end of a shovel handle" growing up in central Utah.[223]

Decolonization movements were of little interest to the profoundly white Mormons, although occasional sparks were ignited by parallel efforts to find "white tribes" in South America whom they believed to be remnants of Book of Mormon populations. Similarly, Utah newspapers published articles reporting archaeologists' efforts to discover a "white tribe of giants" in Central Africa.[224] In 1963, Brigham Young University invited the British ambassador to Ethiopia, Sir Geoffrey Furlonge, to speak on the characteristics of various African tribes. He drew firm genetic distinctions between the Ethiopians, who lacked the "negroid" appearance of other Africans: "Their features are far finer; and . . . are not black." The Somalis, by contrast, were "a lean, dark, hawk-eyed fuzzy-haired Hamitic race" that were "excitable and truculent, but brave and capable of devotion."[225]

Figures like Ottley and Cutler appeared in the press as the modern equivalents of past explorers and missionaries—adventurers who escaped the modern world by stepping backward in time. One newspaper editor fancied that he might join the Peace Corps to teach African natives printing. After "stalking through the African jungle, dodging elephants and lions and stuff, carrying all our worldly goods in packs . . . we arrive at the village. 'Ugh.' Well, after all, if he's a chief, he probably says ugh whether he's red or black."[226] When Rendell Mabey described the hunting methods of the native Africans, he described it as "follow[ing] in a single file (Indian fashion)."[227]

LaMar Williams and other mid-level leaders maintained muted connections with the West African Saints, primarily by providing them with published materials. He began to send "personal copies of the Book of Mormon and other literatures . . . concerning the Church" to the Saints in Ghana.[228] Hungry for literature, they begged Church headquarters: "Many need the Book of Mormon. Kindly send

---

222. "Ends Peace Corps Work in Africa," *Davis County Clipper* (Bountiful, Utah), January 17, 1969, 8. Still, most Mormon youth decided not to participate in the government's Peace Corps program; the evangelizing mission abroad doubled as the international experience for most Mormon youth. It was a "spiritual peace corps . . . [that] joins in protest against the world's ills, but offers by precept and example positive, workable plans for action." See "The Mormon Answer to the Hippies," *Vernal Express*, January 18, 1968, 12.

223. "Evan Thompson Relives Life in Tanzania, East Africa," *Ephraim Enterprise*, May 28, 1970, 7.

224. "Archaeologists Launch Expedition Seeking White Giant Tribe," *Davis County Clipper* (Bountiful, Utah), March 31, 1950, 6.

225. Geoffrey Warren Furlonge, "The Land of Judah on the Horn of Africa," January 21, 1963, in *BYU Speeches of the Year* (1963), 4, 7.

226. "The Ant's Eye View," *Summit County Bee Park Record* (Park City, Utah), March 28, 1963, 2.

227. "Safari in Africa," *Davis County Clipper* (Bountiful, Utah), November 18, 1955, 1.

228. Joseph Dadzie, "The History of the 'Church of Jesus Christ of Latter-Day Saints in Ghana," Dadzie Papers, LDS Church History Library.

more copies." They were "even prepared to pay for their cost."[229] Three months later, Joseph Dadzie, received priesthood and Relief Society manuals as well as copies of the Book of Mormon in the mail.[230]

Due to the efforts of Goddard, Williams, Cutler, and others, American Mormons adopted a more nuanced view of African societies. Though they perpetuated some colonial stereotypes, they also endeavored to expand Mormons' perspective of the global community, recognizing the African continent as such—not merely as an imagined construct filled with lions and cannibals.

But these members too experienced transformation in their own ways. In the 1950s, Goddard was happy that blacks been modernized to the extent that they had a financial stake in the industrialization process. Nigeria had compelled Sonia Johnson to face her own complacency and narrowness of vision. After LaMar Williams looked into the eyes of Nigerian Saints, he knew that the days of the priesthood ban were numbered. They were learning to envision Africa not as the "dark continent" but as the land of "blazing sunshine."

But to categorize Williams, Goddard, Johnson, and others as activists against the priesthood ban at this stage would be incorrect. Generally, they did not question the accepted position of Church authorities; however, they did work within Mormon culture to create a space for a black narrative that had been marginalized for generations.

Africans, unlike African Americans, enjoyed a sovereignty over their own land and culture that African Americans were only now beginning to rediscover. It was a heritage that white Mormons could understand and acknowledge. Even though white Mormons had some understanding of what it meant to have one's land and vision stripped from them, they had drunk deeply of the waters of white, Anglo-Saxon nationalism.

The result? Whether you sat in the Church Office Building at 50 E North Temple or in the stucco homes of Manti, Detroit instilled a fear in white Mormondom that Accra never could.

---

229. Joseph Dadzie, Letter to President of the Church, July 15, 1977.
230. Joseph Dadzie, Autobiography, Joseph Dadzie Papers, LDS Church History Library.

Chapter 5

This Negro Problem:
Mormons and the U.S. Civil Rights Era,
1953–1969

*"It might be that you and I, and all of us in the church, because of
our sins, or because of our lack of thinking upon the great fundamentals that Christ taught, because of not having the Spirit of Christ,
may sometimes be at fault for our limitations."*
—Lowell Bennion, University of Utah Institute (1963)[1]

BYU President Ernest L. Wilkinson was many things: ambitious, productive,
and existentially conservative. Of the many things on his mind (attaining national
respectability for BYU, overseeing the construction of what amounted to a new campus, building a well-staffed law school, etc.), addressing racial injustice was not high
on his priority list. But being the sharp D.C. lawyer that he was, he knew a political
problem when he saw it. In January 1953, Wilkinson tacitly agreed with Church
President David O. McKay "that the relationship of the Church to the colored person
was one of the most pressing problems that had to be faced and resolved."[2]

Throughout the 1950s and '60s, the Southern African American population mobilized to lift racial segregation laws in the South. The African American population
employed many tactics: litigation, boycotts, and public spectacles to raise awareness
about the evils of segregation. In 1954, African Americans took school segregation to
the courts, resulting in the U.S. Supreme Court decision, *Brown v. Board of Education*
(1954), effectively overturning racial segregation laws throughout the country. The
following year blacks in Montgomery, Alabama, boycotted use of the city public bus
system when Rosa Parks, a young black woman and NAACP secretary, refused to sit
in the back of the bus. In 1960, young blacks sat alongside white patrons at the lunch
counter of Woolworth's department store in Greensboro, North Carolina.[3]

---

1. Lowell L. Bennion, qtd. in Mary Lythgoe Bradford, *Lowell L. Bennion: Teacher, Counselor,
Humanitarian*, 249.

2. Ernest L. Wilkinson, Letter to David O. McKay, January 31, 1953.

3. Sound survey texts on the civil rights movement include William H. Chafe, *Civilities and
Civil Rights: Greensboro, North Carolina and the Black Struggle for Freedom;* Taylor Branch, *Parting
the Waters: America in the King Years, 1954–1963;* Nick Kotz, *Judgment Days: Lyndon Baines*

The actions of Southern blacks received national attention and commentary, even in the profoundly white intermountain Mormon corridor. Most Mormons supported legal equality in the abstract but were unsettled by what they interpreted as a mass movement of black Americans trying to compel whites to grant them equality. "Most people in their hearts are for civil rights and tolerance," one small Utah paper opined, "but they don't want Congress ramming it down their throats by law."[4] When nine black students attempted to attend a white school in Little Rock, Arkansas, a newspaper published in a Salt Lake suburb suggested that Arkansas had outwitted the Communists' "prodding of Negro desires for complete racial equality" by "stubbornly but lawfully submitting to the Supreme Court's rulings."[5]

Church leaders continued to look askance at the civil rights movement. In 1957, President J. Reuben Clark instructed Belle Spafford, general president of the Relief Society and a member of the National Council of Women, to "do what she could to keep the [Council] from going on record in favor of . . . negro equality."[6] Utahns responded coolly to the murder of Emmett Till, a Chicago black teenager killed when he flirted with a white woman in Mississippi, by denying that it was a murder at all. Utah's *Green River Journal* uncritically reprinted a column by E. A. Davis, a Tennessee columnist, arguing that Till had brought his death upon himself. Chastising "some folks" who believed that "black people can be made white and white people black by mere law," the column emphasized that this was "the SUICIDE of Emmett Till" and nothing more. By "insulting a white woman in the Magnolia State," Till "committed suicide as surely and certain as though he had leaped from an ailiner [sic] 30,000 feet in the air without a parachute."[7]

Church leaders and members often supported and celebrated racial segregation in word and culture. During a speech at Brigham Young University in August 1954, Apostle Mark E. Petersen warned religious educators that civil rights legislation was only a thinly veiled effort to encourage racial intermarriage. "If I were to marry a Negro woman," Petersen enjoined his listeners, "my children would all be cursed as to the priesthood." If the Saints allowed intermarriage, the consequences would be cataclysmic: "Think what that would do to the work of the Church!"[8] The official Church dance committee, a sub-unit of the Young Men's and Young Women's Mutual Improvement Associations, took care in its manual of 1956–57, to warn dance instructors about the inappropriateness of

Johnson, *Martin Luther King, Jr., and the Laws that Changed America;* and Risa Golubuff, *The Lost Promise of Civil Rights.*

4. "Editorial," *Davis County Clipper* (Bountiful, Utah), February 10, 1957, 2.

5. "Did Little Rock Episode Represent a Backfire of Communistic Strategy," *Murray Eagle,* September 26, 1957, 2.

6. J. Reuben Clark, Office Diary, December 2, 1957, quoted in Gregory A. Prince and Wm. Robert Wright, *David O. McKay and the Rise of Modern Mormonism,* 63.

7. "Comments from Dixie," *Green River [Utah] Journal,* October 6, 1955, 2.

8. Mark E. Petersen, "Race Problems as They Affect the Church," August 27, 1954, 22, microfilm, Perry Special Collections.

black-influenced dancing: "Any of the ugly, crouching styles, or the wild, acrobatic antics of 'Jitterbug' or 'Bop' (a current fad), are entirely out of place in a Church program."[9] The committee felt that the dance combined "the Charleston, the Black Bottom, [and] the Big Apple"—all dances closely associated with African American dance forms.[10] Dance leaders' "job . . . is to set, and hold to, a standard of proper conduct in this and other phases of our dance program." [11] Brigham Young University's first full-time dance instructor, Alma Heaton, also insisted on the importance of teaching students how to dance properly; otherwise, the music and dance of Mormon youth would devolve to "a beat that didn't change more than four times throughout the whole evening and . . . resemble the African stomp dance."[12] Whiteness had become *de rigueur* at the pulpit and on the dance floor.

Yet when Goddard had traveled down the Nile only a few years earlier, he had seen African dance in a different light:

> I am fir[m]ly convinced that "us civilized" moderns could eradicate 90% of our anxiet-ies, neuroses, phobias, psychoses, and repressions if we would only let our hair down occasionally and express our nervous energy as the natives do, freely and naturally, in a gib [sic] dance, where anyone may cavort around in any manner for as long as he pleases. This really is a great release for pent up emotions and frustrated feelings and I'm speaking from experience because I proved the theory by actual experiment.[13]

Predictably, Heaton's perspective tended to dominate Mormon dance culture; in summer 1964, he helped direct a youth conference in Goddard's Los Angeles stake.[14]

Mormon students struggled to come to grips with the priesthood ban. In January 1958, Marion Mills wrote a letter to the *University of Utah Daily Chronicle* asking about "LDS doctrine I have heard," in hopes of finding "a satisfactory source of information."[15] University of Utah student Robert Puzey responded, declaring that "the only problem the Negro has is being a descendant of Cain, cursed by his sin." The *Chronicle* "contacted a high LDS church authority" who confirmed that "LDS doctrine does not state that Negroes are inferior to any other race."[16] Keith Miller, another student, acknowledged that Mormons "answer these questions to

---

9. *LDS Dance Manual, 1956–57,* 29, microfiche. An African American scholar observed of a black jitterbug event in Atlanta: "I thought how often I resented the charges against my people that they were merely happy, carefree dancers. This dancing had been skillful, certainly. But it wasn't free of care. . . . [I]t was defiant of care instead. It was a potent drug, a reefer smoke, a painkiller shot in the arm." Sterling A. Brown, "Jitterbug's Joy," 289.

10. John A. Davis, "The Influence of Africans on American Culture," 76. For the Charleston's African American roots, see also James Weldon Johnson and J. Rosamond Johnson, eds., *The Books of American Negro Spirituals,* 31.

11. *LDS Dance Manual, 1956–57,* 29.

12. Alma Heaton, qtd. in Ward M. Vander Griend, "Alma Heaton: Professor of Fun," 77.

13. John M. Goddard, Letter to Family, January 4, 1951), John M. Goddard Papers, Box 1, fd. 2.

14. "Three-day Conference for Youth Coming Up," *News of the West* [Glendale West Ward Newsletter] 1, no. 6 (June–July 1964): 1.

15. Marion Mills, "Letters to the Editors," *[University of] Utah Daily Chronicle,* January 14, 1958, 2.

16. Keith Puzey, "Letters to the Editor," *[University of] Utah Daily Chronicle,* January 15, 1958, 2.

their own satisfaction by a belief in the pre-existence." However, he assured her, Mormon exaltation is "as obtainable to the Negro as it is to the yellow man or the cinnamon skinned or the orange or what have you. . . . This is basic to our philosophy." He closed by suggesting that "God will reveal when the colored man may receive [the priesthood]." Perhaps, Miller suggested, "man isn't moral enough to receive and live with such an edict."[17]

Later that year, Bruce R. McConkie released his sweeping reference work, *Mormon Doctrine*, which observed matter-of-factly that "negroes are not equal with other races where the receipt of spiritual blessings is concerned." McConkie repeated the now-axiomatic premortality explanation for black skin color, observing: "Those who were less valiant in the pre-existence and who thereby had certain spiritual restrictions imposed upon them during mortality are known to us as the negroes. Such spirits are sent to earth through the lineage of Cain, the mark put upon him for his rebellion against God and his murder of Abel being a black skin." The "present status of the Negro rests purely and simply on the foundation of pre-existence." This inequality "is not of man's origin," McConkie insisted. "It is the Lord's doing, is based on his eternal laws of justice, and grows out of the lack of spiritual valiance of those concerned in their first estate."[18] The 1966 edition echoed this position.[19]

For generations, the Mormon race policy had gone unnoticed by outside observers; that invisibility was no more. In 1959, an anonymous individual wrote the *Los Angeles Tribune*: "Does any one know if there is hope regarding the Mormon racial position on accepting Negroes as members?" He inquired, not as a potential member, but as a taxpayer concerned about the Mormons' tax-exempt status: "If men are taxed equally, they should be saved equally—not according to color of skin."[20]

While Utah's legislature passed no discriminatory laws, segregation was a lived reality for residents and visiting blacks. Three "fine, clean, educated negro boys" visited Salt Lake City in 1955, but Elder Marion D. Hanks, the Assistant to the Quorum of the Twelve, could not find a hotel that would accept them. Hanks's mother, Maude, stepped up, making her home available to the three boys, who slept in the "tiny apartment" during their visit.[21] In 1957, Adam M. Duncan, a state senator, active Mormon, and former missionary to South Africa, proposed anti-segregation legislation that would prohibit the exclusion of anyone "from a public place because of his color or national origin."[22] In 1958,

---

17. Keith Miller, "Letter to the Editor," *[University of] Utah Daily Chronicle*, January 20, 1958, 2.

18. Bruce R. McConkie, *Mormon Doctrine*, (1958), 476–77.

19. Bruce R. McConkie, *Mormon Doctrine*, (1966), 527–28.

20. "Man Wants to Know Mormon Racial Position," *Los Angeles Tribune*, September 25, 1959, 10.

21. Marion D. Hanks, "The Influence of Relief Society in the Home," 570.

22. "Is This 'The Place?'" *[University of] Utah Daily Chronicle*, January 20, 1947, 2; "Segregation in Utah," *[University of] Utah Daily Chronicle*, March 6, 1957, 2. For Duncan's missionary service, see "Transfers," *Cumorah's Southern Messenger* 24, no. 2 (February 1949): 27. While in South Africa, he

he became the chairman of the Utah Advisory Committee to the United States Commission on Civil Rights. Duncan's duty was to carry out the "investigation of and the preparation of reports and recommendations concerning Utah problems and needs" to the federal commission.[23]

When Duncan attempted to enlist Elder Hanks's support for civil rights legislation, Hanks expressed only qualified support: "My experience and sympathies are consonant with yours." But he feared "putting the church into a position where . . . any crusading 'liberals' assail us through our institutional establishments [e.g., Hotel Utah]." But "men of good will and personal worthiness should not be denied normal blessings and facilities."[24]

According to a 1961 study, African Americans in Utah were barred from 12 percent of all restaurants, 72 percent of all hotels, and 80 percent of beauty parlors.[25] A clerk at the Hotel Utah later recalled the words he was instructed to say when African Americans attempted to rent a room: "I am sorry but we are filled to capacity, but I could attempt to obtain a room for you at another hotel."[26] Among those turned away from the city's premier (and Church-owned) hotel, were black politician Adam Powell and singer Marian Anderson, although Anderson was allowed to stay with the understanding that she could use only the freight elevator, not the passenger elevator.[27] Albert Fritz, head of the Salt Lake City NAACP chapter, recalled going to a café where "the waitresses would stand perhaps in a corner in the back of the café, trying to decide which one would tell us they weren't going to serve us."[28] James Gillespie later recalled that in Utah "there was segregation but not violence. If you went to a restaurant in Salt Lake, you'd get put out. If you went to one in Alabama, you could get killed."[29]

An unexpectedly bright note was the decision of some local department stores— both branches of national chains—to publicly integrate. In May 1960, Fritz organized a positive demonstration in front of Kress's and Woolworth's lauding them for

---

interviewed Gen. Jan Smuts, a leading politician and supporter of apartheid, and gave him a Book of Mormon. Smuts insisted that the missionaries "sign your name in the front so that I may remember you." Duncan said: "I have never been so proud in my whole life as that minute when I was writing my name in the front of General Smuts' copy of the Book of Mormon." See A. M. Duncan, "An Interview with 'Mr. South Africa,'" *Cumorah's Southern Messenger* 24, no. 6 (June 1949): 83. When Smuts died in 1950, *Cumorah's Southern Messenger* included his photograph on the front cover and a eulogy declaring that "the history of modern South Africa is the history of Jan Christian Smuts." See "A Son of Africa Has Passed," *Cumorah's Southern Messenger* 25, no. 10 (October 1950): 1–146.

23. "Rights Group Confers in S.L. Today," *Salt Lake Tribune*, July 30, 1960, 14.

24. Marion D. Hanks, Letter to Adam M. Duncan, February 25, 1957.

25. "Status of Utah Negroes Said among Worse in Nation," *Dallas Morning News*, October 31, 1963, 15.

26. Quoted in Linda Sillitoe, *Friendly Fire: The ACLU in Utah*, 21.

27. "Philoshenanigans," *[University of] Utah Daily Chronicle*, October 12, 1955, 2; Dean L. May, *Utah: A People's History*, 145.

28. "Rights," *Deseret News*, January 13, 1985, B4.

29. "King's Name Revives Memories of Struggle," *Deseret News*, January 13, 1985, B1.

their support of integration. Demonstrators handed out pamphlets urging customers to communicate their support of the Salt Lake City branches' racial policies to the corporate headquarters. Perhaps, the pamphlets read, the national office should "conduct their businesses in the South as they do in Salt Lake City."[30]

Some voices from both the mainstream and Mormon dissenting communities served as intermediaries between Church and civil rights leaders. James E. Faust, a stake president and president of the Utah State Bar Association, was invited to serve on President John F. Kennedy's Lawyers Committee for Civil Rights under Law. When Faust asked McKay's permission to participate, McKay "told Brother Faust that he should go and find out what President Kennedy is trying to do." He feared that Kennedy was trying to compel Mormon business owners like hotelier J. Willard Marriott to let blacks conduct business at their establishments.[31]

The committee worked to defend African American clients too poor to afford legal and courtroom costs.[32] In Clarksdale, Mississippi, it mounted a legal offensive against an injunction to prevent integration.[33] Hoping to avoid the taint of coordinating their efforts with civil rights organizations, they opted to recruit the support of Southern bar associations and local volunteers. When the Mississippi Bar Association's president, Sherwood Wise, greeted committee members, he saw them as potential allies in stopping the efforts of leftist attorneys and thanked them for doing the Mississippi Bar "a great favor [by] keep[ing] these zealots off our necks."[34] The committee's purpose, the press repeatedly noted, was "to encourage" attorneys while they "appealed to every state bar association to work closely with local officials."[35] It generally responded to "informal request[s] for assistance."[36] Upon learning of the conservative nature of the lawyers' committee, McKay told Faust that he supported his participation.[37]

Faust accepted the appointment. He also served on the American Bar Association's Special Committee on Civil Rights and Racial Unrest, a seventeen-man group of lawyers that included Rush H. Limbaugh, grandfather of the conservative radio personality. Unlike the Lawyers' Committee, it did little to promote Kennedy's civil rights legislation. Headed by Alfred Schweppe, a Seattle lawyer who had opposed President Dwight D. Eisenhower's deployment of federal troops to force racial integration at Central High School in Little Rock,

---

30. Ardis E. Parshall, "Martin Luther King in Deseret," http://www.keepapitchinin.org/archives/martin-luther-king-in-deseret (accessed October 21, 2013).

31. Prince and Roberts, *David O. McKay*, 68.

32. "Mass. 'Rights' Prisoner to Get RFK Help," *Boston Herald*, October 26, 1963, 21; "Negroes Say Attorneys Hard to Get," *Register-Republic* (Rockford, Ill.), February 19, 1964, 20; David Chappell, *Inside Agitators: White Southerners in the Civil Rights Movement*, 271 note 12.

33. "Lawyers Asked to Aid Integration," *Lakeland [Fla.] Ledger*, August 14, 1963, 3.

34. Sherwood Wise quoted in Sarah Hart Brown, *Three Southern Lawyers in an Era of Fear*, 207.

35. "Suit Attacks Injunction," *[Jackson] Mississippi Free Press*, August 24, 1963, 1; "Moves Fast to Preclude Rights Rifts," *Augusta [Georgia] Chronicle*, July 5, 1964, 1.

36. "Kennedy Asks Lawyers to Enter Allen Case," *Springfield [Mass.] Union*, October 26, 1963, 26.

37. Prince and Wright, *David O. McKay*, 68.

Arkansas,[38] its primary purpose was to "study the grave problems with respect to observance of law and legal processes which have arisen throughout the country on civil rights issues and to make recommendations which will encourage respect by all concerned for, and observance of the rule of law."[39]

Criticism from within the scholarly ranks of Mormonism began to swell. In 1953, Dr. Chauncey Harris, a Logan-born Sovietologist and Mormon at the University of Chicago, told Ernest Wilkinson that the Church's relationship with the black community should be revisited "from the standpoint of the revealed word of the Lord," a perspective Wilkinson thought to be a "very fine attitude." Harris felt that the priesthood ban was a policy enshrouded more in folklore than in revelation. "We have taken too much for granted in interpreting what has been revealed, " he argued, and urged that "the subject is still open for an authoritative interpretation by the President of the Church." Harris knew better than to openly defy Church leadership. But, at the very least, he felt the First Presidency "should reconsider the interpretation of what has been revealed."[40]

Dr. Sterling McMurrin, a prominent Mormon professor of philosophy and John F. Kennedy's U.S. Commissioner of Education, was bolder in his criticisms.[41] In March 1960, McMurrin delivered an "entirely extemporaneous" speech to the NAACP in which he attacked Church leadership for the "morally reprehensible negro doctrine."[42] Though his remarks rankled several high-ranking Church leaders, McKay protected him from excommunication.[43]

Mormon scholars had increasingly come to see the priesthood ban not as evidence of a distant leadership imposing racial strictures on its adherents but as a manifestation of a collective responsibility on the part of the Mormon people. Dr. John L. Sorenson of BYU's anthropology department privately—and gently—criticized McMurrin for failing to place blame where it was due: on the general body of the Saints. "So few realize the degrees which leaders must in turn be followers of the masses. . . . General Authorities have been burned so badly in their efforts at leadership in the past four generations that they are now very hesitant to speak out, perhaps for fear that the members will not follow them." Further, Sorenson observed, even "the favored situation of Indians and Polynesians does not protect them from discrimination." He pointed out wards established especially for American Indians.[44] McMurrin took no issue with such

---

38. "Attorneys Compromise on Rights," *Pittsburgh Post-Gazette*, August 12, 1963, 15.

39. "Board Authorizes Special Committee on Civil Rights and Racial Unrest," 743.

40. Ernest L. Wilkinson, Letter to David O. McKay, January 31, 1953.

41. For McMurrin's appointment to the Kennedy administration, see "Utah's McMurrin Gets School Post," *Omaha [Neb.] World Herald*, February 1, 1961, 20.

42. Sterling M. McMurrin, Speech, March 8, 1960, Sterling M. McMurrin audio collection, Marriott Special Collections.

43. Prince and Wright, *David O. McKay*, 55.

44. John L. Sorenson, Letter to Sterling M. McMurrin, March 9, 1960. Most condemnation of racism had been directed towards anti-Native American rhetoric. Spencer W. Kimball, "The Evil of Intolerance," 103–8.

self-imposed segregation as "there is considerable value in the Indians maintaining their identity as a people and a culture"[45] and affirmed that Sorenson was "right" in his assessment of the "general relationship between the leaders and people." McMurrin asserted, however, that the Mormon people "as a whole are very often ready for more forward-looking leadership than they receive."[46]

Similarly, in September 1961, U.S. Secretary of the Interior Stewart Udall wrote Henry D. Moyle, a senior apostle and future member of the First Presidency, and Hugh B. Brown, a counselor in McKay's presidency, urging them to take proactive measures supporting civil rights. Otherwise, their racial "sentiments will become the subject of widespread public comment and controversy."[47] The First Presidency responded by echoing the long-standing fear that Church leaders must "not welcome Negroes into social affairs, because, if we did, it would lead to intermarriage."[48]

McMurrin was only half-right. While the Saints had begun to be more self-conscious about their relationship to the black community, the larger body of the Utah Mormon population resisted federal civil rights legislation. By now, the Saints had generally accepted the ban as a matter of course. Most Saints resisted civil rights legislation and black priesthood ordination due to a variety of reasons: rank obedience as well as the long-inherited racism absorbed from American society. And as a Latter-day Saint student at the University of Utah wrote to the *Utah Daily Chronicle:* "If we Mormons believe that God is directing our Church, we will carefully avoid counseling or criticizing his policies."[49]

In summer 1963 the John F. Kennedy administration proposed new civil rights legislation. Stephen Holbrook, a young returned missionary turned civil rights activist, and members of the NAACP leaders met with the First Presidency, threatening the Church with a public protest if Church leaders did not clarify their position on civil rights. The NAACP threatened Church leadership by planning a protest staged on Temple Square in conjunction with October 1963 general conference.[50] They hoped to pressure the Church into supporting legislation establishing a fair housing and employment commission in Utah. McKay refused to respond to pressure; Brown told the NAACP that "McKay is a Scot and does not like to have a gun pointed at his head."[51] But when the NAACP made it clear that they would orchestrate an embarrassing public protest during conference weekend, McKay allowed President Brown to deliver a statement on

---

45. Sterling M. McMurrin, Letter to John L. Sorenson, March 18, 1960.

46. Ibid.

47. F. Ross Peterson, "'Do Not Lecture the Brethren': Stewart Udall's Pro-Civil Rights Stance, 1967," 276.

48. Ibid.

49. F. G. Adams, Letter to the Editor, *[University of] Utah Daily Chronicle,* October 10, 1963, 2.

50. Sterling M. McMurrin, "A Note on the 1963 Civil Rights Statement," 60.

51. Hugh B. Brown, qtd. in Glen W. Davidson, "Mormon Missionaries and the Race Problem," Holbrook Papers; draft manuscript, 7.

civil rights at conference. Brown asked Sterling M. McMurrin to assist him in crafting it. When Brown took the stand, he declared that the First Presidency "calls upon all men everywhere, both within and outside the Church, to commit themselves to the establishment of full civil equality for all of God's children."[52] Brown presented the statement independently of the rest of his remarks, suggesting an officiality McKay did not intend.[53]

Brown had been the leading proponent for Church support of civil rights, making him the most logical spokesperson. But he went too far, revealing the private deliberations of the First Presidency. He told a *New York Times* reporter that the Church was "in the midst of a survey looking toward the possibility of admitting Negroes," a comment that infuriated McKay. Brown back-pedaled, saying he had been misquoted; but Turner insisted that the quotations "that appeared in the story were precisely the words spoken by Mr. Brown" in the presence "one of the public information specialists [Theodore Cannon] retained by the Church." Though Turner left Brown's quotation off the record, he would not conceal the conversation entirely and claimed that Brown and the First Presidency were "contemplating a change in its doctrine that would permit Negroes to full participating membership."[54]

The *Utah Daily Chronicle* congratulated the Church on its pro-civil rights stance, even while acknowledging that "the Church may have been under some pressure." Still, it "prefer[red] to believe that the statement was primarily the result of the Church's moral concern about the world's racial situation."[55] The First Presidency's statement prompted the Saints to rethink—but not revise—their state's reputation as the "Eleventh Southern State."[56] With the First Presidency's (albeit tepid) support, Mormons felt emboldened to consider civil rights legislation more seriously. Weeks after Brown's conference address, the Bountiful Women's Republican Club scheduled a special meeting with Adam Duncan, now chairman of Utah's Advisory Committee to the Kennedy Administration's Civil Rights Commission.[57] Duncan had served as a missionary in South Africa where he "realized the vicious folly" of the priesthood ban. He candidly told the *Dallas Morning News* that, while Utah wasn't worse, it "certainly isn't any better" than in neighboring states.[58] He advised national civil libertarians on tactics that he thought had the best chance of success. "You don't slap a Mormon in the face," he told ACLU

52. Hugh B. Brown, *Conference Report of the Church of Jesus Christ of Latter-day Saints,* October 1963, 91.

53. McMurrin, "A Note on the 1963 Civil Rights Statement," 60.

54. Wallace Turner, Letter to Al Johnson, July 9, 1963.

55. "A Step Forward," *[University of]Utah Daily Chronicle,* October 7, 1963, 1.

56. Ibid.

57. "Lady Republicans Schedule Talk on Civil Rights," *Davis County Clipper* (Bountiful, Utah), November 8, 1963, 1.

58. "Status of Utah Negroes Said among Worst in Nation," *Dallas Morning News,* October 31, 1963, 15.

leadership. "You try to talk him out of what he wants in a reasonable way. You don't try to bully him."[59] But Duncan had no luck with the Mormon population. During the 1963 legislative session, only one civil rights measure was passed—the repeal of the state miscegenation ban.[60] When President Lyndon B. Johnson successfully shepherded the Civil Rights Act of 1964 through Congress, President David O. McKay wrote in his diary: "The Civil Rights Bill is now passed and it is the law of the land. Some of it is wrong—the Negro will now have to prove himself."[61]

But it had the desired effect. After hearing the statement, NAACP President Albert Fritz called upon all affiliated parties to "not picket any of the LDS churches or missions as was pending."[62] Nevertheless, while the march on Temple Square did not materialize, Holbrook did help to organize an unaffiliated march outside the Church Administration Building

Like Sorenson, Lowell L. Bennion, director of the LDS Institute at the University of Utah, suggested that the Saints as a body had not sought revelation concerning the state of the blacks:

> God's revelations to us individually and to the church as a whole depend upon our minds, our eagerness, upon our search, upon our questions, upon our moral disturbances. . . . It might be that you and I, and all of us in the church, because of our sins, or because of our lack of thinking upon the great fundamentals that Christ taught, because of not having the Spirit of Christ, may sometimes be at fault for our limitations. It may be that the Lord can't get through to us sometimes on things. Therefore we ought to be thinking and searching and praying even over this Negro problem.[63]

Bennion's colleague at Brigham Young University, Chauncey Riddle—considered to be one of the university's leading philosophers—was more sympathetic to the ban but likewise found it disturbing: "This problem also bothers me. I hope it bothers every Latter-day Saint." He took some solace in knowing that the time would come when "these people will have every opportunity that anyone else has."[64] University of Utah philosophy professor Charles H. Monson hoped that President McKay would establish a non-binding commission to study the "Negro problem" that "could lay the ground work which will enable all Church members to consider the problem intelligently and thus prepare the way in both leaders and members for any revelatory doctrines which may follow."[65]

---

59. Adam Duncan, Letter to ACLU Membership, July 15, 1959, quoted in Sillitoe, *Friendly Fire*, 17.

60. In 1967, the U.S. Supreme Court struck down all anti-miscegenation laws as unconstitutional. For a full treatment of miscegenation law in American history and the significance of *Loving v. Virginia*, see Peggy Pascoe, *What Comes Naturally: Miscegenation Law and the Making of Race in America*, chaps. 8–9.

61. Prince and Wright, *David O. McKay*, 71.

62. "Mormon Leader Asserts Equality," *[University of] Utah Daily Chronicle*, October 7, 1963, 2.

63. Lowell L. Bennion, qtd. in Bradford, *Lowell L. Bennion*, 249.

64. Ibid.

65. Charles H. Monson, "On the Conditions Which Precede Revelation," 160–61.

In June 1963 Apostle Spencer W. Kimball seemed to echo their thinking, declaring that the Lord could "release the ban and forgive the possible error, which brought about the deprivation." Whose error it was, he did not say. But activism would not do: "These smart members who would force the issue, and there are many of them, cheapen the issue and certainly bring into contempt the sacred principle of revelation and divine authority."[66] Kimball was not likely implicating Church leaders, as he said a few sentences later: "I am not sure that there will ever be a change." But he admitted that "direct and positive information" was lacking: "I have wished the Lord had given us a little more clarity in the matter."[67]

While the First Presidency wrangled over how to handle the pressure, the ultra-conservative John Birch Society led the charge against the legislation in Utah. Envisioning itself as a "citizen force capable of defeating the aims of Communism," the John Birch Society saw the civil rights movement primarily as an orchestrated conspiracy to expand federal control over local government.[68] Reed Benson, Apostle Ezra T. Benson's son and head of the state's John Birch Society chapter, took to the Church's Institute of Religion speakers' circuit to oppose the legislation. Kennedy's civil rights package was "ten percent civil rights and ninety percent federal takeover," Benson warned a group of students at the University of Utah's Institute of Religion.[69] Ezra Taft Benson, former U.S. Secretary of Agriculture in the Eisenhower administration and self-appointed Communist watchdog, agreed and compared the legislation to China's "agrarian reform" program of the late 1950s that led to the death of millions of Chinese.[70] The *Vernal Express* also lined up with the Bensons. Kennedy's threat to strip states of federal funding "elevates from a suspicion to a reasonable supposition the increasingly mentioned possibility that the Administration's eagerness for paternalistic spending programs cloaks the lust for unassailable power at the state level as well as the Federal."[71]

The Bensons' argument had been echoed often in the wake of the 1963 legislation. Lloyd Wright, the former president of the American Bar Association from Los Angeles, likewise cited the 90–10 statistic that the Bensons had been using in their speeches; Wright had been a leading figure eliminating anti-Communist litmus tests then required for membership in the Association.[72] And, predictably, Mississippi Governor Ross Barnett echoed the refrain.[73]

---

66. Spencer W. Kimball, Letter to Edward L. Kimball, June 15, 1963, 448.

67. Ibid., 449, 448.

68. "Protecting Our Freedom," *Davis County Clipper* (Bountiful, Utah), March 25, 1960, 3.

69. "Reed Benson Speaks on Birchers; Upholds Civil Rights Battle," *[University of] Utah Daily Chronicle*, October 9, 1963, 1.

70. Prince and Wright, *David O. McKay*, 70.

71. "This Would Be a Switch" (editorial), *Vernal [Utah] Express*, July 4, 1963, 2.

72. Ralph de Toledano, "Civil Rights Is Major Congress Issue," *Sarasota Herald-Tribune*, January 8, 1964, 6; "American Bar Association Drops Its Subversive List Qualification," *Miami Daily News,* October 11, 1955, 19A

73. "New Teeth Planted in Civil Rights Bill," *Miami News*, September 25, 1963, 15A.

Blacks and whites march on South Temple in March 1965 to protest the LDS Church leadership's reticence to actively lobby for civil rights legislation in Salt Lake City. Courtesy Utah State Archives.

Reed Benson was a speaker welcomed throughout Utah, even if controversy enshrouded the society. In September 1963, the Bountiful chapter of the Sertoma Club (an organization committed to assisting the deaf) hosted Benson as a guest speaker where his stated topic was the John Birch Society's activities.[74] He held meetings at Taylor Elementary School in Centerville where he addressed concerns about whether it was a "secret society" and whether society members pay unyielding obedience to its founder, Robert Welch.[75] An Ephraim resident, Clair Erickson, attacked the society, noting that "it amazes me how people are taken in by the protestations of Americanism . . . when their methods too often are the very opposite of the democratic principles of free society." Otherwise "sincere, conservative people are kind of duped by this and don't see the contradiction between the objectives and the methods used."[76]

The struggle of Utah civil rights activists continued apace. In March 1965, the NAACP staged another protest to urge LDS leaders to support the establishment of a fair housing and employment commission in Utah. The NAACP President, Johnie M. Driver, again assured the Saints that "no one questions the right of the LDS Church to hold [a] doctrine of exclusion." But, he continued, "much of the

74. "Sertoma to Host Reed A. Benson," *Davis County Clipper* (Bountiful, Utah), September 6, 1963, 15.

75. "Reed Benson Will Explain Aims of Birch Society," *Davis County Clipper* (Bountiful, Utah), November 15, 1963, 3.

76. "The John Birch Society," *Ephraim Enterprise*, June 9, 1967, 7.

difficulty which Negroes in particular face in gaining access to decent housing and in securing adequate employment in Utah exists because of the official LDS doctrine of exclusion of Negroes from the priesthood in that church." Driver pleaded with the Church to "use your influence for moral justice."[77] The *Deseret News* published an editorial lending its general support for such legislation, without staking out a position on any particular legislation. Holbrook served as a spokesperson for the protestors. Led by Pittsburgh Steelers star and University of Utah alum Roy Jefferson, the march was generally peaceful but also spawned "heated discussions . . . between marchers and observers during the demonstration."[78] That June, Colonel Ray H. Evans, superintendent of the Utah Highway Patrol, ordered that state troopers receive helmets, batons, and riot training.[79] A few days later, the legislature passed measures supporting integrated public accommodations as well as fair employment but killed the housing measure.[80] A Sanpete County Representative noted offhandedly that the legislation was a point "of long discussion."[81]

Meanwhile, Ezra Taft Benson continued his crusade against the encroachment of Communism, which in his mind was best exemplified by the civil rights movement. When the race riots of 1967 exploded in Baltimore, Newark, and Detroit, Benson asked McKay for permission to give a general conference address identifying the movement as a Communist plot to destabilize the American government and install its own puppet. McKay granted permission.[82] The John Birch Society's Manti chapter urged its members to "Support Your Local Police" in opposition to Lyndon B. Johnson's efforts to provide federal aid during riots, expressing alarm that the government was using the riots to install a socialist military regime.[83] Father Francis E. Fenton, a Catholic priest from Connecticut, spoke before a Salt Lake audience, suggesting that the blame for "much of the anarchy" seen in the late 1960s "can be traced to the fact . . . that our churches have not taken an unequivocal stand against the militant godlessness which is Communism."[84] In 1970 a member in Manhattan told his congregation that the

---

77. Johnie M. Driver, "LDS Church Leaders Should Speak Out for Moral Justice," press release, March 9, 1965.

78. "Negro Star Leads Utah Bias Protest," *Spokesman-Review* (Spokane, Wash.), March 9, 1965, 10; see also Blair Howell, "Utah Student Selected as Freedom Rider to Retrace Historic Civil Rights Route," *Deseret News*, April 21, 2011.

79. "New Patrol Chief," *Ogden Standard-Examiner*, March 20, 1965, 2; "They Get Hard Hats," *Deseret News*, July 30, 1965, B7.

80. Robert M. Arbuckle, "Reapportionment—One Party System," *Davis County Clipper* [Bountiful, Utah], March 12, 1965, 1; "Senator Vern Holman Reports on Recent Legislative Session," *Garfield County News*, March 18, 1965, 1; see also Jeffery O. Johnson, "Change and Growth: The Mormon Church and the 1960s," 25.

81. Vance Aagard, "House Notes," *Manti Messenger*, March 18, 1965, 9.

82. bid., 64.

83. "The John Birch Society," *Ephraim Enterprise*, May 12, 1967, 7.

84. "Speak on John Birch Society," *Davis County Clipper* (Bountiful, Utah), May 7, 1971, 6. He also spoke in Manti. "Rev. Fenton Slates Manti Address on Thursday, May," *Ephraim*

tumult was rooted in humankind's failure to understand the nature and identity of God. Humans had made God distant and unknowable: "If God himself ceases to be truly human," he said, "moral decay soon sets in, and more compulsion from above is required to offset this deterioration in individual morality."[85]

Opposition to the civil rights movement in Utah had as much to do with Utah Mormon society's visceral aversion to federal involvement in local affairs as it did with racial matters. Sanpete County Senator G. Stanford Rees assured his constituents that the 1965 legislation "allowed no more freedoms than those by Federal laws and made it so violations would come first under state law and would be prosecuted by the State of Utah which is much better than having the Federal Government enforcing such laws in this state."[86] Utah Mormons seemed to feel that racial integration was but a cover for further-reaching social engineering. Utah schools hosted African American speakers such as news editor Charles E. Smith and former FBI operative Julia Brown who denounced the civil rights movement, declaring that it "is not a Negro movement. It never has been and never will be."[87] In March 1967 another African American woman, Lola Belle Holmes came to Richfield to speak at a John Birch Society event on the subject: "Is the Civil Rights Movement Directed from the Kremlin?"[88]

These black speakers validated everything Benson feared about the civil rights movement. Holmes and Brown both billed themselves as former FBI informants and claimed to have inside information damning the civil rights movement as nothing more than a Communist conspiracy to divide America into a lawless society, ripe for Communist expansion. According to the *Davis County Clipper*, Holmes claimed to have "carried out Moscow orders to gain control of the 'civil rights' movement and to use it as the torch to light a fire of revolution in America."[89]

Both Brown and Holmes had, in fact, served as FBI informants. But Holmes was no apologist for the FBI. According to declassified FBI documents, she was a Communist Party member from 1958 through 1963.[90] She left the bureau under attack for failure to comply with orders she felt were inappropriate. In November 1965, F. J. Baumgarder reported that Brown and Holmes met in Boston where Holmes told Brown that "an Agent or Agents tried to force her into intimacy with Claude Lightfoot, a well-known Communist Party member in Chicago." W. C. Sullivan reported that Holmes had "exhibited some traits of instability." She

Enterprise, May 13, 1971, 4.

85. Unidentified man, Manhattan Second Ward Sacrament Meeting, August 16, 1970, Grant Bethers Audiovisual Collection, AV 3675, tape #20.

86. "Legislators Make Final Reports," *Manti Messenger*, March 18, 1965, 9.

87. "Says Civil Rights Movement Not Negro Movement," *Davis County Clipper* (Bountiful, Utah), November 6, 1970, 20. See also "Will Lecture on Violence Threats," *Davis County Clipper*, October 11, 1968, 11.

88. "Do Communists Run Civil Rights Force," *Davis County Clipper* (Bountiful, Utah), February 24, 1967, 10.

89. Ibid.

90. J. Walter Yeagley, Memo to J. Edgar Hoover, November 4, 1965.

claimed that her past work as an informant had made her unemployable. When interviewed by the FBI, Holmes allegedly admitted that she had made her comments "in a highly emotional condition." The FBI allegedly helped her to find work, but in 1965, she was "discharged . . . when it was found that she had an active case of syphilis." More important to the FBI, Baumgardner wrote, was damage control: "[Brown] should be thoroughly interviewed for detailed information concerning all derogatory statement made by Holmes about the FBI" and "the identities of all persons in whose presence Holmes made the statements should be obtained."[91]

Perhaps the most compelling of the African American John Birch Society speakers was Reverend E. Freeman Yearling who spoke in Centerville in October 1967. He declared that the "NAACP, SCLC [Southern Christian Leadership Conference, CORE [Congress of Racial Equality], SNCC [Student Non-Violent Coordinating Committee] and the like are not interested in Negroes, or the whites, much less Americanism; but their doctrines and their leaders are but tools of the Communists." Yearling served as the national director for the "National Negro Congress of Racial Pride," an organization committed to "encourag[ing] the American Negro, through education, precept, and example to become part of the American answer, not the American problem."[92]

White Utah locals liked to consider themselves as defenders of the black community against the amoral black revolutionaries. In 1967 a Vernal resident attacked supporters of the legislation as "finger-shaking Freuds" who "blaspheme the 99 percent of the black community in our country who work, save, and pray on Sunday whether or not President Johnson requests them to do so."[93] White Mormons sometimes cast themselves as the victims. Folklorists William Wilson and Richard Poulson have documented an account that made its way around Utah Mormon circles about "the kids who were on their way to California and got jumped by some blacks" when the blacks "happened to see their BYU sticker on their car." According to the story, the blacks "beat up the guys and did who knows what to the girls."[94]

In Oakland, California, Roger Bangerter, a ward elders' quorum instructor, expressed qualified sympathy for local black rioters. According to the ward minutes, Bangerter "presented the topic of Joseph Smith running for Pres. Platform-Civil Rights." Bangerter cast the tumult in light of Joseph Smith's 1832 prophecy that "the reminants [sic] of the slaves shall rise up and vex the Gentiles sorely." The prophecy, Bangerter observed, was "not completely fulfilled yet."[95] Some

91. F.J. Baumgardner, Memo to W.C. Sullivan, December 1, 1965.

92. "Truth in Civil Turmoil: Talk," *Davis County Clipper* (Bountiful, Utah), October 20, 1967, 2. See also "Negro Minister Will Speak Here on Civil Turmoil," *The News and Courier*, November 26, 1968, 6A.

93. "That's Sick," *Vernal Express*, August 31, 1967, 3.

94. William ("Bert") Wilson and Richard Poulson, "The Curse of Cain and Other Stories: Blacks in Mormon Folklore," 9.

95. Roger Bangerter, in Minutes of the 11th Quorum of Elders, University II Ward, Oakland, California, June 2, 1968.

weeks later, another instructor, Don Boden, countered with the standard line that the riots violated the Twelfth Article of Faith that citizens are "subject to kings [perhaps significantly he omitted the next word, "presidents"], rulers, and magistrates." But Boden acknowledged the moral dimension to the legality of resistance: "Should we exert civil disobedience if we feel a law is unjust or a court is unjust?" Though the rioters' methods were abhorrent, Boden tacitly acknowledged their grievances to be legitimate.[96]

Meanwhile, in Salt Lake City, the police took harsh measures when they heard rumors that a black mob would be storming Temple Square "armed with machine guns and bombs . . . for the purpose of inciting a riot." Alarmed, McKay encouraged a firm response: "Everything possible must be done to guard that sacred spot." The police cut off all access to Temple Square and monitored closely any blacks who dared to be found in the area. Ethel C. Hale, a social worker and a lead plaintiff in a FCC lawsuit against the Church-owned KSL broadcast station, remembered that moment as being "the most dangerous, most frightening 'monitoring/guarding' action I have ever known." They "saw and heard sheer madness," making it a "nightmare for local black people."[97]

Outside opposition to the priesthood ban increased. In fall 1969, Stanford University publicly boycotted Brigham Young University's sporting events.[98] That October, fourteen University of Wyoming black football players wore black armbands during a game with Brigham Young University, inviting a wave of media scrutiny. A few weeks later, BYU basketball coach Stan Watts explained that he chose not to recruit black athletes because he "won't tell them a bunch of lies." Watts knew "there is no social environment for them around our school or our community and we would be pulling the wool over their eyes if we told them they would be happy here."[99] The Wyoming incident, Wolsey admitted in November 1970, was "the beginning of our problems."[100]

At approximately the same time as the football boycotts, McKay felt the increased heat of public pressure scorching his heels. According to Church architect Richard Jackson, McKay entered the office one day, beside himself with frustration: "I'm badgered constantly about giving the priesthood to the Negro. I've inquired of the Lord repeatedly. That last time I did it was late last night. I was told, with no discussion, not to bring the subject up with the Lord again."[101]

Still, as early as his South Africa visit, McKay had come to identify the ban not as a doctrine or revelation but as a "policy"—a distinction that was important to McKay even if, as Gregory Prince has observed, it was generally lost on his

---

96. Don Boden, in ibid., June 30, 1968.
97. Ethel C. Hale, Letter to ACLU, January 31, 1985, Holbrook Papers.
98. "Mormons Reaffirm Bar on Blacks' Priesthood," *Dallas Morning News*, January 11, 1970, 30.
99. "Could Negro Athletes Be Happy at BYU?" *Sunday Herald* (Provo, Utah), November 2, 1969, 13.
100. Heber Wolsey, Fireside, November 1, 1970.
101. Richard Jackson, qtd. in Prince and Robert Wright, *David O. McKay and the Rise of Modern Mormonism*, 104.

audiences.[102] McMurrin recalls McKay declaring that "there is not now, and there never has been a doctrine in this Church that the Negroes are under a divine curse." Church doctrine specified only "that we have a scriptural precedent for withholding the precedent from the Negro." The ban is "a practice, not a doctrine, and the practice will someday be changed."[103]

How revolutionary were McKay's comments? Perhaps the most remarkable aspect of the ban's intellectual history is the reliably inconsistent nature of its rationales. As early as 1909, Elder Orson M. Rogers, a missionary to South Africa, claimed ignorance as to whether blacks were cursed. It was a theory, he said, which "has been advanced by a few, and not upheld by many." Since the Saints enjoyed no scriptural text describing the origins of Africa's peoples, "we have to consider the theories of men, or form one for ourselves."[104] But his leaders felt otherwise. Heber J. Grant privately justified the ban based on the doctrine of racial cursing, as did George Albert Smith.[105] In 1931 Apostle Joseph Fielding Smith synthesized the past two generations of racial thought in his book, *The Way to Perfection*. In contrast to the more tentative position he had staked out in 1907, Smith now endorsed a premortal explanation for the ban, claiming that the "negro race . . . have been placed under restrictions because of their attitude in the world of spirits."[106] Yet he continued to see the racial ban also as the product of Cain's wickedness: "Not only was Cain called upon to suffer, but because of his wickedness, he became the father of an inferior race." He hoped that "blessings may eventually be given to our negro brethren, for they are our brethren—children of God—not withstanding their black covering emblematical of eternal darkness."[107]

Disagreement and contradiction had defined Mormon discourse on blackness far more than doctrinal reliability. Even Apostle Spencer W. Kimball expressed confusion about exactly why the ban was in place. Knowing these men as he did, McKay's candor with McMurrin revealed the immense complexity of the ban's intellectual genealogy. However committed McKay was to upholding it, he knew as well as anybody that it could not be convincingly justified by anything other than what he believed to be the word of the Lord. Yet relying on the little publicized distinction between "policy" and "doctrine," McKay exercised flexibility in applying it where he could. When a young bride was alleged to have a black grandmother, he allowed the temple sealing to proceed, preferring to "give Miss Marshall the benefit of the doubt." He employed a similar logic for priesthood ordinations, as one General Authority recalled: "If we don't know, give him the benefit of the doubt and go ahead and ordain him."[108]

---

102. Ibid., 77–78.

103. Sterling M. McMurrin, Affidavit, March 6, 1979, qtd. in ibid., 79–80.

104. Elder Orson M. Rogers, "Native Races of South Africa," 625, 627.

105. Lester E. Bush, "Mormonism's Negro Doctrine: An Historical Overview," note 176

106. Joseph Fielding Smith, *The Way To Perfection: Short Discourses on Gospel Themes*, 43.

107. Ibid., 101–2.

108. Prince and Wright, *David O. McKay*, 79

While the web of human rationales and divine silence troubled Church leadership, more political threats loomed for the American Saints. In 1970, Bob Jones University lost its tax-exempt status for refusing to admit African Americans, making it probable that the LDS Church would experience similar scrutiny.[109] Bob Jones University's appeal dragged on for several years; in 1976, the U.S. Supreme Court decided that it "would be wholly incompatible with the concepts underlying tax exemption to grant tax-exempt status to racially discriminatory private educational entities."[110] The Church's sponsorship of the Boy Scouts of America came under fire for reserving the "senior patrol leader" position for the young man in each ward who was serving as the deacons' quorum president.[111]

The troubles bled into the Church's international congregations; in Basingstoke, England, a Mormon congregation wished to acquire a building license to construct a new chapel. In response, a coalition of churches signed a letter of protest requesting that the town council deny the Saints a building permit. Their campaign was successful. Town councilman Len Smart chastised the Church: "The fact that Negroes cannot be ordained to the priesthood of this religion condemns them to a lower level—that of being classified as servants."[112]

Mormon scholars, public figures, and bureaucrats began to revisit the Church's position, albeit through different venues. When George Romney was questioned by a *Meet the Press* reporter on his "attitude . . . toward Negroes," he responded that "a Negro is a child of God just like I am" and that "our most urgent domestic problem is to wipe out human injustice and discrimination against the Negroes."[113] He later told a group of ministers: "If my church prevented me as a public official from doing those things for social justice that I thought right, I would quit the church."[114]

His commitment to civil rights had, in fact, been criticized by high-ranking Church leaders; in January 1964, Apostle Delbert L. Stapley chastised Romney in a private letter for supporting civil rights legislation. While Stapley did "not have any objection to recognizing the Negro in his place and giving him every opportunity for education, for employment, for whatever contribution he can make to society . . . it is not right to force any class or race of people upon those of a different social

109. "Bob Jones U. to Sue U.S. over Tax Status," *Greensboro [N.C.] Daily News*, December 27, 1970, 14.

110. *Bob Jones v. United States*, 461 U.S. 574 (1976). For a fuller discussion of this case, see Bruce R. Hopkins, *Tax-Exempt Organizations and Constitutional Law: Nonprofit Law as Shaped by the U.S. Supreme Court*, 23–24.

111. "Mormons Change Scout Policy," *Seattle Daily Times*, August 2, 1974, 7.

112. "English Town Council Blocks LDS Chapel," *Ogden Standard-Examiner*, July 17, 1971, 3.

113. George Romney, quoted in J. B. Haws, *The Mormon Image in the American Mind*, 40.

114. George Romney, qtd. in Richard Stolley, "A World of Energy, Some Ad-Lib Bumbles," *Life*, March 3, 1967, 74.

order or race classification."[115] Romney took the criticism in stride and remained a participating Mormon all his life.

Angry at the activists who heaped criticism on the Church, a new batch of pro-restriction apologists pushed back. Leading the charge were scholars and activists such as John L. Lund, PhD, and retired U.S. Army Colonel Caleb Shreeve, former University of Michigan military science professor and, by the mid-1970s, a resident of Ogden. Lund's volume, *The Church and the Negro*, perpetuated the premortality narrative: "By operation of some unwritten eternal law with which man is yet unfamiliar, spirits come through parentages for which they are worthy— some as Bushmen of Australia, some as Solomon Islanders, some as Americans, as Europeans, as Asiatics, etc., etc., with all the varying degrees of mentality and spirituality manifest in parents of the different races that inhabit the earth."[116] Lund dismissed the "case of Elijah Abel" as a fluke, one in which Joseph Smith had mistakenly believed him to be white and then revoked the priesthood upon learning of his true racial heritage.[117] He admitted that the "the fact that [Ables] held the Priesthood is . . . a matter of record." But, he continued, "the record needs to be clarified in a very major point." Quoting Zebedee Coltrin's recollection decades later, Lund argued that "once it was discovered that Elijah Abel was of Negroid ancestry, he was dropped from his Priesthood Quorum."[118]

Elijah Ables was becoming a hot spot for Mormons seeking to make sense of the doctrine's history, and Caleb Shreeve made the Ables legacy the primary target of his efforts. Fearful as he was of liberals taking over the Church, he worried that as long as the Ables legacy stood, the First Presidency might cave to public pressure, having fooled themselves into believing that the Church had been following the wrong course over a century.

A distinguished veteran of World War II and the Korean War, recipient of the Purple Heart and former Weber County Democratic Party Chairman, Shreeve's name carried gravitas throughout northern Utah.[119] When Shreeve's brother, Ernest, died, he received a personal condolence letter from Utah governor's Calvin L. Rampton.[120] In 1946, he gave a speech on his wartime experiences at the University of Utah as a "distinguished alumn[us]."[121]

In November 1970 Shreeve sent a "Declaration of Facts" to the First Presidency in order to "reveal several important facts that are not generally

115. Delbert L. Stapley, Letter to George Romney, January 23, 1964.

116. John L. Lund, *The Church and the Negro: A Discussion of Mormons, Negroes, and the Priesthood*, 43.

117. Ibid., 76–78.

118. Ibid., 77.

119. "Third Candidate Seeks to Head County Demos," *Ogden Standard-Examiner*, March 19, 1958, 1B; and University of Michigan, *Register of Students, 1947–1948*, 50.

120. Calvin L. Rampton, Letter to Caleb Shreeve, March 13, 1970, Hyrum Wheelwright Papers (hereafter Wheelwright Papers).

121. "Clubs Plan Joint Lunch," *[University of] Utah Daily Chronicle*, January 31, 1946, 1.

known" regarding "why the Holy Priesthood of God is being denied, or prohibited, to faithful Negro Church members."[122] He blasted Sterling McMurrin's
attacks on the priesthood ban, charging McMurrin with making his statements
"for personal gain or cheap publicity." The attacks of such dissenters, Shreeve
contended, incorporated the language of "vicious left-wing subversives" infused
"with Communist ideologies."[123]

But Shreeve's fears extended far beyond whether a long-dead man held the
priesthood or not. His version of Mormonism fit neatly within the long-established
tradition of Mormon apocalyptic thought. Though claiming to be a committed
patriot, Shreeve's vision of America was undeniably dissolutionist, one in which
America would eventually fall apart at the seams due to political strife. Shreeve
made clear to the First Presidency that he saw George Wallace's segregationist
American Independent Party as the fulfillment of an alleged prophecy of Joseph
Smith that the two major political parties "will go to war and out of these two parties will spring another party which will be the Independent American Party." [124]

Shreeve anticipated the destruction of America with a kind of anxious hope.
Though the Independent American party would eventually gain supremacy, the
United States would become embroiled in foreign wars. Shreeve drew on a
long-standing tradition ascribed to Joseph Smith that when the Constitution
and liberty "hangs by a hair . . . the boys from the mountains will rush forth in
time to save the American army from defeat and ruin." Wallace's party, Shreeve
insinuated, was setting the stage for the Mormon rescue of America from integration and Communist infiltration.[125]

Shreeve's arguments were based on a conflation of Joseph Smith's teaching,
biblical apocalypticism, and Mormon folk doctrine that had endured for generations among Saints cloistered in the Intermountain West. According to Martha
Jane Knowlton Coray, a convert during the Nauvoo period, Joseph Smith had
told a congregation of Saints: "This Nation will be on the very verge of crumbling
to peices [sic] and tumbling to the ground and when the constitution is upon the
brink of ruin this people will be the Staff up[on] which the Nation shall lean and
they shall bear away the constitution away from the very verge of destruction."[126]
Coray recorded these notes on Joseph's discourse in 1840, well before the Saints
had left the Midwest under Brigham Young's leadership. The Saints had strongly
latched onto Joseph Smith's political identity. Shreeve's rendering of Joseph's
"boys from the mountains" comments came from Mosiah Hancock who repro-
duced the comments when he was an elderly man long-settled in Utah.[127] Figures
as varied as Brigham Young, Orson Hyde, Eugene England, and George Romney

122. Caleb Shreeve, Letter to First Presidency, November 25, 1970, Wheelwright Papers.
123. Ibid.
124. Ibid.
125. Caleb Shreeve, compilation of newspaper clippings, Wheelwright Papers.
126. Martha Knowlton Coray, Notebook, July 19, 1840.
127. Mosiah L. Hancock, "The Life Story of Mosiah Lyman Hancock," 29.

Colonel Caleb Shreeve's news clipping montage, ca. 1970. Shreeve, a vocal opponent of activists seeking a change in the priesthood restriction, believed that Alabama Governor George Wallace, a staunch segregationist, helped to fulfill the fabled "White Horse Prophecy" when he ran for president on the American Independent Party's ticket, a party intent on opposing politicians who "dedicate themselves to minority appeasement as the country burns and decays." Courtesy Weber State University Special Collections.

have accepted it as an accurate representation of how Mormonism sees the last days.[128] Shreeve's conspiratorial front matter and shrill tone concealed Shreeve's strength as a public figure and thinker.

---

128. In 1855, Brigham Young said that "when the Constitution of the United States hangs, as it were, upon a single thread, they will have to call for the 'Mormon' Elders to save it from utter destruction; and they will step forth and do it" Brigham Young, February 18, 1855, *Journal of Discourses,* 2:182. Three years later, Orson Hyde, January 3, 1858, suggested that the Constitution might be beyond saving: "The time would come when the Constitution and the country would be in danger of an overthrow; and . . . if the Constitution be saved at all, it will be by the elders of [the LDS] Church" *Journal of Discourses,* 6:152. In 1974, Eugene England, "Hanging by a Thread: Mormons and Watergate," 9–18, suggested that Watergate was the fulfillment of the prophecy, pointing out the important roles that Mormons such as law clerk D. Todd Christofferson and journalist Jack Anderson played in bringing Nixon down. In 1967, George Romney, "A Man's Religion and American Politics: An Interview with Governor Romney," 25, stated that he interpreted the doctrine as saying "that sometime the question of whether we are going to proceed on the basis of the Constitution would arise and at this point government leaders who were Mormons would be involved in answering that question." He felt that the weakening of states' rights indicated

Lund and Shreeve recognized that the priesthood ban was a policy based primarily on historical claims. As such, they took aim at the most problematic figure in the history of the priesthood ban: Elijah Ables. Shreeve agreed with Lund, declaring that this "true DECLARATION OF FACT" should "remove once and for all any and all exceptions for a Negro, because of race, to hold the LDS (Mormon) Priesthood, until the Lord God of Israel, by revelation to his anointed Prophet of the Church, SO DECLARES."[129]

Caleb Shreeve's only piece of evidence came from through an oral tradition allegedly handed down from his ancestor, Thomas A. Shreeve. Born in 1851, Thomas came to Utah at age eighteen, settling in Ogden in August 1880.[130] As a prominent leader and LDS patriarch in Weber County, editor of a youth periodical, *Helpful Visions,* and a lecturer on topics in Church history, Thomas Shreeve's name evoked authenticity.[131]

According to the Shreeve account, Joseph Smith approached Ables "with tears in his eyes" and informed him that he had "been commanded by the Lord to come to you and withdraw from you the Holy Priesthood you now hold." Hurt, Ables allegedly asked what he had done to lose his worthiness; Joseph responded that it was "nothing in this life. . . . [I]t all happened in the pre-existence." Joseph then "put his hands on [Ables'] head and in the authority of his calling withdrew from [him] the Holy Melchizedek Priesthood."[132]

Caleb Shreeve persuaded longtime Ogden City Recorder Donna Adam and Weber County Clerk Wendell Hansen to witness his statement as quoted above and signed by a notary public, Effie McKay Sackett.[133] Months later, Shreeve echoed this family story in a letter to the *Salt Lake Tribune* dismissing concerns over the priesthood ban as "not[h]ing but a tempest in the historical teapot."[134]

---

the weakening of the Constitution: "We are increasingly straining the Constitution and that constitutional government in this country is increasingly in jeopardy" as "the traditional division of government responsibility between state government and the federal government is being eroded." For a thorough analysis of the various sources for the prophecy, see Newell G. Bringhurst and Craig L. Foster, *The Mormon Quest for the Presidency: From Joseph Smith to Mitt Romney,* 282–92.

129. Caleb Shreeve, Letter to First Presidency, November 25, 1970.

130. "Thomas A. Shreeve Dies at Ogden Home," *Salt Lake Telegram,* December 29, 1931, 6.

131. "Thos. A. Shreeve on Book of Mormon," *Ogden Standard,* March 15, 1915, 3; "Shreeve to Talk at 2nd Ward Tomorrow," *Ogden Standard-Examiner,* August 28, 1920, 8; "Joseph Smith to Be Lecture Topic," *Ogden Standard-Examiner,* January 31, 1922, 12; "Patriarch Shreeve to Give Lessons," *Ogden-Standard Examiner,* October 28, 1922, 8; "Book of Mormon Course Offered," *Ogden Standard-Examiner,* May 23, 1927, 10; "Next Lecture on Miracle Subject," *Ogden Standard-Examiner,* May 29, 1927, 30.

132. Caleb Shreeve, Letter to First Presidency, November 25, 1970.

133. For Donna Adam's activities as city recorder, see "There's No Halfway Service in City Recorder's Office," *Ogden Standard-Examiner,* November 5, 1971, 3. See also Shreeve, Letter to First Presidency, November 25, 1970.

134. Caleb Shreeve, "Priesthood Answer," *Salt Lake Tribune,* October 26, 1970, clipping in Wheelwright Papers.

Ironically, Shreeve exhibited remarkable self-awareness about the gaps in his account. "Why wasn't the Priesthood withdrawal officially recorded by Joseph Smith?" he asked. He speculated that Joseph may have been trying to protect the black elder from persecution. Shreeve also acknowledged that the record could have been "lost or destroyed," although "this we do not know." Shreeve also recognizes Ables's late-life missionary service and encouraged the First Presidency to make "a check of Church records . . . to determine if he ever baptized or confirmed any convert while he was on this final mission." But Shreeve, also speaking for his two witnesses, had a hunch that "we, the undersigned, doubt it."[135]

The Shreeve account is emotionally evocative, painting the race restriction as a tragic necessity forced upon an otherwise loving Joseph Smith. However, the account was problematic on a number of levels. The conversation could only have taken place between April 1841 and spring 1842 when Ables left Nauvoo for Cincinnati where he resided until 1853. But aside from Shreeve's century-old account, there is no contemporary documentation to support it.

Additionally, Shreeve leaves a gaping hole in Ables's narrative that obscures documentation problematic to his thesis. According to Shreeve, Ables moved directly from Nauvoo to Salt Lake City. However, Cincinnati branch minutes clearly identify Ables as a priesthood-holding leader of their community. Minutes from a June 1843 meeting provide a detailed accounting of Ables's priesthood activities. He is identified both as a "70" and as an "Elder" at various times throughout the minutes. While it is possible that Ables continued to identify himself as such after leaving Nauvoo, it seems unlikely, since three apostles present at the meeting (Lorenzo Snow, Heber C. Kimball, and Orson Pratt) would have recognized that he was attempting to deceive the members and would have excommunicated him. Since Ables's preaching activities had caused trouble in the white neighborhoods of Cincinnati, he was "advised to visit the coloured population." After all, it seemed fitting to the apostles to follow Joseph Smith's instructions "send men to their . . . native country" as missionaries.[136] Published meeting minutes from June 1845 also identify him as "Elder Elijah Able."[137]

Though sparsely documented, Shreeve's criticisms heralded the controversy that surrounded Ables's status as a priesthood holder. He symbolized not only the debate over the place of blacks in the LDS Church but also, according to Shreeve, a narrative powerful enough to enable Communist factions to attack the Latter-day Saints. "There is a political minority conspiracy gaining momentum," Shreeve warned, and the Saints' "fellowship [in the Church] is a primary target

135. Caleb Shreeve, "A Declaration of Fact," addressed to "All Men of All Nations, Kindred, Tongues, and Races," 1970, Wheelwright Papers. The reference to "we" includes official witnesses Donna Adam and Wendell Hansen, but Shreeve composed the document.

136. Cincinnati Branch Minutes, June 25, 1843; photocopy in my possession courtesy of H. Michael Marquardt.

137. "Cincinnati Branch Minutes," June 1, 1845, *Times and Seasons* 6, no. 10 (June 1, 1845): 915.

for destruction, or subversive change."[138] Shreeve's letter had no discernible impact on the First Presidency, and there is no known documentation of a response.

The Mormon struggle to address the issues of civil rights would haunt the Saints over the coming decade. No one liked to admit it had ever existed. After the searing riots of 1968, Mormons, like much of America, had grown weary of the heat and anger the John Birch Society had peddled even though they were still leery of civil rights activists' push for radical change. By 1975, the John Birch Society had come under sustained attack. Without naming it, Manti resident Alton Stringham said that he "hate[s] these organizations that are eternally criticizing the heads of our government." If only they would "kneel and pray for, instead of criticizing, the leaders of our nation could do a much better job." Greatness, Stringham wrote, has never been "built through criticisms" but "through love and service to our fellow men." He chastised these "organizations" for "fostering hate, fear, and distrust."[139]

Manti resident, Robert C. Keller, picked up on the coded language and said that "only a small percentage" of his community would listen to them. "How apathetic can we get?" he complained. "Water IS pouring in on the ship and the ship is going down fast." Stringham should be grateful that Manti had no organizations "such as the SDS [Students for a Democratic Society] or the Black Panthers."[140] Another Manti John Birch Society member chastised Manti residents for their refusal to listen: "Often those in need of repentance are too far away to hear the call" and stood "in amazement at the complete and total misunderstanding" at his neighbors' attitudes toward of the John Birch Society.[141] Having lost the civil rights battle, the Society moved on to other issues.

The fire of the civil rights era was beginning to die, leaving in its wake a burned-over district in white Mormonism, a community eager to leave behind its decade of embarrassments. The Shreeves and Lunds hoped desperately that they could continue to control the narrative, but their efforts failed them. After all, it would not be Colonel Shreeve but a physician who would catch the First Presidency's ear. A new narrative was in the making.

---

138. Shreeve, Letter to First Presidency, November 25, 1970.
139. "An Open Letter," *Manti Messenger*, September 30, 1971, 4.
140. "An Open Letter," *Manti Messenger*, October 7, 1971, 2.
141. "Letter to the Editor," *Manti Messenger*, April 19, 1973, 5.

Chapter 6

The World Is Ready, 1970–78

"The eyes of our non-Mormon friends are always watching."
—Glendale Ward Newsletter (1970)[1]

"The Lord has granted us the glory and honor we deserve and has granted us the opportunities to become like angels."
—Ghanaian Mormon leader Rebecca Mould
(spring 1978)[2]

Though Church leaders appreciated the comments of black members like Martin, the public discourse surrounding Mormonism had become embroiled in race. Indeed, the Mormon relationship with blacks had heightened Church headquarters' sensitivity to its public image. The Church could not let the issue continue to simmer. It was not going away, and the criticism was only beginning to increase. BYU communications professor Heber Wolsey urged Church leaders to take the initiative on remaking their image: "When an issue like this comes up," he told McKay and others, "it's very easy for it to snowball."[3]

"Everything's Cool"

McKay died on January 18, 1970, and the senior apostle—and therefore his successor—was ninety-three-year-old Joseph Fielding Smith, who was ordained president five days later. Upon learning of the leadership change, Sonia Johnson wrote her mother from Malawi where she was teaching English: "I'm sure the Lord knows what he's about, and I fully sustain President Smith even if he is a bit untactful at times." She sympathized with his brash ways: "I'm hardly the soul of tact myself." Although she hoped that "maybe he'll be a little less dogmatic as President of the Church," she did not really believe it. And perhaps, she felt, the Church needed a hardliner: "The Lord is pretty dogmatic himself. Maybe I'm not dogmatic enough."[4]

---

1. "Youth Fireside," *Second to None* [Glendale Second Ward newsletter] 2, no. 9 (September 1970): 3.
2. Rebecca Mould, qtd. in Samuel Bainson, "An African's Journey," 11.
3. Heber Wolsey, Fireside Address, Manhattan Second Ward, November 1, 1970.
4. Sonia Johnson, Letter to Family, January 30, 1970, Box 1, fd. 16, Sonia Johnson Papers. Unless otherwise noted, all correspondence to and from Sonia Johnson is from this collection.

But Smith proved more flexible than anticipated. Following his work in West Africa, LaMar Williams had been organizing social events for black Latter-day Saints in the United States. But these events did not carry the imprimatur of the Church hierarchy. Hoping for ecclesiastical endorsement of their activities, three black Latter-day Saints—Darius Gray, Eugene Orr, and Ruffin Bridgeforth—met with three apostles on June 8, 1971, about how best to retain black members who were leaving the Church in a steady trickle.[5] The apostles—Gordon B. Hinckley, Boyd K. Packer, and Thomas S. Monson—received permission from the First Presidency to authorize the three black petitioners to establish an official LDS Church auxiliary. Asked to name their new group, the men called themselves the Genesis Group, in hopes of establishing new "beginning" in Mormon race relations.[6]

The Genesis Group was intended to be a social auxiliary, geared toward helping black members feel less isolated in an overwhelmingly white church. Church leaders were wary that the organization would attract undue media attention, and Elder Packer told Genesis members that "things that are young and tender need room to grow, and those who do not belong [should] stand back [and] give them room." The Genesis Group, Packer underscored, "is not a tourist attraction."[7] Meetings tended to be turbulent, since many members had years of disappointment and pain to vent. Bridgeforth acknowledged the difficulties Genesis leaders faced: "We did feel that there would be many problems. We had dissension, and we had people who were dissatisfied. . . . Trying to keep them calm was a constant challenge."[8] When Church leaders tried to speak to the group, the "dissenters would come and try to create problems."[9] In spring 1978, Genesis member Joseph Freeman said that "many white people are hoping for a change, praying that the black[s] will hold the priesthood." For now, Freeman continued, "we're on the right train. Maybe we're not the engineer, but it's better than missing the train."[10]

But the criticism from the 1960s continued apace. Smith died in July 1972, leaving his successor, seventy-three-year-old Harold B. Lee to continue dealing with the media scrutiny. To streamline media inquiries, Lee authorized the establishment of a Public Communications Division (PCD), placed under the direction of Wendell J. Ashton, former managing editor of the *Deseret News* and later, a vice president of Salt Lake City's Gilham Advertising Agency.[11] In 1950, Ashton

---

5. Margaret Blair Young and Darius Gray, Interviewed by Benjamin Crowder, in *The Mormon Artist* 1 (September 2008): 9.

6. "Black Mormons Struggle for Acceptance in Church," *Salt Lake Tribune*, November 4, 2004.

7. J. B. Haws, *The Mormon Image in American Mind: Fifty Years of Public Perception*, 68.

8. Jessie L. Embry, "Separate But Equal? Black Branches, Genesis Groups, or Integrated Wards?" 14–15.

9. Ruffin Bridgeforth, quoted in ibid., 14–15.

10. David Briscoe, "Numbers Declining but Not Devotion," *Winnipeg Free Press,* June 3, 1978, 10.

11. For Ashton's work at Gilham Advertising, see "10 Agencies to Meet on Water Pollution," *Deseret News*, January 15, 1960, 10A; "Ashton Will Head Cancer Drive," *[Provo] Daily Herald*, January 20, 1964, 10.

had also written a history of the *Deseret News*.[12] Lee assigned him the task of improving the Church's image in the public eye, especially in response to criticism over its continued policy of excluding black men from priesthood ordination.[13] "The whole thrust of our department," Ashton later observed, "was to take the initiative and not wait to respond to people seeking information."[14]

Meanwhile, Heber G. Wolsey, a communications professor at Brigham Young University and also assistant to its president for communications—parried attacks in the wake of the University of Wyoming and Stanford University boycotts. Wolsey told some colleagues: "We Mormons are being forced to talk to the non-Mormons," and received the only semi-encouraging response, 'You Mormons don't know how to talk to non-Mormons."[15] In 1969, Wolsey defended BYU as being racially inclusive: "There is no policy at BYU which discriminates against any race or religion in any way." BYU had been willing to play teams regardless of their race: "Persons who arrive at the conclusion that BYU is discriminating should . . . not practice the very thing against BYU that they accuse BYU of doing."[16]

Wolsey took his message to other locales in Mormonism. As BYU student body president Brian Walton told Ernest L. Wilkinson, "The problem will only be remedied by direct communication to the students of other campuses and the public at large."[17] Speaking at a members' fireside in Manhattan in November 1970, Wolsey described the Church's efforts to remake its image. He addressed their concerns about the ban head-on, asserting that he could look anyone "in the eye" and say that the LDS Church "can do more for the black man than any other church on earth." The priesthood exclusion "has nothing to do with what we consider them as human beings and sons and daughters of God."

He assured the Saints that black members of the Church were faithful and happy, illustrating his point with a series of stories about black members who stayed in the Church in spite of their feelings. One of them was a young black named Paul in San Francisco. "Believe me," Wolsey said, "he has a testimony." Challenged after baptism, Paul had told Wolsey, "Some cat said to me, Paul, you can't hold the priesthood." As Wolsey tells it, the Lord spoke to Paul and said: "Paul, everything's cool." The audience laughed.

He told of another black man who had "studied all the religions of the world" and "could honestly say to anybody in the world . . . can look them in the eye and say: 'The Church of Jesus Christ of Latter-day Saints can do more for the black man than any other church on earth." Wolsey reminded the Manhattan Saints of Joseph Smith's anti-slavery sentiments: "Give the poor black man his

12. Wendell J. Ashton, *Voice in the West: Biography of a Pioneer Newspaper* .

13. "Marketing the Mormon Image: An Interview with Wendell J. Ashton," 15–20.

14. Qtd. in Haws, *The Mormon Image in the American Mind*, 77.

15. Ibid.

16. "Stanford U. Closes Door on Cougars," *Ogden Standard-Examiner*, November 13, 1969, 54.

17. Brian Walton, "A University's Dilemma: B.Y.U. and Blacks," 33.

freedom," Wolsey declared, "because one day of freedom on this earth is worth a whole eternity of bondage. Now that's what Joseph Smith taught."[18]

The new image Wolsey cultivated for the Church was no less true than the one that had dominated Mormon society for years. While earlier Saints had repeated Brigham Young's cringe-inducing comments about the black population, Wolsey focused on Utah's quick embrace of the Thirteenth, Fourteenth, and Fifteenth Amendments following the Civil War. It was selective reading, to be sure; but it was no more selective than the past generations who had unquestioningly parroted Brigham Young's racist position.

Wolsey's comments did not go unquestioned. One man asked, What of the Church's "non-involvement" in the civil rights movement? Wolsey reverted to the claims of accepting Church positions on faith. "I don't mean to back away here," he warned, but "we make a mistake . . . when we try to interpret what the Church is doing." When asked to comment on the actual source of the doctrine—whether it was based on "direct revelation" or a "certain amount of tradition that determines the doctrine," Wolsey distanced himself from McKay's premortality explanation: "Is it from the Pearl of Great Price? Is it from the Bible?" Did it come from the idea that "blacks were on the other side of the fence? . . . All these things that go around the church, as far as I can see are not doctrine." Wolsey had ultimately taken the rather courageous position, given the time period, that he did not know the origins of the policy. When a woman, dissatisfied with this fall-back position, asked: "How can you believe something when your whole argument is 'I don't know, but . . .'" Wolsey held his ground: "All I can do is look them in the eye and say: 'I don't know all the answers, but this is [the] doctrine of our church, and we believe that doctrine does come through revelation from God to leaders of our Church." He specified that it was not his place to "second-guess what the brethren do." But Wolsey also made clear who he was not: "I am a representative of BYU," he told the audience—not a Church spokesman, a differentiation that was perhaps too subtle for audiences outside the Mormon corridor.

In October 1970, Brian Walton told a visiting review team from the University of Arizona that "if we had racists at the university, and we do, it was a function of those people being from white America, not a function of their being Mormon."[19] The review team ultimately agreed, concluding that they could "find nothing to indicate that Brigham Young University is a racist institution or that there may be any more or less racism present than at any other school." These

---

18. Heber Wolsey, Fireside Address, Manhattan Second Ward, November 1, 1970. In Joseph Smith's presidential campaign platform, he declared: "Break off the shackles from the poor black man. . . for 'an hour of virtuous liberty on earth is worth a whole eternity o' bondage." See Joseph Smith, *General Smith's Views on the Power and Policy of the Government of the United States*, 17.

19. Walton, "A University's Dilemma," 33.

findings helped BYU win the University of Arizona's goodwill and dampen some of the criticism being heaped upon the Lord's University.[20]

Those who yearned for change were "wonderful people," he assured them, and he obviously responded with sympathy when they approached him with "tears in their eyes," asking him: "Won't you please go home and try to convince the president of your Church to change the doctrine?" He insisted that the Church was guided by living revelation, which had to come from the prophet. There was nothing he could do except acknowledge that his explanations were "not completely satisfying."[21] He hoped that the Saints could reorient the conversation to "talk about the gospel of Jesus Christ," which was "interesting and beautiful."[22] In 1973, Wolsey was promoted to serve as the head of electronic media for the PCD.[23] Five years later, Wolsey replaced Ashton as head of Public Communications.[24]

In the Church's efforts to reorient the conversation, Public Communications released its *Homefront* ad series in 1972, a set of wildly popular television public service vignettes that taught one-topic lessons apiece: the value of honesty, the importance of marriage, spending quality time with children, and the centrality of family to Mormon teachings. Strategically, these well-written and well-acted spots refurbished the Mormon message in a way that took the attention off the grinding conversations about racism. Television stations picked up the ads in order to meet FCC regulations requiring that they air ads promoting the public interest. Drawing on well-known Mormons in show business such as Donny and Marie Osmond, Bill Bixby (from *The Incredible Hulk*), and Gary Burghoff (from *M.A.S.H.*), the PCD placed ads inviting viewers and listeners to call for free materials on the Church's family home evening program.[25] The series won three Emmys, eighteen Clios (the leading international award for advertising), and an honorary award from the National Parents Day Foundation. [26] Ninety-five percent of all television stations carried the ads along with 50 percent of radio stations.[27]

On the ground, local ecclesiastical leaders supported the aggressive image-making campaign albeit with reservations: "The lives of church members are attention getters," a Glendale, California, bishopric told its congregation; "the eyes of our non-Mormon friends are always watching." But "if the convert is sold only on personalities, he has fallen short of the gospel intent. . . . Our purpose is to build firm conviction and testimony above the blast of public or private opinion."[28] By

---

20. Ibid., 35.

21. Wolsey, Fireside Address, Manhattan Second Ward, November 1, 1970,

22. Ibid.

23. "Church Names 2 in Communications Posts," *Deseret News*, February 17, 1973, 3.

24. Orson Scott Card, "Wendell Ashton Called to Publishing Post," 73.

25. Haws, *The Mormon Image in the American Mind*, 79–80.

26. "'Homefront' Ad Series Wins Honors for Mormon Church," *Gettysburg [PA] Times*, August 9, 1995, A8.

27. Haws, *The Mormon Image in the American Mind*, 79.

28. "Bishopric Message," *Second to None* [Glendale Second Ward Newsletter] 2, no. 8 (August 1970): 1. The comment about the "eyes of our non-Mormon friends" comes from "Youth

1976, public affairs representatives for the Church throughout the country numbered over 1,000.[29]

Campaigns to promote family togetherness were not new; as early as 1914,
the First Presidency "advise[d] and urge[d] the inauguration of a 'Home Evening'
throughout the Church, at which time fathers and mothers may gather their boys
and girls about them in the home and teach them the word of the Lord."[30] But
the PCD's campaign indicated a new urgency. "Virtuous Anglo-Saxon woman-
hood," as President McKay styled it, was constantly under attack.[31] Increased
divorce rates were "threatening the stability of the home and the perpetuity of
[the] nation," President McKay warned the Church in April 1964. Marriage
and family received increasing attention as Church leaders positioned it as the
Mormon bastion against a world in chaos. McKay pled with the Saints to realize
that "one of our most precious possessions is our families . . . and, in our present
existence, are worth more than all other social ties."[32] The advertisements drew
an embedded message out of its deeper context and refashioned it as one of
Mormonism's defining and public characteristics, an image all the more painful
for black families longing for their temple blessings.

Before the "*Homefront*" spots, whose popularity dominated the 1970s air-
waves, survey respondents tended to associate the word "Mormon" with polygamy, the Osmonds, the Tabernacle Choir, and racism. In 1982 Ashton told
one interviewer that his publicity team had shifted to place "greater stress on
the family" because people are "more interested in happiness and family life"
than doctrinal disquisitions. "Begin with what they want," Ashton declared,
"and then say, 'We've got the recipe for happiness for you, a divine recipe!'"[33] A
decade earlier in May 1970, General Relief Society President Belle S. Spafford
had spoken directly to her organization's main theme, telling a reporter that
"unless we preserve the family, we are going to have a sorry world."[34] The public relations program worked. As producer Stephen Allen noted, "[after] some
number of years" of Mormon television ads, the survey answers had changed:
"the number one answer was: family. 'You're the Church that believes in
families.'"[35] So successful was the Church's pro-family publicity campaign that
in November 1978, President Spencer W. Kimball gave U.S. President Jimmy
Carter a statue made by local sculptor Dennis Smith called "In the Family

Fireside," *Second to None* 2, no. 9 (September 1970): 3.

29. Cited in Haws, *The Mormon Image in the American Mind*, 81.

30. "Official Announcement," *Liahona: The Elder's Journal* 12, no. 52 (June 22, 1915): 831.

31. David O. McKay, in *Conference Report*, April 1959, 74.

32. Ibid., April 1964, 5.

33. Peggy Fletcher, "A Light Unto the World: Image-Building Is Anathema to Christian
Living," 22.

34. "Preservation of Family—Key to Stability, Leader Says," *[Bannock] Idaho State Journal*,
June 12, 1970, 26.

35. Qtd. in Haws, *The Mormon Image in the American Mind*, 80.

Circle." The statue depicted a father and mother teaching their young child to walk. He commended the Church's message, noting "how much less difficult my own duties would be as president if your mammoth crusade for stable and strong families should be successful."[36]

Indeed, as sociologist Armand Mauss has observed, "the outstanding developments of the 1970s " consisted of "the *respite* granted the Mormon Church over the race issue by its critics."[37] In August 1978, Jan Shipps observed that granting blacks the priesthood "has to do not with America so much as with the world."[38] Indeed, forces both domestic and international had long been forming a constellation that spoke to impending change in the Mormon community.

In December 1973, Harold B. Lee died, leaving in his place Spencer W. Kimball, the man from Thatcher, Arizona. In December 1973, Kimball appeared on the *Today Show,* marking a period when Church leaders began to engage the public more openly. Its traditional response to controversy had been to assume anti-Mormon motivations on the part of journalists who probed the Church's controversial positions regarding race, gender roles, and the state of the family. An increasingly media-savvy leadership, particularly former publicity man, Apostle Gordon B. Hinckley, recognized that familiarity was the key to overcoming the image problems the Church was facing. In 1973, Hinckley happily told the *Ensign* that "there is greater exposure today than ever before. . . . The press, radio, and television have taken note of our work and have reported it more factually and, therefore, more favorably."[39] Hinckley and others were recognizing the value of allowing journalists access to sources—the Church's General Authorities—in other words, to those other than dissenters with an axe to grind.

Brigham Young University continued to reach out to the black community, albeit in measured terms. In March 1976, a black student vice-president was elected to the student council, and Alex Haley, author of the runaway best-seller *Roots* received an honorary doctorate from BYU.[40] The following year, Wendell Ashton observed that the press and public had generally lost interest in racism, having "accepted [the Church] for what our position is."[41] In January 1978, black U.S. Senator Edward Brooke of Massachusetts acknowledged in a BYU forum address

---

36. Qtd. in "Carter Takes Home Warm Feeling," *Deseret News*, November 28, 1978, A2.

37. Armand L. Mauss, "The Fading of the Pharoah's Curse: The Decline and Fall of the Priesthood Ban against Blacks in the Mormon Church," 20; emphasis in original.

38. Jan Shipps, "The Mormons: Looking Forward and Onward," 761.

39. "A Visit with Elder Gordon B. Hinckley about Missionary Work," *New Era,* June 1973, 27.

40. "BYU Honors Author Haley," *[Portland] Oregonian,* August 17, 1977, 20; see also Mauss, "The Fading of the Pharoah's Curse," 22.

41. "Marketing the Mormon Image: An Interview with Wendell J. Ashton," 16.

that "it would be presumptuous and inappropriate for me to insist that the practices of the Mormon Church be altered to fit my preferences."[42]

Dialogues

But even as it appeared the issues were settling down, Church leaders recognized the dangers in not actively shedding the racist image bequeathed by the
1960s. So even though the policy of ordination restriction continued, Church
leaders sought to take virtually every other step they felt theologically possible to
present a message of inclusiveness before the public.

In the late 1960s, a groundswell of scholarly interest in the history of the
priesthood ban sprung up—and it won the attention of top-level Church leaders. In 1967 a young Armand L. Mauss gave voice to the concerns of many liberal Saints: "If one finds the Church's policy on Negroes discomfiting, however,
the 'explanations' for it offered by well-meaning commentators (on all sides) are
often even worse."[43] Mauss included well-meaning liberal Saints in his condemnation: "The 'defenders' are tying the issue to a heritage of American biblical
folklore, while the 'critics' are tying it to the current civil rights controversies.
Neither position is warranted by the standard works, by official pronouncements
of Church leaders, or by the logic of the Church policy itself."[44] He chastised
Mormon theologians for their pretension: "The Lord has been unwilling to provide
us explanations for his judgment in this matter," but "the same cannot be said for
Mormon theologians, whether of the scholarly or the lay variety." But ultimately,
Mauss pled with the civil rights organizations to "get off our backs. . . . No matter
how much racism you think you see in Utah, you can't be sure it has anything
to do with Mormonism." He ascribed any racism to sheer rural insularity.[45] He
condemned "agitation over the 'Negro issue,'" as it would "likely . . . increase the
resistance to change."[46] Change must "come in the Mormon way." Civil rights
activism would not do it. The "freedom of religious *belief must* not be breached,
even in the name of equality."[47]

While Mauss sought to keep the civil rights organizations at arm's length,
Dr. Lester Bush, an army physician stationed in Saigon, had been researching
the origins of the priesthood restriction. When not caring for patients, he pieced
together evidence about the origins of a practice that remained shrouded in mystery. In the spring 1973 edition of *Dialogue*, Bush published a carefully argued
and lengthy article, "Mormonism's Negro Doctrine: An Historical Overview,"
one of the first historical analyses of Mormonism's racial doctrines rooted in primary source documentation.

---

42. Dialogue Editorial Board, "Senator Edward W. Brooke at BYU," 119–20.
43. Armand L. Mauss, "Mormonism and the Negro: Faith, Folklore, and Civil Rights," 20.
44. Ibid., 21; emphasis Mauss's.
45. Ibid., 38.
46. Ibid., 39.
47. Ibid.

Like Caleb Shreeve, Bush fully discussed Elijah Ables's ordination to the priesthood, but Bush took the position that Ables's legitimacy as a priesthood holder could not be responsibly challenged and that he lived and died a devout Latter-day Saint, despite almost brutal efforts by Church leaders like John Taylor to ignore and distance him. Elijah Ables was not the exception, Bush argued; indeed, Ables had been the rule. Joseph Smith had not implemented the priesthood ban, contrary to accepted wisdom. That distinction belonged to Brigham Young. Perhaps the Church could start asking new questions, he hoped, about why it was following the course it was when Church leaders apparently did not fully understand why they were doing it.[48]

Shreeve's fear-based wailing had fallen on deaf ears, but Bush's arguments received widespread attention at 47 E. South Temple.[49] Marion D. Hanks, then Assistant to the Quorum of the Twelve Apostles, later observed that Bush's article "had far more influence than the Brethren would ever acknowledge and that it 'started to foment the pot.'" Edward Ashment, then employed by the Church Translation Department and a scholar of the Book of Abraham, observed Bruce R. McConkie reading the article. Kimball himself also highlighted several sections of the piece.[50]

Eugene England, co-founder of *Dialogue* and now a professor of English at BYU, responded to Bush in the same issue of *Dialogue* by lauding him for the depth of his research while chiding him for failing to acknowledge the "ecclesiastical authority" which England believed the Church alone could wield. "For me," England continued, "that perspective outweighs all the others because I am convinced that ecclesiastically the Church is doing what the Lord has directed, even though morally and spiritually its members may not be." Continuing the arguments that Sorenson and Bennion had made a decade earlier, England concluded that "the Lord wishes a change *could* be made and that we *all* bear responsibility for the fact that it hasn't been made yet." The priesthood ban was in fact "the Mormon cross" that would compel the Saints to purge themselves from the sins they had inherited from their fathers.[51]

Mormonism's virtuoso of the ancient world, Hugh Nibley, considered the priesthood ban to be something of a test in faithfulness: it "puts the Mormons in an embarrassing position." But why shouldn't it? "The Lord has often pushed the Saints into the water to make them swim." Bush's paper, Nibley maintained, exposes the Saints' ignorance about their own theology. Still, the Saints should be wary of applying wordly standards to the kingdom: Nibley "would rather be a doorkeeper in the House of the Lord than mingle with the top brass in the

---

48. Lester E. Bush, "Mormonism's Negro Doctrine: An Historical Overview," 11–68.

49. "New LDS Office Building Nearly Finished," *[Provo] Daily Herald* , June 18, 1972, 32.

50. Lester E. Bush, "'Writing Mormonism's Negro Doctrine': An Historical Overview (1973): Context and Reflections," 266–67. See also Edward L. Kimball, "Spencer W. Kimball and the Revelation on the Priesthood," 56.

51. Eugene England, "The Mormon Cross," 79; emphasis in original.

tents of the wicked." So Nibley called for the Saints to stop philosophizing on the priesthood ban: "Hold your peace," he wrote, quoting Doctrine and Covenants 10:37, "until I shall see fit to make all things known unto the world concerning the matter."[52] Sonia Johnson considered this *Dialogue* issue to be "the best discussion I've ever seen anywhere" on "the Negro question."[53]

"... But by Prayer and Fasting"

In 1961 a young Stephen Holbrook returned from his mission early but continued to work in Republican politics. He had served a mission to Hong Kong and San Francisco during which he looked blacks in the eye and saw for himself the injustice of the ban.[54] He later admitted that his mission experience prompted him "to break with those things I grew up with."[55]

Stephen Holbrook, ca. 1974, a returned missionary and state legislator who had left Mormonism over the priesthood restriction, launched a public campaign for the Mormon community to fast and pray in hopes of the Church leadership receiving a revelation on the topic. Courtesy Utah State Archives.

As a young Republican-turned-social activist, he paid a price to support black civil rights in Utah and in the South. A little over a week after Hugh B. Brown's statement supporting civil rights in October 1963, Holbrook resigned from his post as an aide to Representative Sherman P. Lloyd. "I called Buzz [a nickname for his son, Sherman, Jr.] last night," Lloyd wrote Holbrook, "and he told me that you felt you could not handle your interest in civil rights and put in the time necessary to be on my payroll." Lloyd cautioned Holbrook for drinking too deeply of extremism: "I am not much sold on extreme views on any issues." He did not truly believe

52. Hugh Nibley, "The Best Possible Test," 73–78. Gordon C. Thomasson, an anthropology graduate student, agreed, noting that even "with the addition of Bush's excellent work, final judgments on the priesthood issue are premature at best, and indefensible from a strictly intellectual point of view." Still, he acknowledged, "we are morally bound to work for freedom and equality for all men." Gordon C. Thomasson, "Lester Bush's Historical Overview: Other Perspectives," 69–72.

53. Sonia Johnson, Letter to Harrises, December 9, 1975, Box 1, fd. 21, Johnson Papers.

54. David Briscoe, "Rep. Holbrook: A Legislator Who's Still An Activist," *Deseret News*, March 1, 1975, 10A.

55. "LDS Stand on Blacks Challenged," *Ogden Standard-Examiner*, June 16, 1975, B6.

that Holbrook's "views on civil rights are extreme"; he was just indulging in his "uncontrollable fatherly instinct."[56]

The following summer, Mississippi police arrested Holbrook in Jackson for his activities, exactly where a local had suggested that anyone who believed that "the civil rights movement is not inspired by the devil" was "living in a fool's paradise."[57] Mormon Democratic Senator Frank E. Moss—whose earlier re-election campaign was spearheaded by Kennedy Civil Rights Commission appointee James E. Faust—applauded Holbrook's efforts to his parents: "There are indeed personal risks involved but the idealism of these young people transcends the risks that hover over them. No good cause is ever advanced without a fight and without enduring peril." Moss assured them that they could "take great pride in the action of your son."[58] When Holbrook spoke about his experiences—which he was starting to do with increasing frequency—in Los Angeles, he won the praise of a local medical doctor, Dr. A. Claude Hansen: "Idealism of young people . . . help to keep the world moving forward, and in a sense, counteracts the depraved creatures of Mississippi."[59] He also served as a white spokesperson for the NAACP both in the threatened protest of October 1963 as well as the actual protest of March 1965. In 1974, Holbrook was elected to the Utah House of Representatives from Salt Lake City, thanks to the Supreme Court's removal of residency requirements for voters, a decision that enfranchised University of Utah students. Holbrook prized his position as an activist in power. "Instead of sitting in the university administration building, I'm able to talk with the president as a member of the higher education subcommittee. Instead of picketing for low-income housing," he told the *Deseret News*, "I'm on the Social Services Committee. And instead of talking about redistributing the wealth, I'm on the House Revenue and Taxation Committee where I can do something about it."[60]

In 1975, Holbrook publicly attacked the Church and called for measures to be taken to compel the Church to change its policies. In June 1975, the *Deseret*

56. Sherman Lloyd, Letter to Stephen Holbrook, October 19, 1963, Box 1, fd. 23, Stephen Holbrook Papers.

57. Julia Jennings, Letter to Editor, April 2, 1965, photocopy of clipping from unidentified newspaper, Box 1, fd. 8, Stephen Holbrook Papers.

58. Frank E. Moss, Letter to Dell and Maxine Holbrook, August 24, 1964, Box 1, fd. 5, Stephen Holbrook Papers. Moss had always shown an independent streak; in 1960, he wrote President David O. McKay to complain about McKay's public endorsement of Richard Nixon: "For years we have been striving to convince Americans that our church is outside of and above politics. . . . But your endorsement of one candidate over another brings tumbling down our position of church nutrality [sic] and creates ill will outside as well as inside the church. I am heartsick." Qtd. in D. Michael Quinn, "How the L.D.S. Church Has Influenced Mormon Politicians, and What It Can Teach Us about a Mitt Romney Presidency," *Vanity Fair*, October 15, 2012, http://www.vanityfair.com/politics/2012/10/mormon-politicians-lds-church-romney (accessed April 6, 2014).

59. Dr. A. Claude Hansen, Letter to Stephen Holbrook, September 22, 1964, Box 1, fd. 5, Stephen Holbrook Papers.

60. David Briscoe, "Rep. Holbrook: A Legislator Who's Still An Activist," *Deseret News*, March 1, 1975, 10A.

News carried an Associated Press report in which Holbrook, speaking at an NAACP banquet, allegedly advocated that "outside pressures should be placed on the (Mormon) Church to change its policy."[61] The *Salt Lake Tribune* also summarized his comments as saying that "pressure should be placed on the Church of Jesus Christ of Latter Day Saints, both from within and outside the church, in an effort to change its policy regarding the priesthood."[62]

The comments troubled even civil-rights-minded Democratic Mormon supporters. One Salt Lake City voter, Loren Pearce, lauded Holbrook for his work in lowering tuition at the University of Utah and his support for civil rights legislation, but talk of legal coercion crossed the line. Pearce had "talked to some of the general authorities personally and they are as anxious as you are to see the negro members of the Church receive the priesthood." In fact, he continued, "they are probably more anxious than you because they have a testimony of the importance of the priesthood and what a blessing it is to those who hold it. Keep up your efforts towards 'civil' rights (and I emphasize 'civil')," Pearce implored, "and I will be one of your strongest supporters." But attacking the Church would make Pearce "one of your strongest opponents."[63]

Bruce W. Young, a "young Democrat" from Spanish Fork and talented BYU student, felt similarly aligned with Holbrook in politics but "disturbed" by what he felt were attacks on the Church. Being a Democrat meant that he had "tried to reconcile my idealism with the practical realities of the world, without losing my ideals." That said, he sympathized with Holbrook on a certain level: "I can understand why you feel the way you do. Race does not determine human worth, and unnecessary barriers to understanding and growth should be broken." Young acknowledged that "even though you have made yourself something of an outsider in relation to the Church, you are concerned about the effect, both symbolic and practical, that the Church's practice has on attitudes toward blacks in Utah and the way they are treated." Surely, Holbrook was well-intentioned—at least that's what Young hoped: "You have certain beliefs, certain values, certain ideals, about human beings and their lives; and these values you happen to share, basically, with the Mormon church. . . . You consider them right and true and good." But Young found Holbrook's arrogance insufferable. Young objected to Holbrook's tendency to dictate to Mormons what their deeply rooted beliefs should be, if only because they appealed to a higher authority. He urged Holbrook to recognize that "there must be a higher and more stable source of values, to which our beliefs must correspond roughly in some way if our beliefs are to mean anything at all."[64]

---

61. "He Claims a Misquote," *Deseret News*, June 23, 1965, 5A.

62. "Legislator Urging LDS to Change Black Rule," *Salt Lake Tribune*, June 16, 1975, 7.

63. Loren Pearce, Letter to Stephen Holbrook, June 17, 1975, Box 1, fd. 25, Stephen Holbrook Papers, Utah State Historical Society.

64. Bruce W. Young, Letter to Stephen Holbrook, June 18, 1975, Box 1, fd. 25, Stephen Holbrook Papers.

Regardless of what the Church should do, Young told him, the support of political pressure would not do. Holbrook was not asking Mormons merely to give up the priesthood ban; he was asking them to give up claims to being the divinely led Church:

> If one group of people put pressure on the Mormon Church to change their beliefs in this matter to correspond to those of the first group, then the pressure would succeed . . . in making the Mormon people believe that their Church it is not divinely directed, that it is no more than a human organization, that it has no higher source of values, that it has no higher power to bestow on human beings (though it might then bestow the ghostly remnant of such a supposed power on anyone whom the world says it ought to give it to).[65]

Young went on to Harvard University where he was awarded a PhD in English literature, then returned to teach at Brigham Young University.

Holbrook attracted some high-profile support as well. The old whistleblower, Dr. Lowry Nelson, felt a kinship to the young, bearded activist. "I may have been the first member of the LDS church to lodge a vigorous protest with the First Presidency on the black policy," Nelson wrote fondly, an event that took place "28 years ago tomorrow!" He remembered with satisfaction the impact that his early letters had made: "Thousands of copies of this correspondence [had] circulated sub-rosa," and he happily made sure that Holbrook received copies as well. Recalling his *Nation* article, he assured Holbrook of his belief that "public pressure was the only influence that could finally bring about a change, just as it did in the polygamy case."[66]

But Holbrook had little choice but to soften his comments. The quotation was incorrect, he told the *Deseret News*. "What I said was that U.S. political, military, and economic pressure changed the polygamy policy, but that is not happening now with the Black priesthood question." But he still felt "that people in and out of the Church should urge the Church to use its own processes to solve the problem." Holbrook eschewed "political pressure as was applied to solve the polygamy issue."[67] Fasting and prayer represented "the Mormon way of doing things," Holbrook told the *Tribune* and would help the Saints as a body to resolve the "black priesthood question . . . for the new times in which we live."[68]

Still, he chastised Church leaders for the silence in the heavens: "It's an unspoken fact that they don't get revelations today. . . . [T]he only thing we get is a series of editorials or statements."[69] But within the Church, there still might be hope. If the "Mormon prophet is to receive the revelation," Holbrook concluded, "it will

---

65. Ibid.

66. Lowry Nelson, Letter to Stephen Holbrook, June 25, 1975, Box 1, fd. 25, Stephen Holbrook Papers.

67. "LDS Stand on Blacks Challenged," *Ogden Standard-Examiner*, June 16, 1975, B6.

68. Stephen Holbrook, Letter to Editor, n.d., Box 1, fd. 20, Holbrook Papers. See also Stephen Holbrook, "Revelation Suggestion," *Salt Lake Tribune*, June 25, 1975.

69. Ibid.

require a more earnest effort on the part of both member and non-member to help the church use its own natural and historical process which are part of the Mormon experience."[70] Since "some Mormons use it [the ban] to practice something less than Christian relations with blacks," the policy had "social consequences that I as a member of the Mormon community let go year after year without some kind of initiative."[71] And clearly, someone needed to ask Church leaders to take action. "The right people," Holbrook observed, "ought to ask church leaders to pray, as the church simply cannot go on." Who were the right people? Ideally, "the black Mormons should probably ask, but who are they and where are they?" Being a black Mormon surely was "a pretty masochistic position to be in."[72]

Not long after Holbrook was elected, he came out as gay and founded KRCL FM 90.9, a radio station that sponsored an hour-long program covering news of interest to the LGBT community. KSL helped the station get off the ground by donating equipment. "Never write anyone off," Holbrook said in his later years. "I refuse to be put in a particular box. It keeps me from thinking I know it all."[73]

The Right People

Holbrook was likely unaware of the burgeoning black Mormon narrative that African American Saints were crafting, one story at a time. Several black Mormons commenced a publicity campaign to present their voices to the white Mormon public. "No spectator," black convert Alan Cherry declared, "regardless of how informed he may be, can provide a better witness to the truth about this subject than he who has actually engaged in the experience himself."[74] In his autobiographical conversion account, Cherry assured readers that he "did not

---

70. Stephen Holbrook, Letter to Editor, n.d., Box 1, fd. 20, Holbrook Papers. See also Stephen Holbrook, "Revelation Suggestion," *Salt Lake Tribune*, June 25, 1975.

71. Holbrook, Letter to Editor of *Deseret News*, June 19, 1965, Box 1, fd. 25, Stephen Holbrook Papers. See also "He Claims a Misquote," *Deseret News*, June 23, 1965, 5A.

72. Ibid.

73. Ted McDonough, "Dead Air," *Salt Lake City Weekly*, January 30, 2008, http://www.cityweekly.net/utah/article-12-6491-feature-dead-air-krcl-is-getting-a-corporate-makeover-is-community-radio-done-for.html (accessed April 4, 2014). The *Salt Lake City Weekly* article suggests that Holbrook harbored hostility toward church-owned KSL for ignoring his anti-Vietnam War views in the early 1970s. However, the documentary record indicates that Holbrook felt that Church media outlets had treated his movement with commendable fairness. In summer 1972, he wrote Apostle Gordon B. Hinckley: "I was particularly pleased with the treatment we received at KSL and KBYU. We were offered the most generous amount of time on both of the church owned stations and found the management most cordial, especially at KSL." Stephen Holbrook, Letter to Gordon B. Hinckley, June 23, 1972, Box 2, fd. 17, Stephen Holbrook Papers. For more on Holbrook's activism for the Salt Lake City LGBT community, see Charles Perry, "Let He Who Is without Sin Cast the First Orange: Anita Bryant and the Making of a Gay Rights Movement in Salt Lake City," 6. For Holbrook's quotation on his ideological pragmatism, see "Activists Receive Visionary Awards," *Deseret News*, November 4, 1996, A10.

74. "Black LDS Convert Will Speak Here," *[Boise] Idaho State Journal*, November 8, 1972, 31.

need position or prominence or pride in order to serve." Jesus, after all, had been willing to "stoop down and wash his disciples' feet."[75]

For most Americans, the idea of a "black Mormon" struck them as a contradiction in terms. "I've never met a black Mormon," one Rochester black man told a reporter; "but I've heard about them."[76] The black Mormon identity was in fact beginning to bloom, thanks to a trickle of autobiographies from black members such as Cherry. Wynetta Martin was the first black member of the Mormon Tabernacle Choir. As a young single adult, she had believed "that all churches were relatively void of meaning for me, and I nearly lost all faith in finding my truth, so long locked up inside me!" Raised a Christian in California, she slipped into atheism as an adult when her religious experience had been only a pattern of "rejection . . . by those who belonged and believed."[77] Though she was disaffected from mainstream religion, she forged an autonomous identity, projecting the "image of a full-fledged, independent . . . and very 'with it' single girl."[78] But in bed one night, she saw a vision, one that she would "vow to my death that I saw and heard while wide awake, and while fully in tune with all of my senses."[79]

In this vision, she "lay down in a prison of pillows and stifling bedcovers."[80] Her mouth "became extremely dry," and she "wet her lips fervently" as an "awful and empty black fear crawled persistently throughout my body."[81] Tortured, she "held my head in my hands, and cowered under my covers praying in meaningless, disjointed" sentences, "begging for the terrible anxiety and horror that enveloped me to leave me in peace.[82]" Then, from the depth of her agony, she heard "a voice . . . in the darkness, quietly, serenely, but with the most monumental majesty . . . The voice said, 'BE STILL, AND KNOW THAT I AM GOD.'"[83]

This experience permanently changed her atheism into profound belief in God's existence. Then, during leg surgery, she shared a hospital room with Barbara Weston, a white Mormon "with an infectious laugh" who exuberantly shared with Martin what her life in the Church provided: "It gives us the ground rules to follow in leading a meaningful, happy life with activity, spirituality, and a heck of a lot to live for now and all eternity!!!"[84] After Martin joined the Church in 1966, she came to Utah to attend Brigham Young University as a twenty-something. There, she became the first black member of the Mormon Tabernacle Choir.[85] In 1970 she was hired as a "research consultant on black culture" for

75. Alan Cherry, "A Negro's Life Changed," 2:98.

76. "15,000 See Mormon Pageant Opening," *Post-Standard* (Syracuse, NY), July 25, 1972, 6.

77. Wynetta Mills Martin, *Black Mormon Tells Her Story*, 29.

78. Ibid., 37.

79. Ibid., 36.

80. Ibid., 38.

81. Ibid.

82. Ibid.

83. Ibid., 39.

84. Ibid., 52.

85. "'Black Mormon' Relates Conversion to Church," *Ogden Standard-Examiner*, June 11, 1972, 22.

BYU's nursing program "because many of the girls" had "never talked with any-one of the black race."[86] She seized the "chance to do something for humanity."[87]

"Martin's story," editorialized the *Kansas City Call*, an African American newspa-per, "challenges the commonly held belief that the Mormon church is racist."[88] Eugene England observed that the lives of people such as Martin "made graphically real . . . the truth of patient church service as a means to make a profound change in the 'truth' of the Gospel as it was perceived by others."[89]

In addition to Martin's autobiography, she became a popular speaker for Mormon audiences: "In less than six years," she later wrote, "I have spoken in more than one hundred Sacrament meetings and very close to a hundred fire-sides, in addition to many seminary classes."[90] Her message was simple: "The Gospel is not prejudiced. . . . No matter what church one attends or what race, creed, or nationality we deal with, we will find good and bad people."[91]

Her typical interactions with white Mormons revealed their uncertainty in carrying out interracial dialogue, and she shared them, both for their comedic quality and also as subtle instruction for dealing with mixed-race gatherings. One woman asked Martin if she was from the West Indies. When Martin informed her that she was in fact "a Negro," the flustered woman "was close to collapse."[92] Martin charitably said that the tactless Mormon "was not a vicious woman, but a naïve one."[93] Hostile racism was rare, Martin observed; in fact, white Mormons tended to be "overkind" by way of compensation for how uncomfortable they felt. Another person asked: "What shall I call you—Black, Negro, or Colored?" Martin lightened the mood with a joke: "They could call me anything as long as they spelled my name right!"[94]

As biographer and literary critic Laura Bush has argued, despite Martin's gracious and quick-witted ease, these interactions with the predominantly white Mormon community exhibited a continuing failure to act "without critical aware-ness of a person's skin color and appearance."[95] In Martin's religious community, white Mormons were guilty of what Bush has described as "racial infelicities and insensitivities."[96] The Mormon community, Eugene England finally concluded, suffered from "American contradictions" plus Mormonism's "unique theology . . .

86. Haws, *The Mormon Image in the American Mind*, 67; Gary James Bergera and Ronald Priddis, *Brigham Young University: A House of Faith*, 302.

87. Martin, *Black Mormon Tells Her Story*, 144.

88. Qtd. in Martin, *Black Mormon Tells Her Story*, appendix, n.p.

89. Wynetta Mills Martin, qtd. in Laura Bush, *Faithful Transgressions: Six Twentieth-Century Mormon Women's Autobiographical Acts*, 121.

90. Martin, *A Black Mormon Tells Her Story*, 70.

91. Ibid.,71.

92. Ibid., 59.

93. Ibid.

94. Ibid., 62.

95. Martin, qtd. in Bush, *Faithful Transgressions,*129.

96. Ibid., 131.

which has been in some ways *more racialized* than the rest of American culture."[97] England further noted that the Mormon Church had been "the only church to formally declare a policy that made a distinction by race and to develop a powerfully influential, though unofficial, racialized theology."[98] Yet Martin found fellowship and love among the Mormons: "So many members have welcomed me with open arms, and I don't find the general prejudice that so many think there is in the Mormon Church."[99]

Martin's story resonated widely with the Mormon people, but, tellingly, she was not allowed to speak for herself. Concerned that her autobiography could be interpreted as activism, the publisher, John D. Hawkes, attached an essay to Martin's autobiography entitled: "Why Can't the Negro Hold the Priesthood." With singular tone-deafness, Hawkes reiterated and even developed new aspects of the well-worn preexistence mythos that could not fail to be patronizing. "Some black people are endowed with a great deal of intelligence, some with great abilities and skills. We may be born unequal to them in many aspects." And why? "Because they must have excelled in the pre-existence in those areas and a just God has rewarded them accordingly in this life." Thus, the explanation for all of life's handicaps, abilities, challenges, and even one's purpose in life can always be explained—or explained away—by the premortal realm to which individuals have no conscious access: "There is . . . a reason for all things—and those reasons obviously take us back into the pre-existence."[100] God "does have chosen groups," Hawkes insisted, just as Jesus preached exclusively to the house of Israel. And it was folly to accuse the Mormons of racism since the prophets had declared that black-skinned Polynesians "are not Negroid and are not of the lineage of Cain" and were therefore eligible to hold the priesthood. If the Church were truly "prejudiced against black skin these south sea individuals would never have been ordained into the priesthood."[101] Ultimately, it was out of the Saints' hands: "We have no right to give them the priesthood. It is God's priesthood and not ours."[102]

Indeed, the Church would not countenance members taking the initiative in the ordination of blacks; in spring 1976, Douglas Wallace, a Portland attorney, was excommunicated for ordaining Larry Lester to the priesthood.[103] He proceeded to file a suit with the Bureau of Land Management, claiming that the Church's priesthood restriction invalidated its discounted land purchases from

---

97. Eugene England, "Playing in the Dark: Mormons Writing about Blacks and Blackness," unpublished essay, 4, qtd. in ibid., 133; emphasis in original.

98. Ibid.

99. Ibid., 70.

100. John D. Hawkes, "Why Can't the Negro Hold the Priesthood," appendix to Martin, *Black Mormon Tells Her Story*, 85.

101. Ibid., 90–71.

102. Ibid., 86.

103. "Black Mormon Ordained," *Salina [Kans.] Journal*, April 4, 1976, 32; "Mormons' Ban OK'd by Court," *Oregonian*, October 22, 1976, 8.

the government.[104] In 1979, Wallace commenced a campaign to have the FBI investigate the LDS Church for alleged antitrust law violations.[105] The lawsuits went nowhere (as did his ordination of Lester), but it was a pointed reminder that race was unfinished business.

Aboriginal Ways

Meanwhile, missionaries in Brazil grappled with racial identities with increasing clumsiness and unease. The urgency of deciding men's racial status drained missionary resources. William Grant Bangerter, mission president in the Brazilian Northeast from 1958 to 1963, recollected that discerning African skin color constituted "one of the major preoccupations of the operation of the Brazilian mission."[106] But in most cases, Bangerter believed racial status to be "very difficult to determine," if not outright impossible. Bangerter often resorted to prayer, hoping that God would reveal a candidate's racial status to him.[107] He did not indicate how often this approach provided him any peace of mind.

While Bangerter prayed over race from an office in the Amazon, Robert Hale, an American missionary, navigated the complexities of Mormon and Brazilian racial consciousness further south on the streets of southern Brazil's Passo Fundo. He assisted in making posters about the "ancient American Indians" and used them in their street preaching.[108] When he met a man "of Inca-Spanish descent," he anticipated that the "Book of Mormon should turn out to be quite wonderful to him."[109] In spring 1967 Hales taught a part-native man, St. Portillo, and "read him the scripture that tells of the descendants of Lehi." St. Portillo "grabbed [the] book" and "wanted to read that again." Portillo "was amazed to think he was of Jewish descent." Hales and his missionary companion immediately "gave him the baptismal challenge and he agreed to it." "You should of seen him eat it up," Hale wrote in his journal, "especially the parts about his ancestors."[110]

But black Brazilians created an atmosphere of hyper-vigilance in which largely inexperienced American young men had to scan male converts and investigators for "negro" features. LaMar Williams, still serving on the general Missionary Committee, reported to Apostle Gordon B. Hinckley, also on the committee, that Jerry Curtis, a recently returned missionary, had seen "a negro"—a man identified only as Brother Nascimento—"teaching a priesthood class in the Brazilian South Mission." Curtis was not in the meeting, but as "he returned from the Melchizedek Priesthood meeting into the assembly room, he saw

104. "Mormon Dissident Files Suit," *Oregonian*, May 17, 1977, A12.
105. "Excommunicated Mormon Urges Bell to Probe Church," *Dallas Morning News*, April 11, 1979, 7.
106. William G. Bangerter, *These Things I Know: Autobiography of William Grant Bangerter*, 170.
107. Ibid.
108. Robert M. Hale, Diary, November 13, 1968, LDS Church History Library.
109. Ibid., February 19, 1969.
110. Ibid., May 25, 1967.

Brother Nascimento standing before the group in a teaching position."[111] In another congregation, a fourteen-year-old male convert was interviewed to receive
the priesthood. But, as Mark Grover has told the story, the missionaries claimed
that the boy's "two younger brothers exhibited some negroid physical features"
and, on that basis, objected to the ordination. Without concluding the baptismal interview, the elders visited the home again, this time asking about genealogy and examining family photos. After seeing more visual evidence of African
ancestry, they insisted that the fourteen-year-old could not be ordained.[112] The
missionaries' reactions ran the gamut—from satisfaction that they were following
Church policy, even though it was difficult and unpopular, to intense discomfort
at excluding obviously worthy candidates from ordination, to displacing their
discomfort by blaming the victim.

Since all of the missionaries were young, it is perhaps understandable, though
no less painful, to find them resorting to immature crudeness. Hale felt that black
investigators exhibited an "aboriginal way of acting"; and when they responded
positively to the message, he left frustrated, unable to follow up as he would have
done with a white candidate. "Well, how unsuccessful of a Sunday can you run
across?" he vented to his journal. "Only 3 contacts all day. One was married to a
bugari—a negro, india mix."[113] Loyal as he was, Hales resented the criticism the
Church received for its policy, especially because he was not fully satisfied by the
answers himself. When one investigator, "the Santos girl," had "been receiving
gas from her father about the Mormon view on negroes and polygamy," Hale
dismissed the father's objections as "false and a lack of knowledge."[114] But only
a month later, he pasted in his journal an icon for an oil company, Petrobras,
that depicted a dancing African man wearing a hard hat. Referring to the icon,
Hale laughed to himself: "This hiah litl' Niggah boy iz from da Pe Ro Brass
Ol Company Expo Zishun."[115] Suddenly self-aware, he added uncomfortably:
"Hope none read that."[116]

When black Brazilian converts were taught the six lessons then being sys-
tematized throughout the Church, missionaries presented a "seventh discussion"
in which they explained "certain marvelous teachings of the Church and Gospel
of Jesus Christ." One of these "marvelous teachings" was reserved just for black
members: "Cain and his descendants received a mark which distinguished them
from other people." After reading Moses 7:22 with them, the discussion dialogue

---

111. LaMar Williams, Memo to Gordon B. Hinckley, September 9, 1962.
112. Mark L. Grover, "Religious Accommodation in the Land of Racial Democracy: Mormon
Priesthood and Black Brazilians," 24.
113. Robert Hale, Diary, December 8, 1968.
114. Ibid., July 10, 1968.
115. Ibid., June 8, 1968.
116. Ibid.

told the missionaries to ask: "How are these descendants distinguished from others?" The investigator's simple answer was scripted: "They are black."[117]

The missionaries then explained that "for reasons not fully known to men," these descendants of Cain "are not entitled to the priesthood." Throughout the lesson, the missionaries reiterated at least four times in various ways that the ban was in place because "God revealed that they [blacks] can not receive [priesthood]." But they promised, citing President David O. McKay (who cited Joseph Smith), that they "will receive the priesthood in the future."

The missionary dialogue continued: The policy would change only when "God had revealed [it] to his prophet." The missionaries were also to give the investigator a strict directive: "If you discover that one of your ancestors was a negro," the convert was to inform the presiding authority. The missionaries demanded a verbal commitment: Even under these circumstances, the convert must promise to "remain firm and faithful to the Church and to your covenants with God."[118] When David O. McKay visited Brazil in 1966, he told José Galvão, a black member, that he "might have to wait until the Millennium to be baptized."[119] It was a mixed message of both promise and prohibition. The lesson came to be widely used throughout Latin American missions, although, as Bangerter indicated, mission presidents were allowed to make decisions based on their own judgment.[120]

In the 1960s, Church headquarters had initiated a lineage-screening team to ensure that converts could in fact demonstrate a non-African ancestry. Mission presidents like Bangerter had long experienced the burden of assessing genealogy. Although Brazil was perhaps the most challenging situation, harried mission presidents in other locales also felt ill equipped to determine race in countries with such scant genealogical records. The program veered dangerously close into a public relations embarrassment and a political fiasco, when the Utah Genealogical Society (later the LDS Family History Library) began lobbying Congress for access to the 1900 census records. Even without the still-keen memories of how the Nazis had encouraged genealogical research to target Jews, even those who had been Christians for generations, the LDS priesthood ban prompted some black politicians to stonewall all access.[121] Eventually, the genealogical team faded away, and the First Presidency directed stake and mission units to make racial determinations but with no more helpful resources than before.[122]

---

117. Lineage Lesson, December 1970, Brazil North Mission, LR 959 21, translated by Julianne Parker Weiss, LDS Church History Library.

118. Ibid.

119. José Galvão Oral History, Interviewed by Michael Landon, June 20, 1994, Transcript, 11.

120. Mauss, "The Fading of the Pharoah's Curse," 13.

121. Ibid.

122. First Presidency, Letter to Priesthood Leaders, February 22, 1978, qtd. in Mauss, "The Fading of the Pharoah's Curse," 26.

But reappropriation of responsibility would not suffice. Missionaries were running headlong into a policy no longer viable in the developing world. In 1974, Kimball announced plans for a temple to be constructed in São Paulo, Brazil. The widespread distribution of African genetic influence throughout Brazil had made it virtually impossible to draw strict racial lines between white, black, and others, forcing Church leaders to question the wisdom of building a temple there, even while they recognized the faithful commitment of black and white members alike; Elder LeGrand Richards recalled that "all those people with Negro blood in them have been raising money to build that temple. . . . Brother Kimball worried a lot about it—how the people are so faithful and devoted."[123]

James E. Faust, the International Mission president who had served his mission as a young man in Brazil, told fellow leaders that Brazilians "make blocks for the temple just like anybody else. They have made their monetary contributions for the construction of the temple and they've made their sacrifices just the same as everybody else."[124] Kimball had dreamed for some time about God making a way for the Saints to "throw wide open the doors" to the global community; when he assumed the presidency, it appeared he would have the opportunity to make good on his hopes.[125]

Orphans

But the African Saints continued to toil alone. In the absence of Church assistance, the West Africans sought patronage and care from other parties. Foreign investors tended to be oilmen, like a Mr. E. Allen, a Mormon from Madera, California, and owner of Allen Grease and Oil Company.[126] By January 1974, Mensah's attempt at a Mormon school had failed. Hoping to keep his Mormon experiment afloat, he attempted to win Allen's support so that the Mormon congregations would be able to enjoy "all benefits and facilities" of the Church. Allen presented himself as the embodiment of the American work ethic. Americans did not achieve financial success overnight, he warned. He had achieved affluence as a "businessman who started from scratch."[127] For his part, Clement Osekre, now serving as Mensah's secretary, hoped that Allen was planning "to invest in Ghana to boost the Church and to help the members of the Restored Church in Ghana."[128] Meanwhile, LaMar Williams had been called to serve as mission president in Louisiana, effectively removing him from his increasingly limited mission

123. LeGrand Richards, *Interview with Mormon Apostle LeGrand Richards Concerning the 1978 'Negro' Revelation*, 3–4.

124. Quoted in Mark L. Grover, "The Mormon Priesthood Revelation and the São Paulo, Brazil Temple," 47. The International Mission was the governing body for all areas not incorporated into official mission units.

125. Spencer W. Kimball, Address, ca. 1970, Manhattan Second Ward.

126. "Prospects for Nigeria," August 26, 1965, 24:614.

127. Ibid.

128. Clement Osekre, Letter to LaMar Williams, March 1, 1974.

of representing ardent Ghanaians and Nigerians, who were thus left without any committed advocates within the Church hierarchy.

Clement Osekre explained to LaMar Williams that he expected Allen to benefit Mormons by hiring self-identified Latter-day Saint Ghanians to work in "industries ranging from automotives and communications to even domestic oils."[129] He also petitioned Allen to provide "transportation, church books, old musical instruments, etc. etc.," including much-needed "hand-operated machines, tools, etc."[130] Like most Ghanaians, the Saints struggled with rampant unemployment. Osekre saw Allen as exactly the kind of resource the Mormons were best equipped to provide: wealthy, American, and generous.

On January 29, 1974, Mensah and Allen signed an agreement that enabled Allen to establish a business outlet in Accra.[131] Osekre thought Allen to be "very pious and friendly disposed."[132] But within a few months, Osekre felt betrayed. It became clear that Allen had no intentions of hiring the "would-be converts." Allen's promise, Osekre charged in a description that smacked of black magic, had been sealed by "spells . . . used before and after their departure [with] an altar, a group of white people flanking on it, and a white human head." Osekre swore that "this was revealed to me—Amen."[133] The precise nature of Allen's agreement is unclear. Osekre's own notes indicate that Allen only encouraged the Ghanaians to "be hard working because what they had achieved in the USA was not done in a single day."[134] Mensah hoped Allen would be a "father . . . and a shrewd businessman who has the interest of helping the Ghana Mission."[135]

This episode revealed what could happen if the poverty-stricken Ghanaians were left to their own fragile resources. In November 1977, Mensah offered to "consecrate to the Church" a 2,000 dollar home as a measure of his personal commitment.[136] With no means of patronage or support, the Ghanaians felt little choice but to hope the transcontinental Mormon network would produce an economically self-reliant community, as well as a transcontinental faith movement. Rebecca Mould's secretary, Joseph Dadzie, begged Kimball for guidance: "The Church in Ghana is just like an Orphan who has nobody to care for his welfare."[137]

The problem had now become a top priority for President Spencer W. Kimball, though he continued to deny or delay requests from Ghana for missionaries; James E. Faust, president of the International Mission, which had oversight

129. Ibid., February 21, 1974.

130. Ibid., Letter to E. Allen, February 14, 1974.

131. Clement Osekre, Letter to LaMar Williams, March 1, 1974.

132. Joseph K. Dadzie, "Notes on Discussions with Bros. Allen and Mensah of Madera, Calif., Held on January 19, 1974."

133. Osekre to Williams, March 1, 1974.

134. Joseph K. Dadzie, Notes on Discussions with Bros. Allen and Mensah of Madera, Calif., Held on January 19, 1974.

135. Ibid.

136. Clement Osekre, Letter to Edwin Cannon, November 14, 1977.

137. Joseph Dadzie, Letter to Spencer W. Kimball, July 15, 1977.

for all of Africa but South Africa, regretfully informed Dadzie "that the Church is unable to send any missionaries to that part of the world at this time."[138]

Under these circumstances, the Ghanaians showed remarkable persistence despite the shifting currents. Samuel Bainson, who had been converted by prophetess Rebecca Mould said that "Mould and her group had fasted on Fridays and pleaded with the Lord that their official LDS group in Ghana would be recognized by the Church Headquarters in Salt Lake City as a legitimate group." Bainson later wrote that, in spring 1978, Mould fell "under the influence of the Holy Ghost" and prophesied "that the Lord had poured out unto us the blessings that we had sought for many years." Mould promised the group that the "Lord has granted us the glory and honor we deserve and has granted us the opportunities to become like angels."[139]

In Utah, Kimball had long resisted the prospect of extending priesthood to African American men. "I had a great deal to fight," he later acknowledged; "Myself largely, because I had grown up with the belief that Negroes should not have the priesthood."[140] Like Kimball, Marion G. Romney, Kimball's second counselor in the First Presidency since 1972, had shared Kimball's hesitance to consider changing the Church's policy. Romney promised that he would support any decision the prophet made but personally he "did not expect him [Kimball] to get an answer." Romney acknowledged that if "the decision had been left to me, I would have felt that we've always had that policy and we would stick to it no matter what the opposition." Romney "resisted change in my feelings, but . . . came to accept it slowly." He had "spent eighty years defending the Church position" and felt reticent to change the status quo. "I am a Romney . . . and a stubborn man," he admitted.[141] But Kimball remained open to other possibilities. He told one congregation that he prayed to the Lord that he and other leaders only "want[ed] what is right. . . . We want only the thing that thou dost want, and we want it when you want it and not until."[142]

The new dialogue prompted even Apostle Mark E. Petersen to revisit some of his beliefs about the priesthood restriction. In the spring of 1978, Petersen became aware of a scholarly article, likely Newell G. Bringhurst's "An Ambiguous Decision: The Implementation of Mormon Priesthood Denial for the Black Man—A Re-examination," published in the spring issue of the *Utah Historical Quarterly*. Bringhurst took minor issue with Bush's conclusions; the priesthood ban was not merely "the product of certain racial concepts and prejudices promoted by Brigham Young and others following the death of Joseph Smith," argued Bringhurst. While it was certainly "true that this decision [the imple-

---

138. James E. Faust, Letter to Joseph Dadzie, August 31, 1977.

139. Samuel Bainson, "An African's Journey," 11.

140. Spencer W. Kimball, qtd. in Gerry Avant, "President Kimball Says Revelation Was Clear," 15.

141. Edward L. Kimball, "Spencer W. Kimball and the Revelation on the Priesthood," 64–65 note 196.

142. Spencer W. Kimball, Meeting in Johannesburg South Africa, October 23, 1978, quoted in ibid., 52 note 140.

mentation of the priesthood ban] was, to some extent, the product of church concern with several Mormon-black questions," it had at least as much to do with "less related trends affecting the larger Latter-day Saint movement." And, as Bringhurst took care to emphasize, the implementation of the restriction "did *not* emerge in a direct, clear cut manner." Instead, there was a "basic confusion and ambiguity as to the roots of the controversial Mormon practice." The arguments resonated with Petersen, and on May 25, he recommended that Kimball take the article under consideration in his deliberations.   A few days later, Petersen left for Brazil, just as Kimball commenced the Twelve's deliberations on the issue.[143]

Upon the death of Harold B. Lee, in December 1973 Spencer W. Kimball became president of the LDS Church. Three years earlier, he had shared his hope with the Manhattan Second Ward that the Saints would "convert the world," a sentiment he would repeat again in the years leading up to the revelation.[144] In his address to the Manhattan Second Ward, Kimball prayed that God would "open the gates, throw wide open the doors, to give us visas, to let our missionaries in so that they can bring to a knowledge of the truth those first people who will become the leaders of the nations from then on."[145]

Pentecost

On June 1, 1978, the First Presidency, Quorum of the Twelve, and the First Council of the Seventy met in the upper room of the temple for their regular meeting. (The First Presidency and the Twelve met weekly, joined by the Seventies once a month.) After dealing with the routine business and closing the meeting, Kimball requested that the Twelve remain for a second session as the Seventies left. President Kimball then centered the discussion on the priesthood ban. After all had expressed their views, Kimball asked to lead them in prayer. McConkie later recalled that "the Lord took over and President Kimball was inspired in his prayer, asking the right questions, and . . . for a manifestation."[146] He "told the Lord if it wasn't right, if He didn't want this change to come in the Church," he "would be true to it all the rest of my life" and would "fight the world against it if that's what he wanted."[147] Even for Kimball's commitment to globalization of the Church, this was a line he was willing to draw in the sand.

---

143. Edward L. Kimball, "Spencer W. Kimball and the Revelation on the Priesthood," 54; Newell G. Bringhurst, "An Ambiguous Decision: The Implementation of the Mormon Priesthood Denial for the Black Man—A Re-examination," 48, 63–64; emphasis his. Edward Kimball, "Spencer W. Kimball and the Revelation on the Priesthood," 54 note 148, maintains that the article "almost surely" was Bush's 1973 article; but Bush believes that the article in question was Bringhurst's, not his. Lester Bush, correspondence to Russell Stevenson, May 12, 2014. For Petersen's trip to Brazil during the first week of June, see Leonard J. Arrington, *Adventures of a Church Historian*, 184 note 2.

144. Spencer W. Kimball, Manhattan Second Ward Sacrament Meeting, ca. 1970; Spencer W. Kimball, "When the World Will Be Converted," 3.

145. Kimball, Manhattan Second Ward Sacrament Meeting, ca. 1970.

146. Edward Kimball, "Spencer W. Kimball and the Revelation on the Priesthood," 56.

147. Avant, "President Kimball Says Revelation Was Clear," 15.

Several present described what followed as a miraculous manifestation. First Counselor Ezra Taft Benson wrote in his journal that the Quorum of the Twelve "experienced the sweetest spirit of unity and conviction," as their "bosoms burned with the righteousness of the decision we had made."[148] Apostle Gordon B. Hinckley called it "a quiet and sublime occasion." The revelation changed them: "Not one of us who was present on that occasion was ever quite the same after that," Hinckley acknowledged, nor "has the Church been quite the same."[149] Elder L. Tom Perry felt "something like the rushing of wind." When Kimball arose from his prayer, the apostles saw that he was "visibly relieved and overjoyed."[150] Two apostles were absent during the deliberations: Mark E. Petersen, who had left Brazil for Quito, Ecuador, and Delbert L. Stapley, then ill at LDS Hospital. On June 8, Kimball called Petersen inform him of the decision. Gibbons read the proposed statement, and Petersen expressed his support. The First Presidency also visited Stapley in the hospital. Stapley's response was simple: "I'll stay with the Brethren on this." The agreement of these two apostles rendered the decision unanimous.[151]

Church spokesperson Jerry Cahill of Public Affairs called it a "momentous day, a great day we've lived through today."[152] Dallas-area stake president Arthur Gabriel hadn't been sure "if it would happen in our lifetime or when."[153] Church headquarters buzzed with "an air of excitement and elation."[154] An elderly woman from Mississippi called headquarters to send her thanks: "What a blessing," she kept saying. "What a blessing."[155] In Rockford, Illinois, Latter-day Saint Willis Waite felt "absolutely ecstatic." His colleague, James Giometa, called the event "the single greatest revelation" since the Church's founding in 1830.[156] After the announcement was read to the First Presidency and Quorum of the Twelve, Marion G. Romney told them that he had "changed my position 180 degrees." He declared that he was "not just a supporter of this decision. . . . I am an advocate."[157]

After receiving the revelation, Kimball told the press that it simply was "a different world than it was 20 or 25 years ago. The world is ready for it."[158] Indeed,

148. Sheri Dew, *Ezra Taft Benson: A Biography,* 457.

149. Gordon B. Hinckley, "Priesthood Restoration," 70.

150. Edward Kimball, "Spencer W. Kimball and the Revelation on the Priesthood," 57.

151. Edward Kimball, Working Draft of *Lengthen Your Stride,* 356–57.

152. "Mormons Drop Race Stricture on Priesthood," *State Times [Baton Rouge, LA] Advocate,* June 10, 1978, 1.

153. "'All Worthy Male Members': Mormons to Let Blacks Be Priests," *Dallas Morning News,* June 10, 1978, A17.

154. "Utah 'Jubilant' over Black Friday," *Dallas Morning News,* June 27, 1978, A11.

155. Ibid.

156. Carol Fouke, "Revelation: Blacks May Become Mormon Priests," *Morning Star* [Rockford, Ill.], June 10, 1978, A4.

157. Edward Kimball, "Spencer W. Kimball and the Revelation on the Priesthood," 64.

158. "Not for Women," *Deseret News,* June 13, 1978, 4B.

many Saints worldwide rejoiced upon hearing the news. When Joseph Johnson heard the news in Ghana, he "burst into tears of joy."[159] E. Dale LeBaron, then serving as president of the South African Mission, recalls a black Saint "put[ting] his head in his hands" while he "sob[bed] uncontrollably" and cried out "Thank God! Thank God!"[160] In Mowbray, South Africa, Tessa watched as "Brother Wiseman" administered the sacrament to the all-white congregation. Meyer thought that "the scene should have been familiar to us: black serving white." But this time was different. Tessa felt that "we all wanted to eat the bread from Brother Wiseman's tray." We "would somehow be more cleansed, more holy, more capable of seeing clearly after drinking from his cup." If only "for a moment each heart in that chapel believed utterly that every soul was equal in the eyes of God, and perhaps one more than any other . . . maybe, just maybe, we might all make it to heaven."[161] In Mould's congregation, Bainson, Mould's bass drummer, remembered that "there was great jubilation in the congregation" as they shouted "Praise God, Alleluia" and "Thank you, Jesus." Mould's members "took to the floor dancing and singing praises to the Lord Jesus."[162]

In Brazil, Seventy and second-time mission president W. Grant Bangerter noted that "people didn't respond as they would in the spirit of the Fourth of July" with dancing, singing, or celebration, "but their emotions were very deep." Bangerter saw the Brazilian Saints "heaving great sighs of emotion and raising their eyes to heaven in the spirit of thanksgiving and prayer." Tears poured "freely from their eyes" as they "just quietly tr[ied] to absorb the meaning of all that had taken place."[163] Alfredo Lima Vaz, another black Brazilian, noted that "it helped a lot because many people may have had the desire to come [to church], but did not know how." The black Brazilians "all felt that we were ordained of God." Before the revelation, Gilberto Baroni noted, "missionaries did not look for us." Indeed, black convert Helvécio Martins observed that he had been "conditioned . . . to believe the granting of the priesthood to Blacks would occur only in the millennium."[164] Alfredo Lima Vaz felt that the revelation fundamentally changed the "orientation of missionary work." If missionaries "need[ed] to go to a house of a prostitute, they will baptize her and bring her to the Church."[165]

Jose Galvão learned of the revelation while listening to the British Broadcasting Company radio station, picking up a signal "on AM 1900 overlapping the frequency that you could usually pick up between six and five." Fifteen years later,

---

159. Joseph Johnson, qtd. in E. Dale LeBaron, "Steadfast African Pioneer," 45.
160. E. Dale LeBaron, "Official Declaration 2: Revelation on the Priesthood," 345.
161. Tessa Meyer Santiago, "Brother Wiseman," 71.
162. Bainson, "An African Journey," 11.
163. Mark L. Grover, "The Mormon Priesthood Revelation and the São Paulo, Brazil Temple," 50.
164. Ibid., 49.
165. Gilberto Baroni and Alfredo Lima Vaz, Interview by Michael N. Landon, transcript, 20, June 15, 1994.

Galvão "trie[d] to pick up that signal" but couldn't "seem to find it anymore."[166] When Galvão went to church, he saw that "nobody knew what had happened." He "grabbed one of the people there and said 'Oh my goodness! The MOST IMPORTANT blessing I saw happen this week was the conferring of the priesthood to all men in the world, regardless of race, be it white, black, yellow, or red."[167]

Utah Saints responded with a mixture of relief, apocalyptic rejoicing, and an occasional overtone of bitterness. White Wanship resident Donald Woolstenhulme felt that the revelation indicated the imminence of the Second Coming: "It should be time to start getting your life in order to meet your Maker" since "one of the prophesies concerning the last days would be that blacks would hold the priesthood."[168] Ruffin Bridgeforth agreed, noting that "we are getting close to the end of time, because I think that we perhaps have reached a state of brotherhood."[169]

Yet, as William Wilson and Richard Poulson have indicated, the revelation prompted a recycling of jokes that Mormons had told for generations about black people. Though many understood the event as a "sign of the times," some sought to reappropriate the events to fit with old Mormon narratives. One joke cracked that the Saints needed blacks in the Church during the end times: "Who else are we going to get to carry our bags to Missouri?" Another asked: "How do you know when the millennium is here?" The answer: "When you open the door and hear, 'Hi! Wees you new home teachers."[170]

Even residents of largely Gentile Park City represented a wide range of responses. Annette Ritchie, a pharmacy clerk, thought the revelation was "neat because one of the main goals of our Church is to get everyone involved in Church programs." Others looked beyond the revelatory statement for an explanation. Real estate agent Rocky Smith felt that it was "only fair" and that Church leaders had implemented the new policy as a logical step to expand its recruitment base. "Someday," he noted, "they may even extend the same right to women." In contrast, Betty Sparks, a retiree living in Park City, when asked what she thought about the revelation, responded tersely: "Not much."[171]

Bruce R. McConkie became an ardent defender of the Church's new policy, even as he continued to entertain old racial dogmas about the origins of the races. He confessed to Church leaders' personal struggles to overcome their racial prejudice, noting that they had failed to understand the full import of the words: "All are alike unto God." "We have caught a new vision of their significance," McConkie declared. "Many of us never imagined or supposed that they had the

---

166. Galvão, Interview, 19.

167. Ibid.

168. "Off the Record," *Park [City, Utah] Record,* June 15, 1978, 3.

169. David Briscoe, "Mormon Priesthood Open to Blacks," *[Portland] Oregonian,* June 10, 1978, 1.

170. William Wilson and Richard Poulson, "The Curse of Cain and Other Stories: Blacks in Mormon Folklore," 12.

171. "Off the Record," *Park [City, Utah] Record,* June 15, 1978, 3. The membership status of the aforementioned men and women is unknown.

extensive and broad meaning that they do have." He tellingly noted that Jesus's "prophetic associates . . . were so fully indoctrinated with the concept of having the gospel go only to the house of Israel, that they were totally unable to envision the true significance of his proclamation that after the Resurrection they should go to all the world."[172]

However, McConkie's interpretation of gospel expansion did not take account of the heritage of black Latter-day Saints. No references to Elijah Ables, Walker Lewis, or other black priesthood holders appear in the speech. In McConkie's eyes, priesthood expansion was still founded on a dispensationalist narrative: "The gospel goes to various peoples and nations on a priority basis." The Saints "do not envision the whole reason and purpose behind all of it." And McConkie was still felt it necessary "to suppose and reason that it [the timing of priesthood ordination] is on the basis of our premortal devotion and faith."[173]

Well-aware of the difficult position in which he was now placed, McConkie felt impelled to renounce the priesthood ban even while holding fast to the interpretation he had once declared to be definitive. "Forget everything that I have said," McConkie said, "or what President Brigham Young or President George Q. Cannon or whomsoever has said in days past that is contrary to the present revelation."[174] While not published in the *Ensign* or released before general conference, McConkie's speech was reprinted in several publications for Church educators and was published for public consumption by the Church-owned publishing arm, Deseret Book.[175]

Within a month, a well-funded group calling itself "Concerned Latter-day Saints," headed by Midvale resident Joseph Jensen, paid for a full-page advertisement in the *Salt Lake Tribune* questioning the wisdom of the new revelation. The Church was "throwing away the Book of Mormon and Pearl of Great Price . . . to gain full fellowship with the world and to receive its unqualified praise," Jensen and his followers wrote. They considered themselves to be a "remnant" who would "build up the kingdom upon the earth and usher in the Millennial reign of Christ."[176] But most members had little sympathy with the fundamentalist stance, believing that the revelation marked a new era for the faith.

Both faithful and disaffected saw the declaration as groundbreaking and even apocalyptic. Though a short document, its release had been made possible through a constellation of forces. The success of the civil rights protests had

---

172. Bruce R. McConkie, "All Are Alike Unto God," in *Priesthood* (1981), 132.

173. Ibid.

174. The most accessible version of the speech is Bruce R. McConkie, "All Are Alike Unto God," http://speeches.byu.edu/?act=viewitem&id=1570 (accessed June 13, 2013).

175. The identical text appears in Bruce R. McConkie, "The New Revelation on Priesthood," in *Priesthood* (1981), 126–37; Bruce R. McConkie, "All Are Alike Unto God," in *A Symposium on the Book of Mormon*, 3–5; Bruce R. McConkie, "All Are Alike unto God," *A Charge to Religious Educators*, 152–55.

176. "LDS to Repudiate," Advertisement, *Salt Lake Tribune*, July 23, 1978, A6.

seeped into the Mormon consciousness, compelling Church leaders to walk the awkward border between support for civil rights and the continuing embrace of the priesthood restriction. After the embarrassments of the 1960s, Church leaders needed to contain the fire at home so that it would not stand in the way of growth abroad. Utahns had dragged their feet on civil rights, and now they were paying the price.

Handling image control was a less-than-ideal situation for a faith hoping to focus its message on Jesus Christ and expansion of the missionary effort. The task before the Saints had only begun. And Church leaders faced a wide array of new prospects and challenges, ranging from handling corruption and physical dangers in West Africa to political dilemmas in South Africa to public relations problems in the United States.

Over the generations, racism had metastasized into a major aspect of Mormon society and culture. Now so entrenched, leader and lay member alike faced the pressing need to exorcise the ghosts of Missouri once and for all.

Chapter 7

Repairers of the Breach, 1978–2013

And they that shall be of thee shall build the old waste places: thou
shalt raise up the foundations of many generations; and thou shalt be
called, The repairer of the breach, The restorer of paths to dwell in.
—Isaiah 58:12

In 1987 Apostle Boyd K. Packer, frustrated with the Church's lack of growth in the developing world, exclaimed, "We can't move *there* with all the baggage we produce and carry *here*! We can't move with a 1947 Utah Church!"[1] Indeed, as Phillip Jenkins observed a generation later in 2011, "the era of Western Christianity has passed within our lifetimes."[2]

Mormonism had gone global. Its faltering efforts to expand into Nigeria forgotten in light of the new revelation, Church leaders moved forward aggressively to claim the crop of West African converts. In August 1978, Dr. Merrill J. Bateman, a consultant with the Mars Candy corporation who had experience with the region and Edwin Q. Cannon, former Swiss Mission president (1971–74) and a counselor in the International Mission (1974–84), visited several of the Ghanaian congregations. Both were impressed by their enthusiasm and faith.[3] They gave a positive evaluation to the First Presidency, who in November 1978 called two missionary couples to serve a year-long mission in Ghana and Nigeria: Edwin Cannon and his wife, Janath Russell Cannon,[4] and Rendell N. Mabey and his wife, Rachel Ivins Mabey. After his years as an elephant hunter, Mabey had served as the Swiss Mission president in 1962, which included overseeing white LDS congregations in areas such as Eritrea and Zaire. Mabey was a member of one of Utah's most prominent political families. His father had served as governor; Rendell himself had served as both a speaker of the Utah House of Representatives and as a state senator. Rachel Mabey, the politician's wife, was taken aback by the dingy accommodations

---

1. Boyd K. Packer, "Address to the Church Co-ordinating Committee Meeting," September 8, 1987, cited in Lee Copeland, "From Calcutta to Kaysville: Is Righteousness Color-Coded?" 97.

2. Philip Jenkins, *The Next Christendom: The Coming of Global Christianity,* 3.

3. Bateman had visited Ghana earlier in 1978 at the request of International Mission President James E. Faust. See James P. Bell, "Merrill J. Bateman: Breadth and Depth."

4. Prior to her calling, Cannon had been first counselor in the Relief Society general presidency. In 1992, she co-authored *Women of Covenant: The Story of Relief Society* with Jill Mulvay Derr and Maureen Ursenbach Beecher.

she discovered in her West African hotel; "nothing," she confessed to her journal, "could bring me here but a calling from the Lord."[5]

Embarrassment

Meanwhile, Obinna was growing upset at Church headquarters' unresponsiveness; he pressed the Quorum of the Twelve for answers: "Your long silence about the establishment of the Church in Nigeria is very much embrassing [sic]. . . . The Spirit of God calls us to abide by this church and there is nothing to keep us out."[6] Likely aware of this correspondence, the missionaries went in search of Obinna's congregation immediately upon entering the country. Cannon was asking passersby on the streets when a "woman who happened to hear the town [Owera] we were asking about had her driver lead us there." Upon arrival, Cannon walked through the marketplace, asking for anybody who knew Obinna. When "a man with one arm passed he caught the name of Anthony Obinna & came back saying he knew where he lived." The man rode with the missionaries "& directed us . . . off onto a dirt road back into the 'Bush' where we came upon a village & the main building had a sign painted on it, 'The Church of Jesus Christ of Latter day Saints.'"[7] Obinna had long felt that his Nigerian congregation represented the American church; in 1971, he had drawn an official LDS logo on his Book of Mormon indicating that he represented the "C.J.C. L.D.S. Mission."[8] When Mabey, Cannon, and World Health Organization employee A. Bruce Knudsen[9] baptized nineteen Nigerians, including Obinna, Rachel Mabey rejoiced: "This is our reward. . . . All glory & honor be to Our Heavenly Father who prepared them and these led us to them!"[10] By the end of their missions, Janath Cannon had grown to "feel close to these strong, soft-smiling black women who are so generous with their love."[11]

The American couples began to overcome their initial culture shock and found the local music "contagious." When they were "ringing bells, shaking gourds, & swaying," the American missionaries "joined in the clapping, happy group."[12] Rachel now had the comforting knowledge that the Lord was "guiding us. . . . [W]e see his hand in leading us to these people & preparing them."[13] After spending their first two months in Nigeria, they visited Ghana in December

---

5. Rachel N. Mabey, Diary, November 16, 1978; see also Rendell N. Mabey and Gordon T. Allred, *Brother to Brother: The Story of the Latter-day Saint Missionaries Who Took the Gospel to Africa.*

6. Anthony Obinna, Letter to the Council of the Twelve, September 28, 1978.

7. Rachel Mabey, Diary, November 18, 1978.

8. Anthony Obinna's Book of Mormon Title Page, MS 19820, LDS Church History Library.

9. A. Bruce Knudsen specialized in tropical diseases and had been working in Enugu, Nigeria, researching methods for decreasing the prevalence of mosquitoes. Reed Clegg, "Friends of West Africa: An Opportunity for Service," 95.

10. Rachel Mabey, Diary, November 18, 1978.

11. Janath Cannon, Diary, September 14, 1979.

12. Ibid., November 26, 1978.

13. Ibid.

where they found a warm welcome and the bestowal of culturally significant gifts: elephant chairs and ivory necklaces.[14]

Within six months of the missionaries' arrival, they faced the realities of political instability. During one church service, "two men from the electoral officials arrived to address the congregation and explain the election process," delivering a presentation given to all of Ghana's major churches.[15] A few days later, Lieutenant Jerry Rawlings mounted a coup against the government. Hoping to win the support of Ghanaian religious society, Rawlings made an effort to establish cordial contacts with various religious denominations. Janath Cannon observed that he was "courting the churches" because, as Joseph Johnson, one of the top leaders in the Ghanaian LDS Church, told her, they "have the confidence of the people more than the military has."[16]

With an official American presence, the Church could finally address the ownership of the Mormon branch in both Nigeria and Ghana. The missionaries were troubled to learn that a "unqualified native," left nameless, had set up "some congregations called the Church of Jesus Christ of Latter Saints & who has registered the name with the government of Nigeria." When Rachel Mabey met this "unqualified native," she decided that "he did not have a good spirit."[17] Unlike Obinna and others the American missionaries had met to this point, his congregations had no intention of joining the American hierarchy; he was likely more interested in exploiting the status he would have received from acquiring the name of an American church. Mennie Udorn, a survivor of the Biafran civil war, had refused to join the several Mormon congregations that had cropped up in the 1960s and had written Salt Lake City in 1976 that "they are not to be trusted" since they often "change to other groups, then write as a true organization."[18]

The Cannons and the Mabeys Americanized the West African churches, reconstructing and reorganizing the self-governing faith communities into units within the American Church hierarchy. They immediately replaced Rebecca Mould with Charles Ansah, whom they baptized, ordained to the Melchizidek Priesthood, and called to serve as branch president. The missionaries recognized Mould's charismatic and "motherly" influence and called her as president of the Sekondi Branch Relief Society. Adapting to the new establishment was difficult for this independent woman and her followers, but she seems to have made a good-faith effort to fit into the limitations imposed by the American-style organization. In December 1978, Mould claimed to have "no objections to the new arrangements."[19]

---

14. Isaac Champson, qtd. in Sekondi Branch, Minutes of meeting, December 14, 1978.

15. Janath Cannon, Diary, June 3, 1979.

16. Ibid., June 5, 1979.

17. Rachel Mabey, Diary, November 13 and 26, 1978.

18. Mennie Udorn, Letter to First Presidency, December 3, 1976.

19. Sekondi Branch Meeting Minutes, December 14, 1978.

A few months later, Rachel Mabey taught Mould how to sing the children's hymn, "I Am a Child of God." The song "delighted" Mould,[20] but even so, she fumed over the institutionalization of her congregation. Once able to earn a living as a cleric, Mould found herself jobless. She had no choice but to rely on the goodwill of her followers for her daily sustenance. Emmanuel Kissi recalled that she held fund-raising meetings to "pay her for the use of her building . . . drums were frequently played, which was the Pentecostal way of worshiping and a tradition many members were accustomed to."[21]

Many members still believed in Mould's prophetic authority. One woman asked Janath Cannon "if we had prophetesses in Salt Lake." Cannon responded that "we had a prophet and the Relief Society President." The woman's reply "took [Cannon] back": "Well then, we are really blessed in Ghana—we have prophetesses!" Though Cannon tried to "explain the difference between receiving revelation for the direction of the Church and individuals receiving revelation for their own lives," she made little headway.[22]

The transition proved too difficult for Mould's Mormons. In November 1979, Mould left the Saints, taking most of the Sekondi branch with her. She informed priesthood leaders that "when . . . LDS could not recognize a woman to do the work of God or to lead a Church . . . she could no longer continue with L.D.S Church."[23] Her defection took its toll. By the end of 1979, the branch had shrunk from over 120 to 40.[24]

When senior missionaries Reed and Naomi Clegg arrived in Ghana in late February 1980, Joseph Johnson cast the dust-up in a charitable light, informing the Cleggs that Mould was having "second thoughts about her role" since she "needs the financing, etc.," from member donations.[25] But Mould continued to consider herself to be part of the Mormon body; in 1982, she attended a regional conference in Accra.[26] But the scorned Ghanaians and by-the-book Americans had little desire to acknowledge the legitimacy of what they deemed a schismatic sect. A decade later, Dale LeBaron and Eugene England attempted to interview her about the beginnings of the Church during the transitional phase between the period of autonomous and unauthorized congregations and the imposition of American-style organization, but she refused to comment on her early work

---

20. Rachel Mabey, Diary, January 31, 1979.

21. Ibid. See also Sekondi Branch, Meeting Minutes, February 3, 1979.

22. Janath Cannon, Journal, July 22, 1979.

23. Sekondi Branch Meeting Minutes, November 18, 1979.

24. "Important Dates in Church History—Takoram District," n.d., Danzie Papers.

25. Reed and Naomi Clegg, Letter to Edwin Cannon, February 27, 1980. The Cleggs served in West Africa from 1980 to 1981. A datestamp at the head of the sheet indicates that it was received at the mission office on March 6, 1979.

26. In August 1982, Sylvester Cooper recorded that "Rebecca Mould, the Prophetess, came her with her group" to the regional conference. "They originally joined the church, but fell away as they wanted her to be their leader." Sylvester Cooper, Journal, August 13, 1982.

with the Church.[27] More recently, the LDS Church planned a "Pioneers of '78" celebration in Ghana and invited Mould to attend. She accepted the invitation; however, her health prohibited her from making the trip to Accra.[28]

"The Lord Chose Me"

The struggle of Mormon-black reconciliation was bitter elsewhere in Africa, too. In 1955, South African Julia Mavimbela was left a widow when a car accident killed her husband, John. A noted jazz musician and politician, he had been a member of the African National Congress and was a close friend of Nelson Mandela.[29] The Afrikaaner police not only did little to help but also stole John's belongings from the wrecked car. Angered, Julia struggled to cope with her newly fired hatred of the white establishment. "I was cross," she recalled, in a notable understatement. "I was really cross. And I made my husband a tombstone . . . in such a way that it might be conspicuous from the road to the men who did it." Perhaps that was wrong, Mavimbela acknowledged, but "feelings are feelings."[30]

In 1976, the township of Soweto exploded into riots as the schools were forced to incorporate Afrikaans into their curriculum, the South African postal service removed exclusionary signs from its doors, and, in 1978, hotels and restaurants were required to acquire a license exempting them from certain apartheid laws.[31] But the larger corpus of apartheid law remained firmly in place, including laws requiring churches to acquire multiracial permits before becoming integrated.[32]

As a Soweto native, Mavimbela's hatred for Afrikaaners simmered under the surface, even though she acknowledged to a newspaper reporter in 1977: "Does this mean I should never speak to a white woman? No . . . we must learn to live together."[33] Christianity brought her no consolation. She would "read the word Israel . . . and say, 'It is for the whites. It is not for us. We are not chosen,'" and toss the volume aside in disgust.[34] In retrospect, Mavimbela acknowledged that she "was not yet in a church that could really help me forgive."[35] When she met Mormon missionaries, they taught her that her husband could be baptized posthumously. Mavimbela fell in love with the doctrine, especially since Christian denominations discouraged blacks from entertaining ideas that seemed to resonate with native traditions about spirits and ancestor worship. Mavimbela was baptized in 1981.[36] She

27. Eugene England and E. Dale LeBaron, Comments on Rebecca Mould Interview, May 22, 1988.

28. James Goldberg, Correspondence with Russell Stevenson, March 13, 2014.

29. Mavimbela, Oral History Interview, August 28, 1995, 18. See also Veit Erlmann, *African Stars: Studies in Black South African Performance,* 153.

30. Mavimbela, Oral History Interview, 17.

31. "Subtle Changes in South Africa," *Milwaukee [Wisc.] Journal,* August 16, 1981, 1, 3; "Blacks Gain Expanded Access to Liquor Stores in S. Africa," *Greensboro [N.C.] Daily News,* July 24, 1981, 23.

32. "Defiant Anglicans to Fight Apartheid Despite Cost," *[London] Times,* December 10, 1979, 4.

33. "Women Back Peace, Urge Racial Unity," *San Diego Union,* November 27, 1977, 73.

34. E. Dale LeBaron, "Julia Mavimbela," *Liahona,* March 1995, 43. 42–43

35. Ibid.

36. James B. Allen, "On Becoming a Universal Church," 13–14.

served faithfully twice each week in the Johannesburg Temple.[37] She found support in her Soweto Mormon community, founded the organization, Women for Peace, and later became president of the National Council of Women of South Africa.[38]

American expatriate Andrew Clark, who was working in Johannesburg as a journalist with the *Johannesburg Weekly Mail*, observed that Soweto was "violent even in the best of times."[39] The priesthood revelation marked the second anniversary of violent anti-apartheid riots in Soweto when police gunned down children who were protesting the requirement to speak only Afrikaans in the classroom. President Spencer W. Kimball was under no illusions about the toll that apartheid had exacted on the white Mormon-black relationship in South Africa and confessed that bridging the racial divide would be a "slow, upward haul."[40] Pretoria member Christine DuPlessis admitted, "Another generation made serious mistakes." She told *This People* magazine, "it's up to our generation to correct those mistakes."[41] Tessa Meyer, a white Mormon girl then living in Capetown, South Africa, felt that granting a black member, Solomon Wiseman (whom they affectionately came to call "our Brother Wiseman," a mite better than the term "boy" employed for most blacks in South Africa) equality in the Church also had grave moral implications; for Meyer, it meant that "our white lives were ethically and morally repugnant."[42]

Simultaneously, the South African government was slowly chipping away at apartheid laws.[43] In the 1970s, the Roman Catholics began inching toward integrating their private schools, in spite of government threats to shut them down. Forced to negotiate, the government promised to back off, provided that the schools did not admit any more black students—an agreement several Catholic schools unashamedly violated.[44] But religious schools charged steep rates that most blacks could not hope to afford, leaving most blacks in the townships with textbooks that promoted rank racism and poorly trained teachers.

In 1974, Reginald Nield, a Mormon rugby player from Rhodesia, invited Brigham Young University's variety troupe, "BYU Sounds" to visit the country where they would perform numbers such as "Country Sunshine," "Good Morning, Heartache," and the music of the Carpenters.[45] The proceeds of performance provided "much money" to assist the blacks living in Rhodesia.[46] In 1980, guerrillas took over the Rhodesian government and declared the independent

---

37. Andrew Clark, "The Fading Curse of Cain: Mormonism in South Africa," 42.

38. Mavimbela, Oral History, 21.

39. Clark, "The Fading Curse of Cain," 42. For Clark's occupation, see Mauss, "In Search of Ephraim: Traditional Mormon Conceptions of Lineage and Race," 168 note 113.

40. Ben De Wet, "South Africa: A Different View," n.d., 9, Bateman Temple Papers.

41. David Bly, "Hope in a Torn Land," 31.

42. Tessa Meyer Santiago, "Brother Wiseman," 71.

43. "Blacks May Enter Private Hospitals," *[London] Times*, December 11, 1979, 6.

44. "White Church Schools Jar S. African Regime," *Christian Science Monitor*, April 3, 1978, 4.

45. "BYU Sounds to Africa," *Davis County Clipper* (Bountiful, Utah), May 31, 1974, 30.

46. "Eternal Sealing: Many Miles, Many Years, and Many Blessings," *Deseret News*, April 26, 1975, 25.

state of Zimbabwe. As most white families left, the Nield family stayed behind and served in leadership positions in the Zimbabwean Mormon community.

For proponents of legal action, the 1981 election offered little hope. Nearly a third of Transvaal votes supported the stridently pro-apartheid Herstigte Nasionale Party, its strongest showing in a national election to date. The National Conservative Party also drew decided support.[47] Churches whose international headquarters were in Canada struggled even to hold integrated church services.[48] In 1983, the "coloured branch" of the Dutch Reformed Church began to perform interracial marriages, an act of open rebellion against both the main body of the DRC and the government.[49] Within a week of the election, the LDS Church's Public Communications Division defied the racial violence that was wracking the area by announcing that temple ceremonies would be racially integrated.[50] Hilda Benans, a South African black missionary serving in Alabama, said: "We feel like brothers and sisters."[51] William P. Daniels's daughter, Alice, continued her activity in the Church and expressed gratitude for the opportunity to attend the temple dedication. [52]

Unlike the Catholics and others, the Saints did not participate in the acts of civil disobedience that other religious institutions championed.[53] Indeed, only a week before the LDS announcement, reports of "several thousand blacks rampage[ing] through the streets" had reached the United States.[54] President Gordon B. Hinckley commented on the "dramatic picture of the flames of South Africa," and predicted: "Things may get worse before they get better," but he was confident that "they will get better."[55]

Ben De Wet, then serving as a member of the temple presidency, commented that "permission to proselyte the black people . . . was better accepted here than was expected."[56] As Mormon journalist David Bly observed, "The relative ease with which people of all races mingled at church was heartwarming." Even more, he found "that it was not unusual."[57] In 1986, a man had told Bly, when he was serving a mission in South Africa as a young man, not to use the word *dinsknegte* to describe himself; it literally meant a "servant of the Lord" but had come to be "reserved for black servants and was insulting to whites." Now, this

---

47. Christopher Hill, *Change in South Africa: Blind Alleys or New Directions,* 148–51.

48. Renate Pratt, *In Good Faith: Canadian Churches against Apartheid,* 63–133.

49. "Coloured Church Defies Apartheid Marriage Law," *[London] Times,* March 21, 1983, 5.

50. "Plan New Mormon Temples," *Times-Picayune* (New Orleans), April 18, 1981, 27.

51. "S. African Mormon Missionary Is Doing Work in Alabama," *Plain Dealer* (Cleveland, OH), June 1, 1986, 33.

52. Alice Okkers, Oral History, interviewed by E. Dale LeBaron, July 29, 1988, 8. See also Hal Knight, "Touching Temple Fulfills a Dream for Aged Woman," 10.

53. "S. African Mormon Missionary Is Doing Work in Alabama," *Plain Dealer,* June 1, 1986, 33.

54. "Police Tear Gas Sparks Black Riot in S. Africa," *Dallas Morning News,* April 6, 1981, 4.

55. Ellen Fagg, "LDS Church Bringing Races Together, But Some Obstacles Remain," *Deseret News,* March 13, 1986, A4.

56. De Wet, "South Africa," 9.

57. Bly, "Hope in a Torn Land," 29.

same man had helped to organize a black branch.[58] When G. Phillip Margetts was called as the Capetown South Africa Mission president, baptisms were happening so rapidly—and with poor retention—that the First Presidency directed him to "slow down the work."[59]

But the commitment of black Africans also increased American affection for its newest minority group. In 1992, Sandalamu Chisembe, a black branch president from Zimbabwe, traveled thirty hours to participate in temple services. He spoke no Afrikaans and only a little English. He arrived in Johannesburg on a night of rioting and violence; police dogs and squad cars roamed the streets. The police offered him safe haven for the evening, but Chisembe "insisted that he must contact the temple." The police summoned Reed Webster, a counselor in the Johannesburg Temple presidency, and De Wet to pick him up. Webster and De Wet found "a small black man, about five feet tall carrying a big suitcase." In the letter of introduction he scrawled for himself, he declared that he had "come to the temple to seek for spiritual power, for preaching teaching and doing all the Lord's work." The foreign business elite—which Webster and De Wet resembled—intimidated him: "So many big businessmen around in the buildings where I work," he admitted. When called to be the branch president, he felt humbled: "The Lord chose me."[60]

Racial tensions nevertheless simmered in many of the Church units. Apartheid had played a fundamental role in their economic, social, and religious lives. Granting the priesthood to black men problematized the world they had known. In 1979, Vivien Clark (no known relation to Andrew Clark) joined the Latter-day Saints in Pretoria, her hometown that had long been known as a "stronghold of the apartheid regime." As a longtime critic of apartheid, Clark was "deeply shocked" at the Saints' "open support" for the apartheid system. Clark recalls that a few white Saints even left the Church after they stopped being "all-white meetings." When Clark made public her abhorrence for apartheid, fellow Church members labeled her a Communist. During a Relief Society dinner, she recalls, a "Priesthood leader had drawn the hammer and sickle" on her nametag. After another dinner, one of the women suggested that attendees could "take the scrapings that people had left on their plates" to feed their black servants at home.[61]

Accounts of black-on-black violence provided grist for frightened white Saints' rumor mills. "A picture comes to mind," Clark recalls, "of a sister in her diamonds, curls, and painted nails [who] told . . . how black youths were making black women drink [laundry] softener." She told her story with an "I-told-you-so" quality to highlight "how savage blacks are."[62] Visiting missionaries sympathized

58. Ibid., 30–31.

59. Fagg, "LDS Church Bringing Races Together," A4.

60. Reed Webster, "The Lord Chose Me," n.d (ca. 1992). The article was printed as Reed J. Webster, "Man of Few Words Radiates Serenity," *Deseret News,* January 4, 1992, 11.

61. Vivien Clark, Correspondence with Russell W. Stevenson, November 7, 2013.

62. Ibid., November 8, 2013.

with the mistreatment of blacks but expressed frustration at the blacks' over-eagerness to get "what the whites have, right now."[63] One white Mormon couple expressed fear of "so many Blacks [living] in areas on both sides of them."[64] Some white Mormons believed that the black townships would rise up in vengeance for the generations of abuse.[65] In May 1990, a white Mormon couple allowed a black man to use their telephone to report a nearby break-in. The husband was carrying a gun. The black man seized it, shot the homeowner in the head, and tried to shoot the woman as well. The gun jammed while she ran to the other room. The police arrived at the home and arrested the black man.[66]

Racial conflict occasionally alienated black Saints from much of the black population. The dedication of the Johannesburg Temple was scheduled for August 1985. During that month, approximately 140 people were killed and 2,000 detained during the protests.[67] The day before the dedication, the South African police killed six and wounded twenty.[68] On the day of the dedication, blacks in Soweto held a "stay-away day" in which black militants staged terrorist attacks on the Johannesburg workforce.[69] But Mavimbela "so wanted to be [t]here." She wrapped her child's arm as if he were wounded and told the guards that she needed to take him to the hospital. The device allowed her to pass; but had her deception been uncovered, she "would [have been] killed."[70] Reflecting on the experience, she wondered if "the Lord will forgive me for my little deceit."[71]

Pray for Peace

On the first day of the temple dedication, mobs of black youth attacked the taxi drivers and robbed several gas stations in Soweto.[72] After President Gordon B. Hinckley returned from South Africa, he praised the temple patrons' willingness to "mingl[e] together as brothers and sisters. . . . Those descended from the Dutch who long ago went to that land, those who descended from the British who had fought the Dutch, and also those who came of the native peoples of Africa."[73] De Wet heralded the temple as the "solution to South Africa's chal-

---

63. Carol Howell, qtd in Donovan Howell, Mission Journal, March 11, 1990, LDS Church History Library..

64. Ibid.

65. Mavimbela, Oral History, 30.

66. Carol Donovan, in Donovan Howell Diary, March 25, 1990, LDS Church History Library.

67. "S. Africa Imprisons 27 Leaders," *Plain Dealer*, August 25, 1985, 1.

68. "S. African Children Arrested," *Mobile [Ala.] Register*, August 24, 1985, 1.

69. Julia Mavimbela, quoted in Sheila Bibb., comp., "The Johannesburg South Africa Temple: Historical Background, Construction, Various Events, and Spiritual Experiences Related Thereto," 11.

70. Mavimbela, Oral History, 9.

71. Maurice and Arlene Bateman, Tribute to Julia Mavimbela, July 18, 2000.

72. "South African Police to Take 'Stern Action' against March," *Marietta [Ga.] Journal*, August 25, 1985, 6.

73. Gordon B. Hinckley, "Rejoice in This Great Era of Temple Building," 54.

lenges" and promised the Saints that the temple "would bind us together."[74] The Johannesburg Temple became both a spiritual and social symbol to the South African Saints. When Mavimbela attended the temple, she found "no touch of Afrikaaner. There is no English. There is no Situ or Zulu." She loved "that feeling of oneness [that] you find . . . in the temple."[75] Mavimbela worked to bind the wounds of apartheid, though her words to white Mormons were pointed. She recalled telling white Saints at a regional conference "how I felt when my husband had tragically died, and how the laws of my country wouldn't satisfy me with the truth, because of my color, but how I had found myself moving to a very happy state of life."[76] Malcolm Young, a white Mormon construction contractor had expressed his hard feelings toward the black population in years past, but now testified that the temple made all the difference: "The Lord built a temple here. That tells me the country will not fall apart, that we can live here in peace."[77]

Deseret News reporter Ellen Fagg cast the South African Saints as leaders in racial reconciliation. The Johannesburg Temple was a "symbol of hope" that "God will watch over their land."[78] Sean Covey, then a recently returned missionary from Capetown assured the *News* that for "most of my mission, there wasn't a race problem."[79] Another missionary, Mitch Taylor, said that "the white members used to take the black converts in just like they were family." Any difficulties in racial integration, the *Deseret News* seemed to suggest, lay with blacks' discomfort in meeting with whites.[80] Elder Joseph P. Wirthlin, then area president over Europe and Africa, observed that "it seems to me the church is the answer [to racial discord] in South Africa."[81] Fagg contrasted the Saints to an ordinary South African white woman who fumed against the increased strength of blacks: "I'm still South African. I don't want them living next to me. And I don't want my children going to school with them."[82] Former missionary Mitch Taylor acknowledged that white converts struggled to accept racial integration, recalling one Johannesburg couple telling him that they "just can't feel comfortable being a member of a church where blacks are members."[83]

But entrenched racism sometimes had the flavor of paternalism and white privilege. And not everyone shared the hope of De Wet, Mavimbela, and Fagg. In 1991, Andrew Clark, an American resident of Soweto, observed that South

---

74. De Wet, "South Africa," 9.

75. Mavimbela, Oral History, 21.

76. Clark, "The Fading Curse of Cain," 45.

77. Bly, "Hope in a Torn Land," 31.

78. Fagg, "LDS Church Bringing Races Together," A4.

79. Ibid.

80. Ibid.

81. Ibid., A5.

82. Ellen Fagg, "S. Africa's Scenic Beauty in Sharp Contrast to Its Cultural Strife," *Deseret News*, March 13, 1986, A1.

83. Fagg, "LDS Church Bringing Races Together," A5.

African whites saw "the blacks" as an "omnipresent threat."[84] One Afrikaaner grudgingly accepted integration, grumbling: "I don't like it, but if that's the way the Lord told his prophet, it's got to be and I have to learn to accept it."[85]

Temple President Reed J. Webster acknowledged that some white South African Saints felt uneasy with the changes: "Old ideologies are hard to change with any group, and with the strong dominant South African white, changes are even more difficult. Some had expressed the thought that they were not sure what they would do if the hand of a black man should come through the veil," a reference to Mormon temple rituals. Webster recalled a black ordinance worker "put[ting] his hand through the veil" while "acting in his calling." Meanwhile, "on the other side of the veil," Webster continued, were two white South Africans, both known for being "strongly opinioned" about the racial hierarchy. "What went on in their minds only they know," Webster noted, "but the decision to follow the gospel plan was instantaneous and the work proceeded normally."[86]

Vivien Clark recalls "people pray[ing] all the time for peace in our country… every opening and closing prayer included prayers for peace." Government propaganda, she felt, "had really brainwashed people into believing the Blacks just wanted to annihilate whites."[87] In March 1990, whites in Queenstown "had a special peace march" to protest the ongoing violence. They "marched out to the Black community in the outskirts of town to go to church with them." The local police chief arranged for a strong presence "if anything happened from the march."[88]

The violence was generally "quite removed" from the Mormon missionaries. "Life for us is peaceful," Arlene Bateman wrote her family from the safety of her home.[89] But, she also reminded them, "it IS terrible."[90] Still, they felt as "safe as if we were anywhere in the world." After all, she quipped, "this old terra firma doesn't offer an excess of safety in any of its four corners, does it?"[91] Temple President Reed J. Webster observed that "knifings and shootings are the norm"

---

84. Clark, "The Fading Curse of Cain," 53.

85. Newell G. Bringhurst, "Mormonism in Black Africa: Changing Attitudes and Practices, 1830–1981," 21 note 26.

86. Webster, "Africa's Firsts," in "Reflections on the Great South African Experience," 1.

87. Vivien Clark, Correspondence with Russell Stevenson, November 8, 2013; emphasis hers.

88. Carol Howell, quoted in Donovan Howell, Mission Journal, March 12, 1990. Some reports suggest that Mormon scientist Larry Ford provided South African government officials with biological weapons to be used against the black population. However, weapons researchers associated with the South African government determined that the weapons were "useless." They "come with big talk and fancy stuff and gave us a lot of so-called-dirty tricks materials." But when the material was analyzed, "it came to nothing of substance." Edward Humes, "The Medicine Man," *Los Angeles Magazine*, July 2001, 95–99, 166–68, and Scott Martelle, Jeff Gottlieb, and Jack Leonard, "A Doctor, a Deal Maker, and a Mystery," *Los Angeles Times*, March 20, 2000, http://articles.latimes.com/2000/mar/20/news/mn-10791/2 (accessed June 3, 2013).

89. Arlene Bateman, Letter to Family, April 11, 1991, Maurice Bateman Temple Papers, LDS Church History Library.

90. Arlene Bateman, Letter to family, ca. April 1991.

91. Ibid., Letter to Family, June 9, 1991.

in Johannesburg; after one nighttime shooting, Webster and his wife "agreed that the situation was also beyond our control, punched the pillows a couple times and drifted off into oblivion." Eventually, missionaries moved to a cloistered area called Dukes Flats, widely considered to be "one of the safest areas" of Johannesburg with an adjoining shopping center and closer to the temple.[92] General Authority Richard P. Lindsay had dedicated the complex to be "safe from the influences that seem so pervasive in this country."[93]

When apartheid was finally overturned and Nelson Mandela came to power in 1992, he took special measures to create an atmosphere of forgiveness and tolerance. Notably, in 1995, the Truth and Reconciliation Commission assembled to provide a public venue in which the former South African government officials and black South Africans could engage in a public dialogue in hopes of promoting healing and peace.[94] When Vivien Clark's daughter, Eleanor, met Mandela as an adolescent, she said that meeting him was "like meeting a General Authority." The "peace the man exudes is amazing."[95]

Mormons in Utah wrangled over what to make of the South African regime. In early 1978, U.S. Senator Edward Brooke, speaking at BYU, identified opposition to apartheid as one "cause in which both groups [blacks and Mormons] find merit."[96] Ruth Heidt, a Mormon anti-apartheid activist, credited her fellow Saints for having "strong opinions on this issue" but criticized them for being "unwilling to speak out."[97] Indeed, an *Ensign* article about the Saints in South Africa avoided assessing the morality of apartheid altogether, mentioning matter-of-factly that the government "pursues a policy of apartheid, or separate development for all of the distinctive peoples that make up its population." Though the article's author, Lawrence Cummins, privately grieved over the evils of apartheid, he acknowledged this description to be "simplistic but still reliable."[98]

Mormon political figures winked at the apartheid regime. Centerville resident Carma Jenkins warned that a failure to support South Africa would threaten the American economy and undermine America's moral high ground. "Seventy percent of our strategic metals . . . are available to us only from South Africa and

---

92. Reed J. Webster, "In the Beginning," "Reflections on the Great South African Experience," n.d., ca. 1992, 2, Bateman Temple Papers.

93. Richard Lindsay, Dedicatory Prayer, September 22, 1991, transcript.

94. For discussions of the racial reconciliation process in South Africa and its main actors, see Claire Moon, *Narrating Political Reconciliation: South Africa's Truth and Reconciliation;* Brian Frost, *Struggling to Forgive: Nelson Mandela and South Africa's Search for Reconciliation; Desmond Tutu: Rabble-Rouser for Peace: The Authorized Biography;* and Megan Shore, *Religion and Conflict Resolution: Christianity and South Africa's Truth and Reconciliation Commission.*

95. Eleanor Clark, Correspondence with Russell Stevenson, November 9, 2013.

96. Dialogue Editorial Board, "Senator Edward W. Brooke at BYU," 120.

97. Benjamin Harris, "'In Deed and in Word': The Anti-Apartheid Movement at the University of Utah, 1978–1987," 267–68.

98. Lawrence E. Cummins, "The Saints in South Africa," 4. For Cummins's feelings about apartheid, see Lavina Fielding Anderson, Correspondence with Russell Stevenson, December 24, 2013.

the Soviet Union," Human rights abuses in Communist nations were "far worse than apartheid." Why, she asked, "does our country always show charity towards enemies of human freedom and malice?" She continued to work for American companies in Africa at various times in subsequent years.[99] The heavily Mormon Utah State Legislature hesitated. Congress had long been considering sanctions against the regime, but mining industries—some of them based in Utah—were concerned that sanctions would make business impossible. In 1987, Mormon lobbyist Jeff Flake observed, that if Pieter Botha's government "fell to radical elements from the left . . . we would be deprived of an economic source of these vital minerals." Flake insisted that sanctions would have "a dramatic impact on the black population" as "American companies pull[ed] out," leaving South Africans without access to American subsidies. Flake insisted that opposing the sanctions "coincides with our moral standards."[100] At a Weber State University panel discussion, Ogden Mormon Gary Jaggi declared that "there's a myth that whites (in South Africa) mistreat blacks" and "there are greater freedoms there than in the rest of . . . Africa, much of which is Soviet controlled." His comments invited sharp rebuttals from a Nigerian exchange student who "resented [Jaggi] saying that a lot of Africans are communists." Why is it, he asked Jaggi, "that everyone fighting for his freedom is labeled communist?"[101]

Mormon State Senator Paul Rogers crafted a resolution opposing sanctions against the apartheid government, arguing that sanctions "would have a more direct [and, by implication, negative] impact on the black community in South African than on the white economy" and would "alienate those in the government who have been working toward genuine social reform."[102] U.S. Senator Jake Garn "opposed mandatory sanctions against South Africa" so staunchly that a lobbyist for TransAfrica considered Garn to be a "hopeless cause."[103] Much of the anti-apartheid legislation focused on withholding American funds from Botha's government, a tactic that even some anti-apartheid activists saw as reducing American leverage.[104] When Congress passed anti-apartheid legislation the

99. Carma Jenkins, "Communist Inspired?" *Davis County Clipper* (Bountiful, UT), September 19, 1985, 17.

100. "Jeff Flake Lobbied for Utah Bill Supporting South African Regime," audio recording on YouTube, http://www.youtube.com/watch?v=w7HYMrhU-R0&feature=youtu.be (accessed June 14, 2013).

101. "Angry Emotions Erupt at WSC Meeting," *Davis County Clipper* (Bountiful, UT), February 26, 1987, 3.

102. Resolution 2, Working Bills, Utah State Senate, Utah State Archives, Box 63, fd. 39, http://images.archives.utah.gov/cdm/compoundobject/collection/428/id/144058/rec/7 (accessed August 8, 2013).

103. "Death of South Africa Bill Truly Shameful," *Oregonian* (Portland), October 23, 1984, B5; "Heinz Taken to Task on Economic Sanctions," *Morning Call* (Allentown, PA) July 25, 1984, http://articles.mcall.com/1984-07-25/news/2434721_1_sen-john-heinz-economic-sanctions-black-leaders (accessed December 31, 2013).

104. "Heinz Asked to Pressure S. Africa," *Pittsburgh Post-Gazette*, July 25, 1984, 6.

following year and overruled Reagan's veto, Garn was absent in order to donate a kidney to his diabetic daughter.[105]

"We Must Get Rid of Hate"

In the United States, Church leaders took more rapid steps toward full integration. At the October 1978 general conference following the announcement of Official Declaration—2, no speaker mentioned the revelation directly. Apostle James E. Faust hinted at the Church's new stance when he observed that he "was born with partial color-blindness" and had "learned to love all of the people in the countries where I have been as a missionary, soldier, or General Authority, regardless of the color of their skins."[106] In February 1979, Apostle Howard W. Hunter made the case even more clearly: "Race makes no difference; color makes no difference; nationality makes no difference." The "brotherhood of man is literal," he assured BYU students during a devotional address. He implored the Saints to "lift your vision beyond personal prejudices" to "discover the supreme truth that indeed our Father is no respecter of persons."[107]

Yet as BYU English professor and folklorist Richard C. Poulsen wrote in 1988: "Folkloristic perceptions of blacks have not appreciably changed since 1978."[108] Armand L. Mauss has concluded that the Church struck a "rather ambivalent position . . . in public relations terms since 1978" in its effort to "support some of the political and cultural interests of African Americans" even as it has tried to "live down its own racist past."[109] It would take another generation for these tensions to find any degree of resolution.

Indeed, despite his famous call for the Saints to "forget everything," Bruce R. McConkie continued to associate lineage with premortal worthiness in much of his writings. As the Church's leading scripturalist, his writings continued to serve as a defining source of Mormon thought. Even if he had disavowed the priesthood ban, his arguments continued to influence Mormon perspectives on race and lineage. In 1979, he published a third edition of *Mormon Doctrine* removing all discussion of premortal worthiness and noting only that "in the providences of the Lord the gospel and all its attendant blessings are offered to one nation and people after another."[110] However, in works such as *The Millennial Messiah,* McConkie continued to maintain that premortal worthiness led to an increased enjoyment of favored status: "This is the doctrine of election," McConkie wrote, "[Israelites] were true and faithful in the premortal life, and they earned the right

105. "Reagan Upstaged, But Bows to Veto," *Bangor Daily News* (Maine), October 6, 1986, A10.
106. James E. Faust, "Response to the Call," *Ensign,* November 1978, 20.
107. Howard W. Hunter, "All Are Alike Unto God," 32.
108. Richard C. Poulsen, *Misbegotten Muses: History and Anti-History,* 11.
109. Armand L. Mauss, "Casting Off the 'Curse of Cain,'" 103.
110. Bruce R. McConkie, *Mormon Doctrine,* 3rd ed. (1979), 526.

to be born as the Lord's people and to have the privilege, on a preferential basis, of believing and obeying the word of truth."[111]

The problems of healing past racial wounds were not confined to Church leaders; Mormon scholars felt the need to grapple with the new atmosphere in their own way. Some sought to reconsider the possibility that the ban originated with Joseph Smith. Ronald Esplin questioned Lester Bush's work, suggesting that it was his "feeling that the doctrine was introduced at least by 1843, although it would require additional documentation to raise the possibility from the realm of the probable to the certain."[112]

But most authors sought to redefine Mormonism's racial narrative rather than rescuscitate the old one. Jerald R. Johansen, a former missionary to South Africa and Church Educational System institute instructor, wrote a commentary on the Pearl of Great Price in 1985, a chapter of which was entitled "The Deeper Roots of Black Civilization." In it he echoed the longstanding claim that blacks were the descendants of Cain. Connecting Mormon scripture with the popular miniseries, *Roots,* Johansen wrote that the Pearl of Great Price "tells us of the 'the roots beyond roots' of the great black peoples." Noting that Egyptians "had descended from Ham and Egyptus" and ultimately Cain, he implored the Saints to "look beyond the infamous murderer in the black heritage. . . . [M]an will be punished for his own sins, and not *Cain's* transgressions."[113]

Johansen suggests that Abraham "may have given the Higher Priesthood and the Temple Endowment to the faithful converts—who may have been black," a fact, he acknowledged, that might be "hard for some members of the Church today to accept." With the release of Official Declaration—2, Johansen declared that "we, too, must go to 'strange lands' and teach the descendants of Cain." When they did, the Saints "will be but walking in the footsteps of our great father Abraham."[114]

A 1980 Institute manual suggested that since "black Africans of Ethiopia claim to be descendants of King David through the marriage of King Solomon and the Queen of Sheba," it was "possible that the blood of Israel spread through Africa as well."[115] In 1986, John M. Goddard echoed his affection for "primitive" Africa and celebrated African societies, observing that "when you live with primitives and villagers and observe the quality of their lives compared to what we have in our modern, affluent, technologically advanced societies, you wonder who's really living the most intelligently."[116]

---

111. Bruce R. McConkie, *The Millennial Messiah: The Second Coming of the Son of Man,* 182.

112. Ronald K. Esplin, "Brigham Young and Priesthood Denial to the Blacks: An Alternative View," 399.

113. Jerald Ray Johansen, *A Commentary on the Pearl of Great Price: A Jewel Among the Scriptures,* 95–97.

114. Ibid., 95–97.

115. *Old Testament Student Manual,* 1st ed. (1980), 83.

116. Gary Stockdale and Patricia Campbell, "Interview: John Goddard," 33.

To correct the enduring misconceptions as well as to distance themselves from old doctrines, high-level and local Church leaders engaged in a public relations campaign aimed at black populations both in the United States and abroad. The *Church News* published an unsigned editorial condemning race riots in Miami, declaring that "we must get rid of hate" that "can destroy us, and will, unless we put an end to racial conflict."[117]

In 1989 Elder J. Thomas Fyans, a member of the First Quorum of the Seventy, spoke at an anti-racism symposium sponsored by the Citizens Against Racism. Echoing and expanding upon comments Hugh B. Brown made in 1963, he declared that ideas about racial superiority are "absolutely wrong" and that it is a "moral evil for any person or group of persons to deny any human being the rights to gainful employment, to full educational opportunity, or to every privilege of citizenship." Fyans's comments were public, but the *LDS Church News* published them in a small box tucked toward the back of paper.[118]

Whatever mixed messages endured, the Church's membership generally embraced Church expansion into the black community. The first ordinations of black men to the priesthood occurred within hours of the announcement, the first being Joseph Freeman of Salt Lake City.[119] Nine years later in 1987, integration was adjudged sufficiently successful that the Genesis Group ceased to meet regularly, though in recent years, the custom of monthly Sunday meetings and weekend socials has revived, providing support and sociality for racially mixed marriages—not just black and white, but white-Polynesian and white-Latino.[120]

Church publications began to publish a series of articles celebrating the growth of Mormonism in West Africa. The African story took hold of the Mormon consciousness. Janath Cannon told one correspondent that "more mail [is] received by the missions of the Church in Ghana than by the rest of the International Mission areas put together."[121] In *This People,* a popular magazine targeted at Mormons, Mali's Mobido Diarra was presented to Mormon readers for his timeless sagacity. Journalist Maurine Jensen Proctor took an exotic tack by noting that he "looks . . . like a tribal chieftain" or "perhaps a jungle shaman," even though Modibo was the president of Mali's teachers' union and had spent time in jail for lobbying the government to increase teacher salaries.[122] Mobido would be instrumental in the establishment of the 1985 partnership between

---

117. "Get Rid of Hate," *Deseret News*, May 31, 1980, 16.

118. "Church's Message Is One of Concern for All Men," *LDS Church News*, January 21, 1989, 13.

119. Joseph Freeman, *In the Lord's Due Time.*

120. Jessie L. Embry, "Separate But Equal? Black Branches, Genesis Groups, or Integrated Wards?" 15.

121. Janath Cannon, Letter to "Sister Barrucand," June 24, 1976. The letter was incorrectly dated. Though Cannon could have been aware of Ghana correspondence through her husband's work as president of the International Mission, the letter itself indicates that at the time of writing, Cannon was serving in Nigeria and Ghana. The date almost certainly should have been June 24, 1979.

122. Maurine Jensen Proctor, "Modibo Diarra: Mali Mormon," 22.

the Malian town of Ouelessebougu and the state of Utah that continues to the present.[123] By 2004 the alliance had enabled the digging of eighty-nine water wells, the building of seventeen gardens and twenty-four schools, and the training of eighty-nine health workers.[124] The Saints in West Africa, one *Ensign* article observed, were "humble, truth-seeking Christians who have known little about the Church, except that they need to know more."[125]

The Mabeys and Cannons took pains to spread the word of the African miracle. Delivering lectures and presentations throughout the state, they delighted in detailing the unique blend of religious traditions that made up African Mormonism. "They had collection plates, a lot of Pentecostal hallelujahs, singing, dancing, and drums." Janath Cannon told the *Ensign* that the missionaries couldn't "just go in and say, 'You can't do this.'" The missionaries "had to tell them what they *can* do. . . . They not only have to learn new things, they have to unlearn a lot of old things."[126]

William Lye, Utah State University history professor and vice president of university relations, cast Africa as a continent with "an old and venerable heritage" in an article commissioned by the *Ensign*. He condemned the "legacy of colonialism" even as he celebrated African nations' efforts to "increase[e] their level of literacy: building roads, railways, hospitals, schools, and other facilities; and developing industries geared to their needs."[127] In 1994, former South African Mission President E. Dale LeBaron called the first generation of African converts "gospel pioneers in Africa."[128] Canadian General Authority, physician, and United Nations nutrition adviser Alexander B. Morrison declared that the West Africans were "a people prepared by the Spirit of God." He added that "the time of harvest has come" as the Saints "witness[ed] the dawning of a new day" in Africa: "Our black African brothers and sisters" are "anxious to learn and quick to understand, attentive and responsive, spiritually sensitive, thirsty for the living water and hungry for the bread of life." Truly, Morrison declared, "they long have been in preparation for this day."[129] The narrative the Saints had written for themselves was seamless, with Official Declaration—2 appearing as the culmination of over a century of preparation. The 1978 expansion of Mormonism into Africa was all part of the plan.

Elders Samuel Bainson and Benjamin Sampson-Davis presented an image of African humility and devotion for American Mormon readers. An *Ensign* article observed that "their smiles radiated enthusiasm; their gracious manners spoke well of the education they had received in Ghana; and their clearly articulated

123. Jan Thompson, "Like a Rope Lowered from Heaven," 12–13, 15–16, 19, 21.

124. John M. Mbaku, *Institutions and Development in Africa*, 78.

125. Janet Brigham, "Nigeria and Ghana: A Miracle Precedes the Messengers," 73.

126. Ibid.

127. William Lye, "From Burundi to Zaire: Taking the Gospel to Africa," 14–15. For Lye's qualifications, see Fagg, "LDS Church Bringing Races of South Africa Together," A4.

128. E. Dale LeBaron, "Gospel Pioneers in Africa," 40.

129. Alexander Morrison, "The Dawning of a New Day in Africa," 25.

responses to questions made it obvious that they were ready to serve."[130] African Mormondom excited white American Mormons—seeing a new gospel land open up before their eyes. But Africans and African Americans remained within the realm of the exotic rather than the realm of the normative.

Above all, the West African expansion was depicted as a tidal wave of converts. In 1987, Beverly Campbell, the Church public relations head in Washington, D.C., claimed that "literally whole villages are waiting to be baptized."[131] Rendell and Rachel Mabey described segments of their mission in *This People*, detailing how much the West Africans needed to learn and their efforts to teach them the finer points of American Mormonism. But more importantly, they echoed Campbell's image, speaking of a Mormon message that "spreads so fast we just couldn't handle it." Sometimes, the Cannons grew so weary that they began to "drag our feet."[132] More couples were called to serve in Nigeria and Ghana, including Reed and Naomi Clegg, Frank and Clora Martin, and Victor and Eleanor Bartholomew.[133] Years later, Clegg admitted that he found the calling inconvenient, until Naomi "reminded me that I had long agonized over the status of the blacks in the Church and in our society." Serving in Ghana gave him the opportunity to "put conviction into practice."[134]

Various Church leaders took special care to reach out to the American black community in a variety of high-publicity venues. In 1987, the Twenty-first Ward in Salt Lake City sponsored the Ebony Rose Black History Conference that featured Mary Bankhead, a longstanding black member and descendant of an old black pioneer family.[135] Throughout the 1990s, Church publications presented profiles on black Mormons throughout the United States. On occasion, Church officials drew on the Saints' world-renowned reputation as genealogists to reach out to the black community. In Southern California, the LDS Church co-sponsored an African American genealogical conference featuring Chris Haley, nephew of Alex Haley, as the keynote speaker.[136] Beginning in 1995, LDS genealogists worked tirelessly to compile records for the Freedman's Bank, a bank organized after the U.S. Civil War for freed slaves.[137] But it was not until 1987 that Utah recognized Martin Luther King Day as a holiday worthy of celebration, having previously called it "Human Rights Day."[138]

---

130. Marvin K. Gardner, "Two Elders Called from Ghana," 78.

131. "Mormons Try to Cope with Influx in Africa," *Salina [Kans.] Journal*, March 7, 1987, 16.

132. "Rendell and Rachel Mabey: A Mission to West Africa," 24–37.

133. "Praises Clegg," *Deseret News*, January 14, 1980, A4; Clegg, "Friends of West Africa," 94–95.

134. Clegg, "Friends of West Africa," 94.

135. Armand L. Mauss, *All Abraham's Children: Changing Mormon Conceptions of Race and Lineage*, 245.

136. Ibid., 247.

137. "Freedman's Bank: Boosting Research for African Americans," *LDS Church News*, March 3, 2001, 3.

138. "Martin Luther King to Be Honored with Holiday Celebration," *Davis County Clipper* (Bountiful, Utah), January 15, 1987, 2.

Missionary work expanded into the American urban black population. A surprising symbol of urban black Mormonism was Eldridge Cleaver, the former Minister of Information for the Black Panthers. Cleaver became acquainted with the Church during his exploration of political conservatism and his exposure to Cleon Skousen's political organization, the Freemen Institute. In spring 1981, Skousen was so impressed that he arranged for Cleaver to be a regular lecturer.[139] "I've been very pleased with what I'm finding (with the Mormon Church). . . . I just feel at home," Cleaver told a reporter in 1981.[140] Cleaver had also investigated the theology of the Korean billionaire and self-styled Korean prophet, Sun Myung Moon.

Cleaver's interest in Mormonism struck a nerve for Mormons of all leanings. On December 4, Oakland Mission President Owen K. Earl interviewed Cleaver in preparation for baptism. The mission history reported that Cleaver was "very sincere in his desire to become a member of the Church, and has been ready for some time." Cleaver told Earl that the "Brethren . . . had asked him to postpone it until he had completed his probation, served his community service, and gotten his legal problems behind him," all of which he had done. On December 11, 1983, Carl Loeber baptized Cleaver a member of the LDS Church in the Oakland Stake Center. On the same day that Dennis Lauper, a local humanitarian, prominent member of the community, and bishop of Oakland Third Ward, learned of Cleaver's baptism, he "met with Pres[ident] Earl" to express that he "was very upset about Cleaver coming into the Church." Earl "counseled forgiveness."[141]

Journalist Peggy Fletcher thought Cleaver an opportunist and the Saints his all-too-willing dupes: too often, she wrote, we "measure ourselves by the standards of the world . . . mak[ing] us vulnerable to the manipulations of Eldr[i]dge Cleavers."[142] Skousen signed Cleaver as a Freemen Institute lecturer seven months before his baptism.[143]

In Los Angeles, missionaries began "showing films in parking lots, and just generally talking to people on the streets" of Watts. When the Los Angeles Police Department learned of the missionaries' efforts, they urged the mission presidency to exercise greater caution due to the "dangers in the area." President F. Briton McConkie, Bruce R. McConkie's brother, removed most of the missionaries, although he left two in the area "because they [physically] resembled the

---

139. Newell G. Bringhurst, "Eldridge Cleaver's Passage through Mormonism," 90.

140. Eldridge Cleaver, in "People in the News," *Greensboro [N.C.] Daily News*, April 7, 1981, 9.

141. Oakland Mission Historical Reports, LR 1314/3, December 4, 1983, Box 1, fd. 1. In 1969, Lauper was elected as president of the East Bay Association for Retarded Children (EBARC). Lauper took the helm of the organization during a time of expansion; that same year, the EBARC absorbed several other organizations such as the Mobilized Women of Berkeley (MOBY) and other local groups for children with mental retardation difficulties. See "The LDS Scene," Improvement Era 72, no. 7 (July 1969): 83; and "Children's Retarded Units Will Be Merged," Oakland Tribune, March 14, 1969, 3, http://www.oac.cdlib.org/findaid/ark:/13030/hb421005vz/ (accessed March 7, 2014).

142. Peggy Fletcher, "A Light Unto The World: Image-Building is Anathema to Christian Living," 21.

143. "Cleaver for Change," *Trenton Evening Times*, May 22, 1983, 12.

blacks so much."[144] The mission replaced door-to-door tracting with "telephone tracting" where missionaries made cold calls to residents of the Watts black community. Mission leadership found that contacts "were more willing to . . . talk to a person on the phone, when they will not at the door." The program enabled mission leadership to establish the area's first Mormon congregation in December 1979. Given the demographics, mission leadership took to calling it the "black branch." Robert Lang, a black member for more than twelve years, served as the congregation's first leader.[145]

Briton McConkie enthused over this new program, declaring that "blacks are ready for the gospel, and through the telephone calls by missionaries, these people are being introduced to it and accepting."[146] In June 1980, he arranged for a "special black fireside" in which "various black members were asked to bear their testimony" and tell their conversion stories. Paul Devine, a member of fifteen years and later winner of the Mr. Universe competition, was one of the speakers.[147] The branch was but a provisional organization; Mormon blacks had to face the reality that their faith community continued to be overwhelmingly white. In 1987, the black branch dissolved as Church leaders urged black members to attend their home wards. Devine, who served for a time as the unit's branch president, was grateful it existed as "a means of fellowship for blacks." However, Devine felt "many used it as a crutch . . . and a lot of blacks are still afraid they won't be accepted and treated fairly."[148]

In September 1983, sociologist Armand Mauss delivered a lecture at the Oakland Third Ward Chapel that was "filled to overflowing" on "how we reached the point we now find ourselves at—with the policy changed thru [sic] revelation, after President Kimball went to the Lord about it." Mauss told the Saints that "what we now do with that is much more important than how we got here" and that it is "imperative that we learn to deal with and love one another so that the gospel can have a real impact in the lives of both Whites and Blacks."[149]

The first black sister missionary was Mary Sturlaugson, a native of Chattanooga, Tennessee. Ardently committed to promoting black racial causes, Sturlaugson had long harbored a negative opinion of whites, especially white Mormons. In 1975, she went to college at Dakota Wesleyan University and noticed immediately the scarcity of black people. Initially, she refused to associate with whites; when offered a ride to campus with some white college students, she

---

144. "Telephone Tracting," and "Mission History of the Black Program," 1, 5–7 in California Los Angeles Mission History, 1981, LR 1316, LDS Church History Library. My thanks to Grace Stephenson for directing me to this resource.

145. Ibid., 1, 5–7.

146. Ibid., "Historical Events" (Section B), September 16, 1979.

147. Ibid., "Historical Events" (Section B), June 29, 1980.

148. Russell Chandler, "Door Is Opened: Mormonism: A Challenge for Blacks," *Los Angeles Times*, August 12, 1988.

149. Oakland Mission Historical Reports, LR 1314/3, September 6, 1983, Box 1, fd. 1.

responded curtly that "my daddy did not approve of my being in the company of whites and neither did I."[150] Even when offered a ride with the college president, she responded: "White's still white, and I'm not riding with no honky."[151] While serving on the cheerleading squad, she cheered for teams that had a black player: "My loyalty went to my race first and my school second."[152]

When Sturlaugson first met the Mormon missionaries, she invited them in because, as she later recalled: "I wanted to tell them what I thought of Mormons." After the missionaries invited her to attend church, she screamed: "I'll never attend your stinking church!" When her roommate prodded her, she went but left unimpressed. The missionaries refused to give up: "Day after day they returned with their message, and day after day we told them in no uncertain terms to get lost." On one occasion, she invited them over for dinner, "boiled some water, . . . threw the water on them, closed the door, and laughed." She regularly made "threats on their lives." Finally, she caved, telling the missionaries: "Either you guys are crazy or I am, so come on in so I can be sure it's not me." Though Sturlaugson was skeptical, the humility of the missionaries touched her: "I saw love on those two faces." Over time, "the missionaries' patience and concern" opened "the doors . . . to love and understanding."[153]

In 1976, Sturlaugson joined the Church and transferred to Brigham Young University. Her family threatened to disown her and warned her that joining the LDS Church would make her "a rotten traitor to my race and to my family."[154] In September 1978, she received her mission call to San Antonio, Texas.[155] Like other black Mormons, she gave presentations throughout the country; in September 1983, she gave a presentation in Oakland that was "well received and well attended."[156]

But real progress in the United States was elusive. In 1983, Genesis president Ruffin Bridgeforth acknowledged that "there haven't been a great number of black people to come into the church."[157] BYU football coach LaVell Edward indicated that he was "trying to attract more."[158] In 1985, black BYU defensive back Mark Sherman quipped that Provo, Utah, was a place where "Beaver Cleaver could live and June would be happy." He looked forward to "going back to California and the real world."[159] Another black athlete observed that it was "a whole different atmosphere" than his more cosmopolitan home. He was "doing well . . . but it's

150. Mary Francis Sturlaugson, *A Soul So Rebellious,* 25.

151. Ibid.

152. Ibid., 33.

153. Ibid., 38–40.

154. Ibid., 44.

155. "Black Woman Changed Mind about Mormons," *Aberdeen [S.D.] Daily News,* September 9, 1978, 9.

156. Oakland Mission, Historical Reports, LR 1314/3, September 23, 1983, Box 1, fd. 1.

157. Michael White, "Few Blacks Join Mormons," *Mobile [Ala.] Register,* June 9, 1983, C11.

158. Nick Bertram, "BYU Defies Odds, Builds Powerhouse," *[Portland] Oregonian,* September 14, 1985, E1.

159. Mark Sherman, qtd. in ibid.

something you have to get used to."[160] Van Williams, a black public communications employee, told the Associated Press that, when white members met him, "the first question I get is, 'Where did you play ball?'"[161]

In Barbados, Church missionary work came under sustained accusations of racism from local religious leaders. "No North American cult can be free to fool our people," Reverend Gerry Seale of the Barbados Christian Council declared. Kenneth Zabriskie, president of the LDS West Indies Mission, responded to the attacks directly, declaring that the Saints "are not racist," that they "now do, and always have, accepted people of all races for baptism into the Church as equal candidates for salvation in the Kingdom of God." "We are not racist," he repeated, "we would not be here today if we were."[162] Zabriskie felt that, provided black Mormon communities became self-sustaining units, he could shake off the accusation of racism.

In 1988, the First Presidency issued a statement "repudiat[ing] efforts to deny to any person his or her inalienable dignity and rights on the abhorrent and tragic theory of the superiority of one race or color over another."[163] The statement received little press play, placed as it was in the back of the *Ensign*. But the First Presidency did not use the word "tragic" vainly; racial issues had been the Church's Achilles' heel for five generations.

Though white Mormons across the country expressed elation that they no longer had to carry the burden of the race restriction, many struggled to know *how* to embrace the new position. The ban had left a legacy, the *Marietta Journal* observed "a lingering perception that Mormonism is a faith for whites."[164]

Buses

As McConkie and others were taking special efforts to reach African Americans, white Mormons in Los Angeles expressed their racial anxieties through the political avenue. Understanding white Mormons' struggles with racial integration in Los Angeles requires a discussion of the intricate legal and political developments in regards to the most controversial of California's integration programs: busing.

In 1963, the California Supreme Court ruled in *Jackson v. Pasadena School District* that the state constitution's equal protection clause prohibited both *de jure* (legally sanctioned) and *de facto* (geographically driven) segregation. In

---

160. Bob Lipper, "BYU: Pollsters Converted—for Now," *Richmond [Va.] Times Dispatch*, November 21, 1984, D5.

161. Michael White and Vern Anderson, "Mormons Try to End Racism Reputation," *Marietta [Ga.] Journal*, June 4, 1988, A4.

162. "Controversy Stirs around Mormons in the Caribbean," *The Day* (New London, Conn.), August 31, 1985, A9.

163. "News of the Church: Church Issues Statement on Racial Equality," *Ensign*, February 1988, 74.

164. Ibid.

1976, the State Supreme Court directed the Los Angeles Unified School District to present a plan that would end segregation in all of its manifestations.

The Los Angeles Unified School District instituted a busing program that required white students to ride buses several miles across the city to attend schools dominated by black and Latino students. Los Angeles businessman and former David Thomsen responded by establishing a private school in the area, the Palisades Village School. Enraged by the busing system, Thomsen said that "any politician who thinks I am going to let my children be bused into Watts is crazy." While "Jesse Jackson may be worried about the children of mankind," Thomsen told the press, "I'm worried about my own four."[165] The busing program attracted widespread criticism, winning support from conservative whites throughout the county. Frightened white parents throughout Los Angeles County either placed their children in private schools or arranged to have their children attend in wealthier areas such as Burbank or Santa Monica.

For the previous two years, Democratic State Senator Alan Robbins had been watching the politics of busing closely. Robbins was an unlikely ally of Mormon causes. Raised in racially integrated North Hollywood, he shared the stage with Jane Fonda in favor of the Equal Rights Amendment, a measure that the LDS Church mobilized its women and its funding to defeat.[166] While he had always opposed busing, he had not seen it as a fruitful political issue, even chastising Los Angeles Mayor Tom Bradley in 1977 for "injecting the busing issue into the mayor's race." But Robbins had a keen sense for the trajectory of the political waves. Sensing the opportunity to win a large swath of white conservative voters, he crafted Proposition 1, a constitutional amendment that abolished "obligations or responsibilities which exceed those imposed by the Equal Protection Clause of the 14th Amendment to the United States Constitution." Robbins's efforts were wildly popular. "We love all kids," the Proposition 1 stickers declared. He secured the support of prominent African American voices such as Reverend William Jackson and concerned black parents. "How brutal can we be to impose this action . . . on little children? We'd rather have $100 million spent on books and teaching aids than $100 million spent on busing." A black mother, Eleanor Fitzhugh, feared that busing would turn her neighborhood into a "ghost town." Latino activist Vahac Mardirosian promised area Mexican Americans that, "if parents understand that this process of desegregation ultimately will result in

---

165. Richard Reeves, "Parents Revolt on School Issue," *Lakeland [Fla.] Ledger*, October 11, 1980, 14A.

166. Daniel Martinez-Hosang, "Changing Valence of White Racial Innocence: Black-Brown Unity in the 1970s Los Angeles School Desegregation Struggles," 128. For a fuller treatment of the Mormons' role in the Equal Rights Amendment, see Mary L. Bradford, "Beverly Campbell: Dynamic Spokesperson," 50–54; *The Church and the Proposed Equal Rights Amendment: A Moral Issue*, pamphlet, bound in March 1980 *Ensign*. For a critical treatment juxtaposing the Mormon opposition to the ERA with the nineteenth-century push for Mormon women's equality, see Martha Sonntag Bradley, *Pedestals and Podiums: Utah Women, Religious Authority, and Equal Rights*.

a better future for their children," most "would be willing to live with the additional anxiety."[167]

Drawing on the organizational strength of Bill Butcher and Arnold Forde's political marketing firm, Robbins effectively exploited the existing unease about what many felt was coerced social experimentation. Although Robbins's amendment died in committee hearings in summer 1978, he mounted public support to place it on the ballot in November 1979. Three weeks before Proposition 1 went to ballot, just under 80 percent of voters opposed "busing designed to achieve racial balance."[168] The proposition passed with an overwhelming majority of 68 percent.

For the next eighteen months, the future of the busing program hung in the balance. In February 1980, Governor Edmund Brown vetoed a measure that excluded California from U.S. Supreme Court rulings requiring school districts to prove *de jure* integration. The veto infuriated Robbins: "The governor is going to get this veto shoved right down his throat like nobody's ever had a veto shoved down their throat before."[169] But Robbins failed to win the necessary support in the assembly to override it.[170] The U.S. Supreme Court had determined busing to be constitutional in school districts where *de jure* segregation existed. That summer, the Court went further, saying that if any degree of *de jure* segregation existed, then the court must assume that it exists throughout the district.[171]

Los Angeles Mormons had their own reasons for feeling anxious about the busing program. They hoped the LDS Church would support the leasing of a Los Angeles-area chapel to a group planning to establish a school similar to Thomsen's Pacific Palisades Village. A joke circulating in Mormon circles expressed the Saints' anxiety and resentment: tithing would now be raised to 12 percent "to pay for busing."[172]

In October 1980 Church Commissioner of Education Henry B. Eyring traveled to Los Angeles to investigate. Initially, Eyring's sympathies were for the white children who were "being forced to ride buses." But as Eyring visited the private school ("crammed into the house and bungalows" near the home of late comic Stan Laurel), "ate supper with the driver of the buses," and traveled "with students as they were bused 25 miles," his views of the public education system softened. He "attend[ed] superb classes in an integrated public school" and

---

167. Daniel Martinez-Hosang, "The Triumph of Racial Liberalism: The Demise of Racial Justice," 299.

168. Ibid., 303.

169. "Brown Vetoes Anti-Busing Measure," *Observer-Reporter* (Washington, Pa.), February 5, 1980, B10.

170. "Governor Vetoes Busing Curb, Calls It Unconstitutional," *San Diego Union*, February 5, 1980, 1; "Vote Fails to Override Anti-Busing Bill Veto," *San Diego Union*, April 11, 1980, 3.

171. Otto Kreisher, "Brown Gets Bill Restricting Court Orders on Busing," *San Diego Union*, February 1, 1980, 1.

172. William A. Wilson and Richard C. Poulsen, "The Curse of Cain and Other Stories: Blacks in Mormon Folklore," 12.

learned of the difficulties Pacific Palisades faced in acquiring sufficient land to handle its exploding growth.

The following evening, Eyring and Vaughn J. Featherstone of the Seventy called a special meeting at the Santa Monica Stake Center that drew members from the "San Fernando Valley, Orange County, and all over Los Angeles." Before the meeting, Eyring prayed that he could accomplish three tasks: "teach them the truth; build their faith in their leaders in the priesthood; and help them accept that the Church would not give them Church schools."

Worried that the Los Angeles Saints would push back, Eyring and Featherstone informed the congregation of the decision. But to their surprise, the congregation accepted the decision unhesitatingly. Featherstone promised them that if they "support this decision," the "busing problem will be resolved."[173] The two General Authorities "shed a tear . . . to see them all raise their hands" to sustain the decision of the board.

As of September 1980, resolution seemed distant. Judge William Rehnquist had refused to issue a stay on the Los Angeles busing program.[174] On October 17, Republican Senate candidate Paul Gann expressed exasperated frustration about the court-ordered busing programs to a San Diego City Club: "I don't give a damn what the courts say. It's still not right, and I don't want any part of it, and I would tell people not to have any part of it," though he didn't think he had much power to stop it: "A senator can use his influence on appropriations to see that no money is used to buy those buses for busing," but "it probably won't work."[175] Matters came to a head in December when the California Court of Appeals determined that Proposition 1 was constitutional: "We do not believe a state constitution can be said to violate the Fourteenth Amendment by specifically embracing it."[176]

Though white Saints no longer needed to trouble themselves over the costs of racial integration, the episode revealed that white Mormon suburbia continued to reflect the racial values of the communities in which they lived. While willing to mingle with blacks at Church—if there were blacks in the neighborhood at all—they would not commit resources to ensure integration on the streets and in the schools, even believing that the Church would support what amounted to a racial refuge for white Mormon youth.

Now forced to reconcile their past racial views with the new policy, Mormons had to renegotiate their views, particularly as Mormonism began to spread rapidly throughout black Africa.[177] In Georgia, the *Marietta Journal* praised Church

---

173. All quotations on Eyring's visit to Los Angeles are from Robert I. Eaton and Henry J. Eyring, *I Will Lead You Along: The Life of Henry B. Eyring*, 329–31.

174. "Court Refuses to Halt LA Busing," *Dallas Morning News*, September 14, 1980, A28.

175. "Gann Vows to Fight Forced Busing, But Is Uncertain on How to Halt It," *San Diego Union*, October 18, 1980, A3.

176. *Crawford v. Board of Education*, 113 Cal. App. 3d 633 (1980).

177. Bea Lewis, "Mormons' Worldwide Expansion Finds African Missions Fertile," *Sarasota [Fl.] Herald-Tribune*, March 7, 1987, E6.

leaders for its "stunning success" in proselytizing Africans.[178] Between 1975 and 1980, the black Mormon community grew by 42 percent; but only 19 percent of that growth was among African Americans in the United States.[179] By 1987, black Mormons in South Africa outnumbered Afrikaaners by a ratio of more than 20 to 1.[180] Rank-and-file white Mormons struggled to mend fences they had long been helping to tear down. Rather than recognizing the revelation as a call for introspection and markedly changed behavior, many simply considered it a sign of the times and a relief from an onerous burden.

In 1981, Mould's convert, Samuel Bainson, served as the first African missionary after the issuing of Official Declaration—2. Called to serve in Manchester, England, his experiences illustrate the contradictions of the LDS lived racial experience in a post-Official Declaration world. Two years earlier, Bainson had immigrated to Lagos "without proper legal papers," hoping that the Americans would provide him a job and housing so that he could save money for his education. Shortly after Bainson's baptism, Edwin Cannon informed Joseph Johnson that Bainson had traveled from "from Sekondi [to Lagos] apparently without proper legal papers" and then tried to use the Church network to secure employment, asking District President Roger Curtis "to find him a job and make it possible for him to stay in Nigeria." Cannon urged Johnson to "help the members in Ghana . . . to realize that they cannot go to other Church members expecting them to act as sponsors or patrons without their prior commitment to do so." While "church members are often willing to make great sacrifices to help each other," Bainson could not ask it so freely of members, nor could he cross the porous Ghana-Nigeria border so wantonly.[181]

Perturbed, Edwin Cannon directed Joseph Johnson to "please help the members in Ghana to understand the full meaning of the Twelfth article of faith." But this rebuke for exploiting the Church network did not dampen Bainson's religious commitment. He taught the investigators' class in Lagos and had taught Mormonism freely as a member but he wanted now to preach Mormonism "officially, not as it was done . . . before" through local proselytizing. In February 1981, he received his call to serve in England and entered the MTC two months later. Apostle David B. Haight wondered at the prospects: "Here they are, the first missionaries called from West Africa. They have come to help the Church fulfill its charge to carry the message of hope and salvation to every nation, kindred, tongue, and people. What will flow from here?"[182]

178. White and Anderson, "Mormons Try to End Racism Reputation," *Marietta [Ga.] Journal*, June 4, 1988, 4.

179. Kenneth A. Briggs, "Mormons Perhaps Fastest Growing U.S. Religion," *San Diego Union*, April 2, 1980, 12.

180. Bea Lewis, "Mormons' Worldwide Expansion Finds African Missions Fertile," *Sarasota [Fl.] Herald-Tribune* March 7, 1987, 6E.

181. Edwin Cannon, Letter to Joseph Johnson, September 22, 1979.

182. "First West Africans to Serve Missions," *Deseret News*, February 28, 1981, n.p.

In England, Bainson met a warm welcome. One white Mormon missionary, Paul Huntington, happily wrote in Bainson's journal that he had "learned a great deal from you and have grown to love you." Bainson had "made this door what it is supposed to be." When Bainson received his temple endowment, he observed that "people were so nice to us and all wanted to express to me how proud they were to have me in the house of the Lord." Then on March 20, 1981, he met "the Prophet of God face to face." He was overawed by this man, whom Bainson referred to in reverential terms as "his divinity, Spencer W. Kimball." Bainson felt Kimball's palpable joy. He "kissed me 6 (six) times on the cheek."[183] Bainson rejoiced that President Kimball had "received from the Lord in revelation" to give "the holy Priesthood authority to all worthy male members of the Kingdom of the Lord on earth, of which I have benefitted greatly and [am] so willing to share the blessing of the gospel with others."[184]

Bainson found some white members' praise to be awkward and halting, although he tried to accept it graciously. "Many of the students thought it special to come and shake hands" when he visited the Brigham Young University campus. BYU Professor Dr. Spencer Palmer, he wrote, "just found it special to associate with us, somehow." He saw "people come from all walks of life to have a glimpse of us." One woman struggled to know how best to praise him: "You're just special—all your people."[185]

Bainson felt uncomfortable with the praise. "People think we are famous . . . but I think I need to do more to be part with [of] such recognition given me in the World," he confided to his diary. At times, he "became so dejected and felt so unconfident in myself of the great work ahead." Bainson exercised self-control when the other missionaries teased him, and one of them acknowledged: "Even though we joke around with you and say things about you, you always laugh with us." The missionaries gave Bainson the immature advice that they might have written in high school yearbooks: "Stay cool," and when he returned from his mission, women "will love you because you are such a ladies man."[186]

Even while he was still in the MTC, Bainson's presence moved the local black population. "Today a black American sister of the Church . . . bought four copies of the Book of Mormon and brought them personally to the MTC." She "wrote her testimony in all the copies and added her pictures to be given to our investigators to help them know the truth." Bainson thought it a "special incident for somebody to have love and faith to that extent."[187]

In the United States, the lifting of the ordination ban did not fully resolve the racist issues interwoven with Mormonism. The battle had now shifted to defining not how Mormons should process their pre-78 past but *whether* they

183. Bainson, Journal, March 20, 1981.
184. Ibid.
185. Ibid., March 21, 1981.
186. Ibid., March 22, 1981.
187. Ibid., March 18, 1981.

should remember it at all. In the United States, writers continued to suggest that blacks suffered from the curse of Cain. Conrad Knudson, the author of a conservative commentary accepted that "certain peoples . . . have been cursed." But, Knudson assures his readers, "the Lord has now lifted the curse from all who are willing to repent."[188] By contrast, Eugene England concluded that it had been blacks calling white Mormons to repentance. White Mormons, not blacks, needed redemption from the curse: "The Church's progress in overcoming racism is primarily due to Blacks inside and outside the Church." The Mormon people "are still in denial about the ban." White Saints had "terribly harmed *ourselves*," England concluded, "both morally and spiritually, by the priesthood denial." The ban was allowed to endure "not because *He* was a racist—rather because *we were*." The problem, England found, had been "that we Mormons didn't all follow the prophet."[189]

Church leaders stayed on less controversial ground, focusing instead on the denunciation of past racist teachings. But even then, the most straightforward comments tended to be spoken by members of the Seventies Quorums and less frequently by members of the Twelve and First Presidency. In 1993, Seventy John K. Carmack denounced doctrines of racial inferiority with pointed candor: "We do not believe that any nation, race, or culture is a lesser breed or inferior in God's eyes. Those who believe or teach such doctrine have no authority from either the Lord or his authorized servants."[190] Proactive "tolerance . . . would solve the kinds of problems we still face in the United States and most other nations." Though "thoughtful public policies can assist," only "wide acceptance of the doctrines of Christ and of the attitudes and practices of tolerant people is the ultimate answer." He implored the Saints not to mock others "because of religious, cultural, racial, national, or gender differences." When a member "label[s] a fellow church member an intellectual, a less-active member, a feminist, a South African, an Armenian, a Utah Mormon, or a Mexican," she or he "seemingly provides an excuse to mistreat or ignore that person." Carmack echoed the refrain: "All are alike unto God."[191]

And some black members felt the Mormons were doing a better job of racial integration than most Southern churches. Catherine M. Stokes, a black health-care professional, joined the Church in Chicago in 1979. As a prominent official with the Illinois public health division, she committed herself to healing the racial divide within the Church, to be a "repairer of the breach." On one occasion, a friend cautioned her against attending a Mormon congregation in the South. She responded: "Hey, if they don't do the right thing, I'll call them to repentance.'" Stokes was pleased with what she saw: "Here's this black high councilman and I see black couples sitting around the chapel." When she later attended a Methodist church, there was a "large congregation, maybe 3,000 people" with "nary another black person in the place." "What's the deal here," she probed her

---

188. Conrad Knudson, *Doctrine and Covenants Guidebook*, 306–7.

189. Eugene England, "Becoming a World Religion: Blacks, the Poor—All of Us," 54.

190. John K. Carmack, *Tolerance: Principles, Practices, Obstacles, Limits,* 64.

191. Carmack, qtd. in Chieko N. Okazaki, *Lighten Up!* 22.

friend. "You're telling me not to go to the Mormon Church and I go to yours and I see absolutely no dark except me?" She felt the Methodists should "go down to the Mormon Church and learn how to do this thing."[192]

Truth

Calling for an end to racial bigotry was one thing; full-fledged doctrinal disavowal was another. Though by most outward appearances, Church leaders had made efforts to reach out, they had not taken steps to articulate the realities of the Church's racial past. It remained an uncomfortable specter that all remembered but few wished to speak about.

Feeling that Church leaders had fallen short, some white Mormon intellectuals and public figures took measures to encourage Church leaders to apologize to the black community. In summer 1997, a group of Mormon intellectuals, professionals, and Church leaders gathered in Los Angeles to develop a plan for the Church to disown its 150 years of racism, including a call to cease publication of Bruce R. McConkie's *Mormon Doctrine*. The group included Mormon sociologist Armand Mauss, Seventy Marlin K. Jensen, Church spokesman and lobbyist William Evans, and a local African American couple, David G. and Betty Jackson. The group drew up a proposal in the form of a legal brief to be passed through the channels of Church government.

Believing that he could push the bureaucracy into action, Jackson began to send correspondence to the First Presidency offering suggestions on how they might articulate an apology.[193] When it became obvious that the First Presidency would not respond, he spoke with *Los Angeles Times* reporter Larry Stammer about the discussions. Stammer wrote that "key leaders are debating a proposal to repudiate historic church doctrines that were used to bolster claims of black inferiority."[194] The First Presidency issued a statement denying that either they or the Quorum of the Twelve Apostles had formally discussed the matter, which was technically true.[195] Infuriated, Mauss chastised Jackson for "kill[ing] any chance for such a formal statement of repudiation to occur."[196] Even as the group met, President Gordon B. Hinckley had been distancing the Church hierarchy from the ban, informing media outlets that the era of racial exclusion was "behind us."[197]

---

192. Linda Hoffman Kimball, "Life Is Good: An Interview with Catherine Stokes," 9.

193. Matt Harris, "'People of African Descent Should Not Be Held Accountable for the Deeds of Others': David Jackson, the Mormon Church, and the Quest to Cast Off the Curse of Cain," Presentation Delivered at the Sunstone Symposium, August 1, 2013, Salt Lake City.

194. Larry Stammer, "Mormons May Disavow Old View on Blacks," *Los Angeles Times*, May 18, 1998, A-1.

195. "LDS Church Says Story Is Wrong," *Deseret News*, May 19, 1998, A-1.

196. Armand Mauss, *Shifting Borders and a Tattered Passport: Intellectual Journeys of a Mormon Academic,* 109.

197. Peg McEntee, "Back in 1996, It Was Mike Wallace vs. Gordon B. Hinckley," *Salt Lake Tribune*, April 9, 2012.

Some blacks in Utah also found the move ill advised and unnecessary. "I don't need an apology," Gladys Newkirk told the Mormon History Association during a panel discussion. "That's not going to change or fix anything. We're the results of the apology here."[198] Her husband, Ted Newkirk, agreed, calling on historians to move beyond the issue: "This information can hurt a person's testimony. This information which was good 20 years ago is bad today." Medical researcher and Mormon historian Gregory Prince was "surprised at how strongly they articulated their feelings."[199] Full truth and reconciliation remained an elusive hope. The dance of the past generation was coming to a head; the Saints were only beginning to recognize the degree to which they had collaborated in the racial system of the Mormon Church.

African Zion: Building the Church in Ghana

Over the next decade, the growth of LDS membership in Ghana strained the Church's ability to erect meetingplaces. In 1989, Raymond Tenhoeve, a newly appointed director of physical facilities in Ghana, felt that the Ghanaian mission was "basically running a construction company" and he "signed contract[s] for more plumbing and electrical work."[200] The Associated Press noticed that, as Mormonism expanded into black Africa, they were drawing "newcomers . . . faster than they can be accommodated."[201] Sociologist Rodney Stark observed that the African expansion signified the "rise of a new world religion."[202]

The Ghanaians' intelligence impressed Tenhoeve: "The minds of these Ghanaians are extremely bright, and th[eir] singing ability is fantastic."[203] Tenhoeve did his best to extend a feeling of acceptance to the Ghanaian population: "We know we emanate love to the people we come in contact with," he said in his tape-recorded journal; "the people could feel and see that we have no reservations about them being black." Tenhoeve "never refer[red] to people as blacks." He "call[ed] them Ghanaians and in America, they don't want to be called blacks anymore, but now they want to be called African Americans, which is better yet."[204]

In 1979, Dr. Emmanuel Kissi joined the Church and rose through the ranks of Church leadership, becoming president of the Accra Branch in 1980. By the time Tenhoeve arrived, Kissi was presiding over a larger number of branches as district president. Tenhoeve and others found Kissi's leadership impressive. "President Kiss[i] isn't one who pulls any punches," Tenhoeve noticed. "He tells it like it is."

---

198. Ibid.

199. Ted Newkirk and Greg Prince, qtd. in Bill Broadway, "Black Mormons Resist Apology Talk," *Washington Post*, May 30, 1998, B9.

200. Raymond Tenhoeve, Audio journal, April 22, 1988 and November 3, 1988, transcript, 20, 137, Tenhoeve Papers.

201. "Mormons Try to Cope with Influx in Africa," 16.

202. Rodney Stark, "The Rise of a New World Faith," 18.

203. Tenhoeve, Audio journal, ca. May 1988, transcript, 39.

204. Ibid., January 28, 1989, transcript, 203.

Kissi told "his people . . . what he wanted, and what he expected." If "they couldn't do it, he was going to release and replace them."[205] Tenhoeve tried to tread lightly: "I'm a Brooney [white man]. I just come in as an advisor." Tenhoeve wanted to maintain a hands-off approach. "We should just be the shadow leadership and shouldn't be doing it for them," instructions that mirrored discourse throughout the Church regarding their expansion into African countries.[206]

Tema Branch President Isaac Addy, soon to be president of the Ghanian District, faced similar difficulties in getting members to comply: "You give some-one a responsibility together with some sort of delegation to do something. . . . You end up doing the same job you asked someone to do. Very frustrating but what do you do?"[207] Missionaries' reticence to lead with a firm hand frustrated Addy. When implementing humanitarian programs, Addy complained, "The white missionaries have the tendency of giving in because they do not know the people [and] don't want to offend anyone."[208]

But the clash between American Mormon and Ghanaian cultures rose to the surface quickly. When Mormon missionary Sylvester Cooper attended a meeting with Ghanaian Mormons in 1981, he noted that "a number of them came in their native costumes which was a robe of Kenti cloth draped over one shoulder and down the body" instead of wearing the otherwise universal LDS male cos-tume of white shirts and trousers.[209] The Ghanaian custom of male bare shoul-ders and bare legs at funerals also posed a problem for Addy. However, he insisted that his community accept his dictum: "We have Westernized ourselves so we attend funerals with the Western clothing."[210] Nevertheless, Addy acknowledged that several Ghanaians were leery of Mormons, thinking that they "tend to rob the Ghanaians of their very ancestral cultur[al] heritage."[211]

Polygamy also posed a cultural barrier to Mormon expansion in West Africa. The missionaries could not avoid observing that "polygamy is practiced rather extensively."[212] On LaMar Williams's first early trips to Nigeria, he met several in-terested polygamist investigators, all of them willing to divorce their plural wives to join the Church.[213] Before Williams returned the following year, he asked the First Presidency "concerning interested persons over there who desired to become baptized members and were living in polygamy." McKay directed him "to baptize

205. Ibid., ca. July 1988, transcript, 74.

206. Ibid., January 15, 1989, transcript, 192. See also "Mormons Try to Cope with Influx in Africa," 16.

207. Isaac Addy, Interviewed by E. Dale LeBaron, May 14, 1988, transcript, 31.

208. Ibid., 30.

209. Sylvester Cooper, Journal, November 1, 1981.

210. Addy, Interview, May 14, 1988, transcript, 34.

211. Ibid., 34.

212. Rendell Mabey and Edwin Cannon, Letter to Carlos Asay, February 19, 1979.

213. James B. Allen, "Would-Be Saints: West Africa before the 1978 Priesthood Revelation," 225–26.

and admit them into the Church. They could keep their wives and families that they had at the time of baptism but were not to engage further into this practice."[214]

Having been the United States's most prominent polygamists in the nineteenth-century, American Mormons faced an interesting conundrum in deciding whether to tolerate polygamy in developing countries. It forced Church leaders to reckon with their racial and sexual past even as they looked toward a global future.

Responding to queries from village elders, Mabey and Cannon suggested an inclusive approach: "It is the purpose of this Church to bring families together and not pull them apart." They hoped to welcome polygamists. As long as a man "loves his wives and children and is faithful to them alone in family relationships," believed in the principles of Mormonism, and "will not take another wife (unless the situation changes by death or otherwise so he no longer has a wife on this earth) nor teach polygamy to others," Mabey and Cannon felt that requiring divorce would do more damage than good. They urged International Mission President Carlos Asay to support their decision.[215] But Asay coldly denied their request. "It would not be appropriate at this time to baptize any persons who have more than one wife." This policy could "be changed only by the First Presidency." If a new policy was enacted, they would "be promptly notified."[216]

The missionaries promptly complied with the new order. In 1981, Cannon told Apostle James E. Faust that the missionaries had, in fact, received instructions prior to leaving for Africa that "any case of a worthy individual living in polygamy desiring baptism should be brought to the attention of the General Authorities before baptizing." Allowing for the baptism of polygamists in West Africa would "have implications elsewhere," Cannon warned, "as in the treatment of those who practice polygamy in defiance of both the laws of the land and the direction of Church authority."[217]

Legal conflicts arose as well. Ime Idouk, a member in Nigeria, felt that Bryan Espenschied, appointed president of the West African Mission in 1980, had used duplicitous means to win the support of Nigerian government officials. He is "not a straight forward man," Edouk observed, "and feels that he could come in [and] get things done through the back door." He accused Espenschied of bribing the Dental Association of Nigeria to allow him to set up the Mobile Dental Clinic. Edouk feared Espenschied was losing credibility with responsible local parties and declared that "many things had been done by this man to destroy the work."[218]

The missionaries also needed to take care that newly converted members obey the region's immigration laws. Church leaders instructed local leaders that

---

214. LaMar Williams, Summary Memo, November 21, 1961, LaMar S. Williams Papers, Box 1, fd. 8.

215. Mabey and Cannon to Asay, February 19, 1979.

216. Carlos E. Asay, Letter to the [Rendell and Rachel] Mabeys and the [Edwin and Janath] Cannons, March 5, 1979.

217. Edwin Cannon, Letter to James E. Faust, June 30, 1981.

218. Ime Edouk, Letter to Brother Frank, August 10, 1981.

tribal marriages were no longer valid and needed to be processed through the civil authorities,[219] but Addy complained about Ghanaians' unwillingness to abide by civil marriage law.

Bainson was not the only Mormon to struggle with the delicate political situation of postcolonial West Africa. American missionaries also found themselves taken off-guard as they tried to concentrate on the gospel message during periodic political eruptions in Ghana and Nigeria, even occasionally finding themselves the target of mob hostility. "Drink your oil," Edwin Cannon heard one mob scream during Rawlings's 1979 coup, a reference to the strength of American oil interests such as Shell.[220] In December 1981, political instability surfaced again when Rawlings, now deposed, launched another coup in which "many soldiers [were] killed" while "stray bullets had killed some civilians."[221] Mortar attacks terrorized Mission missionary Sylvester Cooper's neighborhood. On January 1, Cooper and his wife heard "heavy gunfire all day." Sister Cooper stepped away from dinner preparations to comment on a mortar shell that had hit a neighbor's house, observed matter-of-factly, "Gosh, that sounds close," and "then went back to the kitchen." Throughout the day, "shooting continue[d]," making it into "a very uneasy New Year's Day. . . . [W]hat a party!"

Language politics gave the Americans pause when they considered translating pamphlets and the scriptures into tribal languages such as Efik. Mabey and Cannon discouraged the Church Translation Department from selecting one language in which to translate the scriptures and other Church literature. The Nigerian government hoped English could be a "unifying factor" in bringing together the country's competing tribal factions. The Wesleyan Bible Society had labored over Bible translations, but the Nigerian government saw them as political subversives and exiled them from the country. Few Efiks felt motivated to learn how to read their tribal language. English had, after all, become the language of power.[222]

To the Saints' good fortune, they had a government contact that protected them from the more frightening components of the Rawlings regime: Branch President Isaac Addy was Rawlings's older half-brother. He had returned from Great Britain to Ghana in spite of his home country's political instability. "I came to do a cause," Addy later remembered. "When [Mission President] Miles Cunningham calls and says, 'Look, I need somebody of your caliber to do something,' I never hesitate in saying yes."[223]

Better still, Addy had a positive relationship with Rawlings—indeed, he felt "very close to everyone" in the family." Rawlings "knows very well what he is doing," Addy assured E. Dale LeBaron. If Rawlings "happen[ed] to die tomorrow,"

219. Addy, interview, 36.
220. Edwin Cannon, Letter to Oscar McConkie, July 9, 1979.
221. Sylvester Cooper, Journal, December 31, 1981.
222. Mabey and Cannon, Letter to Eb Davis, May 15, 1979.
223. Addy, interview, 28.

Addy noted, "he will die a noble death, die for the cause of his motherland." Addy expected a kind of existential martyrdom for Rawlings: "He knows very well he might lay down his life for his country. . . . It is something I cannot change: his destiny. He is foreordained for that course."[224]

By spring 1989, American missionaries had become the targets for anti-American hostilities. The government established the Provisional National Defence Council (PNDC) to register all religious sects with the National Commission on Culture, hoping that they could control the battling religious sects and perhaps direct public attention against a common enemy. In the Religious Bodies Registration Law, the legislation empowering the council, it was made clear that "every religious body in Ghana" had three months to comply. The Rawlings government established a "Religious Affairs Committee" to advise them, believing that the Commission was protecting the Ghanaians "from the exploitative tendencies of some churches."[225]

Mormons tended to exemplify American opulence in Ghana. They "had a lot of vehicles," U.S. Ambassador Raymond Ewing recalled, "and a fairly high profile."[226] The use of cars had long presented a political problem for Mormon expansion into West Africa. The Nigerian situation illustrates those difficulties. Indeed, since the missionaries' first contact with West Africa, the need for vehicular transportation was well-known among both American missionaries and Nigerian locals. "Cars and special arrangements must be made to go anywhere," missionary Marvin Jones complained in his journal.[227]

Charles Udo-Ete, a leader of the Nigerian congregations, made it clear to the American missionary that he "wants a car" to be able to visit various members in his area.[228] Even before the missionaries arrived, the Nigerians were concerned over Udo-Ete's ability to make contact with the members. In the spring of 1961, the members hoped to purchase a car for him, but they could not: "at present there is no money." The Saints decided to "put this problem of Transport into our daily prayer so that the Lord may give us funds."[229] The Nigerian Saints also hoped to gather enough money "to buy 13 bicycles for our workers" to use "in gospel traveling."[230]

More than six months later, Marvin Jones again recorded their urgent desire for the car. "There is no car," Jones again noted; they "want a car." He could

---

224. Ibid., 5, 27.

225. Walter Suntinger, "Ghana," in P.R. Baehr, Hilde Hey, Jacqueline Smith, and Theresa Swinehart, eds., *Human Rights in Developing Countries: Yearbook1994*, 225.

226. Ambassador Raymond C. Ewing, Interviewed by Charles Stuart Kennedy, November 29, 1993, Association for Diplomatic Studies and Training Oral History Interview Series, http://www.adst.org/OH%20TOCs/Ewing,%20Raymond%20C.toc.pdf (accessed April 18, 2014), 61.

227. Marvin Jones, Diary, October 18, 1961.

228. Ibid., October 22, 1961.

229. Meetings of General Conference of the Church in Nigeria, March 10, 1961, 4,

230. Ibid., 2.

not emphasize it enough: "WANT CAR," he wrote in all caps.[231] But underlying the desire for quality transportation on the barely navigable road-system was also a deep-seated skepticism of American capitalism; one man complained to Marvin Jones and LaMar Williams that, when they finally receive a missionary, they want one "who will stay & not one who is lazy" and reliant on his car all the time.[232] During the missionaries' first meetings in Nigeria, LaMar Williams noticed that "not one" of the Saints "rode in a car."[233] On one occasion a Nigerian Saint with over a decade of experience as a mechanic on foreign cars begged the American missionaries to assist him in attending an American automotive school.[234] In 1974 the Ghanaians offered Mormon businessman, E. Allen, a labor force to help him in the production of automotive products. Cars were a symbol of Western economic strength and dominance, for better and for worse.[235] As Ewing observed, the Mormon problem in Ghana could have easily been called an "American problem."[236]

Worse, prominent anti-Mormon activists Ed Decker and Dave Hunt had released their 1982 documentary, *The God Makers*, in Ghana. Known for its caricatures of Mormon beliefs and depiction of Mormons as a power-hungry cult, the film had gained wide infamy in the United States, offending even Christians who were otherwise opposed to Mormon beliefs. The film was broadcast on Ghanaian television; Rawlings saw the film himself.[237]

A week after the release of the *God Makers* in June 1989, the PNDC cracked down on the Saints and a number of other religious movements (primarily the Jehovah's Witnesses and two local sectarian groups: the Jesus Christ of Dwozulu and Nyame Sompa).[238] The government issued an expulsion order against Tenhoeve and more than ten Mormon missionaries then working in the country, citing the Mormons' history of racism. Public worship services were banned, with native military personnel confiscating all keys to Church buildings and banning any use of Church property. Though worship services could be held in private homes, the Ghanaians Saints needed to exercise discretion.

Meanwhile, in Salt Lake City, Church leaders planned their next moves. Bill Evans, a public affairs staffer, called Catherine Stokes's office with an urgent message to call back immediately.[239] By this point, Stokes had become a liaison between the American black community and the Mormon hierarchy. Stokes was

---

231. Marvin Jones, Diary, October 29, 1961.

232. Ibid.

233. LaMar Williams, Diary, October 22, 1961.

234. Ibid.

235. Clement Osekre, Letter to LaMar Williams, March 1, 1974, Ghana and Nigeria Files, LDS Church History Library.

236. Raymond C. Ewing, Interview, 62. .

237. Ibid., 61.

238. Deportation Order, June 14, 1989, MS 13613, LDS Church History Library.

239. The following events and quotations are from Catherine M. Stokes, Interviewed by Russell Stevenson, April 15, 2014, audio recording in my possession. All emphases Stokes's.

about to leave on a vacation to Yugoslavia to visit Medjugorje. "What does he want?" Stokes remembered thinking. She returned the call, and a grateful Evans requested that Stokes take "a little detour" from her vacation to Ghana. Laughing, Stokes told Evans: "It's not on the way." Evans asked her to hold; Apostle Neal A. Maxwell wanted to talk to her.   Stokes expected the conversation to deteriorate quickly: "Here comes this heavy hand of priesthood authority." But Maxwell was genuinely and generously deferential: "Sister Stokes," he said, "this is *Neal* Maxwell." Stokes did not miss his informal tone. "I apologize for having to ask you this, but it's very important." Though the Church had a backup option out of D.C., Stokes was the Church leaders' "first choice" to meet with Ghanian government officials. But Stokes remained uncertain on the details of her mission to Ghana. She agreed to do it only if she could accompany her traveling companion to the city of Zagreb.

Stokes was told that, after she left her friend in Zagreb, she was to go to the Swiss Air Counter where a ticket to London would be waiting for her. Joseph Muren, head of LDS temporal affairs in England, met Stokes at the airport and explained to her the troubles the Ghanaian LDS community faced. Muren explained that the Ghanaian government wanted to meet some black Latter-day Saints. Muren suggested that Stokes go to Picadilly Circus to purchase a dress to meet with the Ghanaian government officials. But Stokes told Muren that it would not be necessary since she "had the perfect dress." She had packed it the night before even though she "had no reason to put it in there." The dress only needed to be cleaned. Robert Stevenson, a black LDS businessman from Atlanta who had also been an officer in the BYU student government, arrived in London the next day to accompany her. Stokes and Stevenson both acquired visas and left for Accra.

Upon arrival, Isaac Addy met them and took them out of line, essentially bypassing the entire airport security apparatus. "When you have clout in a third world country, you have clout," Stokes said of Addy. But Stokes was glad to see that the LDS Church hierarchy refused to draw on their political and economic influence in the United States. "To our credit," Stokes declared, "the Church turned . . . down" the offers that were coming from Washingtom as well as the Mormons connected with the cocoa trade. "That was a very significant thing for me. . . . [T]here was not the usual politicking." Though Stokes had "nothing against using power and influence," she believed that "when you say you're of God, there's another standard, and that the Church was faithful to that standard was very important to me."[240]

The Church still enjoyed political support from voices with the American political establishment. U.S. Ambassador Raymond C. Ewing "spent a lot of time on the issue," according to his 1993 recollections. "I realized fairly soon that it was probably going to be best to do it in as low key a way as possible."[241] Ewing

---

240. Ibid., 61.
241. Ibid., 62.

hoped to provide means "to allow the Ghanaians to back down and come away from their position of their own volition, rather than by making speeches about the problem." Ewing met several times with Kojo Tsikata, one of Rawlings's confidantes and a member of the PNDC. He also held conversations with Isaac Addy, who himself met often with Tsikata even while avoiding his half-brother entirely. Ewing encouraged the Church to move cautiously: "With a little patience and quiet effort," the Church would find success "rather than by threatening the Ghanaians and exerting public pressure too blatantly in Congress."[242] As Ewing met with Ghanaian government officials, President Jimmy Carter also called upon the Ghanaian government to request that they start a dialogue with Stokes and Stevenson; for all of Carter's concerns about Mormon racism, Carter felt that the Rawlings government had made a mistake.[243]

Stokes, Stevenson, and Elder Robert Sackley, an Australian General Authority with prior Church experience in Nigeria, had a cordial and successful meeting with the National Commissioner on Culture. The commissioner assured the Mormon delegation that LDS Church activities would be allowed again. But he wanted to ensure that the Ghanaian public become aware of the government's change of course. Maxwell had mentioned that, while he did not want a press conference, he would leave the decision up to Stokes and her associates. "What do you mean leave it up to us?" Stokes thought. But she was skeptical of the media: "They never ask sincere questions."

The commissioner responded: "What do you want them to ask?" Stokes wanted only candor and honesty. And she received it. At the press conference, a female reporter asked Stokes about the "magic underwear that makes [Mormons] successful." Stokes laughed: "We wish!" The reporter followed up, asking about the role of women in the Mormon Church. Stokes declared that the role of women "in the world" is that they should be on the "cutting edge of arts, science, education, law, whatever" as well shouldering a "special responsibility for the care and spiritual development of the children." The press hoped she would appear on local television shows, but Stokes was done: "I'm going on vacation." She rejoined her group in Yugoslavia.[244]

Meanwhile, the Saints had been struggling. "They couldn't sing a hymn, they couldn't gather in small groups, they couldn't have the kids' activities." Branch President Stephen Abu recalled: "You could not sing loudly, or you would be picked up."[245] Abu himself was imprisoned when he violated the ban on public

---

242. All Ewing quotations are from Ambassador Raymond C. Ewing, Interviewed by Charles Stuart Kennedy, November 29, 1993, Association for Diplomatic Studies and Training Oral History Interview Series, http://www.adst.org/OH%20TOCs/Ewing,%20Raymond%20C.toc.pdf (accessed April 18, 2014).

243. Douglas Brinkley, *The Unfinished Presidency: Jimmy Carter's Journey Beyond the White House*, 193. See also Stokes, Interview, April 15, 2014.

244. Stokes, Interview, April 15, 2014.

245. Don L. Searle, "Ghana—A Household of Faith," 39.

meetings. Stokes was impressed at how happy the Ghanaian Saints were to see them: "It wasn't the Second Coming but He had sent us to come and help them out."[246] After eighteen months of underground worship, a coalition of religious groups through pleas and negotiations succeeded in lifting the prohibition. In November 1990, Mormon missionaries were allowed back into the country, and the Saints were allowed to hold public meetings and proselytze again. Now that the legal campaign against the Saints was over, a Ghanaian Mormon recalled, "good people wanted to know more about the Church" to see if what they had heard was true.[247]

Growth continued over the next decade at a rapid pace. In April 1998, President Gordon B. Hinckley announced the construction of the Accra Ghana Temple.[248] Missionaries directing the construction liked to think of the project as a truly international one. Interior designer Shirley Katwyk observed that "Colombians did the finish carpentry, the mechanical and electrical workers come from Poland, Russia, and Ireland. All the management of the main contractor came from England, the French laid the floor tile that came from Brazil, and the Americans did the roof, mechanical, electrical, paintings, and special security."[249] They faced skepticism from local government; by calling their structure a "temple," they invoked images of "charismatic, Pentecostal religions that use drums, dancing, laud [sic] singing and noise in their ceremonies"—activities that would be disruptive for neighboring embassies.[250] Between 2000 and 2001, the project stalled, being bounced back and forth between local authorities in Accra and the Federal Planning Board. When Georges Bonnet, director of temporal affairs for the LDS Presiding Bishop's Office for Africa, took over the project in 2001, he succeeded in assuring the jittery boards of the Saints' peaceful intentions.

The temple signified a milestone for the Ghanaian Mormon community, a symbol of the legitimacy they had been seeking for over a generation. In April 2001, Apostle Russell M. Nelson went to Accra to preside at the groundbreaking. Learning that he was a former heart surgeon, the media peppered him with questions, hoping he would promote the building of medical facilities. "I think that the representatives of the media were disappointed in my response,"[251] he commented. That December, Bonnet described the good fortune of discovering "a large quantity of water . . . gushing out at 100 gallons a minute" on the temple site.[252] A decade

246. Ibid.

247. Qtd. in Searle, "Ghana—A Household of Faith," 39.

248. "Mormons Plan to Build Temple in Ghana," *Indiana [Penn.] Gazette*, April 17, 1998, 7.

249. "Project History Log," n.d., Shirley Van Katwyk Papers, LDS Church History Library.

250. Ibid.

251. "Ground Broken for First Temple in West Africa," *LDS Church News*, November 24, 2001, 14.

252. Georges Bonnet, Email to Steve Graham, September 20, 2001, Shirley Katwyk Papers.

later, a member, John Mensah, attended an endowment session at the temple, only to discover his long-lost son sitting a few rows down from him.[253]

As the temple walls rose, anti-Mormon sentiment surfaced again. In 2004, Ghana's English-speaking newspaper, *The Chronicle* accused Church officials of bribing government leaders, saying that "God hates corruption and any church which pays bribes cannot be of God."[254] But "after a few days, the attacks "died out."[255] Construction director Charles Katwyk also struggled with labor issues; in summer 2002, temple laborers mounted a strike. Katwyk responded sharply with summary terminations. All were forced to reapply, but the strike leaders "were not allowed back on site."[256]

The negative publicity did little to dampen the Saints' good spirits. When Hinckley dedicated the structure in January 2004, he heralded the dawning of "a new day in West Africa."[257] He hoped that the temple would symbolize an era of racial reconciliation, noting in his dedicatory prayer that "neither color of skin nor land of birth can separate us."[258] Ghanaian national President John Kufour told LDS Church President Gordon B. Hinckley that the structure ensured that the Church "has gained citizenship in Ghana."[259]

Significantly, American Mormons seemed more comfortable engaging their racial ghosts through the distant Saints of West Africa than in dealing head-on with the generations of racism that remained at home. In 1996, President Gordon B. Hinckley became the first LDS Church President to tour Africa, visiting Mormon hubs in Ghana, Zimbabwe, and South Africa. Two years later, prominent Mormon musicians Peter Breinholt and Nancy Hanson sponsored a benefit concert for Ghanaians.[260] West African Mormons carried an allure and exoticism that American Mormons did not extend so readily to African Americans co-believers.

Somebody Knows

One of the most powerful voices for reconciliation and rediscovery of the black Mormon narrative has been Margaret Blair Young in company with a powerful voice from the Genesis Group, Darius Aidan Gray. As an adolescent, Young had been exposed to racist rhetoric from a seminary teacher. Her father, Dr. Robert W. Blair, was a linguist specializing in central American indigenous

---

253. Susan Warner, "Have Miracles Ceased: The Two John Ekow Mensahs' Story," MS 26893.

254. "Gov't Officials Demand Bribe—Mormon Drops Bombshell," *Chronicle* (Accra, Ghana), Ghana, February 16, 2004, http://www.ghanaweb.com/GhanaHomePage/NewsArchive/artikel. php?ID=51855 (accessed April 15, 2013).

255. March 2003, in "Events of the First Year of Construction," Shirley Van Katwyk Papers.

256. May-June 2002, in "Events of the First Year of Construction," Shirley Van Katwyk Papers.

257. "Ghana Temple Brings Euphoria," *LDS Church News*, January 17, 2004, 14.

258. Gordon B. Hinckley, qtd. in "Brotherhood Exists," *LDS Church News*, January 17, 2004, 11.

259. Ibid., 7.

260. "Breinholt Performs Benefit Concert," *Salt Lake Community College Student Newspaper,* September 29, 1998, 6.

languages (e.g. Guarani and Cakchiquel), and the children had grown up well-accustomed to racial diversity in her home: "There would always be someone in the next room who had dark skin and spoke a language I could not comprehend."[261] She was horrified as a teenager to hear racial slurs, presented both as jokes and also as quasi-doctrine, in her seminary class. When the teacher asked for written feedback on his performance, Margaret strongly suggested that he stop using offensive racial rhetoric. The instructor pointedly, publicly, and solemnly testified that blacks were inherently inferior as spiritual beings. Margaret promptly, with her parents' permission, dropped the class.[262] After a four-year marriage that ended in divorce, she explored the evils of Nazi Germany through the eyes of Latter-day Saints.[263] She had also spent considerable time living in politically unstable Central American countries (e.g., Guatemala).[264] But Young felt increasingly drawn to writing about the black Mormon experience, feeling that "not nearly enough had been said."[265]

In July 1998, Young became acquainted with Genesis Group co-founder Darius Gray after Young had delivered a presentation with former BYU professor Eugene England on the priesthood ban. After the presentation, Young recalled, Darius "hugged me and said, 'Let's write a book.'" In 2000, Young and Gray began writing *Standing on the Promises*, a trilogy of historical novels based on the often-ignored and frequently diminished achievements of black Latter-day Saints, ranging from Joseph Smith's day until the present, with Darius himself as the protagonist of the third volume. Published by Deseret Book, the series popularized the history of the black Mormon experience.[266] They followed up with a widely received documentary in 2008, *Nobody Knows: The Untold Story of Black Mormons*. The volumes coupled with the documentary have received wide acclaim and have won the attention of Mormon readers otherwise unattuned to black Mormon history.

Yet despite the efforts of Young, Gray, and others, relics of old racial dogmas endured. In 2006 Gordon B. Hinckley felt it necessary to chastise priesthood holders for harboring old racial attitudes. "I am advised that even right here among us there is some of this. . . . It seemed to me that we all rejoiced in the 1978 revelation given President Kimball." Hinckley affirmed that "there is no basis for racial hatred among the priesthood of this Church." Those guilty of it

---

261. Margaret Blair Young, "Messiah in Patsun, Guatemala," http://www.patheos.com/blogs/welcometable/2013/12/messiah-in-patsun-guatemala/ (accessed April 3, 2014).

262. Margaret Young, Interviewed by Kylan Rice, September 30, 2012.

263. Margaret Young, *House Without Walls*.

264. Margaret Blair Young, "Household of Faith: Enlarge Thy Borders Forever," http://ldsmag.com/ldsmag/exstories/040220household.html (accessed April 3, 2014).

265. Margaret Young, Interviewed by Lisa Butterworth, February 18, 2013.

266. Margaret Blair Young and Darius Aidan Gray, *Standing on the Promises: Vol. 1: One More River to Cross; Vol. 2: Bound for Canaan; Vol. 3: The Last Mile of the Way*, reprinted in a revised and updated edition in 2013.

needed to "go before the Lord and ask for forgiveness and be no more involved in such." No man, Hinckley said with his gentle gravity, "who makes disparaging remarks concerning those of another race can consider himself to be a true disciple of Christ." Further, Hinckley asked, with remarkable self-indictment: "How can any man holding the Melchizedek Priesthood arrogantly assume that he is eligible for the priesthood whereas another who lives a righteous life but whose skin is of a different color is ineligible?"

Race came up on occasion during Mitt Romney's 2008 presidential campaign, in which John McCain ultimately won the Republican nomination. During Romney's 2012 run as the official GOP candidate, BYU religion professor Randy Bott sent a shockwave through the Mormon community when he told *Washington Post* reporter Jason Horowitz that "blacks not having the priesthood . . . protected [them] from the lowest rungs of hell reserved for people who abuse their priesthood."[267] The comments prompted a wave of introspection within the BYU Religion Department and a firestorm of criticism from without. Acting on non-negotiable instructions, Bott took down his blogsite, even though his commentary would have attracted little attention a generation earlier.

The struggle continues. Eleanor Clark, now a South African expatriate living in America, has observed that she can't count "how many times since I've lived in Utah . . . they [white Church members] start airing their racist viewpoints" once they learn that she is a white South African. While attending BYU, a fellow student commiserated that it was "such a shame what they're doing to your country. . . . [Y]our country has gone downhill since they came to power."[268] The South African experience seared Tessa Meyer, now married with a family She has sent her four children to the "ghetto" schools in her home city of Phoenix so that they would "not be able to know what the majority looks like and . . . have [a] hard time identifying the power structure by the color of a person's skin."[269]

A remarkably important innovation in spreading racial consciousness was the advent of the internet with its ease in making Church-produced statements readily available to massive numbers of people. In March 2013, the scriptures committee, a unit working under the direction of hand-picked LDS scriptorians and General Authorities made the first step toward an official, Church-wide acknowledgment of past racism in conjunction with a new edition of the scriptures in the summer of 2013. The edition announcement was low-key and Church members were not required, or even encouraged, to purchase the new print edition; but anyone who had an e-version of the scriptures received an automatic update. Official Declaration—2 (in the 1981 edition) had previously lacked any introductory material except for the notation that N. Eldon Tanner, first counselor in Spencer K. Kimball's First Presidency, had read it on September

---

267. "The Genesis of a Church's Stand on Race," *Washington Post*, February 28, 2012.
268. Eleanor Clark, Correspondence with Russell Stevenson, January 8, 2013.
269. Tessa Meyer Santiago, "Here's to You, June Williamson," December 28, 2009.

30, 1978, in general conference, which had then canonized it by a "unanimous" vote. The new introduction offered substantial context, quoting the passage, "all are alike unto God" (2 Ne. 26:33), that specified "black and white, bond and free, male and female." It also made the significant concession, long-known among historians and activists but never officially acknowledged: "During Joseph Smith's lifetime, a few black male members of the Church were ordained to the priesthood." The statement further acknowledged that the historical record offered "no clear insights into the origin" of the "practice." It was only known that the "needed" revelation was received and confirmed to Church leaders on June 1, 1978, removing "all restriction with regard to race that once applied to the priesthood."[270] Speaking at the October general conference three months later, Dieter F. Uchtdorf, second counselor in Thomas S. Monson's First Presidency, told the global Mormon audience that "there have been times when members or leaders in the Church have simply made mistakes."[271]

In December 2013, with assistance from the LDS Church History Department, the Publicity Department, and the Mission Department, the Church posted a carefully researched, lavishly footnoted, and thoroughly reviewed essay on "Race and the Priesthood." The essay also included extensive multimedia resources from modern leaders on Mormonism's global dynamics as well as the "doctrine of inclusion." Though the authorship was left unidentified, Darius Gray has indicated that the essay received approval from the First Presidency.[272] The statement's concluding paragraph expressed the strongest denunciation of racism in its history:

> The Church disavows the theories advanced in the past that black skin is a sign of divine disfavor or curse, or that it reflects actions in a premortal life; that mixed-race marriages are a sin; or that blacks or people of any other race or ethnicity are inferior in any way to anyone else. Church leaders today unequivocally condemn all racism, past and present, in any form.[273]

Unlike earlier statements printed in the back of hard-copy publications, these statements posted on the Church's website have received wide readership and publicity—forcing the Saints to grapple with racial discourse to a degree that print media never could. At the same time, Armand Mauss observed that the Mormon community "has traveled from Utah to Galatia to rejoice anew in Paul's declaration to the Saints that the gospel of Christ is for all humankind, and that those who can accept it are all the children of Abraham and of Abraham's God, irrespective of race or lineage."[274]

---

270. "Official Declaration 2," https://www.lds.org/scriptures/dc-testament/od/2, (accessed February 9, 2014), Doctrine and Covenants, summer 2013, pp. 294–95.

271. Dieter F. Uchtdorf, "Come Join with Us," 22.

272. Darius Gray, Lecture at BYU, February 12, 2014, my notes.

273. "Race and the Priesthood," http://www.lds.org/topics/race-and-the-priesthood?lang=eng, posted December 13, 2013 (accessed December 14, 2013).

274. Armand L. Mauss, "From Galatia to Ghana: The Racial Dynamic in Mormon History," 73.

Part 2 of this volume provides touchstone moments in the history of the relationship between the Mormon and black communities. Their pasts and presents haunted each other, afraid of too intimate of an embrace. Troubled, moving, and cathartic, the Mormon-black story represents the struggles between a peculiar mountain sect and the nation's largest racial minority. It is not merely a Mormon story or even an American one; it is a story that extends across the Atlantic and Pacific, from Fiji to Britain and from Brazil to Nigeria. The story of blacks and Mormonism reveals the scope and depth of social, political—and for believing Mormons, providential—forces required to drag twentieth-century white Mormondom free from the grip of the world that the nineteenth century made for them.

Part 2

The Documents

Chapter 8

Making Race in Mormonism, 1833–47

W. W. Phelps Urges Moderation on Slavery (July 1833)

HISTORICAL CONTEXT

The early Latter-day Saints' first exposure to slavery came as they settled in western Missouri. When Joseph Smith visited Jackson County, he freely preached to a "respectable number of negroes."[1] The following year, Joseph Smith received a revelation declaring that "it is not right that a man should be in bondage to another."[2] While the Saints had not embraced the radical abolitionism of activists such as William Lloyd Garrison, they generally found slavery to be a shameful stain on republican government.

More than other Mormons, W. W. Phelps had a long reputation for incendiary rhetoric. As a critic of slavery and a vitriolic anti-Mason, Phelps had few scruples when it came to the printed word. He openly observed that "much is doing towards abolishing slavery, and colonizing the blacks, in Africa."[3] Joseph Smith realized that Phelps's boldness could backfire. George A. Smith quipped that he "considered Phelps the sixth part of an editor, that was a satirist," but "when it came to the cool discretion necessarily instructed to an Editor in the control of American public opinion, the soothing of enmity, he was deficient." George A. would happily "pay Phelps for editing a paper, provided nobody else should have the privilege of reading it." Joseph laughed, agreeing that Phelps had "such severe use of language as to make enemies all the time."[4] In the text below, Phelps attempts to express moderation in support of racial integration.

CITATION

"Free People of Color," *Evening and Morning* Star 2, no. 14 (July 1833): 108.

1. Manuscript History of the Church, A-1, 129, in Richard E. Turley Jr., ed., *Selected Collections from the Archives of the Church of Jesus Christ of Latter-day Saints,* 2 vols., DVD, 1:2.

2. Revelation, December 16–17, http://josephsmithpapers.org/paperSummary/revelation-16-and-17-december-1833-dc-101?p=9 (accessed February 11, 2014).

3. W. W. Phelps, "The Elders Stationed in Zion to the Churches Abroad," *Evening and Morning Star* 2, no. 14 (July 1833): 110.

4. "History of Joseph Smith," in *Millennial Star* 21, no. 7 (February 12, 1859): 107.

DOCUMENT EXCERPT

To prevent any misunderstanding among the churches abroad, respecting Free people of color, who may think of coming to the western boundaries of Missouri, as members of the church, we quote the following clauses from the Laws of Missouri.

SECTION 4. Be it further enacted, That hereafter no free negro or mulatto, other than a citizen of some one of the United States, shall come into or settle in this state under any pretext whatever; and upon complaint made to any justice of the peace, that such person is in his county, contrary to the provisions of this section, he shall cause such person to be brought before him. And if upon examination, it shall appear that such person is a free negro or mulatto, and that he hath come into this state after the passage of this act, and such person shall not produce a certificate, attested by the seal of some court of record in some one of the United States, evidencing that he is a citizen of such state, the justice shall command him forthwith to depart from this state; and in case such negro or mulatto shall not depart from the state within thirty days after being commanded so to do as aforesaid, any justice of the peace, upon complaint thereof to him made may cause such person to be brought before him, and may commit him to the common gaol [sic] of the county in which he may be found, until the next term of the circuit court to be holden in such county. And the said court shall cause such person to be brought before them, and examine into the cause of commitment; and if it shall appear that such person came into the state contrary to the provisions of this act, and continued therein after being commanded to depart as aforesaid, such court may sentence such person to receive ten lashes on his or her bare back, and order him to depart the state; and if he or she shall not so depart, the same proceedings shall be had and punishment inflicted, as often as may be necessary, until such person shall depart the state.

SECTION 5. Be it further enacted, That if any person shall, after the taking effect of this act, bring into this state any free negro or mulatto, not having in his possession a certificate of citizenship as required by this act, [he or she] shall forfeit and pay, for every person so brought, the sum of five hundred dollars, to be recovered by action of debt in the name of the state, to the use of the university, in any court having competent jurisdiction; in which action the defendant may be held to bail, of right, and without affidavit; and it shall be the duty of the attorney-general or circuit attorney of the district in which any person so offending may be found, immediately upon information given of such offence, to commence and prosecute an action as aforesaid.[5]

---

5. The 1820 Missouri state constitution expressly enjoined the Missouri general assembly to "prevent free negroes and mulattos from coming to, and settling in, this state, under any pretext whatsoever." This clause was by far the most controversial in the Constitution. New Hampshire Senator David L. Morril declared that "this [Missouri's] provision . . . is in direct hostility to the Constitution of the United States." In 1826, the city of St. Louis established a police force formed largely to "keep an especial eye upon the negro houses, and other places of rendezvous for slaves and

Slaves are real estate in this and other states, and wisdom would dictate great care among the branches of the church of Christ, on this subject. So long as we have no special rule in the church, as to people of color, let prudence guide; and while they, as well as we, are in the hands of a merciful God, we say: Shun every appearance of evil.

The Early Racialization of White Latter-day Saints (1834)

HISTORICAL INTRODUCTION

Being a Mormon in antebellum America meant more than radical theology; outsiders also assumed that it meant a support for the intermingling of the races. When abolitionist and Oneida Institute [Whitesboro, New York] President Beriah Green, read the following 1835 article, he soundly chastised the reporter for insulting "some of his most intelligent fellow-citizens and devoted fellow Christians."[6]

CITATION

"The Fourth of July," *Commercial Advertiser* (New York), July 5, 1834, 2.

DOCUMENT EXCERPT

The only disturbance, if disturbance it can be called, was at the Chatham Street Chapel.[7] We have been at some pains to ascertain the facts, and we give them as they were, from the relation of a respectable gentleman who was present during the whole of the performance. The Fanatics, it seems have been holding meetings for several successive nights, of the past and present week, preparatory to a factitious phrenzy, adapted to the heats of the season, and to their own excited zeal. . . .

---

coloured people." In 1835, the general assembly cracked down on the free black population even further, requiring all free blacks to acquire a license for residence in the state. In 1838, St. Louis implemented a series of ordinances prohibiting racially integrated social gatherings and establishing curfews for all slaves and most free blacks. Ben Perley Poore, ed., *The Federal and State Constitutions, Colonial Charters, and Other Organic Laws of the United States*, 2:1108; *Abridgement of the Debates of Congress from 1789 to 1856*, 6:691; "An Ordinance Establishing and Regulating a Patrol for this City," February 9, 1826, *Ordinances of St. Louis, Revised, 1828*, 59–62, cited in Daniel Graff, "Race, Citizenship, and the Origins of Organized Labor in Antebellum St. Louis," in Thomas Spencer, ed., *The Other Missouri History: Populists, Prostitutes, and Regular Folk*, 62. See also "An Act Concerning Negroes and Mulattoes," *The Revised Statutes of the State of Missouri* (1835), 413–17.

6. Reverend Beriah Green, "A Review: The Principles of Reform," 47.

7. Founded by Charles Grandison Finney in 1830, the Chatham Street Chapel was a leading site for revivalistic religion, political debates, public education reform, and abolitionist meetings. Finney told his Chatham congregation to expect ridicule for their theological and social radicalism: "Let them say, if they please, that the folks in Chatham Chapel are getting deranged. We need not be afraid of that, if we could live near enough to God to enjoy his Spirit." "Chatham Street," *Commercial Advertiser* (New York City), September 11, 1833, 2; "David Paul Brown," *Spectator* (New York City), June 12, 1834, 1; Charles Grandison Finney, *Lectures on Revivals of Religion*, 59. For a brief history of the origins of the Chatham Street Chapel, see "The Broadway Tabernacle," *Frank Leslie's Sunday Magazine* 4 (July-December 1878): 102.

Much of the excitement was obviously occasioned by the studied admixture of the blacks and whites. The row of seats back of the orchestra were filled *alternately* with blacks and whites—an earnest of the project [of] amalgamation—and a white man in a clerical dress with two "dingy Desdemona's"[8] [went] into a pew, and took his seat between them! These proceedings, so clearly intended to outrage public taste and feeling, produced the results which the projectors of the excitement probably intended. It conduced to the notoriety for which they seek. But it is a notoriety not to be envied. They are less justifiable and more mischievous than the Mormons of the West. They are the Black Mormons of the East.

W. W. Phelps Responds to Attacks (February 1834)

HISTORICAL INTRODUCTION

Newspapers throughout the country read Phelps's remarks as they read the remarks of most abolitionists—as a thinly veiled effort to force racial integration. "The invitation alluded to," the *Missouri Republican* angrily reported, "contained all the necessary directions and cautions to enable the free blacks, on their arrival there, to claim and exercise the rights of citizenship." Phelps tried to backtrack. He immediately released an *Extra,* which he explained would "prevent [blacks] from being admitted as members of the Church," an explanation that clumsily only made matters worse since it implied the existence of a previous welcoming policy. The 1838 "Manuscript History of the Church" reproduces a copy of Phelps's circular.[9]

However, the Manuscript History redacts major passages from Phelps's original notice. The original reads: "Our intention was not only to stop free people of color from emigrating to this state, but to prevent them from being admitted as members of the Church." The edited version deletes the exclusionary portions of the text as follows: "Our intention was ~~not only~~ to stop free people of color from emigrating to this state, ~~but to prevent them from being admitted as members of the Church~~." Later in the text, the words "~~and we say, that none will be admitted into the church~~" were also omitted.[10] By the time this history was composed in 1839, Elijah Ables had joined the faith and gained Joseph's affection. A probable explanation for the strikethroughs is that Joseph Smith refused to allow the history to be composed in a way that would exclude Ables and others like him.

---

8. A racialized reference to Shakespeare's character, Desdemona, from *Othello*—a Venetian woman who had married an Ethiopian man. In antebellum America, Desdemona had been generally been depicted as innocent and virtuous. With the rise of abolitionism, Desdemona came to be seen as an example of a woman who had transgressed racial sensibilities. One popular story is told of a white woman and black man traveling together. When questioned about the propriety of the action, the woman confessed that she "had been reading SHAKESPEARE'S 'Othello,' and fancied herself another *Desdemona*—her sooty lover another moor of Venice." Edward Kahn, "Desdemona and the Role of Women in the Antebellum North," 235–55.

9. Manuscript History of the Church, A-1, 326.

10. Ibid., 332.

CITATION

"The Outrage in Jackson County," *The Evening and the Morning Star* 2, no. 17 (February 1834): 128.

DOCUMENT EXCERPT

Previous to the time when the printing office was demolished, some of the mob sent their negroes to insult and abuse certain young women, who slept in a small cabin adjoining the dwelling where the remainder of the family slept.[11] After repeated attempts to commit insults upon these young women, the parents concluded that it would be unsafe to trust them longer in that situation. Accordingly the young women were put in another bed, and two young men were placed in their stead. After the young men had retired the man of the house was called to the door, and informed by a friend, of the determinations of the mob. This friend also informed him, that as near as he could learn, there would be one or more negroes sent to molest his daughters that night. This was during the excitement while the mob were circulating their secret constitution for signatures. Fortunately, however for the negroes, or their owners, the young men had retired without having this watch-word, and were unprepared with any deadly weapons. In the night they were awoke by the noise occasioned by the negroes whispering and planning without. Directly one made his entrance into the room through the way where the chimney had formerly stood, and was permitted to call the name of one of the young women, and make known his business and intentions when he was seized by the young men, and handled so roughly for a few moments that the demi-infernal when liberated from their grasp, dove head foremost through a wall of stone and bricks that was then remaining of the old chimney.

That the negro did not send himself, is demonstrated from the fact, that whites knew it previous to the time he came, and was informed of [it] by the individual just named. Every person acquainted with the manner in which the blacks are treated in a slave State, know that an act of that kind would cost the slave his own life in an instant, were it possible for the individuals suffering the insult to inflict death: this is no secret among the slaves. And without being encouraged to go, and having a promise of protection from their masters should they be caught, it would be in vain to endeavor to convince the mind, that those blacks would ever attempted an act of so gross a magnitude. And what but an attempt to insult and abuse, could [have] ever prompted any man to encourage any thing of so shameful a nature? What better can we think of a man that will urge his negro to commit unlawful acts, than we could

---

11. Portrayals of African American men as lurking sexual predators circulated throughout the national press. In Connecticut, one newspaper editor expressly connected abolitionism to increasing numbers of black-on-white rapes: "Since [abolitionists'] bowels of mercy began to yearn for the *Negro tribe*, . . . offences of this kind are almost invariably committed by *black men* upon *white girls*." If abolitionism persisted, he argued, "we may expect to hear cases of this kind daily announced." "A Tappanite," *Columbian Register* (New Haven, Conn.), August 31, 1833, 3, and "Depravity," *Philadelphia Inquirer*, December 6, 1830, 2.

were he to attempt the same himself? But these are the men who make such pretensions to virtuous principles, as to complain that the "Mormons" were about to corrupt their society, by the introduction of free negroes and mulattoes into that country.

. . . Here is a set of men in danger of having their public morals corrupted, who make a pretence to religion, and are so far beneath every thing heretofore extant on earth in the form of wickedness, that they will set their Afric colored population to steal into the dwellings of peaceable neighbors and defile the virtuous! They said, "We will ravish your women!"[12] No promise of mercy, ever so solemnly made, has been observed a moment when they saw an opportunity to abuse the persons of their hatred. But on the other side, every act of abuse which they swore to commit, when ever a possibility presented, it was done or attempted. An attempt was made by a gang of these lawless miscreants to abuse a lady who was in the most delicate situation in life, when a part were pursuing her husband to take his life, and others were engaged in pulling down his dwelling round her in the dead hour of the night! These are facts which will stand recorded upon the pages of the history of the inhabitants of the nineteenth century! A century proud of its liberal laws, and its advance in science and religion! Which is entitled to the appelation, Civilized? We talk in our country of savages, whose customs and habits, we say, are such that it is necessary that missionaries should be sent immediately to convert them from their idolatry, and teach them the blessings of civilized life. Is it color that constitutes a savage, or is it the acts of men that appear disgustful, and awake in our breasts feelings of pity and compassion for them?

Elijah Ables's Priesthood Certificate (March 1836)

HISTORICAL INTRODUCTION

As the Saints struggled to adapt to the heated Jackson County environment, prospects looked a little more promising in Kirtland for black Mormons. In September 1832, Elijah Ables, an African American living in Cincinnati, joined the Mormons after hearing the preaching of a local resident, Ezekiel Roberts. He moved to Kirtland where he was ordained an elder in the Melchizedek Priesthood "under the hands of Joseph Smith."[13] Some resisted Joseph Smith's openness. Zebedee Coltrin, one of Joseph's close associates who officiated for Elijah's ritualistic washings and anointings at the Kirtland Temple recalled more than thirty-five years later that he "had never experienced such unpleasant feelings in his life."

---

12. The 1825 Missouri state code provided the following punishment for alleged rape by slaves: "If any negro or mulatto shall . . . commit, or attempt to commit a rape on a white female," he would not be imprisoned but "sentenced to castration, to be performed under the direction of the sheriff, by some skillful person." The law remained in force at the time the Saints were in Missouri. Other crimes would "be punished, at the discretion of the court before whom the conviction shall be had." *Laws of the State of Missouri*, 1:312–13; *The Revised Statutes of the State of Missouri*, 171.

13. Eunice Kinney, Letter to Wingfield Watson, July 5, 1885, photocopy, Perry Special Collections.

He decided that he would refuse to perform any further ordinances for African Americans "unless specifically directed by the Prophet to do so."[14]

By 1838, Elijah Able had won Joseph's affection. It seems likely to me that he ordered his scribe, James Mulholland, to strike out Phelps's exclusionary passages from the Manuscript History. From Joseph Smith's perspective, Elijah's ordination to the Melchizedek Priesthood marked a rejection of Phelps's overreaction in the heat of persecution. The language of Elijah Ables's priesthood certificate uses language identical to other certificates of priesthood ordination. In other words, Ables was ordained to the same priesthood office as Frederick G. Williams, Thomas B. Marsh, and even Joseph Smith himself.[15]

The idea of having a black preacher in a predominantly white congregation was, at the very least, unusual. In 1841, runaway slave Samuel Ward received a Congregationalist preacher's license and directed an all-white congregation in South Butler, a township that was a day's journey from Palmyra, New York.[16] Ward later recalled that his congregation was far removed from the "allurements and deceptions of fashion. . . . They heard a preacher: they supposed and believed that he preached God's truth." The "mere accident of the colour of the preacher was to them a small consideration."[17]

CITATION

Kirtland Elders Certificates, CD, CR 100 401, 75, LDS Church History Library; left justification added.

DOCUMENT EXCERPT:

To Whom It May Concern

This certifies that Elijah Ables has been received into the church of the Latter-day Saints organized on the sixth of April, in the year of our Lord one thousand eight hundred & thirty, & has been ordained an Elder according to the rules & regulations of said church, and is duly authorized to preach the gospel equally to the authority of that Office.[18] From the satisfactory evidence which we have

---

14. Zebedee Coltrin, qtd in L. John Nuttall, Diary, typescript, May 31, 1879, Perry Special Collections.

15. Elders' Certificates for W. W. Phelps, John Whitmer, and Joseph Smith, Kirtland Elders Certificates, CD, 1, 2, 4, 57.

16. Samuel Ward, *Autobiography of a Fugitive Negro: His Anti-Slavery Labours in the United States, Canada, & England*, 31.

17. Ibid., 82–83.

18. When Joseph Smith founded the Church, he (or those acting under his authority) did not ordain all men as Elders in the priesthood but also as "teachers" and "priests." For instance, he ordained Christian Whitmer to be a "teacher of this Church of Christ established & regularly organized in these last days." Joseph Smith's father was ordained to be "a Priest of this Church of Christ." John Whitmer, however, was in fact ordained to be "an apostle of Jesus Christ, an Elder of this Church of Christ." See Michael H. MacKay, Gerrit J. Dirkmaat, Grant Underwood,

of his good moral character, & his zeal for the cause of righteousness, & diligent desire to persuade men to forsake evil & embrace truth, we confidently recommend him to all candid & upright people as a worthy member of society. We, therefore, in the name & by the authority of the Church, grant unto this, our worthy brother in the Lord, this letter of communication as a proof of our fellowship & Esteem: Praying for his success & prosperity in our Redeemer's Cause. Given by a direction of a conference of the Elders of said church Assembled in Kirtland, Geauga County, Ohio, the third day of March, in the year of our Lord, one thousand eight hundred <thirty six>.

Joseph Smith Jr., Chairman
F. G. Williams Clerk.
Kirtland, Ohio, March 31, 1836

Joseph Smith Defends Slavery (April 1836)

HISTORICAL INTRODUCTION

The explosive events in Jackson County that resulted in the Saints' expulsion in the summer of 1833 placed Joseph Smith in a political bind. Should the Latter-day Saints continue to be friendly to the black population, or should they attempt to distance themselves from blacks to avoid the resistance and even violence experienced by abolitionists? April 1836 was only days after Joseph Smith had ordained Elijah Ables to the Melchizedek Priesthood. Joseph's decision was to walk a difficult line—publicly endorsing slavery while continuing to support Elijah Ables in his priesthood calling.

CITATION

Joseph Smith, Letter to Oliver Cowdery, *Messenger and Advocate* 2, no. 7 (April 1836): 288–91.

DOCUMENT EXCERPT

Brother O. Cowdery:

Dear Sir—This place having recently been visited by a gentleman who advocated the principles or doctrines of those who are called abolitionists; if you deem the following reflections of any service, or think they will have a tendency to correct the opinions of the southern public, relative to the views and sentiments I believe, as an individual, and am able to say, from personal knowledge, are the feelings of others, you are at liberty to give them publicity in the columns of the Advocate.[19] I am prompted to this course in consequence, in one respect, of

---

Robert J. Woodford, and William G. Hartley, eds., *Documents: Volume 1, July 1828-June 1831,* 148–50. See also Dan Vogel, *Early Mormon Documents*, 5:357.

19. After Phelps's print shop and press for *The Evening and the Morning Star* in Missouri had been destroyed in 1833, the paper moved to Kirtland, Ohio, under the editorship of Oliver Cowdery.

many elders having gone into the Southern States, besides, there now being many in that country who have already embraced the fulness of the gospel, as revealed through the book of Mormon,—having learned, by experience, that the enemy of truth does not slumber nor cease his exertions to bias the minds of communities against the servants of the Lord, by stiring up the indignation of men upon all matters of importance or interest.

Thinking, perhaps, that the sound might go out, that "an abolitionist" had held forth several times to this community, and that the public feeling was not aroused to create mobs or disturbances, leaving the impression that all he said was concurred in, and received as gospel and the word of salvation[,] I am happy to say, that no violence or breach of the public peace was attempted, so far from this, that all except a very few, attended to their own avocations and left the gentleman to hold forth his own arguments to nearly naked walls.

I am aware, that many who profess to preach the gospel, complain against their brethren of the same faith, who reside in the south, and are ready to withdraw the hand of fellowship because they will not renounce the principle of slavery and raise their voice against every thing of the kind.[20] This must be a tender point, and one which should call forth the candid reflection of all men and especially before they advance in an opposition calculated to lay waste the fall [sic] States of the South, and set loose, upon the world a community of people who might peradventure, overrun our country and violate the most sacred principles of human society, chastity and virtue.

After having expressed myself so freely upon this subject, I do not doubt but those who have been forward in raising their voice against the South, will cry out against me as being uncharitable, unfeeling and unkind—wholly unacquainted with the gospel of Christ. It is my privilege then, to name certain passages from the bible [sic], and examine the teachings of the ancients upon this nature, as the fact is uncontrovertable, that the first mention we have of slavery is found in the holy bible, pronounced by a man who was perfect in his generation and walked

---

But Cowdery was planning to terminate the paper since it had been "designed to be published at Missouri." The newspaper continued from December 1833 until September 1834, when Cowdery ceased production and replaced it with the *Latter-day Saints' Messenger and Advocate*, a title assumed because "the name of this church has lately been entitled the church of the Latter-day Saints." Oliver Cowdery, "Address to the Patrons of the Evening and Morning Star," 1.

20. Joseph Smith is probably referring to stalwart missionaries such as Abraham Smoot and Charles C. Rich. Smoot was born in Owenton, Kentucky, in 1815 and baptized in 1835. In 1820, Owen County was home to just under 200 slaves out of a population of 2,031. By 1840, the slave population had multiplied in accordance with white immigration and totaled over 1,200 out of 8,232. Charles C. Rich was born in nearby Campbell County, Kentucky, where also slaves made up a tiny fraction of the overall population as late as 1847. For the 1820 totals, see William Darby, *Darby's Edition of Brookes' Universal Gazetteer*, 770. For the 1840 totals, see Daniel Haskel and J. Calvin Smith, *A Complete Descriptive and Statistical Gazeteer of the United States of America*, 506. For the Campbell County total, see James McCulloch, *A Dictionary, Geographical, Statistical, and Historical of the Various Countries, Places, and Principal Natural Objects in the World*, 1:525.

with God.[21] And so far from that prediction's being averse from the mind of God it remains as a lasting monument of the decree of Jehovah, to the shame and confusion of all who have cried out against the South, in consequence of their holding the sons of Ham in servitude!

"And he said cursed be Canaan; a servant of servants shall he be unto his brethren. And he said, Blessed be the Lord God of Shem; and Canaan shall be his servant. God shall enlarge Japheth, and he shall dwell in the tents of Shem and Canaan shall be his servant."—Gen. 8:25, 26, 27.

Trace the history of the world from this notable event down to this day, and you will find the fulfilment of this singular prophecy. What could have been the design of the Almighty in this wonderful occurrence is not for me to say; but I can say that the curse is not yet taken off the sons of Canaan, neither will be until it is affected by as great power as caused it to come; and the people who interfere the least with the decrees and purposes of God in this matter, will come under the least condemnation before him; and those who are determined to pursue a course which shows an opposition and a feverish restlessness against the designs of the Lord, will learn, when perhaps it is too late for their own good, that God can do his own work without the aid of those who are not dictated by his counsel. . . .[22]

A Non-Mormon Describes Elijah Ables's Preaching in Canada (1838)

HISTORICAL INTRODUCTION

Probably in the spring of 1838, Elijah left Kirtland to serve a mission in Upper Canada—modern-day Ontario. Known for its large population of former slaves who had run away from U.S. owners, abolitionists boosted the region as "Freedom's Colony in Canada." However, it was also a site of political and military conflict. Since the fall of 1837, Canadian rebels had been organizing against

---

21. Joseph Smith is referencing Noah and his curse of his son Ham that Ham's descendants would be the "servant of servants," an interpretation common to nineteenth-century biblical exegesis. For the best treatment of American Christianity's views of Ham, see Sylvester Johnson, *The Myth of Ham in Nineteenth-century American Christianity: Race, Heathens, and the People of God.*

22. Antislavery gradualism—the argument that slavery ought to be abandoned gradually rather than eradicated immediately—had dominated antislavery discourse since the late eighteenth century. By 1836, however, most American antislavery associations had eschewed gradualist thought. Gradualist thought assumed the inevitable progress of man and the reliability of divine Providence for human betterment, while supporters of immediate abolitionism believed that human society was unpredictable and its future therefore malleable. Joseph Smith argued that emancipation would be a dramatic act of divine Providence, not the product of hubristic abolitionists who felt they could dictate the will of the Lord. In January 1836, leading abolitionist James G. Birney, the abolitionist presidential candidate in 1840 and favorite of Mormon abolitionist Rees E. Price, lectured in Cincinnati on "the influence of slavery on the church and the insufficiency of gradualism." "Anti-Slavery Lectures," *Cincinnati Weekly Herald and the Philanthropist*, January 1, 1836, 6. For a good scholarly treatment of antislavery immediatism, see David Brion Davis, "The Emergence of Immediatism in British and American Antislavery Thought," 209–30.

the British government. By the time Ables arrived in Canada, supportive vigilante groups in upstate New York were beginning to smuggle arms across the St. Lawrence River to assist some Canadians rebels who were seeking to secede from the British Empire. The rebels ardently embraced the American political system, making it dangerous to be an American who came to the attention of British authorities in Upper Canada. Mormon branch president William Burton recalled that the rebellion gave anti-Mormons "a good opportunity" to persecute them. As peculiar Americans that had fixated on talk of an American promised land, the Mormons were ideal political targets for supporters of the Crown. Widely seen as the "far west," Detroit served as a strategically important location for the British, the "Patriots" (rebels), and the American vigilantes who supported them. According to William Burton, they were charged as "rebels, and some were imprisoned [or] brought before magistrates."[23]

John Broeffle, a resident of Williamsburg, Ontario, had several family members who became Mormons and associated with Elijah Ables. In a letter to his aunt, Broeffle describes the activities of this "negro preacher" and relates a close call with a local mob.

CITATION

John Broeffle, Letter to Catherine Beckstead, September 19, 1838, LDS Church History Library.

DOCUMENT EXCERPT

I wrote you that Old Uncle Sandy and Francis[24] with some of their families had become Mormons with some others. They started last June for their Zion in Missouri, a journey or pilgrimage of near two thousand miles. . . . If you remember old William Riley in the eighth concession,[25] you know the last minister left of that society. He was ordained last Spring by Gurley[26] and a negro who was about here to be a preacher for the few left. There are forty some odd of men, women and children gone out of the Becksted connection (as many as 45) and in

---

23. William Burton, Autobiography, 3, MS 1508 1, LDS Church History Library.

24. Alexander ("Sandy") Beckstead (b.1769) was of old upstate New York stock and married Sarah Reddick in 1794/95. They moved with his brother, Francis Beckstead, from New York to Williamsburg, Ontario, in 1807. Alexander and Francis left Williamsburg for Missouri before the end of June 1838. Andrew Jenson, "De Witt," *Historical Record* (Salt Lake City) 7, no. 7 (July 1888): 603.

25. William Riley was a captain in the British military. The "eighth concession" refers to his 200-acre land holdings in the area. His biography is included in J. Smyth Carter, *The Story of Dundas: Being a History of the County of Dundas, from 1784 to 1904*, 438.

26. Born in Bridgewater, New York in 1801, Zenos Gurley joined the Mormons in April 1837 after hearing the preaching of fellow New Yorker James Blakeslee and Truman Gillett. Gurley helped with the relief of the poor Saints driven out of Missouri after the 1838 extermination order of Governor Lilburn H. Boggs. He also collected funds for building the Nauvoo Temple. "Biographical Sketch of Elder Zenos H. Gurley, Sen'r," *The True Latter-day Saints' Herald* 19, no. 1(January 1, 1872): 1–3. See also "Manuscript History of the Church," C-1, April 9, 1838.

all sixty some odd souls left here under the we fear awfully delusive doctrine held by this Mormon sect. They think that Christ will in person reign on the earth there, that all the old prophets will rise with all other dead Christians and be there and beget sons and daughters during a thousand years. And if a man joins them here he must go there immediately if possible. They insist more on the rich ones to go than the poor ones; it appears that money is the greatest object, and they, the men, must get there the best way they can, but if a woman joins them and her husband does not join them in that case the angels will come at the commencement of the millenium (which they say will begin in ten years from last year) and fetch them alive to their Zion, and many other such like absurd things they preach up.[27] The Negro Preacher went off with the last ones two or three days before as there had been about ten men in the night at Uncle Sandies to tar and feather him, but could not find him and Uncle Sandy thought they came for his money and so got his wife to shoot them and they made off and the Negro went soon after. We have heard of them not long since, they were in Michigan then <and the Negro with them>.[28]

A New York Convert Recalls Elijah Ables (1838)

HISTORICAL INTRODUCTION:

When Eunice Ross (later Kinney) first heard Elijah Ables preach in spring 1838, she was a young mother, pregnant with her second child. Impressed by his preaching style, she became a Mormon but was never able to gather with the Saints. After the death or desertion of her first husband, she married Avery Kinney in the 1840s and embraced James Strang as the successor to Joseph Smith. Rumors even circulated that she became pregnant with Strang's child.[29] But she never forgot Elijah Ables. Even in 1891 when she was over ninety years old, she yearned for information on his whereabouts and well-being. "I know of no person living," Eunice wrote nostalgically, "that I would be so glad to see as him.[30]

---

27. Most Mormon missionary work included strong millennialist overtones. When Amos Fuller was serving in Ohio and New York, a man asked if there could be "men standing in this generation that would not away [die] until the Saviour came." Fuller responded that he "knew by the revelation of Jesus Christ" that such was the case. Apostle Orson Hyde unqualifiedly told a congregation in Boston "that the Son of Man will appear in this generation." Orson Hyde, Letter to Editor, *Messenger and Advocate* 2, no. 1 (October 1835): 206. See also Amos Fuller, Journal, January 17, 1838, 26–27.

28. Widely seen as the "far west," Detroit served as a strategically important location. Troops, vigilantes, and rebels centered their efforts on leaving or reaching Detroit. "Authentic from the Detroit Patriots," *Centinel of Freedom*, (Newark, NJ) December 18, 1838, 2; "Important from the Frontier," *Albany [New York] Argus*, December 18, 1838, 2; "Army Orders" and "Michigan—The Western States," both in *Commercial Advertiser[New York City]*. September 17, 1838, 2; and "Frontier Intelligence," *Vermont Phoenix [Brattleboro, Vermont]*, July 13, 1838, 3.

29. Vickie C Speek, *"God Has Made Us a Kingdom": James Strang and the Midwest Mormons*, 115.

30. Kinney, Letter to Wingfield Watson, July 5, 1885, Perry Special Collections.

CITATION

Eunice Kinney, Letter to Wingfield Watson, September 1891, L. Tom Perry Special Collections, Harold B. Lee Library, Brigham Young University, Provo, Utah.

DOCUMENT EXCERPT

In the spring of 1838 I heard the first Gospel sermon by a latter-day Saint.

His name was Elijah Abel; he was ordained by Joseph, the martyred prophet. I was then living in the town of Madrid, Lawrence County, New York.[31] We had never heard of the latter-day Saints until Elder Abel came into the place. I, with my husband,[32] went and heard him preach. Abel was a man without education; it was difficult for him to read his text but when he commenced to preach, the Spirit rested upon him and he preached a most powerful sermon. It was such a Gospel sermon as I had never heard before, and I felt in my heart that he was one of God's chosen ministers, and I verily thought that all those who ever were under the sound of his voice were impressed with the same views. But I soon learned my mistake; when the sermon was ended he gave liberty to anyone that wished to express their feelings either for or against the subject that have been set before him. My husband rose and opposed that bitterly and said many hard things.

After the meeting was closed, the Elder came to my husband[33] putting his hand on his shoulder, says, "Brother where do you live?" My husband told him. He then said to my husband, "tomorrow I will come and see you and have a little chat." He came as he said and he and my husband were soon in conversation. Abel set forth the claims of Joseph Smith to the prophetic office, showing the necessity of the everlasting gospel being restored to prepare a people for the coming of the Son of Man. So the time was drawing near for His coming but He would not come till God had a people prepared to receive him, with all the gifts and blessings that adorned his Church anciently.

My husband opposed him, said that he was under no obligation to receive his message without seeing some sign or miracle performed. Abel then said, "is it a sign that you require for to make you belief [sic]?" He said "yes."

Abel says, "you shall have what you asked, but it will make your heart ache. A curse from God will follow you from this time forward. You will be cursed in your going out and coming in and everything that you put your hand to do will be cursed, and sore affliction will follow you until you repent and humble yourself before God."

---

31. Madrid was small agrarian community with 4,510 residents in 1840. John W. Barber and Henry Howe, *Historical Collections of the State of New York*, 484–85.

32. According to her 1844 certificate for a second marriage, her name was Eunice Ross. No known records definitely indicate her first husband's given name. For her second marriage certificate, see Marriage Certificate of Eunice Ross and Avery Kinney, February 24, 1845, Michigan County Marriages, Berrien, (accessed March 15, 2013).

33. A reference to her first husband, identity unknown.

Well, I have only to say that all was fulfilled to the very letter. The last affliction that came our little boy of three years was taken with the croup. The doctor[34] said that he was in the last stage of the disease and [there] was no hope in his case. My husband then gave up, said that it was enough, burst into a flood of tears, acknowledging his faults saying that he knew that he had been under the influence of evil spirit. He then humbled himself under the mighty hand of God, praying God to forgive him and restore our child, in all things as it should be made known to him.

Suffice it to say that the child got well, and when Elder Abel came again we both went down into the water and was buried with Christ in baptism. When confirmed, great blessings were predicted upon our heads. My husband was to preach the gospel was to become mighty in causing many to believe and obey it. He was also to have the gift of tongues and the interpretation, also the gift of prophecy and the gift of healing the sick. All these things were fulfilled in due time.

But soon after I was baptized I became severely tempted by the power of darkness, and the glorious light that had reflected upon my understanding a short time before had now become darkness, and how great was that darkness! Now, in my view The Book of Mormon was a romance[35] and Joseph was a false prophet and the Elder th[at] baptized me was one of the devil's ministers transformed into a minister of righteousness. And I soon found myself in overwhelming doubts, fears and despair; no language could express the keen anguish that I endured. For one week I could neither eat nor sleep. I thought that if I could only see the Elder I would say many hard things to him.

One Sunday morning very unexpectedly [and to] my great surprise Elder Abel came. As soon as he entered the house, my feelings that I had somewhat changed. After a little conversation, I made an effort to express the feelings and trials that I had had since I was baptized, but I was spellbound. I could not utter the words that I had previously imagined. He only said, "Sister, you have not been tempted as long as the Savior was after he was baptized. He was tempted one way and you in another."

He then said to my husband, "I wish you would circulate an appointment for preaching at three o'clock in the afternoon at the schoolhouse." It was done

---

34. Possibly "Dr. F. Parker," who later served as the censor for the St. Lawrence County Chapter of the New York Medical Society. "Minutes of the St. Lawrence Association," *Universalist Union*, August 18, 1838, 323. See also "Appendix," *Transactions of the Medical Society of the State of New York*, 6:83.

35. Webster (1830) defined a "romance" as "a fabulous relation or story of adventures and incidents designed for the entertainment of readers; a tale of extraordinary adventures, fictitious and often extravagant, usually a tale of love or war, subjects interesting to the sensibilities of the heart or the passions of wonder and curiosity." See Noah Webster, *American Dictionary of the English Language: Exhibiting the Origin, Orthography, Pronunciation, and Definition of Words*, 709.

as he requested. At first I thought I would not go, but when the appointed time came I said to my husband, "I will go and see the coming out of it."

His text was "Think it not strange, brethren, concerning the fiery trials which are to try you as though some strange thing had happened unto you" [1 Pet. 4:12]. I thought the text very appropriate.

While he was preaching, a great and marvelous change came over me. All the doubts and fears and unbelief and the powerful darkness that had so distressed me fled before the light of God's truth like the dew before the sun. The Holy Spirit came upon me and I was in a glorious vision. It was then and there made known to me by the power of God that Joseph Smith was a true Prophet of God, and the <u>Book of Mormon</u> was a sacred record of divine origin, and Elijah Abel was a servant of the most high God. I've never had a doubt of these things from that day to this, and when I think of that glorious event it fills my heart with joy and gratitude to my Heavenly Father for such an expression of his goodness.

After the meeting, Brother Abel explained the cause of his coming so unexpectedly. He was on a mission in Canada and God gave him a vision of my situation and commanded him to come and rebuke the power that was destroying me. He obeyed the command and God's blessing was realized.

Brother Abel now had to leave us and go back to Canada to meet his appointments there, but said that he would come and preach to us again in two weeks. But before the two weeks were up, persecution was raging in a fearful manner. Handbills were pasted up in every direction stating the Mormon Elder had murdered a woman and five children and a great reward was offered for him.[36]

We were members of the Methodist Church[37] at the time we united with the Latter-day Saints, and our Methodist brethren were our greatest persecutors. They said to us, "now, what do you think of your Mormon Elder after committing such a crime?" Said that he would never show himself there again.

I says, "He will come and fill his appointment and God will protect him." They said that just as sure as he did come he would not have the privilege of preaching, for they would nab him too quick, but they knew that he would never be seen there again. When the time was nearly up, Elder Abel came and the house was well filled. After Abel was seated a few moments, he rose and says to the congregation, "my friends, I'm advertised for murdering a woman and five children and a great reward is offered for my person. Now here I am; if anyone has anything to do with me, now is your time. But after I commence my services,

---

36. No evidence has yet been discovered tying Elijah to a murder, nor have I found the report of any murder of a woman and her five children in any contemporary newspapers in the region.

37. The Rosses probably associated with the Potsdam Methodist Church, the nearest congregation. Until 1806, Potsdam had been a part of Madrid and served as the cultural and religious center for the area at the time of Ables's ministry. Barber and Howe, *Historical Collections*, 489–90. See also Thomas F. Gordon, *Gazetteer of the State of New York*, 668.

don't you dare to lay your hands on me." He waited in silence a few moments, and no one moved the tongue or raised the hand.

He then opened the meeting with singing and prayer, and he preached a most powerful sermon. He went home with us to stay for the night. The next day he left unmolested. Before he left us he advised my husband to sell out and go further west to some Branch of the Church where we would have more agreeable society. He said that there was a good branch of Saints about forty miles west and we had better go there. As we were the only ones that obeyed the gospel in the place, he thought it would be hard for us to live our religion alone. So we done as he advised us and it proved a great blessing to us.

We found Elder James Blakesley[38] and family with the Branch. He invited us to move into the house with them. We did so and found them to be the best of Saints.[39] While we were there the power of God was manifested in a won-

---

38. James Blakeslee (1802–66) joined the Mormons in July 1833. In 1835, he moved his family to Upper Canada where he actively preached the necessity of gathering to Missouri. In 1836, he was found guilty of "improper conduct towards one of the sisters," telling her that she "won his affections and that he loved her as much as he did his own wife." Further, he assured her that he "did not think that his own wife would live a great while." The disgusted sister reported Blakeslee's actions to the Twelve, and Blakeslee's elder's license was temporarily suspended. He bounced back quickly, commencing a mission to England in September 1840 where he stayed until March 1841, then returned to upstate New York. James Blakeslee, Letter to "Dear Brethren in the New Covenant," June 11, 1841, *Times and Seasons* 2, no. 18 (July 15, 1841): 482. In the fall of 1841, the Twelve called him to return to Nauvoo, a trip that took him nearly eighteen months to complete. In June 1843, he passed through Cincinnati to assist Elijah Ables with running the dysfunctional Cincinnati branch. By August, he had settled into Nauvoo. Meeting Minutes, June 25, 1843; Joseph Smith III and Heman Smith, *History of the [RLDS] Church of Jesus Christ of Latter-day Saints, 1873–1890*, 4:723. "Letter from J. Blakeslee," *Times and Seasons* 3, no. 8 (February 15, 1842): 696–97. On his return trip, Blakeslee visited Cincinnati where he witnessed Heber C. Kimball, Orson Pratt, and Lorenzo Snow restrict Ables's preaching to the local black population. "Letter from J. Blakeslee," *Times and Seasons* 3, no. 8 (February 15, 1842): 696–97; Meeting Minutes of a Conference in Cincinnati, June 25, 1843, photocopy of holograph in my possession. Despite his own amorous conduct, he lost faith in Joseph Smith when he learned in 1844 of Joseph's polygamy. After Joseph's death, Blakeslee initially supported Sidney Rigdon's claims to leadership and became one of Rigdon's twelve apostles. In 1847, he joined the Strangites, becoming quickly disenchanted when Strang's plural marriage was revealed. In 1857, in association with Zenos Gurley, he helped form a loose organization of Saints (the "New Movement") who had not followed Brigham Young west and who focused hopefully on the principle of familial succession. Their hopes were realized when Joseph Smith III, in response to a Gurley's earnest arguments and a personal revelation agreed in April 1860 to head the group that was later named the Reorganized Church of Jesus Christ of Latter Day Saints. Joseph Smith III, *History of the Church of Jesus Christ of Latter-day Saints: 1844–1872*, 3:756–59. See also William Shepard, "James Blakeslee: The Old Soldier of Mormonism," 113–32.

39. In March 1836, Blakeslee penned a poem: "Behold the man whose tender heart / Expanded with a saviour's love / Wide as eternity expands / His bowels with compassion move . . . / And hastens at his Lord's command / To call his brethren from afar / As volunteers for Zion's land / That in her sorrows they may share." James Blakeslee Record Book, no

derful manner. The sick were healed through his ministration; Sister Blakesley[40] often spoke in tongues and also gave the interpretation, and through the Spirit of prophecy she predicted wonderful events which were all fulfilled in due time.

After remaining there sometime we moved to Michigan, where we remained until after the death of the martyred prophet. While we were in Michigan, I passed through sore afflictions, sometimes wishing my days to be few. But I will pass those things by, and thank God that I yet live to give my testimony to the truth that God has shown me pertaining to the latter-day work.

Jane Manning James Autobiography (1810–93)

HISTORICAL INTRODUCTION

In 1842, Jane Manning came into contact with Charles Wesley Wandell, a missionary preaching in Connecticut. Manning lived as a house servant in the Joseph Fitch household. Dissatisfied with her Presbyterian faith, she joined the Mormons, along with several family members, though there was no congregation of note nearby. As with most Saints, Jane heard the message of gathering to Zion, so she and her family began the grueling journey from Connecticut to Nauvoo the following year. They arrived in Nauvoo in October 1843.

CITATION

Jane Manning James, "Biography of Jane E. Manning James written from her own verbal statement and by her request," holograph, transcribed by Elizabeth J.A. Roundy, 1893, LDS Church History Library.

---

pagination, MS 922 1, LDS Church History Library. Heber C. Kimball called Blakeslee one of the "polished stone[s]" who are "so very . . . smooth in the beginning" but "get badly defaced and spoiled while they are rolling about." Quoted in "History of Joseph Smith," *Millennial Star* 22, no. 10 (March 10, 1860): 151.

40. Louisiana Edmunds Blakesley (1804–76) married James Blakeslee on October 25, 1825. Blakeslee Record Book, 1. While Blakeslee was preaching in upstate New York and Canada, Louisiana became extremely ill. In September 1839, Jonathan Dunham, then serving a mission in Canada, was called to "go lay hands on Sister Blakesley who was in fits." Dunham reported that she was "instantly healed." According to Eunice Kinney, Louisiana accompanied her husband to "investigate the clames of [James] Strang." Louisiana was "very anxious to see Mr. Strang" and "had inquired of the Lord to know the true Prophet." Kinney recalled that "the Lord showed her in vision the man that was to lead the church in Joseph's place, and if James J. Strang is the man I will know him as soon as I set my eyes on him." After seeing Strang, she declared that "he is God's anointed prophet" and "[I] knew him before anyone told me who he was." Blakesley warned Kinney that "there is going to be a great apostasy here in Voree, and those who are now so strongly defending the claims of James will soon deny him and become his bitter enemies." At the time, she didn't believe it; but in 1891, Blakesley declared that "every word Sister Blakesley uttered was fulfilled." Jonathan Dunham, Diary, September 18, 1839, MS 1387, 5, LDS Church History Library. See also Eunice Kinney, Letter to Wingfield Watson, September 1891, holograph, in Wingfield Watson Correspondence, LDS Church History Library.

DOCUMENT EXCERPT

When a child only six years old, I left my home and went to live with a family of white people. Their names were Mr. and Mrs. Joseph Fitch.[41] They were aged people and quite wealthy. I was raised by their daughter.

When about fourteen years old, I joined the Presbyterian Church[42]—yet I did not feel satisfied. It seemed to me there was something more that I was looking for. I had belonged to the [Presbyterian] Church about eighteen months when an Elder of the Church of Jesus Christ of Latter-day Saints, [who] was traveling through our country, preached there. The pastor of the Presbyterian Church forbade me going to hear them as he had heard I had expressed a desire to hear them;[43] nevertheless I went on a Sunday and was fully convinced that it was the true gospel he presented and I must embrace it.[44] The following Sunday I was baptized and confirmed a member of the Church of Jesus Christ of Latter-day Saints.

---

41. The Fitch family had been prominent Fairfield county citizens for several generations. Samuel Fitch II, son of Samuel and Elizabeth Fitch, was the father of Joseph Platt Fitch (1790–1868), who married Emma Sherman in 1816. They had three children: Mary Elizabeth, Sherman, and Harriet A. However, Joseph Platt Fitch would have been in his thirties when Jane began living with them, making it unlikely that he could have been described as "aged." Joseph had an uncle, also named Joseph Platt Fitch (1753-death date unknown). In the 1800 census, a third Joseph Fitch lived in Norwalk, Connecticut, approximately fourteen miles south of Wilton, with his family of nine consisting of one male over age forty-five (Fitch himself) and two females (likely daughters) between ages of sixteen and forty-five. In the 1820 census, a fourth Joseph Fitch maintained a household of seven in New Canaan, approximately eighteen miles from Wilton. The census shows one male over age forty-five (likely Fitch himself) and a daughter between ages sixteen and twenty-six. In 1808, a Joseph Fitch, either the fourth described above or possibly a fifth individual with that name, was among the first members of a Methodist congregation in New Canaan, Connecticut. New Canaan is approximately eight miles from Wilton. Reverend Charles M. Selleck, *Norwalk*, 216; and D. Hamilton Hurd, *History of Fairfield County, Connecticut*, 441. For Joseph Platt Fitch's (1790–1868) death date, see Robert H. Russell, *Wilton, Connecticut: Three Centuries of People, Places, and Progress*, 207. For the records of the other Norwalk and New Canaan candidates for Joseph Fitch, see U.S. Census, 1800, Connecticut, Norwalk, 206, and U.S. Census, 1820, Connecticut, New Canaan, 214.

42. Jane likely attended the Presbyterian congregation that met near Wilton Academy, a private academy in Wilton started by Hawley Olmstead on property donated by Nathan Comstock to the Presbyterian Society of Wilton with the stipulation that it be used strictly for "a school of higher order, and for religious and singing meetings." Hurd, *History of Fairfield County*, 838.

43. This pastor was possibly Samuel Merwin, who had been ordained pastor over a Wilton congregation in March 1832. Jane's brother Isaac told Roundy that Jane had given birth to a son named Sylvester who "was the child of a white man, a preacher, but he could not tell if he was the child of the Presbyterian or a Methodist preacher." See "Quarterly List of Ordinations and Installations," *Quarterly Register and Journal of the American Education Society* (May1832): 336. See also Elizabeth Roundy's editorial notation on p. 23 (the final page) of Elizabeth J. A. Roundy, "Biography of Jane E. Manning James."

44. In Jane's 1905 account, she claimed to have seen Joseph Smith in vision before joining the Church: "After I saw him plain, I was certain he was a prophet because I knew it. . . . Did not have to tell me because I knew him. I knew him when I saw him back in old Connecticut in a

One year after I was baptized, I started for Nauvoo with my mother, Eliza Manning, my brothers Isaac Lewis,[45] and Peter, my sisters, Sarah Stebbins and Angeline Manning, my brother-in-law Anthony Stebbins,[46] Lucinda Manning (a sister-in-law), and myself in the fall of 1840 [sic]. We started from Wilton, Connecticut, and traveled by canal to Buffalo, New York. We were to go to Columbus, Ohio[47] before our fares were to be collected, but they insisted on having the money at Buffalo and would not take us farther. So we left the boat and started on foot to travel a distance of over eight hundred miles.

We walked until our shoes were worn out, and our feet became sore and cracked open and bled until you could see the whole print of our feet with blood on the ground. We stopped and united in prayer to the Lord; we asked God the Eternal Father to heal our feet. Our prayers were answered and our feet were healed forthwith.

When we arrived at Peoria, Illinois, the authorities threatened to put us in jail to get our free papers.[48] We didn't know at first what he meant, for we had never been slaves, but he concluded to let us go. So we traveled on until we came to a river, and as there was no bridge, we walked right into the stream. When we got to the middle, the water was up to our necks but we got safely across. Then it became so dark we could hardly see our hands before us, but we could see a light in the distance, so we went toward it. We found it was an old Log Cabin. Here we

---

vision, saw him plain and knew he was a prophet." "'Aunt' Jane James," *Young Woman's Journal* 16, no. 12 (December 1905):553.

45. Kate B. Carter, *The Negro Pioneer*, 9–13, described both Isaac Lewis and Jane Manning as "servants" who "lived for many years in the household of Joseph Smith."

46. Based on later accounts, it is likely that Anthony Stebbins was a runaway slave. A Reverend Stephen W. Stebbins of West Haven gave the prayer at the 1830 creation of the New Haven congregation in which a Reverend Professor Fitch (likely Eleazar Fitch of Yale College) gave the sermon. The relationship, if any, between Stephen Stebbins, the Fitches, and Anthony is not known. "Installation," *Connecticut Journal* [New Haven], March 30, 1830, 1. After Anthony arrived in Nauvoo, he began to save money to purchase the son he left behind. In doing so, Anthony committed some legal infractions such as selling liquor on the Sabbath. *Ordinances of the City of Nauvoo*, 5, required a license to sell alcohol and forbade the sale of liquor on Sunday. Both violations incurred fines of five dollars per offense. Joseph issued the fine against Anthony. When Anthony begged for mercy, Joseph gave Anthony a horse worth more than $500 to purchase his son's freedom. "Mary Frost Adams," *Young Woman's Journal* 17, no. 12 (December 1906): 538.

47. At the time Columbus was a major canal city connecting Eastern cities with the frontier. Manning's group would have traveled from Buffalo through Cleveland onward to Columbus. From Columbus, steamboats provided transportation to "any river port in the Western States." Samuel Mitchell, *Illinois in 1837*, 64.

48. According to Illinois state law, which was similar to Missouri's law, "No black or mulatto person, not being a citizen of some one of the United States shall be permitted to reside in this state until such person shall produce to the county commissioners' court where he or she is desirous of settling a certificate of his or her freedom which certificate shall be duly authenticated in duly same manner that is required to be done in cases under the acts and judicial proceedings of other states." Any free black without this documentation would be "deemed a runaway slave or servant." *The Revised Laws of Illinois*, 463; *Revised Statutes of the State of Illinois*, 387.

spent the night. The next day we walked for a considerable distance, and stayed that night in a forest out in the open air.

The frost fell on us so heavy, it was like a light fall of snow.[49] We arose early and started on our way walking through that frost with our bare feet, until the sun rose and melted it away. But we went on our way rejoicing, singing hymns, and thanking God for his infinite goodness and mercy to us—in blessing us as he had, protecting us from all harm, answering our prayers, and healing our feet.

In course of time, we arrived at La Harpe, Illinois—about thirty miles from Nauvoo.[50] At La Harpe, we came to a place where there was a very sick child. We administered to it, and the child was healed.[51] I found after the elders had before this given it up, as they did not think it could live.

We had now arrived to our destined haven of rest: the beautiful Nauvoo! Here we went through all kinds of hardship, trial and rebuff, but we at last got to Brother Orson Spencer's.[52] He directed us to the Prophet Joseph Smith's mansion. When we found it, Sister Emma was standing in the door, and she kindly said, "Come in, come in!"

Brother Joseph said to some white sisters that was present, "Sisters, I want you to occupy this room this evening with some brothers and sisters that have just arrived." Brother Joseph placed the chairs around the room and then he went and brought Sister Emma and Dr. Bernhisel[53] and introduced them to us. Brother Joseph took a chair and sat down by me and said, "You have been the head of this little band, haven't you!" I answered, "Yes sir!" He then said, "God bless you! Now I would like you to relate your experience in your travels."

I related to them all I have above stated—and a great deal more minutely, as many incidents has passed from my memory since then. Brother Joseph slapped Dr. Bernhisel on the knee and said, "What do you think of that, Dr.? Isn't that

---

49. In Jane's 1905 interview, she recalled that they "lay in bushes and in barns and outdoors, and traveled until there was a frost just like a snow, and we had to walk on that frost." "'Aunt' Jane James," *Young Woman's Journal* 16, no. 12 (December 1905): 552.

50. Jane's band probably lodged with fellow Latter-day Saints, as a settlement of more than fifty Saints was living there in spring 1841. One resident observed: "The Mormons are getting into this country most too plenty. The people at the east have no idea to what lengths they go in crowding into places where they can get any foothold to make proselytes. There has fifty or more joined them at La Harpe." "The Mormons," *North American* [Philadelphia], June 21,1841, 2.

51. In the Mormon community, healing was not conceptualized as a priesthood ordinance but as a "gift of the spirit" to be exercised by any member (D&C 46:20).

52. A recent convert, Orson Spencer had been baptized in the spring of 1841, shortly before Jane James's arrival at Nauvoo. Jane was probably drawn to the Nauvoo Temple site, which was near Orson Spencer's home. Andrew F. Ehat and Lyndon W. Cook, eds., *The Words of Joseph Smith: The Contemporary Accounts of the Nauvoo Discourses of the Prophet Joseph Smith*, 103. See also Andrew Jenson, *Latter-day Saint Biographical Encyclopedia: A Compendium of Biographical Sketches of Prominent Men and Women in the Church of Jesus Christ of Latter-day Saints*, 1:337–39.

53. John Milton Bernhisel (1799–1881), baptized in New York City and served as bishop over a small branch. He moved to Nauvoo in the spring of 1843. Gwynn Barrett, "Dr. John M. Bernhisel: Mormon Elder in Congress," 147–48.

faith?" The Dr. said, "Well I rather think it is. If it had have been me, I fear I should have backed out and returned to my home!" [Joseph Smith] then said, "God bless you. You are among friends now and you will be protected."

They sat and talked to us awhile, gave us words of encouragement and good counsel.[54] We all stayed there [the Mansion House] one week. By that time, all but myself had secured homes. Brother Joseph came in every morning to say good morning and [see] how we were. During our trip I had lost all my clothes–they were all gone. My trunks were sent by canal [boat] to the care of Charles Wesley Wandell.[55] One large trunk full of clothes of all descriptions–mostly new!

On the morning that my folks all left to go to work, I looked at myself–clothed in the only two pieces I possessed–[and] I sat down and wept. Brother Joseph came into the room as usual, and said, "Good morning. Why [you are] not crying [are you?]?" "Yes sir. The folks have all gone and got themselves homes and I have got none." He said, "Yes you have. You have a home right here, if you want it. You mustn't cry; we dry up all tears here." I said, "I have lost my trunk and all my clothes." He asked how I had lost them. I told him I put them in care of Charles Wesley Wandell and paid him for them and he has lost them. Brother Joseph said, "Don't cry. You shall have your trunk and clothes again."[56] Brother Joseph went out and brought Sister Emma in and said, "Sister Emma, here is a girl that says she has no home. Haven't you a home for her?" "Why yes, if she wants one." He said, "She does." And then he left us. Sister Emma said, "What can you do?" I said, "I can

---

54. In 1905, Jane remembered Joseph's congeniality towards her: "That lovely hand! He used to put it out to me. Never passed me without shaking hands with me wherever I was. . . . I tell you I do wake up in the middle of the night and I just think about Brother Joseph and Sister Emma and how good they was to me." "'Aunt' Jane James," 551.

55. Charles Wesley Wandell (1819–75), baptized in New York in 1837. He taught Jane's group during his mission to Connecticut. He relocated to Nauvoo where he served as a professor at the University of Nauvoo. Wandell apparently became the primary custodian of itinerant black Saints' goods. In December 1843, Albert Gregory charged Wandell for "unchristian-like conduct towards certain colored brethren, by leaving them at Cleveland in Ohio, after having engaged to conduct them to Nauvoo" and failing "to deliver their effects at Nauvoo according to promise." Wandell was "honorably acquitted." Fred Collier, ed., *The Nauvoo High Council Minute Book of the Church of Jesus Christ of Latter-day Saints*, 128. For biographies, see Inez Smith, "Biography of Charles Wesley Wandell," *Journal of History* 3–4 (October 1910/January 1911): 3:455–71, and 4:57–65; Marjorie Newton, *Hero or Traitor: A Biography of Charles Wesley Wandell*.

56. In December 1843, the *Nauvoo Neighbor* ran a notice asking for assistance in locating James's trunk: "About six weeks ago a company of saints arrived in this place escorted by Elder Wandel who had in his charge a trunk belonging to Jane Elizabeth Manning:—Sister Manning was not here then but has since arrived and can obtain no intelligence of her trunk; it is presumed that some one has got it in mistake as there was a number of passengers arrived at the same time. The trunk is about three feet long and covered with a light red hair skin, with the exception of the back, on which there is some white. It is directed 'Jane Elizabeth Manning, Nauvoo.' Whoever shall give such information as shall lead to the discovery of the trunk will be handsomely rewarded by applying to this office." "Lost," *Nauvoo Neighbor*, December 6, 1843, 3. Many thanks to James Goldberg for directing me to this source.

wash, iron, cook, and do housework." "Well," she said, "when you are rested, you may do the washing, if you would just as soon do that." I said, "I am not tired." "Well," she said, "you may commence your work in the morning."

The next morning she brought the clothes down in the basement to wash. Among the clothes, I found brother Joseph's Robes.[57] I looked at them and wondered—[as] I had never seen any before—and I pondered over them and thought about them so earnestly that the spirit made manifest to me that they pertained to the new name that is given the saints that the world knows not of.

I had to pass through Mother Smith's[58] room to get to mine, [and] she would often stop me and talk to me. She told me all Brother Joseph's troubles, and what he had suffered in publishing the Book of Mormon. One morning I met Brother Joseph coming out of his mother's room. He said, "Good morning!" and shook hands with me. I went to his mother's room. She said, "Good morning. Bring me that bundle from my bureau and sit down here." I did as she told me. She placed the bundle [in] my hands and said, "Handle this and then put it in the top drawer of my bureau and lock it up." After I had done it she said, "Sit down. Do you remember that I told you about the Urim and Thummim when I told you about the Book of Mormon? I answered yes ma'am. She then told me I had just handled it. "You are not permitted to see it, but you have been permitted to handle it. You will live long after I am dead and gone and you can tell the Latter-day Saints, that you was permitted to handle the Urim and Thummim."[59]

---

57. A reference to an undergarment that Joseph designed for those who were endowed. Though restricted to an elite circle before Joseph's death, when the Nauvoo Temple was finished, hundreds of the Saints were endowed in the ceremony he had established, which included receiving this garment, which was to be "worn all through life." According to Joseph Smith's bodyguard, James Allred, Joseph commissioned Allred's grandmother, Elizabeth Warner Allred, to make the first garment from "turkey red" muslin. When it was completed, Joseph "held it up before" the congregation , declaring that the garment was "the exact pattern of the one the angel showed him, and was called 'the Garment of the Holy Priesthood.'" Joseph promised the Saints the garment would be a "protection . . . against all physical and spiritual dangers if they were always faithful to the covenants made with the Lord." Eliza M. A. Munson, "The Early Pioneer History of James Allred," n.d., LDS Church History Library. For a fuller treatment, see Colleen McDannell, *Material Christianity: Religion and Popular Culture in America*, 198–218.

58. The widowed Lucy Mack Smith (1775–1856) moved into Joseph Smith's residence in the summer of 1843. Lucy Mack Smith, *Biographical Sketches of Joseph Smith the Prophet and His Progenitors for Many Generations*, 274.

59. When Joseph Smith translated the gold plates received in 1827, he used "the interpreters " (also labeled "Urim and Thummim"), which were with the plates, in the translation process. They consisted of a breastplate and "spectacles" made up of two interlocking bows and transparent stones. In the summer of 1828, the Angel Moroni revoked Joseph's stewardship and repossessed both plates and the Urim and Thummim as a punishment for his decision to give Martin Harris the transcript of the translated portion. Emma Smith Bidamon, Letter to Emma Pilgrim, March 27, 1870, in Dan Vogel, ed., *Early Mormon Documents*, 1:532. When Joseph repented and received the plates again in the fall of 1828, he apparently did not receive the interpreters but instead relied upon his seer stone, which had found while he was digging a well on Mason Chase's property in 1822. The stone was small, "not exactly black, but was rather a dark color." W. D.

Sister Emma asked me one day if I would like to be adopted to them as their child. I did not answer her. She said, "I will wait awhile and let you consider it." She waited two weeks before she asked me again. When she did, I told her, "No Ma'am," because I did not understand or know what it meant. They were always good and kind to me but I did not know my own mind; I did not comprehend.

Soon after, they broke up the mansion and I went to my mother. There was not much work because of the persecutions, and I saw Brother Joseph and asked him if I should go to Burlington and take my sister Angeline with me. He said, "Yes. Go and be good girls, and remember your profession of faith in the everlasting gospel, and the Lord will bless you." We went and stayed three weeks and then returned to Nauvoo. It was during this time that the prophet Joseph and his brother Hyrum was martyred. I shall never forget that time of agony and sorrow.[60] I went to live in the family of Brother Brigham Young.[61] I stayed there until he was ready to emigrate to this valley.[62]

. . . Oh how I suffered of cold and hunger, and the keenest of all was to hear my little ones crying for bread, and I had none to give them; but in all, the Lord was with us and gave us grace and faith to stand at all. I have seen Brother Brigham, Brothers Taylor, Woodruff, and Snow rule this great work and pass on to their rewards, and now Brother Joseph F. Smith. I hope the Lord will spare him, if this [is] his holy will, for many years to guide the Gospel ship to a harbor of safety.

Yours in truth.

Jane Elizabeth James

Purple recalled the stone being "the size of a small hen's egg, in the shape of a high in-stepped shoe." W. D. Purple, "Joseph Smith, The Originator of Mormonism: Historical Reminiscences of the Town of Afton," *Chenango [New York] Union* 30, no. 33 (May 2, 1877), 3. In 1841, Wilford Woodruff noted that he had "the privilege of seeing for the first time in my day the URIM & THUMMIM," suggesting that Joseph's intimate circle also applied the term to the stone as well as to the "spectacles," or the "interpreters." Scott G. Kenney, ed., *Wilford Woodruff's Journal, 1833–1898*, typescript, December 27, 1841, 2:144. Phelps was apparently the first to conflate the "interpreters" with the Old Testament's "Urim and Thummim." "The Book of Mormon," *Evening and the Morning Star* 1 (January 1833): 57. For a full treatment of Joseph Smith's translation methods, see Richard Van Wagoner and Steve Walker, "The Gift of Seeing," 49–68.

60. Jane said of this period that she would have "liked to a died myself. . . . I felt so bad. I could have died, just laid down and died; and I was sick abed." Members of the teachers quorum visited her and exhorted her: "You don't want to die because he did. He died for us, and now we all want to live and do all the good we can." "Aunt' Jane James," *Young Woman's Journal*, 553.

61. Franklin D. Richards confirmed Jane's residence with the Brigham Young family, recording that Jane "had been a faithful Saint & servant in the household of Prest. Brigham Young." Franklin D. Richards, Journal, August 22, 1895, in *Selected Collections*, 2:35.

62. Jane traveled with the Daniel Spencer/Ira Eldredge company, leaving Winter Quarters in June 1847. They arrived in the Salt Lake Valley in September. Jane's travels west were generally peaceful, including "Fife & drumb & fiddle playing" along with "dancing by the Indians." They experienced "comparatively little sickness," and the trip was overall "a very pleasant one." Daniel Spencer, Diary, July 23, 1847, holograph LDS Church History Library; Diana Eldredge Smoot, Autobiography, Perry Special Collections.

Elijah Ables's Preaching Activities Restricted (June 1843)

HISTORICAL INTRODUCTION

Ables moved to Cincinnati in early 1842 for unknown reasons, though it likely involved some kind of missionary labor. It seems probable to me that he was acting in his office as a seventy with the charge to breathe life into the ailing branch in his capacity. Phineas Young and Franklin D. Richards were also serving a mission there where they "resuscitated the few dropping Saints that they found . . . and added to the number until the branch was 56 members when they left."[63]

Ables settled in "Little Africa"—the slums of East Cincinnati.[64] He likely connected with Rees E. Price, a recently baptized Mormon and eccentric philanthropist who also served on the Executive Board of the Ohio Anti-Slavery Society.[65] For the past decade, Cincinnati had been a hotbed for anti-abolitionist mob attacks, making every level of leadership particularly leery of Ables's prominence.[66]

CITATION

Meeting Minutes of a Conference in Cincinnati, June 25, 1843, photocopy in my possession; emphasis and strikeovers in original.

DOCUMENT EXCERPT

Bro. Elder Elijah Ables being called upon made a few remarks Elder Page[67] said he respects a coloured Bro, as such but wisdom forbids that we should introduce before the public Elder O. Pratt sustained the position of Bro. Page. Bro. Ables said he had no disposition to force himself upon an equality with white people and went on to explain a circumstance that had recently occurred Elder Grant[68]

---

63. "Biography of Franklin Dewey Richards," in Manuscript History of the Church, in *Selected Collections*, 1:18.

64. Charles Cist, ed., *Cincinnati Directory for the Year 1842*, 2. See also Nikki Taylor, *Frontiers of Freedom: Cincinnati's Black Community, 1802–1868*, 38.

65. Phineas Young baptized Price on March 13, 1842. Phineas Young, Letter to Brigham Young, March 14, 1842, Brigham Young Office Files, Reel 57.

66. Russell W. Stevenson, *Black Mormon: The Story of Elijah Ables*, chap. 5.

67. John E. Page (1799–1867) joined the Saints in 1833 and was ordained an apostle in 1838 after the Missouri defections of the Johnson brothers and William McLellin. In the summer of 1843, he had been conducting Church business in the eastern states and met Heber C. Kimball and Orson Pratt in Cincinnati, then on a fund-raising mission for the Nauvoo Temple. Joseph Smith, Letter of Introduction for Heber C. Kimball, June 1, 1843, LDS Church History Library; John Quist, "John E. Page: The Apostle of Uncertainty," 53–68.

68. Joshua Grant (1818–51) was the brother of Jedediah M. Grant. Jedediah had handled Ables's earlier disciplinary hearing in Nauvoo in which Ables had been forced to answer charges of alarmism and violence during his mission to Ontario. Joshua had been called as the Cincinnati Branch president in April 1843 but his leadership was not received well. Heber C. Kimball said of the branch that "the Elders are very much like old . . . sheep that get together and Run & and fight each other for mastery." Members had "lent there [sic] support to to [sic] many Heads." Page added that he could "compare it to nothing else but . . . Old Hens quarreling over one

followed he rose to explain his course toward Bro Ables his remarks on the occasion alluded to did not grow out of ill feelings towards Bro. Ables But <u>purely as a matter of policy</u>. . . . [He] thinks perhaps he spoke sharply but still contends for the principle. Bro. Ables arose and insisted that he had been misused.

Bro. Page remarked that there was no excuse for anger or a bad spirit Bro Able said he was sorry inasmuch as he had done wrong (Elder Kimball[69] arose and called upon Bro. Ables to confess before this meeting) boldly and frankly that was the proper course to persue we must cultivate good feelings one to another and any thing short of this will overthrow us Bro. Able arose and made a satisfactory acknowledgement, Elder Kimball deduced therefrom a useful moral, Weed out every bad principle that good seed may take root and bear fruit, viz. Righteousness and peace and Joy in the Holy Ghost.

Elder Ables was called upon to state his wants ~~and~~ by the pres.

Elder John E. Page, arose and made a few remarks concerning the coloured population.

Bro. Pratt arose and stated that the duty of the 12 is to ordain and send men to their ~~own~~ <native> country[70] ~~and own kin~~

Bro. Ables was advised to visit the coloured population

The advice was sanctioned by the conference. Instructions where [sic] then given him concerning his mission

Black Elder Q. Walker Lewis Serves in Boston (1844–47)

HISTORICAL INTRODUCTION:

Ables was not the only black Mormon priesthood holder. In 1842, William Smith baptized a black abolitionist in Lowell, Massachusetts, named Quack Walker Lewis. A barber and committed Saint, Lewis proved to be more devoted

---

nest with one egg in it." See Meeting Minutes of a Conference in Cincinnati, June 25, 1843, photocopy in my possession.

69. Heber C. Kimball had been commissioned to raise funds to construct the Nauvoo Temple. Before arriving in Cincinnati, he dreamed that he was about to take some wheat to a barn but, on closer examination, found that the wheat had become less valuable oats and that the oats had been "all eaten up by . . . rats." He determined that the vermin represented the "Elders and official members who had been in and lain on the Church." He discovered that when the "Twelve came along they could not get anything for the Temple or Nauvoo House." See "History of Joseph Smith," *Millennial Star* 22, no. 10 (March 10, 1860): 151; Joseph Smith, Letter of Introduction for Heber C. Kimball, June 1, 1843, MS 9670, LDS Church History Library.

70. Pratt is referring to the directive Joseph gave Pratt and others before they left for the East: "When you meet with an Arab, send him to Arabia, when you find an Italian, send him to Italy. & a french man, to France; or an Indian, that is suitable. send him among the Indians. & this and that man send them. to the different places where they belong.—Send somebody to Central America and to Spanish America & don't let a single corner of the earth go without a mission." Joseph Smith, Journal, April 19, 1843, in Andrew H. Hedges, Alex D. Smith, and Richard Lloyd Anderson, eds. *Journal, 1841–43*. Vol. 2 in the Journals series. THE JOSEPH SMITH PAPERS. Salt Lake City: Church Historian's Press, 2012., *Journals, Vol. 2, 1841–1843*, 369.

than many of the white priesthood holders. In William Appleby's eyes, he was "an example for his more whiter brethren to follow."[71]

WILFORD WOODRUFF ACCOUNT CITATION

Wilford Woodruff, Letter to Brigham Young, November 16, 1844, Brigham Young Office Files, Reel 56, LDS Church History Library.

DOCUMENT EXCERPT

But I found it different with the Lowell[72] Church, Elder Wm Smith[73] & myself attended a church meeting together there all the mail members resigned their offices in that branch of the Church except one coloured brother who was an elder but the President & Clerk resigned,[74] the reason was a complaint that has saturated my ears in most of the eastern church I have visited but I advised them to hold their stations as they were, & go ahead all would be right if, they did well they would be blessed, they were not accountable for other faults and they did so all kept their places.

WILLIAM APPLEBY ACCOUNT CITATION

William Appleby, Journal, May 19, 1847, LDS Church History Library.

DOCUMENT EXCERPT

Left this Afternoon, for Lowell, where I arrived in about one hour and a half, distance 25. miles. Here I found a branch of the Church of about 20 members in tolerable good standing. Elder [Darius] Lougee[75] presiding. In this Branch there

---

71. For the most thorough account of Lewis's life, see Connell O'Donovan, "The Mormon Priesthood Ban and Elder Q. Walker Lewis: 'An Example for His More Whiter Brethren to Follow,'" 48–100.

72. Many things were different about Lowell, Massachusetts. The city was a large social experiment in religion, human rights, and the industrial revolution. With a dose of hyperbole, one Lowell minister commented: "Among the wonders of the new world, enlightened foreign travelers justly consider the existence of this city as one of the greatest." With its deliberate planning, commitment to Christian ethos, and hard work ethic, Lowell was in the eyes of many a place of "great wonder and distinction." Reverend (Henry) Miles, "Lowell," *Boston Recorder*, June 13, 1844, 96.

73. William Smith ordained Walker Lewis during his mission to the East between October 1843 and 1844. William Appleby, Letter to Brigham Young, June 2, 1847, Brigham Young Office Files, Reel 30. See also O'Donovan, "The Mormon Priesthood Ban and Elder Q. Walker Lewis," 67–68; Calvin P. Rudd, "William Smith, Brother of the Prophet Joseph Smith" (M.A. thesis, Brigham Young University, 1973), 86–88.

74. Probably referring to Varanes Libby, then a twenty-six-year-old "white washer" in Lowell. Wilford Woodruff baptized Libby on October 16, 1844, and he was immediately made branch president. Kenney, *Wilford Woodruff's Diary*, 2:474. He apostatized soon thereafter. Boston Ward 3 Census, https://familysearch.org/pal:/MM9.1.1/MDSC-FBY (accessed January 12, 2014).

75. Darius Longee (1815–1901), then a branch president in Boston, was assigned as a captain of ten in the John Hindley pioneer company and arrived in Utah on September 3, 1855. He preached sermons and sat on council meetings along the way. See references to him in John

is a Coloured Brother, (An Elder ordained by Elder Wm. Smith while he was a member of the Church, contrary though to the order of the Church or the Law of the Priesthood, as the Descendants of Ham are not entitled to that privilege) by the name of Walker Lewis. He appears to be a meek humble man, and an example for his more whiter brethren to follow. At this place there are thousands of girls, working in the Factories, which are the most extensive of any in the United States. The City contains some thirty thousands inhabitants, one fourth perhaps operatives in the mills.[76]

A Mormon-Turned-Radical Abolitionist in Cincinnati (1855)

Historical Introduction

A few months after Elijah Ables moved to Cincinnati in 1842, the Cincinnati Branch attracted a wealthy abolitionist named Rees E. Price.[77] Committed to theocracy and the absolute, immediate, and unequivocal abolition of slavery, Price's presence in the Cincinnati cast a long shadow. As a member of the Executive Board of the Ohio Anti-Slavery Society, Price almost certainly had been targeted in the anti-abolitionist race riots that had roiled Cincinnati in 1836 and 1841. It is also reasonable to suppose that Price assisted with the Underground Railroad. Price's prominence as an abolitionist likely played a role in the Church leaders' June 25, 1843, decision that Elijah should confine his preaching to Cincinnati's black community. Within a few months of this restriction imposed on Elijah, Price defected from the branch and started his own movement in January 1844. Price remained committed to his dream of a theocracy for the remainder of his life.

Price claimed a prophetic mantle. He envisioned the establishment of Zion in his home state of Ohio "in the territory marked by the patriots of 87 [the framers of the Constitution], as seered to the principles of '76."[78] Nearly a decade later, Price was still continuing the fight. In a public letter addressed to his friend William Lloyd Garrison, Price laid out his vision for a theocracy free of slavery. Although he had defected from the Mormons, Price continue to employ Mormon language and political concepts.

Citation

Rees E. Price, Letter to William Lloyd Garrison, in *The Liberator*, June 1, 1855, 87; left justification added.

Parson, Camp Journal, June 24, 1855, LDS Church History Library; and Jemima M. Stookey, "Autobiography of Jemima E. Stookey," 21, LDS Church History Library.

76. Lowell, Massachusetts, was a major site for the textile revolution in New England with factories staffed primarily by young women. For a firsthand account, see Lucy Larcom, *A New England Girlhood: Outlined from Memory.*

77. Phineas Young, Letter to Brigham Young, March 14, 1842, Brigham Young Office Files, Reel 57.

78. "A New Prophet," *Public Ledger* (Philadelphia), January 2, 1844, 3.

Document Excerpt

Democracy, with the help of Constitutional Republicanism, has been tried by the nation, and proved *false* to justice and righteous liberty. The fault is in the element. The vile and ignorant outnumber the virtuous and the wise. The dogma that all men are created (politically) equal is one of the last delusions of "the man of sin." Political rights are acquired "by patient continuance in well-doing," and no two men acquire precisely the same rights.

Governments derive their just powers from God. The Confederacy will be broken to pieces like a potter's vessel, because the Federal Government is unjust. The American institution of slavery has been *tolerated* by the HIGHER POWER (more than a quarter of a century since thy inspiration began the cry, "undo the heavy burden and let the oppressed go free") to *prove* democracy where democracy is most intelligent and free—in the free states,—and where democracy in power is led by men sworn "to establish justice." . . .

The principles of democracy are beastly. The body assumes the sovereign, and the wicked head assumes it lawful to yield obedience to its impulses; and thus, the Federal head says "I have yielded or gave power 'unto a beast' until the purposes of God are fulfilled" in the experiment; for, be assured, the beastly principles of the democratic age will pass away with the elements of the man of sin, and no place be found for them.

A Constitutional Republican Government, elected from above, and guided by Theocracy, is practicable, and will succeed and supplant the democratic federal government in two of the three pieces of the broken confederacy. The other fragment may continue democratic long enough for a contrast.

You are the standard of Abolitionism, and as such, I am in duty bound to pay you high honor. You are a second John the Baptist. Your work is done, and well done. You have shaken the Confederacy to its centre, and made its heart quake with fear of a dissolution, (preceding the enactment of the peace measures of the damned,) and there is nothing more to do under the name of Abolitionist. I would enlist thee in the kingdom of God—a kingdom that shall break in pieces confederated oppressors, establish justice and judgment in the earth, and stand for ever.

I honor the name of Abolitionist. *You* are *the* Abolitionist—I am the Theocrat. . . .

With high regard for thee, I have the honor to be,
Thy fellow-servant,

Rees E. Price.

Elijah Ables Cracks Down on Dissent in Cincinnati (1845)

HISTORICAL INTRODUCTION

The death of Joseph Smith in June 1844 unleashed a wave of organizational chaos throughout the Church. Who was to be the new leader? Several figures made claims to leadership. Joseph Smith's former counselor Sidney Rigdon; a charismatic visionary, James J. Strang; and Joseph Smith's brother, William, counted themselves among the contenders.

The branches throughout southwestern Ohio made their loyalties clear; they were committed to supporting the Twelve. In the summer of 1845, Elder Joseph T. Ball,[79] a Boston African American priesthood leader and former branch president, traveled through the region where he presided over the disfellowshipping of a local white elder, John Bair. Bair had been charged with "teaching things contrary to the Book of Covenants, inconsistent with virtue, which has destroyed the union of the saints and prevented them paying their tithing." Young was surprised at the news of Bair's defection, as he thought that Bair "had been faithful and done much good." Bair quickly repented of his ill-doing, assuring the Saints that he would "receive no doctrine except it comes from the proper source—the Twelve."[80]

But Young had long learned that he needed to root out dissent if it meant preserving the integrity of the Church. He asked Rowland Crispin to send him the names of the southern Ohio dissenters so they could "as soon as consistent come up here that we may know the truth of this matter." Young was more than willing to have "all such characters brot up and cast out of the church that Zion may be made pure."[81] As one of the ordained members of the Quorum of the Seventy who was present in Cincinnati, Elijah Ables played a leading role in carrying out the excommunication of those who were likely Rigdonite sympathizers.

The Cincinnati branch commenced a purge targeted at Rigdonite influence. The Saints had been meeting in the home of James Pugh. After Strang made his claim to Joseph Smith's mantle, Pugh was exuberant: "I rejoice to hear that we have a prophet." Pugh assured Strang that he would use his influence to diminish the authority of the Twelve.[82] Rumors began to circulate that the branch membership had fallen under the sway of the various factions. Ables took immediate action and called for the excommunication of three dissenters, all three of them

---

79. Ball's ordination in Boston was performed under less-than-transparent circumstances. Following Libbe's resignation, George J. Adams and William Smith "took [Ball] off alone & ordained him an High Priest without the knowledge of the Church or anybody." Woodruff called the ordination a "trick" carried out "to gain their point." Wilford Woodruff, Letter to Brigham Young, November 16, 1844, Brigham Young Office Files, Reel 56.

80. John Bair, "Dear Brethren," *Times and Seasons*, 6, no. 12 (July 1, 1845): 949.

81. Brigham Young, Letter to Rowland Crispen, Summer 1845, Brigham Young Office Files, Reel 24.

82. James Pugh, Letter to James E. Strang, March 23, 1846, James Strang Papers, Beinecke Library, Yale University, New Haven, Conn. (hereafter Beinecke Library).

white women. Branch President John Crippin wrote Brigham Young in March 1845 to "correct" reports that "all of the Cincinnati branch ~~had~~ have joined the Rigdonites." Following the purge, Crippin assured Young, "the Branch never flourished as it does at present. . . . [W]e now have peace in our midst."[83]

Citation

"Minutes of a Special Conference of the Cincinnati Branch of the Church of Jesus Christ of Latter-day Saints, held at Elder Pugh's on the 1st day of June, 1845," *Times and Seasons* 6, no. 10 (June 1, 1845): 915; left justification added.

Document Excerpt

The conference met agreeable to previous appointment and was called to order by Elder Crippin. John W. Crippin[84] was appointed President, and George Hales[,] Clerk.[85] The conference was opened by singing and prayer by Abraham Wright.[86] Present—three seventies,[87] two elders, one priest, and two teachers.

The President then laid before them the object of the conference. Elder Elijah Able then preferred a charge against Mrs. Carter, Mrs. Evans,[88] and Miss

---

83. J. W. Crippin, Letter to Brigham Young, March 14, 1845, Brigham Young Office Files, Reel 29.

84. Crippin defected from the leadership of the Twelve in 1849, joining William Smith's sect based in Covington, Kentucky. Crippin composed a hymn in honor of his new-found prophet. "Special Conference," *Melchisedek and Aaronic Herald* 1, no. 4 (June 1849): 4. One of the verses extolled "Prophet William": "Prophet William is the man,/ The Elijah of the Gospel plan,/ Like as Joseph who was slain,/ The faith of Saints remains the same;/ Then when the Savior comes again,/ With Saints we'll rise, with him we'll reign." For text of this hymn, see Joseph Wood, Epistle of the Twelve, 24.

85. George Hales (1822–1907), baptized April 1840. As a skilled printer, Hales worked in the offices of the *Times and Seasons* and the *Nauvoo Neighbor.* In the spring of 1844, Hales and his wife, Sarah Gregory Hales, visited her family in Cincinnati and stayed until the fall of 1845. Kenneth G. Hales, "George Hales: Pioneer Printer," 2008, 1–5, LDS Church History Library.

86. Probably Abraham R. Wright (1811–99), joined the Saints in 1841, ordained an elder April 1, 1844. The above-mentioned *Times and Seasons* article is the only source placing him in Cincinnati in 1845. In 1856 he came to Utah with the Abraham O. Smoot company. By 1859, he had returned to Cincinnati, established a freighting company, and assisted several Saints travel to Utah. "Arrived," *Deseret News*, October 12, 1859, 4; Sarah Myers, "Minersville," *Deseret News*, February 18, 1904, 9.

87. We do not have a complete record of the Seventies living in Cincinnati in June 1845, however, in meeting minutes from a conference in June 1843, three seventies are listed as being present: Branch President Joshua Grant, James Blakeslee, and Elijah Ables. However, Blakeslee was traveling through Cincinnati en route to Nauvoo. See James Blakeslee, Diary, 38–39 in Shepard, "James Blakeslee," 119.

88. Possibly Hannah Evans, who was baptized June 6, 1849. She made a donation in the Cincinnati Branch that year. If correct, Evans had reconciled with the followers of the Twelve by the end of the decade. Baptism List, Edson Whipple Record Book, 1849–1850, MS 861 1, LDS Church History Library. I have not found identifying information on the other two women.

Jane Roberts, for absenting themselves from the meetings of this branch, and speaking disrespectfully of the heads of the church.

It was then moved and seconded that they be expelled from the church, which was done by a unanimous vote. . . . It is with pleasure we inform our brethren and friends that there is more union existing in this branch than there has been for the last three years, for which we give God the glory.

John W. Crippin, Pres.
George Hales, Clerk

Chapter 9

Origins of the Priesthood Ban, 1847–49

Church Leaders Meet William McCary (March 1847)

Historical Introduction

Born a slave in Natchez, Mississippi, McCary[1] ran away as a child and became a musician along the Mississippi River. He joined the Saints in early 1846, converted by Orson Hyde. He lived temporarily in Cincinnati where he started his own brand of Mormonism, drawing predominantly women as converts. Approximately six months later, he arrived in Winter Quarters where he married Lucy Stanton, the "Wife" mentioned in the minutes below. She was a former follower of "Black Pete," an early convert in Kirtland, known for his ecstatic worship practices. McCary and Stanton settled in with the Mormon community.[2] McCary, a talented musician, initially charmed the recently exiled Saints, who welcomed his contributions to Mormon cultural life. A "great fluter & player," McCary gave concerts and wove stories—a sure source of entertainment for a white Mormon population accustomed to black minstrel shows.[3]

Still, several locals were uncomfortable with the cross-race marriage and expressed their dismay freely. In his meeting with Brigham Young and several apostles, McCary explained his views and, more importantly, asked the brethren for protection from racist Saints. Church leaders found McCary amusing and honest. They reassured him that black men had tremendous potential as priesthood holders, noting that "one of our best Elders is an African" and "we don't care about the color." Scribe Thomas Bullock recorded the minutes.

---

1. He would be variously known as William McCray, William McCary, James Warner, William Chubbee, and William McChubby. Wilma King, *Stolen Childhood: Slave Youth in Nineteenth-Century America*, 289–90.

2. Reuben Harmon, Statement, *Startling Revelations: Naked Truths about Mormonism,* edited by Arthur B. Deming, 1, no. 12 (April 1888): 201. See also Mark Lyman Staker, *Hearken O Ye People: The Historical Setting of Joseph Smith's Ohio Revelations,* 84–85.

3. Robert L. Campbell, Diary, March 1, 1847, BYU; see also Juanita Brooks, ed., *On the Mormon Frontier: The Diary of Hosea Stout,* March 30, 1847, 1:244.

CITATION

Meeting Minutes of the Twelve, March 26, 1847, in Richard E. Turley Jr., ed., *Selected Collections from the Archives of the Church of Jesus Christ of Latter-day Saints,* DVD. Provo, Utah: Brigham Young University Press, 2002, 1:18.

DOCUMENT EXCERPT

March 26-1/2 past 7 pm

In Drs. Office, Prest. Young, Kimball,[4] Richards,[5] Lyman,[6] Pratt,[7] Benson,[8] Woodruff,[9] Smith,[10] N.K. Whitney,[11] A. P. Rockwood,[12] G. D. Grant,[13] John

---

4. Heber C. Kimball (1801–68) had been a member of the Church as long as Brigham Young and had served as an apostle since 1835. At this point Kimball was first counselor in the First Presidency. See Stanley B. Kimball, *Heber C. Kimball: Patriarch and Pioneer.*

5. Willard Richards (1804–54), a botanic physician of Thomsonian medicine. His office, an octagonal log structure, was a convenient meeting place for the Twelve while they were at Winter Quarters in the winter of 1846–47.

6. Amasa Mason Lyman (1813–77), baptized in 1832 and called to be a member of the Quorum of the Twelve Apostles after Apostle Orson Pratt's brief defection in the summer of 1842. When Pratt rejoined the Saints, and was restored to the quorum in early 1843, Lyman was removed, but Joseph Smith called him to be a member of the First Presidency. Lyman traveled with Brigham Young westward in the spring of 1847 and branched off en route to pick up the sick detachment from the Mormon Battalion who had wintered in Pueblo, Colorado. See Edward Leo Lyman, *Amasa Mason Lyman, Mormon Apostle and Apostate: A Study in Dedication.*

7. Apostle Orson Pratt (1811–81), brother of Parley P. Pratt, also an apostle, was on a mission in Great Britain in March 1847. Orson Pratt had become a Mormon in September 1830, was ordained an apostle in 1835, and was an autodidact in mathematics and science. See Craig Hazen, *The Village Enlightenment in America: Popular Religion and Science in the Nineteenth Century,* chap. 1. For Parley P. Pratt's whereabouts, see Stephen F. Pratt, "Parley P. Pratt in Winter Quarters and the Trail West," 373–88.

8. Ezra T. Benson (1811–69) joined the Saints in 1840 and was called to fill the position of John E. Page after his 1846 defection. "Ezra Taft Benson," The *Instructor* 80, no. 5 (May 1945): 216–7, 227.

9. Wilford Woodruff (1807–98), baptized in 1833, became an apostle in 1835, and was a member of the Utah Territorial Legislature that legalized slavery. See Thomas G. Alexander, *Things in Heaven and Earth: The Life and Times of Wilford Woodruff, A Mormon Prophet.*

10. George A. Smith (1817–75), Joseph Smith's first cousin, was baptized in 1832 and ordained an apostle in 1839. Smith's photograph collection and family papers, housed at the University of Utah, provide important minutes of meetings on racial questions in the Church as well as the only known portrait of Elijah Ables. "George A. Smith," *Tullidge's Quarterly Magazine* 3, no. 3 (July 1884): 232.

11. Newel K. Whitney (1795–1850) converted in 1830 and was called to be a bishop in Kirtland the following year, a counterpart to Edward Partridge in Missouri. On April 6, 1847, Whitney was set apart as the sole presiding bishop. See D. Michael Quinn, "The Newel K. Whitney Family," 44 and *Manuscript History of the Church,* Vol. 17, p. 81, April 6, 1847, in *Selected Collections,* 1:2.

12. Albert P. Rockwood (1805–79) joined the Saints in 1837 and was a president of the Seventy in March 1847. He served in the Utah Territorial Legislature session that legalized slavery in 1852. See Dean C. Jessee and David J. Whittaker, "The Last Months of Mormonism in Missouri: The Albert Perry Rockwood Journal," 5–41.

13. George D. Grant (1812–76) and his brother, Jedediah Morgan Grant, were baptized in the early 1830s. George was imprisoned with Joseph Smith and others in Richmond, Missouri,

Eldridge,[14] Edson Whipple,[15] T. Bullock,[16] & anoth. man William McCary (the Indian) & his Wife[17]

William McCary[:] I address myself to you as my bro. & my leader. I am satisified by you—& in some places I am hypocritically abused—the bishops have counciled the ppl not to suffer such a Sp[irit] as me in their wigwams. Some say there go the old nigger & his white wife—today some of the Sis⁵say, that is the man that bro. Brigham tells his family to treat with disrespect—if there is any dissatisfac-torʸ & I am not right I will walk right. And to the chalk line—I came in as a red man & want to go out as a red man what am I to depend—if I am wrong I want to walk right, I want you to tell me & then I will tell you what God sent me <here> for—we were all white once, why av. [sic] I the stain now. God has told me to walk

---

in the winter of 1838–39 and was a police officer and watchman in Winter Quarters. His presence and apparent support of McCary would have been reassuring. He came to Utah in 1848, settled in the 13th Ward and later, in Bountiful, where he died of cancer. *Manuscript History of the Church*, November 11, 1838, 9, in *Selected Collections*, 1:2; Brooks, *On the Mormon Frontier*, November 17–19, 1846, 210–21; Ronald W. Walker, "Jedediah and Heber Grant," 46–52. For his approximate birth year and his death year, see Frank Esshom, *Pioneers and Prominent Men of Utah*, 896 and "Demise of George D. Grant," *Salt Lake Herald*, September 21, 1876, 3.

14. There are three candidates: John Eldridge (1) (1804–80s), John S. Eldredge (2) (1821–71), and Alanson Eldredge (3) (unknown). The first candidate, John Eldridge, was born in North Carolina and raised in Indiana; he joined the Church in the early 1830s with his mother and siblings. Dean C. Jessee, ed., "John Taylor Nauvoo Journal," 21, 91 note 41. He came to Utah in 1852 with his wife, Cynthia. That he did not come to Utah until 1852 suggests that he was probably not in Winter Quarters at the time of the McCary incident.The second candidate is John S. Eldredge (1821–71). Some records date his birth at 1830/31; however, this would make him a teenager at the time of the McCary scandal and hardly worthy of Whipple's notice; his death certificate's dating of 1821 is more likely. Born a New Yorker, Eldredge was a member of the Brigham Young vanguard company of 1847. William Clayton, *William Clayton's Journal: A Daily Record of the Original Company of 'Mormon' Pioneers from Nauvoo, Illinois, to the Valley of the Great Salt Lake*, 75–76. He was unmarried during the McCary scandal. In March 1847, he met with McCary and chatted with him casually in Dutch. While Eldredge was certainly present for McCary's initial appearance in Winter Quarters, he had left for the Rocky Mountains by the time Nelson Whipple met McCary in fall 1847. The third candidate is John S. Eldredge's father, Alanson Eldredge. In January 1847, Eldredge served on the high council at Winter Quarters. Manuscript History of the Church, April 6, 1847, 81, *Selected Collections*, 1:2; Meeting Minutes, January 14, 1847, *Selected Collections*, 1:18. However, he was excommunicated six months later. Meeting Minutes, June 13, 1847, *Selected Collections*, 1:19..

15. Edson Whipple (1805–94) was baptized in 1840 and served on the Nauvoo police force. In the fall of 1846, his mother, wife, and child all died of sickness. Whipple left Winter Quarters in April 1847 under the direction of Appleton M. Harmon, who would captain the company in which Elijah Ables crossed the plains. He died in Colonia Juarez, Mexico. Andrew Jenson, *LDS Biographical Encyclopedia*, 3:560–62.

16. Thomas Bullock (1816–1885), official clerk both for Joseph Smith and Brigham Young, had worked as a tax clerk for the British government in Leek, England. Bullock spent the remainder of his life recording meetings, journals, and documents for Church and civic leadership. See Jerald F. Simon, "Thomas Bullock as an Early Mormon Historian," 71–88.

17. Many thanks to Connell O'Donovan for assistance in transcribing this document.

at the lady. I come to lay myself at the foot & God & you for the bal[ance]. I seek the footstool at your feet—dont these backsliders think that I av a feeling I was a nigger. I got baptism I am thankful for it, I'd as like to be a nigger as an Indian as many think they are as are I don't any one to transgress. I am come here for my Salv sake & providing I get this feeling from you I will walk the ri[ght] road. Some say I am as Adam, some as the Indian Prophet—I want the person to come & tell me to my face, providing I behave myself, & you told me to teach all my ppl to obey the K[ingdom] of God. Must I obey you, or must I obey them that don't obey you.

B.Y. Obey me.

McCary: If I am Adam, & we was to say here comes a head jumping along with a head white as wool, they wd. say where is your body?—oh I've left that home (laugh). I am speaking of 4 leg sheep now—to see the head come along & say I am ancient of days & leave body at home is two things—provided ancient of days, comes he must bring his body along—provided I was Adam what wd the ppl do—why theyd be as the dog was with the hot dumpling[18]—if old Fav. was to come—I want to know how many Fa[ther]s & Mo[ther]s to save ppl—we must av. Fa[thers] & mo^s to save ppl. in some wa[y]—now when Adam comes he will bring the lost rib with him—provided the body comes, the Indian av. no oath in their tongue—I ask Jack Redding[19] why he swear—oh says he the white people tell me—Borecale is the same man— they [are] both placed in one body. I av. got as strait hair as any other—look at it, there is no sight in left eye— no hearing in left ear—I want to understand among the 12 whe^r I am protected if I do right. If there is so much fuss about it—that I have a lost rib you give it up

---

18. McCary is alluding to an English proverb referring to an aversion or hesitation to touch. One British short story depicted a preacher being shown a number of secular books. He "turned them over as a dog would a hot dumpling." William Howitt, "The Young Squire," in Joseph Meadows, *Heads of the People: or, Portraits of the English,* 88.

19. Return Jackson Redden (1816–91) joined the Mormons in 1841, had been one of Joseph Smith's bodyguards in Nauvoo, and was a close friend of Orrin Porter Rockwell's. At this time, he was a fugitive from Illinois state authorities. Redding had joined Stephen and William Hodge, Artemus Johnson, and Thomas Brown in a conspiracy to steal wares from Nauvoo non-Mormons. In May 1845, the Hodges, Johnson, and Brown had robbed and killed John Miller and Henry Leisi, two Mennonites living in Lee County, Iowa. When the men returned to Nauvoo, they asked Brigham Young for shelter. He refused, and they threatened to kill him. But where Young would not help, Redding would; he and William Hickman raised $1,000 dollars to cover the gang's legal fees. In July, some of Hodges' non-Mormon witnesses (brothers Aaron and John Long and William Fox a.k.a. Judge Foxx) joined with local Mormons to rob—and, as things would turn out, kill—Colonel George Davenport. One co-conspirator fingered Redding and Orrin Porter Rockwell as participants. When the state militia tried to arrest Redding in October 1845, several local Mormons collaborated in his escape. State authorities searched for Redding for the next two years. He was also said to be the first of the 1847 vanguard company to see the Salt Lake Valley on July 23, 1847. Nita Redden Hampshire, "Biography of Return Jackson Redden"; Esshom, *Pioneers and Prominent Men of Utah,* 1123; Jenson, *LDS Biographical Encyclopedia,* 4:715; Bill Shepard, "Stealing in Mormon Nauvoo," 99–102; Meeting Minutes of the Twelve, October 28, 1845, in *Selected Collections,* 1:18.

there can be no stuffing, one man confesses to be Adam—and the Ancient of Days, Every man is trying to get up a mob to drive me out of the city—there is no man but they speak evil of—they even speak evil of God—you can see & examine—if you ex[amine] my body, see about it & examine for yourself. So long as a white woman is so much in the way, good God why don't they give me a red woman—there is so much modesty, you may have seen a redskin jump into his costume—as my Wife is not ashamed I don't think you will be ashamed.

He put on his Indian costume—D^r. R. felt his ribs

B.Y. What are we to understand by your asking us to ex[amine] you

McCarry: I want to prove whether I av. been here before to be ex^d. I av. come to let you know what I am accused for. I say my body is no more—Ive come here to lay myself bef. you as your servant.

Dr. R. I don't discover any thing novel.

McCarry the ppl are going it all the time some call me adam, some old nigger—I want to know what is the diff.

B.Y. have you one rib more on your right than on your left—

W Mc. That's what I am come here to find out—here's the old rib—(wife)

H.C.K. then you have more on one side than the other

McC—<u>Ah</u> there's it—every one of you have a rib short—not here—but mine is here

B.Y. your body is not what is your mission

McC. All I ask is, will you protect me—I've come here & given myself out to be your servant

B.Y. its nothing to do with the blood for of one blood has God made all flesh, we have to repent & regain we av lost—we av one of the best Elders an African in Lowell—a barber

John Eldridge—brother Lyman you know they pointed me out as dreamer & 6 weeks ago, I dreamed of this very man coming & stripping himself like this

McC I hope now they'l let me <live> in peace now (McCarry dressed himself again) I av now satisfied them & they av satisfied me & if any one molests me I will come to bro. Brigham Thot it well to come & report myself to the heads of the Ch. If I am a donkey, I want to serve God—(Amen BY)

McC. I am very much obliged at meeting you in love & gratitude those that are not my friends I want them to tel me—if you av any thing in your hearts you may as tell me as I shall know all in 48 hours

Mrs. McC. I really want to know whet. you beli[eve] the Bible or not?

BY Sister Lucy[20] in what respect do you mean—in part or parts?

Mrs. McC. Some is fulfilled—some is not translated right—if you certainly bel. the Bible by Joseph's translation

---

20. Lucy McCary was described as being well-educated, "having been brought up with the pale-faces." She spoke with "firmness and dignity" though her "countenance is marked with sadness." "Okah Tubbee," *Massachusetts Spy*, February 21, 1849.

McC. If we dont bel. the bible, we r in a poor place for starters

B.Y. We bel. the bible, & we bel. all truth—tho we have B[ible] B[ook] of Mormon, D&C & without the living oracles—this puts us position of the living oracles—if a man says he bel. Bible, B of Mormon, & D&C, and is not baptized for the remission of sins—he'll be damnd.

McCary suppose I want to make a visit to the Arkansas & take my wife to meet my need—when are Sleep Creaks not all the rest & chiefly inclined to follow—among the Choctaws—why Jesus Christ was born in a stable—does that follow that he had a horses head—I am afraid of ans[wering] questions bec. ppl will take this thing wrong—persons come to me & tell me that the 12 dont teach the Bible & again they ask are you going to the mountains this year—I tell them I never calculate beyond my nose—they ask questions & then answer them themselves & turn away & say I tell them—if any man comes forward & says more than that he tells what is not here—some ask what do you think abt. the D&C—I ask what they think—they tell me then—I say thats enough you av answered the questions yourselves—I am satisfied—I want you to intercede for me I am not a Prest, or a leader of the ppl. but a common bro[ther]—because I am a little shade darker

B.Y. We dont care about the color

McC. Do I hear that from all—(All Aye)

H.C.K don't you feel a good spirit here bro William

McC Yes—thank God There r 2 or 3 men at the end of the camp who want to kill me—I am satisfied in all—with you all—I am coming to lay myself at your feet & if God picks me up—its God & you for it—I mean to travel to the mountain if I only go a mile a day—that is if you dont pick up the load & put it in your pocket (laugh)—I am a Frenchman by trade, but never practice it—(laugh) One man next door to me says I wd. like to be an Indian but I can not speak Choctaw—now I say I dare him to talk American

John Eldridge spoke some Dutch—McCarry talked in reply in Dutch—[21]

He then played on his little thirty six cents flute—he picks no key but Ill put a key to it

McC I have no means nor nothing—you cannot pick up the road & put it in your pocket

B.Y. Suppose we get out to have the council house on monday evening next & give it out for 12 ½ each we want every person to be fitted out—& not have to stay to hunt

McC. I would like them to ~~be~~ come & be satisfied

BY Dont care what the ppl say, shew by your actions that you don't care for what they say. All we do is serve the Lord with all our hearts—

McCarry I help to pick up the cross of Christ—I bel. in the Bible so far as I feel its right—I will take my Bible to my folks & tell them & you may preach 2500 years & they wont believe it (he then ridiculed the American peculiarities of speech) shewed mum, guess so, may be, think so, to be five foolish virgins—& yea, yea, nay, nay &

---

21. McCary reportedly spoke fourteen languages. Ibid.

Amen to be the 5 Wise Virgins—told us of the frog. "knee deep," "knee deep, <"& deeper"> "wants more bacon," more bacon," <"fried bacon,"> & then when they r going to apostatize they sing out "more rum" "more rum," & then asked to part with good feelings & A. Lyman to pray

Lyman made prayer

McCarry I wish you would mention to the Bishops on the South & teach them not to come with one face to me, & not go & tell the brethren not to let me come into their Wigwams. I ask this in the name of God the Father, Jesus Christ the Son, Mary the mother, & the Holy Ghost Amen. We shall get amongst the Royal Family soon, & drink a toast heres to the trouser coon gang & the petticoat coon gang, may the trouser coon gang never be overcome by the petticoat coon gang.

Nelson Whipple Recalls the William McCary Episode (1847)

HISTORICAL INTRODUCTION

Throughout the summer of 1847, McCary had tapped into a desire for a more charismatic strain of Mormonism. He assumed the personality of Adam and taught of the transmigration of spirits in March 1847, but his act wore thin; and within a few weeks of meeting Brigham Young and others, McCary lost the goodwill of the Saints. Realizing that McCary took his identity as "Adam" seriously, they began to question his motives. When it became known that he was practicing his own brand of plural marriage with white women, a mob of white Mormon men chased McCary out of Winter Quarters,

A couple months later, the McCarys appeared again in the Mormon settlement of Springville. Nelson Whipple, a resident of the Springville branch, had just visited Winter Quarters "to see my friends" and returned to Springville to find the branch presidency scandalized by internal accusations of theft. The entire branch presidency was replaced, with Whipple serving as the first counselor. As he was seeking to regain control over the branch, he found the branch was in a "curious fix"; McCary was again pulling the Saints into his movement, and a quickly organized vigilante group sent the McCarys running "on a fast trot" to Missouri. At least one member thought that McCary was dead.[22]

The McCarys initially settled in Jackson County, Missouri, but traveled widely in the East with their Indian minstrel show. McCary called himself Okah Tubbee, and Lucy Stanton adopted the name of Laah Ciel. They performed in the Barnum and Bailey circus in 1848, and the couple recreated the spectacle of their meeting to drum up publicity for their shows. The story, one editorialist jeered, "beats anything that can be found in any cheap, yellow covered book." In spite of McCary's efforts to sell his Indian persona, white news editors were quick to identify him as a "French nigger" named Julius who reportedly admitted that he

---

22. William Warner Major, Letter to Brigham Young, June 16, 1847.

"could do nothing as a nigger but everything as an Indian."[23] The McCarys relocated to Toronto, but McCary's ongoing efforts to practice polygamy earned him an arrest warrant and conviction from Canadian authorities on bigamy charges.[24] For her part, Lucy McCary "the Indian princess" became a doctor in upstate New York in the 1860s and served a prison sentence for performing abortions.[25]

Nelson Whipple produced his autobiography in hopes of presenting "many items of useful information concerning the events that have taken place on earth in my lifetime, which probably is not recorded in any other book."[26] Composed in 1878, Whipple produced the volume over 30 years after the fact. But in general, his documentation of McCary's activities is unparalled and deserves serious attention.

CITATION

Nelson Whipple, Autobiography, 71–73, holograph, MS 5348, LDS Church History Library.

DOCUMENT EXCERPT

When I arrived in this branch [Springville, Iowa] it was in a rather curious fix. A man had been by the name of McCarry [sic]. He was said to be a mulatto or quaterrun who professed to be some great one, and had converted a good many to his kind of religion. It appeared that he understood the slight-of-hand, the black art or that he was a magician or something of the kind, and had fooled the ignorant in that way.

He was in favor of holding his meetings of the men and women separately, saying that his teaching to the men and to the women was entirely different. His talk and pretentions were of the most absurd character, and it would appear that no rational being would adhere to it for a moment, but many did.

He had a number of women sealed to him in his way which was as follows; He had a house in which the ordinance was performed. His wife Lucy Stanton was in the room at the time of the performance, no others were admitted. The form of sealing was for the women to bed with him, in the daytime as I am informed three different times by which they were sealed to the fullest extent.

This order of things continued for a considerable length of time when the secret was revealed by one Mrs. Howard who revolted and ran when she found what the sealing ordanance really was, notwithstanding Mrs. McCarry tried her best to prevent her escape from the house. She went home and told her husband, Mr. Howard of the affair and who they were that had been sealed in that way to the old darkey.

---

23. "Dr. Okah Tubbee, Chief of the Chocktaws!" *[Tallahassee]Floridan and Journal,* October 11, 1851, 1, and "The Celebrated Indian Chief," *Alexandria Gazette,* July 10, 1851, 1. For their efforts at dramatizing the love story, see "Strange Infatuation—Marriage of a White Woman with an Indian at Niagara Falls," *New London [Connecticut] Daily Chronicle,* September 10, 1851, 2.

24. "Okah Tubbee and His Bride," *Trenton [New Jersey] State Gazette,* August 23, 1852, 1.

25. Paul Gilmore, "The Indian in the Museum: Henry David Thoreau, Okah Tubbee, and Authentic Manhood," 25–63.

26. Nelson Whipple, Autobiography, 1, LDS Church History Library.

Howard went forthwith and told Chase,[27] who was a believer in McCarry, and his wife[28] had been through the sealing ordinance. Chase did not of course believe it until his wife acknowledged it and then of course he did. He was very much astonished at the idea and it is said that he did not speak a loud word for about three weeks that anyone knew of. But after a while he became himself, lived with his wife, and does at present.

Others were drawn into strange delusions in some unaccountable way that was a mystery to everybody. The name of the unfortunate persons I will mention. Not to bring disgrace upon them or their posterity but as an item of history.

It was said that Daniel Stanton[29] was a full believer in the nigger prophet as he was called. He denied it but allowed his meetings to be held at his house and his family to attend them and his daughter to marry him, etc. I shall put down his name as one to venture.

Men—Daniel Stanton Sr., Sylvanus Calkins, [30] John Atchinson,[31] Sisson A.

---

27. Sisson Almadoras Chase (1808–1872) was baptized in August 1840 and served a mission to Vermont a few months later. He provided key testimony against Daniel Avery for his role in the 1843 kidnapping of Joseph Smith. In 1850, Congress designated him as an "illegal voter" "List of Illegal Voters at Kanesville," 2:48; Witness List, Hancock County Circuit Court Records, 1843, LDS Church History Library. He and his wife, Miriam Gove Chase, came west with the Daniel Miller/John W. Cooley Company in 1853. Elijah Mayhew, Diary, June 12, 14, 1853. Witness List, Hancock County Circuit Court Records, 1843, LDS Church History Library. In Salt Lake City, he was called as a counselor in the First Ward bishopric. He died in Salt Lake City in 1872. Andrew Jenson, "First Ward," 308. See also Sisson A. Chase, Affidavit, 438–39; Jenson, *LDS Biographical Encyclopedia*, 1:323; "Dead," *Salt Lake Herald*, April 5, 1872, 3.

28. Miriam Gove Chase (1813–1909) was the daughter of Moses Gove and Hannah Chase. She died in Payson, Utah. William Richard Cutter, ed., *Genealogical and Personal Memoirs Relating to the Families of Boston and Eastern Massachusetts*, 3:1385; Death Certificate, November 4, 1909, Salt Lake County Death Records, 1908–1949.

29. Stanton served as a missionary (D&C 75:33), a branch president, and a stake president in Quincy, Illinois. Andrew Jenson, "Quincy, Adams County, Illinois," 739.

30. Whipple's memory is incorrect. In summer 1846, Sylvanus Calkins was inducted as a private into the Mormon Battalion. See, Mormon Battalion, Muster Roll for Company A, October-December 1846, MS 5261; *Roster and Record of Iowa Soldiers*, 6 vols. (Des Moines: Emory H. English, 1911), 6:840. He reached San Diego that winter, was decommissioned by the end of the year, then worked at Sutter's Fort. He left the fort with a company of other Mormons in October 1847; however, rather than going to Utah, he stayed behind and hunted for gold. He went to Utah in 1850, where he met and married Hannah Elizabeth Kilbourn. The Calkins family later moved to Iowa, then to Oregon. Charles Carey, *A General History of Oregon*, 3:253. Whipple likely means Israel Calkins (1766–1848), Sylvanus's father. Israel and his family joined the Church in Freedom, New York, received their endowments in the Nauvoo Temple, and followed the leadership of the Twelve. Israel died in Hamburg, Iowa, near Winter Quarters. According to Hosea Stout, "Mother [Hannah] Calkins" remarried after "her former husband . . . followed off [sic] Wm Chubby the Negro prophet." Brooks, *On the Mormon Frontier*, March 8, 1848, 1:304. For Israel's death, see Mark A. Steele, "Mormon Conversions in Freedom, New York," 47.

31. Likely John Barton Atchison (1823–97), whose wife, Melinda Elizabeth Stanton, was another of Daniel Stanton's daughters. At the time of McCary's preaching, John and Melinda had a two-year-old child. William. Atchison was part of the Echo Canyon campaign of the Utah

Chase,—Eldredge,[32] Jonathon Haywood

Women—Widow Pulsipher and daughter, Meri[a]h Atchison,[33] Harriet Stanton, Caroline Stanton, Constanza Stanton, Mrs. Sisson A. Chase,[34] mother, a woman of upwards of 60 years of age.

As soon as the said McCarry saw that he was found out in his devilment he made his way to Missouri on a fast trot. Bro. Ha[r]mon Cutler[35] determined to shoot him if he could find him for having tried to kiss his girls, but he was gone.[36]

After a while he sent for his wife and Br. Joseph Lish[37] took her to him in Missouri. Charges were preferred against those persons and most of them were cut off from the Church but were again restored to baptism.

War. U.S. Census, 1870, Utah, Washington County, Pannea, 6 index and images, FamilySearch, https://familysearch.org/pal:/MM9.1.1/MNCB-RLC (accessed June 2, 2013), Malinda Atchison in entry for John Atchison. See also Daniel M. Burbank, Journal, October 30, 1857.

32. This man could be John Eldridge (1804–80s), John S. Eldridge (1821–71), or Alanson Eldridge. See discussion above in note 14.

33. Meriah Elizabeth Stanton Atchinson/Atcherson, John Atchison's sister.

34. Likely Amy Scott Chase (1789–1872), then almost sixty. She continued to live with her son, Sisson, in the Salt Lake City First Ward. See U.S. Census, 1860, Utah, Salt Lake County, Salt Lake City, First Ward, 132; U.S. Census, 1870, Utah, Salt Lake County, Salt Lake City, First Ward, 5.

35. Harmon Cutler (1799–1869) was converted in 1839 in upstate New York, probably after hearing James Blakeslee's preaching. Christopher Quinn Cutler, *A Quiet, Faithful, Unobtrusive Follower: The Life and Times of Harmon Cutler,* esp. 35, 85–91. Blakeslee, a resident of the region, was a Mormon elder and a close associate of Elijah Ables's convert, Eunice Ross. His first wife, Susannah Barton Cutler, died in 1840. In 1841, he married Lucy Pettigrew, the daughter of Joseph Smith's associate, David Pettigrew. Ordained a Seventy in Nauvoo, Cutler was friends with his fellow Seventy, Nelson Whipple, and Joseph Young, president of the First Quorum of the Seventy. Young had endorsed Ables's ordination as a Seventy in 1841. Cutler left Nauvoo with the main body of Brighamites in the spring of 1846. In July 1846, Cutler's daughter married Alonzo Raymond who, though ill, accepted Heber C. Kimball's assurance that he would certainly recover if he enlisted in the Mormon Battalion. David Pettigrew, Harmon's father-in-law, also enlisted "as a kind of helmsman" or spiritual leader. Once settled in eastern Nebraska, Cutler claimed nearly 500 acres by squatter's rights. Cutler suffered financial straits. See, Moore, Morton, & Co., Letter to Hiram Dayton and Harmon Cutler, November 23, 1841.

36. Whipple is probably referring to Cutler's daughters, Clarinda (b. 1827), Almira (b. October 13, 1829), and perhaps Anna (April 25, 1831). Clarinda was known for her spunk; she demanded that Willard Richards give her the entirety of Alonzo's pay as a member of the Mormon Battalion "as she was capable of taking care of herself." Cutler, *A Quiet, Faithful, Unobtrusive Follower,* 9 note 28; Journal History, August 24, 1846.

37. Joseph Lish (1804–86) and Harriet Lish (1807–1901), both native New Yorkers, were baptized by George A. Smith while living in Greenwood, Ohio. "George A. Smith," *The Contributor* 4, no. 3 (December 1882): 83. Lish served with Nelson Whipple as a counselor in the Springville Branch presidency. Whipple recalls hand-grinding the corn "in a little mill of Bro. Lishes." In January 1848, he was ordained to be a high priest in the Pottawatomie Branch. Pottawatomie High Priests Minutes, January 2, 1848, 1, *Selected Collections,* 2:19. He left Winter Quarters in 1850, serving as a captain of ten. Once in Utah, he served on the Weber High Council. "Visit of the Presidency to Weber," *Deseret News,* February 8, 1851, 5.

Apostolic Reaction to William McCary (Summer 1847)

HISTORICAL INTRODUCTION

Church leaders received considerable criticism for Hyde's decision to baptize and ordain McCary. In early April McCary left in the wake "of a sermon preached by Elder Orso[n] Hyde against his doctrine."[38] William Smith took particular delight in attacking the Winter Quarters Saints for their racial inclusiveness. After berating Hyde for baptizing McCary, Smith printed a racialized attack on Brigham Young, stating that Joseph Smith had "placed his hands upon Brig Ham Young's head and pronounced these words: 'You are of the lineage of Cain through the loins of Ham.'"[39] Editor Isaac Sheen remarked snidely: "Mr. Hyde's ordination of the Lamanite prophet, alias, the Negro Christ, Adam, &c., the marriage of this black Adam to his white Eve, alias, virgin Mary is well understood here. . . . Can Mr. Hyde tell how many wives this negro has altogether black and white?"[40] McCary's philandering forced the Church leaders to revisit the inclusive policy of Joseph Smith.

While Church leaders had long accepted that blacks suffered from the curse of Ham, they now expanded that view into a rationale for excluding from priesthood ordination. Humiliated by the scandal, Apostles Parley P. Pratt and Orson Hyde came out swinging against McCary. On April 25, 1847, Pratt condemned McCary's activities as a "new thing" in which some bored Saints indulged for variety's sake, stressing that McCary was nothing more than a "black man" whose "blood of Ham" was "cursed as regards to the Priesthood." Made less than a month after Brigham Young's validation of McCary's right to the priesthood, Pratt's comments marked the first time an LDS Church leader had deemed men with black skin "cursed as regards to the Priesthood." The camp clerk, Robert Lang Campbell, recorded the sermons.[41]

PARLEY P. PRATT SERMON CITATION

Parley P. Pratt, sermon transcript, April 25, 1847, found in General Meeting Minutes, *Selected Collections*, 1:18.

DOCUMENT EXCERPT

If people want to follow Strang, go it, want to follow this Black Man who has got the blood of Ham in him which linage was cursed as regards the Priesthood, want to follow a new thing, want to follow a new thing hatch it up for we have only the old thing.

---

38. Lorenzo Brown diary, April 25, 1847, 31, typescript, LDS Church History Library.

39. "Brigham Young's Lineage," *Melchizedek and Aaronic Herald* 1, no. 8 (February 1850): 4.

40. "O. Hyde's Slanders," *Melchizedek and Aaronic Herald* 1, no. 8 (February 1850): 1.

41. On April 25, Campbell recorded that he "attnd[ed] meeting at stand taking minutes" and "attend[ed] high council taking meetings." On May 30, he recorded that he attended a "municipal high council" meeting and took minutes. See Robert Lang Campbell, Journal, April 25 and May 30, 1847, Perry Special Collections.

ORSON HYDE SERMON CITATION:

Orson Hyde,[42] sermon transcript found in Meeting Minutes, May 30, 1847 in *Selected Collections*, 1:18.

DOCUMENT EXCERPT

When will this ppl learn better than to follow after delusive spirits, never. I will recall this. [T]his church is going on & will bring in the bad as well as good & it is necessary that <evil & enthusiastic> kindred spirits raise up to draw those evil & enthusiastic spirits from us, so in this way the Lord leads off the corrupt & the wicked for as they stay with us we are the weaker, mix drops with pure metal & it makes the metal weaker causes the adhesion to be less some imposters have said like John E Page[43] if they were damn'd the Devil would have it to say they were damn'd like gentlemen well it was necessary that an honorable imposter like Strang[44] should raise to take these gentlemen from among us but there are another class who here are not caught with his trap but would go it in a meaner scale. Yes [they] would follow a nigger prophet. Thought I was wrong in baptizing this nigger, but on consideration see it was necessary in order that he should have the opportunity of fulfilling this mission & taking away the tares who were his kindred spirits.

Walker Lewis's Standing in the Church (1847)

HISTORICAL INTRODUCTION

In May 1847, missionary William Appleby visited the LDS branch in Lowell, Massachusetts, where he met Walker Lewis, a black elder who had earned

---

42. Orson Hyde (1805–1878) presents a more complex racial background. In 1843, Joseph Smith criticized Hyde for harboring racist sentiments. When Hyde fumed, "Put them [blacks] on the level, and they will rise above me," Joseph pointed out that the blacks' indignation was justified: "If I raised you to be my equal, and then attempted to oppress you, would you not be indignant?" Joseph Smith, Journal, January 2, 1843, in Dean Jessee, Ronald K. Esplin, and Richard L. Bushman, eds., *Journals, Vol. 2, 1841–1843*, 212.

43. John E. Page (1799–1867), ordained an apostle in July 1838, became a Strangite apostle in April 1846, but by August 1849, had broken with Strang because he felt Strang was overextending his authority. In November 1849, Page affiliated with James Brewster, an apostate during Joseph Smith's lifetime, who claimed communication with Angel Moroni and a book of lost scripture, the Book of Esdras. Apostle John Taylor had denounced Brewster in December 1842, calling his work "a perfect humbug." In 1848, Brewster began to publish *Olive Branch* containing his revealed writings; Page found Brewster's de-emphasis on prophetic authority refreshing. Brewsterism disintegrated in 1852, and Page set apart Granville Hedrick, a figure who had refused to associate with any of the claimants, as the recipient of Joseph Smith's mantle. While he acknowledged Hedrick as a leader, Page never again offered the kind of allegiance he had committed to Joseph. Brewster's newspaper editor, Hazen Aldrich, had recorded Elijah Ables's name as a member who had committed to keep the Word of Wisdom in December 1836. See Roll, First Council of the Seventy, December 27, 1836, CR 3 123, LDS Church History Library; John Quist, "John E. Page: The Apostle of Uncertainty," 53–68. See also Bill Shepard, "Shadows on the Sun Dial," 42, 50.

44. Roger Van Noord, *King of Beaver Island: The Life and Assassination of James Jesse Strang*.

Brigham Young's respect and admiration. Appleby was simultaneously impressed by Lewis's commitment and disgusted at William Smith's willingness to tolerate the mingling of the races. Worse still, Walker's son, Enoch, had married a white woman. Racial admixture—Appleby used the common euphemism "amalgamation"—troubled most Americans, including members of the Church.

CITATION

William Appleby, Letter to Brigham Young, June 2, 1847, Brigham Young Office Files, Reel 30.

DOCUMENT EXCERPT

At this place I found a coloured brother by name of "Lewis," a barber, an Elder in the Church ordained some years ago by Wm. Smith. This Lewis I was informed has also a son who is married to a white girl. and both members of the Church then. Now dear B^r I wish to know if this is the order of God or tolerated in the Church is to ordained Negroes to the Priesthood, and allow amalgamation. If it is I desire to know it, as I have yet got to learn it.

Brigham Young Struggles with Interracial Marriage (1847)

HISTORICAL INTRODUCTION

As Appleby was returning to Winter Quarters from the East, Brigham Young was returning from the vanguard company's epic journey to the Rocky Mountains in the summer of 1847. In Winter Quarters where they endured the winter of 1847–48, lengthy council meetings conducted the Saints' business but also whiled away the time. Appleby's letter questioning Lewis Walker's standing in the Church triggered a complicated discussion, revealing the tangled web of discourse about African Americans, American racism, and Mormon theology. Young had accepted the prevailing scientific thought about the consequences of racial admixture. Edward Long, a white observer of Jamaica, claimed that biracial individuals had intermarried on the island, but "such matches have generally been defective and barren." They seemed to be "in this respect actually of the mule-kind, and not capable of producing them from one another as from a commerce with a distinct White or Black."[45] Prominent biologist Josiah Nott believed that racial intermarriage was not merely repugnant but also fatal to the human race: "Certainly," he said with confidence, "the mulatto" is "no more [a negro]. . . than a mule is a horse."[46] Nott warned that racial intermarriage would render all infertile and lead to the "probable extermination of the two races."[47] Though Young had little in common with either Nott or Edward Long—Nott would

45. Edward Long, *The History of Jamaica, or General Survey of the Antcient and Modern State,* 2:335.
46. Josiah C. Nott, *Two Lectures on the Connection Between the Biblical and Physical History of Man,* 35.
47. Josiah C. Nott, "The Mulatto a Hybrid—Probable Extermination of the Two Races If The Whites and Blacks Are Allowed to Intermarry," 252–57.

have had a roaring laugh at the Mormons—Young had incorporated some of Long's and Nott's views of racial origins into his own theological stew.

Young was willing to embrace blacks holding the priesthood and could even countenance the McCary-Stanton union; after all, they remained childless. But when he learned that Walker Lewis's son, Enoch, had married a white woman and had fathered children, his anger flamed. "They would all av. To be killed." But in the next breath, Young reconsidered, asking aloud: "If a black man & white woman come to you and demand baptism, can you deny them?" But there was a condition: only if they "will be eunuchs for the Kingdom of Heaven's sake" could they "have a place in the Temple." As a believer in Nott's thought, Young knew that sexual intercourse between whites and blacks would result in the ultimate demise of the human race. Brigham Young's enduring loyalty to Joseph Smith continued to impel him towards inclusion.

Interracial marriage whipsawed Young, provoking him to violence in one moment and prodding his conscience toward racial equality the next. This conversation represents the deep contradictions that had formed the core of Brigham Young's racial worldview. Willard Richards took the minutes.

CITATION

Meeting Minutes of Brigham Young and others, *Selected Collections*, 1:18.

DOCUMENT EXCERPT

About ½ past 6 Elder Appleby come into council & presented gold pens & pencil from Col. Kane to the Twelve & give a short description of the State of the Churches in the Eastern Cities[48]

Prest. Young presented Thomas Bulloch with a gold pen as the chief clerk, & a remembrance

Bro Appleby related bro. Waldo's charge agst. Bro. Bates—he considered both parties in the wrong, but rectified it & made peace

Wm. Smith ordained a black man Elder at Lowell & he has married a white girl & they have a child[49]

Prest Young If they were far away from the Gentiles they wd. all av. to be killed—when they mingle it is death to all.[50] If a black man & a white woman come to you &

---

48. William Appleby, Journal, October 15, 1847, recorded that Thomas L. Kane gave him "a check for fifty dollars, to purchase a Dozen Gold pens, &c as a present" for the apostles. Kane directed Appleby to "to select and purchase them, and take them . . . to the camp."

49. Walker Lewis had married Elizabeth Lovejoy (1795-unknown), a free black, in Boston on March 26, 1826. Their son, Enoch Lovejoy Lewis, was born on May 20, 1826. On September 18, 1846, Enoch married a Caucasian woman named Mary Matilda Webster, who gave birth to Enoch R. Lovejoy Lewis Jr. in April 1847. She had probably conceived this child two months before their marriage. Connell O'Donovan, "Mormon Priesthood and Elder Walker Lewis," 48–100.

50. Brigham Young's thought reflects an amalgam of contemporary scientific thought on the fertility of the biracial population. Two doctors, Robert Knox and Josiah Nott, both agreed that the biracial population was sterile. Knox promoted miscegenation as a mechanism for preserving

demand baptism, can you deny them? The law is their seed shall not be amalgamated. Mulattoes r like mules they cant have children, but if they will be eunuchs for the Kingdom of ~~God's~~ Heaven's sake they may have a place in the Temple.[51]

B.Y. The Lamanites r purely of the house of Israel & it is a curse that is to be removed when the fullness of the Gospel comes[52]

O.H[yde].[53] Has taught that if girls marry the half breeds they r throwing themselves away & becoming as one of them

B.Y. It is wrong for them to do so

BY The Pottawatomis will not own a man who has the negro blood in him— that is the reason why the Indians disown the negro prophet[54]

At ½ past 10. H.C.K. retired to bed. Leaving B.Y O.H & W.R[ichards] chatting until one oclock when they also went to bed.

---

a biracial population, insisting that a mixed race "must intermarry with the pure race or perish." Nott, as noted, believed that miscegenation would result in the extermination of both races because biracials were "a degenerate, unnatural offspring, doomed by nature to work out [their] own destruction." Robert Knox, *The Races of Man: A Fragment*, 7; Nott, "The Mulatto," 252–56.

51. In the original minutes, Bullock finished the first paragraph at "amalgamated" and began a new paragraph at "Mulattoes."

52. Since 1830, Mormons have seen themselves as having a special relationship with Native Americans. Mormon poet W. W. Phelps wrote a hymn, "O Stop and Tell Me, Red Man" in which a Native American laments that he "once was pleasant Ephraim" but that his "fathers fell in darkness" and their "race has dwindled to Indian hearts." Emma Smith, comp., *A Collection of Sacred Hymns for the Church of Jesus Christ of Latter-day Saints*, 83. Parley P. Pratt lamented the state of "the poor Indians, the descendants of the ancient prophets!" and asked rhetorically, "Can we behold them unmoved? . . . feed, clothe, instruct them; win, save the remnants of the house of Israel" Qtd. in Juanita Brooks, ed., *Journal of the Southern Indian Mission: Diary of Thomas D. Brown*, 34. Although paternalistic, such sentiments motivated the Saints to adopt humane policies toward Native American tribes. Brigham Young chided the Saints, "If it is right to kill an Indian for stealing, surely in the same principle, it must be an honor to the man who will kill a white thief." First Presidency to Utah Valley Saints, January 8, 1850, Brigham Young Office Files, Reel 24. When missionary Charles Pulsipher was captured by Utes, he reported receiving the gift of speaking their language and exhorted them: "A great many moons ago we was all brothers together and all good friends but through their fighting and shedding blood and living on . . . they had become idle, neglected to raise grain, and live like the white people they had gone down to what they are today but the time had come for them to quit fighting and go to work like we do." Charles Pulsipher, "A True Narrative." Brigham Young instructed, "You must not treat them as your equals, you cannot exalt them by this process. If they are your equals, you cannot raise them up to you." Brigham Young, Letter to Isaac Higbee, October 18, 1849.

53. Orson Hyde (1805–78), a convert of 1831, was one of the original Quorum of the Twelve Apostles, ordained in 1835. Though he left the faith briefly during the Missouri persecutions of 1838, he stayed active for the remainder of his life. Jenson, *LDS Biographical Encyclopedia*, 1:80.

54. Other tribes shared the Pottawatomie concern with racial intermingling. In 1839 and 1858, the Cherokee and Chickasaw Nations passed laws prohibiting black-Indian intermarriage, one tribe calling it a "disgrace to our Nation," punishable by fifty lashes. The Creek and the Cherokee also forbade slaves from owning property and prohibited Afro-Indian children from inheriting their Indian parent's estate. For more on Indian laws prohibiting racial intermingling, see Christina Snyder, *Slavery in Indian Country: The Changing Face of Captivity in Early America*, 210–11; Katja May, *African-Americans and Native Americans in the Cherokee and Creek Nations*, 45–47.

Brigham Young's Explanation of the Priesthood Ban: Three Accounts (1849, 1852, 1900)

HISTORICAL INTRODUCTION

The Saints were settling into their new lives as Israelites in the promised land. Moving west had changed them. The crucible of the wilderness had tribalized them more than ever before. As they struggled to make the wilderness "blossom as a rose," they lacked the patience for the racial pluralism that life in the Eastern states presented to them. Ready to distance themselves from their past, the Saints forged a new identity as God's people—grounded, independent, and white. While the Saints would continue to tolerate Elijah Ables and Jane Manning James as exceptions, that acceptance depended primarily on their personal connection to the Prophet Joseph Smith. Most Saints, and especially the converts who arrived from Great Britain and Scandinavia, saw their faith as white and embraced that identity, no doubt seeing in the local tribes they displaced an uneasy parallel to the marginalized blacks.

On February 13, 1849, at 3:30 P.M, Brigham Young met with Lorenzo Snow, Heber C. Kimball, and other officials in the home of George B. Wallace, second counselor in the presidency of the high priests' quorum. Not all of the Twelve were present, but it was an official meeting for which Thomas Bullock took minutes. Here Brigham Young articulated Mormonism's exclusionary race policy for the first time. While the Saints had tossed around various explanations for black skin—even Joseph Smith suggested that it was the curse of Canaan—these explanations had never been connected with a priesthood ban for black men. For the remainder of the nineteenth century, this conversation loomed over Church leaders' memories as they struggled to determine the exact origins of the policy.

1849 Account

HISTORICAL INTRODUCTION

According to Thomas Bullock's early summary of the meeting, Brigham Young's primary purpose in calling the meeting was to "appoint a committee to lay off the city into wards." Brigham Young and the men opened the meeting with some small talk about mesmerism until Apostle Lorenzo Snow, once a classmate of abolitionists at Oberlin College, interjected by "present[ing] the case of the African Race." He asked about their "chance of redemption" and whether Church leaders would "unlock the door to them." His language suggests that a restriction had already been in place. Thomas Bullock's summary rendition of Young's comments provides the first recorded statement Brigham Young made excluding blacks from the priesthood.

CITATION

Meeting Minutes of the Twelve, February 13, 1849, *Selected Collections*, 1:18, Thomas Bullock, Clerk.

DOCUMENT EXCERPT

Pres. Young explained it very lucidly that the curse remains on them bec[ause] Cain cut off the lives of Abel to hedge up his way & take the lead but the L[ord] has given them blackness, so as to give the children of Abel an opportunity to cult[ivate] his place with his desc[endants] in the [eternal] worlds.

1852 Account

HISTORICAL INTRODUCTION

Wilford Woodruff designated himself as the historian for the Quorum of the Twelve. Upon his appointment, Woodruff enjoined the Quorum to "keep an account of their missions, works, miracles, and the blessings of God unto them." Otherwise, "our friends could not get it correctly before the world" upon their passing.[55]

The summary below is Wilford Woodruff's rendering of the February 13, 1849 Thomas Bullock minutes. It was likely composed in spring 1852 shortly after Woodruff commissioned the Quorum of the Twelve to start compiling their own records.

CITATION

"Record of the Quorum of the Twelve Apostles in the Handwriting of Wilford Woodruff," ca. 1852, in *New Mormon Studies,* CD-ROM. Salt Lake City: Smith Research Associates, 2009.

DOCUMENT EXCERPT

Elder Lorenzo Snow presented the case of the Africans wishing to know the chance of their redemption. Pres[iden]t Young replied with much clearness that the curse remains upon them because Cain cut off the lines of Abel to prevent him & his posterity getting the ascendancy over himself & his generations his own offering not being accepted of God while Abels was. But the Lord has cursed Cain's seed with blackness (sic) & prohibited them the Priesthood that Abel & his progeny may yet come forward & have their dominion place and Blessings in their proper relationship with Cain & his race in a world to come.

1900 Account

HISTORICAL INTRODUCTION

Brigham Young's 1849 comments cast a long shadow over the Church's racial policies of the nineteenth century. When Lorenzo Snow took the helm as president of the Church in 1898, he remembered the conversation he had with Brigham Young nearly fifty years earlier. But his recollection of the conversation also reflects doctrinal developments foreign to Brigham Young's thinking.

---

55. *Wilford Woodruff's Journal,* 4:161–62, December 22, 1852.

Whereas Brigham Young had explicitly denied that black skin was the result of premortal unworthiness, other Church leaders such as Orson Hyde, Orson Pratt, and even his brother, Lorenzo Young, had long accepted the premortal explanation for racial difference. Snow's recollection of the 1849 conversation reveals the degree to which the new theorizing was affecting Mormon rationalizations for the priesthood restriction.[56]

CITATION

Quorum of the Twelve, Meeting Minutes of the Twelve, March 11, 1900, transcript, George Albert Smith Family Papers, Box 78, fd. 7, Marriott Library, University of Utah.

DOCUMENT EXCERPT

President Snow . . . said that he asked President Brigham Young on one occasion why it was that millions and millions of people were cursed with a black skin, and when, if ever, this curse would be removed? President Young explained it to him in this way, but whether the President had had this revealed to him or not, he did not know, or whether he was giving his own personal views or what had been told him by the Prophet Joseph. He said that when Cain slew Abel he fully understood that the effects would not end with the killing of his brother, but that it extended to the spirits in eternity. He said that in the spirit world people were organized as they are here. There were patriarchs standing at the head of certain classes of spirits, and there were certain relationships existing which affected their coming into the world to take tabernacles; as, for instance, when Abel came into the world it was understood by Cain that the class of people he presided over as a prince, if they ever came into the world in the regular way, they would have to come thru him. So with Cain, he was a prince presiding over a vast number of a certain class of spirits, and it was natural that they should come through him, if at all, and therefore when Cain slew Abel he understood that the taking of his brother's life was going to deprive the spirits whom he presided from coming into the world, perhaps for thousands and thousands of years; hence the sin was immense because the effects were immense. Then there was this understanding when the Lord executed judgment upon Cain; the spirits under his leadership still looked up to him, rather than forsake him they were willing: to bear his burdens and share the penalty imposed upon him. This was understood when the curse was pronounced upon him, and it was understood that this curse would remain upon his posterity until the class of spirits presided over by Abel

---

56. Orson Pratt, "The Pre-Existence," *The Seer,* 1, no. 4 (April 1853): 56; Orson Hyde, *Speech of Elder Orson Hyde, Delivered before the High Priests Quorum of Nauvoo, April 27th, 1845, upon the Course and Conduct of Mr. Sidney Rigdon and upon His Merits to His Claim to the Presidency of the Church of Jesus Christ of Latter-day Saints,* 30; *Wilford Woodruff's Journal,* 6:510–511, December 25, 1869.

should have the privilege of coming into the world and taking tabernacles, and then the curse would be removed.

Benjamin Matthews Finds a Runaway
Slave in San Bernadino (March 31, 1849)

HISTORICAL INTRODUCTION

Born in 1819 in Marion County, Alabama, Benjamin Matthews married Temple Weeks, and moved to Mississippi. The Matthews family joined the Saints after hearing the preaching of Elder Benjamin Clapp. In 1844, Matthews served a mission to the Southern States with a fellow Mississippian, William Crosby. During his mission, they baptized South Carolina natives John Daniel Holladay and Catherine Beasley Holladay in Matthews's home county. Matthews returned to the Salt Lake Valley in July 1847 with other Mississippi Saints. He and his family wintered in Salt Lake City and settled on Spring Creek, a few miles from Big Cottonwood Canyon in the spring of 1848, naming their settlement after the Holladays. In the spring of 1849, the Matthews family left the settlement for the gold fields of California.[57]

Meanwhile, with the end of the Mexican-American War, Mormons in the West found themselves under a new government. Instead of being refugees living in Mexican territory, they had to reckon—again—with the Americans. The future of slavery in the territories roiled up Congress; Congressman David Wilmot almost incited a riot by suggesting that the territories newly acquired from Mexico be made free.[58] Though Mormons had generally been opposed to slavery, they had no strong opinion on the matter. So when a runaway slave boy made his way to the Mormon community developing near Sutter's Mill, it forced the Mormons to begin to consider what their relationship should be to the Americans. Fearful of federal encroachment but sympathetic to the boy's plight, the Saints wanted to help the boy without provoking the anger of the federal marshals. The letter below illustrates the moral and political dilemmas that slavery presented to the Mormon people.

CITATION

Benjamin Matthews, Letter to Brigham Young, March 31, 1849, Brigham Young Office Files, Reel 31; left justification added.

---

57. U.S. Census, 1850, California, Sutter County, 60; Andrew Jenson, "Big Cottonwood Precinct," 283; Katherine Holladay Freeman, *Our Family Treasures: Holladay, Christiansen, Greenhalgh, Lebaron,* 26.

58. David Wilmot would later sit on the platform-drafting committee for the Republican Party that identified slavery and polygamy as the "twin relics of barbarism." Richard Poll, "The Mormon Question Enters National Politics," 127; Eric Foner, "The Wilmot Proviso Revisited," 262–79.

DOCUMENT EXCERPT

March the 31, 1849

I take the opportunity of writing you a few lines concerning the business I came here on I am satisfied my self and several others that the Negro boy Belonging to Wm. Smith is here but not comatable yet he has bin see[n] by several persons on Last Saturday the 24 and Sunday he stayed during the knight in this settlement one knight at Roots[59] & the other at McMurtrys[60] I am very well convinced in my own mind that there is people in the company going to California[61] that is knowing to this boys running away and is interested in getting him of[f] and provided the martial does not come I want you to send me

---

59. Jeremiah Root (1802–98), was a bishop in Council Bluffs, Iowa, and was assigned to care for the families of Mormon Battalion soldiers. "Pottawotomie High Council Record, July 24, 1846, in Eugene H. Perkins and Waldo C. Perkins, "'A Room of Round Logs with a Dirt Roof': Ute Perkins' Stewardship to Look after Mormon Battalion Families," 69. Root arrived in Salt Lake with the Heber C. Kimball company in the fall of 1848. He relocated to San Bernardino where he served as a justice of the peace and ran a hotel, the Six Mile House, outside Sacramento. In October 1850, Root's wife took his two-year-old child (listed as C.A.) and $12,000 in gold with the assistance of local miners Henry Fairbanks as well as the Davises—one of whom had been lodging with Root. She was arrested aboard the *Somerset* as she was about to set sail for Panama. Though news reports claimed that Root had taken back his wife, he married a widow, Hannah Peacock, in December. In 1851, he was robbed again, wiping out all of his gold reserves. "An Elopement and Arrest," *Daily [Springfield] Illinois State Journal,* March 19, 1851, 2; "Advertisements," *Sacramento Transcript,* November 5, 1850, 1, and November 6, 1850, 3; "Arrival of the North America," *Spectator* (New York), March 10, 1851, 3; "Another Robbery," *Burlington Hawkeye,* March 27, 1851, 2. By 1855, Root had lost all contact with the Church and later affiliated with the Reorganized movement. "A Lie Nailed," *Morning Herald* (Lexington, Ky.), May 4, 1899, 9; "Report of the 15th Quorum," *Deseret News,* April 13, 1854, 4; "Conferences," *True Latter-day Saints Herald* 22 (June 1, 1875): 348, 351; "Notes from California," *True Latter-day Saints Herald* 23 (October 1, 1876): 592; Charles C. Rich, Diary, May 13–14, 25, and June 21, 1850, *Selected Collections,* 36; Crosby, *No Place to Call Home,* 112. In 1876, an RLDS missionary considered Root to be an "old-time Saint" who had "seen some rough experience as a lover of the truth." Root famously recalled Joseph Smith saying, "If Brigham Young got the lead of the church he would lead it to hell." See also "Experiences and Testimony of Jeremiah Root," 271–73. Census documentation for Jeremiah Root is sometimes unclear. The 1850 census lists a "J. Root" in Sacramento, living with "E. Davis," who had been one of Root's wife's collaborators in the robbery. From 1860 onward, Root is listed as cohabiting with (and presumably married to) a German woman named Sophronia.

60. Likely Samuel McMurtrey (1797–1871). Hailing from Missouri, he and his wife, Julia Ann Morris McMurtrey, traveled west in the Willard Richards company in the fall of 1848. The McMurtreys moved to California in the spring of 1849. In May 1850, the McMurtreys were called to serve a mission to the Society Islands where they shared a three-room complex with Jonathan and Caroline Crosby. The McMurtreys returned in 1851 with the Crosbys following shortly afterward. They lived in San Bernardino until the fall of 1857, then returned to Utah. Crosby recorded that "neither of them could write very well." Crosby, *No Place to Call Home,* 120–22, 485; S. George Ellsworth, "Called to Tubai: Missionary Couples in French Polynesia, 1850," 35.

61. Likely referring to Amasa Lyman's company referenced below.

further orders By Mr. Hopper[62] I think that the Negro Boy called him that come through in A. Lymans Company[63] is knowing to the whole matter there is a good many people going to California that has objections to him going being that he has an owner in Missouri and in fact they think that the Martial[64] will be after him before he crosses Bear River and I could mention names but for fear of being mistaken I will not do it that I think is concerned in this matter.

B. Mathews [sic]
Remains your brother
To B. Young

---

62. Probably William Stevens Hopper (1803–80). Hopper and his wife, Hannah Moore Hopper, were born in Kentucky, joined the Mormons in Illinois, and traveled west with the Heber C. Kimball company in the fall of 1848. In April 1849, Hopper moved to the California gold fields. George S. Higley, *The Higleys and Their Ancestry*, 649; U.S. Census, 1850 California, Sacramento County, Sacramento, 22

63. In early March 1849, the First Presidency commissioned Apostle Amasa A. Lyman "to go to the Pacific with the mail" and to "see after the wheat [the faithful Saints] which may be there or are going." See "An Epistle of the Twelve to President Orson Pratt, and the Church of Jesus Christ of Latter-day Saints in the British Isles," 247.

64. Since 1846, numerous efforts to outlaw slavery in future territories acquired from Mexico had failed. The status of slavery in California remained unclear. On March 23, 1849, Representative Charles Stuart from Michigan said that the fugitive slave law already in place "contains the inference that [slaves] are free when taken into the territories by act of their master." "Speech of Mr. Stuart," *Kalamazoo Gazette*, March 23, 1849, 1–2; "The Slavery Question in California," *Augusta [Georgia] Chronicle*, August 20, 1849, 2.

Chapter 10

White Zion, 1852–1903

Brigham Young Defends Slavery and Publicly Announces the Priesthood Ban (February 1852)

HISTORICAL INTRODUCTION

When the Territorial Legislature first submitted its petition for statehood in 1849, Brigham Young described it as "very nice and clever."[1] Initially, Young had supported a free Utah.[2] But Young urged Apostle Orson Hyde to steer clear of the issue for political reasons. In spite of the general Mormon opposition to slavery, Young "wish[ed] not to meddle with this subject but leave things to their natural course."[3] He had similar advice for John Bernhisel. While Utah would attempt to enter the union as a free territory, Bernhisel should be willing to sacrifice the non-slave holding clause if necessary for "the good of the General Government."[4] In the Compromise of 1850, Congress attempted to solve the tension regarding territorial slavery by allowing each territory to decide its own status.

Even in Utah, the Saints were generally "averse to slavery."[5] In March 1851, Young told one slaveholder that he did not "wish to encourage the sale of blacks in these vallies."[6] A few months later, Brigham Young declared his opposition to a slave Utah: "Shall we lay a foundation for Negro slavery? No, God forbid. And I forbid."[7] Whenever slaves came to the territory, "a devil is raised," Brigham Young observed. "This one is talking, and that one is wondering . . . saying 'do you think

---

1. John Pulsipher, Notebook, n.p., MS 1034, LDS Church History Library.

2. Brigham Young, Letter to William Crosby, March 12, 1851, quoted in William E. Parrish, "The Mississippi Saints," 505.

3. Brigham Young, Letter to Orson Hyde, July 19, 1849, Brigham Young Office Files, Box 16, fd. 17.

4. Brigham Young, Letter to John Bernhisel, October 14, Brigham Young Office Files, Box 16, fd. 18. Unless otherwise noted, all Brigham Young correspondence, cited either by box and folder number or by microfilm reel is in this collection in the LDS Church History Library.

5. Brigham Young, Letter to Orson Hyde, July 19, 1849, Brigham Young Office Files, Box 16, fd. 17.

6. John Turner, *Brigham Young: Pioneer Prophet*, 224.

7. Scott Kenney, ed., *Wilford Woodruff's Journal*, June 1, 1851, 4:31.

its right; I am afraid its not right.'"[8] Such opposition likely came from the British converts such as James Moyle who found a New Orleans market to be "revolting to my feelings" as he saw "the men, women, and children" about "to be sold like cattle or horses." Even though "they had a black skin," Moyle thought to himself, "yet they were human beings." Young considered such views hypocrisy, as he reflected on the abject poverty he witnessed on his mission there: "Though the Enlightened nation England has abolished slavery in her colonies, yet the most damnable slavery exists in the very heart of the nation." Young felt "bold to say that [he]cannot find a black man or woman, in the U.S. that has traveled through the period of his life in hunger in the midst of plenty." He saw "thousands" perish from starvation; "that is meaner slavery than to set them to work in growing cotton, and sugar, &c."[9]

Young fervently hoped to strike a middle position, instructing the Saints that "while slavery may and should exist," particularly among those "naturally designed to occupy the position of 'servant of servants,'" the Saints "must not fall into the other extreme, and make them as beasts of the field." The legislature needed to strike a middle path, neither abusing blacks "nor yet elevat[ing] them . . . to an equality with those whom Nature and Nature's God has indicated to be their masters.[10]

But the Mormons' physical and mental separation from northern political discourse would eventually cause them to reorient their priorities, making opposition to slavery a dispensable political principle. On January 23, 1852, Brigham Young stood before the Utah Territorial Legislature holding in his hand "An Act in Relation to African slavery" as he declared that "inasmuch as we believe in the ordenances [sic] of God, in the Priesthood and order <and decrees> of God, we must in slavery." These were curses "brought upon themselves," Young noted, "and until the curse is removed by him who placed it upon them, they must suffer under its consequences," for Young was "not authorized to remove it." At day's end, Young considered himself to be a "firm believer in slavery." But he considered himself to be something of an egalitarian as well, assuring the all-Mormon legislature that "in short as far as the common comforts of life, salvation, light, truth, enjoyment, and understanding is concerned, the black African has precisely the same privilege as the white man."[11]

As LaJean P. Carruth has recently discovered, Young faced opposition from one of his fellow Church leaders. A few days later, Apostle Orson Pratt denounced Young's speech. "Shall we assume the right," Pratt cried, "without the voice of the Lord speaking to us and commanding us to [allow] slavery into our territory?" Pratt feared that adopting slavery would lose the goodwill of foreign converts:

---

8. "Speach [sic] by Gov. Young in Counsel on a Bill Relating to African Slavery," January 23, 1852, Historian's Office Record of Speeches, CR 100 317, Box 1, fd. 14.

9. Ibid.

10. "Governor's Message," *Deseret News*, January 10, 1852, 1.

11. "Speach [sic] by Gov. Young in Counsel on a Bill Relating to African Slavery," January 23, 1852, Historian's Office Record of Speeches, CR 100 317, Box 1, fd. 14.

the prohibition of slavery "would give us a greater influence among the nations of earth and by that means save them." Pratt later made clear that blacks suffered under a curse, but it was a curse that men did not have the authority to enforce. Pratt enjoined the legislature: "For us to bind the African because he is different from us in color [is] enough to cause the angels in heaven to blush."[12]

The "Act in Relation to Service" passed the legislature on February 4, 1852. Though Pratt's comments had little effect, Young felt it necessary to respond. The following day, Young stood again before the Territorial Legislature to deliver another speech on the subject, the full text of which is reprinted below. Pratt's comments stung, and according to one recorder, Young took care to declare that he considered himself to be "opposed to the system of slavery; its cruelties and abuses were obnoxious to humanity." But as with most matters, Young did not back down: "The negro . . . should serve the seed of Abraham."[13] The following text is drawn from the longhand transcription of scribe George D. Watt.

CITATION

"Speech by Gov. Young in Joint Session of the Legislature Feby 5th 1852 giving his views on slavery," in Historian's Office Reports of Speeches, Box 1, fd. 17, LDS Church History Library.

DOCUMENT EXCERPT

I rise to make a few remarks. The items before the house I do not understand.

The principle of slavery I understand, at least I have self-confidence enough and confidence enough in God to believe I do. I believe still further that a great many others understand it as I do. A great portion of this community have been instructed and have applied their minds to it, and as far as they have, they agree precisely in the principles of slavery. My remarks in the first place will be upon the cause of the introduction of slavery. Long ago mama Eve, our good old mother Eve, partook of the forbidden fruit and this made a slave of her. Adam hated very much to have her taken out of the garden of Eden, and now our old daddy says, I believe I will eat of the fruit and become a slave, too. This was the first introduction of slavery upon this earth; and <there has> not <been> a son or daughter of Adam from that day to this but what were slaves in the true sense of the word.

That slavery will continue until there is a people raised up upon the face of the earth who will contend for righteous principles, who will not only believe in but operate with every power and faculty given to them to help to establish the Kingdom of God, to overcome the devil, and drive him from the earth; then will

---

12. Orson Pratt, Speech Before Territorial Legislature, January 27, 1852, transcribed by LaJean Purcell Carruth from the Pitman shorthand. Quoted in program abstract for LaJean Purcell Carruth, "To bind the African because he is different from us in color enough to cause the angels in heaven to blush": Orson Pratt's Opposition to Slavery in the 1852 Territorial Legislature," paper presented at the Mormon History Association Conference, May 2014, San Antonio.

13. William Knecht and Peter Crawley, comps., *History of Brigham Young,* 113.

this curse be removed. This was the starting point of slavery. Again, after Adam and Eve had partook of the curse, we find they had two sons, Cain and Abel, but which was the oldest I cannot positively say; but this I know, Cain was given more to evil practices than Abel, but whether he was the oldest or not matters not to me. Adam was commanded to sacrifice and offer <up> his offerings to God that placed him into the garden of Eden. Through the faith and obedience of Abel to his Heavenly Father, Cain became <jealous> of him, and he laid a plan to obtain all his flocks; for through his perfect obedience to Father he obtained more blessings than Cain. Consequently[,] he took it into his heart to put able Able [sic] [out] of this mortal existence, after the deed was done, the Lord enquired for Able, and made Cane [sic] own what he had done with him. Now, says the grandfather, I will not destroy the seed of Michal [sic] and his wife, and Cain, I will not kill you nor suffer anyone else to kill you, but I will put a mark upon you. What is that mark? You will see it on the countenance of every African you ever did see upon the face of the earth or ever will see. Now I tell you what I know; when the mark was put upon Cain, Abel's children were in all probability young; the Lord told Cain that he should not receive the blessings of the Priesthood, nor his seed, until the last of the posterity of Abel had received the Priesthood, until the redemption of the earth.[14]

If there never was a prophet or apostle of Jesus Christ [that] spoke it before, I tell you,[15] this people that are commonly called Negroes are <the> children of old Cain.[16] I know they are; I know that they cannot bear rule in the Priesthood, for

14. At this point in the text, scribe and legislator Wilford Woodruff recorded that Brigham Young said "any man having one drop of the seed of Cain in him Cannot hold the Priesthood." Kenney, *Wilford Woodruff's Journal*, January-February 1852, 4:97.

15. Young was likely responding to Pratt's suggestion that there had been no revelation authorizing the adoption of slavery.

16. Compared to most Americans, Mormons were in the minority in attributing the curse to the biblical account of Cain killing Abel. In February 1835, W.W. Phelps queried of the *Messenger and Advocate*: "Is it or is it not apparent from reason and analogy . . . that God causes the Saints, or people that fall away from his church to be cursed in time, with black skin? Was or was not Cain, being marked, obliged to inherit the curse, he and his children forever" See W.W. Phelps, Letter to Oliver Cowdery, *Latter-day Saints' Messenger and Advocate* 1, no. 6 (March 1835): 82. Most Americans attributed black skin to Ham's sin in mocking his father, Noah, while drunk. Reverend Josiah Priest discounted Cain as blacks' progenitor, "as all Cain's race, with all the other races were lost in the flood." Josiah Priest, *Slavery, As It Relates to the Negro, or African Race: Examined in the Light of Circumstances, History and the Holy Scriptures; with an Account of the Origin of the Black Man's Color, Causes of His State of Servitude and Traces of His Character As Well in Ancient As in Modern Times: with Strictures on Abolitionism,* 134. The *Southern Presbyterian Review* dismissed out-of-hand the theory that Cain's skin was ever darkened. "There is not the least evidence that if a mark was set upon Cain, it was transmitted to his descendants." In fact, the *Review* continued, the idea that Cain was cursed with a mark at all was but an "evident mistranslation," since it was God's "intention that he [Cain] should be the parent of a numerous progeny, and the founder of States and cities in the Antediluvian world." Regardless, the *Review* chided those who used the explanations carelessly: "If the Ethiopian hue and features came from the curse of Ham, they do not come from the curse of Cain, and if from the malediction

the curse on them was to remain upon them until the ~~curse was wiped off from the earth~~ residue of the posterity of Michael and his wife receive the blessings, the seed of Cain would have received had they not been cursed, and hold the keys of the Priesthood until the times of the restitution shall come, and the curse be wiped off from the earth and from Michael's seed. Then Cain's seed will be had in remembrance, and the time come when the curse should be wiped off.[17]

Now then in the Kingdom of God on the earth, a man who has the African blood in him cannot hold one jot nor tittle of priesthood; why? Because they are the <true> eternal principles the Lord Almighty has ordained, and who can help it? Men cannot, the angels cannot, and all the powers of earth and hell cannot take it off; but thus saith the Eternal I am, what I am, I take it off at my pleasure, and not one partical [sic] of power can that posterity of Cain have, until the time comes [that] he [the Lord] says he will have it taken away. The time will come when they will have the privilege of all we have the privilege <of> and more.

In the Kingdom of God on the earth the Africans cannot hold one particle of ~~priesthood~~ power in Government. The the [sic] subjects, the rightfull servants of the residue of the children of Adam, and the residue of the children through the benign <influence of the> spirit of the Lord have the privilege of ~~looking~~ seeing to the ~~wants~~ posterity of Cain; inasmuch as it is the Lord's will they should receive the spirit of God by Baptisam [sic], and that is the end of their privilege; and there is not power on earth to give them any more power.

You talk of <the> dark skin. I never saw a white man on earth. I have seen persons whoes [sic] hair came pretty nigh being white, but to talk about white skins, it is something intirely unknown, though some skins are fairer than others. Look at the black eye and the jet black hair we often see upon men and women who are called white. [T]here is no such things as white folks. We are the children of Adam, who receive the blessings, and that is enough for us if we are not quite white.[18]

---

of Cain, then not from that pronounced upon the descendants of Ham." "The Mark of Cain and Curse of Ham," *Southern Presbyterian Review* 3, no. 3 (January 1850): 417. John Jacobus Flournoy, a prominent deaf American and advocate for the disabled, suggested that both Cain's and Ham's sins had brought black skin into the world. "The negroes are twice fallen," he observed, "hence their difference from the rest of mankind; hence their difficulty of civilization, and universal savageism in Africa." Flournoy, *An Essay on the Origin, Habits, &c of the African Race*, 5.

17. Contemporary commentators used similar language to describe racial cursings. In 1808 Pastor Seth Williston spoke of Ham's curse as "a reproach upon his posterity, which is not wiped off to the present day." Seth Williston, Sermon, *The Columbian Preacher. Chambers's Miscellany of Instructive and Entertaining Tracts* claimed that Asante tribesmen believed "that good negroes become white in the future state." "African Discovery," in *Chambers's Miscellany of Instructive and Entertaining Tracts*, 6. Reverend George Burder submitted that the conversion process could be compared to a case where "a blackamore should become white; or a lion become a lamb." George Burder, *Village Sermons*, 71.

18. Young's phrasing is noteworthy, as it suggests Young believed sin to racialize the entirety of the human race. In August 1852 Young encouraged the Saints to "purify yourselves" and "be pure from the crown of the head to the soles of your feet." Then they would "return again as clean as

But let me tell you further. Let my seed mingle with the seed of Cain, and that brings the curse upon me and upon my generations. [W]e will reap the same rewards with Cain.

In the priesthood, I will <tell> you what it will do. Where [sic] the children of ~~men~~ God to mingle there seed with the seed of Cain it would not only bring the curse <of being deprived of the power of the priesthood>[19] upon them ~~also risking themselves slaves~~ but they entail it upon their children after them, and they cannot get rid of it. If a man in an unguarded moment should ~~so~~ commit such a transgression, if he would walk up and say cut off my head, and kill man, woman and child it would do a great deal towards atoning for the sin. Would this be to curse them? No, it would be a blessing to them; it would do them good that they might be saved with their Bre[n] A many <would> shudder should they here us take [sic] about killing folk, but it is one of the greatest blessings to some to kill them, although the true principles of it are not understood.[20]

I would [add] one thing more. It is not in the power of a man on the <face of the> earth to take more life than he can give, that is a proper son of Adam. How many times I have heard it said and how many times has it been reiterated in my ears, and in yours, that to take a life, is to take what you cannot give. This is perfect nonsense. What do I do by taking a man's head off after he is condemned

---

a piece of pure white paper." In 1856, he told of a dream in which Joseph Smith acquired a flock of sheep and goats, the sheep being "white, pure, and clean" and the goats being "of all colors, red, black, white &c. mixed with the sheep; and their sizes, colors, and quality of fleeces seemed to be almost innumerable." When Young told Smith that he had "the strangest flock I ever saw," Joseph responded in his "usual shrewd manner": "They are all good in their places." Young concluded from the dream that "we are trying to train the flock, and to turn goats into sheep, and the spotted, ring-streaked and speckled into beautiful white." Brigham Young, August 28, 1852, *Journal of Discourses*, 6:273 and Brigham Young, April 20, 1856, *Journal of Discourses*, 3:322.

19. This insertion was included in Watt's longhand version of the speech.

20. In 1868, black legislator William Grey attacked an anti-miscegenation clause since it would allow white men to have sexual relationships with black women without serious consequence. Grey suggested that if "any white man shall be found cohabiting with a negro woman, the penalty shall be death." His proposal was partly facetious; the audience responded with "laughter and applause." Acknowledging the problems Grey presented, the legislature still did not ban interracial unions. Arkansas legislator John M. Bradley responded to the proposal: "Let a statute be enacted, based upon this feature of our Constitution, that shall fix the crime and the penalty; and if the penalty be death, as the gentleman suggests, let it be death! I have never be-longed to a bleaching-machinery and do not advocate the bleaching process. . . . It shows me a taste that makes Heaven frown and stinks in the nostrils of man." See *Debates and Proceedings of the Convention Which Assembled at Little Rock, January 7, 1868*, 363–65. For more on violent reactions to interracial unions, see also Charles F. Robinson II, *Dangerous Liaisons: Sex and Love in the Segregated South*, 26–28. For other contemporary examples of language associating one's bloodshed with the purification of one's sins, see Edward Calamy, *God's Free Mercy to England*, 48; "Her Atonement Was in Her Death," *New York Herald*, April 17, 1888, 12; "The Atonement of Blood," *Times-Picayune* (New Orleans), August 21, 1883, 8; and "Blood-Atonement Fanaticism in Arkansas," *[Baltimore] Sun*, April 23, 1881, 4. Additionally, see Stuart Banner, *The Death Penalty: An American History*, 134.

by the law? I put an end to the existence of the mortal taberncall [sic]; but the life still remains. The body and the spirit is only separated, this is all that can be done by any mortal man upon the face of the earth.

Can I give that life? I can; I can make as good tabernacles as any other man, and if you do not believe it <go and> look at my children, therefore that saying is nonsense. We form the tabernacle for the eternal spirit of life that comes from God. We can <only> put an end to the existence of that tabernacle, and this is the principle of sacrifice.

What was the cause of the ancients drawing up hundreds and thousands of bullocks, and Hefiers [sic], and lambs, and doves, and almost every other creature around them, of which they took the best and the fatest [sic], and offered them up as sacrifices unto the Lord. Was it not for the remission of the sins of the people? We read <also> in the New Testament that A man was sacrifised [sic] for the sins of the people. If he had not shed that blood which was given to him in the organization of his body or Tabernacle, you and I could have had no remission of sins. It is the greatest cleansing that could come to some men to shed their blood on the ground, and let it come up before the Lord as an atonement. You nor I cannot take any more life than we can give. If he had not shed that blood which was given to him in the organization of his body or tabernacle, you and I could have had no remission of sins. It is the greatest blessing that could come to some men to shed their blood on the ground, and let it come up to the Lord as an atonement. You nor I cannot take any more life than we can give.

Again to the subject before us, <as to> The men bearing rule,
[line of crossed out illegible text]
[illeg.] not [illeg.] one of the children of old Cain [illeg.] have one partical of right to bear rule in Government affairs from first to last, they have no business there. This privilege was taken from them by their own transgressions, and I cannot help it; and should you or I bear rule, we ought to do it with dignity <and honour> before God.

I am as much oposed to the principle of slavery as any man in the present acceptation or usage of the term. It is [abuse].[21] I am opposed to abusing that which God has decreed, to take a blessing, and make a curse of it. It is a great blessing for to the seed of Adam to have the seed of Cain for servants, but those they serve should use them with all the heart and feeling, as they would use their own children, and their compassion should reach over them and round about them, and treat them as kindly, and with that humane feeling necessary to be shown to mortal beings of the human species. Under these circumstances their blessings in life are greater in proportion than those who have to provide the bread and dinner for them.

We know there is a portion of inhabitants of the earth who dwell in Asia that are Negroes <and> said to be Jews. The blood of Judah has <not only> mingled

---

21. Watt's longhand renders the text ambiguously, making it appear to be "abuses" or "abused."

<illeg> almost with all nations, but also with the blood of Cain, and they have mingled there [sic] seeds together. These Negro Jews may keep up all the outer ordinances of the Jewish religion, they may have the[ir] sacrifices, and they may perform all the releigeous [sic] ceremonies any people on earth could perform, but let me tell you, that the day they consented to mingle there seed with Cainan, the Priesthood was taken away from Judah, and that portion of Judah's seed will never get any rule or blessings of the priesthood until Cain gets it.[22] Let this church which is called the Kingdom of God on the earth, we will summons the first presidency, the twelve, the high Counsel, the Bishoprick, and all the elders of Israel, suppose we summons them to appear here, and here declare that it is right to mingle our seed with the black race of Cain, that this shall come in with with us and be partakers with us of all the blessings God [illeg] has given to us. On that very day, and hour we should do so, the priesthood is taken from this church and kingdom and God leaves us to our fate. The moment we consent to mingle with the seed of Cain, the Church must go to destruction; we should receive the curse which has been placed upon the seed of Cain, and never more be numbered with the children of Adam who are heirs to the priesthood until that curse be removed.

Therefore, I will not consent for one moment to have an African dictate [illeg] me or [illeg] any Breth[n] with regard to [illeg]Church [illeg] or state government. I may vary in my view from others, and they may think I am foolish in the things I have spoken and think that they know more than I do, but I know [that] I know more than they do. If the Africans cannot bear rule and in the church of God, what business have they to bear rule in the state and government affairs of this territory or any others.

I[n] the government afairs [sic] of states and territories and kingdoms, by right God should govern. He should rule over nations and controle [sic] kings. If we suffer the Devil to rule to rule over us, and we shall not accomplish any go<o>d.[23] I

---

22. In 1850, John Bigelow, a traveler to Jamaica, was "astonished to find how little the expression of the Israelitish profile was effected by color." His "imagination could never have combined the sharp and cunning features of Isaac with the thick lipped, careless unthinking countenance of Cudjo; but nature has done it perfectly, if that can be called a combination in which the negro furnishes the color and the Jew all the rest of the expression." John Bigelow, *Jamaica in 1850: Or The Effects of Sixteen Years of Freedom on a Slave Colony,* 15.

23. The suggestion that black skin represented demonic tendencies was an epithet widely since seventeenth-century Anglo-America. Puritan theologian Stephen Charnock declared that the "inclination to sin . . . is incorporated in nature, like blackness in a negro or spots in a leopard." Stephen Charnock, "The Necessity of Regeneration," in Richard Adams and Edward Veal, eds., *The Complete Works of Stephen Charnock*, 3:34. Another author suggested that readers ask "why the Negro is a slave? He's black, not like a Christian." See "On Black Cats," *London Magazine* 5 (March 1822): 285. Calvinist theologian Thomas Williams supposed that during the temptation of Christ, the devil had been depicted with a "Negro complexion" and "if he ever could have occasion for such disguise, it must have been in this instance." Thomas Williams, ed., *The Cottage Bible and Family Expositor,* 18. Author Walter Scott wrote of one of his characters informing a black servant that his "colour . . . is greatly like that of Satan." Walter Scott, "Count Robert of Paris," in *Tales of My Landlord,* 1:173.

want the Lord to rule and be our Governor and and dictator, and we are the [illeg] boys to execute [it]. I shall not consent for a moment to give way to A Gentile spirit of contention, which is the cause of angry [illeg] difference to the alienation of every good feeling. It is for you and I to take a course to bind our feelings together in an everlasting bond of union inasmuch as we love the Lord, [illeg] which we ought to do more than selves. Consequently, I will not consent for a moment to have the children of Cain rule me nor my Bren. No it is not right.

But, say some, is there anything <of this kind> in the Constitution the U.S. has given us? If you will allow me the privilege [of] <telling> right out, it is none of their damned business what we do or say here. What we do it is for them to sanction, and then for us to say what we like about it. It is written right out in the Constitution, "that every free white male inhabitant above the age of twenty-one years," &c. My mind is the same today as when we were pouring over that constitution; any light upon the subject is the same, my judgment is the same, only a little more so. Perhaps I have said enough upon the subject. I have given you the true principles and doctrine. No man can vote for me or my Bre^n in this territory who has not the privilege of acting in church affairs.[24] Every man and woman and child in this territory are citizens; to say the contrary is all nonsense to me. The Indians are Citizens, the Africans are Citizens, and the [J]ews tha[t] come from Asia, that are almost entirely of the blood of Cain. It is our duty to take care of them and administer to them in all the acts of humanity and kindness. They shall have the right of citizenship, but shall not have the right to dictate in church and state matters. . . .

An Act in Relation to Service (1852)

Historical Introduction

The text of the Territorial Slave Act was conventional in many ways. However, it failed to use one word that defined most slave laws in the United States: "slavery." Brigham Young had found the southern slave system to be barbaric, even if he believed that servitude was an honorable occupation for the

---

24. The Utah Territorial Legislature changed course on this point when, in 1867, it ratified an amendment to the Territorial Constitution granting the franchise to "all male citizens of the United States over 21 years of age," likely hoping to win Republican support in Utah's efforts to win statehood. Brigham Young used the vote to express his support for the Fifteenth Amendment. The *Deseret News* editorialized that radical Republican leader Thaddeus Stevens would provide support: "We cannot see how he can do otherwise, and be consistent with his avowed principles." "Equal Rights and Liberty to All," *Deseret News*, February 13, 1867, 4. At the time of the Utah amendment, the Utah legislature was in the minority. Eight states offered blacks the franchise, and the national Republican establishment had proven weak in their support of it. Congress finally passed the amendment in February 1869. See also Brigham Young, Letter to Thomas L. Kane, October 26, 1869, Box 15, fd. 4, Thomas L. Kane Papers, Perry Special Collections; Thomas L. Kane, Letter to Brigham Young, October 13, 1869, Brigham Young Office Files, Box 40, fd. 14, LDS Church History Library. For a discussion of the national fight over the franchise, see Eric Foner, *Reconstruction: America's Unfinished Revolution, 1863–1877*, 446–49.

black population. "Negroes should be used like human beings," Young declared, "and not worse than dumb brutes. For their abuse of that race, the whites will be cursed, unless they repent."[25] When newsman Horace Greeley asked Young about the status of slaves in the territory, Young hedged: "Those laws are printed—you can read them for yourself," he answered obliquely. "If slaves are brought here by their owners in the states, we do not favor their escape from the service of their owners."[26] That certain prominent members of the legislature such as Abraham O. Smoot and Charles C. Rich already owned slaves made the decision relatively straightforward in the eyes of the all-Mormon legislative body.[27] But Young assured Greeley that Utah "will be admitted a free state" since slavery "would prove useless and unprofitable" in Utah.[28]

Also noteworthy is the act's efforts at preventing interracial sexuality, even if it did not address interracial marriages per se. The clause likely was intended to (1) prevent the dreaded mingling of racial lines, and (2) protect African American women from white sexual predators. But in contrast to Young's earlier comments, the law required imprisonment and a fine rather than execution for sexual intercourse with those of African descent.

The act illustrates the Mormon people's awkward attempts at upholding slavery while promoting a nominally benevolent race policy acceptable to most northerners. Originally, the act was entitled "An Act in Relation to African Slavery," with an early draft of the text declaring that blacks in bondage would labor as servants "until the curse of servitude is taken from the descendants of Canaan." To ordinary Saints, the textual splicing was irrelevant; all recognized it to be slavery. In 1934, Charles Nibley recalled that "negro slavery was actually the law of the land and practiced to a small extent . . . in Cache Valley."[29] In 1855, two visitors to Utah "were assured there was but little" of slavery in the Territory, "yet it is there."[30]

But the legislature and Brigham Young knew better than to adopt a slave code that would alienate already anxious northerners. So they crafted the act to

25. Brigham Young, March 8, 1863, *Journal of Discourses*, 10:111.

26. Horace Greeley, *An Overland Journey, from New York to San Francisco, in the Summer of 1859*, 211.

27. Popular understanding of Smoot maintains that Smoot refused to support Joseph Smith's presidential campaign; however, Smoot actively campaigned for Joseph Smith, even reading his "views on the powers and policy of the government . . . for the consideration of all present" during church services in Tennessee. "Minutes of a General Conference," *Times and Seasons* 5, no. 12 (July 1, 1844): 574. The best treatment of Abraham Smoot's complicated views on slavery continues to be Elliot Berlin, "Abraham Owen Smoot."

28. Greeley, *An Overland Journey*, 212.

29. "Reminiscences of Charles W. Nibley," *Improvement Era* 37, no. 10 (October 1934): 598. For a fuller discussion of how parties read the 1852 act, see Nate Ricks, "Ricks's critique of Rich's UHQ article on Utah Servitude/Slavery," *Juvenile Instructor* (blog), http://www.juvenileinstructor.org/responses-ricks-critique-of-richs-uhq-article-on-utah-servitudeslavery/ (accessed April 26, 2014).

30. "The Mormons," *Millennial Star* 17, no. 4 (January 27, 1855): 63.

mirror the language of several northern states by casting slaves as "involuntary servants." Further, the law, Young hoped would "govern . . . those who have made contracts to labour" so that they "may perform their labours according to said contracts." Though Young focused most of his remarks on Africans, he acknowledged that his belief in slavery applied to "slaves that [are] Africans, or that are English, or that [are] Dutch, or ourselves." The passage of the "Act in Relation to Service" was part of a political dance to attract both southern and northern states alike—distancing itself from the slave system while acknowledging the sovereignty of slaveholders over their slaves.[31]

CITATION

"An Act in Relation to Service," in *Acts, Resolutions, and Memorials Passed by the First Annual and Special Sessions of the Legislative Assembly of the Territory of Utah*. Salt Lake City: Brigham Hamilton Young, 1852, 80–82.

DOCUMENT EXCERPT

Sec. 1 *Be it enacted by the Governor and Legislative Assembly of the Territory of Utah,* That any person or persons coming to this Territory and bringing with them servants justly bound to them, arising from special contract or otherwise, said person or persons shall be entitled to such service or labor by the laws of this Territory *Provided,* That he files in the office of the Probate Court, written and satisfactory evidence that such labor or service is due. . . .

Sec. 4 That if any master or mistress shall have sexual or carnal intercourse with his or her servant or servants of the African race, he or she shall forfeit all claim to said servant or servants to the commonwealth; and if any white person shall be guilty of sexual intercourse with any of the African race, they shall be subject, on conviction thereof to a fine of not exceeding one thousand dollars, nor less than five hundred, to the use of the Territory, and imprisonment, not exceeding three years. [32]

Sec. 5 It shall be the duty of masters or to provide for his her or their servants comfortable habitations clothing bedding sufficient food and recreation. And it shall be the duty of the servant in return therefor to labor faithfully all reasonable hours and do such service with fidelity as may be required by his or her master or mistress.

---

31. For the most thorough dissecting of the 1852 act, see Christopher Rich, "The True Policy for Utah: Servitude; Slavery; and 'An Act in Relation to Service,'" 54–74.

32. It is noteworthy that this act did not outlaw interracial marriage per se. No evidence has been found of this law being prosecuted, and a handful of interracial marriages in Utah suggest that the law was not directed at married couples. In 1878, a "full blooded Negro" united himself with "a white haired Scandinavian girl." One observer acknowledged the legitimacy of the union, noting that "in Zion there is no law against it." Interracial marriages would remain legal in Utah territory until 1888. "Off Color," *Salt Lake Tribune,* November 26, 1878, 4. See also Patrick Q. Mason, "The Prohibition of Interracial Marriage in Utah," 108–31.

Sec. 6 It shall be the duty of the master to correct and punish his servant in a reasonable manner when it may be necessary being guided by prudence and humanity and if he shall be guilty of cruelty or abuse or neglect to feed, clothe, or shelter his servants in a proper manner the Probate Court may declare the contract between master and servant or servants void according to the provisions of the fourth section of this act.

Elijah Ables Tells of His Travels West (March 1854)

HISTORICAL INTRODUCTION

Elijah Ables's exact activities in Cincinnati between 1845 and 1853 are largely lost to history. In 1847, he married a young biracial woman named Mary Ann and moved into Cincinnati's German neighborhood. Meanwhile, the Cincinnati branch faced extinction. Dissenters Sidney Rigdon and James J. Strang had made forays into the Mormon community there, leaving Brigham Young's supporters beleaguered as they tried to hold the branch together.

Moreover, in February 1847 William McCary, then a fresh convert, took the Mormon community in Cincinnati by storm, only to leave them scandalized as he would all the Saints in Winter Quarters. "The Black Indian has blown out," Strangite convert Frederick Merryweather[33] wrote James Strang from Cincinnati, "and all his followers are here ashamed."[34] In 1849, Edson Whipple visited Cincinnati while conducting personal business. During his

---

33. F[rederick] Merryweather, Letter to James J. Strang, February 8, 1847, *Zion's Reveille* 2, no. 7 (February 25, 1847): 27. The scandal apparently did not influence Strang's views on blacks holding the priesthood to the same extent that it affected Brigham Young. Two years later, he insisted that there was no race-based priesthood ban in his church: "The impression ha[s] gone forth," he remarked at a New York City meeting, "that a colored man could not hold the priesthood." But this was not true. "The fact that color was a curse was no bar." After all, he observed, "who is there that does not labor under a curse." Shortly after his remarks, he "proposed by revelation that Bro. Walker (colored) be ordained an Elder, which was concurred in unanimously." See "Meetings of a General Conference Held in the City of New York," *Gospel Herald* 4, no. 35 (November 15, 1849): 182.

34. Dr. Frederick Merryweather (ca. 1806-unknown) was a "patent medicine agent," today's equivalent of a pharmaceutical salesman. U.S. Census, Ohio, Hamilton County, Cincinnati, Ward 2, 152. He initially was a follower of Brigham Young. Brigham Young, Letter to Frederick Merryweather, March 4, 1845, Brigham Young Office Files, Reel 24 and Frederick Merryweather, Letter to Brigham Young, March 10, 1850, Brigham Young Office Files, Reel 31. By April 1845, he had defected to join Sidney Rigdon's movement. Heman C. Smith, "Biography of Sidney Rigdon," 180. He next joined the Strangites. Frederick Merryweather, Letter to James Strang, February 8, 1847, *Zion's Reveille* 1, no. 7 (February 25, 1847): 27. By the end of the decade, he had rejoined the Brighamites and played an active role in pushing back against William Smith's movement in Cincinnati. William Smith complained that Merryweather had penned a letter that "slander[s] Joseph [Smith] in the most outrageous manner" and "display[s] far more malice and hatred to the Smith family than the mobocrats did in Joseph's lifetime." "The Brighamite Combination in Cincinnati," *Melchisedek and Aaronic Herald* 1, no. 6 (September 1849): 2. He traveled to Utah in 1861. "Capt. D.H. Cannon's Train," *The Mountaineer*, July 13, 1861, 162. For a commentary on "patent medicine, see *Proceedings of the New Jersey Pharmaceutical*

trip, Whipple felt "the spirit of the gathering rest upon me" as he declared before the "scattered Saints . . . the advantages of gathering, or fleeing to the mountains."[35] But in fact Cincinnati had become a revolving door community of Mormon sects. In 1849, Merryweather told James Blakeslee that a pamphlet sent by Strangite dissident Reuben Miller[36] had "killed every Strangite Mormon in the place" and that "the work under the Presidency of Bro. Strang was all blown up and gone to the shades." Merryweather admitted that he himself had converted back to Brighamite Mormonism.[37]

That same year, Joseph Smith's brother, William Smith, started a religious movement of his own, claiming authority by virtue of his Smith family lineage. With headquarters in Covington, Kentucky, William presented a convenient alternative to those who had little confidence in Brigham Young. William's movement did not last long; in the spring of 1850 (probably April or May), William was accused of seducing the wife of his newspaper editor, Isaac Sheen. He escaped to Cincinnati to stay with his apostle, Henry Nisonger. Nisonger's family was boarding with Elijah Ables.[38] James Blakeslee, a Strangite supporter, wrote that he had "visited from house to house about town" and informed them that there were "about 100 old Mormons in this city who hold with none of the parties."[39] It is possible that Ables was among the hundred.

In the fall of 1853, Elijah cast his allegiance with the Utah Mormons and took his wife and two children to Salt Lake City. The Nisongers left the following year.[40] Nearby present-day Casper, Wyoming, Elijah saw evidence of what he believed to be a murder in the company and felt compelled to communicate the matter to President Brigham Young. Only months before this letter, Brigham Young had denied Elijah Ables his endowment.[41]

Association, 36: Such a man "swoops upon our town with blare of trumpets and peal of bells, with bonfires and calcium lights, with choruses and street lectures."

35. Edson Whipple, Letter to Heber C. Kimball, ca. June 1849, Edson Whipple Notebook.

36. Reuben Miller (1811–82) joined the Strangites in January 1846 and became a stake president but became quickly disaffected when he found that Strang had not been properly ordained to be Joseph Smith's successor: "I came to the conclusion, irresistibly, that I had embraced an error, a delusion, and one that would be handed down on the pages of history, as a monument of his folly and of the corruption and wickedness of the human heart." Reuben Miller, *James J. Strang, Weighed in the Balance of Truth and Found Wanting*, 4. In February 1848, Miller visited Voree, Wisconsin, where he persuaded a few Strangites to be "redeemed and brought to acknowledge the true authority." He called Voree "the capital of Satins [sic] kingdom." Reuben Miller, Letter to Brigham Young, February 23, 1848, Brigham Young Office Files, Reel 30. See also Richard Lloyd Anderson, "Reuben Miller: Recorder of Oliver Cowdery's Reaffirmations," 280–84.

37. James Blakeslee, Letter to Frank Cooper, June 8, 1849, *Gospel Herald*, July 5, 1849, 1.

38. "A Prophetic Family Arrangement," *Covington Daily Union*, June 5, 1850, 2; U.S. Census, Cincinnati, Ohio, Hamilton County, Ward 10, 90.

39. James Blakeslee, Letter to Frank Cooper, June 8, 1849, in *Gospel Herald*, July 5, 1849, 1.

40. Brigham D. Madsen, *Against the Grain: Memoirs of a Western Historian*, 6–7.

41. Quorum of the Twelve, Meeting Minutes, August 26, 1908, typescript, George A. Smith Family Papers, Box 78, fd. 7, Special Collections, Marriott Library, University of Utah.

CITATION

Elijah Ables, Letter to Brigham Young, March 14, 1854, Brigham Young Office Files, Reel 32; left justification added.

DOCUMENT EXCERPT

G.S.L. March 14, 1854

Sir most noble governor man of God With high [r]espect I address you thes[e] lines to inform you about father Bray[42] who came acros[s] the planes with us in Harmons company[43] as far as the last croasing of Plat river[44] and then left our company and came in to Barnes company A merchant train[45] for the sake of more teem and agreed with the two young men that drove his <team> to give them five dollars A pece and give them fifty cents extra every night they stad on guard & came in that company this side of green river as far as mody crick[46] and thare they camped all night & in the morning when preparing to start, Capten Barnes

---

42. Francis Bray (1793–1853) was a sixty-year-old London iron merchant, and Selina Rayson Bray's "dearly beloved" husband. During the trip to New Orleans, the Brays were "most affectionately received by all the Saints." Selina's heart "swelled with gratitude to my Father in Heaven for all his great goodness & mercy unto me." Selina Rayson Bray, Diary, January 20, 1853, 3, LDS Church History Library. She died August 13, 1853. After her death, Bray reportedly "wandered off and was lost." The company "stayed days searching for him but never found him." Lucina Mecham Boren, Journal, in Kate Carter, ed., *Treasures of Pioneer History,* 6: 306.

43. Appleton M. Harmon (1820–77) traveled west with Brigham Young's vanguard company in summer 1847. En route, Harmon made the odometer that William Clayton had conceptualized. He returned to England for a mission in 1850 and served as a company captain during his return trip. Norman E. Wright, "The Mormon Pioneer Odometers," 82–115.

44. In June 1847, the Saints established a ferry service at the "last crossing" of the Platte River. It facilitated river crossing for thousands of Oregon Trail migrants. One non-Mormon considered the ferry to be a "a rather loose affair." The construction of a toll bridge in 1853 put the Mormon ferry out of business. George W. Hunt, *A History of the Hunt Family from the Norman Conquest, 1066 A.D. to the Year 1890,* 22 and Wallace Stegner, *The Gathering of Zion: The Story of the Mormon Trail,* 244.

45. William Barnes (1792–1880) joined the Saints in Great Britain and emigrated to America in 1853. One company member, Cornelius Bagnall, identifies the traveling contingent "as a company of traders belonging to Captain Barnes" and confirms that Bray left the Harmon camp to join with Barnes. Barnes apparently arrived in Utah broke, with his "whole capital stock consist[ing] of ten cents." Cornelius Bagnall, Diary, September 10, 1853, LDS Church History Library; see also Edward W. Tullidge, *Tullidge's Histories: Containing the History of All the Northern, Eastern, and Western Counties of Utah,* 216–17. Bagnall later moved to San Francisco and joined the RLDS Church. "San Francisco," *True Latter-day Saints' Herald,* September 15, 1872, 570.

46. A contemporary described Muddy Creek as a "narrow stream, but in many places quite deep." The "water is clear," he took care to note; its name comes from the "slimy and miry nature of its banks and bed." "Central Route to the Pacific," *Daily Missouri Republican,* December 19, 1853, 1. Mormon emigrant Hezekiah Mitchell observed that Muddy Creek's "water is clear" and had "swift currant" along with "willows and sage brush in abundance." Hezekiah Mitchell, Journal, September 20, 1854, LDS Church History Library.

and Joseph fell out & Barnes discharged Joseph fell out and Joseph came A head with the mail & Davis[47] remained.

So when the teems were about to start Davis came to father Daltons[48] in his wagon to git A cup of coffee for father Bray & stered the coffee up & gave it to father Bray and father Bray remaned there all alone & where the company got A little ahead then Davis & another young man left the company & was not seen by the company until about noon when they came on behind the wagens without father Bray and the general suppsion is that they new new ware father Bray is, Richard was not A member of the church but Davis was but in a state of apostasy & wished to go back to the <old> contry, in the last conversation I had with him & had no mony or means to help him self with & as soon as he could git here and git money or means he would go back & now has fifty dollars in his pockit so [he] sed. He states that he got the mony in this place but no one can say ware [sic]. I beleave it is the Brays mony for I saw him have some at fort Larme[49] & it appeared to be a considerable amount, He also had to servant girls one sarah & the other Elizabeth, Sarah has marred Mr. Belsey since he came to this place. Sister Young & dauter say they saw him have a very large amount of mony & in dressing had very rich aparrel, On the second morning the girls gave another young man named Robert Nesning Mr Brays boots & clothing to put on which leads to shaw that all things were understood about the matter. I am yours respectfully with law and order.

Elijah Ables

Brigham Young Offers to Buy and Free a Slave (January 1861)

Historical Introduction

Though supportive of the abstract principle of black slavery, Brigham Young strove to protect slaves from some of its excesses. In the letter below, Young directs a white sister to sell her black slave, Jerry, to some "kind faithful member." That failing, Young promised to "purchase him and set him at liberty." The slave mentioned was likely sold to Abraham Smoot. He drowned in 1861.[50]

Citation

Brigham Young, Letter to Mrs. David Lewis, January 3, 1860, Box 19, fd. 1; left justification added.

---

47. Possibly William Davis, a captain of ten in the Harmon company. Bagnall, *Journal*, June 16, 1853.

48. Likely John Dalton, who had also left the camp to travel with the Barnes company. Ibid., September 10, 1853.

49. LeRoy R. Hafen, *Fort Laramie and the Pageant of the West, 1834–1890.*

50. Donna Toland Smart, ed., *Mormon Midwife: The 1846–1888 Diaries of Patty Bartlett Sessions*, 286.

DOCUMENT EXCERPT

Great Salt Lake City, January 3, 1860
Mrs. David Lewis
3rd Ward, City

Dear Sister:

I understand that you are frequently importuned to sell your negro man Jerry[51] but that he is industrious and faithful, and desires to remain in this Territory. Under these circumstances, I should certainly deem it most advisable for you to keep him, but should you at any time conclude otherwise and determine to sell him, ordinary kindness would require that you should sell him to some kind faithful member of the Church, that he may have a fair opportunity for doing all the good he desires to do and is capable of doing. I have been told that he is about forty years old, if so, it is not presumable that you will, in case of sale, ask so high a price as you might expect for a younger person. If the price is sufficiently moderate, I may conclude to purchase him and set him at liberty.

Your Brother in the Gospel,
Brigham Young

A Payson Man Inquires about His Racial Status (January 1861)

HISTORICAL INTRODUCTION

In 1861, the Mormons in Utah were far-removed from the war clouds that had enveloped the East. While Brigham Young had long since preached the evils of racial intermarriage and black membership in the priesthood, he had made little effort to systemically implement the doctrines into practice.

The letter below illustrates the racial angst an ordinary Latter-day Saint faced in territorial Utah. N. B. Johnson—full name unknown—struggled to know what having African ancestry might mean. His rhetoric reveals the questions that still loomed about the consequences of having African/"Canaanite" ancestry.

Certain aspects of the letter indicate that there is a social distance between the writer and the Prophet. He incorrectly identifies the Church as "the Church of latter day Saints of Jesus Christ." Also, his request that Young send his reply to his bishop indicates that he did not own a home or land. These features make it likely that N. B. Johnson was Napoleon B. Johnson, a day laborer then working for Parowan City councilman Henry G. Boyle. Johnson lived down the street from Israel Calkins Jr., the son of one of William McCary's followers.[52]

---

51. Sister Lewis might have sold her slave to the Abraham Smoot family. On June 15, 1861, Patty Bartlett Sessions recorded that that a slave named Jerry, the "Smoots['] Negro drowned." Smart, *Mormon Midwife*, 286.

52. U.S. Census, 1860, Utah, Utah County, Payson, "Napoleon Bonaparte Johnson," 253; *The Revised Ordinances of Payson City*, 3.

Citation

N. B. Johnson, Letter to Brigham Young, January 1, 1861, Brigham Young Office Files, Reel 38; ellipses in original; left justification and initial capitals added where needed; sprinkling of misplaced periods as per original.

Document Excerpt

Hon President Brigham Young of the Church of Latter-day Saints of Jessus Christ to your excellence in the holy priesthood I had writen a few lines by way of a question as my mind have bin & are rather embarrasst on the account of some who pretend pretend [sic] to understand all mysteries conserning the following question theirfore after I had Aplied to three diferent Bishop for <an> answer & thea [sic] told me they were not able to to [sic] answered such a question as it was something new to them. . . . Theirfore I was assured by the holy spirit that you could desolve the query wich i hope you will condescend to do. . . . The question as follows am i a lawfull heir or not to the Priesthood my progeny is as follows all on my father's side was <the> white race of man. . . . On my mothers side my great grandmother was near a full Blooded Canaanite my grandmother was about ¾ of the Canaanite my Mothers Father was about one seventh of the Canaanite. . . . Now pleas to let me know. whether I am a legal heir or not to the priesthood. . . . [illegible] Father Morley[53] told me i was in a Blessing he siad [sic] i was of the seed of Ephraim & a legal heir . . . but I hope you you will plead [sic] to give your disesion as it will put an end to all controversy & it was agreeable to thy feelings i would like to see a discorse [on] this subject that is how fair would any legal seed could mix with the Canaanite && then clame an heirship to the priesthood such a discorse <would> give <light> to thousands in Israel or to all the latter day sts. in gen[eral] if you do answer my personal query pleas to direct in care of Bishop Young[54] Payson City

---

53. Isaac Morley (1786–1865) was ordained a patriarch in November 1837, came west with the Saints in 1846, and led the first colonizers to Sanpete in the fall of 1849. His closest interaction with African Americans was with "Black Pete," a black charismatic preacher who had affiliated with the Mormons in Kirtland before Joseph Smith arrived. "Black Pete" probably lived with the Morleys for a brief period. There is no clear indication that "Black Pete" was officially ordained to the priesthood; he claimed to have received his authority through a heavenly manifestation. Morley was also present in Independence when Joseph Smith preached to a "respectable number of negroes." Mark Lyman Staker, *Hearken O Ye People: The Historical Setting of Joseph Smith's Ohio Revelations,* 5–18, 37–92; *Manuscript History of the Church, 1838–1856,* A–1, 129

54. In September 1859, Brigham Young and Ezra T. Benson set apart twenty-year-old Franklin W. Young (ca. 1839–1911) as bishop of the Payson settlement which included about 175 families. Franklin was Lorenzo Young's son and Brigham's nephew. Though "the youngest bishop ever ordained in the Church," the First Presidency assured the Payson Saints that Young was "faithful and prompt in all his duties." However, Franklin felt a "heavy, dark cloud . . . rest over me" and found "much dissatisfaction of late with the bishop" he was replacing—"three party factions, each pulling against the other." Since Young was a "stranger to them all," the factions were able to unite behind him "in a goodly measure." Franklin W. Young, Autobiography, ca. 1916, 67–69; Edward W. Tullidge, "Utah County," 395–96.

I remain your well wisher in the gosple of Jesus Christ
N.B. Johnson

[P.S.] If the Lord permits I yet hope to see you in a proper time face to face as I desire to say some what to thee about my own affairs I was from my boyhood naturally gifted to fore<see> future events both as to myself &C others yet I have bin leed [sic] astray by the spirits of darkness but the God of hope new my heart & showed me my errer for in a nights vision thre[e] diferent times eather thy spirit or your guiding angel or something <in> thy apperance told me of my most secrt sins & warned me in the in [erased] name of Christ <to> flee from the wrath to come yet after all of this I have evil spirits to contend with but the Lord is my helper inasmuch i obay [illegible] his servants. . . . I now conclude

So may the Lord help thee farewell well
N.B. Johnson

I told no persons these things only I said I seen my errer [sic].

A Mormon Dissenter Attacks the Racial Doctrine (April 1870)

HISTORICAL INTRODUCTION

The idea of blacks somehow faltering in the premortal realm had been circulating for several decades; in 1845, Orson Hyde had commented that "those spirits in heaven that lent an influence to the devil, thinking he had a little the best right to govern, but did not take a very active part any way, were required to come into the world and take bodies in the accursed lineage of Canaan; and hence the Negro or African race."[55] Over the next generation, the idea grew in popularity, much to Brigham Young's annoyance. In 1869 Young's brother, Lorenzo, asked "if the Spirits of Negroes were Nutral in Heaven." Young rebuffed him: "There were No Nutral spirits in Heaven at the time of the Rebelion . . . The posterity of Cane are Black Because He Commit Murder. He killed Abel & God set a Mark upon his posterity."[56]

The following year, John S. Lindsay, a prominent stage actor, had joined with anti-Brigham Young dissenter William Godbe to launch a full attack against the Mormon establishment. Initially a faction targeting Brigham Young's protectionist policies in support of the introduction of Eastern capitalism into the territory, the movement soon began to welcome other Eastern intellectual movements, such as spiritualism, alongside scientific racism.[57] In 1870, Godbe,

---

55. Orson Hyde, *Speech of Elder Orson Hyde, Delivered before the High Priests Quorum of Nauvoo, April 27th, 1845, upon the Course and Conduct of Mr. Sidney Rigdon and upon His Merits to His Claim to the Presidency of the Church of Jesus Christ of Latter-day Saints*, 30.

56. Kenney, *Wilford Woodruff's Journal*, 6:510–11, December 25, 1869.

57. The best treatment of William Godbe's movement is Ronald W. Walker, *Wayward Saints: The Godbeites and Brigham Young*.

Elias L. T. Harrison, and Edward W. Tullidge founded a newspaper to counter the Church's stronghold, the *Mormon Tribune,* a name later changed to the *Salt Lake Tribune.*[58]

On April 23, 1870, Lindsay published "The Origin of Races," in which he launched a full-frontal assault on Mormons' conception of racial origins. By modern standards, Lindsay's attacks could be seen as almost as offensive as the racism he was attacking. Lindsay did not reject ideas about racial inequality; he thought of white races as having "nobler and purer blood." Indeed, in cases of racial intermarriage, Lindsay was convinced that "the best and noblest blood . . . keeps the ascendancy" and "never resolves itself into meaner conditions." Lindsay objected to the Mormons' embrace of "ignorance, superstition, and idolatry" in the face of the "lessons of nature and science on this subject. Nature is always true, her laws infallible." Lindsay's article illustrates how racial origins served as a point of contention during the Mormon people's process of integration into the American community.

CITATION

John S. Lindsay, "The Origin of Races," *Mormon Tribune,* April 23, 1870, 130; emphasis in original.

DOCUMENT EXCERPT

The Origin of Races

With the Latter-day Saints, this belief in the origin of the black race is so closely interwoven with the doctrine of the preexistence of man as a spirit that, in examining one theory, touching upon the other will be to some degree unavoidable. Indeed, so inseparably connected are these doctrines in the Mormon faith that, if the one can be shown to be incompatible with the facts of science and grossly improbable to human reason, it may be readily assumed that the other is inconsistent and unreasonable also.

Orthodox Mormonism teaches that the spirits of the black race are such as, at the time of the great warfare in heaven when Lucifer and his hosts were cast out, played an ignoble part, not evincing untainted loyalty on the one hand, nor yet possessing sufficient courage to join with Satan and his band of rebels. To use a homely phrase, now current here, they were "*a-straddle the fence,*" waiting to see which side would conquer and ready to fall over among the victorious and popular party. We are informed that for this ignoble conduct they were condemned to suffer on this earth and pay the penalty of their disloyalty by dwelling in bodies inferior to those of their more loyal brethren—us white folks. In order to effect this, God is said to have cursed Cain with a skin of blackness, thus creating an

---

58. In April 1871, the owners renamed the paper as the *Salt Lake Daily Tribune and Mining Gazette,* soon abbreviated further to the *Salt Lake Tribune.* Edward W. Tullidge, *The History of Salt Lake City and Its Founders,* Appendix, 12.

ignoble lineage through which these spirits were doomed to come in accordance with His divine programme . . .

Cain is said to have been cursed for shedding his brother's blood. This curse is believed to have consisted in God's changing the color of his skin from what was white and beautiful to a loathsome blackness. The Bible, however, does not so inform us; it merely states that God placed a *mark* upon him; and this mark was not put upon him as a curse but to serve him as a *protection*. His real *curse* was, that the earth should not henceforth yield to him her strength— 'A fugitive and a vagabond shalt thou be' etc . . [Genesis 4:12]

Even admitting, to continue the argument, that he was cursed with blackness, it takes something more than a black skin to constitute a true type of the African race. Not only would God have been necessitated to change the color of his skin, but also his form and every feature, to destroy as many characteristics and create in him as many new ones as it takes to make up the essential difference between the white race and the black. Will some of our sage philosophers explain to us how God *might* have accomplished such a seeming impossibility—a miracle only to be surpassed by creating woman out of man's rib? True, it is written that all things are possible with Him. But *how* possible? Surely not in direct violation of His own laws, the laws of Nature.[59] God *cannot* work in antagonism to His own universal laws. In all His wondrous works we beheld the nicest and most complete harmony. What harmony would there be in this? What wisdom? What prescience? God is *manifest* in *all His* works, the impress of infinite wisdom is to be read in all He does; but when men attribute to Infinite Wisdom works which their own puny judgment might overreach, the utility of which their reason can dare to question, 'tis time they assured themselves as to whether He has been the author of such proceedings or not.

Leaving this palpable difficulty as to Cain's transformation for the reader to reason upon, we drift at once upon another equally stupendous in its nature, but the philosophy in connection with which we can better presume to handle because the direct interference of God is withdrawn, and the effect of that interference left to work its own results. It will readily be conceded by all that for Cain's crime he alone was cursed with blackness; and yet how heavy must have been the odium entailed, through that curse, upon his parents and their younger offspring! With what a crushing weight it must have fallen on the innocent *sister* who was doomed to become his *wife*, the mother of his

---

59. Godbeite supporters celebrated scientific inquiry as a vehicle to the true religion that resembled eighteenth-century Deism. William Godbe expressed his faith that the "infallibility of the Creator" could be found as "He has revealed Himself in *His* holy book—the book of universal nature." Godbeite Elias Harrison considered "the grandeur of Nature" to be the God he worshipped; Christianity had served as but a "stepping stone." Walker, *Wayward Saints*, 260, 346.

children, her lovely and innocent nature mingling with his guilty one to give birth to those

> "Who can but suffer many years and die,
> Propagating death, and multiplying murder."[60]

How could the sister's pure soul find affinity in that of her fratricidal brother? Would she not shrink in horror from the embrace of that *elder* brother whose murderous arm had opened wide the door for death to stalk about among humanity, by shedding a *younger* brother's blood?

It is supposed by some that Cain *found* his wife after he went to dwell in the land of Nod; but a careful review of the passage from which such inference is draw, will prove such a supposition unjustifiable; besides the theory of the creation we started with does not admit of the idea at all. If it did it would alter the case a little, for wherever Cain found his wife she must been a *fair* daughter of earth, no curse of blackness resting on *her*. Now the pertinent inquiry comes in, could parents, one *black*, the other *white* beget a genuine African posterity? Nature loudly answers, No. How long would it have taken for this supposed curse upon Cain by amalgamation with the nobler and purer blood of the next of Adam's posterity, to resolve itself back into its first conditions? Let the curious investigate. It is a well-known fact that the best and noblest blood in cases of amalgamation keeps the ascendancy, and where the advantages are equal it never resolves itself into meaner conditions. And yet, in the face of this great natural law, the supporters of this flimsy theory bring a pure African descent from Cain down to the Deluge and even transmit it through the Ark by smuggling in a black woman as the wife of Ham, Noah's son, who, of course, was white,—thus introducing the same difficulties as at first, only *reversing* the color of the parents.

The absurdities of this tradition are sufficient to comprise a volume, and, altogether, too multitudinous to be even touched upon in a hurried article like this, but a consideration of these few more prominent ones will lead the thoughtful reader to that of others.

It was designed, in connection with this subject, to advert to the curse of the Lamanites, but, as space will not permit, suffice it to say that this theory involves the necessity of finding a curse for every tribe or race of men that we consider beneath us in civilization or inferior color.

How much more rational and easy of comprehension are the lessons of nature and science on this subject. Nature is always true, her laws infallible. When will mankind learn to read her great volume of truth spread out before them on every hand, and place a *just* and proper value on *traditions* that have been handed down to them through ages of ignorance, superstition and idolatry?

John S. Lindsay

---

60. Lindsay is paraphrasing Lord Byron's play, *Cain*, in which Cain laments: "Who can but suffer many years, and die / Methinks is merely propagating and multiplying murder." See Lord George Byron, "Cain," in *The Works of Lord Byron, Including His Suppressed Poems*, 370.

Church Leaders Discuss Endowing Ables (May 1879)

Historical Introduction

With Brigham Young's death and the death of Elijah's wife, Mary Ann, Ables not only felt a new incentive to pursue his temple endowment but also thought that Brigham Young's successor, John Taylor, might be friendlier to his cause. Elijah insisted that (1) he held the priesthood worthily and that (2) his ordination and worthiness entitled him to temple blessings. Taylor studied the issue by interviewing two Joseph Smith confidants: Zebedee Coltrin and Abraham O. Smoot, two men who claimed to be intimately familiar with Joseph Smith's views on black people. Coltrin claimed that Joseph Smith had revoked Elijah's ordination, and Smoot said that Joseph Smith had ordered a general restriction on the proselytizing of the slave population. Smoot also confirmed that Joseph had banned all blacks from holding priesthood office. According to family lore, Thomas Shreeve, a member of Elijah Ables's ward, also allegedly claimed that his (Ables's) priesthood had been revoked for racial reasoning.[61]

These minutes provided the foundation for a generations-long tradition in Mormonism that the priesthood ban originated with Joseph Smith. It is noteworthy that, though Brigham Young's son, Brigham Young Jr., was present, his father's views did not appear to play a substantive role in the discussion: it was all about Joseph Smith. President John Taylor's conclusion was that, while Ables's priesthood had been received through the proper channels, it was an innovation of the early Church, a mistake made "before the word of the Lord was fully understood."[62]

Citation

L. John Nuttall Diary and Meeting Minutes, May 31, 1879, typescript, Perry Special Collections. Initial capitals added where needed; scattering of misplaced periods as per original.

Document Excerpt

At the house of Prest A.O. Smoot. Provo City. Utah County Utah—5 p.m. President John Taylor, Elders Brigham Young, A.O. Smoot, Zebedee Coltrin, and L. John Nuttall met, and the subject of ordaining Negroes to the Priesthood was presented. Prest. Taylor said, some parties have said to me that Zebedee Coltrin had talked to the Prophet Joseph Smith on this subject, and they said that he (Coltrin) thought it was not right for them to have the Priesthood, whereupon Joseph Smith said to him that Peter on a certain occasion had a vision wherein he saw heaven opened, and a certain vessel descended unto him, as it had been a great sheet knit at the four corners, and let down to the earth, wherein all manner of four-footed beasts of the earth, and wild beasts, and creeping things, and fowls

---

61. Caleb Shreeve, Declaration of Fact, November 19, 1970.
62. Meeting Minutes, June 4, 1879, in Bringhurst, "Abel and the Changing Status of Blacks," 31.

of the air. And there came a voice to him, Rise, Peter! Kill and eat. But Peter said, Not so Lord, for I have never eaten anything that is common or unclean; and the voice spake unto him again the second time, "What God hath cleansed, that call not thou common." And that the Prophet Joseph then said to Bro. Coltrin as the angel said to Peter, "What God hath cleansed, that call not thou common." (speaking of the Gentiles). Prest. Taylor asked Bro. Coltrin, Did the Prophet Joseph Smith ever make such a statement to you?

Bro. C., No sir, he never said anything of the kind in his life to me.

Pres. T., What did he say?

Bro. C., The spring that we went up in Zion's Camp in 1834 Bro. Joseph sent Bro. J. P. Green[63] and me out south to gather up means to assist in gathering out the Saints from Jackson County, Mo. On our return home we got in conversation about the Negro having a right to the Priesthood—and I took the side he had no right—Bro. Green argued that he had. The subject got so warm between us that he said he would report me to Bro. Joseph when we got home for preaching false doctrine, which doctrine that I advocated was that the Negro could not hold the Priesthood. All right, said I—I hope you will.

When we got home we both went in to Bro Joseph's office together to make our returns and Bro Green was as good as his word and reported to Bro Joseph that I had said that the Negro could not hold the Priesthood—Bro Joseph Kind of dropt his head and rested it on his hand for a minute. And then said Bro Zebedee[64] is right, for the Spirit of the Lord saith the Negro has no right nor cannot hold the Priesthood. He made no reference to scripture at all—but such was his decision—I dont recollect ever having any conversation with him afterwards, but I have heard him say in public, that no person having the least particle of Negro blood can hold the Priesthood Bro Coltrin further said— Bro Abel was ordained a Seventy. because he had labored on the Temple. (it must

---

63. John P. Greene (1793–1844), Brigham Young's brother-in-law, joined the Saints in 1832, participated in Zion's Camp, served a brief mission in Upper Canada where Elijah Ables served in 1838, was a member of the Nauvoo High Council, and executed Joseph Smith's order to destroy the *Nauvoo Expositor.* John P. Greene, Letter to Oliver Cowdery, *Messenger and Advocate* 1, no. 1 (October 1834): 7–8; Richard Lyman Bushman, *Joseph Smith: Rough Stone Rolling,* 540.

64. Zebedee Coltrin (1804–87) had been a committed Mormon since 1831, faithfully attended Joseph Smith's "School of the Prophets" in Kirtland, and was ordained to be a president of the Quorum of the Seventy on February 28, 1835. Coltrin was present at the Kirtland Temple Dedication and testified that he "saw the Lord on high and lifted up and frequently throng the solemn assemblies" and that "the angels of God rested on the temple, and we heard their voices singing heavenly music." In 1866, Brigham Young ordained Coltrin a patriarch in Salt Lake City. Minutes of High Priests Meeting, Spanish Fork, February 5, 1870. During this time, one ailing woman recalled Coltrin "visit[ing] me almost daily, administering to me and blessing me, which was a great help in sustaining me through my sickness." Hannah Last Cornaby, *Autobiography and Poems,* Coltrin also suffered from a speech impediment; Joseph Smith described it as "clipping ½ [his] words." Joseph Smith, Journal, April 19, 1843, in Dean C. Jessee, Ronald K. Esplin, and Richard L. Bushman, eds., *Journals, Vol. 2, 1841–1843,* 369.

have been into the 2nd Quorum)[65] and when the Prophet Joseph learned of his lineage. he was dropped from the quorum and another was put in his place—I was one of the first seven Presidents of the Quorum of Seventies at the time he was dropped–

Prest. Taylor. – Bro Zebedee you are not one of the seven Presidents now. What have you been doing?

Bro C. – I was acting then as one of the 1st seven Presidents of Seventies and was ordered back into the quorum of High Preists [sic]—I can tell you how that thing first started. Bro Winchester[66] and Bro Jared Carter[67] while on the Brick yard at Kirtland—Bro W. A Seventy and Bro Jared a High Priest got to contending which held the highest office. Carter was rebuking him on account of his folly. which he said he had not right to do. as he held a higher Priesthood than he did. and Jared contended he didnt because he was a High Priest—this thing came to the ears of Uncle Joseph Smith. & then they went to the Prophet Joseph with it. The Prophet then enquired of the Lord. and he afterwards directed that we be put back into the Quorum of High Priests and other Men (five) were then ordained to the Presidency of the Seventies and three out of that five apostatized—Bro Joseph Young & Levi Hancock were retained and the other five filled the number—In the washing and Anointing of Bro Abel at Kirtland I anointed him. and while I had my hands upon his head. I never had such unpleasant feelings in my life—and I said I never would again Anoint another person who had Negro blood in him. unless I was commanded by the Prophet to do so.

Prest A. O Smoot said. W.W. Patten[68] Warren Parrish and Thomas B. Marsh were laboring in the Southern States in 1835 & 1836 – there were Negro's who made made [sic] Application for Batizm [sic]. and the question arose with them whether Negro's were entitled to hold the Priesthood—and by those brethren it was decided they would not confer the Priesthood until they had consulted

65. Ables was, in fact, a member of the First Quorum of the Seventy, which is how Coltrin would have known him. First Council of the Seventy Roll, December 27, 1836, CR 3 123.

66. Benjamin Winchester (1817–1901) was baptized in January 1833 and actively defended the Saints against various claims, especially the charge that the Book of Mormon was based on a romance written by Reverend Solomon Spaulding. Coltrin ordained Winchester a seventy in December 1836, and Winchester served a mission in New England from the fall of 1837 to May 1839. Winchester likely had this conversation with Carter in spring or summer 1837 when he was about nineteen. David J. Whittaker, "East of Nauvoo: Benjamin Winchester and the Early Mormon Church," 32–37.

67. Jared Carter (1801–49) was a member of the Kirtland Temple building committee. Fred Collier and William Harwell, eds., *Kirtland Council Minute Book*, 15, 105.

68. Nuttall meant David W. Patten (1799–1838) who served two missions to the South: the first from the fall of 1834 to January 1835 with Warren Parrish, and the second, from the spring of 1836. In the late nineteenth century, Abraham Smoot, one of Patten's converts, circulated an account that Patten had met "a very remarkable personage who had represented himself as being Cain. . . . He wore no clothing but was covered with hair. His skin was very dark." Matthew Bowman, "A Mormon Bigfoot: David Patten's Cain and the Concept of Evil in LDS Folklore," 62–82.

the Prophet Joseph—and subsequently they communicated with him and his decision as I understood, was they were not entitled to the Priesthood, nor yet to be baptized without the consent of their Masters. In after years when I became aquinted [sic] with Joseph Myself in Far West about the year 1838, I received from Joseph substantialy [sic] the same instructions. It was on my application to him what should be done with the Negro in the South as I was preaching to them? He said I could baptize them by consent of their Masters. but [sic] not to confer the Priesthood upon them—These two statements were duly signed by each of these brethren.[69]

Jane Manning James's Campaign to Receive Her Endowment (1880s–1900s)

HISTORICAL INTRODUCTION

As one of the Saints' earliest and most far-traveled black pioneers, Jane James had long enjoyed a close relationship with Church leaders. On the day of Elijah Ables's death, she began a lengthy campaign to receive her temple endowment. Life in Utah had not been easy for her; her husband, Isaac James, had "left her for a white woman" around 1869, and many of her children had either died or imposed serious financial difficulties on her.[70] In 1874 she married Frank Perkins; however, this union was brief and likely born of financial necessity. Her ex-husband, Isaac, finally returned but died in 1891, leaving her both a divorcée and a widow.[71]

In the following correspondence, Jane Manning James provides a voice that echoed mainstream Mormonism even as she lived on its fringes. During her time

69. Warren Parrish (1803–77) served three missions to the South: one each year from 1834 to 1836. On his first mission, Parrish and his companion, David W. Patten, met Abraham Smoot, then gravely ill. Smoot reports that, after hearing the Mormon gospel and believing, Parrish and Patten blessed him to "be healed of my infirmity and become a strong and powerful man. This prediction was verified to the letter." Patten developed a strong relationship with the Saints in the South; when he left during one of his missions, the members "were overwhelmed in tears." On his third mission, he traveled in Ohio, Virginia, Indiana, Illinois, and Kentucky, finally reaching Henry County, Tennessee. He eventually "fell in company with elder Patten, [my] fellow laborer in this part of the Lord's vineyard." While Parrish suffered significant persecution, he was also impressed with "the hospitality and politeness with which I have been treated . . . as a minister of the gospel." Warren Parrish, "Mission in the South," *Messenger and Advocate* 3, no. 2 (November 1836): 404–6. Thomas B. Marsh (1799–1866) served a mission to Illinois, Kentucky, and Tennessee from July 1836 to June 1837, raising funds to assist the Saints in western Missouri. Thomas B. Marsh, Autobiography, 1857, Historian's Office histories of the Twelve, LDS Church History Library.

70. Emily Dow Partridge Journal, January 27, 1875. Many thanks to Brittany Chapman for pointing me to this reference.

71. Ronald Coleman, "'Is There No Blessing for Me?' Jane Manning James, a Mormon African American Woman," in Quintard Taylor and Shirley Ann Wilson Moore, eds., *African American Women Confront the West*, 151.

away from Isaac and after Isaac's death, she pled with Church leaders for her endowment as well as a sealing to Joseph and Emma Smith as their adopted daughter. In May 1894, she received the less-than-welcome compromise of being sealed by proxy to the Smith family as their servant. When she applied again for her endowment that October, President Wilford Woodruff rebuffed her, echoing Brigham Young's earlier reasoning: "this I could not do as it was against the Law of God As Cain killed Abel All the seed of Cain would have to wait for redemption until all the seed that Abel would have had that may come through other men can be redeemed."[72] Like Ables, James was willing to wait for the guard to change before making a new request. Doggedly, James applied again in 1903, this time to Joseph F. Smith. Again, her request was denied. She received her endowment posthumously in 1979.

CITATION

This correspondence was published in Henry J. Wolfinger, "A Test of Faith: Jane Elizabeth James and the Origins of the Utah Black Community," in Clark S. Knowlton, ed., *Social Accommodation in Utah.* Salt Lake City: American West Center Occasional Papers, University of Utah, 1975, 126–47. Terminal punctuation, initial capitals, and left justification added.

DOCUMENT EXCERPT, JANE MANNING JAMES
TO JOHN TAYLOR, 1884

Salt L City Dec 27, 1884
Pres John Taylor
Dear Brother

I cauled [sic] at your house last [T]hursday to have some conversation with you concerning my future salvation. I did not explain my feelings or wishes to you. I realize my race & color & cant expect my Endowments as others who are white. My race was handed down through the flood & God promised Abraham that in his seed all the nations of the earth should be blest & as this is the fullness of all dispensations. Is there no blessing for me?

I with my Fathers family came from Connecticut 42 years the 14th of last Oct. I am the only one of my Fathers family that kept the faith.

You know my history & according to the best of my ability I have lived to all the requairments [sic] of the Gospel. When we reached Nauvoo we were 9 in the family & had traveled 9 hundred miles on foot. Bro Joseph Smith took us in & we staid with him & his family until a few day[s] of his death.

---

72. Kenney, *Wilford Woodruff's Journal,* 9:322, October 16, 1894.

Sister Emma came to me & asked me how I would like to be adopted to them as a Child.[73] I did not comprehend her & she came again. I was so green I did not give her a decided answer & Joseph died & [I] remain as I am. If I could be adopted to him as a child my Soul would be satisfied. I had been in the Church one year when we left the East that was 42 years the 14 of last Oct.

DOCUMENT EXCERPT, JANE MANNING JAMES TO JOSEPH F. SMITH, 1890

Salt Lake City
February 7, 1890

Dear Brother—Please excuse me taking the Liberty of Writing to you—but be a Brother—I am anxious for my Welfare for the future—and has [sic] I hope to be one Bye and Bye, bearing the same name has yourself—I was requested to write to you—Hoping you will please show kindness to me—by answering my questions—Thereby satisfying my mind—

First Has [sic] Brother James has Left me 21 years—And a Coloured Brother, Brother Lewis wished me to be sealed to Him, He has been dead 35 or 36 years[74]—Can I be sealed to him—Parley P. Pratt ordained Him an Elder. When or (how?) can I ever be sealed to Him.—

Second,—Can I obtain my Endowments for my Dead. Also I had the privilege of being baptized for My Dead, in October Last.—

Third, Can I also be adopted in Brother Joseph Smiths the prophet['s] family, I think you are somewhat Acquainted with me—I lived in the prophets family With Emma and others, about a year—and Emma Said Joseph told her to tell me—I could be adopted in their family, she ask me if I should like to. I Did not understand the Law of adoption then—but Understanding it now. Can that be Accomplished and When—

I have heard you attend to the prophets Business in those matters—And so have Written to you for information

Hoping soon to hear from you in these matters—
I remain

Your Sister in the Gospel
Jane E James, Elizabeth
I am Couloured

---

73. In Nauvoo, the Saints were becoming increasingly interested in establishing a web of lateral (and, they hoped, eternal) relationships among its leading families. To facilitate this, members were often sealed to other members, either through polygamy or through adoption. Jonathan Stapley, "Adoptive Sealing Ritual in Mormonism," 53–119.

74. James likely met Walker Lewis (1798–1856), a black Latter-day Saint in Massachusetts (see chap. 8) when he was visiting the Utah Territory in fall 1851. Lewis died from "consumption" (likely tuberculosis) on October 26, 1856. Lowell City [Mass.] Death Register, 1856, 14.

Document Excerpt, Zina D. H. Young
to Joseph F. Smith, 1894

S.L. City Jan 15th 1894

Jane E. James, says, Sister Emma Smith asked her if she would like to be adopted into Joseph Smiths family as a child, & not understanding her meaning said no.

Jane was Born
Wilton Fairfield, Co. Conn

Jane also asked me to ask
If Isaac James & her Brother could also be adopted

Zina D.H. Young[75]

Document Excerpt, Jane Manning James
to Joseph F. Smith, 1903

Mrs Jane Elizabeth James
529 S. 2nd East St.
Salt Lake City
August 31, 1903

President Joseph F Smith
Dear Brother

I take this opportunity of writing to you to ask you if I can get my endowments and also finish the work I have begun for My dead. [A]nd Dear Brother I would like to see and talk with you about it, will you please write to me and tell me how soon, when and where I shall come and I will be there by doing so you will be conferring a great favour.

Your sister in the Gospel

Jane E James

I have enclosed a stamped Envelope for reply.

------

75. Zina D. H. Young (1821–1901) was general president of the Relief Society president at the time of this correspondence. Zina herself had participated in an unconventional sealing when she married Joseph Smith as a plural wife in October 1841, even though she was still married to Henry B. Jacobs. Martha Sonntag Bradley and Mary Brown Firmage Woodward, "Plurality, Patriarchy, and the Priestess: Zina D. H. Young's Nauvoo Marriages," 84–118.

A Mormon Missionary Writes on the Ku Klux Klan (1885)

HISTORICAL INTRODUCTION

Following the Civil War, the Republican Congress commenced to undertake a series of measures to "reconstruct" the South, a society that radical Republicans felt had been so corrupted by slavery that it needed to be remade from the inside out. Some southerners responded to the northern effort by supporting white vigilante groups like the Ku Klux Klan in preventing the black population from voting or acquiring any kind of prominence.

Mormons knew something of the Republican "reconstructing" impulse. After the formation of the predominantly northern Republican Party in 1856, the Utah Territory shared with southern states the distinction of engaging in one of the "twin relics of barbarism": polygamy. Utah knew that whatever animosity existed between southerners and Utahans, both viewed federal authority with hostility.

While the Klan saw Mormons as dangerous threats to the religious establishment, most of the southern Saints felt that the Ku Klux Klan presented a threat to civil rule; a returning missionary warned that the Klan was "very numerous and powerful" and that "no man's life is considered safe whose course is offensive to them."[76] During the early 1880s, the Mississippi Klan effectively pulled the strings of local elections by launching mob attacks on Republicans and independents deemed to be "traitors to their race."[77] Former Klan leaders also led mobs throughout the South against Mormon missionaries.[78] Northern writers occasionally associated the Mormons with the Klan.[79]

Utah found itself besieged with anti-polygamy attacks from all sides. Troubled by how to respond, a Latter-day Saint missionary serving in Mississippi who called himself Horatio both romanticized and condemned the Klan's violence while extolling its efforts to "check . . . many evils that invariably must follow a condition of affairs like that which existed in the South at the close of the war."

CITATION

Horatio, Letter to the Editor, *The Contributor,* 6, no. 9 (June 1885): 328–29. Terminal punctuation and initial capitals added where needed.

---

76. "Returned," *Deseret News,* April 27, 1870, 2.

77. Michael Newton, *The Ku Klux Klan in Mississippi,* 45–60.

78. Patrick Q. Mason, *The Mormon Menace: Violence and Anti-Mormonism in the Postbellum South,* 146–48.

79. "The End of Mormonism," *Daily [Springfield] Illinois State Journal,* January 5, 1871, 2; "An Important Cabinet Meeting," *New York Herald,* November 1, 1871, 6; "Mormon Ku-Klux," *Weekly Journal Miner* (Prescott, AZ), December 16, 1871, 4; "The Mormon Ku-Klux," *Denver Rocky Mountain News,* June 7, 1871, 1.

Document Excerpt

At several of our conferences the colored people have sent representatives to enquire of the Elders if they allowed Cullud folks ter come to de meetins. An answer in the affirmative is always given and occasionally results in a large number of colored people attending service. As a rule too they are very well behaved. They never crowd themselves into the seats which have been prepared but stand at a respectful distance from the place occupied by the whites. For although slavery was abolished more than twenty years ago, the colored man recognizes the fact that the white man will not receive him as a social equal and therefore does not attempt on occasions of this kind to force himself into places where he is not welcome. As the negroes form a circle outside of that formed by the white people, we say at such times we have a conference with a black fringe. But who are those men standing in small groups some distance from the congregation so far away that surely they are not able to hear the remarks of the speakers? An ugly frown is on each face. In a moment we see they are restless filled with wrath and hatred but prevented from doing violence through fear. With a half suppressed shout of mockery they disappear in the woods Those men were the ones who had threatened to do violence to the Mormon Elders if they attempted to hold their conference in the neighborhood who to strike terror into the hearts of the Elders burned the schoolhouse the night preceding the first day of conference. I know of three schoolhouses so destroyed on such occasions and for such a purpose. It was such men as these who posted up notices on the trees near our place of meeting warning us to leave. I here insert a sample of the notices. This particular one was posted on a tree near where we were holding conference in the State of Georgia:

NOTICE

We give you fair worning to get out of Haywood valley the people in that valley have been troubled with you Devils a long time and now we propose to put and end to their troubles by keeping you Mormon Devils [out?] of that part of the country Now we give you warning to get out of Haywood valley by nine o clock pm July the 1th 1883 and never to return again We mean business to you Mormon Devils if you want to preach for the Devil go where his preaching is needed we don t want it in Georgia

Signed good Sitizens

KKK

K. K. K. of course means Ku Klux Klan, a secret organization formed for protection by the people of the South during the period which elapsed between the close of the war of the Rebellion and the readmission of the seceding States unto the Union, usually known as the reconstruction period. At the close of the war the governmental affairs of the southern States were in a chaotic condition. The Confederacy had been overthrown, and it was a question what relation the seceded States held to the Union. There was a split between the President and Congress on this question, which tended greatly to retard the reconstruction of the South. Tennessee was restored to its place in the Union in 1866; but in March of the year following, the ten remaining States which had seceded were divided into five military districts, to be under the control of a governor, appointed by the President. Then came what is now familiarly called "carpetbag rule."[80] The men appointed to administer the laws had no sympathy or interests with the people they were sent to govern, and there were intense feelings of bitterness between the people and the rulers. The negroes who were released from slavery by the Emancipation Proclamation issued by Abraham Lincoln, on the 1st of January, 1863, conceived the idea that they were the equals of their former masters, not only before the law, but also socially.[81] Their presumption was offensive to most of the whites, and they were too frequently encouraged in pursuing an arrogant course by the carpet-bag rulers. As a measure for protection, chiefly against the untoward acts of the negroes, these secret societies were organized, known as the Klu Klux Klans. They were presided over by a president, and sometimes vice-presidents and secretaries were chosen, and other minor officers.[82] Their meetings were held at night, sometimes in a house belonging to one of the Klan, but more frequently in some secluded dell in the woods. Each member of the Klan was sworn to secrecy and had the liberty of entering complaints against those who, in his judgment, were worthy of punishment. The case was heard, and if considered worthy of punishment, the nature and amount was determined, and in a body the Klan proceeded to the domicile of the offender to administer it.[83]

. . . These societies, during the carpet-bag rule in the South, beyond all questioning were a check upon many evils that invariably must follow a condition of affairs like that which existed in the South at the close of the war—with carpet-bag officers filled from the top full of prejudice against the people, to administer the laws, and four millions of slaves turned loose among them, who understood liberty to mean license to do whatever their depraved natures prompted them to

---

80. A common descriptor of northern officials' efforts to govern the postbellum South. The carpetbag symbolized northern opportunists who settled in the South for economic or political gain. One Virginia paper defined a "carpet-bagger" as a "northern thief, who comes South to plunder every white man who is a gentleman of any property or respectability, and get all the offices he can." "The Difference," *Richmond Whig*, September 22, 1868, 1.

81. In January 1867, Pennsylvania Congressman Thaddeus Stevens said, "What is negro equality[?]. . . It means, as understood by honest Republicans, just this much, and no more: every man, no matter what his race or color . . . has an equal right to justice, honesty, and fair play with every other man; and the law should secure him these rights. . . . This doctrine does not mean that a negro shall sit on the same seat or eat at the same table with a white man. . . . [T]he law has nothing to do with it." Beverley Palmer, ed., *The Selected Papers of Thaddeus Stevens*, April 1865-August 1868, 220.

82. Initially started as group of pranksters, the Klan began to develop an official organizational structure in April 1867. Its leadership consisted of "Grand Giants" (assisted by "Goblins") presiding over each "Den" and "Grand Titans" presiding over a conglomerate of Dens. Wyn Wade, *The Fiery Cross: The Ku Klux Klan in America*, 38.

83. The "punishment" typically involved severe beatings or death.

perform.[84] Some of the best men of the South were known to be identified with these organizations during this period. But when the machinery of government was again given into the hands of the people, and there was a prospect of punishment quickly following crime, they withdrew from the organization and issued orders for the <u>Klans</u> to dissolve. But in the meantime, bad men had crept into the societies, and kept them up after there was no necessity for their continuance.[85] The result is they have become a curse to the South—engines of rapine and murder. Happily, however, they are fast becoming things of the past.[86]

B. H. Roberts Suggests a Premortal Origin for the Priesthood Ban (May 1885)

HISTORICAL INTRODUCTION

In the late nineteenth and early twentieth centuries, Brigham H. Roberts was one of Mormonism's most articulate and erudite scholars. He served as president of the Tennessee Conference (District) for the Southern States Mission from 1880 to 1882 and then as mission president from 1883 through 1886.[87]

As the following documents show, Roberts left a troubled and inconsistent legacy on race. Roberts was the thinker who simultaneously believed firmly in racial segregation ("Let not man put together what God has put asunder," he wrote in one lesson manual) even as he struggled to conceptualize God as just—one who would not punish His creations for the sins of their parents. In the process, Roberts helped to solidify the foundation for generations' worth of theological speculation that excluded blacks from the priesthood body—even as he himself

---

84. A Connecticut paper opined that "the nuisance of carpet-bagism breeds the other nuisance of Ku Klux Klans. The death of one will be fatal to the other also." "The Real Story of the Ku Klux Klan," *Norwich [Conn.] Aurora,* June 28, 1871, 2.

85. By 1871, it was widely believed that even former Klan supporters had distanced themselves from the current Klan. One disaffected follower wrote that the original intent was for the "better protection of Southern men from the depredations of robbers turned loose on society after the close of the war. Their object was to protect—not to depredate." When "ruffians and villains assumed the name for the purpose of perpetuating outrages and crimes," the Klan's "dissolution was a necessity." "Ku-Klux Klan," *Columbian Register* (New Haven, Conn.), April 22, 1871, 1. See also "While Such Papers," *New Hampshire Sentinel,* May 11, 1871, 2; "The Ku-Klux Klan," *Albany [N.Y.] Argus,* April 1, 1871, 2; "Ku Klux Klan," *Worcester [Mass.] Daily Spy,* June 23, 1884, 2; "The Ku Klux Klan," *Bismarck [N.D.] Tribune,* March 27, 1885, 4.

86. In 1871, Congress passed the "Ku Klux Klan Act of 1871" which enabled the president to suspend the right to habeas corpus for "unlawful combinations" seeking to deprive citizens "of any rights, privileges, or immunities secured by the Constitution of the United States." *Acts and Resolutions of the United States of America,* 294–95. In 1872, President Ulysses S. Grant dispatched federal troops to South Carolina where they arrested Klan members *en masse.* By the end of Grant's second term, the Ku Klux Klan had been broken as an entity in the South. Foner, *Reconstruction,* 454–56.

87. For a sympathetic biography see Truman G. Madsen, *Defender of the Faith: The B. H. Roberts Story.*

was trying to craft a generous interpretation of a policy that seemed to fly in the face of the just God in which he so firmly believed.

CITATION

B. H. Roberts, "Discourse," *Millennial Star* 57 (July 11, 1895): 434–35.

DOCUMENT EXCERPT

From many scriptures we may infer that spirits, before living in the flesh, had an opportunity of demonstrating their fidelity to God and His laws. . . . Those who stood with Christ and the plan he favored for the salvation of man, formed one extreme, while those who stood with Lucifer and for the plan of salvation devised by him, which was destructive of man's agency, formed the other extreme; between these two extremes every shade of faith, fullness and indifference was exhibited. Only those, however, who wickedly rebelled against God were adjudged to deserve banishment from heaven, and become the devil and his angels. Others there were, who may not have rebelled against God, and yet were so indifferent in their support of the righteous cause of our Redeemer, that they forfeited certain privileges and powers granted to those who were more valiant for God and correct principle. We have, I think, a demonstration of this in the seed of Ham. The first Pharoah—patriarch-king of Egypt—was a grandson of Ham; and "being a righteous man, established his kingdom, and judged his people wisely and justly all his days, seeking earnestly to imitate that order established in the first generation, in the days of the first patriarchal reign, even in the reign of Adam, and also of Noah, his father, who blessed him with the blessings of wisdom, but who *cursed him as pertaining to the Priesthood.*" He[88] being of that lineage by which he could not have right to the Priesthood, notwithstanding the Pharoah would fain claim it from Noah through Ham" [Pearl of Great Price, p. 28; Abr. 1:26–27].

Now why is it that the seed of Ham was cursed as pertaining to the Priesthood? Why is it that his seed "could not have right to the Priesthood?" Ham's wife was named "Egyptus, which in the Chaldaic signifies Egypt which signifies that which is forbidden . . . and thus from Ham sprang that race which preserved the curse in the land" [Pearl of Great Price, p. 28; Abr. 1:23–24]. . . . Was the wife of Ham as her name signifies of a race with which those who held the Priesthood were forbidden to intermarry? Was she a descendant of Cain, who was cursed for murdering his brother? And was it by Ham marrying her, and she being saved from the flood in the ark, that "the race which preserved the curse in the land" was perpetuated? If so, then I believe that race is the one through which it is ordained [that] those spirits that were not valiant in the great rebellion in heaven should come; who through their indifference or lack of integrity to righteousness, rendered themselves unworthy of the Priesthood and its powers, and hence it is withheld from them to this day.

---

88. In the original text, Joseph Smith rendered this text as "Now, Pharoah being…"

CITATION

B. H. Roberts, "What Is Man?" *Deseret Weekly*, March 16, 1895, 387.

DOCUMENT EXCERPT

I believe that conditions in this life are influenced and fixed by the degree of faithfulness, by the degree of development in the pre-existent state. Otherwise the diversified conditions in which men find themselves placed cannot be reconciled with the justice of God. Then how blessed, indeed, some one will exclaim, must they be who are born to riches, who were born to titles, to dukedoms, earldoms, and lordships! How faithful must they have been who inherit these privileges and blessings! whose life is one continual summer, whose existence is as a sea without a ripple! Nay, I pray you, take no such view of it as that. This class that I have described are not the most blessed among men. When you would point to those who are the favored sons of God and who enjoy the best and highest privileges in this life, you must take into account the object for which man came here. That object is to gain an experience. Hence those are the most blessed who live in the midst of conditions that give the widest experience. The favored sons of God are not those furthest removed from trial, from sorrow, from affliction. It is the fate apparently of those whom God most loves that they suffer most, that they might gain the experience for which men came into this world. It is not the smooth seas and the favorable winds that make your best sea-men.

Chapter 11

A Sleep and a Forgetting: Losing the Black Mormon Heritage, 1902–49

"A Man Named Abel": Church Leaders Recollect Denying Elijah Ables and Jane Manning James Their Endowment (January 1902)

HISTORICAL INTRODUCTION

By 1902, Elijah Ables had been dead for nearly two decades. Jane Manning James was aging. Between Brigham Young's personal views, the 1879 investigation, and the fear of blacks that had racked post-bellum America, the image of Ables (rendered "Abel" in the minutes below) was taking a new shape in the collective Mormon mind. The Saints were beginning to transform Elijah Ables from the dynamic preacher who electrified Upper Canada into a one-dimensional figure: a combative black "man named Abel" who couldn't take no for answer. Jane Manning James was treated no differently: instead of an endowment and Smith family sealing, Church leaders devised a special ceremony for her to be sealed as Joseph Smith's "servant."[1]

The priesthood and temple restrictions had altered from the firebrand rhetoric of Brigham Young into a part of how the Mormon hierarchy conducted business. In 1908 Joseph F. Smith, earlier a supporter of Elijah Ables's claims to the priesthood, now declared that his desire and arguments were illegitimate. Having struggled for so long to demonstrate their whiteness to American society, the Mormon mainstream could not afford to give Ables and James a place in the Mormon narrative. As sociologist Maurice Halbwachs observed: "Society tends to erase in its memory everything that might separate individuals or that might distance groups from each other ." Forgetting Ables and James was not a happenstance but a "rational activity that takes its point of departure in the conditions in which the society at the moment finds itself, in other words, the present."[2]

---

1. For more documentation on the sealing, see Franklin D. Richards, Journal, August 22, 1895, MS 2125, 241–242, LDS Church History Library.

2. Maurice Halbwachs, *On Collective Memory*, trans. Lewis A. Coser, 183.

CITATION

Quorum of the Twelve Meeting Minutes, January 2, 1902, George Albert Smith Family Papers, typescript, Box 78, fd. 7, Special Collections, Marriott Library, University of Utah.

DOCUMENT EXCERPT

President Smith . . . said that Presidents Young and Taylor were emphatic in denying to any person receiving the priesthood or endowments who had negro blood in their veins, and he further said that a man named Abel, an octoroon, and who had married a quadroon, applied to President Young for his endowments, he having bean ordained a Seventy and received his patriarchal blessing in the days of the Prophet Joseph, but President Young put him off, and that Brother Abel failed to get his wish gratified by the President. It appeared that a promise was made to him in his patriarchal blessíng to the effect that he should be the welding link between the black and white races, and that he should hold the initiative authority by which his race should be redeemed. [3] He renewed his application to receive his endowments time after time to President Taylor, who at last submitted it to this Council, resulting in a decision unfavorable to Brother Abel. After his death the wife of Isaac James (known as Aunt Jane) asked to receive her own endowments and to be sealed; but President Woodruff, Cannon, and Smith decided that this could not be done, but decided that she might be adopted into the family of the Prophet Joseph Smith as a servant, which was done, a special ceremony having been prepared for the purpose. But Aunt Jane was not satisfied with this, and as a mark of her dissatisfaction she applied again after this for sealing blessings, but of course in vain. [4]

Booker T. Washington's "Views of the 'Mormons'" (June 1913)

HISTORICAL INTRODUCTION

The Mormon people had long been taken with the success of Booker T. Washington and his teachers' college, the Tuskegee Institute. In February 1911, David H. Christensen, superintendent of the Salt Lake City Schools, visited Tuskegee University and was so impressed that he invited Washington to visit Utah.

Washington gave speeches throughout the city to Mormons and non-Mormons alike. He also addressed the city's African American community. The visit was a resounding success. Washington believed that Mormons shared a stirring

---

3. The passage referenced was probably: "Thou shalt be made equal to thy brethren and thy soul be white in eternity and thy robes glittering." See H. Michael Marquardt, *Early Patriarchal Blessings of the Church of Jesus Christ of Latter-day Saints*, 99.

4. For a biography of Jane and transcripts of her repeated petitions to receive her endowment, see Henry J. Wolfinger, "A Test of Faith: Jane Elizabeth James and the Origins of the Utah Black Community," 126–47.

vision of what America ought to be: independent communities committed to economic development and education. Washington had long believed that "there is as much dignity in tilling a field as in writing a poem. It is at the bottom of life we must begin, and not at the top."[5] He saw a kinship between African Americans and the Mormon people. Committed as Mormons were to self-reliance and hard labor, Washington recognized the potential for an important alliance between the Saints and his organization.

The Mormons returned the praise. Washington's memoir, *Up from Slavery*, was sold widely; Relief Societies even placed the text on their book group reading lists. He spoke their language; instead of activism, he promoted hard-boiled pragmatism and adaptation. While no lasting relationship developed between Washington's organization and the Mormon people, this moment illustrates the enduring appeal Mormonism had for those who found themselves disfranchised from American society. Washington felt a kinship with the Saints; he wrote in a subsequent letter that they both believed "that economic progress must go hand in hand with religious progress."[6] Following the visit, Washington wrote Christensen warmly saying: "I shall never forget you nor your people there."[7]

CITATION

Booker T. Washington, "There are Colored Mormons Out in Utah," *New York Age*, April 17, 1913, 1 reprinted in *Improvement Era* 16 (June 1913): 807–8; subheadings eliminated.

DOCUMENT EXCERPT

For a long while I have been anxious to get right into the midst of the Mormons to see kind of people they are, what they look like, what they are doing, and in what respect they are succeeding. I have been spending two of the busiest days that I have ever spent in my life in the very midst of these people. They have been mighty interesting days, and I have seen some mighty interesting people. The leaders of the Mormon Church from President Smith down have gone out of their way to show me kindness and to make my trip here successful.

I am not going to discuss the Mormon religion as I am not a theologian. I shall have to leave that to others. I am always interested in studying and observing people regardless of their religion. One of the Mormon bishops called to see me and from him I got some mighty interesting information that ought to prove of value to our race.

---

5. Booker T. Washington, *Up from Slavery: An Autobiography*, 220.

6. Booker T. Washington, Letter to *New York Age*, March 27, 1913, printed in *New York Age*, April 24, 1913, 2, cited in Louis R. Harlan and Raymond W. Smock, eds., *Booker T. Washington Papers*, 12:152, note 2.

7. Booker T. Washington, Letter to David H. Christensen, March 31, 1913, Frederick Stuart Buchanan Papers, Box 174, fd. 3, Special Collections, Marriott Library.

In speaking of the Mormons, my readers must remember that it was only sixty-six years ago that, led by Brigham Young, 150 people came into this country when it was a wilderness. They traveled in ox carts over a thousand miles from the Missouri River. The Mormon Church itself was organized in New York State only eighty-four years ago. From 150 people, hardy pioneers who entered Utah sixty-six years ago, the number has grown year by year until in Utah there are now over three hundred thousand Mormons, and they have certainly made the desert blossom as a rose. I have never been among a more intelligent, healthy, clean, progressive, moral set of people than these are. All through Utah they have turned the desert into gardens and orchards. Wherever one finds a Mormon colony there he finds evidence of hard work and wealth. . . .

There are two parallels between the Negro and the Mormons. First, as my readers already know, the Mormons were most inhumanly persecuted almost from the first organization of their church. This was especially true in Missouri and Illinois. Hundreds of their followers were put to death. The courts gave them little protection. The mob that either killed or wounded the Mormons was seldom, if ever punished. They were an easy mark for any inhuman brute who wanted to either kill or wound them. Joseph Smith himself, the founder of the church, was murdered in Illinois. But out of this inhuman and unjust treatment grew the strength of these people. The more they were punished the more determined they became to succeed. Without opposition and injustice, I question whether the Mormon church could now be in its present flourishing condition. They were deprived of their property as well as their early years, but the more they were persecuted the closer they banded themselves together and the more determined they were to succeed. Persecutions advertised this little sect to the world. The result was that through persecution their numbers increased instead of being diminished.

The second parallel between the Mormon and the Negro is this. These people, I am sure, have been misrepresented before the world. I have learned by experience and observation that it is never safe to pass final judgment upon a people until one has had an opportunity to get into the real life of those people. The Negro is suffering today just as the Mormons have suffered and are suffering because people from the outside have advertised the worst in connection with Mormon life and they have seldom called attention to the best in connection with the life of the Mormons. And then I have learned, too, that no person outside a race or outside a group of people can ever really know that race or that group of people until he gets into their homes and has a chance to observe their men, their women, and their children and has a chance to partake of their hospitality and get into their inner life. There are many people to-day who consider themselves wise on the condition of the Negro, who are really afraid to go into a negro home, who never go into a Negro church or Sunday school, who have never met colored people in any social circle; hence such people know little about the moral standards and activities of the colored people. The same, I am convinced, is true regarding the Mormons. The people who speak in the most disrespectful terms of these people are those who know least about them.

I am convinced that the Mormons are not an immoral people. No immoral people could have such strong fine bodies as these people nor such vigorous and alert minds as they.[8] It has been my privilege to address schools and universities in nearly every part of America, and I say without hesitation that I have never addressed a college anywhere where the students were more alert, more responsive, more intelligent than is true of the students in these Mormon colleges. I was hardly prepared for the over-generous and rapturous reception that was given me at the State University, the students of which for the most part are Mormons, and I had the same experience in addressing the private schools and other institutions conducted by Mormons.[9]

. . . I think it will interest my readers to know that there are colored Mormons in Utah. I met several of these. Many of them came here in the old days. In fact, Brigham Young brought colored people with him to this country, and they or their descendants have remained. Of course in the old days plural wives were not prohibited by law, but I have made careful inquiry and could find no case where a colored man ever had more than one wife. It seems to have been the custom in the old days that a man could not take a second or third or fourth wife without the consent of his first wife, and I was told that no colored woman in Utah would ever give her consent for her husband to take a second wife.

---

8. Washington's argument drew on emergent theological notions that associated strength and vigor with evangelical Christianity and conservative sexual norms. See Clifford Putney, *Muscular Christianity: Manhood and Sports in Protestant America, 1880–1920.*

9. The "State University" refers to the University of Utah. "The Mormon people value education," a school trustee wrote in 1875. "Their faith imbues them with aspirations of greatness for their children." "Free Schools," *Salt Lake Herald*, April 16, 1875, 3. The nature of these schools is more complex than first glance would suggest. Taxes had been levied for the construction of schoolhouses since the early 1850s; however, the territorial statutes did not allow for the use of tax monies for the payment of teachers' salaries. "Common Schools," *Deseret News*, March 19, 1853, 3. Further, Mormon meetinghouses often doubled as school rooms, much to the annoyance of non-Mormon taxpayers. "Schools and Meeting Houses," *Salt Lake Tribune*, September 7, 1873, 2. One non-Mormon resident "object[ed] to sending them [his children] to Mormon meeting houses. . . . Until the school-tax assessed upon my property is devoted exclusively to the support of public schools, I intend to refuse the payment." "The School Tax," *Salt Lake Tribune*, November 1, 1873, 4. Initially formed in 1850 as the University of Deseret by the State Legislature and, in the words of W. W. Phelps, "the common consent of a generous, good-hearted people," the University of Deseret/Utah closed due to low enrollment in 1853. "The Celebration of the Twenty-Fourth of July," *Deseret News*, July 26, 1851, 1. In 1869, the university reopened at Brigham Young's direction under the stewardship of one of his chief clerks, Dr. John R. Park. Tuition was paid directly to the instructor, but the construction of new buildings drew from taxpayer dollars. "The University of Utah," *Deseret News*, June 9, 1892, 5. In 1892 an amendment added to the University of Deseret's charter renamed the institution the University of Utah and allocated forty acres for its development at its current site. "The New Laws," *Deseret News*, March 19, 1892, 23 and "The University of Utah," *Deseret News*, August 22, 1892, 7.

I met one colored man who came out here in the early days who is now 82 years of age. He is a staunch Mormon and neither the Baptist nor the Methodist church can get a hold of him. He came here from Mississippi. He is a fine looking old fellow, a kind of colored Brigham Young. He has a farm worth $25,000 and lives in the midst of a Mormon colored colony of which he is the leader.[10] I am told that the Mormon church treats the colored people well.

A Black Alabaman Joins the Mormons (1912–38)

HISTORICAL INTRODUCTION

Born and raised in Magnolia, a small Alabama town, Len Hope was a teenager when he first met Mormon missionaries in 1913.[11] Hope was sufficiently literate to read the materials the Mormons left for him. According to Apostle Mark E. Petersen, who met the family in 1936, Hope's appetite for Mormonism was immense; after finishing with the pamphlets, he "wrote to the mission headquarters for a Book of Mormon, and by his own study, converted himself." Hope joined the Church just before serving in World War I and "carried a Book of Mormon with him all through the war." When he returned from the war, he was engaged to marry a local girl named Mary.

Mary's family ribbed her over the union: "I heard you are going to marry that old Mormon boy," her uncle queried. Mary "had not heard anything about the Mormon Church worth while, but it happened to be a Mormon boy that I was to marry."[12] Within a year of the marriage, Mary had read the Book of Mormon; she joined the faith on September 15, 1925. The couple raised nine children together.

Len's baptism stoked the ire of local non-Mormon whites and almost led to his lynching. When the local white members learned of his close call, they told him that

---

10. This individual is almost certainly Samuel Chambers (1831–1929). Born and raised in Mississippi, Chambers joined the faith as a teenage boy in secret. After the Civil War, he saved up money for four years to fund his travel to Utah with his wife. "I did not come to Utah to know the truth of the gospel, but I received it away back where the gospel found me." After his first wife passed away, he married Amanda Leggroan and they settled in Salt Lake City. In 1873 he testified that Mormonism "is not only to the Gentiles but also to the Africans, for I am one of that race. The knowledge I received is from my God. It is a high and holy calling." Chambers soon moved with Amanda to southeast Salt Lake City and found immense success as a farmer, owning thirty acres of land at the time of his passing. When Washington visited Salt Lake City, Chambers had established himself as a leading figure in his ward. One of his home teachers, Mahonri White, observed that Chambers "testified like a man who held the priesthood" and "bore his testimony like an apostle," noting as an aside that Chambers "could holler pretty loud." For a fuller compilation of comments Chambers made in the 1870s, see William G. Hartley, ed., "Saint Without Priesthood: The Collected Testimonies of Ex-Slave Samuel D. Chambers," 13–21.

11. See U.S. Census, 1920, index and images, *FamilySearch*, https://familysearch.org/pal:/MM9.1.1/MX8B-MKQ, Lin [sic] Hope, 1920 (accessed May 02, 2013).

12. Mary L. Hope, Testimony, April 28, 1938, LDS Church History Library.

he could have his name removed from the records, though he could take comfort that his name was "wrote down in Salt Lake and . . . wrote down from heaven."[13]

In the late 1920s, he, his wife, and children moved to Cincinnati, Ohio, along with throngs of other blacks leaving the South to free themselves from segregation laws. Hope committed himself to paying a regular tithe; when he did not have enough, he picked berries and sold them on the streets of Cincinnati to pay it.[14] But disappointingly, they learned that they were not welcome in the same branch where Elijah Ables had put down dissent in loyally supporting the Twelve after Joseph Smith's death. According to Petersen, the branch "met in a group, decided what to do and went to the Branch President, and said that either the Hope family must leave or they would all leave."[15] In 1989, Marion D. Hanks, a member of the First Quorum of the Seventy and a former missionary in Cincinnati, remembered with some understatement that "it had been made known to them that they were not to be there."[16]

Though Petersen expressed his unabashed horror at intermarriage and his unfailing support for racial segregation, he felt compelled to applaud Hope's faithfulness: "He was a man as thoroughly converted to the gospel as anyone I knew." However, he patronizingly added that Hope was evidence of "the great mercy of God" who "allows all men to rise above themselves."[17]

CITATION

Len Hope, "Testimony of Len Hope," April 29, 1938, LDS Church History Library.; left justification added.

DOCUMENT EXCERPT

My reason for being a Mormon and my testimony to the truthfulness of the Gospel of Jesus Christ that has been restored to the earth in the last days Be it known to all the world to all it may concern.

In about the year of 1912 I began to seek religion in the Baptist Church. In the fall of the year the Church had a revival, so I went up to the moruners [sic] bench[18] to be prayed for every day for about two weeks and at night I would go

---

13. Len Hope, Testimony, April 29, 1938, 2, LDS Church History Library.

14. Mark E. Petersen, "Racial Problems as they Affect the Church," 17.

15. Ibid.

16. Jessie L. Embry, "Impact of the LDS 'Negro Policy,'" 45.

17. Petersen, "Racial Problems as they Affect the Church," 16.

18. The "mourning bench" referred to the Methodist innovation of placing a bench at the front of the congregation. One late-nineteenth-century railroad booster noticed in one rural community that the residents used a "mourning bench system": "The people become worked up to the highest pitch of excitement. One after another would rise, and go forward to the 'mourning bench.' This was an inclosed [sic] space immediately in front of the pulpit, and strewn plentifully with straw. Upon this straw, men and women would throw themselves indiscriminately, and roll about in paroxysms of excitement. The loud tones of the teacher's voice would now be mingled with shouts of Amen! Glory to God! Hallelujah! &c., from the congregation; and with groans and cries from the

home and I would go into the cotton field and lie down on my back, looking up to heaven begging our Heavenly Father for religion. I was wet with dew of heaven so I did not get religion in the year of 1912. So in 1913 so as usual at autumn I tried it again. So the elder people would tell me that I must be seeing things also seeing yourself crossing hell on a spider web.[19] So I didn't see any of these things. I decided that I would serve the Lord the rest of my days and live up to all the ruls [sic] and laws of God as far as I understood them. So I was baptized into the Church.

Soon after this I had a dream or a vision that I had to be baptized over again, so that worried me awhile and finally I overcome that living my religion as I had.

Search the scriptures and in them you think you have eternal life so I began to read the Holy Bible late at night and earley [sic] in the morning. Seek and ye shall find; knowledge and it shall be open.

So, in reading I found that to get religion one does not have to see things nor see hell crossing a spider web.

I read "Let the wicked forsake his ways, and the unrighteous man his thoughts and turn unto the Lord and he will abundantly pardon," also I read in Acts II, "When the day of Pentecost was fully come at Peter's preaching they were convinced and asked what should we do to be saved.["] First you must have faith, second repentance, third be baptized, fourth you shall receive the Gift of the Holy Ghost.

So, Jesus Christ said in his teachings that the Holy Ghost lead and guide you into all truth and it will show you things to come.

I was convinced that I must get the Holy Ghost and searching for the light and truth I would read the Bible so much until the people would tell me, "if you

---

persons in the straw." Henry Flint, "Condition of the Western Country Before the Introduction of Railroads," in *The Railroads of the United States; Their History and Statistics, Etc.*, 244.

19. The spider web metaphor for hell has a well-established pedigree in Christian religious thought. In 1861, Reverend Jeremy Taylor was quoted as saying: "For what is thy sin to God's mercy? Even as a spider's web, when the wind blows, it is gone in an instant." Jeremy Taylor, "Of Habitual Sins and Their Remedy," in Reginald Heber, ed., *The Whole Works of the Right Rev. Jeremy Taylor, D.D.*, 225. In 1741, early American minister Jonathan Edwards, in his best-known sermon, "Sinners in the Hands of an Angry God," painted a vivid picture of humankind's fragile spiritual condition: "The God that holds you over the pit of hell, much as one holds a spider, or some loathsome insect over the fire, abhors you. . . . You hang by a slender thread, with the flames of divine wrath flashing about it, and ready every moment to singe it, and burn it asunder." In 1778, London minister John Matlock warned readers: "Woe to apostates, and woe to backsliding, hardened sinners. . . . His hope shall break daily as the spider's web, and his feet shall slip from one transgression to another." Rev. John Matlock, *Apostasy: The Broad way to Hell*, 174. Jarena Lee, an African American evangelist, envisioned hell "covered only, as it were, by a spider's web." Jarena Lee, Autobiography, 1836, 285. In 1926, Southern folklorist Newbell Niles Puckett recorded that "in parts of Georgia they say that if a person has not hung over hell on a spider web that that person has not been converted." Newbell Niles Puckett, *Folk Beliefs of the Southern Negro*, 542.

don't stop reading so much you will go crazy. Already the asylum is full of preachers." But, I would not stop reading or searching for truth.

So I would ask the preacher what should I do to receive the Holy Ghost and the first reply, 'You have the Holy Ghost when you get religion." The second reply, "You have to pray for it." So I decided to the second advece [sic].

So, I went to pray one night for the Holy Ghost. I went into an old house in the woods where the trees and bushes were very thick. I begged our Heavenly Father for the Holy Ghost and I wept very much all night.

Just about the break of day I decided to promise the Lord that I wasn't going to eat or drink until I received the Holy Ghost, but the spirit of the Lord prevailed with me not to make such a promise. I thank the Lord for [sic] guiding hand for the Holy Ghost is only given through the men of God having divine authority.

So at that time I didn't know anything about the Mormon doctrine. All that I heard about them was something bad. They said they believed in many wives and Brigham Young trying to be like God, that could walk on water and that he had a date to walk on the water and had some planks under the water to walk on and some boys removed the planks one day and he fell into the water.[20] So I was just waiting for an answer to my prayer and a good inspired Elder come way off his road into a cotton field and brought me a tract.[21] I think it was the "Plan of Salvation." So my sister gave it to me and said, "Here is a tract the Elder left for you."

So I began to read the tract I knew it was the truth. I soon found that the Elder had been commissioned and whoever they will lay their hands on may receive the Holy Ghost. So being convinced that this was the only true Church I ask the Elders to baptize me. They said, Yes, gladly, but if I were you I would read a little more. So I went back home and set down and ordered the Book of Mormon, The Pearl of Great Price, and the Doctrine & Covenants, and other books and read them, so after this I was called into the World War over Seas.

So being protected by the hands of the Lord serving on the firing lines I barely escaped death. So just as soon as I got back home I had the Elders baptize me and I received the Holy Ghost. I had another vision or dream that the Elders work had been recognized in heaven and my sins had been forgiven and my name was written in heaven. So in a few days a band of white men came to my brother's

---

20. Variations of this story had long circulated about both Joseph Smith and Brigham Young. In 1834, a Susquehanna-area newspaper reported that a "Mormon preacher" had laid "a line of plank . . . in a particular direction completely across the pond, sunk about four inches under the surface of the water." In 1844, the editor of the *Times and Seasons* specifically denounced the tale, referring to it as an "old fabrication" and a "story [that] has been put into requisition to blast our fame." See J. Taylor Hollist, "Walking-on-Water Stories and Other Susquehanna River Folk Tales about Joseph Smith," 36.

21. For most of 1913, the area was beset by severe drought. In September, "spotted rains [had] fallen in Marengo County," but in "some sections showers [were] needed badly." Some had not seen rain for over two months. "Recent Drought Brings Report of Cotton Deterioration from All Parts of the State," *Montgomery Advertiser*, September 9, 1912, 2–3. See also "Bumper Crop Is Promised," *Montgomery Advertiser*, August 11, 1913, 1.

house with rifles and shot guns so they called me saying, "We just want to talk to you." So I went out and they ask me, "Why did you join this Church so you went over to the waters and learned a few things and now you want to join the whites. I said, "No, I was investigating long before I went to war and I found it was the only true Church on earth that is why I joined it." "We want you to go and have your name scratched off the record if not we will hang you up to a limb and shoot you full of holes."[22]

So the next morning I got up and went down to the Church where the Latter-day Saints were holding conference. I had not heard much about per-secution. I rehearsed to the L.D.S. my troubles, so thoes [sic] beautiful smiles they gave me not only put sunshine into their souls but mine also, so they said "Brother Hope we could not scratch your name off if we tried to, for your name is in Salt Lake City and also written in Heaven." So the mob did not come back but if they had come back I could have gladly died for the faith so I know that Joseph Smith is and was a true Prophet of God and God the Father of our spirits and Jesus Christ is the son of God.

My family and I are happy untold so I bear my testimony in the name of Jesus Christ. AMEM [sic]

Len Ross Hope, Sr.
April 29, 1938

The Meeks-Nelson-First Presidency Correspondence (1947)

HISTORICAL INTRODUCTION:

In the summer of 1947, Heber C. Meeks,[23] president of the Southern States Mission, visited Cuba "for the purpose of studying the conditions with a view of doing missionary work in that country." But before missionary work could com-mence, the Church needed to solve what Meeks called "The Problem." Over the past several centuries, white Spaniards, Africans, and natives had intermingled, cre-ating a mixed-race population in which racial distinctions had largely disappeared. After Meeks returned [to mission headquarters in Atlanta, Georgia, he called on Dr. Lowry Nelson, Mormon professor of rural sociology and an expert on Cuba. Formerly a professor at Utah State Agricultural College, he was currently a profes-

---

22. One missionary serving in Alabama wrote that "in the South ninety percent of the people do not own a place of their own and have no way to get one." A few men "with money rule the place and just tell the people what to do." The people "live on a credit system and before the crop is gathered the merchant gets a mortgage on it and the landlord takes what is left." Millard Toone, Letter to Mrs. F. P. Toone, September 2, 1921, Felix Toone Papers, LDS Church History Library.

23. When Heber C. Meeks (1895–1986) became president of the Southern States Mission in 1943, he had served as the executive secretary for the Utah Democratic Party and had held several government positions: civilian representative of the Organization of Military Camps, director of the Federal Home Loan Corporation, and director of the U.S. census for the state of Utah. Heber C. Meeks, Autobiography, MS 7350, LDS Church History Library.

sor at the University of Minnesota where he taught for more than two decades.[24] As a former administrator of Brigham Young University and one of the Church's best-known public intellectuals, Nelson was a leading mind in the Mormon community. He and Meeks were also "old school friends."[25]

Though Nelson had been raised in Utah, Meeks's letter was his first indication that there had been a "fixed" restriction against the black population. "It seems strange to me," he confessed to the First Presidency, "that I should never have before had to face up to this doctrine of the Church relative to the Negro."[26] Nelson knew that earlier leaders had enforced prejudicial policies but had never been brought "face to face with the possibility that the doctrine was finally crystallized."[27] The issue "was rather an academic one to us living in Ferron [his Utah hometown]," he acknowledged, "where there were very few people who had ever seen a Negro, let alone having lived in the same community with them."[28]

In subsequent years, Nelson prided himself on the role he played in exposing Church teachings. He proudly identified himself as "the first member of the LDS church to lodge a vigorous protest with the First Presidency on the black policy." In 1952, he published an article with *The Nation* urging Church leaders "in the spirit of constructive criticism and in the conviction that his church, with so many admirable qualities and achievements to its credit, is faced with a challenge to place itself alongside other groups which are laboring against racial bigotry."[29]

He considered himself to be a daring whistleblower, ready to deal with the consequences of telling the truth. He believed "that public pressure was the only influence that could finally bring about a change, just as it did in the polygamy case."[30] And he made clear to the public that he was venturing onto dangerous territory. "A very real difficulty," he wrote *The Nation*, "is the fact that those who disapprove of the church's attitude have no way of expressing their point of view." Discussions could only take place in what he styled "the Mormon Underground" made up of "generally active" Church members who "rationalize their conduct by weighing the many admirable features of their religion against the features with which they disagree."[31] He likely used this network to distribute copies of his letters from the First Presidency. In 1975, he happily recalled that "thousands of copies of this correspondence circulated sub-rosa at the time."[32]

---

24. Samuel W. Taylor, "The Ordeal of Lowry Nelson and the Mis-Spoken Word," 95.

25. Lowry Nelson, Letter to First Presidency, June 26, 1947.

26. Lowry Nelson, Letter to First Presidency, October 8, 1947.

27. Lowry Nelson, Letter to First Presidency, June 26, 1947.

28. Lowry Nelson, Letter to First Presidency, October 8, 1947.

29. Lowry Nelson, "Mormons and the Negro," *The Nation* 174, (May 24, 1952): 488.

30. Lowry Nelson, Letter to Stephen Holbrook, June 25, 1975, Stephen Holbrook Papers, Box 1, fd. 25.

31. Lowry Nelson, "Mormons and the Negro," *The Nation* 174, (May 24, 1952): 488.

32. Lowry Nelson, Letter to Stephen Holbrook, June 25, 1975, Stephen Holbrook Papers, Box 1, fd. 25.

The correspondence between Meeks, Nelson, and the First Presidency reveals their efforts to negotiate their faith with the racial assumptions they harbored. More pressingly, it also reveals the state of race relations in the United States juxtaposed against racially mixed countries such as Cuba and the prospects for Mormon missionary work in the racial melting pot of Latin America.

CITATION

Heber C. Meeks, Letter to Lowry Nelson, June 20, 1947, Lowry Nelson Papers, Box 4, fd. 2, Merrill-Cazier Library, Utah State University, Logan. All of the correspondence cited in this section is from this location in the Nelson Papers.

HEBER MEEKS TO LOWRY NELSON EXCERPT

. . . I would appreciate your opinion as to the advisability of doing missionary work particularly in the rural sections of Cuba, knowing, of course, our concept of the Negro and his position as to the Priesthood.

Are there groups of pure white blood in the rural sections, particularly in the small communities? If so are they maintaining segregation from the Negroes? The best information we received was that in the rural communities there was no segregation of the races and it would probably be difficult to find, with any degree of certainty, groups of pure white people.

LOWRY NELSON TO HEBER MEEKS, JUNE 26, 1947, EXCERPT

. . . The attitude of the Church in regard to the Negro makes me very sad. Your letter is the first intimation I have had that there was a fixed doctrine on this point. I had always known that certain statements had been made by authorities regarding the status of the Negro, but I had never assumed that they constituted an irrevocable doctrine. I hope no final word has been said on this matter. I must say that I have never been able to accept the idea, and never shall. I do not believe that God is a racist. But if the church has taken an irrevocable stand, I would dislike to see it enter Cuba or any other island where different races live and establish missionary work. The white and colored people get along much better in the Caribbean and most of Latin America than they do in the United States.[33] Prejudice exists, there is no doubt, and the whites in many ways manifest their feelings of superiority, but there is much less of it than one finds in USA, especially in our South. For us to go into a situation like that and preach a doctrine of "white supremacy" would, it seems to me, be a tragic disservice. I am speaking frankly, because I feel very keenly on this question. If world brotherhood and the universal God mean anything, it seems to me they mean equality of races. I fail to see how Mormonism or any other

---

33. Nelson was speaking to the idea of "racial democracy" that had become an identifying feature in Latin American society since the 1930s. In 1933, Brazilian Gilberto Freyre wrote *Casa Grande e Senzala* celebrating the racial mixture that defined Brazilian society. See Edward Eric Telles, *Race in Another America: The Significance of Color in Brazil,* chap. 2.

religion claiming to be more than a provincial church can take any other point of view; and there cannot be world peace until the pernicious doctrine of the superiority of one race and the inferiority of others is rooted out. This is my belief. . . .

I repeat, my frankness or bluntness, as you will, is born of a fervent desire to see the causes of war rooted out of the hearts of men. What limited study I have been able to give the subject leads me to the conclusion that ethnocentrism, and the smugness and intolerance which accompany it, is one of the first evils to be attacked if we are to achieve the goal of peace. . . .

Sincerely,

Lowry Nelson

Heber C. Meeks to the First Presidency, July 23, 1947

Citation

Heber C. Meeks, Report to the First Presidency, July 23, 1947 Heber C. Meeks Papers, MS 1677, Box 2, fd. 10, L. Tom Perry Special Collections, Harold B. Lee Library, Brigham Young University, Provo, Utah.

Document Excerpt

. . . The determining factors, as I analyzed the Cuban situation as to whether missionary work should be carried on among this people, are: 1) the number of pure white (Spanish) blood on the island (2) is the trend toward the preservation of this pure white blood (3) will there be an increase in the pure white blood (4) would an injection of our doctrine into the Cuban situation of no racial discrimination be wise (5) should the gospel be taught to the negro. The major portion of my investigation was to obtain reliable answers to these questions. . . .

There is, no doubt, some of the blood of Israel among the Cubans. Dr. Fortan,[34] who in my opinion, was the outstanding personality we met in Cuba[,] is the son of an Englishman. His father was a practicing physician in Cuba, his mother a Spanish woman of pure white blood.

It was the unanimous opinion of the men we contacted that the lines of race discrimination will be drawn more sharply in the future, and on a broader base between this white group of approximately one million and the colored element. Also, that the pure white group will increase in proportionate numbers over the colored group. There is a definite trend in this direction at the present time.

I am aware that we are doing missionary work in South American countries where there is little or no discrimination against the negro. There we are successfully teaching the gospel to groups free from negro blood. [His report then continued:]

---

34. Dr. Ortelio Martines-Fortan was head of the Sociology Department at the University of Cuba and director of the Finlay Institute, a major immunology research center named after Cuban physician Carlos Finlay. Finlay played a leading role in eradicating yellow fever from Cuba. Mariola Espinosa, *Epidemic Invasions: Yellow Fever and the Limits of Cuban Independence, 1878–1930*, 109–17.

THE NEGRO PROBLEM

The negro situation in Cuba presents a problem. . . . They mingle together freely in all social, business and political activities. They have intermarried freely. There are not available accurate records to determine who has negro blood among the average Cuban. As previously stated, there are approximately one million of the total population that are free from negro blood. The future will see an increase in this group in proportion to total population.

The problem is different than in the South. Here we do not proselyte among the negroes because of race discrimination. The Elders could not socialize with them even to conducting meetings because of public sentiment. The negro convert cannot attend white meetings for the same reason. They cannot carry on Church activities among themselves because they cannot hold the priesthood.

In Cuba there would be no such barriers in proselyting among the negroes. The whites and colored would attend the same meetings. They would socialize in all their religious activities. The Elders could preside over them and socialize with them.

Here the question arises, and this, it seems to me, is all important: what will be the negro's reaction, in a country where there is no race discrimination, to the doctrine that he cannot hold the Priesthood and thus be denied executive leadership in the Church, while his Spanish neighbor may enjoy such a privilege. Would injecting this doctrine into this Cuban situation cause repercussions that may bring the Church in disrespect in that country? May there not be political reaction against such a missionary effort? . . .

The Doctor [Lowry Nelson] seems to have no fear as to any unfavorable reaction against the Church but he feels it would be unfortunate to disturb their present condition of race equality.

We may well ask ourselves the question, would it be a tragedy to teach them the truth. Would it be a disfavor to teach them racial purity? Would not the negro be a happier race if they knew their racial status and enjoyed the blessings of membership in the Church, its purifying influence in their lives—without holding the Priesthood—than in their present tragic plite [sic] in the world[?] Has not the gospel helped the American Negro who accepted of it? In my opinion many of the negroes would accept the gospel and be happy in the church. . . .

I have endeavored to give you such information, without burdening you with too much detail, and make such analysis as would be most helpful to you. I believe I am fully cognizant of the unfavorable factors in doing missionary work among the Cuban people. There is danger of very strong reactions against our doctrine. But I cannot bring myself to recommend—after days of prayerful consideration that we stay out of Cuba. I cannot overcome the feeling that these people are entitled to the truth. I believe there is an intelligent approach to the problem that would bring success to our missionary efforts. I also believe we would be doing a great service to that nation, politically, socially, and spiritually, to put in their hands the Light of the Everlasting Gospel. I am fully aware that you are entitled to the guidance of the Holy Spirit in making the decision. Whatever the Lord directs, we know will be right.

Faithfully your brother,

Heber Meeks
Mission President

FIRST PRESIDENCY TO LOWRY NELSON, JULY 17, 1947, EXCERPT

Dr. Lowry Nelson
Utah State Agricultural College[35]
Logan, Utah

Dear Brother Nelson

As you have been advised, your letter of June 26 was received in due course, and likewise we now have a copy of your letter to President Meeks—. We have carefully considered their contents and are glad to advise you as follows:

We make this initial remark: the social side of the Restored Gospel is only an incident of it; it is not the end thereof.

The basic element of your ideas and concepts seems to be that all God's children stand in equal positions before Him in all things.

Your knowledge of the Gospel will indicate to you that this is contrary to the very fundamentals of God's dealings with Israel dating from the time of his promise to Abraham regarding Abraham's seed and their position vis-à-vis God Himself. Indeed, some of God's children were assigned to superior positions before the world was formed. We are aware that some Higher Critics[36] do not accept this, but the Church does.

---

35. The First Presidency misdirected the letter, believing Nelson was still at Utah State Agricultural College. He had taught at USAC during the first summer term of 1947 but returned to Minnesota in fall of that year. The letter was forwarded to Nelson, but by the time it arrived he was in Europe. See Lowry Nelson, Letters to Heber C. Meeks, June 26, 1947, and First Presidency, October 8, 1947.

36. Since the late nineteenth-century, Church leaders had performed an awkward dance with a sector of the scholarly community that called itself the "Higher Critics," a group of scholars who sought to understand the Bible primarily as a historical rather than inspired document. B. H. Roberts, heretofore the most articulate proponent of the premortality hypothesis, took the claims of critics seriously and even sympathetically. Christendom's "inability to meet in any effectual way the assaults of this New Criticism," Roberts wrote, "must ever be an occasion for . . . humiliation." B. H. Roberts, *A New Witness for God*, 40. President J. Reuben Clark considered "modern criticism" to be a "virus" bent on "destroy[ing] the Bible as an inspired volume." The critics exhibit "acute ingenuity," Clark continued, hoping that by "evilly casting doubt upon the traditionally ascribed authorship of the books of the Bible. . .the books themselves would fall as spurious and worthless." J. Reuben Clark Jr., *On The Way to Immortality and Eternal Life*, 207, 209.

Your position seems to lose sight of the revelations of the Lord touching the preexistence of our spirits, the rebellion in heaven, and the doctrines that our birth into this life and the advantages under which we may be born, have a relationship in the life heretofore.

From the days of the Prophet Joseph even until now, it has been the doctrine of the Church, never questioned by any of the Church leaders, that the Negroes are not entitled to the full blessings of the Gospel.

Furthermore, your ideas, as we understand them, appear to contemplate the intermarriage of the Negro and White races, a concept which has heretofore been most repugnant to most normal-minded people from the ancient patriarchs till now. God's rule for Israel, His Chosen People, has been endogenous.[37] Modern Israel has been similarly directed.

We are not unmindful of the fact that there is a growing tendency, particularly among some educators, as it manifests itself in this area, toward the breaking down of race barriers in the matter of intermarriage between whites and blacks, but it does not have the sanction of the Church and is contrary to Church doctrine.

Faithfully yours,
George Albert Smith
J. Reuben Clark
David O. McKay

A First Presidency Statement on Blacks and the Priesthood (1949)

HISTORICAL INTRODUCTION

In 1869, Brigham and Lorenzo Young had debated whether blacks descended from Cain or had faltered in the pre-mortal life. For three generations, Mormon leaders wrangled over the exact reason for the restriction. Joseph Fielding Smith, the Church's official historian, illustrates the development of explanations. In 1907 he distanced himself from the pre-mortal explanation entirely, telling one inquirer that it "is not the official position of the Church" but "is merely the opinion of men."[38] In 1924, he expressed a greater openness to the theory per se, noting that it was a "reasonable thing" demonstrated "in many passages of scripture." But still, he recommended keeping the explanation abstract: "To dwell upon this topic and point out certain nations as having been cursed because of their acts in the pre-existence enters too much on the realm of speculation." For Smith, it was sufficient to say "that the negro is banned from the Priesthood and the reason some day we may understand."[39]

---

37. Here, the First Presidency is casting the black population as inherently foreign/"exogenous" to the identity of Israel.

38. Joseph Fielding Smith, Letter to Alfred M. Nelson, January 31, 1907, LDS Church History Library.

39. Joseph Fielding Smith "The Negro and the Priesthood," *Improvement Era* 27, no. 6 (April 1924): 565.

Finally, in 1931, Smith offered up his most extensive discussion of the topic in *The Way to Perfection* in which he embraced the premortality theory wholeheartedly, declaring that blacks had been "placed under restrictions because of their attitude in the world of spirits."[40] In October 1947 David O. McKay articulated his support for the premortality theory to Lowry Nelson in terms of chemistry's "law of attraction"—though he, too, acknowledged that the analogy was imperfect. Just as "force[s] acting mutually between particles of matter" tend to "draw them together," so are "individual[s] attracted to the parentage for which they are prepared."[41] As Armand L. Mauss has argued, Joseph Fielding Smith's book became "the template for interpreting all extant Mormon scripture and discourse that had any implications for racial differences or racial policy."[42]

The 1949 statement demonstrated how deeply the premortality explanation had spread throughout the Church; once a folk tale denounced by Brigham Young, now it had become *de rigueur.* When McKay echoed his earlier remarks about the "law of attraction" at the 1954 South African mission conference, one missionary, Curtis Tracy, heralded McKay's words as "so perfect and lovely that you know no one but a prophet of God could utter them."[43] In his *Doctrines of Salvation*, Joseph Fielding Smith wrote: "There is a reason why one man is born black and with other disadvantages, while another is born white with great advantages. The reason is that we once had an estate before we came here, and were obedient; more or less, to the laws that were given us there." Smith still denounced the idea of neutrals in heaven but took care to note that "men receive rewards here based upon their actions there. . . . [T]he Negro, evidently, is receiving the reward he merits."[44] These views represented the mainstream of Mormon thinking for the next two generations.

Two versions of the 1949 document are available. In 1949, the First Presidency consisted of George Albert Smith, David O. McKay, and J. Reuben Clark. The first statement can be found in the Lester Bush papers at the University of Utah, a copy of which would be published in the edited volume, *Neither White Nor Black.* Bush has stated that he "reprinted this statement in its entirety as found in the archives."[45] The Bush version is dated August 17, 1949. The other, a substantially longer version, can be found William E. Berrett's section of John J. Stewart's book, *Mormonism and the Negro,*[46] which is dated to August 17, 1951.

---

40. Joseph Fielding Smith, *The Way to Perfection,* 101.

41. David O. McKay, Letter to Brother [Nelson], November 3, 1947, in Llewelyn R. McKay, ed., *Home Memories of President David O. McKay,* 229.

42. Armand L. Mauss, *All Abraham's Children: Changing Mormon Conceptions of Race and Lineage,* 217.

43. Curtis Tracy, Journal, January 17, 1954, LDS Church History Library.

44. Joseph Fielding Smith, *Doctrines of Salvation,* 1:61, 67.

45. Lester Bush, Letter to Russell Stevenson, May 12, 2014.

46. For details on the publication of *Mormonism and the Negro,* see Jan Shipps, *Sojourner in the Promised Land: Forty Years among the Mormons,* 387; and Eugene England, "'No Respecter of Persons': A Mormon Ethics of Diversity," 89.

Their 1949 statement was never released as a circular, officially read to congregations, or included in James R. Clark's comprehensive six-volume *Messages of the First Presidency* series. It was likely drafted as a letter sent in response to public inquiries.

First Presidency Statement, August 17, 1949, Lester Bush Version

Citation

In the Lester Bush Papers, MS 685, Box 4, fd. 4, Special Collections, Marriott Library, University of Utah. Bush published the statement in *Neither White Nor Black: Mormon Scholars Confront the Race Issue in a Universal Church*, co-edited with Armand L. Mauss, 221.

Document Excerpt

The attitude of the Church with reference to Negroes remains as it has always stood. It is not a matter of the declaration of a policy but of direct commandment from the Lord, on which is founded the doctrine of the Church from the days of its organization, to the effect that Negroes may become members of the Church but that they are not entitled to the priesthood at the present time.[47] The prophets of the Lord have made several statements as to the operation of the principle. President Brigham Young said: "Why are so many of the inhabitants of the earth cursed with a skin of blackness? It comes in consequence of their fathers rejecting the power of the holy priesthood, and the law of God. They will go down to death. And when all the rest of the children have received their blessings in the holy priesthood, then that curse will be removed from the seed of Cain, and they will then come up and possess the priesthood, and receive all the blessings which we now are entitled to."[48]

President Wilford Woodruff made the following statement: "The day will come when all that race will be redeemed and possess all the blessings which we now have."[49]

The position of the Church regarding the Negro may be understood when another doctrine of the Church is kept in mind, namely, that the conduct of spirits in the pre-mortal existence has some determining effect upon the conditions and circumstances under which these spirits take on mortality, and that while the

---

47. In 1954, McKay told Dr. Sterling McMurrin that the priesthood restriction "is a practice, not a doctrine, and the practice some day will be changed." Quoted in Roger O. Porter, "Educator Cites McKay Statement of No Negro Bias in LDS Tenets," *Salt Lake Tribune*, January 15, 1970, B9.

48. Brigham Young, August 19, 1866, *Journal of Discourses*, 11:272.

49. This is a misquotation. In February 1852, Brigham Young made these comments in a speech to the Territorial Legislature. According to Wilford Woodruff, Young said that "the day will Come when all the seed of Cane will be Redeemed & have all the Blessings we have now & a great deal more." Kenney, *Wilford Woodruff's Journal*, January-February 1852, 4:97.

details of this principle have not been made known, the principle itself indicates that the coming to this earth and taking on mortality is a privilege that is given to those who maintained their first estate; and that the worth of the privilege is so great that spirits are willing to come to earth and take on bodies no matter what the handicap may be as to the kind of bodies they are to secure; and that among the handicaps, failure of the right to enjoy in mortality the blessings of the priesthood, is a handicap which spirits are willing to assume in order that they might come to earth. Under this principle there is no injustice whatsoever involved in this deprivation as to the holding of the priesthood by the Negroes.

First Presidency Statement, August 17, 1951, The Berrett Version

DOCUMENT NOTE

The Berrett version includes the entirety of the Bush version but also attaches the following text to the end. In contrast to the Bush copy, Berrett's is dated August 17, 1951, two years later, when the First Presidency consisted of David O. McKay, J. Reuben Clark, and Henry D. Moyle. The text below immediately follows the final paragraph in the Bush copy cited above.

CITATION

William E. Berrett, "The Church and the Negroid People," [an appendix to] John J. Stewart, *Mormonism and the Negro: An Explanation and Defense of the Doctrine of the Church of Jesus Christ of Latter-day Saints in Regard to Negroes and Others of Negroid Blood, with a Historical Supplement,* 1st ed. Orem, Utah: Community Press, 1960, 16–18.

DOCUMENT EXCERPT

Why the Negro was denied the priesthood from the days of Adam to our day is not known. The few known facts about our pre-earth life and our entrance into mortality must be taken into account in any attempt at an explanation.

1. Not all intelligences reached the same degree of attainment in the pre-earth life.

And the Lord said unto me: These two facts do exist, that there are two spirits, one being more intelligent than the other; there shall be another more intelligent than they; I am the Lord thy God, I am more intelligent than they all.

The Lord thy God sent his angel to deliver thee from the hands of the priest of Elkenah.

I dwell in the midst of them all; I now, therefore, have come down unto thee to deliver unto thee the works which my hands have made, wherein my wisdom excelleth them all, for I rule in the heavens above and in the earth beneath, in all wisdom and prudence, over all the intelligences thine eyes have seen from the beginning; I came down in the beginning in the midst of all the intelligences thou hast seen.

Now the Lord had shown unto me, Abraham, the intelligences that were organized before the world was; and among all these there were many of the noble and great ones;

And God saw these souls that they were good, and he stood in the midst of them, and he said:

These I will make my rulers; for he stood among those that were spirits, and he saw that they were good; and he said unto me: Abraham, thou art one of them; thou wast chosen before thou wast born. . . .

And we will prove them herewith to see if they will do all things whatsoever the Lord their God shall command them;

And they who keep their first estate shall be added upon; and they who keep not their first estate shall not have glory in the same kingdom with those who keep their first estate; and they who keep their second estate shall have glory added upon their heads for ever and ever [Abraham 3:19–26].

2. Man will be punished for his own sins and not for Adam's transgression. (2nd Article of Faith.) If this is carried further, it would imply that the Negro is punished or allotted to a certain position on this earth, not because of Cain's transgression, but came to earth through the loins of Cain because of his failure to achieve other stature in the spirit world.

3. All spirits are born innocent into this world. *Every spirit of man was innocent in the beginning; and God having redeemed man from the fall, men became again, in their infant state, innocent before God* [D&C 93:38].

4. The Negro was a follower of Jehovah in the pre-earth life. (There were no neutrals.)

Chapter 12

American Mormons Struggle with Civil Rights, 1953–69

Introduction

The Mormons' effort to define their position with regard to the civil rights of African Americans was uneven at best. White, rural, and insulated, Utah Mormons found the struggle for civil rights to be far-removed and foreign to their experience, a struggle that belonged to the South rather than the West. Following the *Brown v. Board of Education* decision in 1954, the ruling won a single front-page headline whereas the French struggle to fight the Viet Minh in Indo China garnered several.

By the 1950s, Utah Mormons had spent generations striving to shed the racial identities easterners had placed upon them. They had made for themselves a white enclave in the desert where they hoped to be free from the racial difficulties that seemed to trouble the non-Mormon world.

But their perceived racial security proved more imagined than real. As early as 1950, Utahns could sense the changing times. Over the course of the 1960s, the black push for civil rights swept across the nation, and Utah could not shield itself from it. The movement fractured the Mormon community. Mormon civil rights allies such as Adam Duncan and James E. Faust supported the strengthening of civil rights legislation, while returned missionary Stephen Holbrook left the faith and became an NAACP organizer. Even establishment figures expressed diverging views on the topic, with First Counselor Hugh B. Brown supporting civil rights legislation whereas Apostle Ezra Taft Benson expressed hostile skepticism toward civil rights organizers.

The contradictions that defined the positions of Church leaders also manifested themselves throughout Mormon society. Whatever their support of civil rights legislation, many Saints refused to be bullied—again—by compulsive federal action. "The quickest and surest way to kill tolerance," one rural Utah editorialist wrote in 1950, "is to try to make someone tolerant by law."[1] But the *Roosevelt Standard's* editorialist, known only by the initials G.W.H., celebrated Supreme

---

1. "Editorial," *Davis County Clipper*, February 10, 1950, 2.

Court rulings that began to dismantle segregation in the Southern educational system.[2] "Perhaps," it declared, "a new day is dawning for all of America's oppressed minorities—the Jew[,], the Negro, the Oriental, the Mexican, and the Indian." Perhaps, GWH hoped, "their liberation may be in sight"—liberation that any recalcitrant politician would find hard to resist "with a gun pointed in his face."[3]

BYU Professor Alma Heaton on 1950s Mormon Dancing (1981)

HISTORICAL INTRODUCTION

No one knew "fun" like Alma Heaton. Trained at the famed Arthur Murray Dance Studio, Heaton committed himself at an early age to teach people how to dance. "Dancing," Heaton once observed, "is perhaps the most reliable criterion of a nation's temperament."[4] In 1953, Heaton took the position as BYU's first instructor in a recreation program, focusing on teaching dance to young Latter-day Saints. His methods of teaching dance emphasized a "scientific approach" to the promoting of "sound practices and techniques of instruction."[5] Heaton became the leading force for the teaching of dance methods throughout Mormon America.

Dance culture in Mormon America exhibited the white culture Mormons had celebrated for nearly two generations. In 1952, J. Reuben Clark, first counselor in the First Presidency, expressed disapproval of rock and roll, wondering "how far above the tom-tom of the jungle it is"; he was certain that "it is not too far" and that "some of it came out of the voodoo huts."[6] In 1958, the *Deseret News* ran a widely publicized editorial concluding that the "delinquents of today do not know it, but what they need is some training in good music. . . . Hopped up on their diet of 'r & r' [they] need to have their musical beat refined and slowed to an andante." The 1957 handbook for the Mutual Improvement Association, the youth auxiliary for the Church, warned against "any of the crouching styles, or the wild acrobatic antics of 'jitterbug' or 'bop.'"[7]

---

2. G.W.H. is speaking of the following cases: *Sweatt v. Painter* and *McLaurin v. Oklahoma State Regents* (both dealing with segregation in graduate and law schools) and *Henderson v. United States* (dealing with racial segregation in railway cars). Neither case ruled specifically on the constitutionality of the "separate but equal" doctrine found in *Plessy v. Ferguson;* but as G.W.H. observed, the *McLaurin* and *Henderson* cases "ruled, in effect, that segregation is not equality." "Going with the Wind," *Roosevelt Standard,* June 22, 1950, 2. For a full survey of the *Sweatt* case, see Mark V. Tushnet, *Making Civil Rights Law: Thurgood Marshall and the Supreme Court, 1936–1961,* 126-50.

3. "Going with the Wind," *Roosevelt Standard,* June 22, 1950, 2.

4. Alma Heaton, *Ballroom Dance Rhythms: Prepared for the Guidance of Instructor and Student in Ballroom Dancing,* xi.

5. Ibid., vii.

6. J. Reuben Clark, "Home and the Building of Home Life," 792.

7. For these quotations, see Michael D. Hicks, *Mormonism and Music: A History,* 197.

CITATION

Alma Heaton Correspondence, 1981, cited in Ward M. Vander Griend, "Alma Heaton: The Professor of Fun," Ph.D. dissertation, Brigham Young University, 1981, 77.

DOCUMENT EXCERPT

I prophesied when rock dancing came in that one day we'd go back to the original primitive beat. And one reason I prophesied that is because when I started to teach dance, to my kids in the sixth grade, I went around to the teachers and said, "Let me teach your kids to dance." And it was the homeroom philosophy then that one teacher taught every subject, and they didn't know how to teach dancing and they wouldn't let me teach their kids dancing. So I prophesied that dancing would deteriorate back to the original hollow-log sound. And sure enough it did. It wasn't long before all we had was a beat that didn't change more than four times throughout a whole evening and it was loud and the dancing resembled the African stomp dance and it did deteriorate and went right back to the time when dancing was first originated.

Sterling McMurrin Addresses the NAACP (March 1960)

HISTORICAL INTRODUCTION

Sterling M. McMurrin had long defied convention. Raised in Ogden, Utah, and southern California, McMurrin grew up in a devout Mormon home where the dinner conversations "always centered primarily on religion" in which the family was "open, honest, and usually quite critical." By the time McMurrin entered graduate school, he declared himself an agnostic even as he harbored "strong religious sensitivities." He rejected the propositions that Joseph Smith had experienced heavenly visions or that the Book of Mormon accurately represented itself. However, he insisted, even late in life, that he was "intellectually and emotionally constructed with a rather strong religious disposition."[8] As a young man, he taught seminary as well as institute (adult) classes. In 1943, he became director of the LDS Institute at the University of Arizona and completed his PhD from University of Southern California in 1945. The following year, he accepted a post as a professor of philosophy at the University of Southern California. In 1948, he accepted a position as full professor of philosophy at the University of Utah.[9] By this point, he had already become a self-described "heretic" and "stray sheep" from the Church; nevertheless, McMurrin later affirmed, "[I still] love it and defend it."[10] Though he was "critical of the Church," he considered himself to be "for it, not against it."[11]

---

8. L. Jackson Newell, ed., *Matters of Conscience: Conversations with Sterling M. McMurrin on Philosophy, Education, and Religion,* 108.
    9. Ibid., 157.
    10. Ibid., 208.
    11. Ibid., 214.

In March 1960 McMurrin spoke at an NAACP gathering held at the African Methodist Episcopal Church in downtown Salt Lake City, an engagement NAACP President Albert Fritz had struggled to secure for nearly two years. Packing the chapel to standing-room only, McMurrin addressed the topic of "The Mormon Doctrine and the Negro." The speech marked McMurrin's first public foray into the troubled waters of the black-Mormon relationship.

In his address, McMurrin told his listeners that, although the priesthood restriction is "morally reprehensible," his address would seek only to "try to understand the situation, not to condemn it, as condemnatory [as] it may be." Concerned that his speech would be considered a defense of the priesthood restriction, he took care to state that he "frankly deplore[d] the entertainment of such a doctrine and the attitudes that may accompany it in my Church," lest they believe he was "trying to excuse the Mormon people as individuals or as a group [or] the Mormon Church as an institution."

Likely drawing from Fawn Brodie's biography of Joseph Smith, McMurrin suggested that the priesthood restriction could be traced to the difficulties the Saints faced in Missouri as a generally black-friendly community trying to survive in a slave state. McMurrin argued that the Church simply "fell into [its position] unfortunately and thus far, has never been able to extricate itself from [it]." All subsequent explanations that Church leaders offered, McMurrin said, were "shot through with all kinds of ambiguities."

McMurrin maintained that, when dealing with "an institution, especially a Church, of this type, which is highly involved in social matters, economic matters, business and so on, you simply have to recognize that you are not dealing with an institution that can move rapidly in any direction in which ideals may propose that it move." More important, things were changing among the rank-and-file of the Church—"not just . . . the heretics" and "not just . . . those that you might want to call liberals": "This is the attitude of very large numbers of very orthodox, down-the-line Mormons, who simply have a moral sensitivity that dictates to them that this kind of theological nonsense should not be pawned off on the people." Indeed, he noted, even among the leaders, "there is far more of what you might think of as a liberal attitude in the matter than many people would suspect." He predicted that the day would come when the Mormon Church would "dissolve," not "repudiate" the doctrine. McMurrin concluded "that the solution to this whole problem is essentially the solution of time." In some regards, McMurrin thought the priesthood restriction to be "kind of a dead issue" that carried no real meaning for most white Latter-day Saints. McMurrin observed a few days later that "as a religious teaching, it [the priesthood restriction] is an abomination and should be abandoned." But, he continued, "it seems to me that in actual fact it has very little impact one way or the other."[12]

---

12. Sterling M. McMurrin, Letter to John L. Sorenson, March 18, 1960, Sterling M. McMurrin Papers, Box 341, fd. 9, Special Collections, Marriott Library.

The event attracted some of Mormonism's leading establishment figures. Both Mormon historian Thomas C. Romney as well as BYU anthropologist John L. Sorenson attended.[13] Sorenson was impressed with McMurrin's "splendid presentation." Since Sorenson did not have opportunity to chat with McMurrin afterward, he wrote McMurrin, noting that while he could quibble on "a few minor points," he also could "agree about one hundred per cent" with McMurrin's address.[14] D. Arthur Haycock, a secretary to First Presidency Secretary Joseph Anderson also attended. [15]

McMurrin's address also represents perhaps the earliest record of an allusion to President David O. McKay's March 1954 comment that the priesthood restriction "is a practice, not a doctrine, and the practice some day will be changed." According to McMurrin's recollection, McKay also declared that the idea of a "divine curse" was ill-founded: "There is no such doctrine," McMurrin quoted McKay, "and as far as I am concerned there never was." In his NAACP speech, however, he refers to McKay only as one "of the leading officials of the Mormon Church" who believed that "as far as he was concerned, this was not a doctrine of this Church and it never was." McMurrin had long kept his source confidential, feeling that "it would be a lack of propriety" to discuss details of the conversation in public.[16] During the final week of McKay's life, however, McMurrin opened up about the conversation: "I'm willing to discuss it now very frankly," he told the *Tribune*, "because I think President McKay's statement has very great importance to the Mormon people." The quotation received considerable press coverage.[17]

The transcript below comes directly from a digitized version of the reel-to-reel tape available at the Marriott Special Collections at the University of Utah. McMurrin's address offers a whirlwind tour of the prevailing ideas in the Mormon intellectual community as well as in some sectors of the rank-and-file membership of the Church. According to Haycock, McMurrin "spoke fluently, in a friendly, informal style, without any notes"; the ever self-deprecating McMurrin confided that he felt "the talk wasn't very good—completely extemporaneous—

---

13. D. Arthur Haycock, Memo to President Robison, March 8, 1960, LDS Church History Library. Robinson is not otherwise identified nor is there any indication of why Haycock felt he should know about McMurrin's address.

14. John L. Sorenson, Letter to Sterling M. McMurrin, March 9, 1960, McMurrin Papers, Box 341, fd. 9.

15. Haycock to Robison, March 8, 1960.

16. For an example of McMurrin's circumspection, see "Negroes Relegated to Back Pew by Mormons," *Virgin Islands Daily News*, January 4, 1966, 13.

17. The comments received considerable press circulation once McMurrin revealed the source of the quotation. "Educator Cites McKay Statement of No Negro Bias in LDS Tenets," *Salt Lake Tribune*, January 15, 1970, B9; "David O. McKay, Mormon Leader, Dies at Age 96," *Milwaukee Sentinel*, January 19, 1970, 4; "McKay, 96, President of Mormons, Dies," *Schenecdaty [N.Y.] Gazette*, January 19, 1970, 1.

and . . . rather long."[18] Haycock's record represents the only contemporary written account of the speech; graduate student Douglas Monty Trank approached McMurrin about the contents of the Haycock memo, and McMurrin confirmed that "the memo is an accurate account of what he said."[19]

CITATION

Sterling M. McMurrin, transcript of "The Mormon Doctrine and the Negro," Sterling M. McMurrin audio collection, Marriott Library, University of Utah. Transcription by author, capitalization and punctuation standardized, paragraphs added.

DOCUMENT EXCERPT

I'm a member of the Mormon Church and though I'm not especially orthodox in the Mormon religion I feel very close to my Church. I have a very great love for my people. And I feel very keenly the situation in which the Mormon people find themselves, entertaining a religious doctrine of racial discrimination, which certainly is unworthy of a Church, unworthy of a religion, I believe myself, unworthy of what in many respects [is] a great though brief tradition of the Mormon people and certainly unworthy of these people. I feel this very keenly and I frankly deplore the entertainment of such a doctrine and the attitudes that may accompany it in my Church. And I have a very sincere hope that in some way or another this belief will eventually be in some way dissolved in the teachings of the Mormon Church, in the beliefs of the Mormon Church. And whatever practical attitudes that are conducive to what I would regard as immorality in our social life that may result from this doctrine be therefore and thereby overcome.

Now I say this to you not because I came here primarily to make such a statement but so that you will understand very clearly what my views are on this subject. My primary interest is in addressing my comments and, I hope, your thoughts to the problem of the Mormon position with respect to the Negro in the interest of, in some way or another, increasing understanding in the matter. I'm quite sure that the only way to face a situation of this kind is to face it not without genuine idealism and genuine hope that the situation may be changed, but certainly to face it realistically and, by realistically in an attempt to see how it is that the Mormon people became involved in this kind of predicament, what the predicament really amounts to. In other words, to try to understand the situation, not to condemn it, as condemnatory as it may be. I think that condemnation without understanding doesn't get us anywhere.

---

18. Sterling M. McMurrin, Letter to Lowell Bennion, March 22, 1960, qtd. in Douglas Monty Trank, "A Rhetorical Analysis of the Rhetoric Emerging from the Mormon-Black Controversy," 165.

19. Haycock to Robinson, March 8, 1960. See also Trank, "A Rhetorical Analysis," 198 note 38. Though Trank draws from the Haycock memorandum for his remarks, he acknowledges the existence of the recording in the Marriott Library's Special Collections. For a full treatment of the speech, see Trank, "A Rhetorical Analysis," 162–67.

I think it is one of the strange ironies of Mormon history that the presence of the doctrine and the teaching of the Mormon people that discriminates against the Negroes to the extent of denying them full fellowship in the Church should have come about apparently, largely as a result of the fact that, in its early stages, the Mormon Church was for the most part pro-Negro and anti-slavery. And that in its efforts to maintain this position, it moved entirely unwittingly into a kind of trap which was not of its own making but which it fell into unfortunately and thus far has never been able to extricate itself from.

What I have in mind is this. That in the first decade of the Mormon Church, the 1830s, the Mormon doctrine on the Negro moved in the direction in which you now find it. The Mormons were for the most part northern people, people opposed to slavery. And people for that matter who showed at many points, as was the case with Joseph Smith himself, in some of his earlier statements, at many points, very much inclined to favor various kinds of association with the Negroes and certainly to speak very highly of them, of their potentialities. The Mormon people during this decade, which was a very important decade, the first in the history of the Church itself, very important in the development of their thought and attitudes, were in the process of moving as a community from Ohio, a northern state, into Missouri. And as you know, Missouri had been admitted into the Union of States, by what is known as the Missouri Compromise in 1820, and it had, after great debate in the Congress, been admitted as a slave state. And yet it was a slave state that in many ways was in the North. I believe you will find that the Missouri Compromise indicated [in] the so-called Missouri Compromise Law that thereafter slavery would not be tolerated in any new states north of the southern border of Missouri.

This in itself is rather important for the point that I'm going to make. Here in a sense is a slave state that is mixed up with the northern kind of society to some extent. And the Mormons moved into Missouri at the time that the problem of slavery was a very intense one in Missouri. And as strange as it may seem to many of you—I'm sure many of you are better acquainted with this matter than I am but perhaps some of you are not aware of this situation—strange as it may seem, many of the difficulties that the Mormons had in Missouri right from the beginning of their entrance into Missouri and eventually leading to their expulsion from Missouri by force, many of these difficulties arose from the fact that the Mormons indicated as they went into the state, that, to a very considerable degree, they were pro-Negro and anti-slavery. Now this caused them very real difficulties. as for instance, there were already Negroes in the Church, free Negroes. And there was a movement of these free Negroes to move into the Mormon communities in Missouri. As you know, the Mormon religion is essentially a communitarian affair and the Mormons tend to live together. And the Missourians revolted very rigorously against any move on the part of the Mormons to have free negroes come into the state. As a matter of fact, a law had been set up prohibiting that, [a] law from the state legislature . . . . And this is what helped to cause the Mormons trouble in

Missouri. And the trouble was very real trouble, that is, it's trouble that eventuated in murder, and slaughter, and rapine of one kind and another.

. . . I'm not trying to excuse the Mormon people as individuals or as a group, nor the Mormon Church as an institution. I think the position that is taken now and has been taken ever since the beginning of this thing is morally reprehensible, [and I] have no interest whatsoever in excusing it. But I call your attention to this rather interesting fact: that the doctrine seems to have arisen largely out of the Mormons' attempting to get themselves out of a difficult situation that they got themselves into in relationship to the people of Missouri because they did have a rather typical northern, anti-slavery, pro-Negro attitude at that time. I'm well aware that there are instances of the ownership of slaves among the Mormons. And I'm certainly well aware of the fact that there are numerous instances to which all of us could call attention in societies dominated by Mormons of discrimination. And I'm not for a moment, as I say, attempting to excuse the situation but call your attention to the fact that the Mormons did not invent this idea that the Negroes are cursed with a black skin. They didn't invent this idea. They fell into it, it seems to me, when they were grasping for something or other to help them adapt to a most difficult social situation in which they had got themselves.

Now I'm not going to say that not many of them have liked the idea. Because many of them have liked the idea, though I don't think that it has ever been a particularly popular doctrine among the Mormons. It has always been highly ambiguous. Highly ambiguous. I think that the average member of the Mormon Church thinks that he can sit down and tell you what just what the Church's doctrine on the Negro is.

Now in the Mormon Church, what is or is not doctrine is usually decideable by top-level Church officials and they presumably decided in a more or less authoritative manner in reference to revelation, the scripture and so on. But if any Mormon wants to come in for some surprises, possibly some delights, possibly some disappointments, depending upon his view on this matter, he needs to simply write down his interpretation of the doctrine and take it to the leading authorities of his Church and ask them whether or not he has it straight.

He's due for some real surprises if he tries that. Because this is a rather ambiguous thing. It is not clear cut. And it has never been clear cut in the history of the Mormon Church. Some Mormons holding for instance that the Negroes have black skins as a result of the, of the sin of Cain. And other Mormons holding that you can't have a black skin because of a result of someone else's sin; you had to sin yourself in order to have a dark skin. This is a much better view from the standpoint of the Mormons because one of the fundamental principles of the Mormon religion is that no man can be held responsible for another man's sin. If you're going to hold that a black skin is in some way or another the result of sin, you gotta figure out a way for it's being the result of his own sin. This has laid quite a, quite a difficult burden upon most Christian theologies but this is a simple thing for Mormons to handle because they believe in the pre-existence, gives you plenty time to have sinned to your heart's content and to have merited black skin. [laughter]

Now I say, you get Mormons holding these different views. I would like to simply call your attention to the fact that, as ideas in religion go, it's really a much better idea if one must insist and believe that a dark skin, that a dark skin is the result of sin, it is a really much higher level idea, to believe that it's the result of the sin of the dark-skinned person himself rather than someone else's sin. I mean, this is a step forward in many ways, to place the responsibility on the individual.

. . . It's a rather interesting thing that the Mormon theology and the Mormon practice discriminate only against Negroes, [and] not against any other race. This is interesting, you see. It is only with Negroes that the Mormon Church had any kind of experience within the framework of a social situation that could be productive of this kind of a doctrine. Many of you are aware I'm sure that the Mormon Church actually has a most commendable record in the matter of its position—and not only in its theory but also in its practice—with reference to other races than the white race, with the exception of the Negro. I think you will find that it has a very commendable record, for instance, in its attitude toward the Polynesians. It built a temple in the Hawaiian Island along about 1918, 1919, I think, primarily for the Polynesian people. It has a very commendable record with reference to relations with the Japanese people as is evidenced by what went in this part of the country with reference to the Japanese during the past war.[20]

The discrimination is only against the Negroes. It is not a part of the Mormon teaching, nor the Mormon attitude, the Mormon makeup, to be involved in racial discrimination, except in this one instance. I'm not saying that Mormon people feel in the presence of Chinese just as they feel in the presence of typical Anglo-Saxons. But there's no doctrine of discrimination against the Chinese. Or the Iranians.[21] Or the Japanese. Or any other group.

---

20. When the federal government established a Japanese-American relocation center in Abraham, Utah, First Counselor J. Reuben Clark—formerly U.S. Undersecretary of State—strongly disapproved of building the center. D. Michael Quinn, *Elder Statesman: A Biography of J. Reuben Clark*, 323. In November 1942, a Topaz Branch was formed with Warren Richard Nelson, a recently returned missionary from Brazil (likely having been made acquainted with the large Japanese-Brazilian population there), was called as the branch president. "Branch Organized," *Millard County Chronicle*, November 26, 1942, 1. Church authorities generally deplored the internment of the Japanese at Abraham, Utah, site of the "Topaz" internment camp. Richard W. Henderson, Nelson's successor as president of the Topaz branch, told one stakewide assembly that "all mankind regardless of race are all God's children" and that he had "learned to love and respect the unfortunate people at Topaz." He noted that "sixty per cent of them are Americans entitled to rights as such" and that "as Latter day Saints we should recognize them as our brothers and sisters." He also implored white Mormons to only "speak of the people at Topaz as 'Nippons' or 'American Japanese, not 'Japs' as this is an insult to them." "Deseret Stake Conference," *Millard County Chronicle*, January 14, 1943, 1. That Henderson felt it necessary to make such a statement reveals local Mormons' tendency to assume a hostile posture to the local Japanese population.

21. In 1958–59, the State Department asked McMurrin to visit Iran as an adviser at the University of Tehran. McMurrin was not enthusiastic about his trip, even in retrospect. A colleague told him

The reason I'm saying this is that it is a very important key to the nature of the problem, and that is this attitude with respect to the Negroes, the teaching with respect to them is something that is associated you see not with any broad moral or religious principles that supports such a thing, not with any broad theological doctrines that support such a thing, but rather with a social situation in which the Mormons found themselves and which for some cause or another they didn't have the courage to overcome without overcoming it by a moral compromise, coming up with a doctrine that is based upon some very flimsy items in the scripture.

. . . I have discussed this doctrine with some of the leading officials of the Mormon Church. And I find that very often there is far more of what you might think of as a liberal attitude in the matter than many people would suspect. And one of the leading officials of the Church told me not very long ago, and by leading official, I mean one of the General Authorities of the Church, I don't mean a bishop or a stake president somewhere, told me not long ago that he did not believe that the Negroes were under any kind of curse. As far as he was concerned, this was not a doctrine of this Church and it never was.

Well, certainly there are many people who believe that it is and believe that it was. I simply mention this because I'm interested in having the Mormon Church seen in this respect, in the light in which I honestly believe it deserves to be seen. This is not a kind of solid front being set up by an institution against the Negro people but it is an institution which is shot through with all kinds of ambiguities with regard to the problem. And an institution in which there are many people with very genuine liberal ideas and liberal attitudes who simply do not believe the doctrine, who are embarrassed by it. For them it's a problem of how to get rid of it.

. . . I'm being very honest when I say I don't believe the doctrine has very much influence on the attitudes and the conduct on the average Mormon, even the Mormon who believes the doctrine, beyond the exclusion of Negroes in full fellowship. That, of course is, must be must be taken for granted. I'm talking about matters having to do with such problems as civil rights.

In the first place, I think the average Mormon knows that it is not the intention of his Church, now it may have been the intention at various times of some officials in the Mormon Church, but I think I can say this without being in error. It is not the position of the Mormon Church today—I don't know that it ever was—it certainly is not the position of the Mormon Church today that this doctrine on the Negro should be interpreted by the Mormon people as meaning that the Negro should be denied full civil rights. Now of course, you may say if you have the doctrine, it's going to go against the negroes achieving full civil rights, whether that's the intention or not. And I certainly can't argue against that point. My only point is, that it is not the teaching of the Mormon Church to its people. It is not the intention of the Mormon Church in continuing to hold this doctrine: that belief in

---

that Iran was "the most corrupt nation of all the developing nations he'd visited." McMurrin later acknowledged that "he turned out to be right." Newell, *Matters of Conscience,* 247.

the doctrine should lead anyone to any other course of action with regard to the life of the Negro than to prohibit him from having full fellowship in the Church which involves holding the priesthood and admission to the temple.

I think it's only fair to the Church that this be recognized. It is not the official position of the Church to deny civil freedoms to the Negroes. Now if you ask has the Church done what it might have done to get civil freedom for the Negroes, then that's another question. I don't think that it has—[that] is perfectly obvious. And frankly, it makes me very sad that a church which is capable of wielding such power in local politics, in local society, as the Mormon Church is capable of wielding, it makes me very sad to think that it does not use some of this power to further the cause of social justice with respect to the Negroes.

. . . The point that I'm getting at is that there is a great deal of evidence in Mormondom that, as the Mormons have more and more experience with the Negroes, they become less and less satisfied with this Negro doctrine and more and more liberal in their attitude toward the Negroes. Now I've had some experience in this connection. My home is in Los Angeles where there are large numbers of Mormons and where the Mormons have had a good deal to do with the Negroes because there are large numbers of Mormons living in areas in common with Negroes and areas into which Negroes have been moving. Now I've seen this take place in any number of instances with people who[m] I could name to you, if it were appropriate to do so. People who are very conservative, just as conservative in their religious views and in their social practices in matters of this kind as anyone that you could find anywhere in the Mormon Church. And who resisted various kinds of social contacts with Negroes as Negroes moved into their area, Negro children went to school and so on but who eventually not only ceased resisting this sort of thing but as they became acquainted with Negro people, had some experience with them, learned something about them as human beings, it changed their attitudes from negative attitudes to really quite positive attitudes.

. . . So I believe already that the Mormon Church is on the threshold of a new era so to speak in which in all likelihood the Mormon position on the Negro will be somewhat different from what it has been in the past. I hope that this is the case. Large numbers of other Mormons hope that it's the case, even though there are some, of course, who would be quite sure that I am entirely wrong.

Voice [likely of Albert Fritz]: Thank you Dr. McMurrin. [Applause]

Hugh B. Brown on Civil Rights (October 1963)

HISTORICAL INTRODUCTION

Throughout the early 1960s, First Counselor Hugh B. Brown pushed for the First Presidency to issue a statement on civil rights and for expanded missionary work in Nigeria. He even proposed granting Mormonism's "lesser [Aaronic] priesthood" to black male converts.[22]

The civil rights movement had not left Utah untouched, even though it moved at an uneven pace. In 1959, Representative Adam Duncan had managed to shepherd a public accommodations bill, House Bill 16, through the House of Representatives that would illegalize racial discrimination in hotels and restaurants; indeed, the bill received little resistance when aired for discussion at the Governor's Board Room at the Capitol.[23] But as state Senator Sherman P. Lloyd told Duncan, "the majority and minority leaders don't want it on the floor."[24] The bill faded away in committee. The *Deseret News* insisted that "the Negro race is certainly treated no worse in Utah than elsewhere, and most whites and Negroes would mutually agree that treatment here is generally much better."[25] But John F. Kennedy's 1963 civil rights package received cool responses from three out of four representatives in Utah, excepting only Representative Laurence J. Burton. Representative Sherman P. Lloyd, then Stephen Holbrook's boss, refused to support legislation enforcing "access to public accommodations" as it would "constitute a blow to the rights of the states and individuals, with consequences more severe than the hoped-for remedy."[26]

President David O. McKay was equally suspicious of the civil rights movement. Meanwhile, legislation had generally been defanged through political compromise or tabled altogether. Days before the October 1963 general conference, Stephen Holbrook contacted McMurrin, then the U.S. Commissioner of Education, to notify him that the NAACP would be marching on Temple Square. McMurrin urged discretion: "I was entirely sympathetic to the purposes of such a demonstration," McMurrin recalled, but he was "quite sure that such an affair would be counterproductive." McMurrin encouraged Holbrook to arrange a meeting with Church leaders before any protests commenced. Presidents N. Eldon Tanner and Hugh B. Brown met with leaders of the NAACP, who urged Tanner to give voice to the Church's views on civil rights. McMurrin kept the proposed demonstration confidential, as he "felt the Church should take a position on civil rights for minorities and that it should so freely and not under any kind of duress such as would be the case under the threat of a demonstration." When McMurrin attended the NAACP meeting on Friday evening, he "urged that it [the demonstration] be delayed until the end of the Sunday morning session of Conference." McMurrin also believed that the NAACP did not mention

22. Gregory A. Prince, "David O. McKay and Blacks: Building the Foundation for the 1978 Revelation," 148.

23. "Utah Civil Rights Bill Draws No Opposition," *Deseret News*, February 6, 1959, A9; "Civil Rights Bill Passes Utah House," *Deseret News*, March 5, 1959, A1.

24. Linda Sillitoe, *Friendly Fire: The ACLU in Utah*, 22.

25. "Mormons and Civil Rights," *Deseret News*, April 15, 1959, A22.

26. "Utah Congressmen Give Views on New Civil Rights Legislation," *Deseret News*, June 24, 1963, A4.

the possibility of a demonstration to Brown and Tanner, though he acknowledged that he "may be in error on this."[27] The NAACP voted to "g[i]ve the Church enough notice"; but as Fritz told the *Deseret News*, the vote was a close one.[28] That the NAACP was publicly discussing the proposed march makes it almost certain that the Church was aware of its happening.

McKay tasked Brown with delivering the pro-civil rights message with the stipulation that he not attribute the statement to the First Presidency. Brown called Sterling McMurrin for assistance in crafting the statement; McMurrin gladly helped. Brown gave the comments below over the pulpit at the October 1963 general conference. They were met with a mixture of welcome, resistance, and annoyance. The *Deseret News* printed the full text of his remarks.[29] Within days, the University of Utah's student body leaders announced the establishment of a Civil Rights Commission, with Carmen Boyden, Giff Prince, and Mike Soulier as its members.[30]

After the address, other Church leaders backed up Brown's remarks, though with a segregationist touch. Blacks "should be free to choose any kind of employment," Apostle Joseph Fielding Smith told the press two years later, "to go into any kind of business in any field they may choose and to make their lives happy, as it is possible without interference from white men, labor unions, or from any other source." The Church, Smith asserted, would happily stand "in their defense in these privileges."[31]

CITATION

Hugh B. Brown, in *Conference Report of the Church of Jesus Christ of Latter-day Saints,* October 1963, 91.

DOCUMENT EXCERPT

During recent months, both in Salt Lake City and across the nation, considerable interest has been expressed in the position of The Church of Jesus Christ of Latter-day Saints on the matter of civil rights. We would like it to be known that there is in this Church no doctrine, belief, or practice that is intended to deny the enjoyment of full civil rights by any person regardless of race, color, or creed.

We say again, as we have said many times before, that we believe that all men are the children of the same God and that it is a moral evil for any person or group of persons to deny any human being the rights to gainful employment, to full edu-

---

27. Sterling M. McMurrin, "A Note on the 1963 Civil Rights Statement," 61.

28. "Utah Negroes Put Off Civil Rights Marching," *Milwaukee Journal,* October 5, 1963, 4.

29. "Pres. Brown Explains Vital Doctrine," *Deseret News,* October 7, 1963, A1, A5.

30. "Council Issues Declaration on Civil Rights," *[University of] Utah Daily Chronicle,* October 8, 1963, 1. Mike Soulier won "Greek of the Year" award the following spring. See "2 Greeks of the Year Get U. Awards," *Salt Lake Tribune,* May 9, 1964, 30.

31. "Mormon Church Backs Equality for Negroes," *Victoria Advocate,* May 3, 1965, 8.

cational opportunity, and to every privilege of citizenship, just as it is a moral evil to deny him the right to worship according to the dictates of his own conscience.

We have consistently and persistently upheld the Constitution of the United States, and as far as we are concerned this means upholding the constitutional rights of every citizen of the United States.

We call upon all men everywhere, both within and outside the Church, to commit themselves to the establishment of full civil equality for all of God's children. Anything less than this defeats our high ideal of the brotherhood of man.

Joseph Johnson Forms "Mormon" Congregations in Ghana (1964)

HISTORICAL INTRODUCTION

The Mormon community in Ghana lacked official patronage for over fifteen years. Dr. Raphael Abraham Mensah, Joseph Johnson, and Clement Osekre labored to uphold Mormonism with limited materials, guidance, or organization. While the inspiration for the Mormon movement in Ghana was overwhelmingly American—the Book of Mormon, Joseph Smith, and Mormon pamphlets—most of its governance had little oversight from the American Mormons who were still leery of moving too far, too fast with a people who would have to deal with the priesthood ban. By the end of the decade, the Mormon community was struggling to retain its membership; without the promise of "full membership rights," Mensah wrote, the work would be "unstable and lacking in integrity."[32]

Joseph B. Johnson had been "searching for spiritual peace" since he was a young man. When he met Mensah, he "read the testimony of the Prophet Joseph Smith" and "believe[d] it was a great message for the whole world." He, Mensah, Clement Osekre, and a "Prophetess" named Rebecca Mould commenced building a Mormon establishment in Ghana that would struggle—but endure—until American Mormons entered the country in the fall of 1978. "I couldn't help it," Johnson said: "I had to share the message."[33]

CITATION

Joseph Johnson, "History of the Church of Jesus Christ of Latter-day Saints in Ghana," LDS Church History Library.

DOCUMENT EXCERPT

In the early part of February 1964, one Dr. A.F. Mensah, a friend of mine, introduced me to the doctrines of the Church of Jesus Christ of Latter-day Saints.[34]

---

32. Abraham Mensah, Letter to First Presidency, October 21, 1970, Ghana and Nigeria Files, LDS Church History Library.

33. E. Dale LeBaron, "Steadfast Gospel Pioneer," *Ensign,* December 1999, 45.

34. Dr. Raphael Abraham Frank Mensah was running a private school based on the teachings of Mormonism. By 1968, running the Mormon school had become a full-time occupation.

Dr. Mensah had earlier known about the church through a non-Mormon friend in Ireland who kept his tracts or literature of the church.[35] . . . As soon as I got home I started to read the testimony of the Prophet Joseph and consequently I followed up with the pamphlet, "Which Church is Right"[36] and the Book of Mormon. . . . I thereafter started to receive wonderful revelations pertaining to the truthfulness of the Church of Jesus Christ of Latter-day Saints, mainly the fullness of the gospel of Jesus Christ and the Holy Priesthood of God. At that time, I was a member of the Catholic Church and believed then that it was the only true church on the earth. I did not believe then that there could be any other church on earth that could provide answers to the numerous questions that plagued my mind with spiritual and temporal satisfaction. A church that enables me to pursue the course of the straight and narrow path that leads to eternal life. May I share with you some early revelations I had about my calling into the Church. On early morning of March 1964, while I was about to get up to prepare for my daily chores, the Spirit of the Lord fell upon me and my spiritual insight enhanced. I saw the heavens opened and was blessed to see numerous angels with trumpets singing songs of praise to God, our Heavenly Father. In the course of this adoration, I joined in and heard my name called out thrice. I heard a voice from heaven speaking to me saying, "Johnson, if you will take up my word as I will command to your people, I will bless you and bless your land." Trembling with fears, I replied in tears saying, "Lord by thy own help I will do whatsoever Thou would command me." From that day onwards, the Spirit of the Lord constrained me to propagate the Restored Gospel to my people. . . . We met no matter what the weather. We were singing the songs of Zion, using the LDS books and striving to obey all commandments of our Heavenly Father and also learning to emulate the shining examples of the church in America, especially the early pioneers of the Church. . . .

Ezra Taft Benson Attacks the Civil Rights Movement (1967)

HISTORICAL INTRODUCTION

On September 29, 1967, Elder Ezra Taft Benson, Dwight D. Eisenhower's former Secretary of Agriculture and a Mormon apostle, stood in general conference

---

By 1970, Mensah was referring to himself as the "acting president of the Ghana Mission of the Church of Jesus Christ of Latter-day Saints." Mensah, Letter to First Presidency, October 21, 1970, Ghana and Nigeria Files.

35. Mensah had acquired Church literature from Lilian Emile Clark, a Sufi living in St. Agnes, Cornwall, England. Clark was a disciple of Sufi mystic Inayat Khan. In 1914, Khan formed The Sufi Order in the West based in London. In 1923, this organization was renamed "The International Sufi Movement." Khan's movement eschewed the written word as authoritative: "There is one book," he declared, "the sacred manuscript of nature, the only Scripture that can enlighten the reader." When Clark met two sister missionaries, she "received a visitation of a spirit who named himself Moroni son of Mormon" who gave her "prophecies relating the success of their mission and one or two personal prophecies which related to their individual futures." Clark never joined the Mormons, Lilian Clark, Letter, September 25, 1979, Edwin Cannon Papers, Box 1, fd. 2.

36. Mark E. Petersen, *Which Church Is Right?*.

and described the ongoing civil rights movement that Communists were using to overthrow the U.S. government. Tracing Communist racial agitation as far back as 1928, he maintained that racial agitation was but one more trick in the Communist playbook.[37] Riots raging in Detroit, Newark, Washington, D.C., Chicago, and Los Angeles seemed to confirm his suspicion that Communists were planning a black "guerrilla" war on America. Benson cited "knowledgeable Negroes" as his authority.[38]

---

37. In 1928, the Sixth Comintern Congress of the Soviet Communist Party addressed the state of African Americans for the first time in Soviet history. Various black American and Soviet Communists weighed in, with ideas ranging from total dismissal of black American revolutionary activity to the pursuit of "a Negro Soviet republic." Harry Haywood, a black American Communist, offered a more moderate version. He attacked the state of race relations in the American South, suggesting that they lived in a state of "half-feudal bondage." Instead of promoting the establishment of an African Soviet satellite state in the United States, Haywood pushed to agitate for a "national-revolutionary movement" to establish an "independent Negro state." The "Negro Commission" of the Comintern embraced Haywood's position in its publication, "Theses on the Revolutionary Movement in the Colonies and the Semi-Colonies." It stated that the African American Communists "must put forward the slogan of the Right to Self-determination for Negroes." Yet the platform insisted that the plan be orchestrated based on class, rather than race: "Negro Communists must explain to the Negro workers and peasants that only their close union with the white proletariat and joint struggle with them against the American bourgeoisie can lead to their liberation from barbarous exploitation." Quoted in Theodore Draper, *American Communism and Soviet Russia*, 349. For the Soviet position, see Harry Haywood, *Black Communist in the Freedom Struggle: The Life of Harry Haywood*, 152.

38. Benson is likely referring to such African Americans pundits as George Schuyler, Julia Brown, and Lola Belle Holmes. George Schuyler was a widely read black journalist who had become disenchanted with Communism in the 1920s. By 1967, he was one of the most widely read black journalists in the country and a strident critic of Martin Luther King. He called Martin Luther King's 1963 March on Washington a Communist spectacle and dismissed street protests as "nothing but stored up animosity." When King was slated to address a Republican gathering that Schuyler was attending, he walked out, saying simply: "I didn't want to hear that stuff." Race problems, Schuyler argued, could only be solved through "moderation and through innumerable compromises rather than by the use of abrasive tactics that produce irritation and ill-will rather than understanding and co-operation." At the time of Benson's speech, Schuyler served as a regular speaker for the John Birch Society. Brown was an African American woman who claimed to have infiltrated the Communist Party of the United States for nearly ten years. She regularly lectured for the John Birch Society. Julia Brown had testified before the House for Un-American Activities Committee and was said to have identified nearly 125 Communists. While Brown did not believe Martin Luther King Jr. to be a Communist, she did believe that he was "aiding the Communist cause" and "is an enemy to the Negro." Brown acknowledged that there was a "legitimate need for the advancement of civil rights"; she opposed those she believed to be secretly promoting a Communist agenda under the guise of civil rights. In 1966, Brown published an autobiography entitled, *I Testify: My Years as an F.B.I. Undercover Agent*, which one paper called "spectacular, timely, and frightening." In 1978, she testified that if the United States established a holiday for Martin Luther King Jr., "we may as well take down the stars and stripes . . . and replace it with a red flag." Months before Benson's address, Lola Belle Holmes lectured on the subject at the J.A. Taylor Elementary School in Centerville, Utah. She claimed to have "carried out Moscow orders to gain control of the civil rights movement and to use it as the torch to light a fire of revolution in America." For Schuyler's activities, see "Negro Communist Voices Opposition to King," *Oregonian*, April 21, 1966; "King Adept, Dedicated, But Work Gained Little," *Omaha World Herald*, January 7, 1968; "'Civil Rights' Wrong Term, Says Negro," *Seattle Daily Times*, February 12,

The origins of the riots were complex, resulting from a confluence of factors: unemployment, social inequality, ineffective government, and revolutionary agitation. Contemporary observers, however, mostly attributed it to the vitriolic rhetoric disseminated by race leaders in the urban slums. H. Rap Brown, the newly elected chair of the Student Non-violent Coordinating Council (SNCC), had been effective at stoking the flames of riot; in spring 1967, Brown declared before a Detroit congregation that "if Motown [doesn't] come around, we are going to burn you down."[39] Another member of SNCC from Cincinnati told a congregation: "We already had our riot, and we're here to show you how it's done."[40] Later that year, Brown told a black gathering in Cambridge, Maryland: "It is time for Cambridge to explode, baby. Black folks built America. If America doesn't come around, we're going to burn America down, brother."[41]

In August 1967, Brown's threats found fruition when Detroit exploded in violence. Most mainstream observers acknowledged that the riots had been the product of "outside agitators" such as the West Central Organization and the Congress of Racial Equality: "They are men at war," veteran black reporter Louis Lomax wrote of the Detroit rioters, "revolutionaries bent on reducing the nation to ashes."[42] Lomax depicted in vivid detail havoc that professional agitators rained on "a Detroit engulfed in flames, hate, doubt, and racial suspicion. . . . By moonlight, dedicated revolutionaries continued their mission of bringing down the nation's fifth largest city, both physically and spiritually."[43] Lomax warned of total societal disarray: "The bad people are now organized. They are subsidized, trained, and ready."[44] Governor George Romney was "convinced that that [they] couldn't have

---

1966. The best scholarly biography of him is Oscar R. Williams, *George S. Schuyler: Portrait of a Black Conservative.* For Brown's lecture series, see "Ex-FBI Agent Says Reds Using Rights Movement," *Morning Star* (Rockford, Ill.), May 19, 1965, 3; "Amazing Story Told by Undercover Agent," *Wichita Eagle,* January 14, 1968, 32; and Julia Brown in *Hidden Agenda: Anarchy: U.S.A. in the Name of Civil Rights,* G. Edward Griffin. See also "80 Here Identified as Reds at Probe," *[Cleveland] Plain Dealer,* June 5, 1962, 19; "Counterspy Says Reds Infiltrating Churches," *Dallas Morning News,* December 12, 1961, 5; "'Phony' Civil Rights Leader Aiding Reds," *Dallas Morning News,* November 12, 1965, 9; and "Reds Using U.S. Negro," *Omaha World Herald,* April 12, 1965, 2. For a scholarly treatment of Brown's wide-reaching influence, see Veronica Wilson, "To Tell All My People": Race, Representation, and John Birch Society Activist Julia Brown," in Kathleen Blee, ed., *Women of the Right: Comparisons and Interplay Across Borders,* 242–53. On Holmes's visit to Utah, see "Do Communists Run Civil Rights Force," *Davis County Clipper,* (Bountiful, UT) February 24, 1967, 10.

39. Suzanne E. Smith, *Dancing in the Street: Motown and the Cultural Politics of Detroit ,*191.

40. Joshua Bloom and Waldo Martin, *Black against Empire: The History and Politics of the Black Panther Party,* 88.

41. Robert Norrell, *The House I Live In: Race in the American Century ,*254.

42. Louis Lomax, "Outside Revolutionaries Blamed for Detroit Riots," *Dallas Morning News,* August 6, 1967, 1.

43. Louis Lomax, "Looters Helped Agitators," *Dallas Morning News,* August 7, 1967.

44. Louis Lomax, "Philosophy of Black Power Poses Threat of Revolution," *Dallas Morning News,* August 10, 1967, 1.

had what [they] had without some professional involvement," though he was always quick to insist that the agitators exploited rather than created the chaos.[45]

But Benson went further; he saw the riots as a product of global Communism. Heightening fears were reports (unfounded, as it turned out) from the Salt Lake City police that "four car loads of Negroes armed with machine guns and bombs were . . . coming to Salt Lake City for the purpose of inciting a riot and particularly to destroy property on the Temple Block." Frightened, McKay told Hugh B. Brown that "everything possible must be done to guard that sacred spot."[46] Benson approached McKay about making his case in general conference, assuring him that "he would talk on this subject from the viewpoint of bringing peace in our country instead of uprisings of the Negroes in riots, etc."[47] Rattled by the Temple Square scare, McKay approved, and Benson gave his alarmist speech. In response, Vene Dee Turnbull of Carbon County warned that "'racial revolution' has replaced 'workers revolution' as the core of the communist plot to conquer the United States." But, like Benson, she was quick to exonerate the rioting blacks from the charge of Communism: "It means that the Communist scientist has observed that Negro racialism can be ignited into revolt and that such a Negro revolt can produce anarchy as a step to a Communist dictatorship here in America."[48] Haunted by the riots nationwide, the Utah National Guard began highly publicized race riot training exercises.[49]

In 1969, Benson repeated his concerns about a civil rights movement-Communist conspiracy in another speech, "Trade and Treason," authorizing it to be used as a foreword for Wes Andrews's and Clyde Dalton's 1969 volume, *The Black Hammer*. Andrews and Dalton believed government welfare programs were designed "for no other purpose than to debase the Negro spirit, further destroy his already depressed sense of self-reliance, and to accent the Negro's need for complete subservience to the Great White Fathers in Washington." As for civil rights leaders, they were a "breed of vermin that find the brew of America's greatness unpalatable to their demonic appetites."[50] Benson also warned that the Saints "must *not* place the blame upon Negroes" (emphasis his) or participate in "anti-Negro vigilante action" as it "fits perfectly into the Communist plan." The Communists, Benson warned, "are just as anxious to spearhead such anti-Negro actions as they are to organize demonstrations that are calculated to irritate white people."[51] The following text is derived from the September 1967 speech.

---

45. "Aftermath of Detroit Riot," *Morning Star* (Rockford, Ill.), July 30, 1967.

46. Prince and Wright, *David O. McKay and the Rise of Modern Mormonism*, 72.

47. Ibid.

48. "Reds and Riots," letter to the editor, *Deseret News*, October 2, 1967, A12.

49. "Riot Control Tactics Mastered by Guard," *Deseret News*, October 5, 1967, B1.

50. Wes Andrews and Clyde Dalton, *The Black Hammer: A Study of Black Power, Red Influence, and White Alternatives*, 82.

51. Ezra Taft Benson, *Conference Report* (October 1967): 38.

CITATION

Ezra Taft Benson, in *Conference Report of the Church of Jesus Christ of Latter-day Saints,* October 1967, 34–38.

DOCUMENT EXCERPT

There is nothing wrong with civil rights; it is what's being done in the name of civil rights that is alarming.[52] There is no doubt that the so-called civil rights movement as it exists today is used as a Communist program for revolution in America just as agrarian reform was used by the Communists to take over China and Cuba. . . .[53]

. . . First, create hatred. Use any means to agitate blacks into hating whites and whites into hating blacks.[54] Work both sides of the split.[55] Play up and exaggerate real

---

52. Benson's comments closely resemble John Birch Society advertisements. In the October 31, 1965, edition of the *Palm Beach Post,* a local chapter of the society published an advertisement that began: "What's wrong with civil rights? The answer is, nothing!" But, it continued, "there is a great deal wrong with what is being done in the name of civil rights." "What's Wrong with Civil Rights?" *Palm Beach Post,* October 31, 1965, A10.

53. Martin Luther King attracted a broad coalition of civil rights activists, including members of the Communist Party of the United States. King himself largely disavowed Communism, considering it to be "basically evil" even if he felt that "capitalism had outlived its usefulness." Bayard Rustin, his personal secretary, recognized the importance of Communist Party's role in teaching him how to manage logistics and planning: "I learned many of the most important things . . . about organization and detail and writing clearly and the like from my experience as a Communist." While Rustin distanced himself from Communism, another King aide, Hunter Pitts O'Dell, continued his membership well after joining King's organization. When the House Committee on Un-American Activities questioned him about his party affiliation, he responded by asking what the committee "mean[s] by 'the Communist Party'"? After the FBI leaked information revealing O'Dell's membership in the party in 1961, King was forced to remove him from his organization. Jack O'Dell, *Climbin' Jacob's Ladder: The Black Freedom Movement Writings of Jack O'Dell,* 29. See also *Communist Training Operations,* House, 86th Congress, July 21 and 22, 1959; "King Staff Member Called Red Resigns," *Omaha World Herald,* December 2, 1962, 18; Matt Nichter, "The Old Left and the Rise of the Civil Rights Movement," 106; and "Matter of Fact," *Advocate* (Baton Rouge, Lous.), April 16, 1964, 10.

54. In addition to the incendiary remarks from figures such as Brown, agitation came from a variety of community and faith organizations inspired by famed community organizer, Saul Alinsky, such as Reverend Richard Venus's West Central Organization, Reverend Albert Cleage's Black Christian Nationalist Movement, and Father Clement Kern's Detroit-area parish. The West Central Organization was "the first citywide attempt at community organization that was rooted in the concept of self-determination, using the Alinsky model." WCO President, Reverend Harold Featherstone, described his organization as "sort of a Saul Alinsky thing." "Aftermath of Detroit Riot," *Morning Star* (Rockford, Ill.), July 30, 1967, 7; Angela Dillard, *Faith in the City: Preaching Radical Social Change in Detroit,* 222–23, and Todd Shaw, *Now Is the Time! Detroit Black Politics and Grassroots Activism,* 53–55.

55. While there is no evidence of Soviet "double-dealing," the Senate sub-committee on urban violence found that Panther Publications of Boulder, Colorado, sold guerrilla warfare manuals to the Black Panthers and to far right groups such as the Minutemen—organized by Robert de Pugh, a former member of the John Birch Society. By 1968, de Pugh was indicted on federal conspiracy charges for the robbery of a store in Missouri. In fall 1969, FBI agents tracked him to

grievances. If necessary, don't hesitate to manufacture false stories and rumors about injustices and brutality.[56] Create martyrs for both sides.[57] Play upon mass emotions until they smolder with resentment and hatred.

Second, trigger violence. Put the emotional masses into the streets in the form of large mobs, the larger the better. It makes no difference if the mob is told to demonstrate "peacefully" so long as it is brought into direct confrontation with the antagonist. . . .

Third, overthrow established government. . . . Provide leadership and training for guerilla warfare. Institute discipline and terrorism to insure at least passive support from the larger, inactive segment of the population. Train and battle-harden leadership through sporadic riots and battles with police. Finally, at the appointed time, launch an all-out simultaneous offensive in every major city. . . .[58]

---

a small Nevada town. "The All-American Minutemen," *Grito Del Norte* (Las Vegas, Nev.), August 10, 1969, 9; "Minutemen Leader Is Arrested Here," *San Diego Union,* November 11, 1961, 6; "Manuals on Guerrilla Warfare Sold, Senators Told," *Dallas Morning News*, July 1, 1969, 6; "A Most Unusual Publisher," *Palm Beach Post*, April 16, 1972, G2. For background on de Pugh's organization, see Brian Champion, "The Minutemen," *Encyclopedia of Murder and Violent Crime*, edited by Eric Hickey, 314–15.

56. Both parties accused the other of rumor-mongering. In the Supreme Court case, *United States v. Guest,* the white defendants had "caus[ed] the arrest of Negroes by means of false reports" that they had "committed criminal acts." Following the disappearance of three civil rights workers, local politicians initially accused civil rights activists of orchestrating a spectacle. Louisiana State Senator and committed segregationist, Harold Montgomery, crafted a resolution to prohibit "false charges of violence" and the "misrepresentation of facts concerning civil rights movements." These initial accusations proved tragically incorrect when the volunteers' bodies were discovered in August. Some locals had believed that the Communist Party might have killed the workers and then blamed it on segregationists: "It is by no means the first case of such disposition by Communists of their dupes to insure their silence." "Miss. Lawmaker Says Disappearance May Be Hoax," *Springfield [Mass.] Union,* June 26, 1964, 8; "Mississippi Solon Cites Hoax Theory," *Augusta [Maine] Chronicle,* July 23, 1964, 10; "Code of Ethics Bill Sent to Governor for Signature," *Advocate,* July 8, 1964, 10; and Yasuhrio Katagiri, *The Mississippi State Sovereignty Commission: Civil Rights and States' Rights,* 163–67. See also *United States v. Guest,* 383 U.S. 745, 86 S. Ct. 1170, 16 L. Ed. 2d 239 (1966).

57. Political organizing must communicate ideas "concretely," Alinsky argued in 1972. "It is the difference between being informed of the death of a quarter of a million people—which becomes a statistic—or the death of one or two close friends or loved ones or members of one's family." Any given cause must be couched in terms of the specific: "*this* immorality," "*this* slum landlord . . . where *these* people suffer." Saul Alinsky, *Rules for Radicals: A Pragmatic Primer for Realistic Radicals,* 96–97; emphasis his.

58. Southern papers regularly reported that King's ultimate goal was "installing a Communist government in Washington . . . under another party name." "King's Aid to the Enemy," *Augusta Chronicle,* July 5, 1965, 6. See also "The Mails Are Vicious," *Boston Herald,* September 13, 1962, 28; "Matter of Fact," *Advocate* (Baton Rouge, Lous.), April 16, 1964, 10. Benson had earlier repeated these warnings in *The Red Carpet,* Radical black power advocates were giving voice to Benson's fears. When Black Panthers founder Huey Newton (1942–89) was imprisoned for manslaughter, co-founder Stokely Carmichael (1941–98) told him that he would only escape through "armed rebellion, culminating in a race war." See Paul J. Magnarella, "The Black Panther

. . . The planning, direction, and leadership come from the Communists, and most of those are white men who fully intend to destroy America by spilling Negro blood, rather than their own.[59]

First Presidency Policy Statement (December 1969)

HISTORICAL INTRODUCTION

In the wake of the tumult surrounding the civil rights movement in the United States, President David O. McKay saw the need to make a definitive stand (1) declaring the Church's support for equality under the law, and (2) making the case for ecclesiastical sovereignty, even in matters of race. McKay had always felt uneasy about the civil rights movement; the spectacle of mobs in the streets, however peaceful, frightened the older generation of Mormons attuned to the lurking possibility of mob action. McKay was profoundly skeptical about men like Martin Luther King, especially since King had made a conspicuous shift toward socialism in 1967–68. But McKay also knew that the time had long since passed for the Church to remain silent. Eschewing the rhetoric of Benson, Church leadership came down firmly in favor of extending civil rights to all American citizens.

However, Church leaders believed that the priesthood restriction was a different matter. The topic had divided Church leadership deeply, with Ezra Taft Benson and Harold B. Lee drawing a particularly hard line against it. First Counselor Hugh B. Brown and Second Counselor N. Eldon Tanner felt deeply conflicted over the issue. In the late 1960s, Apostle Alvin R. Dyer wrote that Brown had "tried twice to get President McKay to withdraw the withholding of the Priesthood from the Negro, but President McKay refused to move on it." As McKay's health deteriorated, Apostle Harold B. Lee penned a statement declaring the priesthood ban to be a doctrine of the Church "until God reveals his will in this matter." Upon Brown's insistence, the document also con-

---

Party's Confrontation with Ethnicity, Race, and Class," 58. Eldridge Cleaver (1935–98), the Black Panthers' Propaganda Minister, said that if black demands were not met, "war will come . . . not just a race war, which in itself would destroy this country, but a guerrilla resistance movement that will amount to a second Civil War, with thousands of John Browns fighting on the sides of the blacks, plunging America into the depths of its most desperate nightmare on the way to realizing the American dream." Eldridge Cleaver, "Playboy Interview," December 1968, 145.

59. The fear of being manipulated by the white establishment runs deep within African American literature and history. In 1933, former black Communist George Padamore accused the American Communist Party of neglecting the black American community by ignoring the relevant issues: "All this talk about 'championing' and defending the Negro race is a bluff." "An Open Letter to Earl Browder," *The Crisis,* October 1935, 302. Ralph Ellison warned in *Invisible Man* of the dangers of exploitation that blacks faced in associating themselves with any political organization: "All political parties are basically concerned with power and with maintaining power, not with humanitarian issues in the raw and abstract sense." They are not "concerned basically with Negro freedom, but with effecting their own ends." Ralph Ellison, "An Extravagance of Laughter," 542.

tained several passages endorsing civil rights legislation. By the time it was ready to sign, McKay had grown too weak, leaving only Brown and Tanner as signatories.[60]

Notably, the statement made no effort to offer scriptural justification for the ban beyond the existence of tradition. Addressed to virtually every priesthood leader ranging from General Authorities to bishops, this letter took on the aura of authority, setting the tone for a new era in official rationalization—in essence, "we don't know." McMurrin considered the text to be "historic": never before had an "official statement on this matter . . . set forth the policy of the Church so clearly and unambiguously."[61]

The excerpts below quote the letter's most notable passages. In addition to the *Deseret News*, a facsimile of the statement can be found in Douglas Monty Trank's dissertation on Mormon rhetoric about blacks.[62] Additionally, the statement was printed in the February 1970 edition of *Priesthood Bulletin*, the bimonthly publication produced by the Church to disseminate recent changes in policy and doctrine.[63]

CITATION

"Policy Statement of Presidency," December 15, 1969, *Church News* (tabloid-sized weekly section of *Deseret News*), January 10, 1970, 12; left justifcation added.

DOCUMENT EXCERPT

Dear Brethren:

. . . We believe the Negro, as well as those of other races, should have full Constitutional privileges as a member of society, and we hope that members of the Church everywhere will do their part as citizens to see that these rights are held inviolate. Each citizen must have equal opportunities and protection under the law with reference to civil rights.

However, matters of faith, conscience, and theology are not within the purview of the civil law. The first amendment to the Constitution specifically provides that "Congress shall make no law respecting an establishment of religion, or prohibiting the free exercise thereof."

. . . From the beginning of this dispensation, Joseph Smith and all succeeding presidents of the Church have taught that Negroes, while spirit children of a common father, and the progeny of our earthly parents Adam and Eve, were not yet to receive the priesthood, for reasons which we believe are known to God, but which He has not made fully known to man. . .

---

60. Prince and Wright, *David O. McKay*, 100–01.

61. Trank, "A Rhetorical Analysis," 325.

62. Ibid., 315–17.

63. Reed N. Wilcox, Review of *It's You and Me, Lord!* and *Mormonism's Negro Policy: Social and Historical Origins* in *BYU Studies* 11, no. 2 (Winter 1971): 212. For a brief description of the *Priesthood Bulletin*, see Ronald Walker, David J. Whittaker, James B. Allen, *Mormon History*, 219.

. . . Meanwhile, we must strive harder to emulate His Son, the Lord Jesus Christ, whose new commandment it was that we should love one another. In developing that love and concern for one another, while awaiting revelations to come, let us hope that with respect to these religious differences, we may gain reinforcement for understanding and appreciation for such differences. They challenge our common similarities, as children of one Father, to enlarge the out-reachings of our divine souls.

Faithfully your brethren,

THE FIRST PRESIDENCY
By Hugh B. Brown
N. Eldon Tanner

Chapter 13

Reconciliation, then Truth, 1971-2013

Introduction

Still recovering from the struggles of the civil rights era, Church leaders recognized that the Church could no longer allow outsiders to define their positions for them. The unevenness of Church leaders' response to the civil rights movement had created a vacuum in which race had become the all-consuming cloud that hung over the Saints: in news media, at football games, and at general conferences.

The Mormon community responded in a diversity of ways. Black Mormons such as Alan Cherry and Wynetta Martin opened up about their conversion experiences. Meanwhile, blacks in West African "Mormon" congregations continued to toil alone, waiting for official representation. Heber Wolsey, a spokesperson for BYU, launched a public relations offensive to redefine Joseph Smith as a civil rights advocate and to dismiss past explanations employed to justify the restriction.

When Church leaders released the statement in 1978 declaring they had received a revelation dictating a change in the policy, Mormons had to start the long, upward haul of reaching out to a community so long excluded from its membership. A missionary effort began in earnest in Ghana and Nigeria, and the South African Saints began the difficult process of racial integration in the shadow of apartheid. And Mormon intellectuals began to discuss the possibilities of how the Church might approach the issuing of an official denunciation of past doctrines. Over the past decade, the Church has seen the fruits of these efforts. Membership grows at a rapid pace in West Africa; and in 2013, the Church issued a statement on a statement—a statement officially approved by the First Presidency—officially renouncing the doctrines used to justify the restriction.

With the old narrative repudiated, modern Mormons now must come to grips with what the history of racism—and prophetic authority—in their faith means to them. The reconciliation process extends far beyond brokering goodwill between groups; it also includes individual searching and probing, hoping to come to grips with a story that has hung over the Mormons for generations. In the Mormon community, the story is an unparalleled account of an American faith wrestling with a global problem, striving to live up to its global visions.

A Black Mormon's Conversion Story (1971)

HISTORICAL INTRODUCTION

As white Saints worked to shake off the embarrassments and ambiguities of the 1960s, black Saints were also assuming a more public presence in the discourse about blacks and Mormonism. In 1970, Alan Cherry, a recent convert, published his experiences in Hartman Rector Jr.'s two-volume anthology, *No More Strangers.* The following year, Darius Gray, Eugene Orr, and Ruffin Bridgeforth approached Church leaders about how best to retain black members. Wynetta Mills Martin of San Diego published her conversion experience, *Black Mormon Tells Her Story.* Diverse and rich, these public steps demonstrate the various ways in which black Mormon converts of the 1960s experienced this overwhelmingly white religion.

Following high school, Alan Cherry confessed that he had experienced a "terrible tailspin" of sin.[1] He joined the military and began a serious study in search of true religion. One day, Cherry slackened off on his duties to study and was court-martialed for defying orders to return to his labors. Finding himself confined with a Mormon serviceman guilty of drunkenness, the two struck up a conversation, and Cherry's curiosity was piqued. He looked in the library at the religious literature and found a pamphlet by Mark E. Petersen entitled: "Which Church Is Right." The pamphlet seemed to light "a forest fire within me," Cherry wrote. When the pamphlet encouraged him to ask God if Joseph Smith was in fact a prophet of God, "it was just like a gulp in my throat. Boy!" he thought. "It says it right here–just ask God." He was pleased with the prospects: everyone had been telling him about "ideas of truth, but they could never tell you the street address of heaven."[2]

It was not long before Cherry's Mormon friend from the "confinement facility" gave Cherry a *Reader's Digest* article titled "The Spectacular Rise of the Mormon Church." It contained mention of the priesthood restriction. In an excerpt from an article-length version of his memoirs, Cherry describes how he came to grips with being a part of a religion that excluded him from full participation in its ordinances. As he concluded in 1970: "The important thing in God's Kingdom will not be who leads us there, but simply who gets there."[3]

After his baptism on May 9, 1968, he enrolled at Brigham Young University where, as BYU student and vice-president of academics Reed N. Wilcox observed: "His white brothers . . . have showered him with almost apologetic kindness and

---

1. Molly Farmer, "Having Priesthood 'Is My Better Means to Serve,'" [Part 1], *Deseret News*, May 21, 2008, http://www.deseretnews.com/article/705383516/Having-priesthood-is-my-better-means-to-serve.html?pg=all (accessed June 2, 2013).

2. Molly Farmer, "Having Priesthood 'Is My Better Means to Serve," [Part 2], *Deseret News*, May 22, 2008, http://www.deseretnews.com/article/700227876/Having-priesthood-is-my-better-means-to-serve.html?pg=all (accessed May 19, 2014).

3. Alan Cherry, *It's You and Me, Lord!*, 38.

attention in an effort to somehow demonstrate to everyone—and themselves— that they are not racists, that they really like Al Cherry, black Al Cherry."[4] In 1985 Cherry drew a harder line, declaring that the restriction "turned me and perhaps many black Latter-day Saints into shadowy figures who in effect were asked to languish in the shadows to minimize discomfort of other Latter-day Saints. . . . It was an inequality born out of ignorance and mismanagement rather than deliberate disenfranchisement."[5]

CITATION

Alan Cherry, "A Negro's Life Changed," in Hartman Rector Jr. and Connie Rector, *No More Strangers*, 2 vols. Salt Lake City: Deseret Book, 1971, 1:98. Complete: 90–99.

DOCUMENT EXCERPT

". . . I can feel it with my heart more than I can reason it out with my mind. So, if God has spoken to me, who am I to challenge his word just because it may appear as error to other men? I know that most men exist on this earth by the improper use of pride, power, prominence, and position. . . .

But I knew that I had stepped away from the world and sought God, and that he had spoken to me through the Spirit. So how could I dare come back and say to him: "This doctrine is wrong. I won't join your church because I can't have a particular position to which I aspire." Somehow it didn't seem that this attitude would be consistent with the doctrine Christ taught–that he who would be greatest in the kingdom of heaven should be the servant of all. If the greatest man, the Lord himself, would stoop down and wash his disciples' feet and show through serving what true greatness was–the power of love–then I did not need position or prominence or pride in order to serve.

Lester Bush Questions the Origins of the Priesthood Ban (Spring 1973)

HISTORICAL INTRODUCTION

It is rare that works of historical scholarship effect social change. But in 1973, Lester E. Bush, an army medical doctor based in Saigon, found himself entirely dissatisfied with the state of Mormonism's racial discourse. Deciding that a rigorous investigation into the origins of Mormon racism was in order, Bush produced a full scholarly study on the topic.

However, Bush was not the first historian to comment on the origins of the priesthood restriction. In 1967, a young sociology graduate student at Washington State University-Pullman, Armand L. Mauss, observed that "the

---

4. Reed Wilcox, Review of *It's You and Me, Lord!* in *BYU Studies* 11, no. 2 (Spring 1971): 210-11.

5. Jessie L. Embry, *Black Saints in a White Church; Contemporary African-American Mormons*, 52.

chief deterrent to a divine mandate for change is not to be found in any inadequacy among Negroes, but rather in the uneasiness of the Mormon whites, with our heritage of racial folklore."[6] In 1969, Stephen Taggart, a Ph.D. candidate in sociology at Cornell University, wrote a long paper on the topic. The paper included a letter from Sterling M. McMurrin in which he quoted McKay's 1954 comments denying the existence of a black "curse."

Taggart's work was a passionate project for the young man, then stricken with lymphoma. By the summer of 1969, Taggart had become became fully aware that he would die before his work would ever see print. His mother, Pamela, became intimately acquainted with the work; she reported that "during the last months of his life," a driving goal for him was to have "the paper polished and completed." In the foreword for the book, Pamela "hope[d] that this work will be received in the spirit in which it was written—as a constructive criticism of a policy of the Church which seemed to Steve to be hampering implementation of the Church's basic goals." Taggart wrote the work, Pamela recorded, "because he cared for the people of the Church and was committed to the Church's humanitarian and moral ideals."[7] Taggart concluded that "the weight of the evidence suggests that God didn't curse the black man—his white children did."[8] On August 1, 1969, Taggart died, a passing Sterling McMurrin considered to be "a tragic loss to the Church." His essay, Curran declared, was "an excellent piece, a work of honest and competent scholarship."[9] Pamela ensured that the work made its way from an early essay to the academic press.

A few weeks after Taggart's death, President Hugh B. Brown was reading a copy of the work. Brown handed the book to David O. McKay's son, Lawrence McKay, and asked him to confirm McMurrin's claims with his father. When Lawrence took his brother, Llewelyn McKay, to approach the President, Apostle Alvin W. Dyer happened to be standing by. The McKay brothers asked him to stay. As a devoted believer in the scriptural basis for the restriction, Dyer blanched at the implications of the Taggart article. Dyer offered to do a thorough review of the book. He took it home and returned the following week, ready with a top-to-bottom critique. Dyer attacked Taggart's work as "one of the most vicious, untrue articles that has ever been written about the Church."[10] When a member of the BYU student government reviewed the book for *BYU Studies*, he

---

6. Armand L. Mauss, "Mormonism and the Negro: Faith, Folklore, and Civil Rights," in Lester E. Bush, Jr. and Armand L. Mauss, *Neither White Nor Black: Mormon Scholars Confront the Race Issue in a Universal Church* , 23.

7. Pamela Taggart, Foreword to Stephen G. Taggart, *Mormonism's Negro Policy: Social and Historical Origins*, XII-XIII.

8. Stephen Taggart, *Mormonism's Negro Policy: Social and Historical Origins*, 76.

9. Sterling M. McMurrin, Letter to Dr. Llewelyn R. McKay, January 16, 1970, facsimile in Douglas Monty Trank, "A Rhetorical Analysis of the Rhetoric Emerging from the Mormon-Black Controversy," 311, 322.

10. Gregory A. Prince and Wm. Robert Wright, *David O. McKay and the Rise of Modern Mormonism*, 99.

commended its readability but rejected its core thesis by pointing readers to the "Policy Statement of Presidency" published in early 1970.[11] In November 1970 Caleb Shreeve considered the entire discussion subversive: "the dialogue" about race "is nothing but a cover-up," Shreeve informed the First Presidency, intended only to conceal the left wing's agenda to compel "the LDS Church to conform to what they want, or be destroyed, along with other 'establishment institutions.'"[12]

Even after the young man's passing, his work, Gregory Prince has observed, "initiate[ed] an unprecedented storm of controversy" that lasted until McKay's death in January 1970. Bush's piece struck a different chord entirely; times had changed, even in a few short years. In the spring 1973 edition of *Dialogue*, he documented that the restriction was in fact not the product of Joseph Smith but of Brigham Young. Bush had already dismissed Taggart's documentary analysis as unsatisfactory. Though Taggart placed the responsibility on the Saints (and Joseph Smith), Bush demonstrated that the evidence tying the restriction to Joseph Smith failed in the most important regards. For example, Taggart hypothesized that Joseph Smith used the Book of Abraham (1:27) about an Egyptian Pharoah "being of that lineage by which he could not have the right of Priesthood" to justify priesthood denial to blacks. Bush, however, pointed out that this speculation lacks any grounding in the documentary record. But Bush valued Taggart's work for raising "significant questions . . . which subsequent study should attempt to clarify."[13]

Given the longstanding efforts to connect Joseph Smith to the restriction dating back to the late 1870s, Bush's argument was something of an intellectual coup within Mormon intellectual circles. It reverberated not only throughout the Mormon scholarly community but also within the halls of Church headquarters in Salt Lake City. Marion D. Hanks noted that Bush's article "had had far more influence than the Brethren would ever acknowledge. . . . [I]t 'started to foment the pot.'"[14] In 1975 Sonia Johnson, then a Latter-day Saint housewife who had lived in West Africa, assessed the article as the "best discussion I've ever seen anywhere" on "the Negro question."[15]

CITATION

Lester E. Bush Jr., "Mormonism's Negro Doctrine: An Historical Overview," *Dialogue: A Journal of Mormon Thought* 8 (Spring 1973): 11, 26, 48–49.

---

11. Wilcox, Review of *It's You and Me, Lord!*, 211.

12. Caleb Shreeve, Letter to First Presidency, November 25, 1970, Hyrum Wheelwright Papers, Weber State University Special Collections.

13. Lester Bush, "A Commentary on Stephen G. Taggart's *Mormonism's Negro Policy: Social and Historical Origins*," 102.

14. Lester E. Bush, "Writing 'Mormonism's Negro Doctrine: An Historical Overview' (1973): Context and Reflections, 1998," *Journal of Mormon History* 25, no. 1 (Spring 1999): 266.

15. Sonia Johnson, Letter to Alvin and Ida Harris, December 9, 1975, Box 1, fd. 21, Johnson Papers.

DOCUMENT EXCERPT

There once was a time, albeit brief, when a "Negro problem" did not exist for the Church of Jesus Christ of Latter-day Saints. During those early months in New York and Ohio no mention was even made of Church attitudes towards blacks. The gospel was for "all nations, kindreds, tongues and peoples," and no exceptions were made. . . .

Though it is now popular among Mormons to argue that the basis for the priesthood denial to Negroes is unknown, no uncertainty was evident in the discourses of Brigham Young. From the initial remark in 1849 throughout his presidency, every known discussion of this subject by Young (or any other leading Mormon) invoked the connection with Cain as the justification for denying the priesthood to blacks. . . .

Mormon attitudes towards blacks have thus followed an unexpectedly complex evolutionary pattern. When first apparent, these beliefs were sustained by the widely accepted connection of the Negro with Ham and Cain, the acknowledged intellectual and social inferiority of the Negro, his black skin, and the strength of Brigham Young's testimony and/or opinion. With the unanticipated termination of the curse of slavery on Canaan, the death of Brigham Young, increased evidence of Negro capability, and the decline of general support for the traditional genealogy of the blacks, justification of Church policy shifted to the Pearl of Great Price and an interpretation derived from earlier beliefs, and the belief that the policy could be traced through all the presidents of the Church to the Prophet Joseph Smith. By the middle of the twentieth century, little evidence remained for the old concepts of racial inferiority; skin color had also lost its relevance, and the Pearl of Great Price alone was no longer considered a sufficient explanation. Supplementing and eventually surpassing these concepts was the idea that the blacks had somehow performed inadequately in the preexistence. Most recently all of these explanations have been superseded by the belief that, after all, there is no specific explanation for the priesthood policy. Significantly this progression has not weakened the belief that the policy is justified, for there remains the not inconsiderable evidence of over a century of decisions which have consistently denied the priesthood to blacks.

No one, I believe, who has talked with leaders of the contemporary Church can doubt that there is genuine concern over the "Negro doctrine." Nor can there be any question that they are completely committed to the belief that the policy of priesthood denial is divinely instituted and subject only to revelatory change. The not infrequent assumption of critics of Church policy that the demonstration of a convincing historical explanation for modern Church teachings would result in the abandonment of the Negro doctrine is both naive and reflective of a major misunderstanding of the claims of an inspired religion. Yet among the parameters of revelation, careful study has been identified as a conducive, if not necessary, preliminary step (D&C 9:7–8). A thorough study of the history of the Negro doctrine still has not been made. In particular, three fundamental questions have yet to be resolved:

First, do we really have any evidence that Joseph Smith initiated a policy of priesthood denial to Negroes?

Second, to what extent did nineteenth-century perspectives on race influence Brigham Young's teachings on the Negro and, through him, the teachings of the modern Church?

Third, is there any historical basis from ancient texts for interpreting the Pearl of Great Price as directly relevant to the black-priesthood question, or are these interpretations dependent upon more recent (e.g., nineteenth-century) assumptions?

For the faithful Mormon a fourth question, less amenable to research, also poses itself: Have our modern prophets received an unequivocal verification of the divine origin of the priesthood policy, regardless of its history?

The lack of a tangible answer to the fourth question emphasizes even more the need for greater insight into the first three. We have the tools and would seem to have the historical resource material available to provide valid answers to these questions. Perhaps it's time we began.

Official Declaration—2 (October 1978)

HISTORICAL INTRODUCTION

The news was generally well received by the Saints, but it did not come without side effects. The Mormon people were changing. Seen primarily as a North American church with some limited outreach in Latin America, Mormons needed to come to grips with Spencer W. Kimball's vision of a global Mormonism. Over the course of the nineteenth and early twentieth centuries, the Mormon community had left behind Joseph Smith's original vision for a multiethnic Zion.

Official Declaration—2 meant far more than a policy change for the Mormon people; it meant a dramatic embrace of Mormonism as a global identity. "Revelation," Mormon prophet Spencer W. Kimball had written, comes "when a man is on his tip toes, reaching as high as he can for something he knows he needs and there bursts upon him the answer to his problems."[16] Saints across the world remember where they were when they heard the news that the priesthood ban had been lifted. Kimball had long made known his distaste for nationalism and his vision for the establishment of a "universal family" of believers.[17]

But this 1978 vision somehow was different. The issue had weighed heavily on Kimball's mind for months, even taking a toll on his health. In the spring of 1978, fifty-three-year-old junior apostle Boyd K. Packer noticed the burden of this question on the aging Kimball's physical reserves. He begged Kimball: "Why don't you forget this?" Then Packer noticed Kimball's drawn countenance and answered his own question: "Because you can't. The Lord won't let you."[18]

---

16. Edward L. Kimball, "Spencer W. Kimball and the Revelation on the Priesthood," 46.

17. Spencer W. Kimball "When the World Will Be Converted," *Ensign,* October 1974, 7, and "The False Gods We Worship" *Ensign,* June 1976, 3–6.

18. Kimball, "Spencer W. Kimball and the Revelation on the Priesthood," 48.

Kimball was wrestling inner demons. "I had a great deal to fight," Kimball told a reporter for the Church's newspaper. His greatest enemy to the policy change, he acknowledged, was himself: "I had grown up with this thought that Negroes should not have the priesthood and I was prepared to go all the rest of my life until my death and fight for it and defend it as it was." As one Mormon who had been a senior administrator at Harvard suggested, perhaps providence had been at work "preparing us to accept the black man into full Priesthood fellowship."[19] The First Presidency issued the declaration in June 1978, and it was accepted as authoritative during the Saturday morning session of general conference that October.

Citation

N. Eldon Tanner, "Acceptance of Revelation," *Conference Report*, October 1978, 22. See also Doctrine and Covenants (2013 edition), Official Declaration—2, 294–95.

Document Excerpt

. . . As we have witnessed the expansion of the work of the Lord over the earth, we have been grateful that people of many nations have responded to the message of the restored gospel, and have joined the Church in ever-increasing numbers. This, in turn, has inspired us with a desire to extend to every worthy member of the Church all of the privileges and blessings which the gospel affords.

Aware of the promises made by the prophets and presidents of the Church who have preceded us that at some time, in God's eternal plan, all of our brethren who are worthy may receive the priesthood, and witnessing the faithfulness of those from whom the priesthood has been withheld, we have pleaded long and earnestly in behalf of these, our faithful brethren, spending many hours in the Upper Room of the Temple supplicating the Lord for divine guidance.[20]

He has heard our prayers, and by revelation has confirmed that the long-promised day has come when every faithful, worthy man in the Church may receive the holy priesthood, with power to exercise its divine authority, and enjoy with his loved ones every blessing that flows therefrom, including the blessings of the temple. Accordingly, all worthy male members of the Church may be ordained to the priesthood without regard for race or color. Priesthood leaders are instructed to follow the policy of carefully interviewing all candidates for ordination to either the Aaronic or the Melchizedek Priesthood to insure that they meet the established standards for worthiness. . . .[21]

---

19. Chase N. Peterson, qte. in Ibid., 53.

20. Saints outside of Utah followed the developments with intense interest. Nigerian proselyte Anthony Obinna wrote the First Presidency thanking them for "the many hours in the Upper Room of the Temple you spent supplicating the Lord to bring us into the fold." Anthony U. Obinna, Francis I. Obinna, and Raymond I. Obinna to First Presidency, December 1, 1978.

21. The first African American man to be ordained to the priesthood was Joseph Freeman of Salt Lake City on June 10, 1978. Joseph Freeman, *In the Lord's Due Time*, 108.

Fundamentalists Attack the New Policy (July 1978)

HISTORICAL INTRODUCTION

While mainstream Mormons generally reacted with joy and relief to the declaration, it also revealed the factions surrounding the Mormon establishment. H. Byron Marchant, Douglas Wallace, and John Fitzgerald had earlier been excommunicated for their active opposition to the restriction.

Fitzgerald had been disfellowshipped in January 1973 and excommunicated only a few months later for continuing to publicly attack the Church's race restriction policy. His opposition was strictly principled, he told a gathering at the Salt Lake City Public Library: "We can still sustain the authorities in righteousness and still use our free agency." The Saints, he said, "should have the right to disagree."[22] Fitzgerald expressed a willingness to rejoin the faith if his excommunication were revoked but refused to be rebaptized, feeling his baptism had never been truly nullified in the first place.[23]

Prior to the October 1977 general conference, H. Byron Marchant, a chapel janitor, had been notified of a disciplinary hearing. Marchant responded by threatening a protest march around Temple Square. When his bishop informed him of a forthcoming disciplinary hearing,[24] Church leaders delayed the hearing for two weeks. But during the conference, he escalated the tensions by casting a lone dissenting vote against sustaining President Kimball. By mid-October, Marchant had been excommunicated. The following spring, Marchant mounted a civil lawsuit against the Church president but called it off a few hours after the release of the declaration in June 1978.[25] But all three men continued the struggle against the Church well after the release of the restriction.

A year after Mormon feminist Sonia Johnson was excommunicated for her support of the Equal Rights Amendment, Marchant helped Lee Ann Walker, a Salt Lake City attorney, to form Zion's First International Church as a "way station" for Mormons leaving the faith and served as one of the new church's twelve apostles. "These Mormon protestants," Marchant declared alongside Walker, "believe the Mormon prophet and priesthood are unnecessary and are exercising unrighteous dominion in their political activities in opposition to the Equal Rights Amendment to the United States Constitution."[26] The founders officially announced its creation in Liberty Park with the unfurling of a flag heralding the

---

22. "Former Mormon Gives ERA View," *Deseret News*, November 27, 1979, B16.

23. "Mormon 'Revelation' on Blacks Assailed," *Spokane Daily Chronicle*, June 10, 1978, 13.

24. "Mormon Excommunicated, Fired," *Lakeland [Florida] Ledger*, October 16, 1977, 5A. See also "Mormon Cancels Protest After Trial is Postponed," *Prescott [Arizona] Courier*, September 30, 1977, B3.

25. "Dissident Calls Change 'Convenient,'" *Deseret News*, June 10, 1978, A3.

26. "Former Mormons Plan New Church," *The Telegraph* (Nashua, New Hampshire) December 2, 1980, 20.

words "Liberty, Equality, Family."[27] In 1984, Marchant launched a Democratic gubernatorial campaign largely targeted at supporting the E.R.A., decreasing the state's debt, and undermining the influence of the LDS Church.[28]

Unlike the others, Douglas Wallace, an attorney in Vancouver, Washington, went further and ordained a black man, Larry Lester, to the priesthood in April 1976, an event he believed had occurred "as if by Providence." As he "expected," he was excommunicated but "thought that the higher calling was to do what my conscience and the Spirit taught me or told me to do." Wallace commenced a legal campaign to investigate the Church's trusts and dealings with the Bureau of Land Management.[29] Today, Wallace worries about the LDS Church's "ultimate plan of establishing a theocratic government on the land in the United States, taking over the government by default, and building up the Kingdom of God on Earth with the Church leadership being at the head of it."[30]

Fundamentalists lashed out at the declaration. Salt Lake Mormon John Singer attracted national press coverage when he threatened a gunfight with police who were arresting him for his refusal to send his children to schools that "falsely taught that the races are equal."[31] A well-financed group calling itself "Concerned Latter-day Saints" published a full-page advertisement in the *Salt Lake Tribune* (at the cost of more than $2,700) protesting the policy. The text warned that the LDS Church was "moving more and more toward changes that will suit the world." The group's head, Joseph Jensen,[32] told the press that the group's members opted to remain anonymous, being fearful of excommunication since their views "are not in harmony with those of church authorities."[33] The group claimed some two thousand adherents. but I have not been able to find documentation of an official organization.

---

27. Ron Barker, "Pro-ERA Mormons Form New Religious Sect," *Free-Lance Star* (Fredericksburg, Va.), December 1, 1980, 24.

28. "Marchant Attacks Church's Political Influence," *Deseret News*, April 24, 1984, A13.

29. "Excommunicated Mormon Urges Bell to Probe Church," *Dallas Morning News*, April 11, 1979, 7; "Mormon Dissident Files Suit," *Oregonian*, May 17, 1977, A12.

30. "Douglas Wallace Discusses His Book Under the Mormon Tree," YouTube Video, http://www.underthemormontree.com/About_the_Author.html (accessed June 23, 2014).

31. "Bizarre Events Following Black Mormon's Ordination," *Greensboro [North Carolina] Daily News*, September 3, 1978, 13.

32. Joseph L. Jensen (1935–2014) later head of the Apostolic United Brethren, a polygamist break-off sect based in Utah County. See also "Fundamentalist LDS Church Members Object to New Black Preist Doctrine," *The Bulletin* (Bend, Oregon) July 28, 1978, 10; "J. LaMoine Jenson, Utah Polygamist Leader, Dies at 79," *Salt Lake Tribune*, September 4, 2014, http://www.sltrib.com/sltrib/news/58373398-78/jenson-aub-church-watson.html.csp (accessed September 10, 2014); and Christopher Jones, "Repudiating the Pearl of Great Price?: More on Reactions to the 1978 Revelation," Juvenile Instructor [blog], June 17, 2014, http://www.juvenileinstructor.org/curse-to-remain-refuse-to-apostatize-more-on-reactions-to-the-1978-revelations/ (accessed Septermber 10, 2014).

33. Ibid. See also "Fundamentalist LDS Church Members Object to New Black Preist Doctrine," *The Bulletin*, July 28, 1978, 10.

CITATION

"LDS Soon to Repudiate a Portion of Their Pearl of Great Price?" advertisement, *Salt Lake Tribune*, July 23, 1978, A6.

DOCUMENT EXCERPT

Lord Will Send Delusion

It is to be regretted that we have camouflaged the truth, convincing the world and ourselves that we want to play in harmony with its institutions. Wolves always await the departure of the Priesthood shepherds, that they might neutralize the flock. And when we insist enough, the Lord will send us the delusion we have sought.

Once the Saints were willing to burn their own homes and orchards and seek hiding places in the mountains rather than submit to improper governmental or group pressure. Now they generally will sacrifice principle, doctrine, and ordinance to comply with any law of the land. Eager to digress in 1890, the Church crippled her priesthood blessings and power by discarding exalting principles. . . .

There are a few valiant uncompromising men, within and without the official Church, whose integrity leaves no room for changing the doctrines and ordinances, breaking the everlasting covenant, or for presuming to bestow blessings out of season.

These faithful few, under God's direction, shall redeem Zion, build up the kingdom upon the earth and usher in the Millennial reign of Christ. . . .

Where do you stand?

Apostle Bruce R. McConkie Acknowledges
Limitations of Earlier Leadership (August 1978)

HISTORICAL INTRODUCTION

Elder Bruce R. McConkie gave voice to orthodoxy in ways few Church leaders of his time could. Raised in the sleepy coal country of San Juan County, Utah, the collegiate atmosphere of Ann Arbor, and the Mormon heartland of Salt Lake City, McConkie came into his own under a variety of influences, not least of which was a father known for his political connections and prominence as a Church official.

McConkie's hometown of Monticello had not seen a resident black family for years.[34] In 1940, McConkie's father, Oscar, unsuccessfully ran as a Democrat for the governor's office on a platform promising "the principles of equal justice to all men, whether rich or poor, regardless of race, color, or creed."[35]

---

34. In fact the tiny Monticello of McConkie's youth was shrinking in population by the time McConkie reached adolescence, falling from 768 to 496 between 1920 and 1930. *Fifteenth Census of the United States: 1930*, 1105.

35. "Judge McConkie Seeks Governor's Post, Bailiff Enters Attorney General Race," *Deseret News*, May 9, 1940, 1.

As the son of a high-profile public figure in both ecclesiastical and political circles, McConkie grew accustomed to prominence from a young age. He attended law school at the University of Utah and, after graduation, entered the ranks of Church service at an early age; he was called to the First Council of the Seventy at age thirty-one in 1946; by the late 1950s, McConkie enjoyed the status of a senior scriptorian even among fellow Church leaders.

In 1958, McConkie published *Mormon Doctrine,* a weighty tome with entries arranged in alphabetical order which would, he hoped, "teach the doctrines of the gospel in a plain and simple way" and "interpret a host of hard and difficult scriptural passages." He included a passage entitled "Negroes," which reified most clearly the long-standing notions—entertained since the late 1840s—that "the present status of the negro rests purely and simply on the foundation of the pre-existence" and that "negroes are not equal with other races where the receipt of certain spiritual blessings are concerned," particularly the priesthood and temple blessings that flow therefrom."[36] His book was wildly popular, making its way onto bookshelves throughout the Mormon community.

Nearly a decade later, McConkie reiterated these views to a University of Utah Institute of Religion class, noting that God's children "earn the right to be Nephites" and "earn the right to be Lamanites." He acknowledged that blacks "may be the greatest musicians" or they "could have the most persuasive personalities." But because they're "lacking in spirituality, they're Negroes," he told the clearly shocked Mormon college students. "Their lives in this sphere," he said, pointing to his "Plan of Salvation" diorama on the chalkboard, "didn't qualify them for spiritual blessings over here." When a young woman asked how it was that certain blacks had joined the faith in spite of their spiritual ineptitude, McConkie stammered a little, saying that "it's just too complicated" and that they apparently "had enough spirituality so that they accepted the gospel in spite of it over here."[37]

Finally, the "complicated" truth McConkie thought he knew was pulled out from under him. Once a committed opponent of an integrated priesthood, McConkie changed his views when President Spencer W. Kimball requested that he make an in-depth study of the policy's doctrinal underpinnings McConkie's contributions were instrumental in Kimball's deliberations on the subject; he thanked McConkie publicly for the "special support" McConkie had provided during Kimball's deliberations.[38] Still, some of his past ideas endured in subsequent editions of his publications; in 1981, he celebrated that the "ancient curse is no more. The seed of Cain and Ham and Canaan and Egyptus and Pharaoh. . . . All these, Gentile in lineage, may now come and inherit by adoption all the blessings of Abraham, Isaac, and Jacob."[39]

36. Bruce R. McConkie, *Mormon Doctrine,* 1st ed., 476–77.

37. Bruce R. McConkie, Religion Class Lecture to the University of Utah Institute of Religion, October 9, 1967, AV 191, CD 1-3, LDS Church History Library.

38. Kimball, "Spencer W. Kimball and the Revelation on the Priesthood," 46–48.

39. Bruce R. McConkie, "The New Revelation," 128; see also Armand L. Mauss, *All Abraham's Children: Changing Mormon Conceptions of Race and Lineage,* 241.

CITATION

This address was republished in several Church-sponsored volumes; the most accessible is Bruce R. McConkie, "All Are Alike Unto God," August 18, 1978, in *Priesthood.* Salt Lake City: Deseret Book, 1978, 131–32.

DOCUMENT EXCERPT

We have revelations that tell us that the gospel is to go to every nation, kindred, tongue, and people before the Second Coming of the Son of Man. And we have revelations which recite that when the Lord comes he will find those who speak every tongue and are members of every nation and kindred, who will be kings and priests, who will live and reign on earth with him a thousand years. That means, as you know, that people from all nations will have the blessings of the house of the Lord before the Second Coming.

We have read these passages and their associated passages for many years. We have seen what the words say and have said to ourselves, "Yes, it says that, but we must read out of it the taking of the gospel and the blessings of the temple to the Negro people, because they are denied certain things." There are statements in our literature by the early Brethren which we have interpreted to mean that the Negroes would not receive the priesthood in mortality. I have said the same things, and people write me letters and say, "You said such and such, and how is it now that we do such and such?" And all I can say to that is that it is time disbelieving people repented and got in line and believed in a living, modern prophet. Forget everything that I have said, or what President Brigham Young or President George Q. Cannon or whomsoever has said in days past that is contrary to the present revelation. We spoke with a limited understanding and without the light and knowledge that now has come into the world.

We get our truth and our light line upon line and precept upon precept.[40] We have now had added a new flood of intelligence and light on this particular subject, and it erases all the darkness and all the views and all the thoughts of the past. They don't matter any more.

It doesn't make a particle of difference what anybody ever said about the Negro matter before the first day of June of this year, 1978. It is a new day and a new arrangement, and the Lord has now given the revelation that sheds light out into the world on this subject. As to any slivers of light or any particles of darkness of the past, we forget about them. We now do what meridian Israel did when the Lord said the gospel should go to the Gentiles [Acts 10:1–34].

---

40. See, e.g., Isa. 28:10–13; D&C 98:12; D&C 128:21; and 2 Ne. 28:30.

Anthony Obinna Chastises the Twelve (September 1978)

HISTORICAL INTRODUCTION

Nigerian proselyte Anthony Obinna was getting impatient. While Official Declaration—2 had cleared the way for active proselytizing among blacks, the Church had been focused on addressing racial issues at home. After LaMar Williams, one of the few advocates for West African converts at Church headquarters, received a calling to serve as a mission president in the Gulf States in May 1974, West Africans had little choice but to go it alone.

Feeling desperate, the Nigerians pushed Church leadership more aggressively for official recognition. Sorrowfully, Obinna confessed to W. Grant Bangerter that the failure of Church leaders to attend to their needs had made Nigerian Mormons a "laughing stock."[41] On September 19, 1978, Obinna again pressed Bangerter: "I am surprised for not hearing from you for quite a long time and my letters to you are no longer replied to. Should I believe that the preaching of the gospel of Jesus Christ of Latter day Saints is not for Nigerians?"[42] Williams's departure had halted the work in Nigeria. Since he had assumed his post in the Gulf States mission: "every thing appears as dead as a dodo," lamented Obinna.[43] "Sir," another Nigerian urged Edwin Q. Cannon, then president of the International Mission, which had responsibility for Africa, "the ball is in your court, so don't waste time."[44] Frustrated, Obinna took his questions to a higher authority: the Quorum of the Twelve.

CITATION

Anthony Obinna, Letter to Quorum of the Twelve, September 28, 1978, Edwin Q. Cannon Correspondence, LDS Church History Library.

DOCUMENT EXCERPT

Anthony Obinna to Council of Twelve, September 28, 1978 (Umuelem Enyiogugu), [Mbaise-Owerri] Imo State, Nigeria, West Africa
Council of Twelve
Church of Jesus Christ of Latter-day Saints
Salt Lake City, Utah

Dear President,

Your long silence about the establishment of the Church in Nigeria is very much embrassing [sic]. This country should be looked upon as one of the progressive countries of the world.

---

41. Anthony Obinna, Letter to W. Grant Bangerter, October 9, 1976, Edwin Q. Cannon Correspondence.

42. Anthony Obinna, Letter to W. Grant Bangerter, September 19, 1978, Edwin Q. Cannon Correspondence, LDS Church History Library.

43. Ibid.

44. E. D. Ukwat to Edwin Cannon, September 23, 1978, Edwin Cannon Correspondence.

When Christ was teaching people the truth, it can be recalled that many people did not believe him. This church if it is established in Nigeria will work wonders.

Dr. Karl G. Maser continued writing and the Church was brought to his people.[45] There are many people who wanted the Church and it was granted.

Nigeria has an open door for religious denominations.[46] What could hinder this church from having [a] foot hold here?

Did Christ not say—"Go yee [sic] and teach all nations?"

LaMar Williams gave us the lead and since he was on a mission to Gulf States,[47] we do not receive the "Ensign, New Era and the Friend or Church News."

We here are the true sons of God, but colour makes no difference in the service of our Heavenly Father and Christ.

The Spirit of God calls us to abide by this church and there is nothing to keep us out.

May God bless you now and always.
Sincerely, Anthony Obinna

---

45. An "out and out German," Maeser first became familiar with Mormonism when he saw a pamphlet called *Die Mormonen* in Germany. In 1853, he "fell in with a stranger" who told of meeting the Mormons in Denmark. Maeser was able to locate an address for John Van Cott, president of the Scandinavian Mission, who directed him to write to European Mission President Daniel Tyler. Tyler, however, rejected Maeser's requests, believing his questions to be absurd. Maeser passed Tyler's first letter to Van Cott, asking why he had been stonewalled. Only when Van Cott assured Tyler that Maeser's interest was genuine did Tyler begin sending Maeser Mormon literature. Once Tyler saw Maeser's enthusiasm for Mormonism, Tyler felt that it "might be an opening to establish the gospel in the heart of Germany, where it had not been preached for about eighteen hundred years." Maeser devoured all the materials that Tyler sent to him. In fall 1855, the new European Mission president, Franklin D. Richards, sent Elder William Budge to visit Maeser and his friend, Edward Schoenfield. Preaching Mormonism in Maeser's Germany was illegal, making the mission particularly perilous. Maeser and his associates were baptized in October 1855. Maeser and his family emigrated to Utah. In 1875, Karl G. Maeser served as the first president of Brigham Young Academy. A. LeGrand Richards, "Moritz Busch's *Die Mormonen* and the Conversion of Karl G. Maeser," 47–64.

46. Nigeria's 1960 constitution, established when the country declared its independence from the United Kingdom, stated that "no religious community or denomination shall be prevented from providing religious instruction for pupils of that community or denomination in any place of education maintained wholly by that community or denomination." However, Nigeria was deeply divided between the Muslim Hausas in the north and the Christian Ibos in the east. In 1966, a number of Ibo army officers overthrew the government and attempted to redistrict the country with Ibos in power. The northern government rebelled and placed its own leadership at the head of government. When Christians in the east refused to acknowledge the Muslim government's authority and proclaimed themselves the Republic of Biafra, the federal government invaded in a bloody war that ended with Biafra's surrender four years later. Mormon adherent and Biafran Sensen Asianya accused the "Northern Nigeria vandals" of "atrocious and abominable genocide" from Amaoji where he was in a refugee camp. Sensen Asianya, Letter to Mary Cain, February 1, 1969; see also Olayiwola Abegunrin, *Nigerian Foreign Policy under Military Rule: 1966–1999*, chap. 3.

47. For the Williamses mission call, see LaMar S. Williams to Joseph Dadzie, May 8, 1974.

N.B. For eight years now—1971–1978 Our faith is still on trial.

With God on our side we must succeed. I may pray that you ~~you~~ bring this to <the> hearing of the Leading Authorities of the Church.

Thank you for listening.
Anthony Obinna.

President Gordon B. Hinckley Condemns Racism (2006)

HISTORICAL INTRODUCTION

In 2006, President Gordon B. Hinckley devoted the entirety of his address to the priesthood session to a denunciation of racism which had reared its "ugly head." The exact circumstances that prompted this address can only be speculated.

CITATION

Gordon B. Hinckley, "The Need for Greater Kindness," *Ensign*, May 2006, 58–61.

DOCUMENT EXCERPT

Racial strife still lifts its ugly head. I am advised that even right here among us there is some of this. I cannot understand how it can be. It seemed to me that we all rejoiced in the 1978 revelation given President Kimball. I was there in the temple at the time that that happened. There was no doubt in my mind or in the minds of my associates that what was revealed was the mind and the will of the Lord.

Now I am told that racial slurs and denigrating remarks are sometimes heard among us. I remind you that no man who makes disparaging remarks concerning those of another race can consider himself a true disciple of Christ. Nor can he consider himself to be in harmony with the teachings of the Church of Christ. How can any man holding the Melchizedek Priesthood arrogantly assume that he is eligible for the priesthood whereas another who lives a righteous life but whose skin is of a different color is ineligible?

. . . Brethren, there is no basis for racial hatred among the priesthood of this Church. If any within the sound of my voice is inclined to indulge in this, then let him go before the Lord and ask for forgiveness and be no more involved in such.

Official Reaction to a BYU Professor's Racism (February 2012)

HISTORICAL INTRODUCTION

In spite of official Church efforts to exorcise its racial ghosts, many Saints continued to entertain nineteenth-century notions about race and ethnicity. By defining "racism" as something other than what they believed about race, some Saints were able toe the Church's new position without discarding long-held beliefs. In 2012, Dr. Randy Bott, a Brigham Young University professor of religion, gave an interview to *Washington Post* reporter Jason Horowitz. Bott defended the priesthood ban, now thirty-four years in the past, as sparing blacks from a responsibility for which they were not qualified. "What is discrimination?" Bott asked Horowitz rhetorically. "I think that [it] is keeping something from somebody that would be a benefit for them, right? But what if it wouldn't have been a benefit to them? . . . You couldn't fall off the top of the ladder, because you weren't on the top of the ladder. So, in reality the blacks not having the priesthood was the greatest blessing God could give them."[48]

Bott's comments instigated a flurry of negative press attention and a public relations firestorm. Mormon bloggers exploded with denunciations. Dr. Daniel C. Peterson, then a professor of Middle Eastern Studies at Brigham Young University, announced: "[I] distance myself—and my church—from what was said." Peterson "strongly disagree[d] with [Bott], and it doesn't represent Mormonism as I believe and understand Mormonism."[49] Armand L. Mauss, now a senior scholar on Mormon race relations, chastised Bott for indulging in "arm-chair theologizing" that "does enormous damage to the public image of the Church in a time when the Church is trying hard to overcome its historic association with that very kind of folklore."[50] BYU Religious Education Dean Terry Ball assured the press that "the comments attributed to Professor Bott do not reflect the teachings in the classroom at Brigham Young University."[51]

The newly furbished Church Public Affairs Department issued two separate responses distancing themselves from Bott. On February 29, 2012, the LDS Newsroom issued an unsigned statement "in response to news media requests" acknowledging: "It is not known precisely why, how, or when this restriction began in the Church but what is clear is that it ended decades ago. Some have attempted to explain the reason for this restriction but these attempts should be viewed as speculation and opinion, not doctrine."[52] Additionally, the statement distanced the Church from "the positions attributed to BYU professor Randy Bott" in Horowitz's article. On the same day, the Newsroom released the second statement, also unsigned, titled: "Race and the Church: All Are Alike Unto God."

---

48. Jason Horowitz, "The Genesis of a Church's Stand on Race," *Washington Post,* February 28, 2012, http://www.washingtonpost.com/politics/the-genesis-of-a-churchs-stand-on-race/2012/02/22/gIQAQZXyfR_story.html (accessed August 23, 2013).

49. Daniel C. Peterson, "An Unfortunate Attempt to Explain the Pre-1978 Priesthood Ban," *Patheos,* February 28, 2012, http://www.patheos.com/blogs/danpeterson/2012/02/an-unfortunate-attempt-to-explain-the-pre-1978-priesthood-ban.html (accessed June 23, 2014).

50. "From Armand Mauss," *By Common Consent,* February 29, 2012, http://bycommonconsent.com/2012/02/29/from-armand-mauss/ (accessed June 23, 2014).

51. Kate Bennion, "Washington Post Article on Black Priesthood Ban Spurs Concern, Outrage," *BYU Daily Universe,* February 29, 2012, http://universe.byu.edu/2012/02/29/professor-didnt-follow-university-media-policy-when-speaking-with-washington-post/ (accessed June 23, 2014).

52. "Church Statement Regarding 'Washington Post' Article on Race and the Church," http://www.mormonnewsroom.org/article/racial-remarks-in-washington-post-article (accessed. July 30, 2013).

The statement noted that several explanations had been given "with respect to this matter . . . in the absence of direct revelation."[53]

By the Newsroom's own claims, it represents an "official voice from the Church." It seized the "new communication opportunities" of the internet age to disclaim Bott's embarrassing statement.[54]

CITATION

Press Release, "Church Statement Regarding 'Washington Post' Article on Race and the Church," February 29, 2012, http://www.mormonnewsroom.org/article/racial-remarks-in-washington-post-article (accessed July 30, 2013).

DOCUMENT EXCERPT

The positions attributed to BYU professor Randy Bott in a recent *Washington Post* article absolutely do not represent the teachings and doctrines of The Church of Jesus Christ of Latter-day Saints. BYU faculty members do not speak for the Church. It is unfortunate that the Church was not given a chance to respond to what others said.

The Church's position is clear—we believe all people are God's children and are equal in His eyes and in the Church. We do not tolerate racism in any form.

For a time in the Church there was a restriction on the priesthood for male members of African descent. It is not known precisely why, how, or when this restriction began in the Church but what is clear is that it ended decades ago. Some have attempted to explain the reason for this restriction but these attempts should be viewed as speculation and opinion, not doctrine. The Church is not bound by speculation or opinions given with limited understanding.

We condemn racism, including any and all past racism by individuals both inside and outside the Church.

Addition to Official Declaration—2 (2013)

HISTORICAL INTRODUCTION

In March 2013, the Scriptures Division released an updated version of the triple combination that provided new and much less dogmatic chapter summaries to the Book of Mormon (generally attributed to Bruce R. McConkie) and revised headings for the sections of the Doctrine and Covenants that drew on more exact historical backgrounds provided by the mammoth Joseph Smith Papers project of the LDS Historical Department. As part of these revisions, Official Declaration—2 received an expanded heading. Though publicized

---

53. "Race and the Church: All Are Alike Unto God," http://www.mormonnewsroom.org/article/race-church (accessed July 30, 2013).

54. "The Church and New Media: Clarity, Context, and an Official Voice," Mormon Newsroom, http://www.mormonnewsroom.org/article/the-church-and-new-media:-clarity,-context-and-an-official-voice-newsroom-lds.org-full-story>, (accessed August 23, 2013.)

through social media, blogs, and the internet, it generally did not receive much attention at church services, even though all members who had English versions of the scriptures on electronic devices automatically received the updated triple combination. The heading publicly acknowledged that certain black men had been ordained to the priesthood during Joseph Smith's lifetime. Including this information—even as an explanatory note—signaled an official willingness to grapple with this murky aspect of Latter-day Saint history.

CITATION

Heading, Official Declaration—2, March 1, 2013, https://www.lds.org/scriptures/dc-testament/od/2?lang=eng (accessed September 2, 2013).

DOCUMENT EXCERPT

The Book of Mormon teaches that "all are alike unto God," including "black and white, bond and free, male and female" (2 Nephi 26:33). Throughout the history of the Church, people of every race and ethnicity in many countries have been baptized and have lived as faithful members of the Church. During Joseph Smith's lifetime, a few black male members of the Church were ordained to the priesthood. Early in its history, Church leaders stopped conferring the priesthood on black males of African descent. Church records offer no clear insights into the origins of this practice. Church leaders believed that a revelation from God was needed to alter this practice and prayerfully sought guidance. The revelation came to Church President Spencer W. Kimball and was affirmed to other Church leaders in the Salt Lake Temple on June 1, 1978. The revelation removed all restrictions with regard to race that once applied to the priesthood.

Repudiating Past Teachings (December 2013)

HISTORICAL INTRODUCTION

Beginning in November 2013, the LDS Church History Department teamed up with other divisions of the Church to produce a series of well-researched essays addressing topics that had raised controversy in discussions about Mormonism. Over the next six months, nine essays appeared on the topics page section of the www.lds.org website. These essays were: "First Vision Accounts"[55] (November 20, 2013), "Race and the Priesthood"[56] (December 6, 2013), "Plural Marriage and Families in

---

55. "First Vision Accounts," November 20, 2013, https://www.lds.org/topics/first-vision-accounts (accessed June 23, 2014).

56. "Race and the Priesthood," December 6, 2013, https://www.lds.org/topics/race-and-the-priesthood (accessed June 23, 2014).

Early Utah"[57] (December 17, 2013), "Book of Mormon Translation"[58] (December 30, 2013), "Book of Mormon and DNA Studies"[59] (January 31, 2014), "Becoming like God"[60] (February 25, 2014), "Noah"[61] (March 22, 2014), "Same-Sex Attraction"[62] (March 22, 2014), and "Peace and Violence Among 19th-Century Latter-day Saints" (May 13, 2014).[63]

Authored as they were by several parties, the essays were published without attribution but included a note at the end in which "the Church acknowledges the contribution of scholars to the historical content presented in this article" and that "their work is used with permission." With extensive footnoting and citations from serious scholars on each topic, the statements explained each topic in a way that communicated credibility.

The essay, "Race and the Priesthood" offered a concise historical overview of Mormon official attitudes toward blacks and contextualized them against the history of racism in America; it also included extensive multimedia resources including interviews with prominent black Latter-day Saints such as Darius Gray and historical footage of the announcement of the lifting of the priesthood restriction. Unlike the First Presidency statement of 1969, the essay did not claim that "we don't know" the origins of the priesthood restriction.

While the essay was widely welcomed, several voices expressed concern that it did not include a straightforward apology and observed that its lack of attribution left it in a kind of limbo–presumably an official interpretation but lacking the kind of weight an "official declaration" would carry. University of Canterbury lecturer and Mormon blogger Gina Colvin in New Zealand expressed frustration that the statement did not come with an apology nor "with an explanatory letter from the First Presidency, signed by the First Presidency and Quorum of the

---

57. "Plural Marriage and Families in Early Utah," December 17, 2013, https://www.lds.org/topics/plural-marriage-and-families-in-early-utah?lang=eng (accessed June 23, 2014).

58. "Book of Mormon Translation," December 30, 2013, https://www.lds.org/topics/book-of-mormon-translation?lang=eng (accessed June 23, 2014).

59. "Book of Mormon and DNA Studies," January 31, 2014, https://www.lds.org/topics/book-of-mormon-translation?lang=eng, accessed June 23, 2014. For date of posting, see "LDS Church Posts Topic Page on Book of Mormon and DNA Studies," *Deseret News*, http://www.deseretnews.com/article/865595337/LDS-Church-posts-topic-page-on-Book-of-Mormon-and-DNA-studies.html?pg=all (accessed June 23, 2014).

60. "Becoming like God," February 25, 2014, https://www.lds.org/topics/becoming-like-god?lang=eng, (accessed June 23, 2014.)

61. "Noah," March 22, 2014, https://www.lds.org/topics/noah?lang=eng, (accessed June 23, 2014).

62. "Same-Sex Attraction," March 22, 2014, https://www.lds.org/topics/same-gender-attraction?lang=eng (accessed June 23, 2014).

63. "Peace and Violence among 19th-Century Latter-day Saints," May 13, 2014, https://www.lds.org/topics/peace-and-violence-among-19th-century-latter-day-saints?lang=eng (accessed June 23, 2014).

Twelve and backed up with procedures for dealing with those who continue to teach and preach spurious doctrines."[64]

At the time of the essay's release, *Deseret News* reporter Tad Welch wrote that "the First Presidency approves each of the enhanced topic pages." Elder Steven W. Snow, LDS Church Historian and Recorder, likewise announced that "the First Presidency and the Quorum of the Twelve both have been very supportive of this process."[65] Genesis Group co-founder Darius Gray also informed one audience that the First Presidency reviewed the essay twice before approving it for publication.[66] Its final paragraph reads: "Today, the Church disavows the theories advanced in the past that black skin is a sign of divine disfavor or curse, or that it reflects actions in a premortal life; that mixed-race marriages are a sin; or that blacks or people of any other race or ethnicity are inferior in any way to anyone else. Church leaders today unequivocally condemn all racism, past and present, in any form." Dr. Robert A. Rees, a Latter-day Saint professor of religion at the Claremont Graduate Theological Union, celebrated the essay and notes that the final paragraph "erases a century and a half of mythology, misinformation, and misuse of scripture."[67]

CITATION

Multiple authors, "Race and the Priesthood," December 6, 2013, https://www. lds.org/topics/race-and-the-priesthood (accessed December 10, 2013).

DOCUMENT EXCERPT

Today, the Church disavows the theories advanced in the past that black skin is a sign of divine disfavor or curse, or that it reflects actions in a premortal life; that mixed-race marriages are a sin, or that blacks or people of any other race or ethnicity are inferior in any way to anyone else. Church leaders today unequivocally condemn all racism, past and present, in any form.

---

64. Gina Colvin, "Mormons, Mandela, and the Race and Priesthood Statement," *Patheos*, December 8, 2013, http://www.patheos.com/blogs/kiwimormon/2013/12/mormons-mandela-and-the-race-and-priesthood-statement/ (accessed June 23, 2014).

65. Tad Walch, "LDS Church Enhances Web Pages on Its History, Doctrine," http://www.deseretnews.com/article/865592128/LDS-Church-enhances-web-pages-on-its-history-doctrine.html?pg=all (accessed June 23, 2014); and "LDS Blacks, Scholars Cheer Church's Essay on Priesthood," *Deseret News*, June 8, 2014, http://www.deseretnews.com/article/865604750/LDS-blacks-scholars-cheer-churchs-essay-on-priesthood.html?pg=all (accessed June 23, 2014).

66. Darius Gray, lecture delivered at Brigham Young University, February 12, 2014; notes in my possession.

67. Tad Welch, "LDS Blacks, Scholars Cheer Church's Essay on Priesthood," *Deseret News*, June 8, 2014, http://www.deseretnews.com/article/865604750/LDS-blacks-scholars-cheer-churchs-essay-on-priesthood.html?pg=all (accessed June 23, 2014)

Bibliography

Common Abbreviations

Merrill-Cazier Library. Special Collections, Merrill-Cazier Library, Utah State University, Logan.

Perry Special Collections. L. Tom Perry Special Collections and Manuscripts, Harold B. Lee Library, Brigham Young University, Provo, Utah.

LDS Church History Library. Library, Historical Department, Church of Jesus Christ of Latter-day Saints, Salt Lake City, Utah

Journal of Discourses. Cited by name of speaker, date of address, *Journal of Discourses*, 26 vols. (London and Liverpool: LDS Booksellers Depot, 1855–86), volume and page(s).

Journal History. Journal History of the Church of Jesus Christ of Latterday Saints (chronological scrapbook of typed entries and newspaper clippings, 1830–present), LDS Church History Library; Selected Church History Manuscript Collections, http://churchhistorylibrary.lds.org/primo_library/libweb/custom/CHL/pages/collections.jsp.

Note: Titles beginning with numbers are alphabetized as if the number is spelled out. Items beginning with articles are alphabetized under the second word. U.S. Census records are not usually cited separately since the relevant notes contains the specific year, state, county, and town/township/ward.

In the interests of completeness and to make finding a source as easy as possible, some sources are double-cited as, for example, under the name of the editor of a journal and also under the diarist's name.

References

Aagard, Vance. "House Notes." *Manti [Utah] Messenger,* March 18, 1965, 9.

Abegunrin, Olayiwola. *Nigerian Foreign Policy under Military Rule: 1966–1999.* Westport, Conn.: Greenwood Publishing Group, 2003.

Ables, Boyd. Email to Russell Stevenson, June 19, 2013.

Abel/Ables/Abels, Elijah. Elder's Ordination Certificate. Kirtland Elders Certificates, CD, CR 100 41. LDS Church History Library.

_____. Letter to Brigham Young, March 14, 1854. Brigham Young Office Files, Reel 32. LDS Church History Library.

_____. Priesthood Certificate, April 4, 1841, MS 3440, 21. LDS Church History Library.

"Abolition of Polygamy, The." *[Springfield] Illinois State Journal,* April 17, 1870, 1.

Abridgement of the Debates of Congress from 1789 to 1856. 6 vols. New York: D. Appleton and Company, 1858.

Abstract of the Returns of the Fifth Census. Washington, D.C.: Luther M. Cornwall, 1832.

"Act Concerning Negroes and Mulattoes, An." *The Revised Statutes of the State of Missouri.* St. Louis: Missouri General Assembly, 1835.

"Act Concerning Negroes and Mulattoes, An." *The Revised Statutes of the State of Missouri.* St. Louis: Missouri General Assembly, 1835, 413–17.

"Act in Relation to Service, An." In *Acts, Resolutions, and Memorials Passed by the First Annual and Special Sessions of the Legislative Assembly of the Territory of Utah.* Salt Lake City: Brigham H. Young, 1852, 80–82.

"Activists Receive Visionary Awards." *Deseret News*, November 4, 1996, A10.

"Actors Sought to Re-enact Goddard's Nile Adventure." *Daily Herald* (Provo, Utah), October 22, 1975. Clipping in John M. Goddard Papers, Box 3, fd. 3. Perry Special Collections.

Acts and Resolutions of the United States of America. Washington, D.C.: Government Printing Office, 1871.

Adams, F. G. Letter to the Editor. *[University of Utah] Daily Chronicle,* October 10, 1963, 2.

Adams, Hannah. *The History of the Jews: From the Destruction of Jerusalem to the Present Time,* 2 vols. Boston: John Eliot, 1812. Also published in one volume under the same time by London: A. Macintosh, 1840.

Adams, Mary F. "Mary Frost Adams." *Young Woman's Journal* 17, no. 12 (December 1906): 538.

Addy, Isaac. Interviewed by E. Dale Lebaron, May 14, 1988. Transcript. Perry Special Collections.

"Adieu, Kind Friends, Adieu." *Cumorah's Southern Messenger* 28, no. 2 (February 1953): 22.

Advertisement. *Arizona Republican* (Phoenix), June 30, 1905, 6.

Advertisement. *Chicago Daily Tribune*, February 20, 1905, 12.

Advertisements. *Sacramento Transcript*, November 5, 1850, 1, and November 6, 1850, 3.

"African Discovery." In *Chambers's Miscellany of Instructive and Entertaining Tracts.* Edinburgh: William and Robert Chambers, 1847.

"African River Adventure Scheduled for ULAS." *University of Utah Daily Chronicle,* February 17, 1954, 1.

"Aftermath of Detroit Riot." *Morning Star* (Rockford, Mich.), July 30, 1967, 7.

"Against Mormonism." *Daily Inter Ocean* (Chicago), January 25, 1887, 4.

Agu, Charles, B. O. Akpan, E. B. Owo. Welcome Address, n.d. October 1961, Lamar S. Williams Papers, Box 1, fd. 8. LDS Church History Library.

———. Letter to Samuel Uba Oti, November 13, 1964. LaMar S. Williams Papers, Box 1, fd. 8. LDS Church History Library.

———. Welcome Address, Ikot Nsung Congregation. November 3, 1961, LaMar S. Williams Papers, MS 2890, Box 1, fd. 9, LDS Church History Library.

Agbu, Charles. "Welcome Address to Dr. and Mrs. Rytting." June 14, 1975. Edwin Q. Cannon Papers, Box 1, fd. 1. LDS Church History Library.

———. December 1962, LaMar Williams Papers, Box 1, fd. 8. LDS Church History Library.

Akpan, Itah. Letter to Mark E. Petersen, August 28, 1960. LaMar Williams Papers, MS 2015, LDS Church History Library.

Akpan, Ottoman. Letter to LaMar S. Williams, February 16, 1961. LaMar S. Williams Papers, Box 1, fd. 5. LDS Church History Library.

Alexander, Thomas G. *Things in Heaven and Earth: The Life and Times of Wilford Woodruff, A Mormon Prophet.* Salt Lake City: Signature Books, 1993.

Alinsky, Saul. *Rules for Radicals: A Pragmatic Primer for Realistic Radicals,* 2nd ed. New York; Vintage Books, 1972; rpt. under the same title in 1989.

"'All Worthy Male Members': Mormons to Let Blacks Be Priests." *Dallas Morning News*, June 10, 1978, 17A.

"All-American Minutemen, The." *Grito Del Norte* (Las Vegas, Nev.), August 10, 1969, 9.

"Alleged Leaders of Lynching Mob Freed Upon Bail." *News Advocate* (Sanpete, Utah), July 2, 1925, 1.

Allen, James B. "On Becoming a Universal Church." *Dialogue: A Journal of Mormon Thought* 25, no. 1 (Spring 1992): 13–36.

_____. "Would-Be Saints: West Africa before the 1978 Priesthood Revelation." *Journal of Mormon History* 17, no. 1 (Winter 1991): 205–47.

Allen, John. *Desmond Tutu: Rabble-Rouser for Peace: The Authorized Biography.* Chicago: Chicago Review Press, 2008.

"Amazing Story Told by Undercover Agent." *Wichita [Kans.] Eagle*, January 14, 1968, 32.

"American Bar Association Drops Its Subversive List Qualification." *Miami [Fla.] Daily News*, October 11, 1955, 19A.

"Ancestral Data Gathered over 100 Years." *Cumorah's Southern Messenger* 25, no. 7 (July 1950): 103.

Anderson, Joseph. Letter to Lowry Nelson, May 23, 1952. Lowry Nelson Papers, Special Collections, Merrill-Cazier Library, Utah State University, Logan.

Anderson, Lavina Fielding, ed. *Nicholas Groesbeck Smith, 1881–1945: A Documentary History.* Salt Lake City: Privately published for Nicholas Groesbeck Smith Jr. and Marion Burrows Smith, 2000.

_____. "A Ministry of Blessing: Nicholas Groesbeck Smith," *Dialogue: A Journal of Mormon Thought* 31, no. 3 (Fall 1998): 59–78.

_____. Correspondence with Russell Stevenson, December 24, 2013.

Anderson, Richard Lloyd. "Reuben Miller: Recorder of Oliver Cowdery's Reaffirmations." *BYU Studies* 8, no. 3 (1968): 280–84.

"Andes to Amazon Is Second Film." *[Chicago] Daily Herald*, November 14, 1963, 64.

Andrews, Wes, and Clyde Dalton. *The Black Hammer: A Study of Black Power, Red Influence, and White Alternatives.* New York: Desco Press, 1967.

"Angry Emotions Erupt at WSC Meeting." *Davis County Clipper* (Bountiful, Utah), February 26, 1987, 3.

"Another Robbery." *Burlington [Iowa] Hawkeye*, March 27, 1851, 2.

"Another Robbery." *Burlington Hawkeye*, March 27, 1851, 2.

"Answers to Sundry Questions." *Elders Journal of the Church of Jesus Christ of Latterday Saints* 1, no. 2 (May 1838): 29.

"Anti-Slavery Lectures." *Cincinnati Weekly Herald and the Philanthropist*, January 1, 1836, 6.

"Ant's Eye View, The." *Summit County Bee Park Record* (Park City, Utah), March 28, 1963, 2.

Appleby, William Ivins. Autobiography and Journal. LDS Church History Library.

Appleby, William. Letter to Brigham Young, June 2, 1847, Brigham Young Office Files, Reel 30. LDS Church History Library.

Arbuckle, Robert M. "Reapportionment—One Party System." *Davis County Clipper* (Bountiful, Utah), March 12, 1965, 1.

"Archaeologists Launch Expedition Seeking White Giant Tribe." *Davis County Clipper* (Bountiful, Utah), March 31, 1950, 6.

"Army Orders" and "Michigan—The Western States." *Commercial Advertiser (New York City)*, September 17, 1838, 2.

Arrington, Leonard J. "The Search for Truth and Meaning in Mormon History." In D. Michael Quinn, ed., *The New Mormon History.* Salt Lake City, Utah: Signature Books, 1992, 1–11.

_____. *Adventures of a Church Historian.* Urbana: University of Illinois Press, 1998.

_____. *Brigham Young: American Moses.* New York: Alfred Knopf, 1986.

_____. *From Quaker to Latter-day Saint: Bishop Edwin D. Woolley.* Salt Lake City: Deseret Book, 1976.

"Arrival of the North America." *Spectator* (New York), March 10, 1851, 3.

"Arrived." *Deseret News*, October 12, 1859, 4.

"Articles Are Filed by Ku Klux Klan." *Salt Lake Telegram*, November 8, 1924, 2.

Asay, Carlos. Letter to Mabeys [Rendell and Rachel] and Cannons [Edward and Janath], March 5, 1979, Edwin Q. Cannon Papers, MS 21299, Box 1, fd. 2. LDS Church History Library.

Ashton, Wendell J., "Marketing the Mormon Image: An Interview with Wendell J. Ashton." *Dialogue: A Journal of Mormon Thought* 10, no. 3 (Spring 1977): 15–20.

_____. *Voice in the West: Biography of a Pioneer Newspaper.* New York: Duell, Sloan, and Pearce, 1950.

"Ashton Will Head Cancer Drive." *Daily Herald* (Provo, Utah), January 20, 1964, 10.

Asianya, Sensen. Fireside Address at Cedar Rapids, Iowa. Transcript. August 3, 1966, MS 10315, LDS Church History Library.

_____. Letter to Mary Cain, February 1, 1969, MS 10315, LDS Church History Library.

Asmara Branch. Manuscript History, Quarterly Historical Report, July–September 1962, LDS Church History Library.

Asmara Branch, Ethiopia. Melchizedek Priesthood Minutes, LR 10798, 13, LDS Church History Library.

"Association Intelligence." *The Contributor* 4 (June 1883): 359.

"At a Recent Temperance Meeting," *Illinois Weekly Journal*, November 22, 1848, 3.

"At Theatre Next Week." *Park Record*, February 6, 1925, 6.

"Atonement of Blood, The." *Times-Picayune* (New Orleans), August 21, 1883, 8.

Attalla, Maryann. Letter to John M. Goddard, June 10, 1975. Holograph, John M. Goddard Papers, Box 3, fd. 9. Perry Special Collections.

"Attorneys Compromise on Rights." *Pittsburgh Post-Gazette*, August 12, 1963, 15.

"'Aunt' Jane James." *Young Woman's Journal* 16, no. 12 (December 1905): 551–53.

"Authentic from the Detroit Patriots." *Centinel of Freedom*, (Newark, N.J.), December 18, 1838, 2.

Avant, Gerry. "President Kimball Says Revelation Was Clear." *Deseret News*, January 6, 1979, 15.

"Avoidance of Discrimination Act, No. 38 (1957). Qtd. in Kwame Botwe-Asamoah. *Kwame Nkrumah's Politico-Cultural Thought and Politics,* New York: Routledge, 2013, 124.

"Babson's Point of View." *Vernal [Utah] Express*, July 10, 1969, 10.

Bagnall, Cornelius. Diary, 1853. LDS Church History Library.

Bainson, Samuel. "An African's Journey," n.d., Samuel Bainson Papers, LDS Church History Library.

_____. Journal, 1981, Samuel Bainson Papers. LDS Church History Library.

Bair, John. "Dear Brethren." *Times and Seasons* 6, no. 12 (July 1, 1845): 949.

Ball, J. T. "Letter." *The Prophet*, November 9, 1844, 1.

Ballard, Melvin J. "Answering the Call." *Millennial Star* 88, no. 166 (March 18, 1926): 166.

Bangerter, Roger. In University II Ward, Oakland, California, Minutes of the 11th Quorum of Elders, June 2, 1968. LDS Church History Library.

Bangerter, William G. *These Things I Know: The Autobiography of William Grant Bangerter.* Compiled by Cory W. Bangerter. Salt Lake City: Voices and Images, 2013.

Banner, Stuart *The Death Penalty: An American History.* Cambridge, Mass.: Harvard University Press, 2009.

Barber, John W., and Henry Howe. *Historical Collections of the State of New York.* New York: S. Tuttle, 1842.

"Barbrous" [sic]., *Palmyra Register*, August 18, 1819, 2.

Baroni, Gilberto, and Alfredo Lima Vaz. Interviewed by Michael N. Landon. Transcript, June 15, 1994., LDS Church History Library.

Barrett, Gwynn W. "Dr. John M. Bernhisel: Mormon Elder in Congress." *Utah Historical Quarterly* 36, no. 2 (April 1968): 143–67.

Bateman, Arlene. Letters to Family. Maurice Bateman Temple Papers, LDS Church History Library.
>ca. April 1991
>April 11, 1991
>June 9, 1991

Bateman, Maurice, and Arlene Bateman. Tribute to Julia Mavimbela, July 18, 2000, MS 17496, LDS Church History Library.

Baumgardner, F. J. Memo to W.C. Sullivan, December 1, 1965. Photocopies on https://archive.org/details/foia_Holmes_Lola_Belle-HQ-2 (accessed March 15, 2014).

"Beautiful Chapels—A Pressing Need." *Cumorah's Southern Messenger* 24, no. 12 (December 1949): 174.

Beecher, Maureen Ursenbach, ed. "'All Things Move in Order in the City': The Nauvoo Diary of Zina Diantha Huntington Jacobs." *BYU Studies* 19, no. 3 (1979): 285–320.

Belk, Samuel E. Memo to McGeorge Bundy, December 30, 1964. Qtd. in Nina Howland, ed. *Foreign Relations of the United States, 1964–1968: Africa*. Washington, D.C.: Government Printing Office, 1999, 612.

Bell, James P. "Merrill J. Bateman: Breadth and Depth." *BYU Magazine*, March 1996. http://magazine.byu.edu/?act=view&a=517 (accessed January 22, 2014).

Bennion, Lowell. Letter to George Boyd, October 21, 1963. Qtd. in Mary Lythgoe Bradford, *Lowell L. Bennion: Teacher, Counselor, Humanitarian*. Salt Lake City: Dialogue Foundation, 1995, 246.

Benson, Ezra Taft. *Conference Report of the Church of Jesus Christ of Latter-day Saints*, October 1967, 34–39.

_____. *The Red Carpet*. Salt Lake City: Bookcraft, 1962.

Bergera, Gary James, ed. *Autobiography of B. H. Roberts*. Salt Lake City: Signature Books, 2009. Roberts had composed his autobiography in third person; Bergera recast it in first person, a less confusing approach for an *auto*biography.

_____. "The Orson Pratt-Brigham Young Controversies: Conflict within the Quorum, 1853–1868." *Dialogue: A Journal of Mormon Thought* 13, no. 2 (Summer 1980): 7–49.

Bergera, Gary J., and Ronald Priddis. *Brigham Young University: House of Faith*. Salt Lake City: Signature Books, 1985.

Berlin, Elliot. "Abraham Owen Smoot." M.A. thesis, Brigham Young University, 1955.

Bernhisel, John M. Letters to Brigham Young. Brigham Young Office Files, Reel 70. LDS Church History Library.
>March 21, 1850.
>July 3, 1850.
>September 12, 1850.

Berrett, William E. "The Church and the Negroid People." Appendix to John J. Stewart, *Mormonism and the Negro: An Explanation and Defense of the Doctrine of the Church of Jesus Christ of Latter-day Saints in regard to Negroes and others of Negroid Blood, with a Historical Supplement*, 1st ed. Orem, Utah: Community Press, 1960, 16–18.

Bertram, Nick. "BYU Defies Odds, Builds Powerhouse." *[Portland] Oregonian*, September 14, 1985, E1.

Bibb, Sheila, comp. "The Johannesburg South Africa Temple: Historical Background, Construction, Various Events, and Spiritual Experiences Related Thereto." Maurice Bateman Temple Papers, LDS Church History Library.

Bidamon, Emma Smith. Letter to Emma Pilgrim, March 27, 1870. In Dan Vogel, ed., *Early Mormon Documents*, 5 vols. Salt Lake City: Signature Books, 1996–2003, 1:532.

Bigelow, John. *Jamaica in 1850: Or The Effects of Sixteen Years of Freedom on a Slave Colony*. New York: George P. Putnam, 1851.

Bigler, Henry. Journal, 1853. LDS Church History Library.

"Biographical Sketch of Elder Zenos H. Gurley, Sen'r." *The True Latter-day Saints' Herald* 19, no. 1 (January 1, 1872): 1–3.

"Biography of Franklin Dewey Richards." In "Manuscript History of the Church." In *Selected Collections from the Archives of the Church of Jesus Christ of Latterday Saints,* 2 vols. DVD. Provo, Utah: Brigham Young University Press, 2002, 1:18.

"Birth of a Nation at State Saturday." *Salt Lake Telegram,* May 24, 1923, 17.

"'Birth of a Nation' Greatest of All Pictures, Coming to Ides, The." *Grand Valley Times,* May 10, 1918, 8.

"'Birth of a Nation' Has Big Run in Cedar," *Iron County Record,* February 15, 1918, 1.

"Birth of a Nation Is a Production of Great Merit." *Ogden Standard,* March 27, 1916, 5.

"'The Birth of a Nation' Is a Soul-Stirring Spectacle." *Box Elder News,* January 23, 1917, 2.

"'Birth of a Nation' Opens Today at Gem." *Salt Lake Telegram,* February 12, 1922, 14.

"'Birth of a Nation' Scores at American." *Salt Lake Telegram,* December 23, 1921, 6.

"Bishopric Message." *Second to None* (Glendale California Second Ward Newsletter) 2, no. 8 (August 1970): 1.

"Bizarre Events Following Black Mormon's Ordination." *Greensboro [N.C.] Daily News,* September 3, 1978, 13.

"Black LDS Convert Will Speak Here." *[Bannock] Idaho State Journal,* November 8, 1972, 31.

"Black Mormon Ordained." *Salina [Kans.] Journal,* April 4, 1976, 32.

"Black Mormon Relates Conversion to Church." *Ogden Standard-Examiner,* June 11, 1972, 22.

"Black Mormons Keep the Faith." *Dallas Morning News,* April 27, 1978, 14A.

"Black Mormons Struggle for Acceptance in Church." *Salt Lake Tribune,* November 4, 2004. http://www.sltrib.com/faith/ci_2437167 (accessed June 5, 2013).

Black Woman Changed Mind about Mormons." *Aberdeen [S.D.] Daily News,* September 9, 1978, 9.

"Blacks Gain Expanded Access to Liquor Stores in S. Africa." *Greensboro [N.C.] Daily News,* July 24, 1981, 23.

"Blacks May Enter Private Hospitals." *[London] Times,* December 11, 1979, 6.

Blakeslee, James. Diary. Qtd. in William Shepard. "Shadows on the Sun Dial." *Dialogue: A Journal of Mormon Thought* 41, no. 1 (Spring 2008): 34–66.

_____. "Letter from J. Blakeslee." *Times and Seasons* 3, no. 8 (February 15, 1842): 696–97.

_____ Letter to "Dear Brethren in the New Covenant." June 11, 1841. *Times and Seasons* 2, no. 18 (July 15, 1841): 482.

_____. Letter to Frank Cooper, June 8, 1849. *Gospel Herald,* July 5, 1849, 1.

_____s. Record Book. MS 922 1, LDS Church History Library.

"Blames K of C. for Broadside Against Klan." *Salt Lake Telegram,* October 8, 1923, 2.

"Blanding Boy Starts Peace Corps Work." *Times Independent* (Moab, Utah), November 21, 1963, 4.

Blee, Kathleen M. *Women of the Klan: Racism and Gender in the 1920s.* Berkeley: University of California Press, 2009.

"Blessing Upon the Head of Elder LaMar Stevenson Williams, A." Transcript, November 21, 1962. LaMar S. Williams Papers, Box 1, fd. 8, LDS Church History Library.

Blood, Henry H. Letter to Mrs. Leland Larsen, May 2, 1935. Henry H. Blood Papers, Utah State Archives. Qtd. in Kenneth W. Baldridge, "Nine Years of Achievement: The Civilian Conservation Corps in Utah." PhD diss., Brigham Young University, 1971, 338.

"Blood-Atonement Fanaticism in Arkansas." *[Baltimore] Sun],* April 23, 1881, 4.

Bloom, Joshua, and Waldo Martin. *Black against Empire: The History and Politics of the Black Panther Party.* Berkeley: University of California Press, 2012.

Bly, David. "Hope in a Torn Land." *This People,* Summer 1988, 29–31.

"Board Authorizes Special Committee on Civil Rights and Racial Unrest." *American Bar Association Journal* 49, no. 8 (August 1963): 743–44.

"Bob Jones U. to Sue U.S. over Tax Status." *Greensboro [North Carolina] Daily News*, December 27, 1970, 14.

Bob Jones v. United States, 461 U.S. 574 (1976).

Boden, Don. In University II Ward, Oakland, California, Minutes of the 11th Quorum of Elders, June 30, 1968. LDS Church History Library.

Bonnet, Georges. Email to Steve Graham, September 20, 2001. In Shirley Van Katwyk Papers, LDS Church History Library.

"Book of Mormon Course Offered." *Ogden Standard-Examiner*, May 23, 1927, 10.

Boren, Lucina Mecham. Journal. In Kate Carter, comp. and ed., *Treasures of Pioneer History*, 6 vols. Salt Lake City: Daughters of Utah Pioneers, 1952–57, 6:301–48.

Boston Ward 3 Census. https://familysearch.org/pal:/MM9.1.1/MDSC-FBY (accessed July 2013).

"Bountiful News." *Davis County Clipper*, (Bountiful, Utah), December 23, 1955, 15.

Bowman, Matthew. "A Mormon Bigfoot: David Patten's Cain and the Concept of Evil in LDS Folklore." *Journal of Mormon History* 33, no. 3 (Summer 2007): 62–82.

———. *The Mormon People: The Making of an American Faith*. New York: Random House, 2012.

"Boy Scout Drive for Second Ward Monday and Tuesday." *Millard County Progress*, March 12, 1926, 1.

Bradford, Mary L. "Beverly Campbell: Dynamic Spokesperson." *This People* 1 (Summer 1980): 50–54.

———. *Lowell L. Bennion: Teacher, Counselor, Humanitarian*. Salt Lake City: Dialogue Foundation, 1995.

Bradley, Martha Sonntag. *Pedestals and Podiums: Utah Women, Religious Authority, and Equal Rights*. Salt Lake City: Signature Books, 2005.

Bradley, Martha Sonntag, and Mary Brown Firmage Woodward. "Plurality, Patriarchy, and the Priestess: Zina D. H. Young's Nauvoo Marriages." *Journal of Mormon History* 20, no. 1 (Spring 1994): 84–118.

"Branch Notes-Ramah Branch." *Cumorah's Southern Messenger* 32, no. 12 (December 1957): 189.

"Branch Organized." *Millard County Chronicle*, November 26, 1942, 1.

Branch, Taylor. *Parting the Waters: America in the King Years, 1954–1963*. New York: Simon and Schuster, 1989.

Bray, Selina Rayson. Diary, 1853, LDS Church History Library.

Brazil North Mission. Lineage Lesson, December 1970, LR 959 21. Translated by Julianne Parker Weiss. LDS Church History Library.

"Breinholt Performs Benefit Concert." *Salt Lake Community College Student Newspaper*, September 29, 1998, 6.

Briggs, Kenneth A. "Mormons Perhaps Fastest Growing U.S. Religion." *San Diego Union*, April 2, 1980, 12.

Brigham, Janet. "Nigeria and Ghana: A Miracle Precedes the Messengers." *Ensign*, February 1980, 73–76.

Brigham Young, Letter to Isaac Higbee, October 18, 1849, Brigham Young Office Files, Reel 24. LDS Church History Library.

"Brigham Young's Lineage." *Melchizedek and Aaronic Herald* 1, no. 8 (February 1850): 4.

"Brighamite Combination in Cincinnati, The." *Melchizedek and Aaronic Herald* 1, no. 6 (September 1849): 2.

Bringhurst, Newell G. "An Ambiguous Decision: The Implementation of the Mormon Priesthood Denial for the Black Man–A Re-examination." *Utah Historical Quarterly* 46, no. 1 (Winter 1978): 45–64.

_____. "Eldridge Cleaver's Passage Through Mormonism." *Journal of Mormon History* 28 (Spring 2002): 80–110.

_____. "Elijah Abel and the Changing Status of Blacks in Mormonism." *Dialogue: A Journal of Mormon Thought* 12 (Summer 1979): 22–36.

_____. "Mormonism in Black Africa: Changing Attitudes and Practices, 1830–1981." *Sunstone* 6 (May/June 1981): 15–21.

_____. *Saints, Slaves, and Black: The Changing Place of Blacks within Mormonism.* Westport, Conn.: Greenwood Publishing, 1981.

Bringhurst, Newell G., and Craig L. Foster. *The Mormon Quest for the Presidency: From Joseph Smith to Mitt Romney.* Independence, Mo.: John Whitmer Books, 2011.

Bringhurst, Newell G., and Darron T. Smith, eds. *Black and Mormon.* Urbana: University of Illinois Press, 2004.

Brinkley, Douglas. *The Unfinished Presidency: Jimmy Carter's Journey Beyond the White House.* New York: Penguin Books, 1998.

Briscoe, David. "Mormon Priesthood Open to Blacks." *[Portland] Oregonian*, June 10, 1978, 1.

_____. "Numbers Declining but Not Devotion." *Winnipeg [Manitoba, Canada] Free Press*, June 3, 1978, 10.

_____. "Rep. Holbrook: A Legislator Who's Still an Activist." *Deseret News*, March 1, 1975, 10A.

Broadhead, Richard. "Prophets in America circa 1830: Ralph Waldo Emerson, Nat Turner, Joseph Smith." In Reid L. Neilson and Terryl L. Givens, eds. *Joseph Smith, Jr: Reappraisals after Two Centuries.* New York: Oxford University Press, 2009, 13–29.

Broadway, Bill. "Black Mormons Resist Apology Talk." *Washington Post*, May 30, 1998, B–09.

Broadway Tabernacle, The." *Frank Leslie's Sunday Magazine* 4 (July–December 1878): 102.

Broeffle, John. Letter to Catherine Beckstead, September 17, 1838. Photocopy of holograph. LDS Church History Library.

Brooks, Juanita, ed. *Journal of the Southern Indian Mission: Diary of Thomas D. Brown.* Logan: Utah State University Press, 1972.

_____, ed. *On the Mormon Frontier: The Diary of Hosea Stout.* 2 vols. Salt Lake City: University of Utah Press, 2009.

"Brotherhood Exists." *LDS Church News*, January 17, 2004, 11.

Brown, Bill. Letter to John M. Goddard. Holograph, September 15, 1975, John M. Goddard Papers, Box 3, fd. 9. Perry Special Collections.

Brown, David Paul. *Spectator* (New York City), June 12, 1834, 1.

Brown, Hugh B. *Conference Report of the Church of Jesus Christ of Latter-day Saints.* Salt Lake City: Church of Jesus Christ of Latter-day Saints, October 1963, 91–95.

_____. Qtd. in Glen W. Davidson. "Mormon Missionaries and the Race Problem." Draft manuscript, 7, Box 1, fd. 24. Stephen Holbrook Papers, Utah State Historical Society Archives.

_____. "A Message to the Saints of the South African Mission." *Cumorah's Monthly Bulletin* 36, no. 5 (May 1961): 120.

Brown, John. Note. In Franklin B. Sanborn, ed. *The Life and Letters of John Brown: Liberator of Kansas, and Martyr of Virginia.* Boston: Roberts Brothers, 1891.

Brown, Julia. *Hidden Agenda: Anarchy: U.S.A. in the Name of Civil Rights.* Directed by G. Edward Griffin. New York: UFO Tv, 1966.

_____. *I Testify: My Years as an F.B.I. Undercover Agent.* Boston: Western Islands, 1966.

Brown, Karin. Letter to Lori Kennard, Loretta Johnson Papers, August 10, 1993. LDS Church History Library.

Brown, Lorenzo. Diary, 1847. Typescript, LDS Church History Library.

Brown, Samuel. Affidavit, September 5, 1838. In Sidney Rigdon, *An Appeal to the American People: Being an Account of the Persecutions of the Church of Latter-day Saints; and the Barbarities Inflicted on Them by the Inhabitants of the State of Missouri.* 2d ed. Cincinnati, Ohio: Shepard and Stearns, 1840, 17.

Brown, Sarah Hart. *Three Southern Lawyers in an Era of Fear.* Baton Rouge: Louisiana State University Press, 2000.

Brown, Sterling A. "Jitterbug's Joy." In *A Negro Looks at the South.* Edited by John Edgar Tidwell and Mark A. Sanders. New York: Oxford University Press, 2007, 285–91.

Brown Vetoes Anti-Busing Measure." *Observer-Reporter* (Washington, Pa.), February 5, 1980, B-10.

"Bryan and the Boers." *New York Tribune,* October 20, 1899, 8.

Building the Kingdom." *Cumorah's Southern Messenger* 36, no. 10 (October 1961): 265.

"Bumper Crop Is Promised." *Montgomery [Ala.] Advertiser,* August 11, 1913, 1.

Burbank, Daniel M. Journal, October 30, 1857, LDS Church History Library.

Burder, George. *Village Sermons.* London: Religious Tract Society, 1849.

Burton, William. Autobiography, MS 1508 1. LDS Church History Library.

Bush, Laura. *Faithful Transgressions: Six Twentieth-Century Mormon Women's Autobiographical Acts.* Logan: Utah State University, 2004.

Bush, Lester E. Email to Russell Stevenson, May 12, 2014.

_____. "Mormonism's Negro Doctrine: An Historical Overview." *Dialogue: A Journal of Mormon Thought* 8, no. 1(Spring 1973): 11–68. Rpt. in Lester E. Bush Jr. and Armand L. Mauss, eds. *Neither White Nor Black: Mormon Scholars Confront the Race Issue in a Universal Church.* Midvale, Utah: Signature Books, 1984, 53–129.

_____. "'Writing Mormonism's Negro Doctrine': An Historical Overview (1973): Context and Reflections." *Journal of Mormon History* 25, no. 1 (Spring 1999): 229–71.

Bush, Lester E., and Armand L. Mauss, eds. *Neither White Nor Black: Mormon Scholars Confront the Race Issue in a Universal Church.* Midvale, Utah: Signature Books, 1984.

Bushman, Richard Lyman. *Joseph Smith: Rough Stone Rolling.* New York: Alfred A. Knopf, 2005.

"Business and the Stock Market." *Vernal [Utah] Express,* February 5, 1970, 3.

"By Their Fruits." *Deseret News,* May 29, 1965, 17.

Byron, Lord George. "Cain." In *The Works of Lord Byron, Including His Suppressed Poems.* Paris: A. and W. Galignani, 1827.

"BYU Adds Major in Agricultural Economics." *Washington County News* (St. George), August 15, 1935, 1.

"BYU Honors Author Haley." *[Portland] Oregonian,* August 17, 1977, 20.

"BYU Sounds to Africa." *Davis County Clipper* (Bountiful, Utah), May 31, 1974, 30.

Calamy, Edward. *God's free Mercy to England.* London: Christopher Meredith, 1642.

"Called on Mission." *Uintah Basin Standard,* April 25, 1963, 1.

Campbell, Robert L. Diary, 1847. Perry Special Collections.

Cannon, Edwin Q. Letter to Joseph Johnson, September 22, 1979. Edwin Q. Cannon Papers, Box 1, fd. 2, LDS Church History Library.

_____. Letters, Edwin Q. Cannon Papers. Box 1, fd. 2. LDS Church History Library.
to James E. Faust, June 30, 1981
to Joseph Johnson, September 22, 1979
to Oscar McConkie, July 9, 1979

Cannon, Janath [Russell], Diary, 1978–79. LDS Church History Library.

_____. Diary, 1979, LDS Church History Library.

_____. Letter to "Sister Barrucand." June 24, 1976, [sic; should be 1979] Edwin Q. Cannon Papers, Box 1, fd. 2.

"Cannon's Volley at Supreme Court." *Salt Lake Tribune,* July 19, 1879, 4.

"Cape District." *Cumorah's Southern Cross* 6, no. 3 (March 1932): 46.

"Cape District." *Cumorah's Southern Cross* 7, no. 3 (March 1933): 46.

"Capt. D. H. Cannon's Train." *The Mountaineer*, July 13, 1861, 162.

Card, Orson Scott. "Wendell Ashton Called to Publishing Post." *Ensign,* January 1978, 73.

Carey, Charles. *History of Oregon*, 3 vols. Chicago: Pioneer Historical Publishing Company, 1922.

Carmack, John K. *Tolerance: Principles, Practices, Obstacles, Limits.* Salt Lake City: Bookcraft, 1993.

Carter, J. Kameron. *Race: A Theological Account.* New York: Oxford University Press, 2008.

Carter, J. Smyth. *The Story of Dundas: Being a History of the County of Dundas, from 1784 to 1904.* Iroquois, Ontario: St. Lawrence News Publishing House, 1905.

Carter, Kate B., ed. and comp. *The Negro Pioneer.* Salt Lake City: Daughters of Utah Pioneers, 1965.

"Carter Takes Home Warm Feeling." *Deseret News*, November 28, 1978, A2.

"Celebrated Indian Chief, The." *Alexandria Gazette*, July 10, 1851, 1.

"Celebration of the Twenty-Fourth of July, The." *Deseret News*, July 26, 1851, 1.

"Central Route to the Pacific." *Daily Missouri Republican* (St. Louis), December 19, 1853, 1.

Chafe, William H. *Civilities and Civil Rights: Greensboro, North Carolina and the Black Struggle for Freedom.* New York: Oxford University Press, 1981.

Champion, Brian. "The Minutemen." *Encyclopedia of Murder and Violent Crime.* Edited by Eric Hickey, New York: Sage, 2003, 314–15.

Champson, Isaac. Sekondi Branch, Minutes of meeting, December 14, 1978.

Chandler, Russell. "Door Is Opened: Mormonism: A Challenge for Blacks." *Los Angeles Times*, August 12, 1988. http://articles.latimes.com/1988-08-12/news/mn-204_1_several-black-mormons (accessed January 8, 2013).

Chapman, Brittany, ed. *Carry On: The Personal Writings of Ruth May Fox.* Salt Lake City: University of Utah Press, forthcoming.

Chappell, David. *Inside Agitators: White Southerners in the Civil Rights Movement.* Baltimore, Md.: Johns Hopkins University Press, 1996.

"Charges against Accused Lynching Leaders Dropped." *News Advocate* (Price, Utah), September 10, 1925, 1.

Charnock, Stephen. "The Necessity of Regeneration." In Richard Adams and Edward Veal, eds. *The Complete Works of Stephen Charnock,* 5 vols. Edinburgh: James Nichol, 1865, 3:7–81.

Chase, Miriam Gove. Death Certificate, November 4, 1909, Utah, Salt Lake County Death Records, 1908–1949. Holograph on FamilySearch, certificate #004139806 (accessed February 1, 2014).

Chase, Sisson A. Affidavit, *Millennial Star* 28, no. 22 (July 14, 1860): 438–39.

"Chatham Street." *Commercial Advertiser* (New York City), September 11, 1833, 2.

Cherry, Alan. "A Negro's Life Changed." In Hartman Rector Jr. and Connie Rector, eds. *No More Strangers*, 2 vols. Salt Lake City: Deseret Book, 1971, 2:90–99.

"Children to Stage 'Birth of a Nation.'" *Salt Lake Telegram*, November 9, 1926, 13.

"Children's Retarded Units Will Be Merged." *Oakland [Calif.] Tribune,* March 14, 1969, 3.

Christensen, Niels C. Journal, October 5, 1860. http://history.lds.org/overlandtravels/trailExcerptMulti?lang=eng&pioneerId=24377&sourceId=4915 (accessed August 28, 2013).

_____. Journal, October 5, 1860. http://history.lds.org/overlandtravels/trailExcerptMulti?lang=eng&pioneerId=24377&sourceId=4915 (accessed August 28, 2013).

Chukwu, Ambrose. "They're Importing Ungodliness." *Nigerian Outlook,* March 5, 1963, 3, FN 1907, Butler Library, Columbia University.

"The Church and New Media: Clarity, Context, and an Official Voice." Mormon Newsroom. http://www.mormonnewsroom.org/article/the-church-and-new-media:-clarity,-context-and-an-official-voice-newsroom-lds.org-full-story (accessed August 23, 2013).

The Church and the Proposed Equal Rights Amendment: A Moral Issue Pamphlet. Salt Lake City: Church of Jesus Christ of Latter-day Saints, 1980. Bound as centerfold of March 1980 *Ensign.*

"Church Moves On, The." *Improvement Era* 66, no. 3 (March 1963): 195.

"Church Names 2 in Communications Posts." *Deseret News*, February 17, 1973, 3.

"Church Statement Regarding 'Washington Post' Article on Race and the Church." http:// www.mormonnewsroom.org/article/racial-remarks-in-washington-post-article (accessed July 30, 2013).

"Church's Message Is One of Concern for All Men." *LDS Church News*, January 21, 1989, 13.

Cincinnati Branch Minutes, June 25, 1843. Photocopy in my possession courtesy of H. Michael Marquardt.

"Cincinnati Branch Minutes, June 1, 1845." *Times and Seasons* 6, no. 10 (June 1, 1845): 915.

"City Teacher Wins Long Foreign Trip." *Seattle Daily Times*, April 26, 1958.

"Civil Rights Bill Passes Utah House." *Deseret News*, March 5, 1959, A1.

"'Civil Rights' Wrong Term, Says Negro." *Seattle Daily Times*, February 12, 1966.

Clark, Andrew. "The Fading Curse of Cain: Mormonism in South Africa." *Dialogue: A Journal of Mormon Thought* 27, no. 4 (Winter 1994): 41–56.

Clark, Eleanor. Letters to Russell Stevenson, January 8 and November 9, 2013. Transcript in my possession.

Clark, J. Reuben Jr. *On The Way to Immortality to Eternal Life.* Salt Lake City: Deseret Book, 1949.

Clark, J. Reuben. "Home and the Building of Home Life." *Relief Society Magazine* 39, no. 12 (December 1952): 790–97.

Clark, Lilian Emile. Letter, September 25, 1979, Edwin Q. Cannon Papers, Box 1, fd. 2. MS 18052 LDS Church History Library.

Clark, Lilian. Letter to Loretta Johnson, June 3, 1962. Loretta Johnson Papers, LDS Church History Library.

Clark, Vivien. Correspondence with Russell Stevenson, November 7–8, 2013.

Clayton, Myron D. Letter to John Goddard, February 29, 1972, John M. Goddard Papers, Box 3, fd. 9, Perry Special Collections.

Clayton, William. *William Clayton's Journal: A Daily Record of the Original Company of "Mormon" Pioneers from Nauvoo, Illinois, to the Valley of the Great Salt Lake.* Salt Lake City: Deseret News, 1921.

Cleaver, Eldridge. Qtd. in "People in the News." *Greensboro [N.C.] Daily News*, April 7, 1981, 9.

———. *Target Zero: A Life in Writing.* Edited by Kathleen Cleaver. New York: Macmillan, 2007. Includes interview pubished in *Playboy*, December 1968, 144–70.

"Cleaver for Change." *Trenton [N.J.] Evening Times*, May 22, 1983, 12.

Clegg, Reed. "Friends of West Africa: An Opportunity for Service." *Dialogue: A Journal of Mormon Thought* 19, no. 1 (Spring 1986): 94–106.

Clegg, Reed, and Naomi Clegg. Letter to Edwin Q. Cannon, February 27, 1980 [received at the mission office on March 6, 1979]. Edwin Q. Cannon Papers, Box 1, fd. 2. LDS Church History Library.

"Club Members Hear Reports on Foreign Visits." *Vernal [Utah] Express*, April 11, 1968, 5.

"Club Members." *Winona Republican-Herald*, May 17, 1949, 4.

"Clubs Plan Joint Lunch." *[University of Utah] Daily Chronicle*, January 31, 1946, 1.

"Code of Ethics Bill Sent to Governor for Signature." *Advocate* (Baton Rouge, La.), July 8, 1964, 10.

Cole, Olen. *The African-American Experience in the Civilian Conservation Corps.* Gainesville: University Press of Florida, 1999.

Coleman, Ronald. "'Is There No Blessing for Me?' Jane Elizabeth Manning James, a Mormon African American Woman." In Quintard Taylor and Shirley Ann Vilson Moore, eds.

African-American Women Confront the West. Norman: University of Oklahoma Press, 2008, 144–77.

"College to Award Degrees during Ceremony June 11." *Ogden Standard-Examiner*, June 5, 1966, 11.

Collier, Fred, ed. *The Nauvoo High Council Minute Book of the Church of Jesus Christ of Latter-day Saints*. Hanna, Utah: Collier's Publishing, 2005.

――――, ed. *The Teachings of Brigham Young 3, 1852–1854*. Hanna, Utah: Collier Publications, 1987.

Collier, Fred, and William Harwell, eds. *Kirtland Council Minute Book*. Salt Lake City: Collier's Publishing, 1996.

"Colored Film on Congo at College Tonight." *Los Angeles Tribune*, April 8, 1960, 8.

"Coloured Church Defies Apartheid Marriage Law." *[London] Times*, March 21, 1983, 5.

Coltrin, Zebedee. Autobiographical Sketch as written by Thomas Martell. Typescript. LDS Church History Library.

――――. Qtd. in L. John Nuttall, Diary, 1879. Typescript. Perry Special Collections.

"Comments from Dixie." *Green River [Utah] Journal*, October 6, 1955, 2.

"Common Schools." *Deseret News*, March 19, 1853, 3.

Communist Training Operations. House of Representatives, 86th Congress, July 21–22, 1959. Washington, D.C.: Government Printing Office, 1959.

"Condition of Utah, The." *National Aegis*, April 1, 1857, 2.

"Conference Minutes." *Times and Seasons* 5, no. 13 (July 15, 1844): 1.

"Conference Minutes." *Times and Seasons* 6, no. 5 (March 15, 1845): 842.

"Conference Minutes." *Times and Seasons* 6, no. 10 (June 1, 1845): 915.

Conference Report of the Church of Jesus Christ of Latter-day Saints. Salt Lake City: Church of Jesus Christ of Latter-day Saints, semi-annual.

"Conferences." *True Latter-day Saints Herald* 22 (June 1, 1875): 348–51.

Conquest, Robert. *The Great Terror: A Reassessment*, 2nd ed. New York: Oxford University Press, 1990.

Constitution and Bye[Sic]-Laws of the Church of Jesus Christ of Latter-day Saints, The. Aba, Nigeria: Apex Printing Works, n.d.

"Constitution of the Church of Jesus Christ of Latter-day Saints, April 27, 1969." Joseph K. Dadzie Papers. LDS Church History Library.

"Controversy Stirs around Mormons in the Caribbean." *The Day* (New London, Conn.), August 31, 1985, A9.

Cooper, Sylvester, Journal, 1981–82. LDS Church History Library.

Copeland, Lee. "From Calcutta to Kaysville: Is Righteousness Color-Coded?" *Dialogue: A Journal of Mormon Thought* 21 (Fall 1988): 89–99.

Coray, Martha Knowlton. Notebook, July 19, 1840, LDS Church History Library.

Cornaby, Hannah Last. *Autobiography and Poems*. Salt Lake City: J. C. Graham and Company, 1881.

"Correspondence of Albany Argus." *Sun* (Pittsfield, Mass.). November 7, 1848, 3.

"Correspondence." *Millennial Star* 26 (December 10, 1864): 797.

"Could Negro Athletes Be Happy at BYU?" *Herald*, Sunday edition, (Provo, Utah), November 2, 1969, 13.

"Council Issues Declaration on Civil Rights." *[University of] Utah Daily Chronicle*, October 8, 1963, 1.

"Counterspy Says Reds Infiltrating Churches." *Dallas Morning News*, December 12, 1961, 5.

"Court Refuses to Halt LA Busing." *Dallas Morning News*, September 14, 1980, 28A.

Cowdery, Oliver. "Address to the Patrons of the Evening and Morning Star." *Evening and Morning Star* 2, no. 24 (September 1834): 1.

Cowley, Matthew. "You Are the Leaven." *Cumorah's Southern Messenger* 27, no. 7 (July 1952): 105.

_____, ed. *Wilford Woodruff: History of His Life and Labors as Recorded in His Daily Journals.* Salt Lake City: Deseret News, 1909.

Crawford v. Board of Education, 113 Cal. App. 3d 633 (1980).

Crippin, J. W. Letter to Brigham Young, March 14, 1845. Brigham Young Office Files, Reel 29. LDS Church History Library.

Crosby, Caroline Barnes. *No Place to Call Home: The 1807–1857 Life Writings of Caroline Barnes Crosby, Chronicler of Outlying Mormon Communities.* Edited by Edward Leo Lyman. Logan: Utah State University Press, 2005.

Cummins, Lawrence E. "The Saints in South Africa." *Ensign*, March 1973, 4–10.

Cumorah G and G Ball." *Cumorah's Southern Messenger* 25, no. 12 (December 1950): 187.

Curbelo, Nestor. *The History of the Mormons in Argentina.* Salt Lake City: Greg Kofford Books, 2009.

Cutler, Christopher Quinn. *A Quiet, Faithful, Unobtrusive Follower: The Life and Times of Harmon Cutler.* San Bernardino, Calif.: Self-published, 2012.

Cutter, William Richard, ed. *Genealogical and Personal Memoirs Relating to the Families of Boston and Eastern Massachusetts,* 3 vols. New York: Lewis Historical Publishing, 1908.

_____. Death Certificate, November 4, 1909, Salt Lake County Death Records, 1908–1949.

Dadzie, Joseph. Autobiography. Joseph Dadzie Papers, LDS Church History Library.

_____. "The History of the Church in Ghana and Takoradi." Joseph Dadzie Papers, LDS Church History Library.

_____. "The History of the 'Church of Jesus Christ of Latter-day Saints in Ghana." Joseph Dadzie Papers, LDS Church History Library.

_____. Letter to President of the Church [Spencer W. Kimball], July 15, 1977. Joseph Dadzie Papers, LDS Church History Library.

_____. "Notes on Discussions with Bros. Allen and Mensah of Madera, Calif., Held on January 19, 1974." Ambassador Hotel, Madera, California. Ghana and Nigeria Files, LDS Church History Library.

_____. "Timeline." Joseph Dadzie Papers, LDS Church History Library.

Darby, William. *Darby's Edition of Brookes' Universal Gazetteer.* Philadelphia: Benjamin Warner, 1828.

Davies, Laura. Letter to John Goddard, June 1, 1975. Holograph, John M. Goddard Papers, Box 3, fd. 9. Perry Special Collections.

"David O. McKay, Mormon Leader, Dies at Age 96." *Milwaukee Sentinel*, January 19, 1970, 4.

"David Paul Brown." *Spectator* (New York City), June 12, 1834, 1.

Davidson, Glen W. "Mormon Missionaries and the Race Problem." Draft manuscript, n.d., Box 1, fd. 24, Stephen Holbrook Papers, Utah State Historical Society Archives.

Davidson, Karen Lynn, Richard L. Jensen, and David J. Whittaker, eds. *Histories—Vol. 2: Assigned Histories, 1831–1847.* Vol. 2 in the Histories series of the THE JOSEPH SMITH PAPERS. General editors Dean C. Jessee, Ronald K. Esplin, and Richard Lyman Bushman. Salt Lake City: Church Historian's Press, October 2012.

Davidson, Karen Lynn, David J. Whittaker, Mark Ashurst-McGee, and Richard L. Jensen. *Histories—Vol. 1: Joseph Smith Histories, 1832–1844.* Vol. 1 in the Histories series of THE JOSEPH SMITH PAPERS. General editors Dean C. Jessee, Ronald K. Esplin, and Richard Lyman Bushman. Salt Lake City: Church Historian's Press, 2011.

Davis, David Brion. "The Emergence of Immediatism in British and American Antislavery Thought." *Mississippi Valley Historical Review* 49, no. 2 (1962): 209–30.

Davis, John A. "The Influence of Africans on American Culture." *Annals of the American Academy of Political and Social Science* 354 (July 1964): 75–83.

de Toledano, Ralph. "Civil Rights Is Major Congress Issue." *Sarasota [Fla.] Herald Tribune,* January 8, 1964, 6.

De Wet, Ben. "The Great South African Experience." ca. 1992. Maurice Bateman Temple Papers, LDS Church History Library.

_____. "South Africa: A Different View." n.d., Maurice Bateman Temple Papers, LDS Church History Library.

"Dead." *Salt Lake Herald,* April 5, 1872, 3.

"Death of South Africa Bill Truly Shameful." *[Portland] Oregonian,* October 23, 1984, B5.

Debates and Proceedings of the Convention Which Assembled at Little Rock, January 7, 1868. Little Rock: J. G. Price, 1868.

"Decade Later: Freedman's Bank Still Connecting Families, A." *Deseret News,* February 16, 2002. http://www.deseretnews.com/article/765551111/A-decade-later-Freedmans-Bank-still-connecting-families.html?pg=all (accessed May 16, 2014).

"Defiant Anglicans to Fight Apartheid Despite Cost." *[London] Times,* December 10, 1979, 4.

DeGruchy, John W. *The Church Struggle in South Africa.* 2d ed. London: Fortress Press, 2004.

Deming, Arthur B. *Startling Revelations!: Naked Truths about Mormonism* 1, no. 2 (1888): 201–4. The two numbers were published in Oakland, California, by Deming and Co.

"Demise of George D. Grant." *Salt Lake Herald,* September 21, 1876, 3.

"Depravity." *Philadelphia Inquirer,* December 6, 1830, 2.

Derr, Jill Mulvay, Janath Russell Cannon, and Maureen Ursenbach Beecher. *Women of Covenant: The Story of Relief Society.* Salt Lake City: Deseret Book, 1992.

Derr, Jill Mulvay, and Karen Lynn Davidson, eds. *Eliza R. Snow: The Complete Poetry.* Provo, Utah: Brigham Young University/Salt Lake City: University of Utah Presses, 2009.

"Deseret Stake Conference." *Millard County Chronicle,* January 14, 1943, 1.

"Details of Utah News." *Boston Post,* June 8, 1857, 2.

Dew, Sheri. *Ezra Taft Benson: A Biography.* Salt Lake City: Deseret Book, 1989.

Dialogue Editorial Board. "Senator Edward W. Brooke at BYU." *Dialogue: A Journal of Mormon Thought* 11, no. 2 (Summer 1978): 119–20.

"Diary of Eliza Maria 'Partridge' Lyman, The." MSS 1217, Perry Special Collections.

"Did Little Rock Episode Represent a Backfire of Communistic Strategy?" *Murray [Utah] Eagle,* September 26, 1957, 2.

"Died." [Jeremiah Root] *San Francisco Call,* February 28, 1898.

"Difference, The." *Richmond Whig,* September 22, 1868, 1.

"Different Colors of the Jews, The." *Deseret News,* November 16, 1850, 4.

Dillard, Angela. *Faith in the City: Preaching Radical Social Change in Detroit.* Ann Arbor: University of Michigan Press, 2007.

"District Highlights." *Cumorah's Southern Messenger* 13, no. 10 (October 1939): 157.

"District Highlights." *Cumorah's Southern Messenger* 27, no. 5 (May 1952): 76.

"Do Communists Run Civil Rights Force." *Davis County Clipper* (Bountiful, Utah), February 24, 1967, 10.

"Doctor, a Deal, and a Mystery, A." *Los Angeles Times,* March 20, 2000. http://articles.latimes.com/2000/mar/20/news/mn-10791/2 (accessed June 3, 2013).

Dorsett, Lyle W. "Slaveholding in Jackson County, Missouri." *Missouri Historical Society Bulletin* 20, no. 1 (1963): 25–37.

Doxey, Roy W. "The Mormons and the Negro." *The Nation,* August 16, 1952, inside front cover.

"Dr. Lowry Nelson Speaker at Seminary Commencement." *Iron County [Utah] Record,* April 18, 1931, 1.

"Dr. Okah Tubbee, Chief of the Chocktaws!" *[Tallahassee] Floridan and Journal,* October 11, 1851, 1.

Draper, Theodore. *American Communism and Soviet Russia.* Piscataway, N.J.: Transaction Publishers, 1960.

Driver, Johnie M. "LDS Church Leaders Should Speak Out for Moral Justice." Press release, March 9, 1965, Box 1, fd. 29. Stephen Holbrook Papers, Utah State Historical Society Archives.

Duncan, Adam M. "An Interview with 'Mr. South Africa.'" *Cumorah's Southern Messenger* 24, no. 6 (June 1949): 82–83, 91.

_____. Letter to ACLU Membership, July 15, 1959, Quoted in Linda Sillitoe. *Friendly Fire: The ACLU in Utah.* Salt Lake City: Signature Books, 1996, 17.

Dunham, Jonathan. Diary, 1839. MS 1387 5, LDS Church History Library.

Dunklin, Daniel. Letter to W. W. Phelps and Others, July 18, 1836. In "Manuscript History of the Church," A-1, 748. http://josephsmithpapers.org/paperSummary/history-1838-1856-volume-b-1-1-september-1834-2-november-1838?p=202#!/paperSummary/history-1838-1856-volume-b-1-1-september-1834-2-november-1838&p=202 (accessed May 17, 2014).

Eaton, Robert I., and Henry J. Eyring, *I Will Lead You Along: The Life of Henry B. Eyring.* Salt Lake City: Deseret Book, 2013.

"Editorial." *Davis County Clipper* (Bountiful, Utah), February 10, 1950, 2.

Edouk, Ime. Letter to Brother Frank, August 10, 1981. Edwin Q. Cannon Papers, Box 1, fd. 2. LDS Church History Library.

"Educator Cites McKay Statement of No Negro Bias in LDS Tenets." *Salt Lake Tribune,* January 15, 1970, B9.

Ehat, Andrew F., and Lyndon W. Cook, eds. *The Words of Joseph Smith: The Contemporary Accounts of the Nauvoo Discourses of the Prophet Joseph Smith.* Provo, Utah: BYU Religious Studies Center, 1980.

"Eighth General Epistle." *Latter-day Saints' Millennial Star* 15 (February 19, 1853): 115.

"80 Here Identified as Reds at Probe." *Plain Dealer* (Cleveland, Ohio), June 5, 1962, 19.

"Elder Goddard Sets Congo Exploration." *Deseret News,* May 12, 1956, 6.

Elders in the Land of Zion to the Church of Christ Scattered Abroad, The." *Evening and Morning Star* 1, no. 2 (July 1832): 12.

"Elders in the South African Mission." *Cumorah's Monthly Bulletin* 1, no. 5 (October 15, 1927): front matter.

Elders' Certificates for W. W. Phelps, John Whitmer, and Joseph Smith. Kirtland Elders Certificates, CD, 1, 2, 4, 57. LDS Church History Library.

"Eleven Arrested on Charge of Murder in Lynching of Negro." *News Advocate* (Price, Utah), June 25, 1925, 1.

"Elks Minstrels Fun." *Evening Bulletin* (Honolulu), March 9, 1906, 3.

Ellison, Ralph. "An Extravagance of Laughter." In John F. Callahan, ed. *The Collected Essays of Ralph Ellison.* New York: Random House, 1995, 491785.

Ellsworth, George. "Called to Tubai: Missionary Couples in French Polynesia, 1850." *Ensign,* October 1989, 35–39.

"Elopement and Arrest, An." *Daily [Springfield] Illinois State Journal,* March 19, 1851, 2.

Embry, Jessie L. *Black Saints in a White Church: Contemporary African-American Mormons.* Salt Lake City: Signature Books, 1994.

_____. "Impact of the LDS 'Negro Policy.'" In *Black Saints in a White Church,* edited by Jessie L. Embry. Salt Lake City: Signature Books, 1994, 37–78.

_____. "Separate But Equal? Black Branches, Genesis Groups, or Integrated Wards?" *Dialogue: A Journal of Mormon Thought* 23, no. 1 (1992): 11–37.

"End of Mormonism, The." *Daily [Springfield] Illinois State Journal,* January 5, 1871, 2.

"Ends Peace Corps Work in Africa." *Davis County Clipper* (Bountiful, Utah), January 17, 1969, 8.

England, Eugene. "Becoming a World Religion: Blacks, the Poor—All of Us." *Sunstone* 21, no. 2 (June–July 1998): 49–60.

_____. "Hanging by a Thread: Mormons and Watergate." *Dialogue: A Journal of Mormon Thought* 9, no. 2 (Summer 1974): 9–18.

_____. "The Mormon Cross." *Dialogue: A Journal of Mormon Thought* 8, no. 1 (Spring 1973): 78–86.

_____. "'No Respecter of Persons': A Mormon Ethics of Diversity." *Dialogue: A Journal of Mormon Thought* 27, no. 4 (1994): 79–100.

_____. "Playing in the Dark: Mormons Writing about Blacks and Blackness." Unpublished essay. Qtd. in Laura Bush, *Faithful Transgressions: Six Twentieth–Century Mormon Women's Autobiographical Acts.* Logan: Utah State University Press, 2004.

England, Eugene, and E. Dale LeBaron. Comments on Rebecca Mould Interview, May 22, 1988. Perry Special Collections.

"English Family to Live in Tridell." *Vernal [Utah] Express*, June 15, 1949, 1.

"English Town Council Blocks LDS Chapel." *Ogden Standard-Examiner*, July 17, 1971, 3.

"Epistle of the Twelve to President Orson Pratt, and the Church of Jesus Christ of Latter-day Saints in the British Isles, An." *Latter-day Saints Millennial Star* 11, no. 16 (March 9, 1849): 247.

Ereba, Joseph. Letter to Missionary Department, November 30, 1976, Edwin Q. Cannon Papers, Box 1, fd. 1, LDS Church History Library.

Erlmann, Veit. *African Stars: Studies in Black South African Performance.* Chicago: University of Chicago Press, 1991.

Ertman, Martha M. "Race Treason: The Untold Story of America's Ban on Polygamy." *Columbia Journal of Gender and Law* 19, no. 2 (2010): 351–54.

"Escalante Chit-Chat." *Garfield County News*, September 19, 1963, 1.

Esiem, Elijah. Letter to LaMar Williams, May 30, 1960, LaMar S. Williams Papers, Box 1, fd. 5. LDS Church History Library.

Espinosa, Mariola. *Epidemic Invasions: Yellow Fever and the Limits of Cuban Independence, 1878–1930.* Chicago: University of Chicago Press, 2009.

Esplin, Ronald K. "Brigham Young and Priesthood Denial to the Blacks: An Alternative View." *BYU Studies* 19, no. 3 (1979): 394–402.

Esshom, Frank. *Pioneers and Prominent Men of Utah.* Salt Lake City: Utah Pioneers Book Publishing Company, 1913.

"Eternal Sealing: Many Miles, Many Years, and Many Blessings." *Deseret News*, April 26, 1975, 25.

"Evan Thompson Relives Life in Tanzania, East Africa." *Ephraim [Utah] Enterprise*, May 28, 1970, 7.

"Events of the First Year of Construction," May 2002–May–June 2002. In Shirley Van Katwyk Papers, LDS Church History Library.

Ewing, Raymond C. Interviewed by Charles Stuart Kennedy, November 29, 1993. Association for Diplomatic Studies and Training Oral History Interview Series. http://www.adst.org/OH%20TOCs/Ewing,%20Raymond%20C.toc.pdf (accessed April 18, 2014).

"Ex-Editor's Saturday Talk, An." *Deseret News*, February 25, 1893, 14.

"Ex-FBI Agent Says Reds Using Rights Movement." *Morning Star* (Rockford, Mich.), May 19, 1965, 3.

"Ex-Pilot Tours Africa in Canoe." *Pampa Daily News*, August 1, 1950, 2.

"Excommunicated Mormon Urges Bell to Probe Church." *Dallas Morning News*, April 11, 1979, 7.

"Experiences and Testimony of Jeremiah Root." *Autumn Leaves* 10, no. 6 (June 1897): 271–73.

"Exploring African Wonderlands." *Daily Herald* (Provo, Utah), March 23, 1969, 10.

"Extract from Heber C. Kimball's Journal" *Woman's Exponent* 10, no. 2 (June 15, 1881): 9.

"Ezra Taft Benson." *Instructor* 80, no. 5 (May 1945): 216–17, 227.

"F. Goodriches Receive New Assignment." *Vernal [Utah] Express*, January 17, 1963, 13.

Fadiman, Anne. "John Goddard: 108 Adventures Down, 19 Go go." *Life* 9 (February 1986): 19–21.

———. "LDS Church Bringing Races Together, But Some Obstacles Remain." *Deseret News*, March 13, 1986, A4–A5.

Fagg, Ellen. "S. Africa's Scenic Beauty in Sharp Contrast to Its Cultural Strife." *Deseret News*, March 13, 1986, 1A.

"Famed Explorer to Speak and Show Movies." *Garfield County News*, January 28, 1954, 1.

Faringer, Gunilla. *Press Freedom in Africa*. Westport, Conn: Greenwood Press, 1991.

Farmer, Molly. "Having Priesthood 'Is My Better Means to Serve.'" *Deseret News*, May 21, 2008. http://www.deseretnews.com/article/705383516/Having-priesthood-is-my-better-means-to-serve.html?pg=all (accessed June 2, 2103).

Faulring, Scott H., ed. *An American Prophet's Record: The Diaries and Journals of Joseph Smith*. Salt Lake City: Signature Books,1989.

Faust, James E. Letter to Joseph Dadzie, August 31, 1977. Joseph Dadzie Papers. LDS Church History Library.

———. "Response to the Call." *Ensign*, November 1978, 20.

"15,000 See Mormon Pageant Opening." *Post-Standard* (Syracuse, N.Y.), July 25, 1972, 6.

Fifteenth Census of the United States: 1930. Washington, D.C.: Government Printing Office, 1931.

"Fifty-First Annual Conference." *Salt Lake Herald* April 7, 1881, 3.

"Film to Portray Eventful Trip down Nile River." *Ogden-Standard Examiner*, March 17, 1953, 12.

Finney, Charles Grandison. *Lectures on Revivals of Religion*. New York: Leavitt, Lord, & Co., 1835.

First Council of the Seventy, Roll, December 27, 1836, CR 3 123, LDS Church History Library.

"First Integrated Church." *Florence [Fla.] Times Daily*, November 3, 1962, 2.

First Presidency (David O. McKay, J. Reuben Clark, Henry D. Moyle). Letter to Glen Fisher, March 21, 1960. Glen Fisher Correspondence. LDS Church History Library.

———. Letter to Rulon Howells, June 29, 1935, Rulon Howells Missionary Papers, LDS Church History Library.

———. Letter to Lowry Nelson, July 17, 1947. Lowry Nelson Papers, Box 4, fd. 2, Merrill-Cazier Library, Utah State University, Logan.

——— (George Albert Smith, J. Reuben Clark, and David O. McKay). Letter to Lowry Nelson, November 12, 1947. Special Collections, Merrill-Cazier Library, Utah State University, Logan.

———. Letter to Priesthood Leaders, February 22, 1978. Qtd. in Armand L. Mauss. "The Fading of the Pharoah's Curse: The Decline and Fall of the Priesthood Ban against Blacks in the Mormon Church." *Dialogue: A Journal of Mormon Thought* 14, no. 3 (Autumn 1981): 26.

———. Letter to Utah Valley Saints, January 8, 1850. Brigham Young Office Files, Reel 24.

———. "Statement," August 17, 1949., In Lester E. Bush Papers, Box 4, fd. 4. Special Collections. Marriott Library, University of Utah. Published in Lester E. Bush and Armand L. Mauss, eds. *Neither White Nor Black: Mormon Scholars Confront the Race Issue in a Universal Church*. Midvale, Utah: Signature Books, 1984, 221.

——— "Statement." December 15, 1969. *Deseret News*, December 18, 1969.

"First Time in Ventura County." *Press-Courier* (Oxnard, Calif.), June 2, 1958, 6.

"First West Africans to Serve Missions." *Deseret News*, February 28, 1981.

Fisher, Glen. Reminiscences, n.d. Glen Fisher Correspondence, MS 18205, LDS Church History Library.

Fitzpatrick, Sheila. "Revisionism in Retrospect: A Personal View." *Russian Review* 67, no. 3 (Fall 2008): 683–94.

Fletcher, Peggy. "A Light Unto The World: Image-Building is Anathema to Christian Living" *Sunstone* 7, no. 4 (July-August 1982): 16–23.

Flint, Henry. *The Railroads of the United States; Their History and Statistics, Etc.* Philadelphia: John E. Potter and Company, 1868.

Flourney, J. Jacobus. *An Essay on the Origin, Habits, &c of the African Race.* New York: J. Jacobus Flourney, 1835.

Fluhman, J. Spencer. *"A Peculiar People": Anti-Mormonism and the Making of Religion in Nineteenth-Century America.* Chapel Hill: University of North Carolina Press, 2012.

Foner, Eric. *Reconstruction: America's Unfinished Revolution, 1863–1877.* New York: HarperCollins, 2002.

_____. "The Wilmot Proviso Revisited." *Journal of American History* 56, no. 2 (September 1969): 262–79.

"Forrest Goodrich Chosen for LDS Mission." *Vernal Express*, October 4, 1951, 8.

"42 Negroes in Jail." *Jonesboro [Ark.] Weekly Sun*, December 29, 1909, 1.

"Forum Will Show Film on Turkey." Tucson [Ariz.] Daily Citizen, February 9, 1967, 29.

Fotheringham, Don. Letter to the Editor." *Manti Messenger*, April 19, 1973, 5.

Foucault, Michel. "BodyPower." In Colon Gordon, ed. *Power/Knowledge: Selected Interviews and Other Writings, 1972–1977.* New York: Pantheon Books, 1980.

_____. *Discipline and Punish: The Birth of the Prison*, 2d ed. New York: Random House, 2012.

_____. *"Society Must Be Defended": Lectures at the College De France.* New York: Picador, 1997.

Fouke, Carol. "Revelation: Blacks May Become Mormon Priests." *Morning Star* (Rockford, Ill.), June 10, 1978, A4.

"Fourth of July, The." *Commercial Advertiser* (New York), July 5, 1834, 2.

Frampton, T. Ward. "'Some Savage Tribe': Race, Legal Violence, and the Mormon War of 1838." *Journal of Mormon History* 40, no. 1 (Winter 2014): 175–207.

Free Country, A." *Constitution* (Middletown, Conn.), June 18, 1856, 2.

"Free People of Color." *Evening and Morning Star* 2, no. 14 (July 1833): 108.

"Free Schools." *Salt Lake Herald*, April 16, 1875, 3.

"Freedman's Bank: Boosting Research for African-Americans." *LDS Church News*, March 3, 2001, 3.

Freeman, Joseph. *In the Lord's Due Time.* Salt Lake City: Bookcraft, 1979.

Freeman, Katherine Holladay. *Our Family Treasures: Holladay, Christiansen, Greenhalgh, Lebaron.* Self-published. https://dcms.lds.org/delivery/DeliveryManagerServlet?dps_pid=IE61405 (accessed November 24, 2014). LDS Family History Library.

Fritz, Albert B. Letter to Sterling McMurrin, February 27, 1960. Sterling M. McMurrin Papers, Box 341, fd. 9. Special Collections, Marriott Library.

"From Utah." *Newark [N.J.] Daily Advertiser*, April 6, 1857, 2.

"From Utah." *Weekly Wisconsin Patriot*, April 18, 1857, 1.

"Frontier Intelligence." *[Brattleboro] Vermont Phoenix*, July 13, 1838, 3.

Frost, Brian. *Struggling to Forgive: Nelson Mandela and South Africa's Search for Reconciliation.* London: HarperCollins, 1998.

Fuente, Alejandro De La. *Nation for All: Race, Inequality, and Politics in Twentieth-Century Cuba.* Chapel Hill: University of North Carolina Press, 2011.

Fuller, Amos. Journal, 1838. Holograph. Perry Special Collections.

"Fundamentalist LDS Church Members Object to New Black Priest Doctrine." *The Bulletin* (Bend, Ore.), July 28, 1978, 10.

Furlonge, Geoffrey. "The Land of Judah on the Horn of Africa." January 21, 1963. *BYU Speeches of the Year*. Provo, Utah: Brigham Young University, 1963.

Galvão, Jose. Oral History Transcript. Interviewed by Michael Landon, June 20, 1994. LDS Church History Library.

"Gann Vows to Fight Forced Busing, But Is Uncertain on How to Halt It." *San Diego Union*, October 18, 1980, A3.

Gardner, Marvin K. "Two Elders Called from Ghana." *Ensign*, April 1981, 78.

Gaskin, Shereeze (Bellville, South Africa). Letter to Joseph B. Rogers, November 11, 1992. MS 17809, LDS Church History Library.

Gates, Susa Young. *Surname Book and Racial History: A Compilation and Arrangement of Genealogical and Historical Data for Use by the Students and Members of the Relief Society of the Church of Jesus Christ of Latter-day Saints*. Salt Lake City: General Board of the Relief Society, 1918.

"Gathering, The." *Evening and the Morning Star* 1, no. 6 (November 1832): 45.

"Genealogy Message." *Cumorah's Southern Messenger* 27, no. 8 (August 1952): 124.

General Church Meeting Minutes. March 26, April 25, May 23, and December 2, 1847, Box 1, fds. 52, 53, and 59. In Richard E. Turley, ed. *Selected Collections from the Archives of the Church of Jesus Christ of Latter-day Saints*. Provo, Utah: BYU Religious Studies Center, 2002, DVD 18.

General Church Minutes. February 13, 1849, Box 2, fd. 8. In Richard E. Turley, ed. *Selected Collections from the Archives of the Church of Jesus Christ of Latter-day Saints*. Provo, Utah: BYU Religious Studies Center, 2002, DVD 18.

"Genesis of a Church's Stand on Race, The." *Washington Post*, February 28, 2012. http://www.washingtonpost.com/politics/the-genesis-of-a-churchs-stand-on-race/2012/02/22/gIQAQZXyfR_story.html (accessed June 17, 2013).

"George A. Smith." *The Contributor* 4, no. 3 (December 1882): 81–86.

"George A. Smith." *Tullidge's Quarterly Magazine* 3, no. 3 (July 1884): 232–52.

Gerlach, Larry. *Blazing Crosses in Zion: The Ku Klux Klan in Utah*. Logan: Utah State University Press, 1982.

"Get Rid of Hate." *Deseret News*, May 31, 1980, 16.

Getty, J. Arch. *Origins of the Great Purges: The Soviet Communist Party Reconsidered*. Cambridge, England: Cambridge University Press, 1987.

"Yank, 2 Pals End up Nile Dinghy Trip." *Omaha World Herald*, June 27, 1951, 16.

"Ghana Temple Brings Euphoria." *LDS Church News*, January 17, 2004, 14.

Gilmore, Paul. "The Indian in the Museum: Henry David Thoreau, Okah Tubbee, and Authentic Manhood." *Arizona Quarterly* 54, no. 2 (1998): 25–63.

"Girls Who Want Husbands." *Deseret News*, April 18, 1855, 5.

Gish, Steven. *Desmond Tutu: A Biography*. Westport, Conn.: Greenwood Press, 2004.

Givens, Terryl L. *By the Hand of Mormon: The American Scripture that Launched a New World Religion*. New York: Oxford University Press, 2002.

———. *The Viper on the Hearth: Mormons, Myths, and the Construction of Heresy*. New York: Oxford University Press, 1996.

Givens, Terryl L., and Matthew J. Grow. *Parley P. Pratt: The Apostle Paul of Mormonism*. New York: Oxford University Press, 2011.

Glendale (California) West Ward. Manuscript History and Historical Reports, October 28, 1956. LR 3211 2, LDS Church History Library.

Goddard, John M. "Congo Journal." 1956. Typescript, John M. Goddard Papers, Box 1, fd. 6. Perry Special Collections.

———. "Q&A response." *New Era*, July 1974, 10.

_____. "Kayaks down the Nile, Part I." *Improvement Era* 62, no. 10 (October 1959): 736–39, 760, 762.

Goddard, John M. "Kayaks Down the Nile." *National Geographic Magazine* 72, no. 5 (May 1955): 697–723.

_____. Letters to Family, all holograph, all in John M. Goddard Papers, Box 1, fd. 1, Perry Special Collections.
January 10, 1950
September 20, 1950
September 21, 1950
n.d.(prob. ca. October 1950
October 3, 1950
October 12, 1950
October 25, 1950
October 26, 1950. Note: typescript contains more information than the holograph.
November 1, 1950
November 20, 1950
December 30, 1950
January 4, 1951 (December–January inclusive)
January 10, 1951
January 11, 1951
April 27, 1951
May 15, 1951
July 20, 1951

Goddard, John, and Pearlyne Crowley wedding photograph. http://gatheringgardiners. blogspot.com/2012/05/1920-1970-glendale-ca.html (accessed January 21, 2014).

"Goddard Congo Films Scheduled for Building Fund." *Sunday Herald* (Provo, Utah), March 20, 1960, 9A.

"Goddard Film to Feature Scenic Trip." *University of Utah Daily Chronicle*, March 25, 1955, 1.

"Goddard to Narrate Film Here Sunday." *Carroll [Iowa] Daily Times Herald*, March 15, 1963, 1.

"Going with the Wind." *Roosevelt [Utah] Standard*, June 22, 1950, 2.

Goldberg, James. Correspondence with Russell Stevenson, March 13, 2014.

Golubuff, Risa. *The Lost Promise of Civil Rights.* Cambridge. Mass.: Harvard University Press, 2010.

"Good Suggestion, A." *Saginaw [Michigan] News*, August 27, 1881, 1.

Gooren, Henri. "The Dynamics of LDS Growth in Guatemala, 1948–1998." *Dialogue: A Journal of Mormon Thought* 34, no. 3 (Fall 2004): 55–75.

Gordon, Sarah Barringer. *The Mormon Question: Polygamy and Constitutional Conflict in Nineteenth-Century America.* Chapel Hill: University of North Carolina Press, 2002.

Gordon, Thomas F. *Gazetteer of the State of New York.* Philadelphia: T. M. and F. G. Collins, 1836.

"Gospel Preached through Music." *Cumorah's Southern Messenger* 24, no. 5 (May 1949): 70.

"Governor Vetoes Busing Curb, Calls It Unconstitutional." *San Diego Union*, February 5, 1980, 1.

"Governor's Message." *Deseret News*, January 10, 1852, 1–2.

"Gov't Officials Demand Bribe—Mormon Drops Bombshell." *The [Accra] Chronicle*, February 16, 2004. http://www.ghanaweb.com/GhanaHomePage/NewsArchive/artikel. php?ID=51855 (accessed December 18, 2013).

"Grand Instigators of the New York Riots." *Liberator* (Boston, Mass.), July 26, 1834, 119.

Gray, Darius. Lecture at BYU, February 12, 2014. Notes in my possession.

"Greek Student Learns American Way of Farming." *Vernal (Utah) Express*, November 2, 1950, 1.

Greeley, Horace. *An Overland Journey, from New York to San Francisco, in the Summer of 1859.* New York: C. M. Saxton, Barker, and Company, 1860.

Green, Beriah. "A Review: The Principles of Reform." *The Quarterly Anti-Slavery Magazine* 1 (October 1835): 34–67.

Greene, John P. Letter to Oliver Cowdery. *Messenger and Advocate* 1, no. 1 (October 1834): 7–8.

Griend, Ward M. Vander. "Alma Heaton: Professor of Fun." PhD diss., Brigham Young University, 1981.

"Ground Broken for First Temple in West Africa." *LDS Church News*, November 24, 2001, 14.

Grover, Mark L. "The Maturing of the Oak: The Dynamics of LDS Growth in Latin America." *Dialogue: A Journal of Mormon Thought* 38, no. 2 (Summer 2005): 79–104.

_____. "The Mormon Church and German Immigrants in Southern Brazil: Religion and Language." *Jahrbuch für Geschichte von Staat: Wirtschaft und Gesellschaft Lateinamerikas* 26 (1989): 299–306.

_____. "The Mormon Priesthood Revelation and the São Paulo, Brazil Temple." *Dialogue: A Journal of Mormon Thought* 23, no. 1 (Spring 1990): 39–53.

_____. "Religious Accommodation in the Land of Racial Democracy: Mormon Priesthood and Black Brazilians." *Dialogue: A Journal of Mormon Thought* 17, no. 3 (Autumn 1984): 23–34.

"Growing Power of Mormonism." *[Portland] Oregonian*, June 17, 1902, 12.

Hafen, LeRoy R. *Fort Laramie and the Pageant of the West, 1834–1890.* Lincoln: University of Nebraska Press, 1938.

Hale, Ethel C. Letter to ACLU, January 31, 1985, Box 2, fd. 18. Stephen Holbrook Papers, Utah State Historical Society Archives.

Hale, Robert M. Diary, 1967–69. LDS Church History Library.

Hales, Kenneth G. "George Hales: Pioneer Printer." Unpublished manuscript, 2008. LDS Church History Library.

_____. *George Hales: Pioneer Printer.* N.p.: Self-published, n.d.

Hales, Stephanie. Facebook post, August 24, 2013. https://www.facebook.com/stephanie.hales.39/posts/322956557850322 (accessed January 22, 2014; screenshot in my possession.)

Hammond, John J. *A Divided Mormon Zion: Northeastern Ohio or Western Missouri.* N.p.: Published by Xlibris for John Hammond, 2012.

Hampshire, Nita Redden. "Biography of Return Jackson Redden." MSS 945, Perry Special Collections.

Hancock, Levi Ward. "The Life of Levi W. Hancock." Typescript. Perry Special Collections.

Hancock, Mosiah L. "The Life Story of Mosiah Lyman Hancock." Typescript, 1970. Perry Special Collections.

Hanks, Marion D. "The Influence of Relief Society in the Home." *Relief Society Magazine* 42, no. 1 (January 1955): 566–75.

_____. Letter to Adam M. Duncan, February 25, 1957, Box 2, fd. 18. In Linda Sillitoe Papers, Special Collections, Marriott Library.

_____. "The Influence of Relief Society in the Home." *Relief Society Magazine* 42, no. 1 (January 1955): 566–76.

Hansen, A. Claude. Letter to Stephen Holbrook, September 22, 1964, Box 1, fd. 5. Stephen Holbrook Papers, Utah State Historical Society Archives.

_____. Letter to Stephen Holbrook, September 22, 1964, Box 1, fd. 5, Stephen Holbrook Papers, Utah State Historical Society Archives.

Hansen, Debra Gold. "The Boston Female Anti-Slavery Society and the Limits of Gender Politics." In Jean Fagan Yellin and John C. Van Lorne, eds. *The Abolitionist Sisterhood:*

Women's Political Culture in Antebellum America. Ithaca: Cornell University Press, 1994, 45–100.

Hardy, John. *History of the Trials of Elder John Hardy before the Church of Latter Day Saints in Boston*. Boston: Conway and Company, 1844.

Harlan, Louis R., and Raymond W. Smock, eds. *The Booker T. Washington Papers: 1912–1914*, 14 vols. Urbana: University of Illinois Press, 1982.

Harmon, Reuben. [Statement.] *Startling Revelations: Naked Truths about Mormonism*. Edited by Arthur B. Deming, 1, no. 12 (April 1888): 201.

Harris, Benjamin. "'In Deed and in Word': The Anti-Apartheid Movement at the University of Utah, 1978–1987." *Utah Historical Quarterly* 75, no. 3 (Summer 2007): 258–76.

Harris, Matt. "'People of African Descent Should Not Be Held Accountable for the Deeds of Others': David Jackson, the Mormon Church, and the Quest to Cast Off the Curse of Cain." Paper, Sunstone Symposium, August 1, 2013, Salt Lake City.

Hartley, William G. "Saint without Priesthood: The Collected Testimonies of Ex-Slave Samuel Chambers." *Dialogue: A Journal of Mormon Thought* 12, no. 2 (Summer 1979): 13–21.

Haskel, Daniel, and J. Calvin Smith. *A Complete Descriptive and Statistical Gazeteer of the United States of America*. New York: Sherman and Smith, 1843.

Hawkes, John. "Why Can't the Negro Hold the Priesthood." In Wynetta Mills Martin, *Black Mormon Tells Her Story*. Salt Lake City: Hawkes Publication, 1972, 85–91.

Haws, J. B. *The Mormon Image in American Mind: Fifty Years of Public Perception*. New York: Oxford University Press, 2013.

Haycock, D. Arthur. Memo to President Robison, March 8, 1960, LDS Church History Library.

Haywood, Harry. *Black Communist in the Freedom Struggle: The Life of Harry Haywood*. Edited by Gwendolyn Hall. St. Paul: University of Minnesota Press, 2012.

Haven, Jesse. Diaries. LDS Church History Library.

Hazen, Craig. *The Village Enlightenment in America: Popular Religion and Science in the Nineteenth Century*. Urbana: University of Illinois Press, 2000.

"He Claims a Misquote." *Deseret News*, June 23, 1965, 5A.

Heading, Official Declaration—2, March 2013. https://www.lds.org/scriptures/dc-testament/od/2?lang=eng (accessed September 2, 2013).

Heaton, Alma. *Ballroom Dance Rhythms: Prepared for the Guidance of Instructor and Student in Ballroom Dancing*. Dubuque, Iowa: W. C. Brown, 1958.

Hedges, Andrew H., Alex D. Smith, and Richard Lloyd Anderson, eds. *Journals, Vol. 2, December 1841–April 1843*. Vol. 2 of the Journal series of THE JOSEPH SMITH PAPERS. General editors Dean C. Jessee, Ronald K. Esplin, and Richard Lyman Bushman. Salt Lake City: Church Historian's Press, 2011.

Heifitz, Ronald A. *Leadership without Easy Answers*. Cambridge, Mass.: Harvard University Press, 1994.

"Heinz Asked to Pressure S. Africa." *Pittsburgh Post-Gazette*, July 25, 1984, 6.

"Heinz Taken to Task on Economic Sanctions." *Morning Call* (Allentown, Penn.), July 25, 1984. http://articles.mcall.com/1984-07-25/news/2434721_1_sen-john-heinz-economic-sanctions-black-leaders (accessed December 31, 2013).

Henderson, Richard W. Qtd. in "Deseret Stake Conference." *Millard County Chronicle*, January 14, 1943, 1.

Henderson v. United States. 339 U.S. 816 (1950).

Henry, Patrick. "Letter on Slavery." *Palmyra Register*, December 29, 1819, 3.

"Her Atonement Was Her Death." *New York Herald*, April 17, 1889, 12.

Hickey, Eric, ed. *Encyclopedia of Murder and Violent Crime*. Thousand Oaks, Calif.: Sage, 2003.

Hicks, Michael D. *Mormonism and Music: A History.* Urbana: University of Illinois Press, 2003.

Hidley, John H. "Race and Rights: Part I." *[University of] Utah Daily Chronicle,* October 1, 1963, 2.

Higley, George S. *The Higleys and Their Ancestry: An Old Colonial Family.* New York: D. Appleton and Company, 1896.

Hill, Christopher. *Change in South Africa: Blind Alleys or New Directions.* New York: Rowman and Littlefield, 1983.

Hilliard, David, and Donald Weise, eds. *The Huey P. Newton Reader.* New York: Seven Stories Press, 2002.

Hinckley, Gordon B. "The Church and New Media: Clarity, Context, and an Official Voice." Mormon Newsroom, http://www.mormonnewsroom.org/article/the-church-and-new-media:-clarity,-context-and-an-official-voice-newsroom-lds.org-full-story (accessed August 23, 2013).

_____. "The Need for Greater Kindness." *Ensign,* May 2006, 58–61.

_____. "Priesthood Restoration." *Ensign,* October 1988, 69–72.

_____. "Rejoice in This Great Era of Temple Building." *Ensign,* November 1985, 53–60.

"Historical Events." (Section B). September 16, 1979; June 29, 1980.

"History of George A. Smith." In George A. Smith Papers, Box 1, fd. 1. In Richard E. Turley, ed. *Selected Collections from the Archives of the Church of Jesus Christ of Latter-day Saints.* Provo, Utah: BYU Religious Studies Center, 2002, 1:18.

"History of Joseph Smith." *Millennial Star*
21, no. 7 (February 12, 1859): 107.
22, no. 10 (March 10, 1860): 151.

"History of Robert Gardner, Jr., Written by Himself." Perry Special Collections.

"History of the South African Mission, The." *Cumorah's Southern Messenger* 32, no. 10 (October 1957): 152–57.

"History of the Southern States Mission." *Latter-day Saints Southern Star* 1, no. 18 (April 1, 1899): 138–39.

History of the Church of Jesus Christ of Latter-day Saints. Edited by B. H. Roberts, 2d ed. rev. 6 vols., 1902–12, Vol. 7, 1932. Rpt., Salt Lake City: Deseret Book, 1980 printing.

Holbrook, Stephen. Letter to Editor of *Deseret News,* June 19, 1965, Box 1, fd. 25. Stephen Holbrook Papers, Utah State Historical Society Archives.

_____. Letter to Editor, n.d., Box 1, fd. 20. Stephen Holbrook Papers, Utah State Historical Society Archives.

_____. Letter to Gordon B. Hinckley, June 23, 1972, Box 2, fd. 17, Stephen Holbrook Papers, Utah State Historical Society Archives.

_____. "Revelation Suggestion." *Salt Lake Tribune,* June 25, 1975. Clipping in Hyrum Wheelwright Papers, Stewart Library, Weber State University, Ogden, Utah.

"Holiday Week Marked by Parties and Numerous Get-Togethers." *Ogden-Standard Examiner,* November 26, 1950, 2B.

Hollist, J. Taylor. "Walking-on-Water Stories and Other Susquehanna River Folk Tales about Joseph Smith." *Mormon Historical Studies* 6, no. 1 (Spring 2005): 35–52.

"Home Economist Slates 2-Year Indonesian Stay." *Deseret News,* March 8, 1957, 8.

"'Homefront' Ad Series Wins Honors for Mormon Church." *Gettysburg [Penn.] Times,* August 9, 1995, A8.

Hope, Len. Autobiography, LDS Church History Library.

_____. "Testimony of Len Hope." April 29, 1938. LDS Church History Library.

Hope, Mary L. Testimony, April 28, 1938. LDS Church History Library.

Hopkins, Bruce R. *Tax-Exempt Organizations and Constitutional Law: Nonprofit Law as Shaped by the U.S. Supreme Court.* Hoboken, N.J.: Wiley and Sons, 2012.

Horatio, Letter to the Editor, *The Contributor* 6, no. 9 (June 1885): 32829.

Horne, Dennis. *Latter Leaves in the Life of Lorenzo Snow*. Spanish Fork, Utah: Cedar Fort, 2013.

Horowitz, Jason. "The Genesis of a Church's Stand on Race." *Washington Post*, February 28, 2012. http://www.washingtonpost.com/politics/the-genesis-of-a-churchs-stand-on-race/2012/02/22/gIQAQZXyfR_story.html (accessed August 23, 2013).

House Committee on Un-American Activities. *Communist Training Operations*. House of Representatives, 86th Congress, July 21–22, 1959. Washington, D.C.: Government Printing Office, 1960.

Howell, Blair. "Utah Student Selected as Freedom Rider to Retrace Historic Civil Rights Route." *Deseret News*, April 21, 2011. http://www.deseretnews.com/article/705371083/Utah-student-selected-as-Freedom-Rider-to-retrace-historic-civil-rights-route.html?pg=all (accessed May 9, 2013).

Howell, Carol. In Donovan Howell, Mission Journal, 1989–90, LDS Church History Library.

Howitt, William. "The Young Squire." In Joseph Meadows, *Heads of the People: or, Portraits of the English*. Philadelphia: Carey and Hart, 1841, 81–90.

Howland, Nina, ed. *Foreign Relations of the United States, 1964–1968: Nigeria*. Washington, D.C.: Government Printing Office, 1999.

Humes, Edward. "The Medicine Man." *Los Angeles Magazine*, July 2001, 95–99, 166–68.

Hunt, George W. *A History of the Hunt Family from the Norman Conquest, 1066 A.D. to the Year 1890*. Boston: McDonald, Gill, and Company, 1890.

Hunter, Howard W. "All Are Alike Unto God." *BYU Speeches of the Year*. Provo, Utah: Brigham Young University Press, 1980.

Hurd, D. Hamilton. *History of Fairfield County, Connecticut*. Philadelphia: J. W. Lewis and Co., 1881.

Hyde, Joseph Smith. *Orson Hyde*. Salt Lake City: n.pub., 1933.

Hyde, Orson. Letter to Editor. *Messenger and Advocate* 2, no. 1 (October 1835): 206.

_____. Sermon transcript. In General Meeting Minutes, May 30, 1847. In Richard E. Turley, ed. *Selected Collections from the Archives of the Church of Jesus Christ of Latter-day Saints*. Provo, Utah: BYU Religious Studies Center, 2002, 1:18.

_____. *Speech of Elder Orson Hyde, Delivered before the High Priests Quorum of Nauvoo, April 27th, 1845, upon the Course and Conduct of Mr. Sidney Rigdon and upon His Merits to His Claim to the Presidency of the Church of Jesus Christ of Latter-day Saints*. City of Joseph [Nauvoo], Ill: John Taylor, 1845.

"I Can't Let You Talk to Them, George. You'll Snow Them," *Life*, May 5, 1967, 823.

"Idaho Klan to Go after Bootleggers." *Ogden Standard*, January 1, 1923, 1.

"Important Cabinet Meeting, An." *New York Herald*, November 1, 1871, 6.

"Important Dates in Church History—Takoram District." n.d. Joseph Dadzie Papers. LDS Church History Library.

"Important from the Frontier." *Albany [N.Y.] Argus*, December 18, 1838, 2.

Inaugural Minutes, June 12, 1960. LaMar S. Williams Papers, Box 1, fd. 9. LDS Church History Library.

"Incestuous Marriages." *Jackson [Mich.] Citizen*, April 5, 1870, 4.

"Indignant at Smoot's Action." *Pittsburgh Press*, February 13, 1903, 11.

"Installation." *[New Haven] Connecticut Journal* March 30, 1830, 1.

"Is This 'The Place?'" *[University of Utah] Chronicle*, January 20, 1947, 2.

James, Jane Manning. "Biography of Jane E. Manning James written from her own verbal statement and by her request." Holograph. Transcribed by Elizabeth J. A. Roundy, 1893. LDS Church History Library.

"Jeff Flake Lobbied for Utah Bill Supporting South African Regime." Audio recording on YouTube. http://www.youtube.com/watch?v=w7HYMrhU-R0&feature=youtu.be (accessed June 14, 2013).

Jenkins, Carma. "Communist Inspired? "*Davis County Clipper* (Bountiful, Utah), September 19, 1985, 17.

Jenkins, Phillip. *The Next Christendom: The Coming of Global Christianity.* New York: Oxford University Press, 2011.

Jennings, Julia. Letter to Editor, April 2, 1965. Photocopy of clipping from unidentified newspaper, Box 1, fd. 8, Stephen Holbrook Papers, Utah State Historical Society Archives.

Jensen, Robin Scott, Robert J. Woodford, and Steven C. Harper, eds., *Manuscript Revelation Books, Facsimile Edition*, Vol. 1 in the Revelations and Translations series of THE JOSEPH SMITH PAPERS. General editors Dean C. Jessee, Ronald K. Esplin, and Richard Lyman Bushman. Salt Lake City: Church Historian's Press, October 2009.

Jensen, Robin Scott, Richard E. Turley Jr., and Riley M. Lorimer, eds. *Revelations and Translations, Vol. 2: Published Revelations*. Vol. 2 in the Revelations and Translations series of THE JOSEPH SMITH PAPERS. General editors Dean C. Jessee, Ronald K. Esplin, and Richard Lyman Bushman. Salt Lake City: Church Historian's Press, 2011.

Jenson, Andrew. "Big Cottonwood Precinct." *Historical Record* 6, nos. 9–12 (December 1887): 283.

_____. "De Witt." *Historical Record* 7, no. 7 (July 1888): 603–8.

_____. "First Ward." *The Historical Record* 6, nos. 9–12 (December 1887): 308.

_____. *Latterday Saint Biographical Encyclopedia: A Compendium of Biographical Sketches of Prominent Men and Women in the Church of Jesus Christ of Latterday Saints.* 4 vols. Salt Lake City: Andrew Jenson History Company, 1901–30; rpt. Salt Lake City, Western Epics, 1971.

_____. "Quincy, Adams County, Illinois." *The Historical Record* 8, nos. 2–3 (March 1889): 733–39.

_____, ed. "South American Mission Manuscript History and Historical Reports, 1925–35." LR 8458 2. LDS Church History Library.

Jessee, Dean C., ed. "John Taylor['s] Nauvoo Journal." *BYU Studies* 23, no. 3 (1983): 1–105.

Jessee, Dean C., Mark Ashurst-McGee, and Richard L. Jensen, eds. *Journals, Vol. 1: 1832–1839*, Vol. 1 of the Journals series of THE JOSEPH SMITH PAPERS. General editors Dean C. Jessee, Ronald K. Esplin, and Richard Lyman Bushman. Salt Lake City: Church Historian's Press, 2008.

Jessee, Dean C., and David J. Whittaker. "The Last Months of Mormonism in Missouri: The Albert Perry Rockwood Journal." *BYU Studies* 28 (Winter 1988): 5–41.

Johansen, Jerald Ray. *A Commentary on the Pearl of Great Price: A Jewel Among the Scriptures.* Salt Lake City: Cedar Fort, 1985.

"John Birch Society, The." *Ephraim [Utah] Enterprise*, June 9, 1967, 7.

"John M. Goddard Presents." *Daily Herald* (Provo, Utah), March 25, 1973, 23.

"Johnny Young's Plea." *New York Herald*, February 17, 1881, 6.

Johnson, James Weldon, and J. Rosamond Johnson. *The Books of American Negro Spirituals.* New York: Da Capo Press, 2009.

Johnson, Jeffery O. "Change and Growth: The Mormon Church and the 1960s." *Sunstone* 17, no. 1 (June 1994): 25–29.

Johnson, Joseph. Autobiography, LDS Church History Library.

_____. "History of the Church of Jesus Christ of Latter-day Saints in Ghana." ca. 1985. LDS Church History Library.

_____. Qtd. in E. Dale LeBaron, "Steadfast African Pioneer." *Ensign*, December 1999, 45–49.

Johnson, Loretta. Journal, March 24, 1962. Loretta Johnson Papers, LDS Church History Library.

Johnson, N. B. Letter to Brigham Young, January 1, 1861. Reel 38, Brigham Young Office Files. LDS Church History Library.

Johnson, Nephi. Autobiography. http://history.lds.org/overlandtravels/trailExcerptMulti?lang =eng&pioneerId=24377&sourceId=4923 (accessed August 28, 2013).

Johnson, Sonia [Harris]. Letters to Harrises/Harris/Alvin and Ida Harris, Sonia Johnson Papers, Box 3, fds. 10–11. Special Collections, Marriott Library, University of Utah.
> October 23, 1965
> February 5, 1966
> March 24, 1966
> July 16, 1966
> August 28, 1966
> January 30, 1970, Box 1, fd. 16
> December 9, 1975, Box 1, fd. 21
> July 20, 1978, Box 42, fd. 12

Johnson, Sylvester. *The Myth of Ham in Nineteenth-Century American Christianity: Race, Heathens, and the People of God.* New York: Palgrave Macmillan, 2004.

Jones Marvin. Letters to Dorothy Buckley, Marvin Jones Papers, LDS Church History Library:
> October 26, 1961
> November 2, 1961,

_____. Diary, 1961, LDS Church History Library.

"Joseph Smith to Be Lecture Topic." *Ogden Standard-Examiner*, January 31, 1922, 12.

Journal History of the Church of Jesus Christ of Latter-day Saints (chronological scrapbook), LDS Church History Library; cited by date in notes.

"Judge McConkie Seeks Governor's Post, Bailiff Enters Attorney General Race." *Deseret News*, May 9, 1940, 1.

Kahn, Edward. "Desdemona and the Role of Women in the Antebellum North." *Theatre Journal*, 60, no. 2 (May 2008): 235–55.

Kalu, Ogbu. *African Pentecostalism: An Introduction.* New York: Oxford University Press, 2008.

Kampala Uganda Group. General Minutes, MS 13691 11, November 15, 1970, and March 14, 1971, LDS Church History Library.

Kane, Thomas L. Letter to Brigham Young, October 13, 1869. Brigham Young Office Files, Box 40, fd. 14, LDS Church History Library.

Kasdorf, Hans. *Design of My Journey: An Autobiography.* Fresno: Center for Mennonite Brethren Studies, 2004.

Katagiri, Yashurio. *The Mississippi State Sovereignty Commission: Civil Rights and States' Rights.* Jackson: University Press of Mississippi, 2001.

Katwyk, Shirley. See Shirley Van Katwyk. Papers, LDS Church History Library.

Kellogg, Heather M. "Shades of Gray: Sonia Johnson's Life through Letters and Autobiography." *Dialogue: A Journal of Mormon Thought* 29, no. 2 (Summer 1996): 77–86.

Kennedy Asks Lawyers to Enter Allen Case." *Springfield [Mass.] Union,* October 26, 1963, 26.

Kenney, Scott G., ed. *Wilford Woodruff's Journal, 1833–1898.* Typescript, 9 vols. Midvale, Utah: Signature Books, 1983–85.

"Khumalo Inspires 'Sarafina!'" and "Stage Production Better than Movie." Both in *Mobile Register*, October 2, 1992.

"Killing of Thos. Coleman Monday Night, The." *Union Vedette*, December 15, 1866, 2.

Kimball, Edward L. "Spencer W. Kimball and the Revelation on the Priesthood." *BYU Studies* 47, no. 2 (2008): 5–78.

_____. Working Draft of *Lengthen Your Stride: The Presidency of Spencer W. Kimball*. Salt Lake City: Benchmark Books, 2009.

Kimball, Heber C. Letter of Introduction by Joseph Smith, June 1, 1843, MS 9670. LDS Church History Library.

Kimball, Linda Hoffman. "Life Is Good: An Interview with Catherine Stokes." *Exponent II* 26, no. 3 (Spring 2003): 9.

Kimball, Spencer W. Address, ca. 1970. Manhattan Second Ward, audiocassette 13, Grant Bethers Audio Recordings Collection. Transcription by Russell Stevenson. LDS Church History Library.

_____. "The Evil of Intolerance." *Conference Report*, April 1954, 103–8.

_____. "The False Gods We Worship" *Ensign*, June 1976, 3–6.

_____. Letter to Edward L. Kimball, June 15, 1963. In Edward L. Kimball, ed. *The Teachings of Spencer W. Kimball, Twelfth President of the Church of Jesus Christ of Latter-day Saints*. Salt Lake City: Bookcraft, 1982, 448.

_____. Meeting in Johannesburg South Africa, October 23, 1978, quoted in Edward L. Kimball, "Spencer W. Kimball and the Revelation on the Priesthood." *BYU Studies* 47, no. 2 (2008): 52 note 140.

_____. "Weep, O World, For the Indian." *Conference Report of the Church of Jesus Christ of Latter-day Saints*, April 1947, 143–52.

_____. "When the World Will Be Converted." Adapted from an address to Regional Representatives, April 4, 1974, *Ensign*, October 1974, 3–7.

Kimball, Stanley B. *Heber C. Kimball: Patriarch and Pioneer*. Urbana: University of Illinois Press, 1986.

"King Adept, Dedicated, But Work Gained Little." *Omaha [Neb.] World Herald*, January 7, 1968.

"King Staff Member Called Red Resigns." *Omaha [Neb.] World Herald*, December 2, 1962, 18.

King, Wilma. *Stolen Childhood: Slave Youth in Nineteenth-century America*. Bloomington: Indiana University Press, 2011.

King's Aid to the Enemy." *Augusta [Maine] Chronicle*, July 5, 1965, 6.

"King's Name Revives Memories of Struggle." *Deseret News*, January 13, 1985, B1.

Kinney, Eunice Ross. Letters to Wingfield Watson. Holograph. Perry Special Collections.
July 5, 1885
September 1891

Kinney, Eunice Ross. Marriage Certificate of Eunice Ross and Avery Kinney, February 24, 1845, Michigan County Marriages, Berrien, Michigan.

Kirtland Elders Certificates. CD. CR 100 41, 75, LDS Church History Library.

"Kiwanis Will Hear 'Des. News.' Editor." *Davis County Clipper* (Bountiful, Utah), July 15, 1955, 1.

"Klan in a Day's Uproar, The." *Ogden Standard*, June 26, 1924, 4.

"Klan Lecture Given Here." *Ogden Standard-Examiner*, March 26, 1924, 2.

Klein, Alan. *Growing the Game: The Globalization of Major League Baseball*. New Haven, Conn.: Yale University Press, 2006.

Knecht, William L., and Peter L. Crawley, eds. *History of Brigham Young*. Berkeley, Calif.: MassCal Associates, 1974.

Knight, Hal. "Touching Temple Fulfills a Dream for Aged Woman." *LDS Church News*, March 7, 1981, 10.

Knox, Robert. *The Races of Man: A Fragment*. Philadelphia: Lea and Blanchard, 1850.

Knudson, Conrad. *Doctrine and Covenants Guidebook*. Spanish Fork: Cedar Fort, 1999.

Kotkin, Stephen. *Magnetic Mountain: Stalinism as a Civilization*. Berkeley: University of California Press, 1997.

Kotz, Nick. *Judgment Days: Lyndon Baines Johnson, Martin Luther King, Jr., and the Laws that Changed America.* New York: Houghton Mifflin, 2005.

Kreisher, Otto. "Brown Gets Bill Restricting Court Orders on Busing." *San Diego Union,* February 1, 1980, 1.

"Ku Klux Klan, Fully Organized in Salt Lake; Serves Public Notice That Lawless Element Will Be Punished." *Salt Lake Telegram,* February 7, 1922, 2.

"Ku Klux Klan, The." *Bismarck [N.D.] Tribune,* March 27, 1885, 4.

"Ku Klux Klan." *Worcester [Mass.] Daily Spy,* June 23, 1884, 2.

"Ku Klux Klan's Warning to Its Victims." *Logan Republican,* March 25, 1916, 5.

"Ku-Klux Klan, The." *Albany [N.Y.] Argus,* April 1, 1871, 2.

"Ku-Klux Klan." *Columbian Register* (New Haven, Conn.), April 22, 1871, 1.

"Labor in Civilization." *The Prophet,* September 28, 1844, 1.

"Lady Republicans Schedule Talk on Civil Rights." *Davis County Clipper* (Bountiful, Utah), November 8, 1963, 1.

Larcom,Lucy. *A New England Girlhood: Outlined from Memory.* Boston: Houghton Mifflin, 1889.

Larsen, Mrs. Leland. Letter to Henry H. Blood, April 26, 1935, Henry H. Blood Papers, Utah State Archives. Qtd. in Kenneth W. Baldridge. "Nine Years of Achievement: The Civilian Conservation Corps in Utah." PhD diss., Brigham Young University, 1971, 338.

Laws of the State of Missouri, 2 vols. St. Louis: E. Charles, 1825.

"Lawyers Asked to Aid Integration." *Lakeland [Fla.] Ledger,* August 14, 1963, 3.

"LDS Church Says Story Is Wrong." *Deseret News,* May 19, 1998. http://www.deseretnews.com/article/630911/LDS-Church-says-story-is-wrong.html?pg=all (accessed September 10, 2013).

"LDS Church Says Story Is Wrong." *Deseret News,* May 19, 1998, A-1. http://www.deseretnews.com/article/630911/LDS-Church-says-story-is-wrong.html?pg=all (accessed September 10, 2013).

LDS Dance Manual, 1956–57. Salt Lake City: General Boards of the Mutual Improvement Association, 1956. Microfiche. LDS Church History Library.

"LDS Missionary to Speak Wednesday." *Winona [Minn.] Republican-Herald,* May 14, 1949, 13.

"LDS Scene, The." *Improvement Era* 72, no. 7 (July 1969): 83.

"LDS Stand on Blacks Challenged." *Ogden Standard-Examiner,* June 16, 1975, 6B.

"LDS to Repudiate." Advertisement. *Salt Lake Tribune,* July 23, 1978, A6.

"Leadership Fete Planned at B.Y.U." *Milford News,* January 25, 1934, 1.

Leary, James P., ed. *Wisconsin Folklore.* Madison: University of Wisconsin Press, 1999.

LeBaron, E. Dale. "Gospel Pioneers in Africa." *Ensign,* August 1990, 40–43.

_____. "Julia Mavimbela." *Liahona,* March 1995, 43–48.

_____. "Official Declaration 2: Revelation on the Priesthood." In *Sperry Symposium Classics: The Doctrine and Covenants.* Edited by Craig K. Manscill. Provo, Utah: BYU Religious Studies Center, 2004, 332–46.

_____. "Steadfast African Pioneer." *Ensign,* December 1999, 45–49.

Lee, Jarena. Autobiography, 1836. In *American Lives: An Anthology of Autobiographical Writing.* Edited by Robert Sayre. Madison: University of Wisconsin Press, 1994, 281–98.

Lee, John D. Journal, 1842. MS 2092. LDS Church History Library.

"Legislator Urging LDS to Change Black Rule." *Salt Lake Tribune,* June 16, 1975, 7.

"Lehi Locals and Personals." *American Fork Citizen,* March 11, 1916, 5.

Lentz, Richard Glen, and Karla K. Gower. *The Opinions of Mankind: Racial Issues, Press, and Propaganda in the Cold War.* Columbia: University of Missouri Press, 2011.

Lewis, Bea. "Mormons' Worldwide Expansion Finds African Missions Fertile." *Sarasota [Fla.] Herald-Tribune* March 7, 1987, 6E.

"Lie Nailed, A." *Morning Herald* (Lexington, Ky.), May 4, 1899, 9.

"Life and Testimony of Mary E. Lightner, The." *Utah Genealogical and Historical Magazine* 17 (July 1926): 1–44.

"Linda Pierce Will Marry Ted C. Olsen." *Vernal [Utah] Express*, May 26, 1966, 4.

Lindsay, John S. "The Origin of Races." *Mormon Tribune*, April 23, 1870, 130.

Lindsey, Richard P. Dedicatory Prayer, September 22, 1991. Transcript. Maurice Bateman Temple Papers, LDS Church History Library.

Lingle, Earl R. Letter to John M. Goddard, March 7, 1972. Holograph, John M. Goddard Papers, Box 3, fd. 9. Perry Special Collections.

"Lion's Club Planning Minstrel Show." *Iron County Record*, October 14, 1935, 4.

Lipper, Bob. "BYU: Pollsters Converted—for Now." *Richmond [Va.] Times Dispatch*, November 21, 1984, D5.

"List of Agents." *The Prophet*, August 17, 1844, 2.

"List of Illegal Voters at Kanesville." In *Miscellaneous Documents Printed by Order of the House of Representatives*, 2 vols. Washington, D.C.: William M. Belt, 1850, 2:48.

"Little Dictator of Salt Lake, The." *Broad Ax*, March 14, 1896, 1.

"Little Nigger Baby." *Juvenile Instructor* 55, no. 1 (January 1920): 44.

Littlefield, Lyman O. *Reminiscences of Latter-day Saints: Giving an Account of Much Individual Suffering Endured for Religious Conscience.* Logan, Utah: Utah Journal Co., 1888.

Llife, John. *The African Poor: A History.* Cambridge, England: Cambridge University Press, 1987.

————. *The African Poor: A History.* Cambridge, England: Cambridge University Press, 1987.

Lloyd, Sherman. Letter to Stephen Holbrook, October 19, 1963, Box 1, fd. 23, Stephen Holbrook Papers, Utah State Historical Society Archives.

"Local Couple to Teach School in Morocco." *Davis County Clipper* (Bountiful, Utah), September 26, 1958, 4.

"Location Selected, A." *Utah Journal*, July 27, 1889, 4.

Lomax, Louis. "Looters Helped Agitators." *Dallas Morning News*, August 7, 1967.

————. "Outside Revolutionaries Blamed for Detroit Riots." *Dallas Morning News*, August 6, 1967, 1.

————. "Philosophy of Black Power Poses Threat of Revolution." *Dallas Morning News*, August 10, 1967, 1.

London, Jack. *The Star Rover.* New York: Grosslet and Dunlap, 1914.

Long, Edward *The History of Jamaica, or General Survey of the Antient and Modern State*, 3 vols. London, Ontario, Canada: T. Lowndes, 1774. Rpt. London, Ontario McGill-Queens Press, 2002.

"Lost." *Nauvoo Neighbor*, December 6, 1843, 3.

Lowell Conference (November 3, 1844)" and "Religious Notices." Both "in *The Prophet*, November 9, 1844, 2–3.

"Lowry Nelson to Preside Over Timp. Council." *Manti [Utah] Messenger*, October 10, 1930, 1.

Lund, John L. *The Church and the Negro: A Discussion of Mormons, Negroes, and the Priesthood.* Salt Lake City: Self-published, 1967.

Lye, William. "From Burundi to Zaire: Taking the Gospel to Africa." *Ensign,* March 1980, 10–15.

Lyman, Edward Leo. *Amasa Mason Lyman, Mormon Apostle and Apostate: A Study in Dedication.* Salt Lake City: University of Utah Press, 2009.

————, ed. *No Place to Call Home: The 1807–1857 Life Writings of Caroline Barnes Crosby, Chronicler of Outlying Mormon Communities.* Logan: Utah State University Press, 2005.

Lyman, Eliza Maria Partridge. Autobiography. Typescript. Perry Special Collections.

Mabey, Rachel N. Diary, 1978–79. LDS Church History Library.

Mabey, Rendell N., and Gordon T. Allred. *Brother to Brother: The Story of the Latter-day Saint Missionaries Who Took The Gospel to Africa*. Salt Lake City: Bookcraft, 1984.

Mabey, Rendell, and Edwin Q. Cannon. Letter to Carlos Asay, February 19, 1979, Edwin Q. Cannon Papers, MS 21299, Box 1, fd. 2. LDS Church History Library.

_____. Letter to EB Davis, May 15, 1979. Edwin Q. Cannon Papers, Box 1, fd. 2. LDS Church History Library.

"Mabey Shows African Safari." *Davis County Clipper* (Bountiful, Utah), December 9, 1960, 10.

MacKay, Michael Hubbard, Gerrit J. Dirkmaat, Grant Underwood, Robert J. Woodford, and William G. Hartley, eds. *Documents—Vol. 1: July 1828–June 1831*. Vol. 1 in the Documents series of THE JOSEPH SMITH PAPERS. General editors Dean C. Jessee, Ronald K. Esplin, and Richard Lyman Bushman. Salt Lake City: Church Historian's Press, 2013.

MacLean, Nancy K. *Behind the Mask of Chivalry: The Making of the Second Ku Klux Klan*. New York: Oxford University Press, 1994.

Madsen, Brigham D. *Against the Grain: Memoirs of a Western Historian*. Salt Lake City: Signature Books, 1998.

Madsen, Truman G. *Defender of the Faith: The B. H. Roberts Story*. Salt Lake City: Bookcraft, 1980.

Magnarella, Paul J. "The Black Panther Party's Confrontation with Ethnicity, Race, and Class." In Santosh C. Sasha, ed. *The Politics of Ethnicity and National Identity*. New York: Peter Lang, 2007, 52–65.

Mahlungu, Moses. "I Waited Fourteen Years," In E. Dale LeBaron, ed. *All Are Alike Unto God*. Salt Lake City: Bookcraft, 1990, 153–61.

"Mails Are Vicious, The." *Boston Herald*, September 13, 1962, 28.

Major, William Warner. Letter to Brigham Young, June 16, 1847, Brigham Young Office Files, Reel 30, LDS Church History Library.

"Man of Little Monkey Business, A." *Monday Magazine* (Provo, Utah), April 7, 1975, 17.

"Man Wants to Know Mormon Racial Position." *Los Angeles Tribune*, September 25, 1959, 10.

"Manuals on Guerrilla Warfare Sold, Senators Told." *Dallas Morning News*, July 1, 1969, 6.

"Manuscript History of the Church," A-1, 1838–56; Manuscript History of the Church, C-1, April 9, 1838. In Richard E. Turley, ed. *Selected Collections from the Archives of the Church of Jesus Christ of Latter-day Saints*. Provo, Utah: BYU Religious Studies Center, 2002, *Selected Collections*, 1:2.

"Mark of Cain and Curse of Ham, The." *Southern Presbyterian Review* 3, no. 3 (January 1850): 415–26.

"Marketing the Mormon Image: An Interview with Wendell J. Ashton." *Dialogue: A Journal of Mormon Thought* 10, no. 3 (Spring 1977): 15–20.

Marquardt, H. Michael. *Early Patriarchal Blessings of the Church of Jesus Christ of Latter-day Saints*. Salt Lake City: Smith-Pettit Foundation, 2007.

Marriage Certificate of Eunice Ross and Avery Kinney, February 24, 1845, Michigan County Marriages, Berrien, Michigan.

Marsh, Thomas B. Autobiography, 1857. In Historian's Office. Histories of the Twelve, LDS Church History Library.

Martelle, Scott, Jeff Gottlieb, and Jack Leonard. "A Doctor, a Deal Maker, and a Mystery." *Los Angeles Times*, March 20, 2000. http://articles.latimes.com/2000/mar/20/news/mn-10791/2 (accessed June 3, 2013).

"Martin Luther King to Be Honored with Holiday Celebration." *Davis County Clipper* (Bountiful, Utah), January 15, 1987, 2.

Martin, Wynetta Mills. *Black Mormon Tells Her Story*. Salt Lake City: Hawkes Publication, 1972.

Martinez-Hosang, Daniel. "Changing Valence of White Racial Innocence: Black-Brown Unity in the 1970s Los Angeles School Desegregation Struggles." In Josh Kun and Laura Pulido, eds., *Black and Brown in Los Angeles: Beyond Conflict and Coalition.* Berkeley: University of California Press, 2013, 115–42.

Martinez-Hosang, Daniel. "The Triumph of Racial Liberalism, The Demise of Racial Justice." In Joseph E. Lowndes, Julie Iovkov, and Dorian T. Warren, eds. *Race and American Political Development.* New York: Routledge, 2012, 299–303.

"Mary Frost Adams." *Young Woman's Journal* 17, no. 12 (December 1906): 538.

Mason, Patrick Q. *The Mormon Menace: Violence and Anti-Mormonism in the Postbellum South.* New York: Oxford University Press, 2011.

_____. "The Prohibition of Interracial Marriage in Utah, 1888–1963." *Utah Historical Quarterly* 76, no. 2 (Spring 2008): 108–31.

"Mass. 'Rights' Prisoner to Get RFK Help." *Boston Herald*, October 26, 1963, 21.

Matlock, John. *Apostasy: The Broad way to Hell.* London: John Matlock, 1778.

"Matter of Fact." *Advocate* (Baton Rouge, La.), April 16, 1964, 10.

Matthews, Benjamin. Letter to Brigham Young, March 31, 1849. Brigham Young Office Files, Reel 31. LDS Church History Library.

Mattice, Seth. Journal, 1946–47. LDS Church History Library.

Mauss, Armand L. *All Abraham's Children: Changing Mormon Conceptions of Race and Lineage.* Urbana: University of Illinois Press, 2003.

_____. "Casting Off the 'Curse of Cain.'" In Newell G. Bringhurst and Darron T. Smith, eds. *Black and Mormon.* Urbana: University of Illinois Press, 2004, 82–115.

_____. "The Fading of the Pharoah's Curse: The Decline and Fall of the Priesthood Ban against Blacks in the Mormon Church." *Dialogue: A Journal of Mormon Thought* 14, no. 3 (Autumn 1981): 10–45.

_____. "In Search of Ephraim: Traditional Mormon Conceptions of Lineage and Race." *Journal of Mormon History* 25, no. 1 (1999): 131–73.

_____. "Mormonism and the Negro: Faith, Folklore, and Civil Rights." *Dialogue: A Journal of Mormon Thought* 2, no. 4 (Winter 1967): 19–39.

_____. *Shifting Borders and a Tattered Passport: Intellectual Journeys of a Mormon Academic.* Salt Lake City: University of Utah Press, 2012.

Mavimbela, Julia, Oral History. Interviewed by Francine Russell Bennion and Matthew Heiss, August 28, 1995, Provo, Utah. LDS Church History Library.

Mavimbela, Julia. Qtd. in Sheila Bibb, comp. "The Johannesburg South Africa Temple: Historical Background, Construction, Various Events, and Spiritual Experiences Related Thereto." Maurice Bateman Temple Papers, LDS Church History Library.

May, Dean L. *Utah: A People's History.* Salt Lake City: University of Utah Press, 1987.

May, Katja. *African-Americans and Native Americans in the Cherokee and Creek Nations.* New York: Taylor and Francis, 1996.

Mayhew, Elijah. Diary, 1853. Holograph. LDS Church History Library.

Mbaku, John M. *Institutions and Development in Africa.* Trenton, N.J.: Africa World Press, 2004.

McCary, Lucy, writing as Laah Tubbee. *A Sketch of the Life of Okah Tubbee.* Toronto, Ontario: Henry Stephens, 1852.

McConkie, Bruce R. "All Are Alike Unto God." Printed in:
    A Charge to Religious Educators. Salt Lake City: Church of Jesus Christ of Latter-day Saints, 1982, 152–55.
    In *Priesthood.* Salt Lake City: Deseret Book, 1981, 126–37.
    In *A Symposium on the Book of Mormon.* Salt Lake City: The Church of Jesus Christ of Latter-day Saints 1979; rpt. 1981, 3–5.

_____. *The Millennial Messiah: The Second Coming of the Son of Man.* Salt Lake City: Bookcraft, 1982.

_____. *Mormon Doctrine.* Salt Lake City: Bookcraft,
first ed., 1958.
second ed., 1966. Rpt. 1979.

_____. Religion Class Lecture to the University of Utah Institute of Religion, October 9, 1967, AV 191, CD 1–3, LDS Church History Library.

McCulloch, James. *A Dictionary, Geographical, Statistical, and Historical of the Various Countries, Places, and Principal Natural Objects in the World,* 2 vols. New York: Harper and Brothers, 1843.

McDannell, Colleen. *Material Christianity: Religion and Popular Culture in America.* New Haven, Conn.: Yale University Press, 1995.

McDonald, David L. "The Individual Sacrament Cup." *Young Woman's Journal* 23, no. 4 (April 1912): 216–17.

McDonough, Ted. "Dead Air." *Salt Lake City Weekly,* January 30, 2008. http://www.cityweekly. net/utah/article-12-6491-feature-dead-air-krcl-is-getting-a-corporate-makeover-is-community-radio-done-for.html (accessed April 4, 2014).

McEntee, Peg. "Back in 1996, It Was Mike Wallace vs. Gordon B. Hinckley." *Salt Lake Tribune,* April 9, 2012. http://www.sltrib.com/sltrib/news/53880923-78/wallace-hinckley-mcentee-church.html.csp (accessed November 28, 2013).

"McKay, 96, President of Mormons, Dies." *Schenecdaty [N.Y.] Gazette,* January 19, 1970, 1.

McKay, David O. Diaries. Special Collections. Marriott Library.

_____. *Conference Report:*
April 1959, 71–75.
April 1964, 3–7.

_____. Letter to Lowell Bennion and Students at the University of Utah, November 3, 1947. In Llewelyn R. McKay, comp. *Home Memories of President David O. McKay.* Salt Lake City: Deseret Book, 1956, 226–31.

McKay, Llewelyn R. *Home Memories of President David O. McKay.* Salt Lake City: Deseret Book, 1956.

McKay, Michael H., Gerrit J. Dirkmaat, Grant Underwood, Robert J. Woodford, and William G. Hartley, eds. *Documents: Volume 1, July 1828–June 1831.* In Dean C. Jessee, Ronald K. Esplin, and Richard L. Bushman, general eds. The Joseph Smith Papers. Salt Lake City: Church Historian's Press, 2013.

McLaurin v. Oklahoma State Regents. 339 U.S. 637 (1950).

McMurrin, Sterling M. Letter to Lowell Bennion, March 22, 1960. Qtd. in Douglas Monty Trank, "A Rhetorical Analysis of the Rhetoric Emerging from the Mormon-Black Controversy." PhD diss., University of Utah, 1973, 165.

McMurrin, Sterling M. Letter to John L. Sorenson, March 18, 1960. McMurrin Papers, Box 341, fd. 9. Special Collections, Marriott Library.

_____. "A Note on the 1963 Civil Rights Statement." *Dialogue: A Journal of Mormon Thought* 12, no. 2 (Summer 1978): 60–63.

_____. "A Note on the 1963 Civil Rights Statement." *Dialogue: A Journal of Mormon Thought* 12, no. 2 (Summer 1979): 60–63.

McMurrin, Sterling M., and L. Jackson Newell. *Matters of Conscience: Conversations with Sterling M. McMurrin on Philosophy, Education, and Religion.* Edited by L. Jackson Newell. Salt Lake City: Signature Books, 1996.

Meeks, Heber C. Autobiography, 1980–1982. MS 7350, LDS Church History Library.

_____. Letter to Lowry Nelson, June 20, 1947. Lowry Nelson Papers, Box 4, fd. 2, Merrill-Cazier Library, Utah State University, Logan.

———. "Report on Visit to Cuba," July 23, 1947. Heber C. Meeks Papers, MS 1677, Box 2, fd. 10, Perry Special Collections. Also catalogued as Report to the First Presidency dated June 26, 1947, with the same call number.

Meeting Minutes. Unit not specified. ca. 1972. Joseph Dadzie Papers, LDS Church History Library.

"Meetings of a General Conference Held in the City of New York." *Gospel Herald* 4, no. 35 (November 15, 1849): 182.

Meeting Minutes of the Twelve (also catalogued as "of Brigham Young and Others"). In Richard E. Turley, ed. *Selected Collections from the Archives of the Church of Jesus Christ of Latter-day Saints.* Provo, Utah: BYU Religious Studies Center, 2002, 1:18.

June 25, 1843

October 28, 1845

January 14, 1847

March 26, 1847

June 13, 1847

February 13, 1849

Meeting Minutes of a Conference in Cincinnati, June 25, 1843. Photocopy in my possession.

Meik, Vivien. "Is Mormonism the Remedy." *Cumorah's Southern Messenger* 22, no. 8 (August 1947): 111–12.

"Members and the Mission, The." *Cumorah's Southern Messenger* 32, no. 8 (August 1957): 122.

Mensah, Raphael Abraham Frank. Letter to First Presidency, October 21, 1970. Ghana and Nigeria Files, LDS Church History Library.

Merryweather, F[rederick]. Letter to James J. Strang, February 8, 1847, *Zion's Reveille* 2, no. 7 (February 25, 1847): 27.

Merryweather, Frederick. Letter to Brigham Young, March 10, 1850, Brigham Young Office Files, Reel 31. LDS Church History Library.

"M.I.A. Road Show Proves Pleasing." *Iron County Record*, January 31, 1935, 4.

Miles, Henry. "Lowell." *Boston Recorder*, June 13, 1844, 96.

Miller, Keith. "Letter to the Editor." *[University of Utah] Daily Chronicle*, January 20, 1958, 2.

Miller, Reuben. *James J. Strang, Weighed in the Balance of Truth and Found Wanting.* Burlington, Wisc.: Reuben Miller, 1846.

———. Letter to Brigham Young, February 23, 1848. Brigham Young Office Files, Reel 30, LDS Church History Library.

Mills, Marion. "Letter to the Editor." *[University of Utah] Daily Chronicle*, January 14, 1958, 2.

"Minstrels Entertain." *Daily News-Democrat* (Huntington, Indiana), February 18, 1905, 1.

"Minutemen, The." *Encyclopedia of Murder and Violent Crime.* edited by Eric Hickey. New York: Sage, 2003, 314–15.

"Minutemen Leader Is Arrested Here." *San Diego Union,* November 11, 1961, 6.

"Minutes of a General Conference." *Times and Seasons*, July 1, 1844, 572.

"Minutes of a General Conference." *Times and Seasons*, July 1, 1844, 572.

"Minutes of the General Conference of the Church in Nigeria, March 10, 1961. LaMar S. Williams Papers, Box 1, fd. 9. LDS Church History Library.

"Minutes of High Priest Meeting, Spanish Fork, Utah, February 5, 1870.

"Minutes of a Special Conference of the Cincinnati Branch of the Church of Jesus Christ of Latter-day Saints, held at Elder Pugh's on the 1st day of June, 1845." *Times and Seasons* 6, no. 10 (June 1, 1845): 915.

Miscellaneous Documents Printed by Order of the House of Representatives, 2 vols. Washington, D.C.: William M. Belt, 1850.

"Miss. Lawmaker Says Disappearance May Be Hoax." *Springfield [Mass.] Union,* June 26, 1964, 8.

"Mission President's Message." *Cumorah's Southern Messenger* 28, no. 2 (February 1953): 18.

"Mississippi Solon Cites Hoax Theory." *Augusta [Maine] Chronicle* July 23, 1964, 10.

"Missouri and Slavery." *Palmyra Register*, December 6, 1820, 3.

Mitchell, Hezekiah. Journal, September 20, 1854. LDS Church History Library.

_____. "Central Route to the Pacific." *Daily [St. Louis] Missouri Republican*, December 19, 1853, 1.

Mitchell, Samuel. *Illinois in 1837.* Philadelphia: S. Augustus Mitchell, 1837.

Monson, Charles H. "On the Conditions Which Precede Revelation." *Dialogue: A Journal of Mormon Thought* 2, no. 3 (Autumn 1967): 159–61.

Monson, Thomas S. "Mark E. Petersen: A Giant among Men." *Ensign*, March 1984, 6–13.

Moon, Claire. *Narrating Political Reconciliation: South Africa's Truth and Reconciliation.* Lanham, Md.: Lexington Book, 2008.

Moore, Morton, & Co. Letter to Hiram Dayton and Harmon Cutler, November 23, 1841. LDS Church History Library.

"The Mormon Answer to the Hippies." *Vernal [Utah] Express*, January 18, 1968, 12.

Mormon Battalion, Muster Roll for Company A, October–December 1846, MS 5261. Holograph. LDS Church History Library.

"Mormon Church Backs Equality for Negroes." *Victoria [Tex.] Advocate*, May 3, 1965, 8.

"Mormon Dissident Files Suit." *[Portland] Oregonian*, May 17, 1977, A12.

"Mormon Elder to Give Talk on Foreign Tour." *Winnipeg [Manitoba] Tribune*, January 11, 1949, 7.

"Mormon Ku-Klux, The." *Denver Rocky Mountain News*, June 7, 1871, 1.

"Mormon Ku-Klux, The." *Weekly Journal Miner* (Prescott, Ariz.), December 16, 1871, 4.

"Mormon Leader Asserts Equality." *[University of] Utah Daily Chronicle*, October 7, 1963, 2.

"Mormon Problem, The." *San Francisco Bulletin*, March 16, 1869, 1.

"Mormonaires' Attract Bloemfontein Audiences." *Cumorah's Southern Messenger* 24, no. 9 (September 1949): 128.

"Mormonism in Africa." *Salt Lake Tribune*, January 11, 1879, 6.

"Mormonism in South Africa." *Millennial Star* 32, no. 42 (October 18, 1870): 668–69.

"Mormonites—Nullification, The." *National Gazette* (Philadelphia), August 22, 1833, 3.

"Mormons and Civil Rights." *Deseret News*, April 15, 1959, A22.

"Mormons Change Scout Policy." *Seattle Daily Times*, August 2, 1974, 7.

"Mormons Drop Race Stricture on Priesthood." *State Times [Baton Rouge, La.] Advocate*, June 10, 1978, 1.

"Mormons in Utah, The." *Boston Traveler*, April 14, 1857, 2.

"Mormons Plan to Build Temple in Ghana." *Indiana [Pa.] Gazette*, April 17, 1998, 7.

"Mormons Reaffirm Bar on Blacks' Priesthood." *Dallas Morning News*, January 11, 1970, 30.

"Mormons, The." *Millennial Star* 17, no. 4 (January 27, 1855): 63.

"Mormons, The." *North American* (Philadelphia), June 21,1841, 2.

"Mormons Try to Cope with Influx in Africa." *Salina [Kans.] Journal*, March 7, 1987, 16.

"Mormons." *Daily Inter Ocean* (Chicago), October 27, 1889, 4.

"Mormons: The Black Saints of Nigeria." *Time,* June 18, 1965, 72.

"'Mormons' Ban OK'd by Court." *[Portland] Oregonian,* October 22, 1976, 8.

Morrison, Alexander. "The Dawning of a New Day in Africa." *Ensign*, November 1987, 25–26.

"Moses Mahlangu—The Conversion Power of the Book of Mormon." https://www.lds.org/pages/moses-mahlangu-the-conversion-power-of-the-book-of-mormon?lang=eng&country=afe (accessed December 29, 2013).

Moss, Frank E. Letter to Dell and Maxine Holbrook, August 24, 1964, Box 1, fd. 5, Stephen Holbrook Papers, Utah State Historical Society Archives.

"Most Barbarous Scene, A." *Rochester Telegraph,* August 1, 1820, 3.

Most Unusual Publisher, A." *Palm Beach Post*, April 16, 1972, G2.

"Moves Fast to Preclude Rights Rifts." *Augusta [Georgia] Chronicle*, July 5, 1964, 1.

Mowbray [South Africa] Cottage Meeting. Minutes, 1921–23. LR 5689, LDS Church History Library.

Moyer, Jonathan H. "Dancing with the Devil: The Making of the Mormon-Republican Pact." Ph.D. diss., University of Utah, 2009.

Moyle, James Henry. Reminiscences, 1886, LDS Church History Library.

"Mrs. Artiburn Discharged." *Deseret News*, November 21, 1901, 8.

Munson, Eliza M. A. "The Early Pioneer History of James Allred." n.d. LDS Church History Library.

"Murder Victim Is Buried at Former Home in Sanpete." *News Advocate* (Price, Utah), June 25, 1925, 1.

Muster Roll for Company A, MS 5261, LDS Church History Library.

Myers, Sarah. "Minersville." *Deseret News*, February 18, 1904, 9.

"Mysterious Dark Continent, The." *Cumorah's Southern Messenger* 36, no. 10 (October 1961): 260–61.

"Naturalization of Mormons, The." *Salt Lake Tribune*, July 13, 1889, 6.

"Negro Communist Voices Opposition to King." *[Portland] Oregonian*, April 21, 1966.

"Negro Minister Will Speak Here on Civil Turmoil." *The News and Courier* (Charleston, S.C.), November 26, 1968, 6A.

"Negro Mormons," *Galveston [Texas] Tri-Weekly News*, March 16, 1870, 2.

"Negro Star Leads Utah Bias Protest." *Spokesman-Review* (Spokane, Wash.), March 9, 1965, 10.

"Negroes and Heaven." *Deseret News*, December 17, 1903, 4.

"Negroes Relegated to Back Pew by Mormons." *Virgin Islands Daily News*, January 4, 1966, 13.

"Negroes Say Attorneys Hard to Get." *Register-Republic* (Rockford, Ill.), February 19, 1964, 20.

Nelson, Lowry. *In the Direction of His Dreams: Memoirs*. New York: Philosophical Library, 1985.

———. Letters to First Presidency, Special Collections, Merrill-Cazier Library, Utah State University, Logan, Utah:
June 26, 1947
October 8, 1947

———. Letter to Stephen Holbrook, June 25, 1975, Box 1, fd. 25, Stephen Holbrook Papers, Utah State Historical Society Archives.

———. Letter to Heber Meeks, June 26, 1947, Heber C. Meeks Papers, MS 1677, Box 1, fd. 4, Perry Special Collections.

———. "Mormons and the Negro." *The Nation*, May 24, 1952, 488.

"Nelson to Head U.S.A.C. Station." *Salt Lake Telegram*, December 12, 1935, 13.

"New Africa Means Diplomacy Problems." *[University of] Utah Daily Chronicle*, February 27, 1963, 2.

"New Jerusalem." *Evening and the Morning Star* 1, no. 5 (October 1832): 39.

"New Laws, The." *Deseret News*, March 19, 1892, 23.

"New LDS Office Building Nearly Finished." *[Provo] Daily Herald*, June 18, 1972, 32.

"New Patrol Chief." *Ogden [Utah] Standard-Examiner*, March 20, 1965, 2.

"New Prophet, A." *Public Ledger* (Philadelphia), January 2, 1844, 3.

"New Teeth Planted in Civil Rights Bill." *Miami [Fla.] News*, September 25, 1963, 15A.

Newell, L. Jackson, ed. *Matters of Conscience: Conversations with Sterling M. McMurrin on Philosophy, Education, and Religion*. Midvale, Utah: Signature Books, 1996. Newell's interviews with McMurrin.

Newell, Quincy, ed. "The Autobiography and Interview of Jane Manning James." *Journal of Africana Religions* 1, no. 2 (2013): 251-70.

Newkirk, Ted, and Greg Prince. Qtd. in Bill Broadway, "Black Mormons Resist Apology Talk." *Washington Post*, May 30, 1998, B9.

News Notes from All Parts of Utah." *Davis County Clipper* (Bountiful, Utah), July 4, 1924, 2.

News of the Church: Church Issues Statement on Racial Equality." *Ensign*, February 1988, 74.

"News, The." *Salt Lake Tribune*, October 6, 1893, 5.

Newton, Marjorie. *Hero or Traitor: A Biography of Charles Wesley Wandell*. Independence, Mo.: Independence Press, 1992.

Newton, Michael. *The Ku Klux Klan in Mississippi: A History*. Jefferson, N.C.: McFarland and Company, 2010.

"Next Lecture on Miracle Subject." *Ogden Standard-Examiner*, May 29, 1927, 30.

"Next Senator from Missouri, The." *Washington Sentinel*, September 9, 1854, 2.

Ngerna, Mbongeni, and William Nicholson. *Sarafina!* Film. Directed by Darrell Roodt. Miramax Films/BBC. September 18, 1992.

Nibley, Hugh. "The Best Possible Test." *Dialogue: A Journal of Mormon Thought* 8, no. 1 (Spring 1973): 73–78.

Nichter, Matt. "The Old Left and the Rise of the Civil Rights Movement." PhD diss., University of Wisconsin-Madison, 2005.

Nigerian General Conference Minutes, March 10, 1961. LaMar S. Williams Papers, Box 1, fd. 9. LDS Church History Library.

"Nile River Film to Be Shown in Cedar City." *Iron County Record*, March 12, 1953, 1.

"1960 Annual Merit Badge Pow-Wow." *Daily Herald* (Provo, Utah), March 3, 1960, 9.

"No Negro Need Apply." *Columbus [Ga.] Daily Enquirer*, April 14, 1883, 1.

"No Room for Blacks." *Salt Lake Tribune*, November 1, 1903, 8.

Noble, Antonette C. "Utah's Defense Industries and Workers in World War II." *Utah Historical Quarterly* 59, no. 4 (1991): 365–79.

Norr, Marriner K. "Genealogy in South Africa." *Cumorah's Southern Messenger* 24, no. 12 (December 1949): 180.

Norrell, Robert. *The House I Live In: Race in the American Century*. New York: Oxford University Press, 2005.

"North Notes." *Ephraim Enterprise*, December 3, 1970, 9.

"Not for Women." *Deseret News*, June 13, 1978, 4B.

"Notes from California." *True Latter-day Saints Herald* 23 (October 1, 1876): 592.

Nott, Josiah C. "The Mulatto a Hybrid—Probable Extermination of the Two Races If The Whites and Blacks Are Allowed to Intermarry." *The American Journal of the Medical Sciences* 6 (July 1843): 252–57.

_____. *Two Lectures on the Connection Between the Biblical and Physical History of Man* New York: Bartlett and Welford, 1849.

Notten, Eleonore Van. *See* Van Notten, Eleanore.

Nuttall, L. John. Diary and Meeting Minutes, 1879. Typescript. Perry Special Collections.

"O. Hyde's Slanders." *Melchizedek and Aaronic Herald* 1, no. 8 (February 1850): 1.

Oakland (California) Mission. Historical Reports, LR 1314/3, Box 1, fd. 1. LDS Church History Library:
September 6, 1983
September 23, 1983
December 4, 1983

Oates, Stephen. *The Fires of Jubilee: Nat Turner's Fierce Rebellion*. New York: HarperCollins, 2009.

Obinna, Anthony. Letter to W. Grant Bangerter, September 19, 1978. Edwin Q. Cannon Correspondence. LDS Church History Library.

_____. Letter to the Council of the Twelve, September 28, 1978. Edwin Q. Cannon Papers. LDS Church History Library.

_____. Title Page of personal copy of Book of Mormon, MS 19820, LDS Church History Library.

Obinna, Anthony Uzodimma. "Voice from Nigeria." *Ensign*, December 1980, 28–30.

Obinna, Anthony U., Francis I. Obinna, and Raymond I. Obinna. Letter to First Presidency, December 1, 1978. In Edwin Q. Cannon Correspondence, LDS Church History Library.

Obot, A. D., S.U.E. Ekanem, O. Usoroh, and M. E. Akpan. Letter to LaMar S. Williams, November 15, 1961, LaMar S. Williams Papers, Box 1, fd. 9. LDS Church History Library.

"Off Color." *Salt Lake Tribune*, November 26, 1878, 4.

"Off the Record." *Park [City, Utah] Record*, June 15, 1978, 3.

"Official Announcement." *Liahona: The Elder's Journal* 12, no. 52 (June 22, 1915): 831.

Official Declaration—2. Heading. https://www.lds.org/scriptures/dc-testament/od/2?lang=eng (accessed September 2, 2013 and February 9, 2014).

"Officials of Resettlement Administration." *Salt Lake Telegram*, August 15, 1935, 13.

"Okah Tubbee." *Massachusetts Spy*, February 21, 1849.

"Okah Tubbee." *Telescope* (Manchester, N.H.), January 20, 1849.

"Okah Tubbee and His Bride." *Trenton [New Jersey] State Gazette*, August 23, 1852, 1.

Okazaki, Chieko N. *Lighten Up!* Salt Lake City: Deseret Book, 1993.

Okkers, Alice. Oral History. Interviewed by E. Dale LeBaron, July 29, 1988. In E. Dale LeBaron African Oral History Collection, Box 17, fd. 1, Perry Special Collections.

Okoro, Moses. Speech transcript, November 12, 1961, LaMar S. Williams Papers, Box 1, fd. 9. LDS Church History Library.

Okpon, E. J. Letter to District Office, June 24, 1960, LaMar S. Williams Papers, Box 1, fd. 9. LDS Church History Library.

Old Testament Student Manual, 1st ed. Salt Lake City: Church of Jesus Christ of Latter-day Saints, 1980.

Oman, Nathan. "Natural Law and the Rhetoric of Empire: *Reynolds v. United States*, Polygamy, and Imperialism." William and Mary Law School Research Paper. http://papers.ssrn.com/sol3/papers.cfm?abstract_id=1560015## (accessed October 13, 2013).

"On Black Cats." *London Magazine* 5 (March 1822): 285.

"On the Common Origin of the Human Races." *Debow's Review* 17 (1854): 25–39.

"On Tour with the President." *Cumorah's Southern Messenger* 23, no. 11 (November 1948): 114.

"One Baptism May Eventually Lead to Many Conversions." *Church News*, June 14, 1980, 23.

"One Man's Life of No Regrets," *Life*, March 24, 1972, 66.

"Open Letter, An." *Manti Messenger*, September 30, 1971, 4.

"Open Letter, An." *Manti Messenger*, October 7, 1971, 2.

"Open Letter to Earl Browder, An." *The Crisis*, October 1935, 302.

"Ordinance Establishing and Regulating a Patrol for This City, An." February 9, 1826. *Ordinances of St. Louis, Revised, 1828*, 59–62. Qtd. in Daniel Graff, "Race, Citizenship, and the Origins of Organized Labor in Antebellum St. Louis." In Thomas Spencer, ed., *The Other Missouri History: Populists, Prostitutes, and Regular Folk*. Columbia: University of Missouri Press, 2004.

Ordinances of the City of Nauvoo. Nauvoo, Ill.: Joseph Smith, 1842.

"Origin of Races, The." *Salt Lake Tribune*, April 23, 1870, 130.

"Origin of the Polynesians." *Deseret News*, January 15, 1898, 4.

Orsi, Robert. "Everyday Miracles: The Study of Lived Religion." In *Lived Religion in America: Towards a History of Practice*. Edited by David D. Hall. Princeton, N.J.: Princeton University Press, 1997, 3–21.

Osekre, Clement. Letter to E. Allen, February 14, 1974. Ghana and Nigeria Files, LDS Church History Library.

_____. Letter to Edwin Q. Cannon, November 14, 1977. Edwin Q. Cannon Papers, Box 1, fd. 1, LDS Church History Library.

_____. Letter to Rebecca Mould, September 11, 1972. Dadzie Papers. LDS Church History Library.

_____. Letters to LaMar Williams. Ghana and Nigeria Files, LDS Church History Library.
February 21, 1974
March 1, 1974.

"Our Coloured Brethren." *The Contributor* 7, no. 1 (October 1885): 32–33. Published under the same title in *The Phrenological Journal and Science of Health* 81, no. 52 (November 1885): 260–62.

"Our Coloured Brethren." *The Contributor* 7, no. 1 (October 1885): 32–33.

"Outrage in Jackson County, The." *The Evening and the Morning Star* 2, no. 17 (February 1834): 128.

"Outrages of Brigham Young." *Rock River [Rockford, Ill.] Democrat*, April 14, 1857, 2.

O'Dell, Jack. *Climbin' Jacob's Ladder: The Black Freedom Movement Writings of Jack O'Dell*. Berkeley: University of California Press, 2009.

O'Donnal, John Forrest. *Pioneer in Guatemala: The Personal History of John Forrest O'Donnal*. Salt Lake City: Shumway Family Services, 1997.

O'Donovan, Connell. "Joseph T. Ball." In "Early Boston Mormons and Missionaries, A to I, 1831–1860." http://www.connellodonovan.com/boston_mormonsA-I.pdf (accessed May 16, 2014).

_____. "The Mormon Priesthood Ban and Elder Q. Walker Lewis: 'An Example for His More Whiter Brethren to Follow.'" *John Whitmer Historical Association Journal* 26 (2006): 48–100.

_____. "Three Newly Discovered Early Black Mormon Women." http://rationalfaiths.com/three-newly-discovered-early-black-mormon-women/ (accessed February 11, 2014).

O'Toole, James M. *Passing for White: Race, Religion, and the Healy Family, 1820–1920*. Amherst: University of Massachusetts Press, 2002.

Palmer, Beverly, ed. *The Selected Papers of Thaddeus Stevens: April 1865–August 1868*. Pittsburg, Pa.: University of Pittsburg Press, 1998.

Palmer, William R. Qtd. in "Pioneers of Southern Utah: Robert Gardner." *The Instructor* 79, no. 8 (August 1944): 382–85.

Papanikolas, Helen. *The Peoples of Utah*. Salt Lake City: Utah State Historical Society, 1976.

Parker, F. "Minutes of the St. Lawrence Association." *Universalist Union*, August 18, 1838, 323.

Parrish, Warren. "Mission in the South." *Messenger and Advocate* 3, no. 2 (November 1836): 404–6.

Parrish, William E. "The Mississippi Saints." *The Historian* 50 (August 1988): 489–506.

Parshall, Ardis E. "Eminent Women: Anna Charlotte Eldridge Hinkle Chidester and Charlotte Coray." http://www.keepapitchinin.org/2012/01/02/eminent-women-anna-charlotte-eldridge-hinkle-chidester-and-charlotte-corday/ (accessed February 23, 2014).

_____. "Martin Luther King in Deseret." http://www.keepapitchinin.org/archives/martin-luther-king-in-deseret/ (accessed October 21, 2013).

Parson, John. Camp Journal, June 24, 1855. LDS Church History Library.

Partridge, Emily Dow. Journal, 1875. LDS Church History Library.

_____. "Reminiscences of Emily Dow Partridge Young." April 7, 1884. Typescript. Perry Special Collections.

Pascoe, Peggy. *What Comes Naturally: Miscegenation Law and the Making of Race in America*. New York: Oxford University Press, 2010.

"Patriarch Shreeve to Give Lessons." *Ogden-Standard Examiner*, October 28, 1922, 8.

Paulos, Michael H. Caricatured and Made Hideous in Cartoons: Political Cartooning and the Reed Smoot Hearings." In J. Michael Hunter, ed. *Mormons and Popular Culture: The Global Influence of an American Phenomenon*. New York: Praeger, 2013, 121–43.

Pearce, Loren. Letter to Stephen Holbrook, June 17, 1975, Box 1, fd. 25. Stephen Holbrook Papers, Utah State Historical Society.

Pearson, Howard. "Mormon Missionary Baseball Team Makes Friends in South Africa." *Deseret News*, January 23, 1937, 3.

"Peculiar People, A." *Cumorah's Southern Messenger* 32, no. 7 (July 1957): 101.

Pegram, Thomas. *One Hundred Percent American: The Rebirth and Decline of the Klan in 1920s America*. New York: Ivan R. Dee, 2011.

"People We Want to Know More About—Dr. Virginia Cutler." *Improvement Era*, February 1970, 51–52.

"Performed Caesarian Section." *Salt Lake Tribune*, February 28, 1902, 3.

Perkins, Eugene H., and Waldo C. Perkins. "'A Room of Round Logs with a Dirt Roof': Ute Perkins' Stewardship to Look after Mormon Battalion Families." *Mormon Historical Studies* 1, no. 1 (Spring 2000): 61–72.

Perkins, Phyllis. Letter to John M. Goddard, May 15, 1975. Holograph, John M. Goddard Papers, Box 3, fd. 9. Perry Special Collections.

Perry, Charles. "Let He Who Is without Sin Cast the First Orange: Anita Bryant and the Making of a Gay Rights Movement in Salt Lake City." M.A. thesis, University of Utah, 2008.

Petersen, Mark E. "Race Problems as They Affect the Church." August 27, 1954. Microfilm, Perry Special Collections.

———. *Which Church Is Right?* Salt Lake City: Deseret News Press, 1955. Rpt. under the same title in 1963.

Peterson, Ross F. "'Do Not Lecture the Brethren': Stewart Udall's Pro-Civil Rights Stance, 1967." *Journal of Mormon History* 25, no. 1 (Spring 1999): 272–87.

Phelps, W. W. "The Book of Mormon." *Evening and Morning Star* 1 (January 1833): 57.

———. "The Elders Stationed in Zion to the Churches Abroad." *Evening and Morning Star* 2, no. 14 (July 1833): 110.

———. Extra of *Evening and the Morning Star*, July 1833. Photocopy of original. LDS Church History Library.

———. "O Stop and Tell Me, Red Man." In [Emma Hale Smith, comp.]. *A Collection of Sacred Hymns for the Church of Jesus Christ of Latter-day Saints*. Kirtland, Ohio: Frederick G. Williams and Co., 1835, #83.

Philoshenanigans." *[University of Utah] Daily Chronicle*, October 12, 1955, 2.

"'Phony' Civil Rights Leader Aiding Reds." *Dallas Morning News*, November 12, 1965, 9.

Pickens, William. "One Negro in Heaven Mormons Tell Pickens." *The Afro-American*, March 3, 1928, 6.

"Plan New Mormon Temples." *Times-Picayune* (New Orleans), April 18, 1981, 27.

Plessy v. Ferguson. 163 U.S. 537 (1896).

Pocock, Roger. "My Most Exciting Adventure." *Denver Post*, December 11, 1910, 59.

"Police Tear Gas Sparks Black Riot in S. Africa." *Dallas Morning News*, April 6, 1981, 4.

"Policy Statement of Presidency." December 15, 1969. *LDS Church News*, January 10, 1970, 12.

Poll, Richard D. "The Mormon Question Enters National Politics, 1850–1856." *Utah Historical Quarterly* 25 April 1957): 117–31.

Poore, Ben Perley, ed. *The Federal and State Constitutions, Colonial Charters, and Other Organic Laws of the United States*. 2 vols. Washington, D.C.: Government Printing Office, 1878.

Porter, Roger O. "Educator Cites McKay Statement of No Negro Bias in LDS Tenets." *Salt Lake Tribune*, January 15, 1970, B9.

Posel, Deborah. *The Making of Apartheid, 1948–1961.* New York: Oxford University Press, 1997.

Post, Stephen. Journal, 1836. LDS Church History Library.

Pottawatomie High Council Record, 1846. In Eugene H. Perkins and Waldo C. Perkins. "'A Room of Round Logs with a Dirt Roof:' Ute Perkins' Stewardship to Look After Mormon Battalion Families." *Mormon Historical Studies* 1, no. 1 (Spring 2000): 61–72.

Pottawatomie High Priests Minutes, January 2, 1848, 1. In Richard E. Turley, ed. *Selected Collections from the Archives of the Church of Jesus Christ of Latter-day Saints.* Provo, Utah: BYU Religious Studies Center, 2002, 2:19.

Poulsen, Richard C. *Misbegotten Muses: History and Anti-History.* New York: Peter Lang, 1988.

Powell, Allan Kent, ed. *Utah History Encyclopedia.* Salt Lake City: University of Utah Press, 1994.

"Praises Clegg." *Deseret News,* January 14, 1980, 4A.

Pratt, Orson. "The Pre-Existence." *The Seer* 1, no. 4 (April 1853): 56.

Pratt, Parley P. *Late Persecution of the Church of Jesus Christ, of Latter-day Saints; Inflicted by the State of Missouri upon the Mormons.* Detroit: Dawson and Bates, 1839.

———. *Late Persecutions of the Church of Jesus Christ, of Latterday Saints; Ten Thousand American Citizens Robbed, Plundered, and Banished; Others Imprisoned, and Others Martyred for Their Religion. With a Sketch of Their Rise, Progress and Doctrine.* New York: J. W. Harrison, 1840.

———. Sermon transcript, April 25, 1847. General Meeting Minutes. In Richard E. Turley, ed. *Selected Collections from the Archives of the Church of Jesus Christ of Latter-day Saints.* Provo, Utah: BYU Religious Studies Center, 2002, 1:18.

Pratt, Renate. *In Good Faith: Canadian Churches against Apartheid.* Waterloo, Ontario: Wilfrid Laurier University Press, 1997.

Pratt, Stephen F. "Parley P. Pratt in Winter Quarters and the Trail West." *BYU Studies* 24, no. 3 (1984): 373–88.

"Pres. Brown Explains Vital Doctrine." *Deseret News,* October 7, 1963, A1, A5.

"Preservation of Family—Key to Stability, Leader Says." *[Bannock] Idaho State Journal,* June 12, 1970, 26.

Price, Rees E. Letter to William Lloyd Garrison. In *The Liberator,* June 1, 1855, 87.

Priest, Josiah. *Bible Defence of Slavery: Or The Origin, History, and Fortunes of the Negro Race.* Glasgow, Ky.: W. S. Brown, 1853.

Priest, Josiah. "On the Common Origin of the Human Races." *Debow's Review* 17, no. 1 (July 1854): 25–39.

———. *Slavery, As It Relates to the Negro, or African Race: Examined in the Light of Circumstances, History and the Holy Scriptures; with an Account of the Origin of the Black Man's Color, Causes of His State of Servitude and Traces of His Character As Well in Ancient As in Modern Times: with Strictures on Abolitionism.* Albany, N.Y.: C. Van Benthuysen, 1843.

"Priesthood Corner." *Cumorah's Southern Messenger* 32, no. 3 (March 1957): 39.

Prince, Gregory A. "David O. McKay and Blacks: Building the Foundation for the 1978 Revelation." *Dialogue: A Journal of Mormon Thought* 35, no. 1 (Spring 2002): 145–53.

Prince, Gregory A., and Wm. Robert Wright. *David O. McKay and the Rise of Modern Mormonism.* Salt Lake City: University of Utah Press, 2005.

Proceedings of the New Jersey Pharmaceutical Association. Jersey City, N.J.: Times Printing Company, 1871.

Proctor, Maurine Jensen. "Modibo Diarra: Mali Mormon." *This People* 15, no. 2 (Summer 1994): 22–27.

Program for "The Devine [sic] Order of Mount Tabborar Service." August 22, 1971. Dadzie Papers, LDS Church History Library.

"Project History Log." n.d. See Shirley Van Katwyk.

"Prophetic Family Arrangement, A." *Covington Daily Union*, June 5, 1850, 2.

"Prospects for Nigeria." August 26, 1965. In *Foreign Relations of the United States, 1964–1968*, 34 vols. Washington, D.C.: Government Printing Office, 1995, 24:614.

"Protect Your Birthright." *Cumorah's Southern Messenger* 35, no. 4 (April 1960): 97.

"Protecting Our Freedom." *Davis County Clipper* (Bountiful, Utah), March 25, 1960, 3.

"Protecting Our Freedom." *Davis County Clipper* (Bountiful, Utah), March 25, 1960, 3.

Puckett, Newbell Niles. *Folk Beliefs of the Southern Negro*. Chapel Hill: University of North Carolina Press, 1926.

Pugh, James. Letter to James E. Strang, March 23, 1846. James Strang Papers, Beinecke Library, Yale University, New Haven, Conn.

Pulsipher, Charles. "A True Narrative." Zerah Pulsipher Papers. MS 753 2, LDS Church History Library.

Pulsipher, John. Notebook, 1849, 1855. Microfilm of holograph. MS 1034. LDS Church History Library.

Purple, W. D. "Joseph Smith, The Originator of Mormonism: Historical Reminiscences of the Town of Afton." *Chenango [New York] Union* 30, no. 33 (May 2, 1877), 3. Rpt. in Richard L. Saunders, ed. *Dale Morgan on the Mormons: Collected Works, Part 2, 1949–1970*. Norman: University of Oklahoma Press, 2013, 192–97.

Putney, Clifford. *Muscular Christianity: Manhood and Sports in Protestant America, 1880–1920*. Cambridge, Mass.: Harvard University Press, 2009.

Puzey, Keith. "Letters to the Editor." *[University of Utah] Daily Chronicle*, January 15, 1958, 2.

Quarterly List of Ordinations and Installations." *Quarterly Register and Journal of the American Education Society* 4 (May 1832): 335–36.

Quashigah, E. K. "Legislating Religious Liberty: The Ghanaian Experience." *Brigham Young University Law Review* 2 (1999): 589–93.

"Quincy, Adams County, Illinois." In Andrew Jenson, ed., *The Historical Record* 8, nos. 2–3 (March 1889): 739.

Quinn, D. Michael, ed. *The New Mormon History*. Salt Lake City: Signature Books, 1992.

Quinn, D. Michael *Elder Statesman: A Biography of J. Reuben Clark*. Salt Lake City: Signature Books, 2002.

———. "The Newel K. Whitney Family." *Ensign*, December 1978, 42–45.

———. "How the L.D.S. Church Has Influenced Mormon Politicians, and What It Can Teach Us About a Mitt Romney Presidency." *Vanity Fair*, October 15, 2012. http://www.vanityfair.com/politics/2012/10/mormon-politicians-lds-church-romney (accessed April 6, 2014).

Quist, John. "John E. Page: The Apostle of Uncertainty." *Journal of Mormon History* 12 (1985): 53–68.

[Quorum of the Twelve] Meeting Minutes, October 24, 1946. Adam S. Bennion Papers. Special Collections, Marriott Library.

Quorum of the Twelve. Meeting Minutes, January 2, 1902. George Albert Smith Family Collection. Box 78, fd. 7, Special Collections, Marriott Library.

Quorum of the Twelve, Meeting Minutes, August 26, 1908. Typescript, George A. Smith Family Papers, Box 78, fd. 7, Special Collections, Marriott Library, University of Utah.

"Race and the Priesthood." http://www.lds.org/topics/race-and-the-priesthood?lang=eng (accessed December 27, 2013).

"Race Riot Threatened at Magnolia, Alabama." *Macon [Ga.] Telegraph*, December 21, 1909, 2.

"Ramah Branch." *Cumorah's Southern Messenger* 30, no. 2 (February 1955): 31.

Rampton, Calvin L. Letter to Caleb Shreeve, March 13, 1970. Hyrum Wheelwright Papers, Stewart Library, Weber State University, Ogden, Utah.

"Reagan Upstaged, But Bows to Veto." *Bangor [Maine] Daily News*, October 6, 1986, A10.

"Real Story of the Ku Klux Klan, The." *Norwich [Conn.] Aurora,* June 28, 1871, 2.

"Recent Drought Brings Report of Cotton Deterioration from All Parts of the State." *Montgomery [Ala.] Advertiser,* September 9, 1912, 2-3.

"Record of the Quorum of the Twelve Apostles in the Handwriting of Wilford Woodruff." ca. 1852, *New Mormon Studies,* CD-ROM. Salt Lake City: Smith Research Associates, 2009.

"Reds and Riots." Letter to the editor. *Deseret News,* October 2, 1967, A12.

"Reds Using U.S. Negro." *Omaha World Herald,* April 12, 1965, 2.

"Reed Benson Speaks on Birchers; Upholds Civil Rights Battle." *[University of] Utah Daily Chronicle,* October 9, 1963, 1.

"Reed Benson Will Explain Aims of Birch Society." *Davis County Clipper* (Bountiful, Utah), November 15, 1963, 3.

Rees, Robert A. "Black African Jews, The Mormon Denial of Priesthood to Blacks, and Truth and Reconciliation." *Sunstone,*October 2004, 62–67.

Reeve, Paul. "From Not White to Too White: The Historical Evolution of a 'Mormon Race.'" Paper presented at the Mormon History Association, annual conference, 2013, Kaysville, Utah. Notes in my possession.

Reeves, Richard. "Parents Revolt on School Issue." *Lakeland Ledger,* October 11, 1980, 14A.

"Regulating the Mormonites." *Niles' Weekly Register* 9, no. 3 (September 14, 1833): 47–48.

Relief Society. Minutes Pretoria [Ward], Transvaal Stake, 1972. LR 7191 14. LDS Church History Library.

Relief Society. Minutes Durban Branch, South Africa. LR 2382 14. LDS Church History Library.

"Religious Notices." *The Prophet,* December 21, 1844, 3.

"Reminiscences of Charles W. Nibley." *Improvement Era* 37, no. 10 (October 1934): 597–98.

"Reminiscences of Emily Dow Young Partridge." April 7, 1884. Typescript. Perry Special Collections.

"Rendell and Rachel Mabey: A Mission to West Arica." *This People,* Sesquicentennial Issue (1980): 24–37.

"Rendell Mabey Sets Second African Trip." *Davis County Clipper,* (Bountiful, Utah), August 8, 1958, 1.

"Report of the 15th Quorum." *Deseret News,* April 13, 1854, 4.

Resolution 2, Working Bills, Utah State Senate, Utah State Archives, Box 63, fd. 39. http://images.archives.utah.gov/cdm/compoundobject/collection/428/id/144058/rec/7 (accessed August 8, 2013).

"Returned." *Deseret News,* April 27, 1870, 2.

"Revelation, December 16–17, 1833. http://josephsmithpapers.org/paperSummary/revelation-16-and-17-december-1833-dc-101?p=9 (accessed February 11, 2014).

Revised Laws of Illinois, The. Vandalia, Ill.: Greiner and Sherman, 1833.

Revised Ordinances of Payson City, The. Provo, Utah: Enquirer Company, 1893.

Revised Statutes of the State of Illinois. Springfield, Ill.: William Walters, 1845.

Revised Statutes of the State of Missouri, The. St. Louis: Missouri General Assembly, 1835.

"Rialto." *Jewish Chronicle,* November 7, 1924, 11.

Rich, Charles C. Diary, 1850. In Richard E. Turley, ed. *Selected Collections from the Archives of the Church of Jesus Christ of Latter-day Saints.* Provo, Utah: BYU Religious Studies Center, 2002, DVD 36.

———. Diary, May 13–14, 25, and June 21, 1850. In Richard E. Turley, ed. *Selected Collections from the Archives of the Church of Jesus Christ of Latter-day Saints.* Provo, Utah: BYU Religious Studies Center, 2002, DVD 36.

Rich, Christopher. "The True Policy for Utah: Servitude; Slavery; and 'An Act in Relation to Service.'" *Utah Historical Quarterly* 80, no. 1 (Winter 2012): 54–74.

Rich, Sarah DeArmon Pea. "Autobiography." In Daughters of Utah Pioneers Lesson Committee, comp. *An Enduring Legacy*, 12 vols. Salt Lake City: Daughters of Utah Pioneers, 1978–89, 5:189–222.

_____. "Journal of Sarah De Armon Pea Rich." Transcribed by Alice M. Rich. Perry Special Collections.

Richards, A. LeGrand. "Moritz Busch's *Die Mormonen* and the Conversion of Karl G. Maeser." *BYU Studies* 45, no. 4 (2006): 47–64.

Richards, Franklin D. Journal, 1895. MS 2125. In Richard E. Turley, ed. *Selected Collections from the Archives of the Church of Jesus Christ of Latter-day Saints.* Provo, Utah: BYU Religious Studies Center, 2002, 2:35.

Richards, LeGrand. *Interview with Mormon Apostle LeGrand Richards Concerning the 1978 'Negro' Revelation.* Phoenix, Ariz.: Bobwitte, 1978.

Richards, Willard. Journal, Willard Richards Papers. Holograph in Richard E. Turley, ed., *Selected Collections from the Archives of the Church of Jesus Christ of Latter-day Saints.* Provo, Utah: Brigham Young University Press, 2002, 1:31.

Ricks, Nathaniel. "A Peculiar Place for a Peculiar Institution: Slavery and Sovereignty in Early Territorial Utah." M.A. thesis, Brigham Young University, 2007.

Ricks, Nate. "Ricks's Critique of Rich's UHQ Article on Utah Servitude/Slavery." *Juvenile Instructor* (blog). http://www.juvenileinstructor.org/responses-ricks-critique-of-richs-uhq-article-on-utah-servitudeslavery/(accessed April 26, 2014).

Rigdon, Sidney, et al. Petition Draft, ca. 1838-39. http://joseph smithpapers.org/paperSummary/sidney-rigdon-js-et-al-petition-draft-tothe-publick-circa-1838%E2%80%931839#5 (accessed August 11, 2013).

"Rights Group Confers in S.L. Today." *Salt Lake Tribune*, July 30, 1960, 14.

"Rights." *Deseret News*, January 13, 1985, B4.

"Riot Control Tactics Mastered by Guard." *Deseret News*, October 5, 1967, B1.

"Robbery and Lynching." *Nauvoo Neighbor* 1, no. 4 (April 3, 1844): 2.

Roberts, Brigham H. *A Comprehensive History of the Church of Jesus Christ of Latter-day Saints, Century I.* 6 vols. 1930. Rpt., Provo, Utah: Brigham Young University Press, 1965 printing.

_____. "Discourse by Elder B. H. Roberts." *Millennial Star* 57 (July 11, 1895): 434–35.

_____. *A New Witness for God.* Salt Lake City: George Q. Cannon and Sons, 1895.

_____. *The Seventy's Course in Theology: First Year.* Salt Lake City: Deseret News, 1907.

_____. "To The Youth in Israel." *The Contributor* 6, no. 8 (May 1885): 29499.

_____. "What Is Man?" *Deseret Weekly*, March 16, 1895, 387.

Roberts, David. *Devil's Gate: Brigham Young and the Great Mormon Handcart Tragedy.* New York: Simon and Schuster, 2008.

Robinson, Charles F., II. *Dangerous Liaisons: Sex and Love in the Segregated South.* Little Rock: University of Arkansas Press, 2006.

Rogers, Orson M. "Native Tribes of South Africa," *Improvement Era* 12, no. 8 (June 1909): 625–26

Roll, First Council of the Seventy, December 27, 1836, CR 3 123, LDS Church History Library.

Romig, Rollo. "'Julie through the Looking Glass': The Rise and Fall of the Mormon TV Commercial." *New Yorker*, January 20, 2012. http://www.newyorker.com/online/blogs/culture/2012/01/mormon-public-service-announcements.html (accessed June 3, 2013).

Romney, George. "A Man's Religion and American Politics: An Interview with Governor Romney." *Dialogue: A Journal of Mormon Thought* 2, no. 3 (Autumn 1967): 23–38.

"Romney Heads 'Rights' March," *Plain Dealer* (Cleveland, Ohio), June 30, 1963, 5-AA.

Root, Jeremiah. "Experiences and Testimony of Jeremiah Root." *Autumn Leaves* 10, no. 6 (June 1897): 271–73.

Roster and Record of Iowa Soldiers. 6 vols. Des Moines: Emory English, 1911.

Roundy, Elizabeth J. A. *See* James, Jane Manning.

Rowe, Peter. Letter to John Goddard, March 2, 1975. Holograph. John M. Goddard Papers, Box 3, fd. 9. Perry Special Collections.

Rudd, Calvin P. "William Smith, Brother of the Prophet Joseph Smith." M.A. thesis, Brigham Young University, 1973.

Russell, Robert H. *Wilton, Connecticut: Three Centuries of People, Places, and Progress.* Wilton, Conn.: Wilton Historical Society, 2004.

"S. Africa Imprisons 27 Leaders." *[Cleveland] Plain Dealer,* August 25, 1985, 1.

"S. African Children Arrested." *Mobile [Ala.] Register,* August 24, 1985, 1.

"S. African Mormon Missionary Is Doing Work in Alabama." *Plain Dealer* (Cleveland, Ohio), June 1, 1986, 33.

Sachs, William. *The Transformation of Anglicanism: From State Church to Global Communion.* Cambridge, England: Cambridge University Press, 2002.

"Safari in Africa." *Davis County Clipper,* November 11, 1955, 1. Series continued: November 18, 1955, 1; November 25, 1955, 1.

Salm, Steven J., and Toyin Falola. *Culture and Customs of Ghana.* Westport, Conn.: Greenwood Press, 2002.

Salt Lake City Tenth Ward. Minutes, March 10, 1912, LR 9051 11, Reel #2, LDS Church History Library.

"Salt Lake Ku Klux Officers Deny Threats." *Salt Lake Telegram,* March 9, 1922, 2.

"Sam Verge Is Killed by Angry Mob at Demopolis." *Montgomery [Ala.] Advertiser,* August 5, 1912, 1.

"San Francisco." *True Latter-day Saints' Herald,* September 15, 1872, 570.

Sanborn, Franklin B., ed. *The Life and Letters of John Brown: Liberator of Kansas, and Martyr of Virginia.* Boston: Roberts Brothers, 1891.

Santiago, Tessa Meyer. "Brother Wiseman." *BYU Studies* 35, no. 2 (1995): 69–72.

———. "Here's to You, June Williamson." Blog post, December 28, 2009. http://tms-giraffesmakemelaugh.blogspot.com/2009/12/heres-to-you-june-williamson.html (accessed February 9, 2014).

Saunders, Richard L., ed. *Dale Morgan on the Mormons: Collected Works, Part 2, 1949-1970.* Norman: University of Oklahoma Press, 2013.

"Says Civil Rights Movement Not Negro Movement." *Davis County Clipper* (Bountiful, Utah), November 6, 1970, 20.

Schaer, Zola. "N'Gamiland Adventure." *Cumorah's Southern Messenger* 15, no. 2 (February 1941): 22–23, 30.

"School Tax, The." *Salt Lake Tribune,* November 1, 1873, 4.

"Schools and Meeting Houses." *Salt Lake Tribune,* September 7, 1873, 2.

Scott, Peter Dale, and Jonathan Marshall. *Cocaine Politics: Drugs, Armies, and the CIA.* Berkeley: University of California Press, 1991.

Scott, Walter. *Count Robert of Paris.* Novel reprinted in Vol. 1 of series, *Tales of My Landlord,* 3 vols. Paris: A. and W. Galigani, 1832.

Scott, Walter. "On Black Cats." *London Magazine* 5 (March 1822): 285–87.

Seale, Bobby. *Seize the Time: The Story of the Black Panther Party and Huey P. Newton.* Baltimore, Md.: Black Classic Press, 1991.

Searle, Don L. "Ghana—A Household of Faith." *Ensign,* March 1996, 34–42.

"Segregation in Utah." *[University of Utah] Chronicle,* March 6, 1957, 2.

"Seifert Rites." *Davis County Clipper* (Bountiful, Utah), February 12, 1960, 6.

Sekondi Branch. Meeting Minutes, 1978–79. Joseph Dadzie Papers., LDS Church History Library.

Selleck, Charles M. *Norwalk.* Norwalk, Conn.: Charles M. Selleck, 1896.

"Senator Vern Holman Reports on Recent Legislative Session." *Garfield County [Utah] News*, March 18, 1965, 1.

"Sertoma to Host Reed A. Benson." *Davis County Clipper* (Bountiful, Utah), September 6, 1963, 15.

"Sets Congo Expedition." *Cumorah's Southern Messenger* 31, no. 6 (June 1956): 83.

Seventies Council, Los Angeles Stake, March 8, 1975. Holograph. In John M. Goddard Papers, Box 3, fd. 9. Perry Special Collections.

"Shapley Teacher On Her Way to Big Adventures." *Corsicana Daily Sun* (Navarro, Tex.), June 25, 1958, 7.

Sharp, Ida. Notebook, September 20–21, 1947. LDS Church History Library.

Shaw, Diane. *City Building on the Eastern Frontier: Sorting the New Nineteenth-Century City.* Baltimore, Md.: Johns Hopkins University Press, 2004.

Shaw, Todd. *Now Is the Time! Detroit Black Politics and Grassroots Activism.* Durham, N.C.: Duke University Press, 2009.

Shepard, Bill. "Shadows on the Sun Dial." *Dialogue: A Journal of Mormon Thought* 41, no. 1 (Spring 2008): 34–66.

———. "Stealing in Mormon Nauvoo." *John Whitmer Historical Association Journal* 23 (2003): 99–102.

Shepard, William. "James Blakeslee: The Old Soldier of Mormonism." *John Whitmer Association Journal* 17 (1997): 113–32.

Shipps, Jan. "The Mormons: Looking Forward and Onward." *Christian Century*, August 16–23, 1978, 761–66.

———. *Sojourner in the Promised Land: Forty Years among the Mormons.* Urbana: University of Illinois Press, 2000.

Shore, Megan. *Religion and Conflict Resolution: Christianity and South Africa's Truth and Reconciliation Commission.* Surrey, England: Ashgate Publishing, 2009.

"Short Report on the Ghana Mission, A." September 10, 1973. In Ghana and Nigeria Files, MS 16493, LDS Church History Library.

Shreeve, Caleb. Compilation of newspaper clippings. Hyrum Wheelwright Papers, Stewart Library, Weber State University, Ogden, Utah.

———. "A Declaration of Fact." Addressed to "All Men of All Nations, Kindred, Tongues, and Races," November 19, 1970. In Hyrum Wheelwright Papers, Special Collections, Stewart Library, Weber State University, Ogden, Utah.

———. Letter to First Presidency, November 25, 1970. Hyrum Wheelwright Papers, Special Collections, Stewart Library, Weber State University, Ogden, Utah.

———. "Priesthood Answer." *Salt Lake Tribune*, October 26, 1970. Clipping in Hyrum Wheelwright Papers, Special Collections, Stewart Library, Weber State University, Ogden, Utah.

"Shreeve to Talk at 2nd Ward Tomorrow." *Ogden Standard-Examiner*, August 28, 1920, 8.

"Signs Point to Romney as Victor in Michigan." *Dallas Morning News*, October 9, 1962, 5.

Sillitoe, Linda. *Friendly Fire: The ACLU in Utah.* Salt Lake City: Signature Books, 1996.

———. Papers. Special Collections, Marriott Library. University of Utah.

Simon, Jerald F. "Thomas Bullock as an Early Mormon Historian." *BYU Studies* 30, no. 1 (Winter 1990): 71–88.

"Slavery in Utah." *Broad Ax*, March 25, 1899, 1.

"Slavery Question in California, The." *Augusta [Ga.] Chronicle*, August 20, 1849, 2.

Smart, Donna T., ed. *Mormon Midwife: The 1846–1888 Diaries of Patty Bartlett Sessions.* Logan: Utah State University Press, 1997.

Smith (Sister). "God, Grant Us Strength." *Cumorah's Southern Messenger* 28, no. 9 (September 1953): 132.

Smith, Bathsheba Bigler Wilson. Autobiography. Photocopy of holograph and typescript. Perry Special Collections.

Smith, Emma, comp. *A Collection of Sacred Hymns for the Church of Jesus Christ of Latter-day Saints*. Kirtland, Ohio: Frederick G. Williams and Co., 1835.

Smith, George Albert, and J. Reuben Clark. Statement, August 17, 1949, Lester E. Bush Papers, Box 4, fd 4. Special Collections, Marriott Library.

Smith, Heman C. "Biography of Sidney Rigdon." *Journal of History* 4, no. 2 (April 1911): 171–81.

Smith, Inez. "Biography of Charles Wesley Wandell." *Journal of History*, 3 (October 1910): 455–71; 4 (January 1911): 4:57–65.

Smith, Joseph, Jr., et al. *History of the Church of Jesus Christ of Latter-day Saints*. Edited by B. H. Roberts, 2d ed. rev. 6 vols., 1902–12, Vol. 7, 1932. Rpt., Salt Lake City: Deseret Book, 1980 printing.

_____. *General Smith's Views of the Powers and Policy of the Government of the United States*. Nauvoo, Ill.: John Taylor, 1844.

_____. *Joseph Smith Tells His Own Story*. Salt Lake City: Church of Jesus Christ of Latter-day Saints, 1959.

_____. Letter to Oliver Cowdery. *Messenger and Advocate* 2, no. 7 (April 1836): 288–91.

_____. Letter of Introduction for Heber C. Kimball, June 1, 1843. LDS Church History Library.

_____. "Views of the Powers and Policy of the Government of the United States." Rpt., *Deseret News*, August 19, 1851, 2, 8.

Smith, Joseph, III, and Heman C. Smith. *History of the Reorganized Church of Jesus Christ of Latter Day Saints, 1805–1890*. 4 vols. Independence: Herald House, 1896. Continued by F. Henry Edwards as *The History of the Reorganized Church of Jesus Christ of Latter Day Saints*, Vols. 5–8. Independence: Herald House, 1897–1903. 3rd ed. 1908.

Smith, Joseph F. *Conference Report*. Salt Lake City: Church of Jesus Christ of Latter-day Saints, April 1905, 83–86.

Smith, Joseph Fielding. *Doctrines of Salvation*, 3 vols. Salt Lake City: Deseret Book, 1954–56.

_____. Letter to Alfred M. Nelson, January 31, 1907, MS 14591, LDS Church History Library.

_____. "The Negro and the Priesthood." *Improvement Era* 27, no. 6 (April 1924): 565.

_____. *The Way To Perfection: Short Discourses on Gospel Themes*. Salt Lake City: Genealogical Society of Utah, 1931.

Smith, Lucy Mack. *Biographical Sketches of Joseph Smith the Prophet and His Progenitors for Many Generations*. Liverpool: S. W. Richards, 1853.

Smith, Nicholas G. Address notebook. MS 8861, Reel #3, LDS Church History Library.

Smith, Nicholas Grosbeck. Diaries. Transcribed in Lavina Fielding Anderson, ed. *Nicholas Groesbeck Smith, 1881–1945: A Documentary History*. Salt Lake City: Privately published for Nicholas Groesbeck Smith Jr. and Marion Burrows Smith, 2000.

Smith, Suzanne E. *Dancing in the Street: Motown and the Cultural Politics of Detroit*. Cambridge, Mass: Harvard University Press, 2009.

Smith, William. "Judas Iscariot's Lineage," *Melchisedek and Aaronic Herald*, 1, no. 8 (February 1850): 2.

Smith, William B. *The Color Line: A Brief in Behalf of the Unborn*. New York: McClure, Phillips & Co., 1905.

Smoot, Diana Eldredge. Autobiography. Perry Special Collections.

Snow, A. H. [Alphonzo Houtz]. Letter to Editor, March 15, 1882.

Snow, Eliza R. *See also* Derr, Jill Mulvay.

Snyder, Christina. *Slavery in Indian Country: The Changing Face of Captivity in Early America.* Cambridge, Mass.: Harvard University Press, 2010.

"Social Life of the Zone," *Canal Record*, April 13, 1910, 261.

"Society in the South." *Deseret News*, November 18, 1885, 14.

"Son of Africa Has Passed, A." *Cumorah's Southern Messenger* 25, no. 10 (October 1950): Cover, 146.

"Songs, Jokes, Sketches, and Dances by Elks." *Indianapolis News*, March 2, 1907, 13.

Sorenson, Asael. Letter to Frank Meyers, June 7, 1956. MS 6677, LDS Church History Library.

Sorenson, John L., Letter to Sterling M. McMurrin, March 9, 1960. McMurrin Papers, Box 341, fd. 9, Special Collections, Marriott Library.

Souders, Michael. "Preaching the Restored Gospel: John Nicholson's Homiletic Theories for Young Mormons," *Rhetorica: A Journal of the History of Rhetoric* 27, no. 4 (Autumn 2009): 420–46.

"South African Mission." *Cumorah's Southern Messenger* 27, no. 3 (March 1952): 38.

"South African Police to Take 'Stern Action' against March." *Marietta [Ga.] Journal*, August 25, 1985, 6.

"South African Police to Take 'Stern Action' against March." *Marietta [Ga.] Journal*, August 25, 1985, 6.

South American Mission. Manuscript History and Historical Reports, 1925–35. LR 8458 2, LDS Church History Library.

Spafford, Horatio Gates, ed. *A Gazetteer of the State of New York.* Albany, N.Y.: B. D. Packard, 1824.

Spanish Fork. Minutes of High Priests Meeting, February 5, 1870. LDS Church History Library.

Speach [sic] by Gov. Young in Joint Session of the Legislature Feby 5th 1852 Giving His Views on Slavery." In Historian's Office Reports of Speeches, Box 1, fd. 17, LDS Church History Library.

"Special Conference." *Melchisedek and Aaronic Herald* 1, no. 4 (June 1849): 4.

"Spectacular Rise of the Mormon Church, The." *Reader's Digest*, February 1967, 78–82.

"Speech of Mr. Stuart." *Kalamazoo Gazette*, March 23, 1849, 1–2.

Speek, Vickie C. *"God Has Made Us a Kingdom": James Strang and the Midwest Mormons.* Salt Lake City: Signature Books, 2006.

Spencer, Daniel. Diary, 1847. Holograph. LDS Church History Library.

St. Lawrence County Chapter of the New York Medical Society. "Minutes of the St. Lawrence Association." *Universalist Union*, August 18, 1838, 323.

"Step Forward, A." *[University of] Utah Daily Chronicle*, October 7, 1963, 1.

Staker, Mark Lyman. *Hearken O Ye People: The Historical Setting of Joseph Smith's Ohio Revelations.* Salt Lake City: Greg Kofford Books, 2009.

Stammer, Larry. "Mormons May Disavow Old View on Blacks." *Los Angeles Times*, May 18, 1998. http://articles.latimes.com/1998/may/18/news/mn-51047 (accessed September 10, 2013).

"Stanford U. Closes Door on Cougars." *Ogden Standard-Examiner*, November 13, 1969, 54.

Stapley, Delbert L. Letter to George Romney, January 23, 1964. http://www.boston.com/news/daily/24/delbert_stapley.pdf (accessed December 27, 2013).

Stapley, Jonathan A. "Adoptive Sealing Ritual in Mormonism." *Journal of Mormon History* 37, no. 3 (Summer 2011): 53–119.

Stark, Rodney. "The Rise of a New World Faith." *Review of Religious Research* 26, no. 1 (September 1984): 18–27.

"Status of Utah Negroes Said among Worse in Nation." *Dallas Morning News*, October 31, 1963, 15.

Steele, Mark A. "Mormon Conversions in Freedom, New York." *Mormon Historical Studies* 8, nos. 1–2 (Spring/Fall 2007): 39–52.

Stegner, Wallace, *The Gathering of Zion: The Story of the Mormon Trail.* Lincoln: University of Nebraska Press, 1992.

Stenhouse, T.B.H. *The Rocky Mountain Saints: A Full and Complete History of the Mormons, from the First Vision of Joseph Smith to the Last Courtship of Brigham Young.* New York: D. Appleton, 1873.

"Step Forward, A." *[University of] Utah Daily Chronicle*, October 7, 1963, 1.

Stevens, Thaddeus. In *The Selected Papers of Thaddeus Stevens*, 1865–68. Pittsburgh. University of Pittsburgh Press, 1998.

Stevenson, Kent. Interviewed by Russell Stevenson, December 27, 2013. Notes in my possession.

Stevenson, Russell W. *Black Mormon: The Story of Elijah Ables.* Afton, Wyo.: PrintStar for Author, 2013.

_____. "Mo-rientalism: Mizra Khan and Mormon identity in India." June 2013. Unpublished manuscript.

Stewart, John J. *The Eternal Gift: The Story of the Crucifixion and Resurrection of the Christ.* Orem, Utah: Community Press, 1960.

_____. *For God So Loved the World.* Salt Lake City: Deseret Book, 1966.

_____. *How You Gain a Testimony.* Logan, Utah: Bookmark, 1962.

_____. *The Glory of Mormonism.* Salt Lake City: Mercury Publishing, 1963.

_____. *George Washington and the Mormons.* Salt Lake City: Deseret Book, 1967.

_____. *Joseph Smith: Democracy's Unknown Prophet.* Salt Lake City: Mercury Publishing, 1960.

_____. *The Miracles of Christmas.* Salt Lake City: Deseret Book, 1965.

_____. *Mormonism and the Negro: An Explanation and Defense of the Doctrine of the Church of Jesus Christ of Latter-day Saints in regard to Negroes and Others of Negroid Blood, with a Historical Supplement.* Orem, Utah: Bookmark, 1960. This first edition was self-published (under the name of Bookmark), but Community Press reprinted it that same year, publishing two editions.

_____. *Mormonism v. Communism.* Salt Lake City: Mercury, 1961.

_____. *Remembering the McKays: A Biographical Sketch with Pictures of David O. and Emma Ray McKay.* Salt Lake City: Deseret Book, 1970.

Stewart, John J., and William E. Berrett. *Mormonism and the Negro: An Explanation and Defense of the Doctrine of the Church of Jesus Christ of Latter-day Saints in Regard to Negroes and Others of Negroid Blood, with a Historical Supplement.* Orem, Utah: Community Press, 1967, followed by a 3rd ed., and a 4th (fall 1978). I cite only the Bookmark first edition.

Stockdale, Gary, and Patricia Campbell. "Interview: John Goddard." *Metamorphisis* 4, no. 2 (Summer 1986): 24–33, 54–64.

Stokes, Catherine M. Interviewed by Russell Stevenson, April 15, 2014. Audio recording in my possession.

Stolley, Richard. "A World of Energy, Some Ad-Lib Bumbles." *Life*, March 3, 1967, 74.

Stone, Eileen Hallet. *Hidden History of Utah.* Charleston, S.C.: History Press, 2013.

Stookey, Jemima M. *Autobiography of Jemima E. Stookey.* Clover, Utah: Paul and Gwenevere Stookey, 1971.

"Stop Gambling Here!" *Salt Lake Telegram*, July 16, 1916, 2.

"Strange Infatuation—Marriage of a White Woman with an Indian at Niagara should be Niagara Falls." *New London [Connecticut] Daily Chronicle,* September 10, 1851, 2.

Stum, Robert W. "Photographer Wins Office, Awards with State Group." *Daily Herald* (Provo, Utah), September 10, 1954, 4.

Sturlaugson, Mary Francis. *A Soul So Rebellious.* Salt Lake City: Deseret Book, 1980.

"Subtle Changes in South Africa." *Milwaukee [Wisc.] Journal*, August 16, 1981, 1, 3.

"Suit Attacks Injunction." *[Jackson] Mississippi Free Press*, August 24, 1963, 1.

"Summoned." *Deseret News*, November, 16 1940, 9.

Suntinger, Walter. "Ghana." In P. R. Baehr, Hilde Hey, Jacqueline Smith, and Theresa Swinehart, eds. *Human Rights in Developing Countries: Yearbook 1994*. Boston, Mass.: Kluwer Law and Taxation Publishers, 1994.

Sweatt v. Painter. 339 U.S. 629 (1950).

Taggart, Stephen. *Mormonism's Negro Policy: Social and Historical Origins*. Salt Lake City: University of Utah Press, 1970.

"Talk with Brigham Young, A." *Charleston Courier*, August 9, 1869, 4.

Tanner, N. Eldon. "Acceptance of Revelation." *Conference Report*, October 1978, 22.

"Tappanite, A." *Columbian Register* (New Haven, Conn.), August 31, 1833, 3.

Taylor, Jeremy. "Of Habitual Sins and Their Remedy." In Reginald Heber, ed. *The Whole Works of the Right Rev. Jeremy Taylor, D.D.*, 10 vols. London: Longman, 1861.

Taylor, Nikki. *Frontiers of Freedom: Cincinnati's Black Community, 1802–1868*. Athens: Ohio University Press, 2005.

"Telephone Tracting." and "Mission History of the Black Program." 1, 5–7. California Los Angeles Mission History, 1981. LR 1316, LDS Church History Library.

"Television." *Redlands [Calif.] Daily Facts*, September 1, 1965, 16.

Telles, Edward Eric. *Race in Another America: The Significance of Color in Brazil*. Princeton, N.J.: Princeton University Press, 2004.

"10 Agencies to Meet on Water Pollution." *Deseret News*, January 15, 1960, 10A.

Tenhoeve, Raymond. Audio journal, 1988–89. Transcript. LDS Church History Library.

"That's Sick." *Vernal [Utah] Express*, August 31, 1967, 3.

"Theater Gossip." *Evening Independent* (St. Petersburg, Fla.), July 19, 1927, 4.

Themba, Cam. *The Will to Die*. London: Heinemann Educational Books, 1972.

"There's No Halfway Service in City Recorder's Office." *Ogden Standard-Examiner*, November 5, 1971, 3.

"They Get Hard Hats." *Deseret News*, July 30, 1965, B7.

"Things Politically." *Park [City, Utah] Record*, August 29, 1924, 1.

"Third Candidate Seeks to Head County Demos." *Ogden Standard-Examiner*, March 19, 1958, 1B.

"Thirty Citizens to Be Summoned for Grand Jury." *News Advocate* (Price, Utah), July 9, 1925, 1.

"This Would Be a Switch." Editorial. *Vernal [Utah] Express*, July 4, 1963, 2.

"Thomas A. Shreeve Dies at Ogden Home." *Salt Lake Telegram*, December 29, 1931, 6.

Thomas, Martha Pane Jones. Autobiographical sketch. In Daniel Stillwell Thomas Family History. Perry Special Collections.

Thomasson, Gordon C. "Lester Bush's Historical Overview: Other Perspectives." *Dialogue: A Journal of Mormon Thought* 8, no. 1 (Spring 1973): 69–72.

Thompson, Jan. "Like a Rope Lowered from Heaven." *This People* 15, no. 2 (Summer 1994): 12–13, 15–16, 19, 21.

Thomson, Alex. *U.S. Foreign Policy towards Apartheid South Africa, 1948–1994*. New York: Palgrave Macmillan, 2008.

"Thos. A. Shreeve on Book of Mormon." *Ogden Standard*, March 15, 1915, 3.

"Three-Day Conference for Youth Coming Up." *News of the West* (Glendale West Ward Newsletter) 1, no. 6 (June–July 1964): 1.

"Three Paddle Down the Nile for 9 Months." *Anniston Star*, July 29, 1951, 16,

"Thuggee and Mormonism." *Salt Lake Tribune*, January 6, 1877, 2.

Thurman, Wallace. Letter to William Rapp, n.d. Qtd. in Eleonore Van Notten, *Wallace Thurman's Harlem Renaissance*. Amsterdam, The Netherlands: Rodopi, 1994.

_____. "Quoth Brigham Young: This is the Place." In Tom Lutz and Susanna Ashton, eds. *These "Colored" United States: African American Essays from the 1920s.* New Brunswick, N.J.: Rutgers University Press, 1996.

"Thursday." *Independent Star-News*, January 13, 1963; television pullout.

"'Tis Truly Said That Fools Rush In Where Angels Fear to Tread." *Murray [Utah] Eagle*, September 12, 1957, 2.

"To Explore Nile." *Greeley [Colo.] Daily Tribune*, September 6, 1950, 11.

"To the Colored People of Utah." *Broad Ax*, August 31, 1895, 1.

Toone, Millard. Letter to Mrs. F. P. Toone, September 2, 1921. Felix Toone Papers, LDS Church History Library.

"'Totalitarian Sect, A': Youth Group Wants to Kick Mormons Out of Russia." October 31, 2012. http://www.rferl.org/content/pro-kremlin-group-wants-mormons-out-of-russia/24757052.html (accessed December 5, 2013).

Tracy, Curtis. Journal, 1954., LDS Church History Library.

Transactions of the Medical Society of the State of New York. 6 vols. Albany: J. Munsell, 1846. Appendix.

"Transfers." *Cumorah's Southern Messenger* 24, no. 2 (February 1949): 27.

"Travel Film to Be Seen by Forum." *Tsucon [Ariz.] Daily Citizen*, February 7, 1964, 44.

"Travelogue Program." *Independent* (Long Beach, Calif.), October 5, 1967, P2.

"Tremont Temple Hall." *Boston Evening Transcript*, November 16, 1848, 3.

"Tridell." *Vernal [Utah] Express*, May 16, 1963, 12.

"Trio in Canoe Explore Entire Nile for First Time in 4,200-Mile Trip." *Kane [Pa.] Republican*, September 6, 1951, 10.

"Troop Sponsors Church Benefit." *San Bernadino County Sun*, September 29, 1955, 48.

"Trouble in the Transvaal, The." *New Haven [Conn.] Register*, September 5, 1899, 6.

"Trouble with Birthdays, The." *Deseret News*, September 28, 1972, 1E.

"Truth in Civil Turmoil: Talk." *Davis County Clipper* (Bountiful, UT), October 20, 1967, 2.

Tubbee, Laah. *A Sketch of the Life of Okah Tubbee.* Springfield, Mass.: H. S. Taylor, 1848.

_____. *See also* McCary, Lucy.

Tullidge, Edward W. *The History of Salt Lake City and Its Founders.* Salt Lake City: Edward W. Tullidge, 1886.

_____. *Tullidge's Histories: Containing the History of All the Northern, Eastern, and Western Counties of Utah.* Salt Lake City: Juvenile Instructor, 1889.

_____. "Utah County." *Tullidge's Quarterly Magazine* 4, no. 3 (April 1885): 395–96.

"Turks and the Mormons, The." *Washington Sentinel*, May 7, 1854, 2.

Turley, Richard E., ed. *Selected Collections from the Archives of the Church of Jesus Christ of Latter-day Saints.* 2 vols. Provo, UT: Brigham Young University Press, 2002.

Turner, JeanAnne. Letter to John M. Goddard, April 30, 1975. Holograph. John M. Goddard Papers, Box 3, fd. 9. Perry Special Collections.

Turner, John. *Brigham Young: Pioneer Prophet.* Cambridge, Mass.: Belknap Press, 2013.

Turner, Orasmus. *History of the Pioneer Settlement of Phelps & Gorham's Purchase and Morris' Reserve.* Rochester, N.Y.: William Alling, 1852.

_____. *History of the Pioneer Settlement of Phelps & Gorham's Purchase and Morris' Reserve.* Rochester, N.Y.: William Alling, 1852.

Turner, Wallace. Letter to Al Johnson (Riverton, Utah), July 9, 1963, Box 1, fd. 23, Utah State Archives, Salt Lake City.

Tushnet, Mark V. *Making Civil Rights Law: Thurgood Marshall and the Supreme Court, 1936–1961.* New York: Oxford University Press, 1994.

"TV Last Night." *Boston Daily Record*, May 12, 1959, 18.

"Tweedle." *Plain Dealer* (Cleveland, Ohio), November 16, 1853, 2.

"20th Century Reveals Program for 1956–1957." *Oshkosh [Wisc.] Daily Northwestern,* August 23, 1956, 24.

"Two Big Attractions Coming to Milford." *Beaver County News,* November 9, 1917, 1.

"Two Elders Appointed to Work Genealogy." *Cumorah's Southern Messenger* 25, no. 7 (July 1950): 107.

"2 Greeks of the Year Get U. Awards." *Salt Lake Tribune,* May 9, 1964, 30.

"2,000 Mormons to Trek." *Omaha World Herald,* April 13, 1901, 1.

Uchtdorf, Dieter F. "Come Join with Us." *Ensign,* November 2013, 22, http://www.lds.org/general-conference/2013/10/come-join-with-us?lang=eng (accessed December 17, 2013).

Udoh, Timothy. Letter to LaMar Williams, August 25, 1960, LaMar Williams Papers, MS 2015, LDS Church History Library.

Udorm, Mennie. Letters to First Presidency. In Edwin Q. Cannon Papers, Box 1, fd. 1. LDS Church History Library.
November 9, 1976
December 3, 1976

Ukwat, E. D., Letter to Edwin Q. Cannon, September 23, 1978. In Edwin Q. Cannon Correspondence, Box 1, fd. 1. LDS Church History Library.

Ulibarri, Richard O. "Utah's Ethnic Minorities: A Survey." *Utah Historical Quarterly* 40 (Summer 1972): 210-32.

Ulrich, Laurel Thatcher. "Family Scriptures." *Dialogue: A Journal of Mormon Thought* 20, no. 2 (Summer 1987): 119–27.

Umah, Gaskon. Letter to LaMar Williams, January 10, 1961, LaMar S. Williams Papers, Box 1, fd. 5. LDS Church History Library.

United States v. Guest, 383 U.S. 745, 86 S.Ct. 1170, 16 L.Ed., 2d 239 (1966).

University II Ward, Oakland, California. Minutes of the 11th Quorum of Elders, 1968. LR 6349 13,, LDS Church History Library.

University of Michigan, *Register of Students, 1947–1948,* 50, no. 20. Ann Arbor: University of Michigan, 1948.

"University of Utah, The." *Deseret News,* June 9, 1892, 5.

"University of Utah, The." *Deseret News,* August 22, 1892, 7.

"Urim and Thummim" and "The Book of Mormon." *Evening and the Morning Star* 1 (January 1833): 57.

"Utah Civil Rights Bill Draws No Opposition." *Deseret News,* February 6, 1959, A9.

"Utah Congressmen Give Views on New Civil Rights Legislation." *Deseret News,* June 24, 1963, A4.

"Utah, Deaths and Burials, 1888–1946." Index, *FamilySearch.* https://familysearch.org/pal:/MM9.1.1/F85D-6MN (accessed May 10, 2013).

"Utah Negroes Put Off Civil Rights Marching." *Milwaukee Journal,* October 5, 1963, 4.

"Utah Territory—Mormonism." *Weekly Advocate* (Baton Rouge, La.), March 25, 1860, 4.

"Utah 'Jubilant' over Black Friday." *Dallas Morning News,* June 27, 1978, 11A.

"Utah." *Boston Courier,* May 14, 1860, 2.

"Utah," *American Traveller,* May 15, 1857, 4.

"Utah's Good Will and Martin Luther King Jr. Get Their Day." *Deseret News,* February 13, 1986, 1A.

"Utah's McMurrin Gets School Post." *Omaha [Neb.] World Herald,* February 1, 1961, 20.

Van Katwyk, Shirley, comp. "Project History Log." n.d. In Shirley Van Katwyk Papers, LDS Church History Library.

Van Noord, Roger. *King of Beaver Island: The Life and Assassination of James Jesse Strang.* Urbana: University of Illinois, 1988.

Van Notten, Eleonore. *Wallace Thurman's Harlem Renaissance.* Amsterdam, The Netherlands: Rodopi, 1994.

Van Wagoner, Richard S. ed. *The Collected Discourses of Brigham Young,* 5 vols. Salt Lake City: Signature Books, 2009.

Van Wagonen, Richard, and Steve Walker. "The Gift of Seeing." *Dialogue: A Journal of Mormon Thought* 15, no. 2 (Summer 1982): 49–68.

"Violence Hit by Thousands." *San Diego Union,* March 10, 1965, 1.

"Virginia Cutler—Her Heart Is Where the Home Is." *Ensign,* July 1985, 36.

"Vision of Brigham Young, February 17, 1847. Reel 87, Brigham Young Office Files. LDS Church History Library.

"Visit of the Presidency to Weber." *Deseret News,* February 8, 1851, 5.

"Visit with Elder Gordon B. Hinckley about Missionary Work, A." *New Era,* June 1973, 27–28.

Vogel, Dan, ed. *Early Mormon Documents,* 5 vols. Salt Lake City: Signature Books, 1996–2003.

"Voice from the Southern States." *Deseret News,* April 19, 1882, 7.

"Vote Fails to Override Anti-Busing Bill Veto." *San Diego Union,* April 11, 1980, 3.

Wade, Wyn. *The Fiery Cross: The Ku Klux Klan in America.* New York: Oxford University Press, 1987.

Walker, Ronald G. "Jedediah and Heber Grant." *Ensign,* July 1979, 46–52.

Walker, Ronald W. *Wayward Saints: The Godbeites and Brigham Young.* Urbana: University of Illinois Press, 1998.

Walker, Ronald W., Richard E. Turley, and Glen M. Leonard. *Massacre at Mountain Meadows: An American Tragedy.* New York: Oxford University Press, 2007.

Walker, William Holmes. *The Life Incidents and Travels of Elder William Holmes Walker and His Association with Joseph, the Prophet.* Bountiful, Utah: Elizabeth Jane Walker Piepgrass, 1943.

Wallace, Thurman. "Quoth Brigham Young: This Is the Place." Reprinted in Tom Lutz and Susanna Ashton, eds. *These "Colored" United States: African American Essays from the 1920s.* New Brunswick, N.J.: Rutgers University Press, 1996, 266–67.

Walton, Brian. "A University's Dilemma: B.Y.U. and Blacks." *Dialogue: A Journal of Mormon Thought* 6, no. 1 (Spring 1970): 30–36.

Wandell, Charles Wesley. "To The Elders Laboring in the State of New York." *The Prophet,* June 1, 1844, 2.

Ward, Samuel. *Autobiography of a Fugitive Negro: His Anti-Slavery Labours in the United States, Canada, & England.* London: John Snow, 1855.

Warner, Susan. "Have Miracles Ceased: The Two John Ekow Mensahs' Story." MS 26893. LDS Church History Library.

Washington, Booker T., Letter to David H. Christensen, March 31, 1973. In Frederick Stuart Buchanan Papers, Box 173, Special Collections, Marriott Library.

_____. "There are Colored Mormons Out in Utah." *New York Age,* April 17, 1913, 1. Rpt. in *Improvement Era* 16 (June 1913): 8078.

_____. *Up from Slavery: An Autobiography.* New York: Doubleday, 1907.

_____. "Views of the Mormons." *Improvement Era* 16 (June 1913): 807–8.

Waterman, Bryan, and Brian Kagel. *The Lord's University: Freedom and Authority at BYU.* Salt Lake City: Signature Books, 1998.

Watson, Elden, ed. *Orson Pratt Journals.* Salt Lake City: Elden J. Watson, 1975.

"Weber College Lists High Honor Students." *Ogden Standard-Examiner,* July 1, 1964, 19.

Webster, Noah. *American Dictionary of the English Language: Exhibiting the Origin, Orthography, Pronunciation, and Definition of Words.* New York: S. Converse, 1830.

Webster, Reed J. "In the Beginning." n.d., ca. 1992. In Maurice Bateman Temple Papers, LDS Church History Library.

_____."Reflections on the Great South African Experience." ca. 1992. Maurice Bateman Temple Papers, LDS Church History Library.

Webster, Reed. "The Lord Chose Me." n.d, ca. 1992. Maurice Bateman Temple Papers, LDS Church History Library. Published as Reed J. Webster. "Man of Few Words Radiates Serenity." *Deseret News,* January 4, 1992, 11.

Webster's Academic Dictionary. New York: American Book Company, 1895.

"West Bountiful." *Davis County Clipper,* December 25, 1964, 11.

Westergren, Bruce N., ed. *John Whitmer: From Historian to Dissident.* Salt Lake City: Signature Books, 1995.

"What Is Religion?" *New York Herald,* May 11, 1879, 10.

"What You Ought to Know about the Church of Jesus Christ of Latter-day Saints." *Nigerian Outlook,* June 26, 1963, 5. James Allen, "Would-Be Saints," 231, misdates this article at June 16, 1963.

"What's Wrong with Civil Rights?" Advertisement. *Palm Beach Post,* October 31, 1965, A10.

Wheelwright, Hyrum. Papers. Stewart Library, Weber State University, Ogden, Utah.

"While Such Papers." *[Keene] New Hampshire Sentinel,* May 11, 1871, 2.

Whipple, Edson. Autobiography. Holograph, MS 5348. LDS Church History Library. Also catalogued as "History of Nelson Whipple," under the same call number.

_____. Baptism List. In Edson Whipple Record Book, 1849–1850. MS 861 1, LDS Church History Library.

_____. Letter to Heber C. Kimball, ca. June 1849. Edson Whipple Notebook, MS 861 1, LDS Church History Library.

_____. Record Book, 1849–1850. Microfilm of holograph. MS 861 1. LDS Church History Library.

White, Michael. "Few Blacks Join Mormons." *Mobile [Ala.] Register,* June 9, 1983, 11-C.

White, Michael, and Vern Anderson. "Mormons Try to End Racism Reputation." *Marietta [Ga.] Journal,* June 4, 1988, 4A.

"White Church Schools Jar S. African Regime." *Christian Science Monitor,* April 3, 1978, 4.

White Plague and Weak Bodies, The." *Good Health* 43, no. 12 (December 1908): 696.

Whitmer, John. *John Whitmer: From Historian to Dissident.* Edited by Bruce N. Westergren. Salt Lake City: Signature Books, 1995.

Whitmer, John, and W. W. Phelps, Letter to Brethren, July 29, 1833. Joseph Smith Collection, LDS Church History Library.

Whittaker, David J. "East of Nauvoo: Benjamin Winchester and the Early Mormon Church." *Journal of Mormon History* 21, no. 2 (Fall 1995): 31–83.

Wilcox, Reed N. Review of *It's You and Me, Lord!* and *Mormonism's Negro Policy: Social and Historical Origins.* In *BYU Studies* 11, no. 2 (Winter 1971): 210–12.

Wilkinson, Ernest L. Letter to David O. McKay, January 31, 1953. Adam S. Bennion Papers, Box 9, fd. 7. Special Collectins, Marriott Library.

"Will Lecture on Violence Threats." *Davis County Clipper* (Bountiful, Utah), October 11, 1968, 11.

Willey, W. W. Letter to Editor. *Davis County Clipper* (Bountiful, Utah), April 4, 1947, 5.

Williams, LaMar S., Diary/Journal, 1961, 1964, LDS Church History Library.

_____. Letter to Itah Akpan, November 16, 1960. LaMar S. Williams Papers, Box 1, fd. 6. LDS Church History Library.

_____. Letter to I. A. Emuldamu, July 23, 1963, Edwin Q. Cannon Papers, MS 21299, Box 1, fd. 1. LDS Church History Library.

_____. Letter to Joseph Dadzie, May 8, 1974. Joseph Dadzie Papers, LDS Church History Library.

_____. Letter to First Presidency, May 3, 1961, Box 1, fd. 7. LDS Church History Library.

_____. Letter to Marvin Jones, November 8, 1961. Marvin Jones Papers, LDS Church History Library.

_____. Letter to Charles Udo-Ete, January 31, 1961, LaMar S. Williams Papers, Box 1, fd. 6. LDS Church History Library.

_____. Memo to Gordon B. Hinckley, September 9, 1962, LaMar S. Williams Papers, Box 1, fd. 12. LDS Church History Library.

_____. Statement, n.d. LaMar S. Williams Papers, Box 1, fd. 9. LDS Church History Library.

_____. Summary Memo, November 21, 1961. LaMar S. Williams Papers, Box 1, fd. 8. LDS Church History Library.

Williams, Oscar R. *George S. Schuyler: Portrait of a Black Conservative.* Nashville: University of Tennessee Press, 2007.

Williams, Thomas, ed., *The Cottage Bible and Family Expositor.* London: W. Simpkin and R. Marshall, 1828.

Williston, Seth. "Sermon," *The Columbian Preacher.* Catskill, N.Y.: Nathan Elliot, 1808.

Wilson, Veronica. "To Tell All My People': Race, Representation, and John Birch Society Activist Julia Brown." In Kathleen Blee, ed. *Women of the Right: Comparisons and Interplay across Borders.* University Park: Pennsylvania State University Press, 2012, 242–53.

Wilson, William ("Bert"), and Richard Poulson, "The Curse of Cain and Other Stories: Blacks in Mormon Folklore." *Sunstone,* (November–December 1980), 9–12.

Wise, Sherwood. Qtd. in Sarah Hart Brown, *Three Southern Lawyers in an Era of Fear.* Baton Rouge: Louisiana State University Press, 2000, 207.

Witness List, Hancock County Circuit Court Records, 1843, LDS Church History Library.

Wolfinger, Henry J. "A Test of Faith: Jane Elizabeth James and the Origins of the Utah Black Community." In Clark S. Knowlton, ed. *Social Accommodation in Utah.* Salt Lake City: American West Center Occasional Papers, University of Utah, 1975, 126–47.

Wolpe, Howard. *Urban Politics in Nigeria: A Study of Port Harcourt.* Berkeley: University of California Press, 1974.

Wolsey, Heber. Fireside Address, Manhattan Second Ward. November 1, 1970. Grant Bethers Audio Recordings Collection, cassette 14. LDS Church History Library.

"Women Back Peace, Urge Racial Unity." *San Diego Union,* November 27, 1977, 73.

"Women Cited for Accomplishments in '56." *Deseret News,* December 11, 1956, 28.

Wood, Joseph. *Epistle of the Twelve.* Milwaukee: Sentinel and Gazette Steam Press Print, 1851.

Woodruff, Abraham O. Journal. Abraham O. Woodruff Collection, Box 1, fd. 3, Perry Special Collections.

Wilford Woodruff's Journal, 1833–1898. Edited by Scott G. Kenney. Typescript, 9 vols. Midvale, Utah: Signature Books, 1983–85.

Woodruff, Wilford. Letter to Brigham Young. Brigham Young Office Files, Reel 56., LDS Church History Library.

October 9, 1844

November 16, 1844

_____. *See also* Kenney, Scott G.

Wright, Norman E. "The Mormon Pioneer Odometers." *BYU Studies* 37, no. 1 (1997): 82–115.

"WSC Plans Travelogue on Nile Trip." *Ogden-Standard Examiner,* April 4, 1973, 9B.

Yalof, David. *Prosecution among Friends: Presidents, Attorneys General, and Branch Wrongdoing.* College Station: Texas A&M Press, 2012.

"Yank Will Make Record Canoe Trip." *Miami [Okla.] Daily News-Record,* August 1, 1950, 1.

Yeagley, J. Walter. Memo to J. Edgar Hoover, November 4, 1965. Photocopies posted on https://archive.org/details/foia_Holmes_Lola_Belle-HQ-2 (accessed March 15, 2014).

Young, Brigham. Letters. All in Brigham Young Office Files, LDS Church History Library. Also see separate citations for other correspondence
    to John Bernhisel, October 14, 1849, Box 16, fd. 18
    to Rowland Crispen, Summer 1845. Brigham Young Office Files, Reel 24.
    to Isaac Higbee, October 18, 1849.
    to Orson Hyde, July 19, 1849, Box 16, fd. 17
    to Mrs. Lewis, January 3, 1860, Box 19, fd. 1
    to Frederick Merryweather, March 4, 1845, Reel 24
_____. Letter to William Crosby, March 12, 1851. In William E. Parrish, "The Mississippi Saints." *The Historian* 50, no. 4 (August 1988): 505.
_____. Letter to John Eldridge, March 14, 1854. In Richard E. Turley, ed. *Selected Collections from the Archives of the Church of Jesus Christ of Latter-day Saints.* Provo, Utah: BYU Religious Studies Center, 2002, 21:467.
_____. Letter to Thomas L. Kane, October 26, 1869. Thomas L. Kane Collection, Box 15, fd. 4. Perry Special Collections.
_____. "Vision, February 17, 1847." Reel 87, Brigham Young Office Files. LDS Church History Library.
Young, Bruce W. Letter to Stephen Holbrook, June 18, 1975, Box 1, fd. 25. Stephen Holbrook Papers, Utah State Historical Society Archives.
Young, Emily [Dow] P[artridge]. Autobiography, Typescript. Perry Special Collections.
_____. "Reminiscences of Emily Dow Partridge Young." April 7, 1884. Typescript. Perry Special Collections.
Young, Franklin W. Autobiography, 1916. MS 1148. LDS Church History Library.
Young, Margaret Blair. *House Without Walls.* Salt Lake City: Deseret Book, 1991.
_____. "Household of Faith: Enlarge Thy Borders Forever." http://ldsmag.com/ldsmag/exstories/040220household.html (accessed April 3, 2014).
_____. Interviewed by Lisa Butterworth. Feminist Mormon Housewives. Audio podcast, February 18, 2013. http://feministmormonhousewivespodcast.org/category/margaret-blair-young/ (accessed June 2, 2013).
_____. Interviewed by Kylan Rice. *A Thoughtful Faith.* Audio podcast, September 30, 2012. http://www.athoughtfulfaith.org/podcast/AThoughtfulFaith-007-MargaretYoung. mp3 (accessed June 2, 2013).
_____."Messiah in Patsun, Guatemala." http://www.patheos.com/blogs/welcometable/2013/12/messiah-in-patsun-guatemala/ (accessed April 3, 2014).
Young, Margaret Blair, and Darius A. Gray. Interviewed by Benjamin Crowder. *The Mormon Artist* 1 (September 2008): 3–11.
_____. Interviewed by John Dehlin. *Mormon Matters.* Audio podcast. April 12, 2006. http://mormonstories.org/mormon-stories-026-blacks-and-the-lds-priesthood-an-interview-with-darius-gray-and-margaret-young/ (accessed June 2, 2013).
_____. *Standing on the Promises: Vol. 1: One More River to Cross; Vol. 2: Bound for Canaan; Vol. 3 (The Last Mile of the Way.* Salt Lake City: Deseret Book, 2000, 2002, 2003 respectively. Rpt. in a revised and updated edition in 2013. Provo, Utah: Zarahemla Books, 2013.
Young, Phineas. Letter to Brigham Young, March 14, 1842. Brigham Young Office Files, Reel 57. LDS Church History Library.
"Your Ward and Branch Activities." *Cumorah's Southern Messenger* 45, no. 5 (May 1970): 130.
"Youth Fireside." *Second to None* (Glendale California Second Ward newsletter), 2, no. 9 (September 1970): 3.

Index

About the Author

Russell Stevenson is an independent historian and author of *Black Mormon: The Story of Elijah Ables*. He has also been published in the *Journal of Mormon History*, *Dialogue*, and Oxford University Press's *American National Biography Series*. He currently resides in East Lansing, Michigan.

Also available from
GREG KOFFORD BOOKS

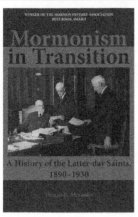

Mormonism in Transition: A History of the Latter-day Saints, 1890–1930, 3rd ed.

Thomas G. Alexander

Paperback, ISBN: 978-1-58958-188-3

More than two decades after its original publication, Thomas G. Alexander's Mormonism in Transition still engages audiences with its insightful study of the pivotal, early years of the Church of Jesus Christ of Latter-day Saints. Serving as a vital read for both students and scholars of American religious and social history, Alexander's book explains and charts the Church's transformation over this 40-year period of both religious and American history.

For those familiar with the LDS Church in modern times, it is impossible to study Mormonism in Transition without pondering the enormous amount of changes the Church has been through since 1890. For those new to the study of Mormonism, this book will give them a clear understanding the challenges the Church went through to go from a persecuted and scorned society to the rapidly growing, respected community it is today.

Praise for Mormonism in Transition:

"A must read for any serious student of this 'peculiar people' and Western history." – STANLEY B. KIMBALL, *Journal of the West*

"Will be required reading for all historians of Mormonism for some time to come." – WILLIAM D. RUSSELL, *Journal of American History*

"This is by far the most important book on this crucial period in LDS history." – JAN SHIPPS, author of *Mormonism: The Story of a New Religious Tradition*

"A work of careful and prodigious scholarship." – LEONARD J. ARRINGTON, author of *Brigham Young: American Moses*

"Clearly fills a tremendous void in the history of Mormonism." – Klaus J. Hansen, author of *Mormonism and the American Experience*

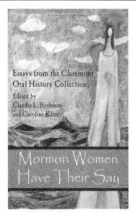

Mormon Women Have Their Say: Essays from the Claremont Oral History Collection

Edited by Claudia L. Bushman and Caroline Kline

Paperback, ISBN: 978-1-58958-494-5

The Claremont Women's Oral History Project has collected hundreds of interviews with Mormon women of various ages, experiences, and levels of activity. These interviews record the experiences of these women in their homes and family life, their church life, and their work life, in their roles as homemakers, students, missionaries, career women, single women, converts, and disaffected members. Their stories feed into and illuminate the broader narrative of LDS history and belief, filling in a large gap in Mormon history that has often neglected the lived experiences of women. This project preserves and perpetuates their voices and memories, allowing them to say share what has too often been left unspoken. The silent majority speaks in these records.

This volume is the first to explore the riches of the collection in print. A group of young scholars and others have used the interviews to better understand what Mormonism means to these women and what women mean for Mormonism. They explore those interviews through the lenses of history, doctrine, mythology, feminist theory, personal experience, and current events to help us understand what these women have to say about their own faith and lives.

Praise for *Mormon Women Have Their Say*:

"Using a variety of analytical techniques and their own savvy, the authors connect ordinary lives with enduring themes in Latter-day Saint faith and history." --Laurel Thatcher Ulrich, author of *Well-Behaved Women Seldom Make History*

"Essential. . . . In these pages, Mormon women will find *ourselves*." --Joanna Brooks, author of *The Book of Mormon Girl: A Memoir of an American Faith*

"The varieties of women's responses to the major issues in their lives will provide many surprises for the reader, who will be struck by how many different ways there are to be a thoughtful and faithful Latter-day Saint woman." --Armand Mauss, author of *All Abraham's Children: Changing Mormon Conceptions of Race and Lineage*

Common Ground—Different Opinions:
Latter-day Saints and Contemporary Issues

Edited by Justin F. White
and James E. Faulconer

Paperback, ISBN: 978-1-58958-573-7

There are many hotly debated issues about which many people disagree, and where common ground is hard to find. From evolution to environmentalism, war and peace to political partisanship, stem cell research to same-sex marriage, how we think about controversial issues affects how we interact as Latter-day Saints.

In this volume various Latter-day Saint authors address these and other issues from differing points of view. Though they differ on these tough questions, they have all found common ground in the gospel of Jesus Christ and the latter-day restoration. Their insights offer diverse points of view while demonstrating we can still love those with whom we disagree.

Praise for *Common Ground—Different Opinions*:

"[This book] provide models of faithful and diverse Latter-day Saints who remain united in the body of Christ. This collection clearly demonstrates that a variety of perspectives on a number of sensitive issues do in fact exist in the Church. . . . [T]he collection is successful in any case where it manages to give readers pause with regard to an issue they've been fond of debating, or convinces them to approach such conversations with greater charity and much more patience. It served as just such a reminder and encouragement to me, and for that reason above all, I recommend this book." — Blair Hodges, Maxwell Institute

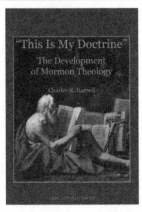

"This is My Doctrine": The Development of Mormon Theology

Charles R. Harrell

Hardcover, ISBN: 978-1-58958-103-6

The principal doctrines defining Mormonism today often bear little resemblance to those it started out with in the early 1830s. This book shows that these doctrines did not originate in a vacuum but were rather prompted and informed by the religious culture from which Mormonism arose. Early Mormons, like their early Christian and even earlier Israelite predecessors, brought with them their own varied culturally conditioned theological presuppositions (a process of convergence) and only later acquired a more distinctive theological outlook (a process of differentiation).

In this first-of-its-kind comprehensive treatment of the development of Mormon theology, Charles Harrell traces the history of Latter-day Saint doctrines from the times of the Old Testament to the present. He describes how Mormonism has carried on the tradition of the biblical authors, early Christians, and later Protestants in reinterpreting scripture to accommodate new theological ideas while attempting to uphold the integrity and authority of the scriptures. In the process, he probes three questions: How did Mormon doctrines develop? What are the scriptural underpinnings of these doctrines? And what do critical scholars make of these same scriptures? In this enlightening study, Harrell systematically peels back the doctrinal accretions of time to provide a fresh new look at Mormon theology.

"*This Is My Doctrine*" will provide those already versed in Mormonism's theological tradition with a new and richer perspective of Mormon theology. Those unacquainted with Mormonism will gain an appreciation for how Mormon theology fits into the larger Jewish and Christian theological traditions.

Women at Church: Magnifying LDS Women's Local Impact

Neylan McBaine

Paperback, ISBN: 978-1-58958-688-8

Women at Church is a practical and faithful guide to improving the way men and women work together at church. Looking at current administrative and cultural practices, the author explains why some women struggle with the gendered divisions of labor. She then examines ample real-life examples that are currently happening in local settings around the country that expand and reimagine gendered practices. Readers will understand how to evaluate possible pain points in current practices and propose solutions that continue to uphold all mandated church policies. Readers will be equipped with the tools they need to have respectful, empathetic and productive conversations about gendered practices in Church administration and culture.

Praise for *Women at Church*:

"Such a timely, faithful, and practical book! I suggest ordering this book in bulk to give to your bishopric, stake presidency, and all your local leadership to start a conversation on changing Church culture for women by letting our doctrine suggest creative local adaptations—Neylan McBaine shows the way!" — Valerie Hudson Cassler, author of *Women in Eternity, Women of Zion*

"A pivotal work replete with wisdom and insight. Neylan McBaine deftly outlines a workable programme for facilitating movement in the direction of the privileges and powers promised the nascent Female Relief Society of Nauvoo." — Fiona Givens, co-author of *The God Who Weeps: How Mormonism Makes Sense of Life*

"In her timely and brilliant findings, Neylan McBaine issues a gracious invitation to rethink our assumptions about women's public Church service. Well researched, authentic, and respectful of the current Church administrative structure, McBaine shares exciting and practical ideas that address diverse needs and involve all members in the meaningful work of the Church." — Camille Fronk Olson, author of *Women of the Old Testament* and *Women of the New Testament*

Dead Wood and Rushing Water: Essays on Mormon Faith, Culture, and Family

Boyd Jay Petersen

Paperback, ISBN: 978-1-58958-658-1

For over a decade, Boyd Petersen has been an active voice in Mormon studies and thought. In essays that steer a course between apologetics and criticism, striving for the balance of what Eugene England once called the "radical middle," he explores various aspects of Mormon life and culture—from the Dream Mine near Salem, Utah, to the challenges that Latter-day Saints of the millennial generation face today.

Praise for *Dead Wood and Rushing Water*:

"*Dead Wood and Rushing Water* gives us a reflective, striving, wise soul ruminating on his world. In the tradition of Eugene England, Petersen examines everything in his Mormon life from the gold plates to missions to dream mines to doubt and on to Glenn Beck, Hugh Nibley, and gender. It is a book I had trouble putting down." — Richard L. Bushman, author of *Joseph Smith: Rough Stone Rolling*

"Boyd Petersen is correct when he says that Mormons have a deep hunger for personal stories—at least when they are as thoughtful and well-crafted as the ones he shares in this collection." — Jana Riess, author of *The Twible* and *Flunking Sainthood*

"Boyd Petersen invites us all to ponder anew the verities we hold, sharing in his humility, tentativeness, and cheerful confidence that our paths will converge in the end." — Terryl. L. Givens, author of *People of Paradox: A History of Mormon Culture*

Hearken, O Ye People:
The Historical Setting of Joseph
Smith's Ohio Revelations

Mark Lyman Staker

Hardcover, ISBN: 978-1-58958-113-5

2010 Best Book Award - John Whitmer Historical Association

2011 Best Book Award - Mormon History Association

More of Mormonism's canonized revelations originated in or near Kirtland than any other place. Yet many of the events connected with those revelations and their 1830s historical context have faded over time. Mark Staker reconstructs the cultural experiences by which Kirtland's Latter-day Saints made sense of the revelations Joseph Smith pronounced. This volume rebuilds that exciting decade using clues from numerous archives, privately held records, museum collections, and even the soil where early members planted corn and homes. From this vast array of sources he shapes a detailed narrative of weather, religious backgrounds, dialect differences, race relations, theological discussions, food preparation, frontier violence, astronomical phenomena, and myriad daily customs of nineteenth-century life. The result is a "from the ground up" experience that today's Latter-day Saints can all but walk into and touch.

Praise for *Hearken O Ye People*:

"I am not aware of a more deeply researched and richly contextualized study of any period of Mormon church history than Mark Staker's study of Mormons in Ohio. We learn about everything from the details of Alexander Campbell's views on priesthood authority to the road conditions and weather on the four Lamanite missionaries' journey from New York to Ohio. All the Ohio revelations and even the First Vision are made to pulse with new meaning. This book sets a new standard of in-depth research in Latter-day Saint history."

-Richard Bushman, author of *Joseph Smith: Rough Stone Rolling*

"To be well-informed, any student of Latter-day Saint history and doctrine must now be acquainted with the remarkable research of Mark Staker on the important history of the church in the Kirtland, Ohio, area."

-Neal A. Maxwell Institute, Brigham Young University

CPSIA information can be obtained
at www.ICGtesting.com
Printed in the USA
BVOW11s0930120816

458829BV00002B/26/P